CBSE Term II 2022

Mathematics Standard

Class X

Complete Theory Covering NCERT

Case Based Questions

Short/Long Answer Questions

3 Practice Papers with Explanations

Authors
Vishal Kumar Mehta
Alok Sharma

arihant

ARIHANT PRAKASHAN (School Division Series)

arihant

ARIHANT PRAKASHAN (School Division Series)

ॐ **Administrative & Production Offices**

Regd. Office
'Ramchhaya' 4577/15, Agarwal Road, Darya Ganj, New Delhi -110002
Tele: 011- 47630600, 43518550

ॐ **Head Office**
Kalindi, TP Nagar, Meerut (UP) - 250002, Tel: 0121-7156203, 7156204

ॐ **Sales & Support Offices**
Agra, Ahmedabad, Bengaluru, Bareilly, Chennai, Delhi, Guwahati, Hyderabad, Jaipur, Jhansi, Kolkata, Lucknow, Nagpur & Pune.

ॐ **ISBN :** 978-93-25796-60-7

ॐ **PRICE :** ₹200.00

PO No : TXT-XX-XXXXXXX-X-XX

Published by Arihant Publications (India) Ltd.

For further information about the books published by Arihant, log on to www.arihantbooks.com or e-mail at info@arihantbooks.com

Follow us on   

Contents

Watch Free Learning Videos

Subscribe **arihant** You Tube Channel

☑ Video Solutions of CBSE Sample Papers
☑ Chapterwise Important MCQs
☑ CBSE Updates

Syllabus

CBSE Term II Class XII

One Paper   **Max Marks: 40**

No.	Units	Marks
I.	Algebra (Cont.)	10
II.	Geometry (Cont.)	09
III.	Trigonometry (Cont.)	07
IV.	Mensuration (Cont.)	06
V.	Statistics & Probability (Cont.)	08
	Total	**40**
	Internal Assessment	**10**
	Total	**50**

UNIT-I ALGEBRA

1. Quadratic Equations (10 Periods)

Standard form of a quadratic equation $ax^2 + bx + c = 0$, $(a \neq 0)$. Solutions of quadratic equations (only real roots) by factorisation, and by using quadratic formula. Relationship between discriminant and nature of roots. Situational problems based on quadratic equations related to day to day activities (problems on equations reducible to quadratic equations are excluded)

2. Arithmetic Progressions

Motivation for studying Arithmetic Progression Derivation of the nth term and sum of the first n terms of AP and their application in solving daily life problems. (Applications based on sum to n terms of an AP. are excluded)

UNIT-II GEOMETRY

3. Circles

Tangent to a circle at point of contact

1. (Prove) The tangent at any point of a circle is perpendicular to the radius through the point of contact.
2. (Prove) The lengths of tangents drawn from an external point to a circle are equal.

4. **Constructions**
    1. Division of a line segment in a given ratio (internally).
    2. Tangents to a circle from a point outside it.

UNIT-III TRIGONOMETRY

5. **Some Applications of Trigonometry**

    HEIGHTS AND DISTANCES-Angle of elevation, Angle of Depression.
    Simple problems on heights and distances. Problems should not involve more than two right triangles. Angles of elevation / depression should be only 30°, 45°, 60°.

UNIT-IV MENSURATION

6. **Surface Areas and Volumes**
    1. Surface areas and volumes of combinations of any two of the following: cubes, cuboids, spheres, hemispheres and right circular cylinders/cones.
    2. Problems involving converting one type of metallic solid into another and other mixed problems. (Problems with combination of not more than two different solids be taken).

UNIT-V STATISTICS & PROBABILITY

5. **Statistics**

    Mean, median and mode of grouped data (bimodal situation to be avoided). Mean by Direct Method and Assumed Mean Method only

Internal Assessment	Marks	Total Marks
Periodic Test	3	
Multiple Assessments	2	10 Marks
Portfolio	2	for the
Student Enrichment Activities-practical work	3	Term

CBSE Circular

Exam Scheme Term I & II

केन्द्रीय माध्यमिक शिक्षा बोर्ड

(शिक्षा मंत्रालय, भारत सरकार के अधीन एक स्वायत संगठन)

CENTRAL BOARD OF SECONDARY EDUCATION

(An Autonomous Organisation under the Ministryof Education, Govt. of India)

CBSE/DIR (ACAD)/2021

Date: July 05, 2021
Circular No: Acad-51/2021

All the Heads of Schools affiliated to CBSE

Subject: Special Scheme of Assessment for Board Examination Classes X and XII for the Session 2021-22

COVID 19 pandemic caused almost all CBSE schools to function in a virtual mode for most part of the academic session of 2020-21. Due to the extreme risk associated with the conduct of Board examinations during the second wave in April 2021, CBSE had to cancel both its class X and XII Board examinations of the year 2021 and results are to be declared on the basis of a credible, reliable, flexible and valid alternative assessment policy. This, in turn, also necessitated deliberations over alternative ways to look at the learning objectives as well as the conduct of the Board Examinations for the academic session 2021-22 in case the situation remains unfeasible.

CBSE has also held stake holder consultations with Government schools as well as private independent schools from across the country especially schools from the remote rural areas and a majority of them have requested for the rationalization of the syllabus, similar to last year in view of reduced time permitted for organizing online classes. The Board has also considered the concerns regarding differential availability of electronic gadgets, connectivity and effectiveness of online teaching and other socio-economic issues specially with respect to students from economically weaker section and those residing in far flung areas of the country. In a survey conducted by CBSE, it was revealed that the rationalized syllabus notified for the session 2020-21 was effective for schools in covering the syllabus and helped learners in achieving learning objectives in a less stressful manner.

In the above backdrop and in line with the Board's continued focus on assessing stipulated learning outcomes by making the examinations competencies and core concepts based, student-centric, transparent, technology-driven, and having advance provision of alternatives for different future scenarios, the following schemes are introduced for the Academic Session for Class X and Class XII 2021-22.

Special Scheme for 2021-22

A. Academic session to be divided into 2 Terms with approximately 50% syllabus in each term:

The syllabus for the Academic session 2021-22 will be divided into 2 terms by following a systematic approach by looking into the interconnectivity of concepts and topics by the Subject Experts and the Board will conduct examinations at the end of each term on the basis of the bifurcated syllabus. This is done to increase the probability of having a Board conducted classes X and XII examinations at the end of the academic session.

B. The syllabus for the Board examination 2021-22 will be rationalized similar to that of the last academic session to be notified in July 2021. For academic transactions, however, schools will follow the curriculum and syllabus released by the Board vide Circular no. F.1001/CBSE-Acad/Curriculum/2021 dated 31 March 2021. Schools will also use alternative academic calendar and inputs from the NCERT on transacting the curriculum.

C. Efforts will be made to make Internal Assessment/ Practical/ Project work more credible and valid as per the guidelines and Moderation Policy to be announced by the Board to ensure fair distribution of marks.

Details of Curriculum Transaction

- Schools will continue teaching in distance mode till the authorities permit in-person mode of teaching in schools.
- **Classes IX-X: Internal Assessment** (throughout the year-irrespective of Term I and II) would include the *3 periodic tests, student enrichment, portfolio and practical work/ speaking listening activities/ project.*
- **Classes XI-XII: Internal Assessment** (throughout the year-irrespective of Term I and II) would include end of topic or unit tests/ exploratory activities/ practicals/ projects.
- Schools would create a student profile for all assessment undertaken over the year and retain the evidences in digital format.
- CBSE will facilitate schools to upload marks of Internal Assessment on the CBSE IT platform.
- Guidelines for Internal Assessment for all subjects will also be released along with the rationalized term wise divided syllabus for the session 2021-22.The Board would also provide additional resources like sample assessments, question banks, teacher training etc. for more reliable and valid internal assessments.

केन्द्रीय माध्यमिक शिक्षा बोर्ड

(शिक्षा मंत्रालय, भारत सरकार के अधीन एक स्वायत संगठन)

CENTRAL BOARD OF SECONDARY EDUCATION

(An Autonomous Organisation under the Ministryof Education, Govt. of India)

Term I Examinations:

- At the end of the first term, the Board will organize **Term I Examination** in a flexible schedule to be conducted between November-December 2021 with a window period of 4-8 weeks for schools situated in different parts of country and abroad. Dates for conduct of examinations will be notified subsequently.

- The Question Paper will have Multiple Choice Questions (MCQ) including case-based MCQs and MCQs on assertion-reasoning type. Duration of test will be **90 minutes** and it will cover only the rationalized syllabus of **Term I only** (i.e. approx. 50% of the entire syllabus).

- Question Papers will be sent by the CBSE to schools along with marking scheme.

- The exams will be conducted under the supervision of the External Center Superintendents and Observers appointed by CBSE.

- The responses of students will be captured on OMR sheets which, after scanning may be directly uploaded at CBSE portal or alternatively may be evaluated and marks obtained will be uploaded by the school on the very same day. The final direction in this regard will be conveyed to schools by the Examination Unit of the Board.

- Marks of the **Term I** Examination will contribute to the final overall score of students.

Term II Examination/ Year-end Examination:

- At the end of the second term, the Board would organize **Term II or Year-end Examination** based on the rationalized syllabus of Term II only (i.e. approximately 50% of the entire syllabus).

- This examination would be held around **March-April 2022** at the examination centres fixed by the Board.

- The paper will be of **2 hours duration** and have questions of different formats (case-based/ situation based, open ended- short answer/ long answer type).

- In case the situation is not conducive for normal descriptive examination a **90 minute MCQ based exam** will be conducted at the end of the Term II also.

- Marks of the Term II Examination would contribute to the final overall score.

केन्द्रीय माध्यमिक शिक्षा बोर्ड

(शिक्षा मंत्रालय, भारत सरकार के अधीन एक स्वायत संगठन)

CENTRAL BOARD OF SECONDARY EDUCATION

(An Autonomous Organisation under the Ministryof Education, Govt. of India)

Assessment / Examination as per different situations

A. In case the situation of the pandemic improves and students are able to come to schools or centres for taking the exams.

Board would conduct Term I and Term II examinations at schools/centres and the theory marks will be distributed equally between the two exams.

B. In case the situation of the pandemic forces complete closure of schools during November-December 2021, but Term II exams are held at schools or centres.

Term I MCQ based examination would be done by students online/offline from home - in this case, the weightage of this exam for the final score would be reduced, and weightage of Term II exams will be increased for declaration of final result.

C. In case the situation of the pandemic forces complete closure of schools during March-April 2022, but Term I exams are held at schools or centres.

Results would be based on the performance of students on Term I MCQ based examination and internal assessments. The weightage of marks of Term I examination conducted by the Board will be increased to provide year end results of candidates.

D. In case the situation of the pandemic forces complete closure of schools and Board conducted Term I and II exams are taken by the candidates from home in the session 2021-22.

Results would be computed on the basis of the Internal Assessment/Practical/Project Work and Theory marks of Term-I and II exams taken by the candidate from home in Class X / XII subject to the moderation or other measures to ensure validity and reliability of the assessment.

In all the above cases, data analysis of marks of students will be undertaken to ensure the integrity of internal assessments and home based exams.

Dr. Joseph Emmanuel
Director (Academics)

CHAPTER 01

Quadratic Equations

In this Chapter...

- Quadratic Equation and its Solutions
- Solution of a Quadratic Equation by Factorisation
- Solution of a Quadratic Equation by Quadratic Formula
- Relationship between Discriminant and Nature of Roots

An equation of the form $ax^2 + bx + c = 0$ is called **quadratic equation** in variable x, where a, b and c are real numbers and $a \neq 0$.

e.g. $2x^2 + x - 100 = 0$, $-x^2 + 1 + 300x = 0$,

$4x - 3x^2 + 7 = 0$, $4x^2 - 25 = 0$ are quadratic equations.

The form $ax^2 + bx + c = 0$, $a \neq 0$ is called the **standard form of a quadratic equation**.

To express a quadratic equation in its standard form, write the terms of given equation in the descending order of their degrees.

e.g. $3x^2 + x + 2 = 0$ and $x^2 - 2x + 6 = 0$, are in standard form whereas, $x^2 - 3 + 4x = 0$ and $x + x^2 + 8 = 0$ are not in their standard form.

Method to Check Whether a Given Equation is Quadratic or Not

To check whether a given equation is quadratic or not, first write the given equation in its simplest form and then compare the equation with the standard form of a quadratic equation,

i.e. $ax^2 + bx + c = 0$, $a \neq 0$.

If the given equation follows the form of quadratic equation $(ax^2 + bx + c = 0, a \neq 0)$, then it is a quadratic equation otherwise not.

Solutions or Roots of a Quadratic Equation

All the values of variable which satisfy the given quadratic equation, are called roots or zeroes or solutions of given quadratic equation.

In other words, a real number α is said to be a root or zero or solution of a quadratic equation $ax^2 + bx + c = 0$, $a \neq 0$, if $a(\alpha)^2 + b(\alpha) + c = 0$.

Any quadratic equation can have atmost two roots.

Method to Check Whether the Given Value is a Solution of the Given Quadratic Equation

Let $p(x) = 0$ be the given quadratic equation and $x = \alpha$ be the given value of x.

To check whether $x = \alpha$ is a solution of the given equation or not, use the following steps

Case I Write the given equation in the form, $p(x) = 0$.

Case II Now, put $x = \alpha$ in $p(x)$. If $p(\alpha) = 0$, then $x = \alpha$ is the solution of given equation, otherwise not.

Method to Determine An Unknown Constant in a Quadratic Equation when its Solution or Root is Given

I. Sometimes, given quadratic equation involves one unknown constant and its solution or root is given. Then, to find the value of unknown constant, we put the value of root or solution in given quadratic equation and simplify it to get the required unknown constant.

II. Sometimes, quadratic equation involves two unknown constants and its both roots are given. Then, to find unknowns we put both roots one-by-one in the quadratic equation and get two linear equations in two unknowns. On solving these equations, we get the required values of unknown constants.

Solution of a Quadratic Equation by Factorisation

To find the solution of a quadratic equation by factorisation method, we use the following steps.

Step I Write the given equation in standard form i.e. $ax^2 + bx + c = 0$ (if not given in standard form) and find the value of a, b and c.

Step II Find the product of a and c and write it as a sum of its two factor such that sum is equal to b. i.e. write $ac = p \times q$ and $p + q = b$ where, p and q are factors of ac.

Step III Put the value of b obtained from step II in given equation and write it LHS as product of two linear factors.

Step IV Now, equate each factor equal to zero and get desired roots of given quadratic equation.

Solution of a Quadratic Equation by Quadratic Formula

In a quadratic equation $ax^2 + bx + c = 0$, $a \neq 0$, if $b^2 - 4ac \geq 0$, then the roots of the quadratic equation are given by

$$x = \frac{-b \pm \sqrt{b^2 - 4ac}}{2a} \text{ or } x = \frac{-b \pm \sqrt{D}}{2a}$$

where, $D = b^2 - 4ac$ is known as **discriminant**. This result is known as **quadratic formula** or **Sridharacharya formula**.

Relationship between Discriminant and Nature of Roots

The nature of roots depends upon the value of the discriminant D, whereas, D can be zero, positive or negative, so three cases may arise.

Case I When $D = 0$ i.e. $b^2 - 4ac = 0$.

If $D = b^2 - 4ac = 0$, then $x = \frac{-b \pm 0}{2a} \Rightarrow x = -\frac{b}{2a}, -\frac{b}{2a}$

So, the quadratic equation has **two equal real roots** or repeated roots or coincident roots.

Case II When $D > 0$ i.e. $b^2 - 4ac > 0$.

If $D = b^2 - 4ac > 0$, then $x = \frac{-b + \sqrt{D}}{2a}$ and $\frac{-b - \sqrt{D}}{2a}$

So, the quadratic equation has **two distinct real roots.**

Case III When $D < 0$ i.e. $b^2 - 4ac < 0$.

If $D = b^2 - 4ac < 0$, then $\sqrt{D}$ can not be evaluated as square root of negative value is not defined.

So, the quadratic equation has **no real roots** or **imaginary roots** or we can say that roots of quadratic equation does not exist. This can be explained using the flow chart.

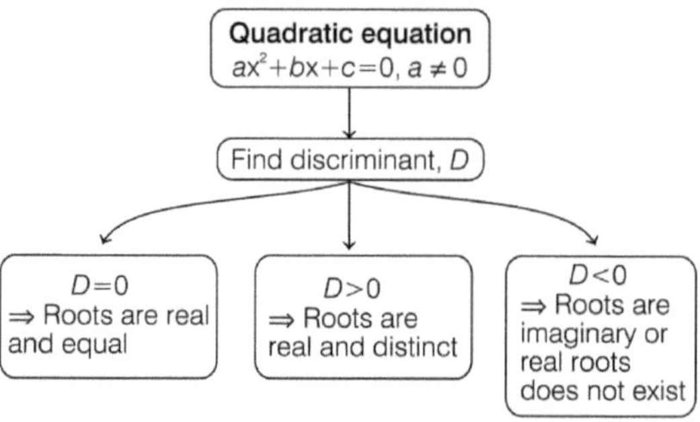

Method to Determine The Value of Unknown when Nature of Roots is Given

If nature of roots of a quadratic equation is given and quadratic equation involves an unknown. Then to find the value of unknown, first we find the value of discriminant in terms of unknown. After that use the given condition i.e. $D > 0$ or $D = 0$ or $D < 0$ and simplify it.

Some Important Points

(i) Three consecutive numbers are $x, (x+1)$ and $(x+2)$, respectively.

(ii) Three consecutive even and odd numbers are $2x, (2x+2), (2x+4)$ and $(2x+1), (2x+3), (2x+5)$, respectively.

(iii) **Pythagoras theorem,**

$$(\text{Hypotenuse})^2 = (\text{Perpendicular})^2 + (\text{Height})^2$$

(iv) Area of triangle $= \frac{1}{2} \times \text{Base} \times \text{Height}$

(v) Area of right angled triangle

$$= \frac{1}{2} \times \text{Base} \times \text{Perpendicular}$$

(vi) Area of rectangle $= \text{Length} \times \text{Breadth}$

(vii) Perimeter of rectangle $= 2 \times (\text{Length} + \text{Breadth})$

(viii) Speed $= \dfrac{\text{Distance}}{\text{Time}}$

(ix) Two-digit number $= 10x + y$, where x and y are the digits of ten's place and unit place, respectively.

On reversing the digits, new number $= 10y + x$

(x) If speed of stream be x km/h and speed of boat in still water be y km/h. Then speed of boat in upstream $= (y - x)$ km/h and speed of boat in downstream $= (y + x)$ km/h.

Solved Examples

Example 1. Check whether the following equations are quadratic or not.

(i) $x + \dfrac{3}{x} = x^2$

(ii) $2x^2 - 5x = x^2 - 2x + 3$

(iii) $x^2 - \dfrac{1}{x^2} = 5$

(iv) $x^2 - 3x - \sqrt{x} + 4 = 0$

Sol. (i) Given that, $x + \dfrac{3}{x} = x^2$

$\Rightarrow \qquad x^2 + 3 = x^3$

$\Rightarrow \qquad x^3 - x^2 - 3 = 0$

Which is not of the form $ax^2 + bx + c$, $a \ne 0$.

Thus, the equation is not a quadratic equation.

(ii) Given that, $2x^2 - 5x = x^2 - 2x + 3$

$\Rightarrow \qquad 2x^2 - x^2 - 5x + 2x - 3 = 0$

$\Rightarrow \qquad x^2 - 3x - 3 = 0$

Which is of the form $ax^2 + bx + c$, $a \ne 0$.

Thus, the equation is a quadratic equation.

(iii) Given that, $x^2 - \dfrac{1}{x^2} = 5$

$\Rightarrow \qquad x^4 - 1 = 5x^2$

$\Rightarrow \qquad x^4 - 5x^2 - 1 = 0$

Which is not of the form $ax^2 + bx + c$, $a \ne 0$.

Thus, the equation is not a quadratic equation.

(iv) Given that, $x^2 - 3x - \sqrt{x} + 4 = 0$

Which is not of the form $ax^2 + bx + c$, $a \ne 0$.

Thus, the equation is not a quadratic equation.

Example 2. Which of the following are the roots of $3x^2 + 2x - 1 = 0$?

(i) $x = -1$

(ii) $x = \dfrac{1}{3}$

(iii) $x = -\dfrac{1}{2}$

(iv) $x = 2$

Sol. Given equation is of the form $p(x) = 0$, where

$$p(x) = 3x^2 + 2x - 1 \qquad \qquad \ldots(i)$$

(i) On putting $x = -1$ in Eq. (i), we get

$p(-1) = 3(-1)^2 + 2(-1) - 1$

$= 3 - 2 - 1 = 0$

So, $x = -1$ is a root of the given quadratic equation.

(ii) On putting $x = \dfrac{1}{3}$ in Eq. (i), we get

$p\left(\dfrac{1}{3}\right) = 3\left(\dfrac{1}{3}\right)^2 + 2\left(\dfrac{1}{3}\right) - 1$

$= \dfrac{1}{3} + \dfrac{2}{3} - 1$

$= \dfrac{1 + 2 - 3}{3} = 0$

So, $x = \dfrac{1}{3}$ is a root of the given equation.

(iii) On putting $x = -\dfrac{1}{2}$ in Eq. (i), we get

$p\left(-\dfrac{1}{2}\right) = 3\left(-\dfrac{1}{2}\right)^2 + 2\left(-\dfrac{1}{2}\right) - 1$

$= \dfrac{3}{4} - 1 - 1$

$= \dfrac{3}{4} - 2 = \dfrac{3 - 8}{4} = \dfrac{-5}{4} \ne 0$

So, $x = -\dfrac{1}{2}$ is not a root of the given equation.

(iv) On putting $x = 2$ in Eq. (i), we get

$p(2) = 3(2)^2 + 2(2) - 1$

$= 12 + 4 - 1 = 15 \ne 0$

So, $x = 2$ is not a root of the given equation.

Example 3. In each of the following equations, find the value of unknown constant(s) for which the given value(s) is (are) solution of the equations.

(i) $x^2 - k^2 = 0$; $x = 0.3$

(ii) $3x^2 + 2ax - 3 = 0$; $x = \dfrac{-1}{2}$

Sol. (i) We have, $x^2 - k^2 = 0$, here k is unknown.

Since, $x = 0.3$ is a solution of given equation, so it will satisfy the given equation,

On putting $x = 0.3$ in the given equation, we get

$(0.3)^2 - k^2 = 0$

$\Rightarrow \qquad k^2 = (0.3)^2$

$\Rightarrow \qquad k = \pm\, 0.3$

(ii) We have, $3x^2 + 2ax - 3 = 0$, here a is unknown.

Since, $x = -\dfrac{1}{2}$ is a solution of given equation, so it will satisfy the given equation.

On putting $x = -\dfrac{1}{2}$ in the given equation, we get

$3\left(-\dfrac{1}{2}\right)^2 + 2a\left(-\dfrac{1}{2}\right) - 3 = 0$

$\Rightarrow \qquad \dfrac{3}{4} - a - 3 = 0$

$\Rightarrow \qquad a = \dfrac{3}{4} - 3$

$\Rightarrow \qquad a = \dfrac{3 - 12}{4} = -\dfrac{9}{4}$

Example 4. Find the roots of the quadratic equation $2x^2 + \dfrac{5}{3}x - 2 = 0$ by factorisation method.

Sol. Given equation is $2x^2 + \dfrac{5}{3}x - 2 = 0$

On multiplying by 3 both sides, we get
$$6x^2 + 5x - 6 = 0$$
$$\Rightarrow \qquad 6x^2 + (9x - 4x) - 6 = 0$$
$$\text{[by splitting the middle term]}$$
$$\Rightarrow \qquad 6x^2 + 9x - 4x - 6 = 0$$
$$\Rightarrow \qquad 3x(2x + 3) - 2(2x + 3) = 0$$
$$\Rightarrow \qquad (2x + 3)(3x - 2) = 0$$

Now, $\qquad 2x + 3 = 0$
$$\Rightarrow \qquad x = -\dfrac{3}{2}$$
and $\qquad 3x - 2 = 0$
$$\Rightarrow \qquad x = \dfrac{2}{3}$$

Hence, the roots of the equation $2x^2 + \dfrac{5}{3}x - 2 = 0$ are $\dfrac{-3}{2}$ and $\dfrac{2}{3}$.

Example 5. Solve the quadratic equation by factorisation method.
$$3\sqrt{2}x^2 - 5x - \sqrt{2} = 0$$

Sol. Given equation is $3\sqrt{2}\,x^2 - 5x - \sqrt{2} = 0$
$$3\sqrt{2}\,x^2 - (6x - x) - \sqrt{2} = 0$$
$$\text{[by splitting the middle term]}$$
$$3\sqrt{2}x^2 - 6x + x - \sqrt{2} = 0$$
$$3\sqrt{2}x^2 - 3\sqrt{2} \cdot \sqrt{2}x + x - \sqrt{2} = 0$$
$$\Rightarrow \qquad 3\sqrt{2}\,x(x - \sqrt{2}) + 1(x - \sqrt{2}) = 0$$
$$\Rightarrow \qquad (x - \sqrt{2})(3\sqrt{2}x + 1) = 0$$

Now, $\qquad x - \sqrt{2} = 0 \Rightarrow x = \sqrt{2}$
and $\qquad 3\sqrt{2}\,x + 1 = 0$
$$\Rightarrow \qquad x = -\dfrac{1}{3\sqrt{2}} = \dfrac{-\sqrt{2}}{6}$$

Hence, the roots of the equation $3\sqrt{2}x^2 - 5x - \sqrt{2} = 0$ are $-\dfrac{\sqrt{2}}{6}$ and $\sqrt{2}$.

Example 6. Find the sum of the roots of the equation,
$$\left[\dfrac{1}{x - 3} - \dfrac{1}{x + 5} = \dfrac{1}{6}\right].$$

Sol. Given $\left[\dfrac{1}{x - 3} - \dfrac{1}{x + 5}\right] = \dfrac{1}{6}$
$$\Rightarrow \qquad \dfrac{x + 5 - (x - 3)}{(x - 3)(x + 5)} = \dfrac{1}{6}$$

$$\Rightarrow \qquad \dfrac{x + 5 - x + 3}{(x - 3)(x + 5)} = \dfrac{1}{6} \Rightarrow 8 \times 6 = (x - 3)(x + 5)$$
$$\Rightarrow \qquad 48 = x^2 + 2x - 15$$
$$\Rightarrow \qquad x^2 + 2x - 63 = 0$$
$$\Rightarrow \quad x^2 + 9x - 7x - 63 = 0 \qquad \text{[by splitting the middle term]}$$
$$\Rightarrow \quad x(x + 9) - 7(x + 9) = 0$$
$$\Rightarrow \qquad (x - 7)(x + 9) = 0$$
$$\Rightarrow \qquad x = 7 \text{ and } x = -9$$
$$\therefore \text{Sum of roots} = 7 + (-9) = -2$$

Example 7. Using the quadratic formula, solve the quadratic equation.
$$x^2 + 2\sqrt{2}x - 6 = 0.$$

Sol. Given equation is $x^2 + 2\sqrt{2}\,x - 6 = 0$.

On comparing with $ax^2 + bx + c = 0$, we get
$$a = 1, \ b = 2\sqrt{2} \text{ and } c = -6$$

By quadratic formula, $x = \dfrac{-b \pm \sqrt{b^2 - 4ac}}{2a}$
$$= \dfrac{-(2\sqrt{2}) \pm \sqrt{(2\sqrt{2})^2 - 4(1)(-6)}}{2(1)}$$
$$= \dfrac{-2\sqrt{2} \pm \sqrt{8 + 24}}{2}$$
$$= \dfrac{-2\sqrt{2} \pm \sqrt{32}}{2} = \dfrac{-2\sqrt{2} \pm 4\sqrt{2}}{2}$$
$$= \dfrac{-2\sqrt{2} + 4\sqrt{2}}{2}, \ \dfrac{-2\sqrt{2} - 4\sqrt{2}}{2}$$
$$= \sqrt{2}, \ -3\sqrt{2}$$

So, $\sqrt{2}$ and $-3\sqrt{2}$ are the roots of the given equation.

Example 8. Find discriminant of the quadratic equation $3x^2 + 4x - 5 = 0$.

Sol. Comparing the given quadratic equation
$$3x^2 + 4x - 5 = 0$$

with standard quadratic equation $ax^2 + bx + c = 0$, we get
$$a = 3, \ b = 4 \text{ and } c = -5$$
$$\therefore \text{ Discriminant } (D) = b^2 - 4ac$$
$$= (4)^2 - 4 \times (3) \times (-5) = 16 + 60 = 76$$

Example 9. Check whether the quadratic equation has real roots. If real roots exist, find them
$$8x^2 + 2x - 3 = 0$$

Sol. Given equation is $8x^2 + 2x - 3 = 0$.

On comparing with $ax^2 + bx + c = 0$, we get
$$a = 8, \ b = 2 \text{ and } c = -3$$
$$\therefore \text{Discriminant, } D = b^2 - 4ac$$
$$= (2)^2 - 4(8)(-3)$$
$$= 4 + 96 = 100 > 0$$

Therefore, the equation $8x^2 + 2x - 3 = 0$ has two distinct real roots as the discriminant greater than zero.

Thus roots, $x = \dfrac{-b \pm \sqrt{D}}{2a} = \dfrac{-2 \pm \sqrt{100}}{16} = \dfrac{-2 \pm 10}{16}$

$$= \dfrac{-2 + 10}{16}, \dfrac{-2 - 10}{16}$$

$$= \dfrac{8}{16}, -\dfrac{12}{16} = \dfrac{1}{2}, -\dfrac{3}{4}$$

Example 10. Find the nature of roots of the quadratic equation $3x^2 - 4\sqrt{3}x + 4 = 0$.

If the roots are real, find them. **[CBSE 2020 (Standard)]**

Sol. Given quadratic equation is
$$3x^2 - 4\sqrt{3}x + 4 = 0$$

Compare with standard quadratic equation
$$ax^2 + bx + c = 0, \text{ we get}$$
$$a = 3, b = -4\sqrt{3} \text{ and } c = 4$$

Now, discriminant $= b^2 - 4ac$

$$= (-4\sqrt{3})^2 - 4 \times 3 \times 4$$

$$= 48 - 48 = 0$$

Hence, roots are real and equal.

By using Sridharacharya formula,
$$x = \dfrac{-b \pm \sqrt{D}}{2a}$$

$$= \dfrac{-(-4\sqrt{3}) \pm \sqrt{0}}{2 \times 3}$$

$$= \dfrac{4\sqrt{3}}{2 \times 3} = \dfrac{2\sqrt{3}}{3}$$

Hence, roots of given quadratic equation are $\dfrac{2\sqrt{3}}{3}$ and $\dfrac{2\sqrt{3}}{3}$.

Example 11. State whether the following quadratic equations have two distinct real roots. Justify your answer.

(i) $x^2 - 3x + 4 = 0$

(ii) $2x^2 + x - 1 = 0$

(iii) $2x^2 - 6x + \dfrac{9}{2} = 0$

Sol. (i) Given equation is $x^2 - 3x + 4 = 0$.

On comparing with $ax^2 + bx + c = 0$, we get
$$a = 1, b = -3 \text{ and } c = 4$$

∴ Discriminant,
$$D = b^2 - 4ac = (-3)^2 - 4(1)(4)$$
$$= 9 - 16 = -7 < 0$$

i.e. $\qquad D < 0$

Hence, the equation $x^2 - 3x + 4 = 0$ has no real root.

(ii) Given equation is $2x^2 + x - 1 = 0$

On comparing with $ax^2 + bx + c = 0$, we get
$$a = 2, b = 1 \text{ and } c = -1$$

∴ Discriminant,
$$D = b^2 - 4ac = (1)^2 - 4(2)(-1)$$
$$= 1 + 8 = 9 > 0 \text{ i.e. } D > 0$$

Hence, the equation $2x^2 + x - 1 = 0$ has two distinct real roots.

(iii) Given equation is $2x^2 - 6x + \dfrac{9}{2} = 0$.

On comparing with $ax^2 + bx + c = 0$, we get
$$a = 2, b = -6 \text{ and } c = \dfrac{9}{2}$$

∴ Discriminant, $D = b^2 - 4ac$

$$= (-6)^2 - 4(2)\left(\dfrac{9}{2}\right)$$

$$= 36 - 36 = 0$$

i.e. $D = 0$

Hence, the equation $2x^2 - 6x + \dfrac{9}{2} = 0$ has equal and real roots.

Example 12. The quadratic equation $x^2 - 4x + k = 0$ has distinct real roots, if $k = 4$. Why or why not?

Sol. Given quadratic equation is $x^2 - 4x + k = 0$

Compare with standard equation $ax^2 + bx + c = 0$, we get
$$a = 1, b = -4 \text{ and } c = k$$

The condition for distinct real root is $b^2 - 4ac > 0$

$$\Rightarrow \qquad (-4)^2 - 4 \times 1 \times k > 0$$

$$\Rightarrow \qquad 16 - 4k > 0$$

$$\Rightarrow \qquad 16 > 4k$$

$$\Rightarrow \qquad k < \dfrac{16}{4} \Rightarrow k < 4$$

Example 13. Find the value of k, for which the quadratic equation $(k + 4)x^2 + (k + 1)x + 1 = 0$ has equal roots. **[CBSE 2020 (Standard)]**

Sol. Given, quadratic equation is
$$(k + 4)x^2 + (k + 1)x + 1 = 0$$

Compare with $ax^2 + bx + c = 0$, we get
$$a = k + 4, b = k + 1 \text{ and } c = 1$$

Condition for equal roots, $b^2 - 4ac = 0$

∴ $\qquad (k + 1)^2 - 4 \times (k + 4)(1) = 0$

$\Rightarrow \qquad k^2 + 1^2 + 2k - 4k - 16 = 0$

$\qquad\qquad\qquad [\because (a + b)^2 = a^2 + b^2 + 2ab]$

$\Rightarrow \qquad k^2 - 2k - 15 = 0$

$\Rightarrow \qquad k^2 - (5 - 3)k - 15 = 0$

$\qquad\qquad\qquad$ [by splitting middle term]

$\Rightarrow \qquad k^2 - 5k + 3k - 15 = 0$

$\Rightarrow \qquad k(k - 5) + 3(k - 5) = 0$

$\Rightarrow \qquad (k + 3)(k - 5) = 0$

$\Rightarrow \qquad k = -3, 5$

Example 14. The denominator of a fraction is 3 more than its numerator. The sum of the fraction and its reciprocal is $\dfrac{29}{10}$. Find the fraction.

Sol. Let numerator $= x$

Then denominator $= x + 3$

$\therefore$ The fraction is the form of $\dfrac{x}{x + 3}$

According to the question,

$$\dfrac{x}{x + 3} + \dfrac{x + 3}{x} = \dfrac{29}{10}$$

$$\Rightarrow \qquad \dfrac{x^2 + (x + 3)^2}{x(x + 3)} = \dfrac{29}{10}$$

$$\Rightarrow \qquad 10(x^2 + x^2 + 9 + 6x) = 29(x^2 + 3x)$$

$$\Rightarrow \qquad 20x^2 + 60x + 90 = 29x^2 + 87x$$

$$\Rightarrow \qquad 9x^2 + 27x - 90 = 0$$

$$\Rightarrow \qquad x^2 + 3x - 10 = 0 \qquad \text{[divide by 9]}$$

$$\Rightarrow \qquad x^2 + 5x - 2x - 10 = 0 \qquad \text{[by splitting middle term]}$$

$$\Rightarrow \qquad x(x + 5) - 2(x + 5) = 0$$

$$\Rightarrow \qquad (x + 5)(x - 2) = 0$$

$$\Rightarrow \qquad x + 5 = 0 \text{ and } x - 2 = 0$$

$$\Rightarrow \qquad x = -5 \text{ and } x = 2$$

Example 15. Find a natural number whose square diminished by 84 is equal to thrice of 8 more than the given number.

Sol. Let n be a required natural number.

Square of a natural number diminished by $84 = n^2 - 84$

And thrice of 8 more than the natural number $= 3(n + 8)$

Now, by given condition,

$$n^2 - 84 = 3(n + 8)$$

$$\Rightarrow \qquad n^2 - 84 = 3n + 24$$

$$\Rightarrow \qquad n^2 - 3n - 108 = 0$$

$$\Rightarrow \qquad n^2 - 12n + 9n - 108 = 0$$

$$\text{[by splitting the middle term]}$$

$$\Rightarrow \qquad n(n - 12) + 9(n - 12) = 0$$

$$\Rightarrow \qquad (n - 12)(n + 9) = 0$$

$$\Rightarrow \qquad n = 12$$

$$[\because n \neq -9 \text{ because } n \text{ is a natural number}]$$

Hence, the required natural number is 12.

Example 16. If Zeba were younger by 5 yr than what she really is, then the square of her age (in years) would have been 11 more than five times her actual age, what is her age now?

Sol. Let the actual age of Zeba $= x$ yr

Her age when she was 5 yr younger $= (x - 5)$ yr

Now, by given condition,

Square of her age $= 11$ more than five times her actual age

$$(x - 5)^2 = 5 \times \text{actual age} + 11$$

$$\Rightarrow \qquad (x - 5)^2 = 5x + 11$$

$$\Rightarrow \qquad x^2 + 25 - 10x = 5x + 11$$

$$\Rightarrow \qquad x^2 - 15x + 14 = 0$$

$$\Rightarrow \quad x^2 - 14x - x + 14 = 0 \qquad \text{[by splitting the middle term]}$$

$$\Rightarrow \qquad x(x - 14) - 1(x - 14) = 0$$

$$\Rightarrow \qquad (x - 1)(x - 14) = 0$$

$$\Rightarrow \qquad x = 14$$

[here, $x \neq 1$ because her age is $x - 5$. So, $x - 5 = 1 - 5 = -4$ i.e. age cannot be negative]

Hence, required Zeba's age now is 14 yr.

Example 17. A two-digit number is such that the product of its digit is 35. When 18 is added to the number the digits interchange their places. Find the number.

Sol. Let the ten's digit number be x.

According to the question,

Product of the digits $= 35$

i.e. Ten's digits $\times$ Unit digit $= 35$

$$\Rightarrow \text{Units digit} = \dfrac{35}{x}$$

$\therefore$ Two digit number $= 10x + \dfrac{35}{x}$

Also it is given that if 18 is added to the number, the digits gets interchange.

$$\therefore \qquad 10x + \dfrac{35}{x} + 18 = 10 \times \dfrac{35}{x} + x$$

$$\Rightarrow \qquad \dfrac{10x^2 + 35 + 18x}{x} = \dfrac{350 + x^2}{x}$$

$$\Rightarrow \qquad 9x^2 + 18x - 315 = 0$$

$$\Rightarrow \qquad x^2 + 2x - 35 = 0 \qquad \text{[divide by 9]}$$

$$\Rightarrow \qquad x^2 + 7x - 5x - 35 = 0$$

$$\Rightarrow \qquad x(x + 7) - 5(x + 7) = 0$$

$$\Rightarrow \qquad (x - 5)(x + 7) = 0$$

$$\Rightarrow \qquad x = 5, -7$$

But a digit can never be negative.

So, $x = -7$ is rejected.

$\therefore$ The required number is

$$10 \times 5 + 5 = 50 + 5$$

$$= 55$$

Chapter Practice

PART 1

Objective Questions

• Multiple Choice Questions

1. Which of the following is a quadratic equation?

[NCERT Exemplar]

(a) $x^2 + 2x + 1 = (4 - x)^2 + 3$

(b) $-2x^2 = (5 - x)\left(2x - \dfrac{2}{5}\right)$

(c) $(k + 1)\, x^2 + \dfrac{3}{2}x = 7$, where $k = -1$

(d) $x^3 - x^2 = (x - 1)^3$

2. Which of the following is not a quadratic equation?

[NCERT Exemplar]

(a) $2(x - 1)^2 = 4x^2 - 2x + 1$ (b) $2x - x^2 = x^2 + 5$

(c) $(\sqrt{2}x + \sqrt{3})^2 = 3x^2 - 5x$ (d) $(x^2 + 2x)^2 = x^4 + 3 + 4x^2$

3. If a number x is added to twice its square, then the resultant is 21. Then the quadratic representation of this statement is

(a) $2x^2 - x + 21 = 0$ (b) $2x^2 + x - 21 = 0$

(c) $2x^2 - x - 20 = 0$ (d) None of these

4. Which of the following equations has 2 as a root?

(a) $x^2 - 4x + 5 = 0$ (b) $x^2 + 3x - 12 = 0$

(c) $2x^2 - 7x + 6 = 0$ (d) $3x^2 - 6x - 2 = 0$

5. If $\dfrac{1}{2}$ is a root of the equation $x^2 + kx - \dfrac{5}{4} = 0$, then the value of k is

[NCERT Exemplar]

(a) 2   (b) −2   (c) $\dfrac{1}{4}$ (d) $\dfrac{1}{2}$

6. Which of the following equation has root as 3?

(a) $x^2 - 5x + 6 = 0$ (b) $-x^2 + 3x - 3 = 0$

(c) $\sqrt{2}\, x^2 - \dfrac{3}{\sqrt{2}}x + 1 = 0$ (d) $3x^2 - 3x + 3 = 0$

7. 0.2 is a root of the equation $x^2 - 0.4 = 0$?

[NCERT Exemplar]

(a) True   (b) False

(c) Can't determined   (d) None of these

8. A quadratic equation with integral coefficient has integral roots.

(a) True   (b) False

(c) Can't determined   (d) None of these

9. If $b = 0, c < 0$, then the roots of $x^2 + bx + c = 0$ are numerically equal and opposite in sign.

[NCERT Exemplar]

(a) True   (b) False

(c) Can't determined   (d) None of these

10. The roots of the quadratic equation $x^2 - 8x - 20 = 0$ are

(a) 5, −4   (b) −4, 5   (c) 10, −2   (d) −10, 2

11. Which constant must be added and subtracted to solve the quadratic equation $9x^2 + \dfrac{3}{4}x - \sqrt{2} = 0$.

[NCERT Exemplar]

(a) $\dfrac{1}{8}$ (b) $\dfrac{1}{64}$ (c) $\dfrac{1}{4}$ (d) $\dfrac{9}{64}$

12. Solve $12x^2 + 5x - 3 = 0$.

(a) $\dfrac{1}{3}, \dfrac{4}{3}$ (b) $\dfrac{1}{2}, \dfrac{3}{4}$ (c) $-\dfrac{1}{3}, \dfrac{3}{4}$ (d) $\dfrac{1}{3}, -\dfrac{3}{4}$

13. The discriminant of the quadratic equation $x^2 - 4x + 1 = 0$ is

[CBSE 2013]

(a) $2\sqrt{3}$ (b) 4   (c) 12   (d) 16

14. If the discriminant of the equation $6x^2 - bx + 2 = 0$ is 1, then the value of b is

[CBSE 2012]

(a) 7   (b) −7

(c) Both (a) and (b)   (d) None of these

15. Value(s) of k for which the quadratic equation $2x^2 - kx + k = 0$ has equal roots is/are

[NCERT]

(a) 0   (b) 4   (c) 8   (d) 0, 8

16. The quadratic equation $2x^2 - \sqrt{5}x + 1 = 0$ has

(a) two distinct real roots   (b) two equal real roots

(c) no real roots   (d) more than 2 real roots

17. If the discriminant of the equation $kx^2 - 3\sqrt{2}x + 4\sqrt{2} = 0$ is 14, then the value of k is

(a) $\sqrt{2}$ (b) $\dfrac{1}{3\sqrt{2}}$ (c) $\dfrac{1}{\sqrt{2}}$ (d) $\dfrac{1}{4\sqrt{2}}$

18. Which of the following equations has two distinct real roots?   **[NCERT Exemplar]**

(a) $2x^2 - 3\sqrt{2}x + \dfrac{9}{4} = 0$ (b) $x^2 + x - 5 = 0$

(c) $x^2 + 3x + 2\sqrt{2} = 0$ (d) $5x^2 - 3x + 1 = 0$

19. Which of the following equations has no real roots?

(a) $x^2 - 4x + 3\sqrt{2} = 0$ (b) $x^2 + 4x - 3\sqrt{2} = 0$

(c) $x^2 - 4x - 3\sqrt{2} = 0$ (d) $3x^2 + 4\sqrt{3}x + 4 = 0$

20. $(x^2 + 1)^2 - x^2 = 0$ has   **[NCERT Exemplar]**

(a) four real roots   (b) two real roots

(c) no real roots   (d) one real root

21. The sum of the squares of three consecutive integers is 110, then the smallest positive integer is   **[NCERT Exemplar]**

(a) 6   (b) 5   (c) 7   (d) 4

22. A line segment AB is 8 cm in length. AB is produced to P such that $BP^2 = AB \cdot AP$. Then, the length of BP is   **[NCERT Exemplar]**

(a) $5(\sqrt{5} + 1)$ (b) $\sqrt{5} + 1$

(c) $4(\sqrt{5} + 1)$ (d) $\sqrt{3} + 1$

23. One year ago, a man was 8 times as old as his son. Now, his age is equal to the square of his son's age. Present age of man is

(a) 49 yr   (b) 37 yr

(c) 59 yr   (d) 39 yr

• Case Based MCQs

24. Raj and Ajay are very close friends. Both the families decide to go to Ranikhet by their own cars. Raj's car travels at a speed of x km/h while Ajay's car travels 5 km/h faster than Raj's car. Raj took 4 h more than Ajay to complete the journey of 400 km.   **[CBSE Question Bank]**

(i) What will be the distance covered by Ajay's car in two hours?

(a) $2(x + 5)$ km   (b) $(x - 5)$ km

(c) $2(x + 10)$ km   (d) $(2x + 5)$ km

(ii) Which of the following quadratic equation describe the speed of Raj's car?

(a) $x^2 - 5x - 500 = 0$ (b) $x^2 + 4x - 400 = 0$

(c) $x^2 + 5x - 500 = 0$ (d) $x^2 - 4x + 400 = 0$

(iii) What is the speed of Raj's car?

(a) 20 km/h   (b) 15 km/h

(c) 25 km/h   (d) 10 km/h

(iv) How much time took Ajay to travel 400 km?

(a) 20 h   (b) 40 h   (c) 25 h   (d) 16 h

(v) How much time took Raj to travel 400 km?

(a) 15 h   (b) 20 h   (c) 18 h   (d) 22 h

25. The speed of a motor boat is 20 km/h. For covering the distance of 15 km the boat took 1 h more for upstream than downstream.   **[CBSE Question Bank]**

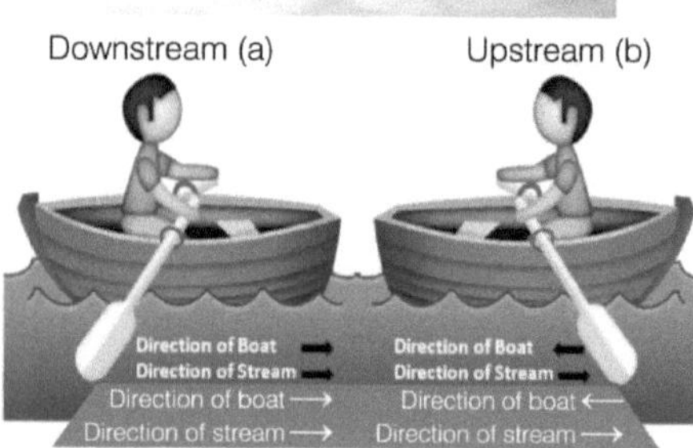

(i) Let speed of the stream be x km/h, then speed of the motorboat in upstream will be

(a) 20 km/h   (b) $(20 + x)$ km/h

(c) $(20 - x)$ km/h   (d) 2 km/h

(ii) What is the relation between speed, distance and time?

(a) Speed $= \dfrac{\text{Distance}}{\text{Time}}$

(b) Distance $= \dfrac{\text{Speed}}{\text{Time}}$

(c) Time $=$ Speed $\times$ Distance

(d) Speed $=$ Distance $\times$ Time

(iii) Which is the correct quadratic equation for the speed of the current ?

(a) $x^2 + 30x - 200 = 0$ (b) $x^2 + 20x - 400 = 0$

(c) $x^2 + 30x - 400 = 0$ (d) $x^2 - 20x - 400 = 0$

(iv) What is the speed of current ?

(a) 20 km/h   (b) 10 km/h

(c) 15 km/h   (d) 25 km/h

(v) How much time boat took in downstream?

(a) 90 min   (b) 15 min

(c) 30 min   (d) 45 min

26. By quadratic formula, the roots of the quadratic equation $ax^2 + bx + c = 0$, $a \neq 0$ are given by

$$x = \frac{-b \pm \sqrt{b^2 - 4ac}}{2a} \quad \text{or} \quad x = \frac{-b \pm \sqrt{D}}{2a}$$

where, $D = b^2 - 4ac$ is called *discriminant*.

(i) The roots of the quadratic equation $8x^2 - 22x - 21 = 0$ are

(a) $-\dfrac{7}{2}, -\dfrac{3}{4}$ (b) $\dfrac{7}{2}, \dfrac{3}{4}$

(c) $\dfrac{7}{2}, -\dfrac{3}{4}$ (d) $-\dfrac{7}{2}, \dfrac{3}{4}$

(ii) The discriminant of $x^2 + x + 7 = 0$ is

(a) 27   (b) -27
(c) $\sqrt{27}$ (d) $\sqrt{-27}$

(iii) Roots of $4x^2 - 2x = 3$ are

(a) Real and distinct   (b) Real and equal
(c) Imaginary   (d) More than two real roots

(iv) The value of k for which $4x^2 + kx + 9 = 0$ has real and equal roots is

(a) 12   (b) -12
(c) Both (a) and (b)   (d) None of these

(v) The least positive value of k for which $x^2 + kx + 16 = 0$ has real roots, is

(a) 18   (b) 4
(c) 2   (d) 8

27. Seven years ago, Varun's age was five times the square of Swati's age. Three years hence, Swati's age will be two-fifth of Varun's age.

(i) If seven years ago, Swati's age be x yr, then Varun's age is

(a) $(5x - 7)^2$ yr   (b) $5x^2$ yr
(c) $(5x^2 + 7)$ yr   (d) $(5x^2 - 7)$ yr

(ii) After three years, Swati's age is

(a) $(x + 3)$ yr   (b) $(x - 3)$ yr
(c) $(x + 7)$ yr   (d) $(x + 10)$ yr

(iii) The quadratic equation related to the given problem is

(a) $2x^2 - x - 6 = 0$ (b) $5x^2 - x + 6 = 0$
(c) $3x^2 - 2x + 5 = 0$ (d) $7x^2 - 3x + 1 = 0$

(iv) Present age of Varun's is

(a) 27 yr   (b) 20 yr
(c) 30 yr   (d) 37 yr

(v) If Swati's present age 10 yr, then present age of Varun's is

(a) 40 yr   (b) 47 yr
(c) 45 yr   (d) 52 yr

Subjective Questions

• Short Answer Type Questions

1. Check whether the following are quadratic equations or not.

(i) $(x - 1)(x + 2) = (x - 3)(x + 1)$

(ii) $(x + 2)^2 = 4(x + 3)$

2. If $x = \dfrac{1}{\sqrt{3}}$ is root of the equation

$Px^2 + (\sqrt{3} - \sqrt{2})x - 1 = 0$, then find the value of $P^2 + 1$.   **[NCERT Exemplar]**

3. In each of the following equations, determine the value of k for which the given value is a solution of the equation.

(i) $kx^2 + 2x - 3 = 0$, $x = 2$

(ii) $x^2 + 2ax - k = 0$, $x = -a$

4. Find the value of k in the following equations

(i) $x^2 - 2kx - 6 = 0$, when $x = 3$

(ii) $x^2 - kx - \dfrac{5}{4} = 0$, when $x = \dfrac{1}{2}$

5. Determine whether $x = \dfrac{-1}{2}, x = \dfrac{1}{3}$ are the solutions of the given equation $6x^2 - x - 2 = 0$, or not.

6. Solve the quadratic equation by factorisation method.

$$4\sqrt{3}x^2 + 5x - 2\sqrt{3} = 0$$

7. Solve for $x : \dfrac{16}{x} - 1 = \dfrac{15}{x+1}; x \neq 0, -1.$

8. Find the roots of the equation $ax^2 + a = a^2x + x.$ **[CBSE 2012]**

9. Solve for x, $\sqrt{6x + 7} - (2x - 7) = 0$ **[CBSE 2016]**

10. Find the numerical difference of the roots of equation $x^2 - 7x - 18 = 0$.   **[CBSE 2015]**

11. Using the quadratic formula, solve the quadratic equation.

$$\sqrt{3}x^2 + 11x + 6\sqrt{3} = 0$$

12. If the discriminant of the equation $5x^2 - sx + 4 = 0$ is 1, then find the value of s.

13. Show that $(x^2 + 1)^2 - x^2 = 0$ has no real roots.

[**NCERT Exemplar**]

14. Find the value of k for which the quadratic equation $2x^2 - kx + k = 0$ has equal roots.   [**NCERT Exemplar**]

15. Find the values of k for which the equation $9x^2 + 3kx + 4 = 0$ has real roots.

16. If the equation $(1 + m^2)x^2 + (2mc)x + (c^2 - a^2) = 0$ has equal roots, then prove that $c^2 = a^2(1 + m^2)$.

17. The sum of two numbers is 11 and the sum of their reciprocals is $\dfrac{11}{28}$. Find the numbers.

[**CBSE 2013**]

18. In a cricket match. Harbhajan took three wickets less than twice the number of wickets taken by Zaheer. The product of the numbers of wickets taken by these two is 20. Represent the above situation in the form of a quadratic equation.

[**CBSE 2015**]

• Long Answer Type Questions

19. If $x = 2$ and $x = 3$ are roots of the equation $3x^2 - 2ax + 2b = 0$, then find the values of a and b.

20. Find the nature of roots of the following quadratic equations. If the real roots exist, then also find the roots.

(i) $4x^2 + 12x + 9 = 0$ (ii) $3x^2 + 5x - 7 = 0$

21. Find the value of k for which the given equation has equal roots.

$$(k - 12)\,x^2 + 2(k - 12)\,x + 2 = 0$$

22. If $x = -2$ is a root of the equation $3x^2 + 7x + p = 0$. Find the values of k, so that the roots of the equation $x^2 + k(4x + k - 1) + p = 0$ are equal.   [**CBSE 2015**]

23. Find two consecutive odd natural numbers, sum of whose squares is 130.   [**CBSE 2013**]

24. A piece of cloth costs ₹ 200. If the piece was 5 m longer and each metre of cloth costs ₹ 2 less, the cost of the piece would have remained unchanged. How long is the piece and what is the original rate per metre?   [**CBSE 2015**]

25. The difference of two numbers is 4. If the difference of their reciprocals is $\dfrac{4}{21}$, the find the two numbers.   [**CBSE 2008**]

26. The perimeter of a right angled triangle is 70 units and its hypotenuse is 29 units we would like to find the length of the other sides.

27. The sum of the reciprocals of Anjali's age 3 yr ago and 5 yr from now is $\dfrac{1}{3}$. Find the present age of Anjali.

28. A two-digit number is such that the product of the digits is 12. When 36 is added to the number the digits interchange their places. Find the two-digit number.

29. "John and Janvi together have 45 marbles. Both of them lost 5 marbles each and the product of the number of marbles they now have, is 124. Find out how many marbles they had to start with?"

30. The hypotenuse of right angled triangle is 6 m more than twice the shortest side. If the third side is 2 m less than the hypotenuse, then find all sides of the triangle.   [**CBSE 2020 (Standard)**]

31. At present Asha's age (in years) is 2 more than the square of her daughter Nisha's age. When Nisha grows to her mother's present age. Asha's age would be one year less than 10 times the present age of Nisha. Find the present ages of both Asha and Nisha.   [**NCERT Exemplar**]

32. The speed of a boat in still water is 15 km/h. It can go 30 km upstream and return downstream to the original point in 4 h and 30 min. Find the speed of stream.

33. Two water taps together can fill a tank in $1\dfrac{7}{8}$ h. The tap with longer diameter takes 2 h less than the tap with smaller one to fill the tank separately. Find the time in which each tap can fill the tank separately.   [**CBSE 2019**]

• Case Based Questions

34. In the centre of a rectangular lawn of dimensions $50\ \text{m} \times 40\ \text{m}$, a rectangular pond has to be constructed, so that the area of the grass surrounding the pond would be $1184\ \text{m}^2$

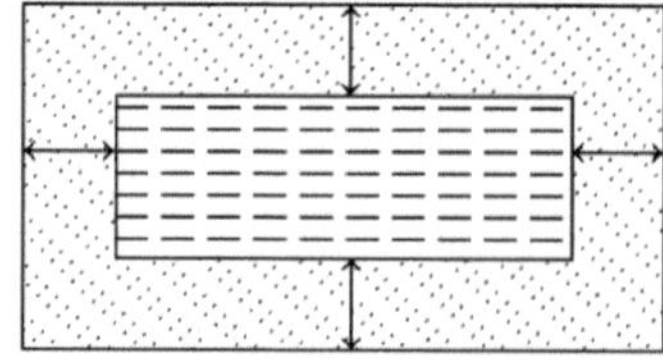

(i) If the distance between pond and lawn is x m. Find the length and breadth of rectangular pond.

(ii) Find the quadratic equation related to the given problem.

(iii) Find the length and breadth of the pond.

SOLUTIONS

Objective Questions

1. (d) (a) Given that,
$$x^2 + 2x + 1 = (4 - x)^2 + 3$$
$$\Rightarrow \quad x^2 + 2x + 1 = 16 + x^2 - 8x + 3$$
$$\Rightarrow \quad 10x - 18 = 0$$
which is not of the form $ax^2 + bx + c = 0, a \neq 0$.
Thus, the equation is not a quadratic equation.

(b) Given that, $-2x^2 = (5 - x)\left(2x - \dfrac{2}{5}\right)$
$$\Rightarrow \quad -2x^2 = 10x - 2x^2 - 2 + \dfrac{2x}{5}$$
$$\Rightarrow \quad 50x + 2x - 10 = 0$$
$$\Rightarrow \quad 52x - 10 = 0$$
which is also not a quadratic equation.

(c) Given that, $x^2(k + 1) + \dfrac{3}{2}x = 7$
Given, $\qquad\qquad k = -1$
$$\Rightarrow \quad x^2(-1 + 1) + \dfrac{3}{2}x = 7$$
$$\Rightarrow \quad 3x - 14 = 0$$
which is also not a quadratic equation.

(d) Given that, $x^3 - x^2 = (x - 1)^3$
$$\Rightarrow \quad x^3 - x^2 = x^3 - 3x^2(1) + 3x(1)^2 - (1)^3$$
$$[\because \ (a - b)^3 = a^3 - b^3 + 3ab^2 - 3a^2b]$$
$$\Rightarrow \quad x^3 - x^2 = x^3 - 3x^2 + 3x - 1$$
$$\Rightarrow \quad -x^2 + 3x^2 - 3x + 1 = 0 \Rightarrow 2x^2 - 3x + 1 = 0$$
which represents a quadratic equation because it has the quadratic form $ax^2 + bx + c = 0, a \neq 0$.

2. (d) (a) Given that, $2(x - 1)^2 = 4x^2 - 2x + 1$
$$\Rightarrow \quad 2(x^2 + 1 - 2x) = 4x^2 - 2x + 1$$
$$\Rightarrow \quad 2x^2 + 2 - 4x = 4x^2 - 2x + 1$$
$$\Rightarrow \quad 2x^2 + 2x - 1 = 0$$
which represents a quadratic equation because it has the quadratic form $ax^2 + bx + c = 0, a \neq 0$.

(b) Given that, $2x - x^2 = x^2 + 5$
$$\Rightarrow \quad 2x^2 - 2x + 5 = 0$$
which also represents a quadratic equation because it has the quadratic form $ax^2 + bx + c = 0, a \neq 0$.

(c) Given that, $(\sqrt{2} \cdot x + \sqrt{3})^2 = 3x^2 - 5x$
$$\Rightarrow \quad 2 \cdot x^2 + 3 + 2\sqrt{6} \cdot x = 3x^2 - 5x$$
$$\Rightarrow \quad x^2 - (5 + 2\sqrt{6})x - 3 = 0$$
which also represents a quadratic equation because it has the quadratic form $ax^2 + bx + c = 0, \ a \neq 0$.

(d) Given that, $(x^2 + 2x)^2 = x^4 + 3 + 4x^2$
$$\Rightarrow \quad x^4 + 4x^2 + 4x^3 = x^4 + 3 + 4x^2$$
$$\Rightarrow \quad 4x^3 - 3 = 0$$
which is not of the form $ax^2 + bx + c = 0, a \neq 0$.
Thus, the equation is not quadratic.
This is a cubic equation.

3. (b) Let the number be x.
Then according to the given condition,
$$2x^2 + x = 21$$
$$\Rightarrow \quad 2x^2 + x - 21 = 0$$

4. (c) (a) Substituting $x = 2$ in $x^2 - 4x + 5$, we get
$$(2)^2 - 4(2) + 5 = 4 - 8 + 5 = 1 \neq 0.$$
So, $x = 2$ is not a root of $x^2 - 4x + 5 = 0$.

(b) Substituting $x = 2$ in $x^2 + 3x - 12$, we get
$$(2)^2 + 3(2) - 12$$
$$= 4 + 6 - 12 = -2 \neq 0$$
So, $x = 2$ is not a root of $x^2 + 3x - 12 = 0$.

(c) Substituting $x = 2$ in $2x^2 - 7x + 6$, we get
$$2(2)^2 - 7(2) + 6 = 2(4) - 14 + 6$$
$$= 8 - 14 + 6 = 14 - 14 = 0$$
So, $x = 2$ is root of the equation $2x^2 - 7x + 6 = 0$.

(d) Substituting $x = 2$ in $3x^2 - 6x - 2$, we get
$$3(2)^2 - 6(2) - 2 = 12 - 12 - 2 = -2 \neq 0$$
So, $x = 2$ is not a root of $3x^2 - 6x - 2 = 0$.

5. (a) Since, $\dfrac{1}{2}$ is a root of the quadratic equation $x^2 + kx - \dfrac{5}{4} = 0$.

Then, $\left(\dfrac{1}{2}\right)^2 + k\left(\dfrac{1}{2}\right) - \dfrac{5}{4} = 0$
$$\Rightarrow \quad \dfrac{1}{4} + \dfrac{k}{2} - \dfrac{5}{4} = 0$$
$$\Rightarrow \quad \dfrac{1 + 2k - 5}{4} = 0$$
$$\Rightarrow \quad 2k - 4 = 0$$
$$\Rightarrow \quad 2k = 4$$
$$\Rightarrow \quad k = 2$$

6. (a) (a) Given that, $x^2 - 5x + 6 = 0$
Put $x = 3$, we get
$$(3)^2 - 5(3) + 6 = 9 - 15 + 6 = 0$$
Hence, $x = 3$ is a root of the equation.

(b) $-x^2 + 3x - 3 = 0$
Put $x = 3$, we get
$$-(3)^2 + 3(3) - 3 = -9 + 9 - 3 = -3 \neq 0$$
Hence, $x = 3$ is not a root of the equation.

(c) $\sqrt{2}\,x^2 - \dfrac{3}{\sqrt{2}}x + 1 = 0$
Put $x = 3$, we get
$$\sqrt{2}(3)^2 - \dfrac{3(3)}{\sqrt{2}(3)} + 1$$

$\Rightarrow 9\sqrt{2} - \dfrac{9}{\sqrt{2}} + 1 = \dfrac{9}{\sqrt{2}} + 1 \neq 0$

Hence, $x = 3$ is not a root of the equation.

(d) $3x^2 - 3x + 3 = 0$

Put $x = 3$, we get

$3(3)^2 - 3(3) + 3 = 27 - 9 + 3 = 21 \neq 0.$

Hence, $x = 3$ is not a root of the equation.

7. (b) False, since 0.2 does not satisfy the equation i.e. $(0.2)^2 - 0.4 = 0.04 - 0.4 \neq 0.$

8. (b) False, consider the quadratic equation $2x^2 + x - 6 = 0$ with integral coefficient. The roots of the given quadratic equation are -2 and $\dfrac{3}{2}$ which are not integrals.

9. (a) Given that, $b = 0$ and $c < 0$ and quadratic equation

$$x^2 + bx + c = 0 \qquad \text{...(i)}$$

Put $b = 0$ in Eq. (i), we get

$$x^2 + 0 + c = 0$$

$\Rightarrow \qquad x^2 = -c \qquad \begin{bmatrix} \text{here, } c > 0 \\ \therefore \quad -c > 0 \end{bmatrix}$

$\therefore \qquad x = \pm \sqrt{-c}$

So, the roots of $x^2 + bx + c = 0$ are numerically equal and opposite in sign.

10. (c) Given, quadratic equation is $x^2 - 8x - 20 = 0$, which is already in its standard form.

On comparing it with $ax^2 + bx + c = 0$, we get

$$a = 1, \ b = -8 \text{ and } c = -20$$

Here, $\quad ac = 1 \times (-20) = -20.$

Here, ac has $-$ve sign,

So, let $p = -10$ and $q = 2$ as $p \times q = -20$ and $p + q = -8$

$\therefore \qquad x^2 - 8x - 20 = 0$

$\Rightarrow \quad x^2 - 10x + 2x - 20 = 0$

$\Rightarrow \quad x(x - 10) + 2(x - 10) = 0$

$\Rightarrow \qquad (x - 10)(x + 2) = 0$

Now, put $x - 10 = 0$ or $x + 2 = 0$

$\Rightarrow \qquad x = 10$ or $x = -2$

Thus, 10 and -2 are the required roots of a given quadratic equation.

11. (b) Given equation is $9x^2 + \dfrac{3}{4}x - \sqrt{2} = 0.$

$$(3x)^2 + \dfrac{1}{4}(3x) - \sqrt{2} = 0$$

On putting $3x = y$, we have

$$y^2 + \dfrac{1}{4}y - \sqrt{2} = 0$$

$$y^2 + \dfrac{1}{4}y + \left(\dfrac{1}{8}\right)^2 - \left(\dfrac{1}{8}\right)^2 - \sqrt{2} = 0$$

$$\left(y + \dfrac{1}{8}\right)^2 = \dfrac{1}{64} + \sqrt{2}$$

$$[\because (a + b^2) = a^2 + b^2 + 2ab]$$

$$\left(y + \dfrac{1}{8}\right)^2 = \dfrac{1 + 64 \cdot \sqrt{2}}{64}$$

Thus, $\dfrac{1}{64}$ must be added and subtracted to solve the given equation.

12. (d) Given quadratic equation is $12x^2 + 5x - 3 = 0.$

On comparing the given equation with $ax^2 + bx + c = 0$, we get $a = 12, \ b = 5$ and $c = -3$

On substituting the values of $a = 12, \ b = 5$ and $c = -3$ in quadratic formula,

$$x = \dfrac{-b \pm \sqrt{b^2 - 4ac}}{2a}, \text{ we get}$$

$$x = \dfrac{-5 \pm \sqrt{(5)^2 - 4 \times 12 \times (-3)}}{2 \times 12}$$

$\Rightarrow \qquad x = \dfrac{-5 \pm \sqrt{25 + 144}}{24}$

$$= \dfrac{-5 \pm \sqrt{169}}{24}$$

$$= \dfrac{-5 \pm 13}{24}$$

Now, $\quad x = \dfrac{-5 + 13}{24} = \dfrac{8}{24} = \dfrac{1}{3} \qquad$ [taking +ve sign]

Or $\quad x = \dfrac{-5 - 13}{24} = -\dfrac{18}{24} = -\dfrac{3}{4} \qquad$ [taking $-$ve sign]

Hence, the roots of the given equation are $\dfrac{1}{3}$ and $-\dfrac{3}{4}.$

13. (c) Given quadratic equation is $x^2 - 4x + 1 = 0.$

On comparing with $ax^2 + bx + c = 0$, we get

$$a = 1, \ b = -4 \text{ and } c = 1$$

Now, discriminant $(D) = b^2 - 4ac$

$$= (-4)^2 - 4 \times 1 \times 1$$

$$= 16 - 4 = 12$$

14. (c) Given, $6x^2 - bx + 2 = 0$

On comparing with $Ax^2 + Bx + C = 0$, we get

$$A = 6, \ B = -b \text{ and } C = 2$$

We know that,

Discriminant, $D = B^2 - 4AC$

$\Rightarrow \qquad 1 = (-b)^2 - 4 \times 6 \times 2 \qquad$ [given, $D = 1$]

$\Rightarrow \qquad 1 = b^2 - 48$

$\Rightarrow \qquad b^2 = 49$

$\Rightarrow \qquad b = \pm 7 \qquad$ [taking square root on both sides]

Hence, the required value of b is -7 or 7.

15. (d) Given equation is $2x^2 - kx + k = 0$

On comparing with $ax^2 + bx + c = 0$, we get

$$a = 2, \ b = -k \text{ and } c = k$$

For equal roots, the discriminant must be zero.

i.e. $\qquad D = b^2 - 4ac = 0$

$\Rightarrow \qquad (-k)^2 - 4(2)k = 0$

$$\Rightarrow \qquad k^2 - 8k = 0$$
$$\Rightarrow \qquad k\,(k - 8) = 0$$
$$\therefore \qquad k = 0,\, 8$$

Hence, the required values of k are 0 and 8.

16. (c) Given equation is $2x^2 - \sqrt{5}x + 1 = 0$.

On comparing with $ax^2 + bx + c = 0$, we get
$$a = 2,\, b = -\sqrt{5} \text{ and } c = 1$$

$\therefore$ Discriminant,
$$D = b^2 - 4ac$$
$$= (-\sqrt{5})^2 - 4 \times (2) \times (1) = 5 - 8 = -3 < 0$$

Since, discriminant is negative, therefore quadratic equation $2x^2 - \sqrt{5}x + 1 = 0$ has no real roots i.e. imaginary roots.

17. (d) Given quadratic equation is
$$kx^2 - 3\sqrt{2}x + 4\sqrt{2} = 0$$

On comparing with
$$ax^2 + bx + c = 0, \text{ we get}$$
$$a = k,\, b = -3\sqrt{2} \text{ and } c = 4\sqrt{2}$$

$\because$ Discriminant, $D = b^2 - 4ac$
$$\Rightarrow \qquad 14 = (-3\sqrt{2})^2 - 4 \times k \times 4\sqrt{2}$$
$$\Rightarrow \qquad 14 = 18 - 16\sqrt{2}k$$
$$\Rightarrow \qquad 16\sqrt{2}k = 4$$
$$\Rightarrow \qquad k = \frac{1}{4\sqrt{2}}$$

18. (b)

(a) Given equation is $2x^2 - 3\sqrt{2}x + 9/4 = 0$, we get

On comparing with $ax^2 + bx + c = 0$
$$a = 2,\, b = -3\sqrt{2} \text{ and } c = 9/4$$
Now, $D = b^2 - 4ac$
$$= (-3\sqrt{2})^2 - 4(2)(9/4)$$
$$= 18 - 18 = 0$$

Thus, the equation has real and equal roots.

(b) The given equation is $x^2 + x - 5 = 0$

On comparing with $ax^2 + bx + c = 0$, we get
$$a = 1,\, b = 1 \text{ and } c = -5$$
The discriminant of $x^2 + x - 5 = 0$ is
$$D = b^2 - 4ac = (1)^2 - 4(1)(-5)$$
$$= 1 + 20 = 21$$
$$\Rightarrow \qquad b^2 - 4ac > 0$$

So, $x^2 + x - 5 = 0$ has two distinct real roots.

(c) Given equation is $x^2 + 3x + 2\sqrt{2} = 0$

On comparing with $ax^2 + bx + c = 0$, we get
$$a = 1,\, b = 3 \text{ and } c = 2\sqrt{2}$$
Now, $D = b^2 - 4ac = (3)^2 - 4(1)(2\sqrt{2})$
$$= 9 - 8\sqrt{2} < 0$$

$\therefore$ Roots of the equation are not real.

(d) Given equation is, $5x^2 - 3x + 1 = 0$

On comparing with $ax^2 + bx + c = 0$, we get
$$a = 5,\, b = -3,\, c = 1$$
Now, $D = b^2 - 4ac = (-3)^2 - 4(5)(1) = 9 - 20 < 0$

Hence, roots of the equation are not real.

19. (a) (a) The given equation is $x^2 - 4x + 3\sqrt{2} = 0$.

On comparing with $ax^2 + bx + c = 0$, we get
$$a = 1,\, b = -4 \text{ and } c = 3\sqrt{2}$$

The discriminant of $x^2 - 4x + 3\sqrt{2} = 0$ is
$$D = b^2 - 4ac$$
$$= (-4)^2 - 4(1)(3\sqrt{2})$$
$$= 16 - 12\sqrt{2} = 16 - 12 \times (1.41)$$
$$= 16 - 16.92 = -0.92$$
$$\Rightarrow \qquad b^2 - 4ac < 0$$

(b) The given equation is $x^2 + 4x - 3\sqrt{2} = 0$

On comparing the equation with $ax^2 + bx + c = 0$, we get
$$a = 1,\, b = 4 \text{ and } c = -3\sqrt{2}$$
Then, $D = b^2 - 4ac = (4)^2 - 4(1)(-3\sqrt{2})$
$$= 16 + 12\sqrt{2} > 0$$

Hence, the equation has real roots.

(c) Given equation is $x^2 - 4x - 3\sqrt{2} = 0$

On comparing the equation with $ax^2 + bx + c = 0$, we get
$$a = 1,\, b = -4 \text{ and } c = -3\sqrt{2}$$
Then, $D = b^2 - 4ac = (-4)^2 - 4(1)(-3\sqrt{2})$
$$= 16 + 12\sqrt{2} > 0$$

Hence, the equation has real roots.

(d) Given equation is $3x^2 + 4\sqrt{3}x + 4 = 0$.

On comparing the equation with $ax^2 + bx + c = 0$, we get
$$a = 3,\, b = 4\sqrt{3} \text{ and } c = 4$$
Then, $D = b^2 - 4ac = (4\sqrt{3})^2 - 4(3)(4)$
$$= 48 - 48 = 0$$

Thus, the equation has real roots.

Hence, $x^2 - 4x + 3\sqrt{2} = 0$ has no real roots.

20. (c) Given equation is $(x^2 + 1)^2 - x^2 = 0$
$$\Rightarrow \qquad x^4 + 1 + 2x^2 - x^2 = 0$$
$$[\because (a + b)^2 = a^2 + b^2 + 2ab]$$
$$\Rightarrow \qquad x^4 + x^2 + 1 = 0$$
$$\text{Let} \qquad x^2 = y$$
$$\therefore \qquad (x^2)^2 + x^2 + 1 = 0$$
$$\Rightarrow \qquad y^2 + y + 1 = 0$$

On comparing with $ay^2 + by + c = 0$, we get
$$a = 1,\, b = 1 \text{ and } c = 1$$
Discriminant, $D = b^2 - 4ac$
$$= (1)^2 - 4(1)(1)$$
$$= 1 - 4 = -3$$

Since, $\qquad D < 0$

$\therefore \qquad y^2 + y + 1 = 0$ i.e. $x^4 + x^2 + 1 = 0$

or $(x^2 + 1)^2 - x^2 = 0$ has no real roots.

21. (b) Let the smallest integer be x. Then, three consecutive integers are $x, x + 1, x + 2$.

From the question,

$x^2 + (x + 1)^2 + (x + 2)^2 = 110$

$\Rightarrow \qquad x^2 + x^2 + 1 + 2x + x^2 + 4 + 4x = 110$

$\Rightarrow \qquad 3x^2 + 6x - 105 = 0$

$\therefore \qquad x = \dfrac{-6 \pm \sqrt{6^2 - 4 \cdot 3 \cdot (-105)}}{2 \times 3}$ [using formula]

$\qquad = \dfrac{-6 \pm \sqrt{36 + 1260}}{6}$

$\qquad = \dfrac{-6 \pm \sqrt{1296}}{6} = \dfrac{-6 \pm 36}{6}$

$\qquad = \dfrac{-6 + 36}{6}, \dfrac{-6 - 36}{6} = \dfrac{30}{6}, \dfrac{-42}{6} = 5, -7$

When $x = 5$,

$\qquad x + 1 = 5 + 1 = 6$

$\qquad x + 2 = 5 + 2 = 7$

When $x = -7$

$\qquad x + 1 = -7 + 1 = -6$

$\qquad x + 2 = -7 + 2 = -5$

$\therefore$ Three consecutive integers are $5, 6, 7$ or $-7, -6, -5$.

Hence, smallest positive integer is 5.

22. (c) Let $BP = x$ cm

Then, $AP = AB + BP = (8 + x)$ cm

$$\underset{A \qquad\qquad\qquad\qquad B \quad P}{\bullet\!\!-\!\!-\!\!-\!\!\overset{8\text{ cm}}{-\!\!-\!\!-\!\!-\!\!-\!\!-}\!\!-\!\!\bullet\!\!-\!\!\overset{x\text{ cm}}{-\!\!-\!\!-\!\!-}\!\!\bullet}$$

Now, $BP^2 = AB \cdot AP \Rightarrow x^2 = 8 \cdot (8 + x)$

$\Rightarrow \quad x^2 - 8x - 64 = 0$

$\therefore \qquad x = \dfrac{-(-8) \pm \sqrt{(-8)^2 - 4 \cdot 1 \cdot (-64)}}{2}$

or $\qquad x = \dfrac{8 \pm \sqrt{64 \times 5}}{2}$

$\qquad = \dfrac{8 \pm 8\sqrt{5}}{2} = 4 \pm 4\sqrt{5}$

But the length of BP is positive.

So, $x = (4 + 4\sqrt{5})$ cm $= 4(\sqrt{5} + 1)$ cm

23. (a) Let present age of his son $= x$ yr

One year ago, his son's age $= (x - 1)$ yr

One year ago, man's age $= 8(x - 1)$ yr

$\qquad\qquad\qquad\qquad = (8x - 8)$ yr

Present age of man $= (8x - 8 + 1)$ yr

$\qquad\qquad\qquad\qquad = (8x - 7)$ yr

According to the question,

$\qquad 8x - 7 = x^2 \Rightarrow x^2 - 8x + 7 = 0$

which is the required quadratic equation.

Now, $x^2 - 7x - x + 7 = 0$ [by factorisation]

$\Rightarrow x(x - 7) - 1(x - 7) = 0$

$\Rightarrow \qquad (x - 7)(x - 1) = 0$

$\Rightarrow \ x - 7 = 0$ or $x - 1 = 0$

$\Rightarrow \qquad\qquad x = 7$ or $x = 1$

But $x = 1$ is not possible because if $x = 1$, then present age of the son and father are same.

So, $x = 7$.

Hence, present age of his son $= 7$ yr

and present age of man $= 8 \times 7 - 7 = 49$ yr.

24. (i) (a) Given, Raj's car travel at a speed of x km/h. Then Ajay's car travels a distance in one hour is $(x + 5)$ km. Therefore, Ajay's car travels a distance in two hours is $2(x + 5)$ km.

(ii) (c) $\because$ Time $= \dfrac{\text{Distance}}{\text{Speed}}$

Time taken by Ajay and Raj to complete the 400 km journey

$$t_1 = \frac{400}{x + 5} \text{ and } t_2 = \frac{400}{x}$$

According to the question,

$$t_2 = t_1 + 4$$

$\therefore \qquad\qquad \dfrac{400}{x} = \dfrac{400}{x + 5} + 4$

$\Rightarrow \qquad\qquad \dfrac{100}{x} = \dfrac{100}{x + 5} + 1$ (divide by 4)

$\Rightarrow \qquad 100(x + 5) = 100x + x(x + 5)$

$\Rightarrow \qquad 100x + 500 = 100x + x^2 + 5x$

$\Rightarrow \qquad x^2 + 5x - 500 = 0$

(iii) (a) Consider the quadratic equation $x^2 + 5x - 500 = 0$

On comparing with $ax^2 + bx + c = 0$, we get

$\qquad\qquad a = 1, b = 5$ and $c = -500$

$\because \qquad x = \dfrac{-b \pm \sqrt{b^2 - 4ac}}{2a}$

$\qquad = \dfrac{-5 \pm \sqrt{(5)^2 - 4 \times (1)(-500)}}{2 \times 1}$

$\qquad = \dfrac{-5 \pm \sqrt{25 + 2000}}{2} = \dfrac{-5 \pm \sqrt{2025}}{2}$

$\qquad = \dfrac{-5 \pm 45}{2} = \dfrac{-50}{2}, \dfrac{40}{2} = -25, 20$

Since, speed cannot be negative, so we consider only, $x = 20$.

Hence, speed of Raj's car is 20 km/h.

(iv) (d) To travel 400 km, time taken by Ajay

$$t_1 = \frac{400}{(x + 5)} = \frac{400}{20 + 5} = \frac{400}{25} = 16\,\text{h}$$

(v) (b) To travel 400 km, time taken by Raj,

$$t_2 = \frac{400}{x} = \frac{400}{20} = 20\,\text{h}$$

25. (i) (c) Since, the speed of stream be x km/h and speed of motorboat is 20 km/h. Therefore, the speed of motorboat in upstream will be $(20 - x)$ km/h.

(ii) (a) The relation between speed, distance and time is
$$\text{Speed} = \frac{\text{Distance}}{\text{Time}}$$

(iii) (c) $\because \ \text{Time} = \dfrac{\text{Distance}}{\text{Speed}}$

Here, distance = 15 km/h

Speed of motorboat in downstream $= (20 + x)$ km/h

and speed of motorboat in upstream $= (20 - x)$ km/h

Time taken by motorboat in downstream and upstream are $t_1 = \dfrac{15}{20 + x}$ h and $t_2 = \dfrac{15}{20 - x}$ h.

According to the question,
$$t_2 = 1 + t_1$$
$$\therefore \qquad \frac{15}{20 - x} = 1 + \frac{15}{20 + x}$$
$$\Rightarrow \qquad \frac{15}{20 - x} - \frac{15}{20 + x} = 1$$
$$\Rightarrow \quad 15\,(20 + x - 20 + x) = (20 + x)(20 - x)$$
$$\Rightarrow \qquad 15(2x) = 400 - x^2$$
$$\Rightarrow \qquad x^2 + 30x - 400 = 0$$

(iv) (b) Consider quadratic equation,
$$x^2 + 30x - 400 = 0$$
$$\Rightarrow \qquad x^2 + (40 - 10)x - 400 = 0$$
$$\Rightarrow \qquad x^2 + 40x - 10x - 400 = 0$$
$$\Rightarrow \qquad x(x + 40) - 10\,(x + 40) = 0$$
$$\Rightarrow \qquad (x - 10)\,(x + 40) = 0$$
$$\Rightarrow \qquad x = 10, -40$$

Since, speed cannot be negative, so we consider only positive value.
$$\therefore \qquad x = 10$$

Hence, speed of current is 10 km/h.

(v) (c) The time taken by motorboat in downstream
$$t_1 = \frac{15}{20 + x}$$
$$= \frac{15}{20 + 10} = \frac{15}{30} = \frac{1}{2}\,\text{h} = 30 \text{ min}$$

26. (i) (c) Given quadratic equation is
$$8x^2 - 22x - 21 = 0$$

On comparing the given equation with
$$ax^2 + bx + c = 0, \text{ we get}$$
$$a = 8, \, b = -22 \text{ and } c = -21$$

By quadratic formula,
$$x = \frac{-(-22) \pm \sqrt{(-22)^2 - 4 \times 8 \times (-21)}}{2 \times 8}$$
$$= \frac{22 \pm \sqrt{484 + 672}}{16} = \frac{22 \pm \sqrt{1156}}{16}$$
$$\Rightarrow \qquad x = \frac{22 \pm 34}{16} = \frac{11 \pm 17}{8}$$

Now, $\qquad x = \dfrac{11 + 17}{8} = \dfrac{28}{8} = \dfrac{7}{2}$ [taking + ve sign]

or $\qquad x = \dfrac{11 - 17}{8} = -\dfrac{6}{8} = -\dfrac{3}{4}$ [taking − ve sign]

Hence, the roots of the given equation are $\dfrac{7}{2}$ and $-\dfrac{3}{4}$.

(ii) (b) Given quadratic equation is $x^2 + x + 7 = 0$.

On comparing with $ax^2 + bx + c$, we get
$$a = 1, \, b = 1 \text{ and } c = 7$$

Now, discriminant $(D) = b^2 - 4ac = 1^2 - 4 \times 1 \times 7$
$$= 1 - 28 = -27$$

(iii) (a) Given equation is $4x^2 - 2x - 3 = 0$

On comparing with $ax^2 + bx + c = 0$, we get
$$a = 4, \, b = -2 \text{ and } c = -3$$
$$\therefore \ \text{Discriminant } (D) = b^2 - 4ac$$
$$= (-2)^2 - 4 \times 4 \times (-3) = 4 + 48 = 52 > 0$$

So, $4x^2 - 2x = 3$ has two distinct real roots.

(iv) (c) Given equation is $4x^2 + kx + 9 = 0$.

On comparing with $ax^2 + bx + c = 0$, we get
$$a = 4, \, b = k \text{ and } c = 9$$

Now, $\qquad D = b^2 - 4ac$
$$= k^2 - 4 \times 4 \times 9 = k^2 - 144$$

Since, roots of given equation are real and equal.
$$\therefore \qquad D = 0$$
$$\Rightarrow \quad k^2 - 144 = 0 \Rightarrow k^2 = 144$$
$$\Rightarrow \qquad k = \pm 12$$

(v) (d) Given equation is $x^2 + kx + 16 = 0$

On comparing with $ax^2 + bx + c = 0$, we get
$$a = 1, \, b = k \text{ and } c = 16$$

Now, $\quad D = b^2 - 4ac$
$$= k^2 - 4 \times 1 \times 16 = k^2 - 64$$

Since, roots of given equation are real.
$$\therefore \qquad D \geq 0$$
$$\Rightarrow \quad k^2 - 64 \geq 0$$
$$\Rightarrow \qquad k^2 \geq 64$$
$$\Rightarrow \qquad k \geq 8 \text{ and } k \leq -8$$

Hence, positive least value of k is 8.

27. (i) (b) Seven years ago,

Swati's age $= x$ yr

Varun's age $= 5x^2$ yr

(ii) (d) Swati's present age $= (x + 7)$ yr

and Varun's present age $= (5x^2 + 7)$ yr

After three years, we have

Swati's age $= (x + 7 + 3) = (x + 10)$ yr

Varun's age $= (5x^2 + 7 + 3) = (5x^2 + 10)$ yr

(iii) (a) According to the question,
$$x + 10 = \frac{2}{5}\,(5x^2 + 10)$$
$$\Rightarrow \qquad 2x^2 - x - 6 = 0$$

(iv) (a) Now, $\qquad 2x^2 - x - 6 = 0$

$\Rightarrow \quad 2x^2 - 4x + 3x - 6 = 0$

$\Rightarrow 2x(x - 2) + 3(x - 2) = 0$

$\Rightarrow \qquad (2x + 3)(x - 2) = 0$

$\Rightarrow \qquad x = -\dfrac{3}{2}, 2$

$\therefore \qquad x = 2 \qquad$ [$\because$ age can't negative]

$\Rightarrow$ Present age of Varun's $= (5x^2 + 7)$ yr

$\qquad = (5 \times 4 + 7)$ yr

$\qquad = (20 + 7)$ yr

$\qquad = 27$ yr

(v) (d) Here, Swati's present age $= 10$ yr

$\Rightarrow \qquad x + 7 = 10$

$\Rightarrow \qquad x = 3$

So, Varun's present age $= (5x^2 + 7)$ yr

$\qquad = 5(3)^2 + 7$

$\qquad = 45 + 7 = 52$ yr

Subjective Questions

1. (i) Given, $(x - 1)(x + 2) = (x - 3)(x + 1)$ $\qquad$ ...(i)

$\text{LHS} = (x - 1)(x + 2) = x^2 + 2x - x - 2$

$\qquad = x^2 + x - 2$

$\text{RHS} = (x - 3)(x + 1) = x^2 + x - 3x - 3$

$\qquad = x^2 - 2x - 3$

On substituting these values in Eq. (i), we get

$\qquad x^2 + x - 2 = x^2 - 2x - 3$

$\Rightarrow \quad x^2 - x^2 + x + 2x - 2 + 3 = 0$

$\Rightarrow \qquad 3x + 1 = 0$

It is not of the form $ax^2 + bx + c = 0, a \neq 0$.

As $a = 0$ and it is an equation of degree 1.

Hence, the given equation does not represent a quadratic equation.

(ii) Given, $(x + 2)^2 = 4(x + 3)$ $\qquad$ ...(ii)

$\qquad x^2 + 4 + 4x = 4x + 12$

$\qquad [\because (a + b)^2 = a^2 + b^2 + 2ab]$

$\Rightarrow \qquad x^2 + 4x - 4x + 4 - 12 = 0$

$\Rightarrow \quad x^2 - 8 = 0$ or $x^2 + 0x - 8 = 0$

It is of the form $ax^2 + bx + c = 0, a \neq 0$.

Hence, given equation represents a quadratic equation.

2. Given equation is

$\qquad Px^2 + (\sqrt{3} - \sqrt{2})x - 1 = 0$

and $x = \dfrac{1}{\sqrt{3}}$ is a root of the equation.

$\therefore \quad P\left(\dfrac{1}{\sqrt{3}}\right)^2 + (\sqrt{3} - \sqrt{2})\dfrac{1}{\sqrt{3}} - 1 = 0$

$\Rightarrow \qquad \dfrac{P}{3} + \dfrac{\sqrt{3} - \sqrt{2} - \sqrt{3}}{\sqrt{3}} = 0$

$\Rightarrow \qquad \dfrac{P}{3} - \dfrac{\sqrt{2}}{\sqrt{3}} = 0$

$\Rightarrow \qquad P = \dfrac{\sqrt{2}}{\sqrt{3}} \times 3$

$\Rightarrow \qquad P = \sqrt{2} \times \sqrt{3} = \sqrt{6}$

$\therefore \qquad P^2 + 1 = (\sqrt{6})^2 + 1$

$\qquad = 6 + 1 = 7$

3. (i) We have,

$\qquad kx^2 + 2x - 3 = 0$, here k is unknown.

Since, $x = 2$ is a solution of given equation, so it will satisfy the given equation.

On putting $x = 2$ in the given equation, we get

$\qquad k(2)^2 + 2(2) - 3 = 0$

$\Rightarrow \qquad 4k + 4 - 3 = 0$

$\Rightarrow \qquad 4k + 1 = 0$

$\Rightarrow \qquad k = \dfrac{-1}{4}$

(ii) We have, $x^2 + 2ax - k = 0$, here k is unknown.

Since, $x = -a$ is a solution of given equation, so it will satisfy the given equation.

On putting $x = -a$ in the given equation, we get

$\qquad (-a)^2 + 2a(-a) - k = 0$

$\Rightarrow \qquad a^2 - 2a^2 - k = 0$

$\Rightarrow \qquad -a^2 - k = 0$

$\Rightarrow \qquad k = -a^2$

4. (i) Given quadratic equation is

$\qquad x^2 - 2kx - 6 = 0$ $\qquad$ ...(i)

Since, $x = 3$ is one of the root of the given quadratic equation. Then, it satisfies the given equation.

So, put $x = 3$ in Eq. (i), we get

$\qquad (3)^2 - 2k(3) - 6 = 0$

$\Rightarrow \qquad 9 - 6k - 6 = 0$

$\Rightarrow \qquad 6k = 3$

$\Rightarrow \qquad k = \dfrac{1}{2}$

(ii) Given quadratic equation is

$\qquad x^2 - kx - \dfrac{5}{4} = 0$

Put $x = \dfrac{1}{2}$, we get

$\qquad \left(\dfrac{1}{2}\right)^2 - k\left(\dfrac{1}{2}\right) - \dfrac{5}{4} = 0$

$\Rightarrow \qquad \dfrac{1}{4} - \dfrac{k}{2} - \dfrac{5}{4} = 0$

$\Rightarrow \qquad \dfrac{1 - 2k - 5}{4} = 0$

$\Rightarrow \qquad 2k = -4$

$\Rightarrow \qquad k = -2$

5. Given equation is in the form $p(x) = 0$, where

$\qquad p(x) = 6x^2 - x - 2$ $\qquad$ ...(i)

On putting $x = \dfrac{-1}{2}$ in Eq. (i), we get

$$p\left(\frac{-1}{2}\right) = 6\left(\frac{-1}{2}\right)^2 - \left(\frac{-1}{2}\right) - 2$$

$$= \frac{6}{4} + \frac{1}{2} - 2 = \frac{6+2-8}{4} = \frac{8-8}{4}$$

$$\Rightarrow \quad p\left(\frac{-1}{2}\right) = 0$$

So, $x = \dfrac{-1}{2}$ is a solution of the given equation.

Now, on putting $x = \dfrac{1}{3}$ in Eq. (i), we get

$$p\left(\frac{1}{3}\right) = 6\left(\frac{1}{3}\right)^2 - \left(\frac{1}{3}\right) - 2$$

$$= 6 \times \frac{1}{9} - \frac{1}{3} - 2 = \frac{6}{9} - \frac{1}{3} - 2$$

$$= \frac{6-3-18}{9} = \frac{-15}{9} \neq 0$$

$$\Rightarrow \quad p\left(\frac{1}{3}\right) \neq 0$$

So, $x = \dfrac{1}{3}$ is not a solution of the given equation.

6. Given, $4\sqrt{3}x^2 + 5x - 2\sqrt{3} = 0$.

On comparing with standard form of quadratic equation

i.e. $ax^2 + bx + c = 0$, we get

$$a = 4\sqrt{3}, b = 5 \text{ and } c = -2\sqrt{3}$$

Here, $ac = 4\sqrt{3} \times (-2\sqrt{3}) = -24$

Then, factors of ac are 8 and -3.

$$\therefore \quad 4\sqrt{3}x^2 + (8-3)x - 2\sqrt{3} = 0$$

$$\Rightarrow \quad 4\sqrt{3}x^2 + 8x - 3x - 2\sqrt{3} = 0$$

$$\Rightarrow \quad 4x(\sqrt{3}x + 2) - \sqrt{3}(\sqrt{3}x + 2) = 0$$

$$\Rightarrow \quad (4x - \sqrt{3})(\sqrt{3}x + 2) = 0$$

$$\Rightarrow \quad 4x - \sqrt{3} = 0$$

$$\text{and} \quad \sqrt{3}x + 2 = 0$$

$$\Rightarrow \quad x = \frac{\sqrt{3}}{4}$$

$$\text{or} \quad x = \frac{-2}{\sqrt{3}}$$

Hence, roots of equation $4\sqrt{3}x^2 + 5x - 2\sqrt{3} = 0$ are $\dfrac{\sqrt{3}}{4}$ and $\dfrac{-2}{\sqrt{3}}$.

7. Given, $\dfrac{16}{x} - 1 = \dfrac{15}{x+1}$

$$\Rightarrow \quad \frac{16}{x} - \frac{15}{x+1} = 1 \Rightarrow \frac{16(x+1) - 15x}{x(x+1)} = 1$$

$$\Rightarrow \quad 16x + 16 - 15x = x^2 + x$$

$$\Rightarrow \quad x^2 = 16$$

$$\Rightarrow \quad x^2 = \pm 4$$

Hence, the roots are 4 and -4.

8. Given that, $ax^2 + a = a^2x + x$

$$\Rightarrow \quad ax^2 - a^2x - x + a = 0$$

$$\Rightarrow \quad ax(x - a) - 1(x - a) = 0$$

$$\Rightarrow \quad (ax - 1)(x - a) = 0$$

$$\Rightarrow \quad x = \frac{1}{a}, a$$

9. Given that, $\sqrt{6x + 7} - (2x - 7) = 0$

$$\Rightarrow \quad \sqrt{6x + 7} = 2x - 7$$

On squaring both sides, we get

$$6x + 7 = (2x - 7)^2$$

$$6x + 7 = 4x^2 + 49 - 28x$$

$$\Rightarrow \quad 4x^2 - 34x + 42 = 0$$

$$\Rightarrow \quad 2x^2 - 17x + 21 = 0 \qquad \text{[divide by 2]}$$

$$\Rightarrow \quad 2x^2 + 14x + 3x + 21 = 0$$

$$\Rightarrow \quad 2x(x + 7) + 3(x + 7) = 0$$

$$\Rightarrow \quad (2x + 3)(x + 7) = 0$$

$$\Rightarrow \quad x = -\frac{3}{2}, -7$$

10. Given equation is $x^2 - 7x - 18 = 0$

$$\Rightarrow \quad x^2 - 9x + 2x - 18 = 0$$

$$\Rightarrow x(x - 9) + 2(x - 9) = 0$$

$$\Rightarrow \quad (x + 2)(x - 9) = 0$$

$$\Rightarrow \quad x = -2, 9$$

So, the roots of given equation are -2 and 9.

$\therefore$ Required numerical difference of the roots

$$= 9 - (-2) = 11$$

11. The given equation is $\sqrt{3}x^2 + 11x + 6\sqrt{3} = 0$.

On comparing with $ax^2 + bx + c = 0$, we get

$$a = \sqrt{3}, b = 11 \text{ and } c = 6\sqrt{3}$$

On substituting the values of a, b and c in the quadratic formula,

$$x = \frac{-b \pm \sqrt{b^2 - 4ac}}{2a}$$

$$\Rightarrow \quad x = \frac{-11 \pm \sqrt{(11)^2 - 4(\sqrt{3})(6\sqrt{3})}}{2(\sqrt{3})}$$

$$= \frac{-11 \pm \sqrt{121 - 72}}{2\sqrt{3}}$$

$$= \frac{-11 \pm \sqrt{49}}{2\sqrt{3}}$$

$$= \frac{-11 \pm 7}{2\sqrt{3}}$$

$$\Rightarrow \quad x = \frac{-11 + 7}{2\sqrt{3}} = \frac{-4}{2\sqrt{3}} = \frac{-2}{\sqrt{3}} \qquad \text{[taking +ve sign]}$$

$$\text{and} \quad x = \frac{-11 - 7}{2\sqrt{3}} = \frac{-18}{2\sqrt{3}} = \frac{-9}{\sqrt{3}} \qquad \text{[taking −ve sign]}$$

Hence, $\dfrac{-2}{\sqrt{3}}$ and $\dfrac{-9}{\sqrt{3}}$ (or $\dfrac{-2\sqrt{3}}{3}$ and $-3\sqrt{3}$) are the required solutions of the given equation.

12. Given equation is $5x^2 - sx + 4 = 0$

On comparing with $ax^2 + bx + c = 0$, we get

$$a = 5,\ b = -s\ \text{and}\ c = 4$$

$\therefore$ Discriminant $(D) = b^2 - 4ac$

$$= (-s)^2 - 4 \times 5 \times 4$$

$$= s^2 - 80$$

Given, $\qquad D = 1$

$\Rightarrow \qquad s^2 - 80 = 1$

$\Rightarrow \qquad s^2 = 81$

$\Rightarrow \qquad s = \pm\, 9$

13. Given that,

$$(x^2 + 1)^2 - x^2 = 0$$

$\Rightarrow \qquad (x^2 + 1)^2 = x^2 \Rightarrow x$

$\Rightarrow \qquad x^2 + 1 = \pm\, x$

$\Rightarrow \qquad x^2 \mp x + 1 = 0$

On comparing with $ax^2 + bx + c$, we get

$$a = 1,\ b = \mp\, 1\ \text{and}\ c = 1$$

$\therefore \qquad D = b^2 - 4ac$

$$= (\mp\, 1)^2 - 4 \times 1 \times 1$$

$$= 1 - 4 = -3 < 0$$

$\therefore$ It has no real roots.

14. Given equation is $2x^2 - kx + k = 0$

On comparing with $ax^2 + bx + c = 0$, we get

$$a = 2,\ b = -k\ \text{and}\ c = k$$

$\therefore \qquad D = b^2 - 4ac$

$$= (-k)^2 - 4 \times 2 \times k$$

$$= k^2 - 8k$$

Since, the given equation has equal roots.

$\therefore \qquad\qquad D = 0$

$\Rightarrow \qquad k^2 - 8k = 0$

$\Rightarrow \qquad k\,(k - 8) = 0$

$\Rightarrow \qquad k = 0,\ 8$

15. Given quadratic equation is

$$9x^2 + 3kx + 4 = 0$$

On comparing with $ax^2 + bx + c = 0$, we get

$$a = 9,\ b = 3k\ \text{and}\ c = 4$$

Now, $D = b^2 - 4ac = (3k)^2 - 4(9)(4)$

$$= 9k^2 - 144$$

Since, roots of given equation are real.

$\therefore \quad D \geq 0 \Rightarrow 9k^2 - 144 \geq 0$

$\Rightarrow \qquad 9(k^2 - 16) \geq 0$

$\therefore \qquad k^2 - 16 \geq 0 \qquad\qquad [\because 9 \neq 0]$

$\Rightarrow \qquad k^2 - (4)^2 \geq 0$

$\Rightarrow \qquad (k - 4)(k + 4) \geq 0 \qquad [\because a^2 - b^2 = (a - b)(a + b)]$

$\Rightarrow \qquad k \leq -4\ \text{or}\ k \geq 4$

16. Given equation is

$$(1 + m^2)x^2 + (2mc)x + (c^2 - a^2) = 0$$

On comparing with $Ax^2 + Bx + C = 0$, we get

$$A = (1 + m^2),\ B = 2mc\ \text{and}\ C = (c^2 - a^2)$$

Since, the given equation has equal roots.

$\therefore \quad$ Discriminant, $D = 0 \Rightarrow B^2 - 4AC = 0$

$\Rightarrow \qquad (2mc)^2 - 4(1 + m^2)(c^2 - a^2) = 0$

$\Rightarrow \quad 4m^2c^2 - 4(c^2 - a^2 + m^2c^2 - m^2a^2) = 0$

$\Rightarrow \quad m^2c^2 - (c^2 - a^2 + m^2c^2 - m^2a^2) = 0 \ \text{[dividing by 4]}$

$\Rightarrow \quad m^2c^2 - c^2 + a^2 - m^2c^2 + m^2a^2 = 0$

$\Rightarrow \qquad\qquad -c^2 + a^2 + m^2a^2 = 0$

$\Rightarrow \qquad\qquad -c^2 + a^2(1 + m^2) = 0$

$\Rightarrow \qquad\qquad -c^2 = -a^2(1 + m^2)$

$\Rightarrow \qquad\qquad c^2 = a^2(1 + m^2) \qquad$ **Hence proved.**

17. Let one number be x.

Then, another number $= (11 - x)$

$$[\because \text{sum of two numbers} = 11,\ \text{given}]$$

According to the question,

$$\frac{1}{x} + \frac{1}{(11 - x)} = \frac{11}{28}$$

$\Rightarrow \qquad \dfrac{11 - x + x}{x(11 - x)} = \dfrac{11}{28}$

$\Rightarrow \qquad x(11 - x) = 28$

$\Rightarrow \qquad x^2 - 11x + 28 = 0$

$\Rightarrow \qquad x^2 - (7 + 4)x + 28 = 0$

$\Rightarrow \qquad x^2 - 7x - 4x + 28 = 0$

$\Rightarrow \qquad x(x - 7) - 4(x - 7) = 0$

$\Rightarrow \qquad (x - 7)(x - 4) = 0$

$\Rightarrow \qquad x = 4\ \text{or}\ x = 7$

When $x = 4$, then $11 - x = 11 - 4 = 7$

When $x = 7$, then $11 - x = 11 - 7 = 4$

Hence, the numbers are 4 and 7.

18. Let the number of wickets taken by Zaheer in a cricket match are x, then number of wickets taken by Harbhajan

$$= 2x - 3$$

According to the question,

$$x\,(2x - 3) = 20$$

$\Rightarrow \qquad 2x^2 - 3x = 20$

$\Rightarrow \qquad 2x^2 - 3x - 20 = 0$

19. Given, $3x^2 - 2ax + 2b = 0 \qquad\qquad\qquad ...(i)$

Here, a and b are unknown constants. Since, $x = 2$ and $x = 3$ are the solutions of given equation, so it will satisfy the given equation.

On putting $x = 2$ and $x = 3$ one-by-one,

in Eq. (i), we get

$$3(2)^2 - 2a \times (2) + 2b = 0$$

$\Rightarrow \qquad 3 \times 4 - 4a + 2b = 0$

$\Rightarrow \qquad 12 - 4a + 2b = 0$

$\Rightarrow \qquad -2(2a - b - 6) = 0$

$\Rightarrow \qquad\qquad 2a - b = 6 \qquad [\because -2 \neq 0] \;\;...(ii)$

and $\qquad 3(3)^2 - 2a \times 3 + 2b = 0$

$\Rightarrow \qquad\qquad 27 - 6a + 2b = 0$

$\Rightarrow \qquad\qquad 6a - 2b = 27 \qquad\qquad ... (iii)$

On multiplying Eq. (ii) by 2 and then subtract it from Eq. (iii), we get

$$6a - 2b - 4a + 2b = 27 - 12$$

$\Rightarrow \qquad\qquad 2a = 15 \Rightarrow a = \dfrac{15}{2}$

On substituting $a = \dfrac{15}{2}$ in Eq. (ii), we get

$$2 \times \dfrac{15}{2} - b = 6$$

$\Rightarrow \qquad\qquad 15 - b = 6$

$\Rightarrow \qquad\qquad b = 15 - 6 = 9$

$\Rightarrow \qquad\qquad b = 9$

Hence, the required values of a and b are 15/2 and 9, respectively.

20. (i) Given quadratic equation is

$$4x^2 + 12x + 9 = 0$$

On comparing with $ax^2 + bx + c = 0$, we get

$$a = 4, \, b = 12 \text{ and } c = 9$$

Now, $\quad D = b^2 - 4ac = (12)^2 - 4(4)(9)$

$$= 144 - 144 = 0$$

Since, $D = 0$, so given quadratic equation has two equal and real roots which are given by

$$x = \dfrac{-b \pm \sqrt{D}}{2a} = \dfrac{-12 \pm 0}{2(4)}$$

$\Rightarrow \qquad x = \dfrac{-12 + 0}{8} \text{ or } x = \dfrac{-12 - 0}{8}$

$\Rightarrow \qquad x = -\dfrac{3}{2} \text{ or } x = -\dfrac{3}{2}$

Hence, the roots are $\dfrac{-3}{2}$ and $-\dfrac{3}{2}$.

(ii) Given quadratic equation is

$$3x^2 + 5x - 7 = 0$$

On comparing with $ax^2 + bx + c = 0$, we get

$$a = 3, \, b = 5 \text{ and } c = -7$$

Now, $D = b^2 - 4ac = (5)^2 - 4(3)(-7) = 25 + 84 = 109$

Since, $D > 0$, so given quadratic equation has two distinct real roots which are given by

$$x = \dfrac{-b \pm \sqrt{D}}{2a} = \dfrac{-5 \pm \sqrt{109}}{2(3)}$$

$\Rightarrow \qquad x = \dfrac{-5 + \sqrt{109}}{6} \qquad [\text{taking +ve sign}]$

or $\qquad x = \dfrac{-5 - \sqrt{109}}{6} \qquad [\text{taking -ve sign}]$

Hence, the roots are $\dfrac{-5 + \sqrt{109}}{6}$ and $\dfrac{-5 - \sqrt{109}}{6}$.

21. Given quadratic equation is

$$(k - 12) x^2 + 2(k - 12) x + 2 = 0$$

On comparing with $ax^2 + bx + c = 0$, we get

$$a = k - 12, \, b = 2(k - 12) \text{ and } c = 2$$

Now, $\quad D = b^2 - 4ac$

$$= [2(k - 12)]^2 - 4(k - 12)(2)$$

$$= 4(k - 12)^2 - 8(k - 12)$$

$$= (k - 12)[4(k - 12) - 8]$$

$$= (k - 12)(4k - 48 - 8)$$

$$= (k - 12)(4k - 56)$$

Since, roots of given equation are equal.

$\therefore \qquad\qquad D = 0$

$\Rightarrow \qquad (k - 12)(4k - 56) = 0$

$\Rightarrow \qquad k - 12 = 0 \text{ or } 4k - 56 = 0$

$\Rightarrow \qquad k = 12 \text{ or } k = \dfrac{56}{4}$

$\Rightarrow \qquad k = 12 \text{ or } k = 14$

But $k = 12$ does not satisfy the given equation because if $k = 12$, then coefficients of x^2 and x become zero.

Hence, required value of k is 14.

22. Given equation is $3x^2 + 7x + p = 0$

Since, $x = -2$ is a root of the given equation, so it will satisfy the given equation.

On putting $x = -2$ in the given equation, we get

$$3(-2)^2 + 7(-2) + p = 0$$

$\Rightarrow \qquad\qquad 12 - 14 + p = 0$

$\Rightarrow \qquad\qquad -2 + p = 0$

$\Rightarrow \qquad\qquad p = 2$

On putting $p = 2$ in $x^2 + k(4x + k - 1) + p = 0$, we get

$$x^2 + k(4x + k - 1) + 2 = 0$$

$\Rightarrow \qquad x^2 + 4kx + (k^2 - k + 2) = 0$

On comparing with $ax^2 + bx + c = 0$, we get

$$a = 1, \, b = 4k \text{ and } c = k^2 - k + 2$$

$\therefore \qquad\qquad D = b^2 - 4ac$

$$= (4k)^2 - 4 \times 1 \times (k^2 - k + 2)$$

$$= 16k^2 - 4k^2 + 4k - 8$$

$$= 12k^2 + 4k - 8$$

Since, roots are equal.

$\therefore \qquad\qquad D = 0$

$\Rightarrow \qquad 12k^2 + 4k - 8 = 0 \qquad [\text{divide by 4}]$

$\Rightarrow \qquad\qquad 3k^2 + k - 2 = 0$

$\Rightarrow \qquad 3k^2 + 3k - 2k - 2 = 0$

$\Rightarrow \qquad 3k(k + 1) - 2(k + 1) = 0$

$\Rightarrow \qquad (3k - 2)(k + 1) = 0$

$\Rightarrow \qquad\qquad k = \dfrac{2}{3}, -1$

23. Let two consecutive odd natural numbers are x and $x + 2$.
Then according to the given condition,

$$x^2 + (x + 2)^2 = 130$$
$$\Rightarrow \quad x^2 + x^2 + 4x + 4 = 130$$
$$\Rightarrow \quad 2x^2 + 4x - 126 = 0$$
$$\Rightarrow \quad x^2 + 2x - 63 = 0 \qquad \text{[divide by 2]}$$
$$\Rightarrow \quad x^2 + 9x - 7x - 63 = 0$$
$$\Rightarrow \quad x(x + 9) - 7(x + 9) = 0$$
$$\Rightarrow \quad (x - 7)(x + 9) = 0$$
$$\Rightarrow \quad x = 7, -9$$

Since, natural number cannot be negative.
So, we neglect $x = -9$.
Thus, $x = 7$ and $x + 2 = 7 + 2 = 9$
Hence, two consecutive odd numbers are 7 and 9.

24. Let the length of piece be x m.

Then, rate $= ₹ \dfrac{200}{x}$ per m

Now, new length $= (x + 5)$ m
Since, the cost remains same.

$\therefore$ New rate $= ₹ \dfrac{200}{x + 5}$ per m

According to the given condition,

$$\dfrac{200}{x + 5} = \dfrac{200}{x} - 2$$
$$\Rightarrow \quad \dfrac{200}{x + 5} = 2\left(\dfrac{100 - x}{x}\right)$$
$$\Rightarrow \quad 100x = (x + 5)(100 - x)$$
$$\Rightarrow \quad 100x = 100x - x^2 + 500 - 5x$$
$$\Rightarrow \quad x^2 + 5x - 500 = 0$$
$$\Rightarrow \quad x^2 + 25x - 20x - 500 = 0$$
$$\Rightarrow \quad x(x + 25) - 20(x + 25) = 0$$
$$\Rightarrow \quad (x - 20)(x + 25) = 0$$
$$\Rightarrow \quad x = 20, -25$$

Since, length of piece cannot be negative, so neglect $x = -25$.
Thus, $x = 20$

Now, rate $= \dfrac{200}{x} = \dfrac{200}{20} = ₹\, 10$

Hence, length of piece is ₹ 20 m and rate per metre is ₹ 10.

25. Let first number be x.
Then, second number $= x + 4$

$$[\because \text{ difference of two numbers } = 4]$$

According to the question,

$$\dfrac{1}{x} - \dfrac{1}{x + 4} = \dfrac{4}{21}$$
$$\Rightarrow \quad \dfrac{(x + 4) - x}{x(x + 4)} = \dfrac{4}{21} \Rightarrow \dfrac{4}{x^2 + 4x} = \dfrac{4}{21}$$
$$\Rightarrow \quad x^2 + 4x = 21 \Rightarrow x^2 + 4x - 21 = 0$$
$$\Rightarrow \quad x^2 + (7 - 3)x - 21 = 0 \Rightarrow x^2 + 7x - 3x - 21 = 0$$
$$\Rightarrow \quad x(x + 7) - 3(x + 7) = 0 \Rightarrow (x - 3)(x + 7) = 0$$
$$\Rightarrow \quad x = -7, 3$$

When $x = -7$, then second number $= -7 + 4 = -3$
When $x = 3$, then second number $= 3 + 4 = 7$
Hence, two numbers are $-7, -3$ or $3, 7$.

26. Let one side $= x$.

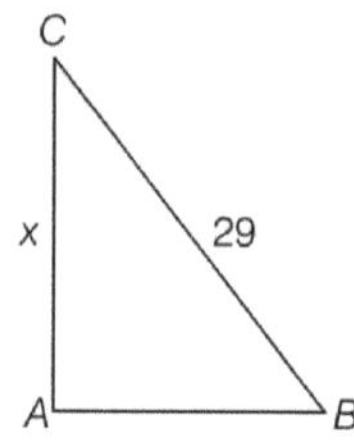

Now, perimeter of a triangle,

$$70 = x + 29 + AB$$
$$\Rightarrow \quad AB = 70 - 29 - x = 41 - x.$$

In right $\triangle ABC$, use Pythagoras theorem,

$$BC^2 = AC^2 + AB^2$$
$$\Rightarrow \quad (29)^2 = x^2 + (41 - x)^2$$
$$\Rightarrow \quad 841 = x^2 + 1681 + x^2 - 82x$$
$$\Rightarrow \quad 2x^2 - 82x + 840 = 0$$
$$\Rightarrow \quad x^2 - 41x + 420 = 0 \qquad \text{[divide by 2]}$$
$$\Rightarrow \quad x^2 - 21x - 20x + 420 = 0$$
$$\Rightarrow \quad x(x - 21) - 20(x - 21) = 0$$
$$\Rightarrow \quad (x - 20)(x - 21) = 0$$
$$\Rightarrow \quad x = 20, 21$$

Hence, length of other sides of a $\triangle ABC$ are 20 units, 21 units.

27. Let present age of Anjali be x yr.

$\therefore$ Anjali's age 3 yr ago $= (x - 3)$ yr
and Anjali's age 5 yr from now $= (x + 5)$ yr
According to the question,

$$\dfrac{1}{x - 3} + \dfrac{1}{x + 5} = \dfrac{1}{3}$$
$$\Rightarrow \quad \dfrac{x + 5 + x - 3}{(x - 3)(x + 5)} = \dfrac{1}{3}$$
$$\Rightarrow \quad \dfrac{2x + 2}{x^2 - 3x + 5x - 15} = \dfrac{1}{3}$$
$$\Rightarrow \quad 3(2x + 2) = x^2 + 2x - 15$$
$$\Rightarrow \quad 6x + 6 = x^2 + 2x - 15$$
$$\Rightarrow \quad x^2 + 2x - 15 - 6x - 6 = 0$$
$$\Rightarrow \quad x^2 - 4x - 21 = 0,$$

which is the required quadratic equation.
Now, by factorisation method, we get

$$x^2 - 7x + 3x - 21 = 0$$
$$\Rightarrow \quad x(x - 7) + 3(x - 7) = 0$$
$$\Rightarrow \quad (x - 7)(x + 3) = 0$$
$$\Rightarrow \quad x - 7 = 0 \text{ or } x + 3 = 0$$
$$\Rightarrow \quad x = 7 \text{ or } x = -3$$

But $x = -3$ is not possible because age cannot be negative.
$\therefore \quad x = 7$
Hence, Anjali's present age is 7 yr.

28. Let the ten's digit of the number be x.

According to the question,

Product of the digits $= 12$

i.e. Ten's digit $\times$ Unit's digit $= 12$

$\Rightarrow \qquad$ Unit's digit $= \dfrac{12}{x} \qquad$ [$\because$ ten's digit $= x$]

$\therefore \qquad$ Two-digit number $= 10x + \dfrac{12}{x}$

Also, it is given that if 36 is added to the number, the digits get interchange.

$\therefore \qquad 10x + \dfrac{12}{x} + 36 = 10 \times \dfrac{12}{x} + x$

$\Rightarrow \qquad 10x^2 + 12 + 36x = 120 + x^2$

$\Rightarrow \qquad 9x^2 - 108 + 36x = 0$

$\Rightarrow \qquad x^2 + 4x - 12 = 0 \qquad$ [divide both sides by 9]

which is the required quadratic equation.

By factorisation method, we get

$\qquad x^2 + 6x - 2x - 12 = 0$

$\Rightarrow \qquad x(x + 6) - 2(x + 6) = 0$

$\Rightarrow \qquad (x + 6)(x - 2) = 0$

$\Rightarrow \qquad x + 6 = 0$ or $x - 2 = 0$

$\Rightarrow \qquad x = -6$ or $x = 2$

But a digit can never be negative.

So, $x = 2$.

Hence, the required two-digit number

$\qquad = 10 \times 2 + \dfrac{12}{2} = 20 + 6 = 26$

29. Given, John and Janvi together have 45 marbles.

Let John has x marbles.

Then, number of marbles Janvi has $= 45 - x$

$\because$ Both of them lost 5 marbles each.

$\therefore$ The number of marbles John has $= x - 5$

and the number of marbles Janvi has $= 45 - x - 5 = 40 - x$

Now, product of the number of marbles $= 124$

$\therefore \qquad (x - 5)(40 - x) = 124$

$\Rightarrow \qquad 40x - x^2 - 200 + 5x = 124$

$\Rightarrow \qquad -x^2 + 45x - 200 - 124 = 0$

$\Rightarrow \qquad -x^2 + 45x - 324 = 0$

$\Rightarrow \qquad x^2 - 45x + 324 = 0 \qquad$ [multiplying by (-1)]

which is the required quadratic equation.

Now, by factorisation method, we get

$\qquad x^2 - 36x - 9x + 324 = 0$

$\Rightarrow \qquad x(x - 36) - 9(x - 36) = 0$

$\Rightarrow \qquad (x - 36)(x - 9) = 0$

$\Rightarrow \qquad x - 36 = 0$ or $x - 9 = 0$

$\Rightarrow \qquad x = 36$ or $x = 9$

when John has 36 marbles, then

Janvi has $= 45 - 36 = 9$ marbles.

when John has 9 marbles, then

Janvi has $= 45 - 9 = 36$ marbles.

30. Let length of the shortest side $= x$ m.

Then, hypotenuse $= (2x + 6)$ m and

$\qquad$ third side $= (2x + 6 - 2)$ m $= (2x + 4)$ m

By Pythagoras theorem,

$\qquad (2x + 6)^2 = x^2 + (2x + 4)^2$

$\qquad$ [$\because$ (Hypotenuse)^2 = (Perpendicular)^2 + (Base)^2]

$\Rightarrow 4x^2 + 24x + 36 = x^2 + 4x^2 + 16x + 16$

$\qquad$ [$\because (a + b)^2 = a^2 + 2ab + b^2$]

$\Rightarrow x^2 + 4x^2 + 16x + 16 - 4x^2 - 24x - 36 = 0$

$\Rightarrow \qquad x^2 - 8x - 20 = 0$

By quadratic formula,

$\qquad x = \dfrac{-(-8) \pm \sqrt{(-8)^2 - 4 \times 1 \times (-20)}}{2 \times 1}$

$\left[\because x = \dfrac{-b \pm \sqrt{b^2 - 4ac}}{2a}; \text{ here } a = 1, b = -8 \text{ and } c = -20\right]$

$\Rightarrow \qquad x = \dfrac{8 \pm \sqrt{64 + 80}}{2} \Rightarrow x = \dfrac{8 \pm \sqrt{144}}{2}$

$\Rightarrow \qquad x = \dfrac{8 \pm 12}{2}$

$\Rightarrow \qquad x = \dfrac{8 + 12}{2}$ or $x = \dfrac{8 - 12}{2}$

$\Rightarrow \qquad x = \dfrac{20}{2}$ or $x = \dfrac{-4}{2}$

$\Rightarrow \qquad x = 10$ or $x = -2$

But length of side cannot be negative.

$\therefore \qquad x = 10$

Hence, shortest side is 10 m, hypotenuse is $2 \times 10 + 6 = 26$ m and third side $= 2 \times 10 + 4 = 24$ m.

31. Let Nisha's present age be x yr.

Then, Asha's present age $= x^2 + 2 \qquad$ [by given condition]

Now, when Nisha grows to her mother's present age.

Then, Asha's age will be $[(x^2 + 2) - x]$ yr.

Again by given condition,

Age of Asha = One year less than 10 times the present age of Nisha

$\qquad (x^2 + 2) + \{(x^2 + 2) - x\} = 10x - 1$

$\Rightarrow \qquad 2x^2 - x + 4 = 10x - 1$

$\Rightarrow \qquad 2x^2 - 11x + 5 = 0$

$\Rightarrow \qquad 2x^2 - 10x - x + 5 = 0$

$\Rightarrow \qquad 2x(x - 5) - 1(x - 5) = 0$

$\Rightarrow \qquad (x - 5)(2x - 1) = 0$

$\therefore \qquad x = 5$

$\left[\text{here, } x = \dfrac{1}{2} \text{ cannot be possible, because at } x = \dfrac{1}{2},\right.$

$\left. \text{Asha's age is } 2\dfrac{1}{4} \text{ yr which is not possible}\right]$

Hence, required age of Nisha $= 5$ yr

and required age of Asha $= x^2 + 2$

$\qquad = (5)^2 + 2 = 25 + 2 = 27$ yr

32. Let speed of the stream $= x$ km/h

Given, speed of boat in still water $= 15$ km/h

$\therefore$ Speed of boat upstream $= (15 - x)$ km/h

and speed of boat downstream $= (15 + x)$ km/h

According to the question,

$$\frac{30}{15 - x} + \frac{30}{15 + x} = 4\frac{1}{2}$$

$$\left[\because \text{time} = \frac{\text{distance}}{\text{speed}} \text{ and distance} = 30 \text{ km} \right.$$

$$\left. \text{and also, 4h 30 min} = \left(4 + \frac{30}{60}\right) \text{h} = 4\frac{1}{2}\text{h} \right]$$

$$\Rightarrow \qquad \frac{30(15 + x) + 30(15 - x)}{(15 - x)(15 + x)} = \frac{9}{2}$$

$$\Rightarrow \qquad \frac{450 + 30x + 450 - 30x}{(15)^2 - x^2} = \frac{9}{2}$$

$$\left[\because (A - B)(A + B) = A^2 - B^2 \right]$$

$$\Rightarrow \qquad \frac{900}{225 - x^2} = \frac{9}{2}$$

$$\Rightarrow \quad \frac{900 \times 2}{9} = 225 - x^2 \Rightarrow 200 = 225 - x^2 \Rightarrow x^2 = 25$$

$$\Rightarrow \qquad x = \pm 5 \quad \text{[taking square root on both sides]}$$

But speed cannot be negative.

$\therefore \ x = 5$

Hence, speed of stream is 5 km/h.

33. Let the time taken by smaller tap to fill tank completely $= x$ h

So, volume of tank filled by smaller tap in 1 h $= \dfrac{1}{x}$

Volume of tank filled by larger tap in 1 h $= \dfrac{1}{x - 2}$

Now, time taken by both taps to fill $= 1\dfrac{7}{8} = \dfrac{15}{8}$ h

Tank filled by smaller tap in $\dfrac{15}{8}$ h $= \dfrac{1}{x} \times \dfrac{15}{8} = \dfrac{15}{8x}$

Tank filled by larger tap in $\dfrac{15}{8}$ h $= \dfrac{1}{x - 2} \times \dfrac{15}{8} = \dfrac{15}{8(x - 2)}$

Therefore, $\dfrac{15}{8x} + \dfrac{15}{8(x - 2)} = 1 \ \Rightarrow \ \dfrac{15}{8}\left[\dfrac{1}{x} + \dfrac{1}{x - 2}\right] = 1$

$$\Rightarrow \qquad \frac{2(x - 1)}{x^2 - 2x} = \frac{8}{15} \Rightarrow 15(x - 1) = 4(x^2 - 2x)$$

$$\Rightarrow \qquad 15x - 15 = 4x^2 - 8x$$

$$\Rightarrow \qquad 23x = 4x^2 + 15$$

$$\Rightarrow \qquad 4x^2 - 23x + 15 = 0$$

By using quadratic formula

$$x = \frac{-(-23) \pm \sqrt{(-23)^2 - 4 \cdot 4 \cdot 15}}{2 \cdot 4} \Rightarrow x = \frac{23 \pm \sqrt{529 - 240}}{8}$$

$$\Rightarrow \qquad x = \frac{23 \pm \sqrt{289}}{8} \Rightarrow x = \frac{23 \pm 17}{8}$$

Taking positive sign, $x = \dfrac{23 + 17}{8} = \dfrac{40}{8} = 5$

Taking negative sign, $x = \dfrac{23 - 17}{8} = \dfrac{6}{8} = \dfrac{3}{4}$

When, $x = 5$

Time taken by smaller tap $= 5$ h

Time taken by larger tap $= x - 2 = 5 - 2 = 3$ h

When, $x = \dfrac{3}{4}$

Time taken by smaller tap $= \dfrac{3}{4}$ h

Time taken by larger tap $= x - 2$

$$= \frac{3}{4} - 2 = \frac{-5}{4}, \text{ which is not solution.}$$

Hence, time taken by smaller tap $= 5$ h and time taken by larger tap $= 3$ h.

34. (i) Given that a rectangular pond has to be constructed in the centre of a rectangular lawn of dimensions 50 m $\times$ 40 m.

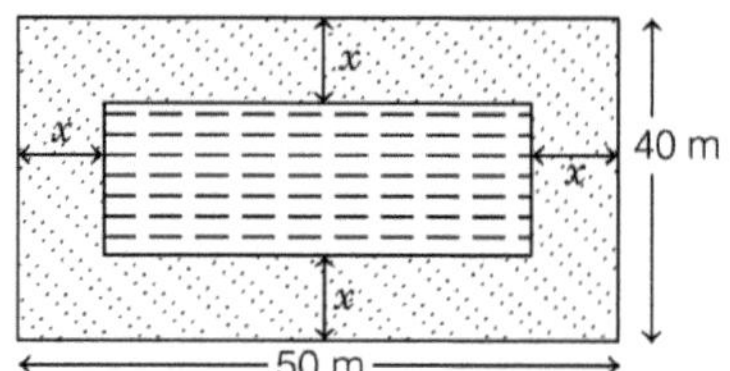

Now, length of rectangular lawn

$$(l_1) = 50 \text{ m}$$

and breadth of rectangular lawn

$$(b_1) = 40 \text{ m}$$

$\therefore$ Length of rectangular pond

$$(l_2) = 50 - (x + x) = 50 - 2x$$

and breadth of rectangular pond

$$(b_2) = 40 - (x + x) = 40 - 2x$$

(ii) Given, area of the grass surrounding the pond $= 1184$ m^2

$\therefore$ Area of rectangular lawn $-$ Area of rectangular pond

$$= \text{Area of grass surrounding the pond}$$

$$l_1 \times b_1 - l_2 \times b_2 = 1184$$

$$\qquad [\because \text{area of rectangle} = \text{length} \times \text{breadth}]$$

$$\Rightarrow \qquad 50 \times 40 - (50 - 2x)(40 - 2x) = 1184$$

$$\Rightarrow \quad 2000 - (2000 - 80x - 100x + 4x^2) = 1184$$

$$\Rightarrow \qquad 80x + 100x - 4x^2 = 1184$$

$$\Rightarrow \qquad 4x^2 - 180x + 1184 = 0$$

$$\Rightarrow \qquad x^2 - 45x + 296 = 0 \quad \text{[divide by 4]}$$

(iii) Now, $x^2 - 4.5x + 296 = 0 \Rightarrow x^2 - 37x - 8x + 296 = 0$

$$\text{[by splitting the middle term]}$$

$$\Rightarrow x(x - 37) - 8(x - 37) = 0$$

$$\Rightarrow \qquad (x - 37)(x - 8) = 0$$

$$\therefore \qquad x = 8$$

[at $x = 37$, length and breadth of pond are -24 and -34, respectively but length and breadth cannot be negative. So, $x = 37$ cannot be possible]

$\therefore$ Length of pond $= 50 - 2x = 50 - 2(8)$

$$= 50 - 16 = 34 \text{ m}$$

and breadth of pond $= 40 - 2x$

$$= 40 - 2(8) = 40 - 16 = 24 \text{ m}$$

Hence, required length and breadth of pond are 34 m and 24 m, respectively.

Chapter Test

Multiple Choice Questions

1. Is -8 a solution of the equation
$3x^2 + 8x + 2 = 0$? **[NCERT Exemplar]**
(a) Yes
(b) No
(c) Cannot be determined
(d) None of the above

2. Solve the quadratic equation
$$x^2 - 14x + 24 = 0$$ **[CBSE 2013]**
(a) 2, 12
(b) 3, 8
(c) 8, 3
(d) None of these

3. The roots of a equation $2x^2 + 5\sqrt{2}x + 5 = 0$ are
(a) $\dfrac{-5\sqrt{2} \pm \sqrt{5}}{2}$
(b) $\dfrac{-5\sqrt{2} \pm \sqrt{10}}{4}$
(c) $\dfrac{-5\sqrt{2} \pm \sqrt{10}}{5}$
(d) None of these

4. The quadratic equation $7y^2 - 4y + 5 = 0$ has
(a) Real and distinct
(b) Real and equal
(c) Imaginary
(d) More than 2 real roots

5. If a number is added to twice its square, then the resultant is 21. The quadratic representation of this situation is **[CBSE 2014, 15]**
(a) $2x^2 + x - 21 = 0$
(b) $2x^2 + x + 21 = 0$
(c) $2x^2 - x + 21 = 0$
(d) $2x^2 - x - 21 = 0$

Case Study MCQs

6. Sohan is preparing for UPSC exam. For this, he has to practice the chapter of quadratic equations. So, he started with factorisation method.

Let two roots of $ax^2 + bx + c$ be p and q.
$$\therefore \quad ac = p \times q \text{ and } p + q = b$$

Now, factorize each of the following quadratic equations and find the roots.

(i) $x^2 - 10x + 21 = 0$
(a) 9, 3
(b) 21, 1
(c) 3, 7
(d) 3, 9

(ii) $15y^2 - 41y - 14 = 0$
(a) $\dfrac{3}{7}, \dfrac{2}{3}$
(b) $\dfrac{3}{5}, \dfrac{7}{2}$
(c) $\dfrac{2}{3}, \dfrac{7}{5}$
(d) $\dfrac{2}{5}, \dfrac{7}{3}$

(iii) $21x^2 - 2x + \dfrac{1}{21} = 0$
(a) 21, 3
(b) $\dfrac{1}{21}, \dfrac{1}{21}$
(c) $-21, \dfrac{1}{21}$
(d) $\dfrac{1}{21}, \dfrac{3}{21}$

(iv) $6x^2 - 31x + 40 = 0$
(a) $\dfrac{5}{2}, \dfrac{8}{3}$
(b) $-\dfrac{5}{2}, -\dfrac{8}{3}$
(c) $-\dfrac{5}{2}, \dfrac{3}{8}$
(d) $\dfrac{2}{3}, \dfrac{5}{8}$

(v) $3x^2 + 2\sqrt{5}x - 5 = 0$
(a) $2\sqrt{5}, -\sqrt{5}$
(b) $\sqrt{5}, -\dfrac{\sqrt{5}}{3}$
(c) $-\sqrt{5}, 3\sqrt{5}$
(d) $-\sqrt{5}, \dfrac{\sqrt{5}}{3}$

Short Answer Type Questions

7. Find the roots of the equation $x^2 + 182 = 27x$

8. Find the roots of the quadratic equation
$$a^2b^2x^2 + b^2x - a^2x - 1 = 0$$ **[CBSE 2012, 11]**

9. If the roots of the equation $x^2 + 2cx + ab = 0$ are real and unequal, then prove that the equation $x^2 - 2(a + b)x + a^2 + b^2 + 2c^2 = 0$ has no real roots.

Long Answer Type Questions

10. If $x = -5$ is a root of the quadratic equation $2x^2 + px - 15 = 0$ and the quadratic equation $p(x^2 + x) + k = 0$ has equal roots, then find the value of k. **[CBSE 2016]**

11. A rectangular park is to be designed whose breadth is 3 m less than its length. Its area is to be 4 sq m more than the area of a park that has already been made in the shape of an isosceles triangle with its base as the breadth of the rectangular park and of altitude 12 m. Find its length and breadth of the rectangular park.

Answers

1. (b) **2.** (a) **3.** (b) **4.** (c) **5.** (a) **6.** (i) (c) (ii) (d) (iii) (b) (iv) (a) (v) (d)

7. 13 , 14   **8.** $x = +\dfrac{1}{b_2}, -\dfrac{1}{a_2}$ **10.** 7/4

11. Length $= 7\,m$ and Breadth $= 4\,m$

For Detailed Solutions
Scan the code

Arithmetic Progressions

In this Chapter...

- Arithmetic Progression
- nth Term of an AP
- Sum of n-Term of an AP
- Arithmetic Mean

Sequence Some numbers arranged in definite order, according to a definite rule are said to form a sequence.

Progression Sequences which follow a definite pattern are called progressions.

Arithmetic Progression

An Arithmetic Progression (AP) is a list of numbers in which each term is obtained by adding a fixed number to the preceding term except the first term.

This fixed number is called the **common difference** (d) of the AP. It can be positive, negative or zero.

In other words, a list of numbers $a_1, a_2, a_3, ..., a_n$ is called an arithmetic progression (AP), if there exists a constant number d (called common difference) such that

$$a_2 - a_1 = d$$
$$a_3 - a_2 = d$$
$$a_4 - a_3 = d$$
$$\vdots$$
$$a_n - a_{n-1} = d \text{ and so on.}$$

Each of the number in this list is called a **term**.

In general, $a, a + d, a + 2d, a + 3d, ...$ represent an arithmetic progression, where a is the **first term** and d is the **common difference**. This is called general form of an AP.

If number of terms in an AP is finite, then it is called a **finite AP**, otherwise it is called an **infinite AP** and such AP's do not have a last term.

Method to Check an AP When a List of Numbers is Given

Sometimes, a list of numbers or sequence is given and we have to check that this sequence is an AP or not. For this, we find the differences of consecutive terms. If these differences are same, then given list of numbers or sequence is an AP, otherwise not.

Method to Write an AP When First Term and Common Difference are Given

To write an AP, the minimum information required to know the first term a and the common difference d of the arithmetic progression. Then, we put the values of a and d in $a, a + d, a + 2d, a + 3d, ...$ to get the required AP.

nth Term of an AP

If the first term of an AP is 'a' and its common difference is 'd', then its nth term is given by the formula

$$a_n = a + (n-1)d$$

The nth term of an AP is also called its general term.

In an AP, nth term is known as last term of an AP and it is denoted by l, which is given by the formula

$$l = a + (n-1)d$$

nth Term from the End of an AP

Let 'a' be the first term, 'd' be the common difference and 'l' be the last term of an AP, then nth term from the end can be found by the formula

$$n\text{th term from the end} = l - (n-1)d$$

Selection of Terms in an AP

Number of terms	Terms	Common difference
3	$a-d,\ a,\ a+d$	d
4	$a-3d, a-d, a+d, a+3d$	$2d$
5	$a-2d, a-d, a, a+d, a+2d$	d

Sum of First n-Terms of an AP

If first term of an AP is 'a' and its common difference is 'd', then the sum of its first n terms S_n, is given by the formula

$$S_n = \frac{n}{2}[2a + (n-1)d]$$

or

$$S_n = \frac{n}{2}[a + a_n]$$

where, $a_n = n$th term of an AP.

(i) If l is the last term of an AP having n terms, then sum of all the terms is given by this formula

$$S_n = \frac{n}{2}[a + l]$$

(ii) If S_n and S_{n-1} are the sums of first n and $(n-1)$ terms of an AP respectively, then its nth term a_n is given by

$$a_n = S_n - S_{n-1}$$

Arithmetic Mean

If a, b and c are in AP, then b is known as arithmetic mean of a and c, i.e. $b = \dfrac{a+c}{2}$.

Solved Examples

Example 1. Examine that the sequence 13, 10, 7, 4,... is an AP.

Sol. Given, AP is 13, 10, 7, 4, ...

Here, $a_1 = 13, a_2 = 10, a_3 = 7, a_4 = 4, \ldots\ldots$

Here, we have $a_2 - a_1 = 10 - 13 = -3$,

$$a_3 - a_2 = 7 - 10 = -3,$$
$$a_4 - a_3 = 4 - 7 = -3 \text{ and so on.}$$

Since, difference of any two consecutive terms is same. So, the given sequence is an AP.

Example 2. Find the common difference of the following AP's.

(i) $3, -2, -7, -12, \ldots$

(ii) $11, 11, 11, 11, \ldots$

(iii) $5\dfrac{1}{2}, 9\dfrac{1}{2}, 13\dfrac{1}{2}, 17\dfrac{1}{2} \ldots\ldots$

Sol. (i) Given, AP is $3, -2, -7, -12, \ldots$

Here, $a_1 = 3, a_2 = -2, a_3 = -7, a_4 = -12$ and so on.

$\therefore$ Common difference $(d) = a_2 - a_1 = -2 - 3 = -5$

(ii) Given, AP is $11, 11, 11, 11, \ldots$

Here, $a_1 = 11, a_2 = 11, a_3 = 11, a_4 = 11$ and so on.

$\therefore$ Common difference $(d) = a_2 - a_1 = 11 - 11 = 0$

(iii) Given, AP is $5\dfrac{1}{2}, 9\dfrac{1}{2}, 13\dfrac{1}{2}, 17\dfrac{1}{2}, \ldots\ldots$

Here, $a_1 = 5\dfrac{1}{2}, a_2 = 9\dfrac{1}{2}, a_3 = 13\dfrac{1}{2}, a_4 = 17\dfrac{1}{2}$ and so on.

$\therefore$ Common difference $(d) = a_2 - a_1 = 9\dfrac{1}{2} - 5\dfrac{1}{2}$

$$= \dfrac{19}{2} - \dfrac{11}{2} = \dfrac{8}{2} = 4$$

Example 3. Write an AP having 4 as the first term and -3 as the common difference.

Sol. Given, first term $(a) = 4$ and common difference $(d) = -3$

On putting the values of a and d in general form

$a, a + d, a + 2d, a + 3d, \ldots$, we get

$$4, 4 - 3, 4 + 2(-3), 4 + 3(-3), \ldots$$
$$4, 1, 4 - 6, 4 - 9, \ldots \text{ or } 4, 1, -2, -5, \ldots$$

Which is the required AP.

Example 4. Find the 20th term of the sequence $7, 3, -1, -5 \ldots$

Sol. Given, sequence is $7, 3, -1, -5, \ldots$.

Here, $3 - 7 = -4, -1 - 3 = -4, -5 + 1 = -4$ and so on.

So, given sequence is an AP, in which $a = 7$ and $d = -4$.

Since, nth term, $a_n = a + (n-1)d$

On putting $n = 20$, we get

$$a_{20} = a + (20-1)d = 7 + 19(-4) \qquad [\because a = 7, d = -4]$$
$$= 7 - 19 \times 4 = 7 - 76 = -69$$

Hence, 20th term of given sequence is -69.

Example 5. How many terms are there in the sequence 3, 6, 9, 12, ..., 111?

Sol. Given, sequence is 3, 6, 9, 12, ..., 111.

Here, $6 - 3 = 9 - 6 = 12 - 9 \ldots = 3$

So, it is an AP with first term, $a = 3$ and common difference, $d = 3$. Let there be n terms in the given sequence.

Then, $\qquad n$th term $= 111$

$$\Rightarrow \qquad a + (n-1)d = 111 \qquad [\because a_n = (a + (n-1)d)]$$
$$\Rightarrow \qquad 3 + (n-1) \times 3 = 111$$
$$\Rightarrow \qquad 3(1 + n - 1) = 111$$
$$\Rightarrow \qquad n = \dfrac{111}{3} \Rightarrow n = 37$$

Hence, the given sequence contains 37 terms.

Example 6. Which term of the AP: 21, 18, 15,... is -81?

Sol. Given, AP is 21, 18, 15,....

Here, $a = 21$ and $d = 18 - 21 = -3$

Let nth term of given AP be -81

Then, $\qquad a_n = -81$

$$\Rightarrow \qquad a + (n-1)d = -81 \qquad [\because a_n = a + (n-1)d]$$

On putting the values of a and d, we get

$$21 + (n-1)(-3) = -81 \Rightarrow 21 - 3n + 3 = -81$$
$$\Rightarrow \qquad 24 - 3n = -81 \Rightarrow -3n = -81 - 24 = -105$$
$$\Rightarrow \qquad n = \dfrac{-105}{-3} = 35$$

Hence, 35th term of given AP is -81.

Example 7. How many numbers of two digits are divisible by 7?

Sol. Two-digits numbers are 10, 11, 12, 13, 14, 15,..., 97, 98, 99 in which only 14, 21, 28,..., 98 are divisible by 7.

Here, $21 - 14 = 28 - 21 \ldots = 7$.

So, this list of numbers forms an AP, whose first term $(a) = 14$, common difference $(d) = 7$.

Let there are n terms in the above sequence, then $a_n = 98$

$$\Rightarrow \qquad a + (n-1)d = 98 \qquad [\because a_n = a + (n-1)d]$$
$$\Rightarrow \qquad 14 + (n-1)7 = 98 \Rightarrow 14 + 7n - 7 = 98$$
$$\Rightarrow \qquad 7n = 91 \Rightarrow n = \dfrac{91}{7} = 13$$

Hence, 13 numbers of two digits are divisible by 7.

Example 8. Determine the 10th term from the end of the AP : 4, 9, 14, ..., 254.

Sol. Given, AP is 4, 9, 14,..., 254.

Here, $\qquad l = $ last term $= 254$

$\qquad d = $ common difference $= 9 - 4 = 5$

$\therefore$ 10th term from the end $= l - (10-1)d = l - 9d$

$$= 254 - 9 \times 5 = 254 - 45 = 209$$

Alternate Method

On reversing the given AP, new AP is 254, ..., 14, 9, 4.

Here, first term $(a) = 254$ and

common difference $(d) = 4 - 9 = -5$

Now, 10th term of new AP $= a_{10}$

$$= 254 + (10 - 1)(-5)$$
$$= 254 - 9 \times 5 = 209$$

Hence, 10th term from the end of given AP is 209.

Example 9. Determine the general term of an AP whose 7th term is -1 and 16th term is 17.

Sol. Let a be the first term and d be the common difference of the AP, whose 7th term is -1 and 16th term is 17.

Since, $a_7 = -1$ and $a_{16} = 17$

$\therefore$ We have, $a + (7 - 1)d = -1 \Rightarrow a + 6d = -1$ ...(i)

and $\qquad a + (16 - 1)d = 17 \Rightarrow a + 15d = 17$ ...(ii)

$$[\because a_n = a + (n - 1)d]$$

On subtracting Eq. (i) from Eq. (ii), we get

$$a + 15d - a - 6d = 17 + 1$$
$$\Rightarrow \qquad 9d = 18 \Rightarrow d = 2$$

On substituting $d = 2$ in Eq. (i), we get

$$a + 6 \times 2 = -1$$
$$\Rightarrow \qquad a + 12 = -1$$
$$\Rightarrow \qquad a = -13$$

Hence, general term,

$$a_n = a + (n - 1)d$$
$$= -13 + (n - 1)2 \quad [\because a = -13 \text{ and } d = 2]$$
$$= -13 + 2n - 2 = 2n - 15$$

Example 10. Find four numbers in AP whose sum is 20 and the sum of whose squares is 120.

Sol. Let the numbers be $a - 3d$, $a - d$, $a + d$ and $a + 3d$.

Then, according to the given condition, we have

$$(a - 3d) + (a - d) + (a + d) + (a + 3d) = 20 \qquad ...(i)$$

and $(a - 3d)^2 + (a - d)^2 + (a + d)^2 + (a + 3d)^2 = 120$ ...(ii)

From Eq. (i), we get

$$4a = 20 \Rightarrow a = 5$$

From Eq. (ii), we get

$$a^2 + 9d^2 - 6da + a^2 + d^2 - 2ad + a^2 + d^2 + 2ad$$
$$+ a^2 + 9d^2 + 6ad = 120$$
$$\Rightarrow \qquad 4a^2 + 20d^2 = 120$$
$$\Rightarrow \qquad a^2 + 5d^2 = 30$$
$$\Rightarrow \qquad 25 + 5d^2 = 30 \quad [\because a = 5]$$
$$\Rightarrow \qquad 5d^2 = 5 \Rightarrow d^2 = 1 \Rightarrow d = \pm 1$$

If $d = 1$, then the numbers are 2, 4, 6, 8 and if $d = -1$, then the numbers are 8, 6, 4, 2.

Hence, the numbers are 2, 4, 6, 8 or 8, 6, 4, 2.

Example 11. A sum of ₹ 2000 is invested at 7% simple interest per year. Calculate the interest at the end of each year. Do these interest form an AP? If so, then find the interest at the end of 20th year making use of this fact.

Sol. Given, initial money $P = ₹\ 2000$

Rate of interest, $R = 7\%$ per year; Time, $T = 1, 2, 3, 4,...$

We know that, simple interest is given by the following formula

$$SI = \frac{PRT}{100}$$

$\therefore SI$ at the end of 1st year $= \dfrac{2000 \times 7 \times 1}{100} = ₹\ 140$

SI at the end of 2nd year $= \dfrac{2000 \times 7 \times 2}{100} = ₹\ 280$

SI at the end of 3rd year $= \dfrac{2000 \times 7 \times 3}{100} = ₹\ 420$

Thus, required list of numbers is 140, 280, 420, ...

Here, $280 - 140 = 420 - 280 ... = 140$

So, above list of numbers forms an AP, whose first term $(a) = 140$ and common difference $(d) = 140$.

Now, SI at the end of 20th year will be equal to 20th term of the above AP.

$\because a_{20} = a + (20 - 1)d = 140 + 19 \times 140 = 140 + 2660 = 2800$

Hence, the interest at the end of 20th year will be ₹ 2800.

Example 12. Each year, a tree grow 5 cm less than the preceding year. If it grew by 1m in the first year, then in how many years will it have ceased growing? **[CBSE 2015]**

Sol. Given that, tree grow 5 cm or 0.05 m less than preceding year.

$\therefore$ The following sequence can be formed.

$$1, (1 - 0.05), (1 - 2 \times 0.05), ..., 0$$

i.e. $\quad$ 1, 0.95, 0.90, ... ,0 which is an AP.

Here, $\quad a = 1$, $d = 0.95 - 1 = -0.05$ and $l = 0$

Let $\qquad l = a_n = a + (n - 1)d$

Then, $\qquad 0 = 1 + (n - 1)(-0.05)$
$$\Rightarrow \qquad (n - 1)(0.05) = 1$$
$$\Rightarrow \qquad n - 1 = \frac{1}{0.05}$$
$$\Rightarrow \qquad n - 1 = \frac{1}{5} \times 100$$
$$\Rightarrow \qquad n - 1 = 20$$
$$\Rightarrow \qquad n = 21$$

Hence, in 21 yr, tree will have ceased growing.

Example 13. The eighth term of an AP is half its second term and the eleventh term exceeds one-third of its fourth term by 1. Find the 15th term. **[NCERT Exemplar]**

Sol. Let a and d be the first term and last term of an AP. Then,

$$a_8 = \frac{1}{2}a_2 \text{ and } a_{11} = \frac{1}{3}a_4 + 1$$

$\Rightarrow \quad a + (8 - 1)d = \dfrac{1}{2}[a + (2 - 1)d]$

and $\quad a + (11 - 1)d = \dfrac{1}{3}[(a + (4 - 1)d) + 1]$

$\Rightarrow \qquad a + 7d = \dfrac{1}{2}(a + d)$

and $\qquad a + 10d = \dfrac{1}{3}[(a + 3d) + 1]$

$\Rightarrow 2a + 14d - a - d = 0$

and $\qquad 3a + 30d = a + 3d + 1$

$\Rightarrow \qquad a + 13d = 0 \qquad \qquad$ ...(i)

and $\quad 2a + 27d - 1 = 0 \qquad \qquad$ ...(ii)

On solving Eqs. (i) and (ii), we get

$$a = -13, d = 1$$

$\therefore \qquad a_{15} = a + (15 - 1)(1)$

$$= -13 + 14 = 1$$

Example 14. The fourth term of an AP is 11. The sum of the fifth and seventh terms of the AP is 24. Find its common difference. **[CBSE 2015]**

Sol. Let a be the first term and d be the common difference. Then,

$$a_4 = 11 \Rightarrow a + (4 - 1)d = 11$$

$\Rightarrow \qquad a + 3d = 11 \qquad \qquad$ ...(i)

Also, given $a_5 + a_7 = 24$

$\Rightarrow \quad a + (5 - 1)d + a + (7 - 1)d = 24$

$\Rightarrow \qquad a + 4d + a + 6d = 24$

$\Rightarrow \qquad 2a + 10d = 24$

$\Rightarrow \qquad a + 5d = 12 \qquad$ [divide by 2] ...(ii)

On subtracting Eq. (i) from Eq. (ii), we get

$$2d = 1 \Rightarrow d = \frac{1}{2}$$

Hence, common difference is $\frac{1}{2}$.

Example 15. Find the sum of the first 22 terms of the AP : $8, 3, - 2, ...$

Sol. Given, AP is $8, 3, - 2, ...$

Here, first term, $(a) = 8$

Common difference, $(d) = 3 - 8 = -5$ and $n = 22$

$\because$ Sum of first n terms, $(S_n) = \dfrac{n}{2}[2a + (n - 1)d]$

$\therefore$ Sum of first 22 terms, $(S_{22}) = \dfrac{22}{2}[2 \times 8 + (22 - 1) \times (-5)]$

$$= 11[16 + 21 \times (-5)]$$

$$= 11[16 - 105]$$

$$= 11(-89) = -979$$

Hence, sum of first 22 terms of an AP is -979.

Example 16. Find the sum of first 24 terms of an AP, whose nth term is given by $a_n = 3 + 2n$.

Sol. Given, nth term of an AP, $a_n = 3 + 2n$

Clearly, sum of first 24 terms, (S_{24})

$$= \frac{24}{2}(a + a_{24}) = 12(5 + 51)$$

$[\because a_1 = 3 + 2 = 5$ and $a_{24} = 3 + 2 \times 24 = 3 + 48 = 51]$

$$= 12 \times 56 = 672$$

Example 17. If the sum of first 10 terms of an AP is 140 and the sum of first 16 terms is 320, then find the sum of first m terms.

Sol. Let the first term of this AP be a and common difference be d.

Given, sum of first 10 terms, $(S_{10}) = 140$

$\Rightarrow \qquad \dfrac{10}{2}[2a + (10 - 1)d] = 140 \Rightarrow 2a + 9d = \dfrac{140}{5}$

$$\left[\because S_n = \frac{n}{2}[2a + (n - 1)d]\right]$$

$\Rightarrow \qquad 2a + 9d = 28 \qquad \qquad$ ...(i)

Also, given sum of first 16 terms, $(S_{16}) = 320$

$\Rightarrow \qquad \dfrac{16}{2}[2a + (16 - 1)d] = 320$

$\Rightarrow \qquad 2a + 15d = \dfrac{320}{8} \Rightarrow 2a + 15d = 40 \qquad$ ...(ii)

On subtracting Eq. (i) from Eq. (ii), we get

$$6d = 12 \Rightarrow d = 2$$

On putting $d = 2$ in Eq. (i), we get

$$2a + 9(2) = 28 \Rightarrow 2a = 28 - 18$$

$\Rightarrow \qquad a = \dfrac{10}{2} = 5$

Thus, $a = 5$ and $d = 2$.

Hence, sum of first m terms, $(S_m) = \dfrac{m}{2}[2a + (m - 1)d]$

$$= \frac{m}{2}[2(5) + (m - 1)2] = m[5 + (m - 1)]$$

$$= m(5 + m - 1) = m(m + 4) = m^2 + 4m$$

Example 18. Find the sum of all three-digit natural numbers, which are multiples of 11. **[CBSE 2009]**

Sol. All three-digit natural numbers, multiples of 11 are $110, 121, 132, ..., 990$.

Here, common difference, $121 - 110 = 132 - 121 = ... = 11$.

So, it is an AP with first term, $a = 110$, common difference, $d = 11$ and last term, $l = 990$.

Let $\qquad \qquad l = a_n = a + (n - 1)d$

$\therefore \qquad \qquad 990 = 110 + (n - 1) \times 11$

$\Rightarrow \qquad \qquad 990 = 110 + 11n - 11$

$\Rightarrow \qquad \qquad 11n = 891 \Rightarrow n = 81$

$\because \qquad \qquad S_n = \dfrac{n}{2}[a + l]$

$\therefore \qquad \qquad S_{81} = \dfrac{81}{2}[110 + 990]$

$$= \frac{81}{2} \times 1100 = 81 \times 550 = 44550$$

Example 19. If S_n, the sum of first n terms of an AP is given by $S_n = 3n^2 - 4n$, find the nth term. **[CBSE 2019]**

Sol. Given, $\qquad S_n = 3n^2 - 4n \qquad \qquad$ ...(i)

On replacing n by $(n - 1)$ in Eq. (i), we get

$$S_{n-1} = 3(n - 1)^2 - 4(n - 1)$$

nth term of the AP $a_n = S_n - S_{n-1}$

$\therefore \qquad a_n = (3n^2 - 4n) - [3(n - 1)^2 - 4(n - 1)]$

$\Rightarrow \qquad a_n = 3[n^2 - (n - 1)^2] - 4[n - (n - 1)]$

$\Rightarrow \qquad a_n = 3[n^2 - n^2 + 2n - 1] - 4[n - n + 1]$

$\Rightarrow \qquad a_n = 3(2n - 1) - 4$

$\Rightarrow \qquad a_n = 6n - 3 - 4 \Rightarrow a_n = 6n - 7$

Thus, the nth term of the AP $= 6n - 7$.

Chapter Practice

Objective Questions

• **Multiple Choice Questions**

1. Which of the following form of an AP?

[**NCERT Exemplar**]

(a) $-1, -1, -1, -1, \ldots$ (b) $0, 2, 0, 2, \ldots$

(c) $1, 1, 2, 2, 3, 3, \ldots$ (d) $\dfrac{1}{2}, \dfrac{1}{3}, \dfrac{1}{4}, \ldots$

2. Which of the following is not an AP?

[**CBSE 2020 (Standard)**]

(a) $-1.2, 0.8, 2.8, \ldots$

(b) $3, 3+\sqrt{2}, 3+2\sqrt{2}, 3+3\sqrt{2}, \ldots$

(c) $\dfrac{4}{3}, \dfrac{7}{3}, \dfrac{9}{3}, \dfrac{12}{3}, \ldots$

(d) $\dfrac{-1}{5}, \dfrac{-2}{5}, \dfrac{-3}{5}, \ldots$

3. If $-\dfrac{5}{7}, a, 2$ are consecutive terms in an Arithmetic Progression, then the value of 'a' is

[**CBSE 2020 (Standard)**]

(a) $\dfrac{9}{7}$ (b) $\dfrac{9}{14}$

(c) $\dfrac{19}{7}$ (d) $\dfrac{19}{14}$

4. The common difference of an AP, whose nth term is $a_n = (3n + 7)$, is

(a) 3   (b) 7

(c) 10   (d) 6

5. The value of x for which $2x, (x + 10)$ and $(3x + 2)$ are the three consecutive terms of an AP, is

[**CBSE 2020 (Standard)**]

(a) 6   (b) -6

(c) 18   (d) -18

6. The value of p for which $(2p + 1), 10$ and $(5p + 5)$ are three consecutive terms of an AP is

(a) -1 (b) -2

(c) 1   (d) 2

7. The first four terms of an AP whose first term is -2 and the common difference is -2, are

[**NCERT Exemplar**]

(a) $-2, 0, 2, 4$ (b) $-2, 4, -8, 16$

(c) $-2, -4, -6, -8$ (d) $-2, -4, -8, -16$

8. Let a be a sequence defined by $a_1 = 1$, $a_2 = 1$ and $a_n = a_{n-1} + a_{n-2}$ for all $n > 2$, then the value of $\dfrac{a_4}{a_3}$ is

(a) $\dfrac{2}{3}$ (b) $\dfrac{5}{4}$ (c) $\dfrac{4}{5}$ (d) $\dfrac{3}{2}$

9. If an AP have 8 as the first term and -5 as the common difference and its first three terms are $8, A, B$, then $(A + B)$ is equal to

(a) 0   (b) -1

(c) 1   (d) 2

10. In an AP, if $d = -4$, $n = 7$ and $a_n = 4$, then a is equal to

(a) 6   (b) 7

(c) 20   (d) 28

11. The 11th term of an AP $-5, \dfrac{-5}{2}, 0, \dfrac{5}{2}, \ldots$

[**NCERT Exemplar**]

(a) -20 (b) 20

(c) -30 (d) 30

12. The 21st term of an AP whose first two terms are -3 and 4, is

[**NCERT Exemplar**]

(a) 17   (b) 137

(c) 143   (d) -143

13. If the 2nd term of an AP is 13 and 5th term is 25, what is its 7th term?

(a) 30   (b) 33

(c) 37   (d) 38

14. Which term of an AP : 21, 42, 63, 84, ... is 210?

[**NCERT Exemplar**]

(a) 9th   (b) 10th

(c) 11th   (d) 12th

15. If the common difference of an AP is 5, then what is $a_{18} - a_{13}$?
- (a) 5
- (b) 20
- (c) 25
- (d) 30

16. What is the common difference of an AP in which $a_{18} - a_{14} = 32$? **[NCERT Exemplar]**
- (a) 8
- (b) -8
- (c) -4
- (d) 4

17. Two APs have the same common difference. The first term of one of these is -1 and that of the other is -8. The difference between their 4th terms is **[NCERT Exemplar]**
- (a) -1
- (b) -8
- (c) 7
- (d) -9

18. If 7 times the 7th term of an AP is equal to 11 times its 11th term, then its 18th term will be
- (a) 7
- (b) 11
- (c) 18
- (d) 0

19. The 4th term from the end of an AP $-11, -8, -5, ..., 49$ is
- (a) 37
- (b) 40
- (c) 43
- (d) 58

20. Which term of the AP 5, 15, 25, ... will be 130 more than its 31st term?
- (a) 42
- (b) 44
- (c) 46
- (d) 48

21. The number of terms of an AP 5, 9, 13, ..., 185 is **[NCERT Exemplar, CBSE 2020 (Standard)]**
- (a) 31
- (b) 51
- (c) 41
- (d) 46

22. The sum of AP, sequence $-37, -33, -29, \ldots\ldots$ upto 12 term is
- (a) 180
- (b) -180
- (c) 170
- (d) -170

23. The sum of first 16 terms of the AP 10, 6, 2, ... is **[NCERT Exemplar]**
- (a) -320
- (b) 320
- (c) -352
- (d) -400

24. If the first term of an AP is -5 and the common difference is 2, then the sum of the first 6 terms is
- (a) 0
- (b) 5
- (c) 6
- (d) 15

25. In an AP, if $a = 1$, $a_n = 20$ and $S_n = 399$, then n is equal to
- (a) 19
- (b) 21
- (c) 38
- (d) 42

26. The sum of first five multiples of 3 is **[NCERT Exemplar]**
- (a) 45
- (b) 55
- (c) 65
- (d) 75

• **Case Based MCQs**

27. In a flower bed, there are 43 rose plants in the first row, 41 in the second, 39 in the third and so on.

(i) If there are 11 rose plants in the last row, then number of rose required are
- (a) 16
- (b) 15
- (c) 17
- (d) 10

(ii) Difference of rose plants in 7th row and 13th row is
- (a) 11
- (b) 12
- (c) 13
- (d) 14

(iii) If there are x rose plants in 15 rose, then x is equal to
- (a) 10
- (b) 12
- (c) 13
- (d) 15

(iv) The rose plants in 6th row is
- (a) 35
- (b) 37
- (c) 33
- (d) 31

(v) The total number of rose plants in 5th and 8th row is
- (a) 64
- (b) 54
- (c) 46
- (d) 45

28. The sum of the first five terms of an AP and the sum of the first seven terms of the same AP is 167. The sum of the first ten terms of this AP is 235.

(i) Let first term and common difference of an AP be a and d, respectively. Then pair of linear equations for given problem is
- (a) $13a + 31d = 167, 2a + 9d = 47$
- (b) $13a + 31d = 169, 2a + 9d = 45$
- (c) $12a + 31d = 167, 2a + 9d = 47$
- (d) $12a + 31d = 169, 2a + 9d = 45$

(ii) Common difference of given AP is
- (a) 5
- (b) 7
- (c) 9
- (d) 11

(iii) First term of given AP is
- (a) 3
- (b) 4
- (c) 2
- (d) 1

(iv) Fourth term of the AP is
- (a) 15
- (b) 16
- (c) 17
- (d) 18

(v) Sum of first twenty terms is
- (a) 970
- (b) 990
- (c) 950
- (d) 980

29. India is competitive manufacturing location due to the low cost of manpower and strong technical and engineering capabilities contributing to higher quality production runs. The production of TV sets in a factory increases uniformly by a fixed number every year. It produced 16000 sets in 6th year and 22600 in 9th year.

Based on the above information, answer the following questions:

(i) Find the production during first year.
  (a) 4000 sets   (b) 5000 sets
  (c) 6000 sets   (d) 7000 sets

(ii) Find the production during 8th year.
  (a) 48000 sets   (b) 20400 sets
  (c) 43000 sets   (d) None of these

(iii) Find the production during first 3 years.
  (a) 20000 sets   (b) 25000 sets
  (c) 31000 sets   (d) 21600 sets

(iv) In which year, the production is ₹ 29200.
  (a) 11   (b) 12
  (c) 10   (d) 8

(v) Find the difference of the production during 7th year and 4th year.
  (a) 5500   (b) 6700
  (c) 5400   (d) 6600

30. Your friend Veer wants to participate in a 200 m race. He can currently run that distance in 51 seconds and with each day of practice it takes him 2 seconds less. He wants to do in 31 seconds.

[CBSE Question Bank]

(i) Which of the following terms are in AP for the given situation?
  (a) 51, 53, 55....   (b) 51, 49, 47....
  (c) − 51, − 53, − 55....   (d) 51, 55, 59...

(ii) What is the minimum number of days he needs to practice till his goal is achieved?
  (a) 10   (b) 12
  (c) 11   (d) 9

(iii) Which of the following term is not in the AP of the above given situation?
  (a) 41   (b) 30
  (c) 37   (d) 39

(iv) If nth term of an AP is given by $a_n = 2n + 3$, then common difference of an AP is
  (a) 2   (b) 3
  (c) 5   (d) 1

(v) The value of x, for which $2x, x + 10, 3x + 2$ are three consecutive terms of an AP, is
  (a) 6   (b) − 6
  (c) 18   (d) − 18

31. Your elder brother wants to buy a car and plans to take loan from a bank for his car. He repays his total loan of ₹ 118000 by paying every month starting with the first installment of ₹ 1000. If he increases the installment by ₹ 100 every month, answer the following :

[CBSE Question Bank]

(i) The amount paid by him in 30th installment is
  (a) 3900   (b) 3500
  (c) 3700   (d) 3600

(ii) The amount paid by him in the 30 installments is
  (a) 37000   (b) 73500
  (c) 75300   (d) 75000

(iii) What amount does he still have to pay after 30th installment?
  (a) 45500   (b) 49000
  (c) 44500   (d) 54000

(iv) If total installments are 40, then amount paid in the last installment?
  (a) 4900   (b) 3900
  (c) 5900   (d) 9400

(v) The ratio of the 1st installment to the last installment is
  (a) 1 : 49   (b) 10 : 49
  (c) 10 : 39   (d) 39 : 10

PART 2
Subjective Questions

• Short Answer Type Questions

1. Justify whether it is true to say that

$-1, \dfrac{-3}{2}, -2, \dfrac{5}{2}, \ldots$ forms an AP as $a_2 - a_1 = a_3 - a_2$.

[NCERT Exemplar]

2. Find the values of a, b and c if it is given that the numbers a, 7, b, 23, c are in AP. [CBSE 2020 (Standard)]

3. The angles of a triangle are in AP. The greatest angle is twice the least. Find all the angles of the triangle.

[NCERT Exemplar]

4. The taxi fare after each km, when the fare is ₹ 15 for the first kilometre and ₹ 8 for each additional kilometre, does not form an AP as the total fare (in ₹) after each kilometre is 15, 8, 8, 8, … . Is the statement true? Give reasons.

5. Determine k, so that $k^2 + 4k + 8$, $2k^2 + 3k + 6$ and $3k^2 + 4k + 4$ are three consecutive terms of an AP.

[NCERT Exemplar]

6. Show that $(a - b)^2, (a^2 + b^2)$ and $(a + b)^2$ are in AP.

[CBSE 2020 (Standard)]

7. Find the 11th term from the last term (towards the first term) of the AP 12, 8, 4, .., -84.

[CBSE 2020 (Standard)]

8. For the AP $-3, -7, -11, \ldots$ can we find directly $a_{30} - a_{20}$ without actually finding a_{30} and a_{20}? Give reason for your answer. [NCERT Exemplar]

9. Is 0 a term of the AP 31, 28, 25,…? Justify your answer.

10. If four numbers are in AP such that their sum is 50 and the greatest number is 4 times the least, then find the numbers.

11. Find the 20th term of the AP whose 7th term is 24 less than the 11th term, first term being 12.

[NCERT Exemplar]

12. If the 9th term of an AP is zero, then prove that its 29th term is twice its 19th term.

13. The 16th term of an AP is 1 more than twice its 8th term. If the 12th term of an AP is 47, then find its nth term.

14. Find the 19th term of the following sequence.

$$t_n = \begin{cases} n^2, & \text{where } n \text{ is even} \\ n^2 - 1, & \text{where } n \text{ is odd} \end{cases}$$

[CBSE 2015]

15. Split 207 into three parts such that these are in AP and the product of the two smaller parts is 4623.

[NCERT Exemplar]

16. Find the 12th term from the end of the AP $-2, -4, -6, \ldots, -100$. [NCERT Exemplar]

17. How many numbers lie between 10 and 300, which divided by 4 leave a remainder 3?

18. If m times the mth term of an AP is equal to n times its nth term, show that the $(m + n)$th term of the AP is zero.

19. Find the sum of first 20 terms of the following AP sequence 1, 4, 7, 10, ……

20. Which term of the AP : 120, 116, 112, … is first negative term? [CBSE 2012]

21. How many terms of AP 18, 16, 14, … should be taken, so that their sum is zero? [CBSE 2013]

22. Find the sum of first 8 multiples of 3. [CBSE 2018]

23. Subha Rao started work in 1995 at an annual salary of ₹ 5000 and received an increment of ₹ 200 each year. In which year did his income reach ₹ 7000?

[NCERT Exemplar]

24. Ramkali saves ₹ 5 in the first week of a year and then increased her weekly savings by ₹ 1.75. If in the nth week, her weekly saving becomes ₹ 20.75. Find n. [NCERT Exemplar]

25. If $\dfrac{1 + 3 + 5 + \ldots \text{upto } n \text{ terms}}{2 + 5 + 8 + \ldots \text{upto } 8 \text{ terms}} = 9$, then find the value of n.

26. In an AP, if $S_n = 3n^2 + 5n$ and $a_k = 164$, then find the value of k. [NCERT Exemplar]

27. Find the sum $(-5) + (-8) + (-11) + \ldots + (-230)$.

[CBSE 2020 (Standard)]

28. Sum of the first n terms of an AP is $5n^2 - 3n$. Find the AP and also find its 16th term. [CBSE 2010]

29. The sum of the first n terms of an AP whose first term is 8 and the common difference is 20, is equal to the sum of first $2n$ terms of another AP whose first term is -30 and the common difference is 8. Find the value of n. [NCERT Exemplar]

30. Find the sum of 10 terms of an AP.

$$\sqrt{2}, \sqrt{8}, \sqrt{18}, \sqrt{32}, \ldots,$$

31. Find the sum of all multiples of 7 lying between 500 and 900.

32. Find the sum of all the two digit numbers which leave the remainder 2 when divided by 5. [CBSE 2019]

33. If S_n denotes the sum of first n terms of an AP, then prove that $S_{12} = 3(S_8 - S_4)$.   **[NCERT Exemplar]**

34. Find the sum of last ten terms of the AP 8, 10, 12,..., 126.   **[NCERT Exemplar]**

35. Find the sum of the first 100 natural numbers.   **[CBSE 2020 (Standard)]**

36. Find the sum of first seven numbers which are multiples of 2 as well as of 9.   **[NCERT Exemplar]**

37. For an AP, it is given that the first term $(a) = 5$, common difference $(d) = 3$, and the nth term $(a_n) = 50$. Find n and sum of first n terms (S_n) of the AP.   **[CBSE 2020 (Standard)]**

38. Find the sum of first 16 terms of an Arithmetic Progression whose 4th and 9th terms are -15 and -30, respectively.   **[CBSE 2020 (Standard)]**

39. If the sum of first 14 terms of an Arithmetic Progression is 1050 and its fourth term is 40, find its 20th term.   **[CBSE 2020 (Standard)]**

• Long Answer Type Questions

40. If the nth terms of the two AP's 9, 7, 5, ... and 24, 21, 18, ... are the same, then find the value of n. Also, that term.   **[NCERT Exemplar]**

41. The 26th, 11th and the last terms of an AP are, 0, 3 and $-\dfrac{1}{5}$, respectively. Find the common difference and the number of terms.   **[NCERT Exemplar]**

42. The 4th term of an AP is zero. Prove that the 25th term of the AP is three times its 11th term.   **[CBSE 2016]**

43. If the mth term of an AP is $\dfrac{1}{n}$ and nth term is $\dfrac{1}{m}$, then show that its mnth term is 1.

44. In an AP given that the first term $(a) = 54$, the common difference $(d) = -3$ and the n th term $(a_n) = 0$, find n and the sum of first n terms (S_n) of the AP.   **[CBSE 2020 (Standard)]**

45. Solve $1 + 4 + 7 + 10 + ... + x = 287$.   **[CBSE 2020 (Standard)]**

46. Solve the equation:
$$1 + 5 + 9 + 13 + ... + x = 1326$$
[CBSE 2020 (Standard)]

47. Find the sum
(i) $1 + (-2) + (-5) + (-8) + ... + (-236)$

(ii) $\left(4 - \dfrac{1}{n}\right) + \left(4 - \dfrac{2}{n}\right) + \left(4 - \dfrac{3}{n}\right) + ...$ upto n terms.   **[NCERT Exemplar]**

48. Find the sum of the two middle most terms of an AP $-\dfrac{4}{3}, -1, -\dfrac{2}{3}, ..., 4\dfrac{1}{3}$.

49. Find the sum of first 17 terms of an AP whose 4th and 9th terms are -15 and -30, respectively.

50. The sum of first n terms of three AP's are S_1, S_2 and S_3. The first term of each AP is unity and their common differences are 1, 2 and 3, respectively. Prove that
$$S_1 + S_3 = 2S_2.$$
[CBSE 2016]

51. If the sum of first four terms of an AP is 40 and that of first 14 terms is 280. Find the sum of its first n terms.   **[CBSE 2019]**

52. The ratio of the 11th term to the 18th term of an AP is $2 : 3$. Find the ratio of the 5th term to the 21st term and also the ratio of the sum of the first five terms to the sum of the first 21 terms.   **[NCERT Exemplar]**

53. The sum of four consecutive numbers in AP is 32 and the ratio of the product of the first and last terms to the product of two middle terms is $7 : 15$. Find the numbers.   **[CBSE 2020 (Standard)]**

54. Show that the sum of an AP whose first term is a, the second term b and the last term c, is equal to
$$\dfrac{(a + c)(b + c - 2a)}{2(b - a)}.$$
[NCERT Exemplar]

55. How many terms of the AP 20, $19\dfrac{1}{3}$, $18\dfrac{2}{3}$, ... must be taken, so that their sum is 300?

• Case Base Questions

56. Kanika was given her pocket money on Jan 1st, 2008. She puts ₹ 1 on day 1, ₹ 2 on day 2, ₹ 3 on day 3 and continued doing so till the end of the month. From this money into her piggy bank, she also spent ₹ 204 of her pocket money and found that at the end of the month she still had ₹ 100 with her.   **[NCERT Exemplar]**

(i) How much Kanika take till the end of the month from pocket money?

(ii) How much was pocket money for the month?

(iii) What is the amount saved by Kanika, till January 13th, 2008?

SOLUTIONS

Objective Questions

1. (a) (a) Here, $t_1 = -1$, $t_2 = -1$, $t_3 = -1$ and $t_4 = -1$

Now, $t_2 - t_1 = -1 + 1 = 0$

$t_3 - t_2 = -1 + 1 = 0$

$t_4 - t_3 = -1 + 1 = 0$

Clearly, the difference of successive terms is same, therefore given list of numbers forms an AP.

(b) Here, $t_1 = 0$, $t_2 = 2$, $t_3 = 0$ and $t_4 = 2$

Now, $t_2 - t_1 = 2 - 0 = 2$

$t_3 - t_2 = 0 - 2 = -2$

$t_4 - t_3 = 2 - 0 = 2$

Clearly, the difference of successive terms is not same, therefore given list of numbers does not form an AP.

(c) Here, $t_1 = 1$, $t_2 = 1$, $t_3 = 2$ and $t_4 = 2$

Now, $t_2 - t_1 = 1 - 1 = 0$

$t_3 - t_2 = 2 - 1 = 1$

$t_4 - t_2 = 2 - 2 = 0$

Clearly, the difference of successive terms is not same, therefore given list of numbers does not form an AP.

(d) $\dfrac{1}{2}, \dfrac{1}{3}, \dfrac{1}{4}, \ldots$

Here, $t_1 = \dfrac{1}{2}$, $t_2 = \dfrac{1}{3}$ and $t_3 = \dfrac{1}{4}$

Now, $t_2 - t_1 = \dfrac{1}{3} - \dfrac{1}{2} = \dfrac{2-3}{6} = -\dfrac{1}{6}$

$t_3 - t_2 = \dfrac{1}{4} - \dfrac{1}{3} = \dfrac{3-4}{12} = -\dfrac{1}{12}$

Clearly, the difference of successive terms is not same, therefore given list of numbers does not form an AP.

2. (c) The condition for given series is not AP is the common difference of two consecutive terms is not constant.

(a) We have, $-1.2, 0.8, 2.8, \ldots$

Here, $a_1 = -1.2$, $a_2 = 0.8$, $a_3 = 2.8$

Now, $a_2 - a_1 = 0.8 - (-1.2) = 2.0$

and $a_3 - a_2 = 2.8 - 0.8 = 2$

Thus, given series is an AP.

(b) We have, $3, 3 + \sqrt{2}, 3 + 2\sqrt{2}, 3 + 3\sqrt{2}, \ldots$

Here, $a_1 = 3$, $a_2 = 3 + \sqrt{2}$, $a_3 = 3 + 2\sqrt{2}$

Now, $a_2 - a_1 = 3 + \sqrt{2} - 3 = \sqrt{2}$

and $a_3 - a_2 = 3 + 2\sqrt{2} - (3 + \sqrt{2}) = \sqrt{2}$

Thus, given series is an AP.

(c) We have, $\dfrac{4}{3}, \dfrac{7}{3}, \dfrac{9}{3}, \dfrac{12}{3}, \ldots$

Here, $a_1 = \dfrac{4}{3}$, $a_2 = \dfrac{7}{3}$, $a_3 = \dfrac{9}{3}$

Now, $a_2 - a_1 = \dfrac{7}{3} - \dfrac{4}{3} = \dfrac{3}{3} = 1$

$a_3 - a_2 = \dfrac{9}{3} - \dfrac{7}{3} = \dfrac{2}{3}$

Thus, given series is not an AP, as common difference is not constant.

(d) We have, $\dfrac{-1}{5}, \dfrac{-2}{5}, \dfrac{-3}{5}, \ldots$

Here, $a_1 = -\dfrac{1}{5}$, $a_2 = -\dfrac{2}{5}$, $a_3 = \dfrac{-3}{5}$

Now, $a_2 - a_1 = -\dfrac{2}{5} - \left(\dfrac{-1}{5}\right) = -\dfrac{1}{5}$

$a_3 - a_2 = \dfrac{-3}{5} - \left(-\dfrac{2}{5}\right) = \dfrac{-3}{5} + \dfrac{2}{5} = -\dfrac{1}{5}$

Thus, given series is an AP.

Hence, in the given options, option (c) is not an AP.

3. (b) Given, $-\dfrac{5}{7}, a, 2$ are consecutive terms in AP.

$\therefore \quad a - \left(-\dfrac{5}{7}\right) = 2 - a \quad [\because \text{In AP}, a_2 - a_1 = a_3 - a_2]$

$\Rightarrow \quad 2a = 2 - \dfrac{5}{7} \Rightarrow 2a = \dfrac{9}{7} \Rightarrow a = \dfrac{9}{14}$

4. (a) Given, nth term of an AP is

$a_n = (3n + 7)$

$\therefore$ The common difference of an AP $= a_n - a_{n-1}$

$= (3n + 7) - [3(n - 1) + 7]$

$= 3n + 7 - (3n + 4) = 7 - 4 = 3$

5. (a) If a, b, c are in AP, then $b = \dfrac{a+c}{2} \quad [\because b - a = c - b]$

Given, $2x, (x + 10)$ and $(3x + 2)$ are in AP.

$\therefore \quad x + 10 = \dfrac{2x + (3x + 2)}{2}$

$\Rightarrow \quad x + 10 = \dfrac{5x + 2}{2} \Rightarrow 2x + 20 = 5x + 2$

$\Rightarrow \quad 5x - 2x = 20 - 2 \Rightarrow 3x = 18$

$\Rightarrow \quad x = \dfrac{18}{3} = 6$

6. (d) Let $a_1 = 2p + 1$, $a_2 = 10$ and $a_3 = 5p + 5$.

Given that three consecutive terms are in AP.

$\therefore \quad a_2 - a_1 = a_3 - a_2$

$\Rightarrow \quad 10 - (2p + 1) = 5p + 5 - 10$

$\Rightarrow \quad 10 + 10 = 5p + 5 + 2p + 1$

$\Rightarrow \quad 20 = 7p + 6$

$\Rightarrow \quad 7p = 20 - 6$

$\Rightarrow \quad 7p = 14$

$\Rightarrow \quad p = \dfrac{14}{7} = 2$

7. (c) Let the first four terms of an AP are $a, a + d, a + 2d$ and $a + 3d$.

Given, that first term, $a = -2$ and common difference, $d = -2$, then we have an AP as follows

$-2, -2 - 2, -2 + 2(-2), -2 + 3(-2)$ i.e. $-2, -4, -6, -8$

8. (d) We have, $a_1 = 1$, $a_2 = 1$ and $a_n = a_{n-1} + a_{n-2}$ for all $n > 2$

On putting $n = 3$ and 4, we get

$a_3 = a_2 + a_1 = 1 + 1 = 2$

$a_4 = a_3 + a_2 = 2 + 1 = 3$

Now, $\dfrac{a_4}{a_3} = \dfrac{3}{2}$

9. (c) Given, first term $(a) = 8$, common difference $(d) = -5$

On putting the values of a and d in general form,

$a, a + d, a + 2d, a + 3d, ...$, we get

$$8, 8 - 5, 8 + 2(-5), 8 + 3(-5), ... \text{ or } 8, 3, -2, -7, ...$$

On comparing with given terms $8, A, B, ...$, we get

$$A = 3, B = -2$$

$\therefore \quad A + B = 3 + (-2) = 3 - 2 = 1$

10. (d) In an AP, $\quad a_n = a + (n - 1) d$

$\Rightarrow \quad 4 = a + (7 - 1)(-4) \quad$ [by given condition]

$\Rightarrow \quad 4 = a + 6(-4) \Rightarrow 4 + 24 = a$

$\therefore \quad a = 28$

11. (b) Given AP, $-5, -\dfrac{5}{2}, 0, \dfrac{5}{2}, ...$

Here, $\ a = -5, d = \dfrac{-5}{2} + 5 = \dfrac{5}{2}$

$\therefore \quad a_{11} = a + (11 - 1) d \quad [\because a_n = a + (n - 1) d]$

$$= -5 + (10) \times \dfrac{5}{2} = -5 + 25 = 20$$

12. (b) Given, first two terms of an AP are $a = -3$ and $a + d = 4$.

$\Rightarrow \quad -3 + d = 4$

Common difference, $d = 7$

$\therefore \quad a_{21} = a + (21 - 1) d [\because a_n = a + (n - 1) d]$

$$= -3 + (20) \, 7$$

$$= -3 + 140 = 137$$

13. (b) Given, $a_2 = 13$ and $a_5 = 25$

$\Rightarrow \quad a + (2 - 1) d = 13 \quad [\because a_n = a + (n - 1) d]$

and $\quad a + (5 - 1) d = 25$

$\Rightarrow \quad a + d = 13 \quad\quad\quad ...(i)$

and $\quad a + 4 d = 25 \quad\quad\quad ...(ii)$

On subtracting Eq. (i) from Eq. (ii), we get

$$3d = 25 - 13 = 12 \Rightarrow d = 4$$

From Eq. (i), $a = 13 - 4 = 9$

$\therefore \quad a_7 = a + (7 - 1) d = 9 + 6 \times 4 = 33$

14. (b) Let nth term of the given AP be 210.

Here, first term, $a = 21$

and common difference,

$$d = 42 - 21 = 21 \text{ and } a_n = 210$$

$\because \quad a_n = a + (n - 1) d$

$\Rightarrow \quad 210 = 21 + (n - 1) 21$

$\Rightarrow \quad 210 = 21 + 21n - 21$

$\Rightarrow \quad 210 = 21n \Rightarrow n = 10$

Hence, the 10th term of an AP is 210.

15. (c) Given, the common difference of AP i.e. $d = 5$

Now, $a_{18} - a_{13} = a + (18 - 1) d - [a + (13 - 1) d]$

$$[\because a_n = a + (n - 1) d]$$

$$= a + 17 \times 5 - a - 12 \times 5 = 85 - 60 = 25$$

16. (a) Given, $\quad\quad\quad a_{18} - a_{14} = 32$

$\Rightarrow \quad a + (18 - 1) d - [a + (14 - 1) d] = 32 \quad [\because a_n = a + (n - 1) d]$

$\Rightarrow \quad a + 17d - a - 13d = 32$

$\Rightarrow \quad 4d = 32$

$\therefore \quad d = 8$

Which is the required common difference of an AP.

17. (c) Let the common difference of two APs are d_1 and d_2, respectively.

By condition, $\quad d_1 = d_2 = d \quad\quad\quad ...(i)$

Let the first term of first AP $(a_1) = -1$

and the first term of second AP $(a_2) = -8$

We know that, the nth term of an AP, $T_n = a + (n - 1) d$

$\therefore$ 4th term of first AP, $T_4 = a_1 + (4 - 1) d = -1 + 3d$

and 4th term of second AP, $T_4{'} = a_2 + (4 - 1) d = -8 + 3d$

Now, the difference between their 4th terms is

$$|T_4 - T_4{'}| = (-1 + 3d) - (-8 + 3d)$$

$$= -1 + 3d + 8 - 3d = 7$$

Hence, the required difference is 7.

18. (d) According to the question,

$$7a_7 = 11 a_{11}$$

$\Rightarrow \quad 7[a + (7 - 1) d] = 11[a + (11 - 1) d]$

$$[\because a_n = a + (n - 1) d]$$

$\Rightarrow \quad 7(a + 6 d) = 11(a + 10 d)$

$\Rightarrow \quad 7a + 42 d = 11a + 110 d$

$\Rightarrow \quad 4a + 68 d = 0$

$\Rightarrow \quad 4(a + 17d) = 0$

$\Rightarrow \quad a + 17d = 0 \quad\quad\quad ...(i)$

$\therefore$ 18th term of an AP, $a_{18} = a + (18 - 1) d$

$$= a + 17d = 0 \quad\quad [\text{from Eq. (i)}]$$

19. (b) We know that, the n th term of an AP from the end is

$$a_n = l - (n - 1) d \quad\quad\quad ...(i)$$

Here, $l =$ Last term and $l = 49 \quad\quad$ [given]

Common difference, $d = -8 - (-11)$

$$= -8 + 11 = 3$$

From Eq. (i), $a_4 = 49 - (4 - 1) \, 3 = 49 - 9 = 40$

20. (b) We have, $a = 5$ and $d = 10$

$\therefore \quad a_{31} = a + 30d = 5 + 30 \times 10 = 305$

Let nth term of the given AP be 130 more than its 31st term.

Then, $\quad\quad a_n = 130 + a_{31}$

$\Rightarrow \quad a + (n - 1)d = 130 + 305$

$\Rightarrow \quad 5 + 10(n - 1) = 435$

$\Rightarrow \quad 10(n - 1) = 430$

$\Rightarrow \quad n - 1 = 43$

$\Rightarrow \quad n = 44$

Hence, 44th term of the given AP is 130 more than its 31st term.

21. (d) Given, AP sequence is 5, 9, 13, ..., 185.

Here, first term $a = 5$

Common difference, $d = 9 - 5 = 4$

and last term, $l = 185$

$\because \quad\quad l = a + (n - 1)d$

$\therefore \quad\quad 185 = 5 + (n - 1)4$

$\Rightarrow \quad\quad 180 = (n - 1)4$

$\Rightarrow \quad (n - 1) = \dfrac{180}{4}$

$\Rightarrow \quad (n - 1) = 45$

$\Rightarrow \quad n = 45 + 1 \Rightarrow n = 46$

22. (b) Given sequence is

$$-37, -33, -29, \ldots\ldots \text{ upto 12 terms}$$

Here $a = -37$, $d = -33 - (-37) = 4$

$$\therefore \quad S_n = \frac{n}{2}[2a + (n-1)d]$$

$$\therefore \quad S_{12} = \frac{12}{2}[2 \times (-37) + (12-1)4]$$

$$= 6[-74 + 44]$$

$$= 6 \times (-30) = -180$$

23. (a) Given, AP is $10, 6, 2, \ldots$

Here, first term $a = 10$, common difference, $d = -4$

$$\therefore \quad S_{16} = \frac{16}{2}[2a + (16-1)\,d]$$

$$\left[\because S_n = \frac{n}{2}\{2a + (n-1)\,d\} \right]$$

$$= 8[2 \times 10 + 15(-4)]$$

$$= 8(20 - 60) = 8(-40) = -320$$

24. (a) Given, $a = -5$ and $d = 2$

$$\therefore \quad S_6 = \frac{6}{2}[2a + (6-1)\,d]$$

$$\left[\because S_n = \frac{n}{2}\{2a + (n-1)\,d\} \right]$$

$$= 3[2(-5) + 5(2)]$$

$$= 3(-10 + 10) = 0$$

25. (c) $\because \quad S_n = \frac{n}{2}[2a + (n-1)\,d]$

$$399 = \frac{n}{2}[2 \times 1 + (n-1)\,d]$$

$$798 = 2n + n(n-1)\,d \qquad \ldots\text{(i)}$$

and $\quad a_n = 20$

$\Rightarrow \quad a + (n-1)\,d = 20 \qquad [\because a_n = a + (n-1)\,d]$

$\Rightarrow \quad 1 + (n-1)\,d = 20 \Rightarrow (n-1)\,d = 19 \qquad \ldots\text{(ii)}$

Using Eq. (ii) in Eq. (i), we get

$$798 = 2n + 19n$$

$$\Rightarrow \quad 798 = 21n$$

$$\therefore \quad n = \frac{798}{21} = 38$$

26. (a) The first five multiples of 3 are 3, 6, 9, 12 and 15.

Here, first term, $a = 3$, common difference, $d = 6 - 3 = 3$ and number of terms, $n = 5$

$$\therefore \quad S_5 = \frac{5}{2}[2a + (5-1)\,d]$$

$$\left[\because S_n = \frac{n}{2}\{2a + (n-1)\,d\} \right]$$

$$= \frac{5}{2}[2 \times 3 + 4 \times 3]$$

$$= \frac{5}{2}(6 + 12) = 5 \times 9 = 45$$

27. (i) (c) Number of rose plants in 1st, 2nd and 3rd row $\ldots\ldots$ are 43, 41, 39, $\ldots\ldots$

So, it forms an AP with first term,

$a = 43$ and common difference,

$d = 41 - 43 = -2$

Let n be the number of rows required.

$$\therefore \quad a_n = 11$$

$$\Rightarrow \quad a + (n-1)\,d = 11$$

$$\Rightarrow \quad 43 + (n-1)(-2) = 11$$

$$\Rightarrow \quad -2(n-1) = -32$$

$$\Rightarrow \quad n - 1 = 16 \Rightarrow n = 17$$

(ii) (b) Number of rose plants in 7th row $= a_7$

$$= a + 6d = 43 + 6(-2) = 43 - 12 = 31$$

Number of rose plants in 13th row $= a_{13}$

$$= a + 12d = 43 + 12(-2) = 43 - 24 = 19$$

$\therefore$ Required difference $= 31 - 19 = 12$

(iii) (d) Here, $n = 15$

$$\therefore \quad a_{15} = a + 14d = 43 + 14(-2) = 43 - 28 = 15$$

(iv) (c) Number of rose plants in 6th row

$$= a_6 = a + 5d$$

$$= 43 + 5(-2)$$

$$= 43 - 10 = 33$$

(v) (a) Number of rose plants in 5th row

$$= a_5 = a + 4d$$

$$= 43 + 4(-2)$$

$$= 43 - 8 = 35$$

Number of rose plants in 8th row

$$= a_8 = a + 7d$$

$$= 43 + 7(-2)$$

$$= 43 - 14 = 29$$

$\therefore$ Required sum $= 35 + 29 = 64$

28. (i) (c) Let the number of terms of AP be n.

$\because$ Sum of first n terms of an AP,

$$S_n = \frac{n}{2}[2a + (n-1)\,d] \qquad \ldots\text{(i)}$$

$\therefore$ Sum of first five terms of an AP,

$$S_5 = \frac{5}{2}[2a + (5-1)\,d] \qquad [\text{from Eq.(i)}]$$

$$= \frac{5}{2}(2a + 4d) = 5(a + 2d)$$

$$\Rightarrow \quad S_5 = 5a + 10d \qquad \ldots\text{(ii)}$$

and sum of first seven terms of an AP,

$$S_7 = \frac{7}{2}[2a + (7-1)\,d]$$

$$= \frac{7}{2}[2a + 6d] = 7(a + 3d)$$

$$\Rightarrow \quad S_7 = 7a + 21d \qquad \ldots\text{(iii)}$$

Now, by given condition,

$$S_5 + S_7 = 167$$

$$\Rightarrow \quad 5a + 10d + 7a + 21d = 167$$

$$\Rightarrow \quad 12a + 31d = 167 \qquad \ldots\text{(iv)}$$

Given that, sum of first ten terms of this AP is 235.

$$\therefore \quad S_{10} = 235$$

$$\Rightarrow \quad \frac{10}{2}[2a + (10-1)\,d] = 235$$

$$\Rightarrow \quad 5(2a + 9d) = 235$$

$$\Rightarrow \quad 2a + 9d = 47 \qquad \ldots\text{(v)}$$

(ii) (a) On multiplying Eq. (v) by 6 and then subtracting it into Eq. (iv), we get

$$12a + 54d = 282$$
$$12a + 31d = 167$$
$$\underline{ - - -}$$
$$23d = 115$$

$$\Rightarrow \qquad d = 5$$

(iii) (d) Now, put the value of d in Eq. (v), we get

$$2a + 9(5) = 47 \Rightarrow 2a + 45 = 47$$
$$\Rightarrow \qquad 2a = 47 - 45 = 2 \Rightarrow a = 1$$

(iv) (b) $a_4 = a + 3d$
$$= 1 + 3(5) = 1 + 15 = 16$$

(v) (a) Sum of first twenty terms of this AP,

$$S_{20} = \frac{20}{2}[2a + (20 - 1)d]$$
$$= 10[2 \times (1) + 19 \times (5)] = 10(2 + 95)$$
$$= 10 \times 97 = 970$$

Hence, the required sum of its first twenty terms is 970.

29. (i) (b) Let the production of TV sets in first year be 'a' units. Then, production in the next consecutive years are $a + d, a + 2d, \ldots$.

Thus, we get the sequence, $a, a + d, a + 2d, \ldots$

This is an AP sequence, whose first term $= a$ and common difference $= d$.

Given, $T_6 = 16000$ and $T_9 = 22600$

$$\therefore \qquad a + (6 - 1)d = 16000$$
$$\text{and} \qquad a + (9 - 1)d = 22600 \qquad [\because T_n = a + (n - 1)d]$$
$$\Rightarrow \qquad a + 5d = 16000 \qquad \ldots(i)$$
$$\text{and} \qquad a + 8d = 22600 \qquad \ldots(ii)$$

On subtracting Eq. (i) from Eq. (ii), we get

$$3d = 22600 - 16000$$
$$\Rightarrow \qquad 3d = 6600$$
$$\Rightarrow \qquad d = 2200$$

Put $d = 2200$ in Eq. (i), we get

$$a + 5 \times 2200 = 16000$$
$$\Rightarrow \qquad a = 16000 - 11000 = 5000$$

Hence, the production during first year is 5000 sets.

(ii) (b) The production during 8th year is

$$T_8 = a + (8 - 1)d$$
$$= 5000 + 7 \times 2200$$
$$= 5000 + 15400 = 20400$$

Hence, production during 8th year is 20400 sets.

(iii) (d) The production during first 3 years,

$$S_3 = \frac{3}{2}[2a + (3 - 1)d]$$
$$= \frac{3}{2}[2 \times 5000 + 2 \times 2200]$$
$$= 3[5000 + 2200]$$
$$= 3 \times 7200 = 21600$$

(iv) (b) Let in nth year, the production is 29200

$$\because \qquad T_n = a + (n - 1)d$$
$$\therefore \qquad 29200 = 5000 + (n - 1)2200$$
$$\Rightarrow \qquad (n - 1)2200 = 24200$$

$$\Rightarrow \qquad (n - 1) = \frac{24200}{2200}$$
$$\Rightarrow \qquad n - 1 = 11 \Rightarrow n = 12$$

Hence, production is ₹ 29200 in 12th year.

(v) (d) The difference of the production during 7th year and 4th year $= T_7 - T_4$

$$= a + (7 - 1)d - [a + (4 - 1)d]$$
$$= 6d - 3d = 3d = 3 \times 2200 = 6600$$

30. (i) (b) In first day, Veer takes 51 seconds to complete the 200 m race. But in each day he takes 2 seconds lesser than the previous days.

Thus, AP series will formed

$$51, 49, 47, \ldots$$

(ii) (c) Since, Veer wants to achieve the race in 31 seconds. Let Veer takes n days to achieve the target.

$$\therefore \qquad T_n = a + (n - 1)d$$

Here, $a = 51$, $d = 49 - 51 = -2$

$$\therefore \qquad 31 = 51 + (n - 1)(-2)$$
$$\Rightarrow \qquad (n - 1)2 = 20 \Rightarrow (n - 1) = 10 \Rightarrow n = 11$$

Hence, he needs minimum 11 days to achieve the goal.

(iii) (b) In an AP series, we get the series of odd terms. Hence, term 30 is not an AP.

(iv) (a) Given, $a_n = 2n + 3$

$$\therefore \text{Common difference} = a_{n+1} - a_n$$
$$= 2(n + 1) + 3 - (2n + 3)$$
$$= 2n + 2 + 3 - 2n - 3 = 2$$

(v) (a) Given, terms $2x$, $x + 10$, $3x + 2$ are in AP.

$$\therefore \qquad x + 10 = \frac{2x + (3x + 2)}{2}$$
$$\Rightarrow \qquad 2x + 20 = 5x + 2 \Rightarrow 3x = 18 \Rightarrow x = 6$$

31. (i) (a) Since, he pays first installment of ₹ 1000 and next consecutive months he pay the installment are 1100, 1200, 1300, ...

Thus, we get the AP sequence,

$$1000, 1100, 1200, \ldots$$

Here, $a = 1000$, $d = 1100 - 1000 = 100$

Now, $T_{30} = a + (30 - 1)d$
$$= 1000 + 29 \times 100 = 1000 + 2900 = 3900$$

Hence, the amount paid by him in 30th installment is ₹ 3900.

(ii) (b) Now, $S_{30} = \dfrac{30}{2}[2a + (30 - 1)d]$

$$= 15(2 \times 1000 + 29 \times 100)$$
$$= 15(2000 + 2900)$$
$$= 15 \times 4900 = ₹ 73500$$

(iii) (c) After 30th installment, he still have to pay

$$= 118000 - 73500 = 44500$$

(iv) (a) The amount in last 40th installment is

$$T_{40} = a + (40 - 1)d$$
$$= 1000 + 39 \times 100$$
$$= 1000 + 3900 = ₹ 4900$$

(v) (b) The ratio of 1st installment to the last installment is $\dfrac{1000}{4900}$ i.e. $\dfrac{10}{49}$.

Subjective Questions

1. Here, $a_1 = -1$, $a_2 = \dfrac{-3}{2}$, $a_3 = -2$ and $a_4 = \dfrac{5}{2}$

Now,
$$a_2 - a_1 = \dfrac{-3}{2} + 1 = -\dfrac{1}{2}$$
$$a_3 - a_2 = -2 + \dfrac{3}{2} = -\dfrac{1}{2}$$
$$a_4 - a_3 = \dfrac{5}{2} + 2 = \dfrac{9}{2}$$

Clearly, the difference of successive terms is not same, although, $a_2 - a_1 = a_3 - a_2$ but $a_3 - a_2 \neq a_4 - a_3$, therefore it does not form an AP.

2. Given, sequence a, 7, b, 23, c is an AP.

Since, a, 7, b is in AP.

$\therefore \qquad 7 = \dfrac{a+b}{2} \qquad \left[\because \text{If } x, y, z \text{ in AP, then, } y = \dfrac{x+z}{2} \right]$

$\Rightarrow \qquad a + b = 14 \qquad \qquad \text{...(i)}$

Since, 7, b, 23 is in AP.

$\therefore \qquad b = \dfrac{7+23}{2} \Rightarrow b = \dfrac{30}{2} \Rightarrow b = 15 \qquad \text{...(ii)}$

Since, b, 23, c is in AP.

$\therefore \qquad 23 = \dfrac{b+c}{2}$

$\Rightarrow \qquad 23 \times 2 = 15 + c \qquad [\text{from Eq. (ii), } b = 15]$

$\Rightarrow \qquad c = 46 - 15$

$\Rightarrow \qquad c = 31$

Put $b = 15$ in Eq. (i), we get
$$a + 15 = 14$$
$\Rightarrow \qquad a = 14 - 15$
$\Rightarrow \qquad a = -1$

Hence, values of a, b and c are respectively -1, 15 and 31.

3. Let the angles are $(a-d)°$, $a°$, $(a+d)°$.

Then, we get $(a-d) + a + (a+d) = 180$

and $\qquad \qquad a + d = 2(a-d)$

$\Rightarrow \qquad 3a = 180° \Rightarrow a = 60°$

and $\qquad 60° + d = 2(60° - d)$

$\Rightarrow \qquad 60° + d = 120° - 2d$

$\Rightarrow \qquad 3d = 60°$

$\Rightarrow \qquad d = 20°$

$\therefore$ The angles of an AP are
$$a - d = 60° - 20° = 40°$$
$$a = 60°$$

and $\qquad a + d = 60° + 20° = 80°$

Hence, angles of an AP are $40°$, $60°$, $80°$.

4. No, because the total fare (in ₹) after each kilometre is 15, $(15 + 8)$, $(15 + 2 \times 8)$, $(15 + 3 \times 8)$,... or 15, 23, 31, 39,...

Let $\quad t_1 = 15$, $t_2 = 23$, $t_3 = 31$ and $t_4 = 39$

Now, $\qquad t_2 - t_1 = 23 - 15 = 8$
$$t_3 - t_2 = 31 - 23 = 8$$
$$t_4 - t_3 = 39 - 31 = 8$$

Since, all the successive terms of the given list have same difference i.e. common difference $= 8$

Hence, the total fare after each killometre form an AP.

5. Since, $k^2 + 4k + 8$, $2k^2 + 3k + 6$ and $3k^2 + 4k + 4$ are consecutive terms of an AP.

$\therefore \quad 2k^2 + 3k + 6 - (k^2 + 4k + 8) = 3k^2 + 4k + 4$
$$- (2k^2 + 3k + 6) = \text{Common difference}$$

$\Rightarrow \quad 2k^2 + 3k + 6 - k^2 - 4k - 8 = 3k^2 + 4k + 4 - 2k^2 - 3k - 6$

$\Rightarrow \qquad \qquad k^2 - k - 2 = k^2 + k - 2$

$\Rightarrow \qquad -k = k \Rightarrow -2k = 0 \Rightarrow k = 0$

6. Let $a_1 = (a-b)^2$, $a_2 = a^2 + b^2$ and $a_3 = (a+b)^2$.

Now, $\quad a_2 - a_1 = a^2 + b^2 - (a-b)^2$
$$= a^2 + b^2 - (a^2 + b^2 - 2ab) = 2ab \qquad \text{...(i)}$$

and $\quad a_3 - a_2 = (a+b)^2 - (a^2 + b^2)$
$$= a^2 + b^2 + 2ab - (a^2 + b^2) = 2ab \qquad \text{...(ii)}$$

From Eqs. (i) and (ii), we get
$$a_2 - a_1 = a_3 - a_2$$

Hence, given terms are in AP.

7. Given, sequence of an AP is 12, 8, 4, ..., -84.

Here, first term is $a = 12$

Common difference is $d = 8 - 12 = -4$ and last term, $l = -84$

The nth term from the last term of an AP is $l - (n-1)d$.

$\therefore$ The 11th term from the last term of an AP
$$= l - (11-1)d$$
$$= -84 - (10) \times (-4)$$
$$= -84 + 40 = -44$$

8. $\because$ nth term of an AP, $a_n = a + (n-1)d$

$\therefore \qquad a_{30} = a + (30-1)d = a + 29d$

and $\qquad a_{20} = a + (20-1)d = a + 19d \qquad \text{...(i)}$

Now, $\quad a_{30} - a_{20} = (a + 29d) - (a + 19d) = 10d$

and from given AP common difference,
$$d = -7 - (-3) = -7 + 3 = -4$$

$\therefore \qquad a_{30} - a_{20} = 10(-4) = -40 \qquad [\text{from Eq. (i)}]$

9. Let 0 be the nth term of given AP i.e. $a_n = 0$.

Given that, first term $a = 31$,

Common difference, $d = 28 - 31 = -3$

The nth term of an AP, is $a_n = a + (n-1)d$

$\Rightarrow \qquad \qquad 0 = 31 + (n-1)(-3)$

$\Rightarrow \qquad 3(n-1) = 31 \Rightarrow n - 1 = \dfrac{31}{3}$

$\therefore \qquad n = \dfrac{31}{3} + 1 = \dfrac{34}{3} = 11\dfrac{1}{3}$

Since, n should be positive integer. So, 0 is not a term of the given AP.

10. Let four numbers in AP are a, $a+d$, $a+2d$, $a+3d$. Then,

$(a) + (a+d) + (a+2d) + (a+3d) = 50 \Rightarrow 4a + 6d = 50$

$\Rightarrow \qquad \qquad 2a + 3d = 25 \qquad \qquad \text{...(i)}$

and $\qquad \qquad (a+3d) = 4(a)$

$\Rightarrow \qquad \qquad a = d \qquad \qquad \text{...(ii)}$

On solving Eq. (i) and Eq. (ii), we get
$$a = d = 5$$

$\therefore$ The four numbers in AP are
$$a = 5, a + d = 5 + 5 = 10$$
$$a + 2d = 5 + 10 = 15, a + 3d = 5 + 15 = 20$$

Hence, four numbers in AP are 5, 10, 15 and 20.

11. Let the first term, common difference and number of terms of an AP are a, d and n, respectively.

Given that, first term $(a) = 12$.

Now by condition,

$$7\text{th term}\,(T_7) = 11\text{th term}\,(T_{11}) - 24$$
$$[\because n\text{th term of an AP},\ T_n = a + (n-1)\,d]$$
$$\Rightarrow \qquad a + (7-1)\,d = a + (11-1)\,d - 24$$
$$\Rightarrow \qquad a + 6d = a + 10d - 24$$
$$\Rightarrow \qquad 24 = 4d \Rightarrow d = 6$$
$$\therefore\ 20\text{th term of AP},\ T_{20} = a + (20-1)\,d = 12 + 19 \times 6 = 126$$

Hence, the required 20th term of an AP is 126.

12. Let the first term, common difference and number of terms of an AP are a, d and n, respectively.

Given that, 9th term of an AP, $T_9 = 0$

$$[\because n\text{th term of an AP},\ T_n = a + (n-1)\,d]$$
$$\Rightarrow\ a + (9-1)\,d = 0 \Rightarrow a + 8d = 0 \Rightarrow a = -8d \qquad \text{... (i)}$$

Now, its 19th term, $T_{19} = a + (19-1)\,d$

$$= -8d + 18d \qquad \text{[from Eq. (i)]}$$
$$\Rightarrow \qquad T_{19} = 10d \qquad \text{... (ii)}$$

and its 29th term, $T_{29} = a + (29-1)\,d$

$$= -8d + 28d \qquad \text{[from Eq. (i)]}$$
$$= 20d = 2 \times (10d)$$
$$\Rightarrow \qquad T_{29} = 2 \times T_{19} \qquad \text{[from Eq. (ii)]}$$

Hence, its 29th term is twice its 19th term.　　**Hence proved.**

13. Let first term and common difference of an AP are a and d.

According to the given condition,

$$a_{12} = 47$$
$$\Rightarrow \qquad a + 11d = 47 \qquad \text{...(i)}$$
$$\text{and} \qquad a_{16} = 1 + 2a_8 \qquad \text{[by given condition]}$$
$$\Rightarrow\ [a + (16-1)d] = 1 + 2[a + (8-1)d]$$
$$\Rightarrow \qquad a - d = -1 \qquad \text{...(ii)}$$

On solving Eqs. (i) and (ii), we get

$$d = 4 \text{ and } a = 3$$
$$\therefore \qquad a_n = 3 + (n-1)\,4 = 4n - 1$$

14. We have, $t_n = \begin{cases} n^2, & \text{where } n \text{ is even} \\ n^2 - 1, & \text{where } n \text{ is odd} \end{cases}$

For 19th term, i.e. for $n = 19$ which is odd, we take

$$t_n = n^2 - 1 = (19)^2 - 1 = 360$$

15. Let the three parts of the number 207 are $(a - d)$, a and $(a + d)$, which are in AP.

Now, by given condition,

$$\text{Sum of these parts} = 207$$
$$\Rightarrow \qquad a - d + a + a + d = 207$$
$$\Rightarrow \qquad 3a = 207$$
$$a = 69$$

Given that, product of the two smaller parts $= 4623$

$$\Rightarrow \qquad a\,(a - d) = 4623$$
$$\Rightarrow \qquad 69 \cdot (69 - d) = 4623 \Rightarrow 69 - d = 67$$
$$\Rightarrow \qquad d = 69 - 67 = 2$$
$$\text{So,} \qquad \text{first part} = a - d = 69 - 2 = 67,$$
$$\text{second part} = a = 69$$
$$\text{and} \qquad \text{third part} = a + d = 69 + 2 = 71,$$

Hence, required three parts are 67, 69, 71.

16. Given AP, $-2, -4, -6, ..., -100$

Here, first term $(a) = -2$, common difference $(d) = -4 - (-2) = -2$ and the last term $(l) = -100$.

We know that, the nth term a_n of an AP from the end is $a_n = l - (n-1)\,d$, where l is the last term and d is the common difference.

$\therefore$ 12th term from the end,

$$a_{12} = -100 - (12 - 1)\,(-2)$$
$$= -100 + (11)\,(2) = -100 + 22 = -78.$$

Hence, the 12th term from the end is -78.

17. Here, the first number is 11, which divided by 4 leave remainder 3 between 10 and 300. Last term before 300 is 299, which divided by 4 leave remainder 3.

$\therefore$ Required AP is 11, 15, 19, 23, ..., 299

Here, first term $(a) = 11$, common difference $d = 15 - 11 = 4$

$$\because \qquad n\text{th term},\ a_n = a + (n-1)\,d = l \qquad \text{[last term]}$$
$$\Rightarrow \qquad 299 = 11 + (n-1)\,4$$
$$\Rightarrow \qquad 299 - 11 = (n-1)\,4$$
$$\Rightarrow \qquad 4\,(n-1) = 288 \Rightarrow (n-1) = 72$$
$$\therefore \qquad n = 73$$

18. Let first term of an AP is a and common difference is d.

The nth term of an AP is

$$a_n = a + (n-1)d$$

According to the given condition,

$$m \times a_m = n \times a_n$$
$$\therefore\ m \times [a + (m-1)d] = n \times [a + (n-1)d]$$
$$\Rightarrow \qquad a(m - n) = [(n^2 - m^2) + (-n + m)]d$$
$$\Rightarrow \qquad a(m - n) = [(n - m)(n + m) + (m - n)]d$$
$$\Rightarrow \qquad a = [-(n + m) + 1]\,d \qquad \text{...(i)}$$
$$[\text{divide both sides by } m - n]$$

Now, $(m + n)$th term of an AP is

$$a_{m+n} = a + (m + n - 1)d$$
$$= [-(n + m) + 1]d + (m + n - 1)d$$
$$= 0 \qquad\qquad \textbf{Hence proved.}$$

19. Given, AP sequence is 1, 4, 7, 10, ... whose first term is $a = 1$ and common difference, $d = 4 - 1 = 3$.

$\because$ Sum of n terms of an AP is

$$S_n = \frac{n}{2}[2a + (n-1)d]$$
$$\therefore \qquad S_{20} = \frac{20}{2}[2 \times 1 + (20 - 1) \times 3] \qquad \text{[put, } d = 3]$$
$$= 10\,[2 + 19 \times 3] = 10\,[2 + 57] = 590$$

Hence, sum of the first 20 terms of an AP is 590.

20. Given sequence in AP is 120, 116, 112, ...

Here, $a = 120$, $d = 116 - 120 = -4$

The nth term of an AP is

$$a_n = a + (n-1)\,d$$
$$a_n = 120 + (n-1)\,(-4)$$

For, first negative term, $a_n < 0$

$$\therefore \qquad 120 + (n-1)\,(-4) < 0$$
$$\Rightarrow \qquad 4\,(n-1) > 120$$
$$\Rightarrow \qquad (n-1) > 30$$
$$\Rightarrow \qquad n > 31$$

$\therefore$ The first negative term is 32.

21. Here, $a = 18$ and $d = -2$

Let n terms are taken, so that their sum is zero.

Then, we have

$$S_n = 0$$

$$\Rightarrow \quad \frac{n}{2}[2a + (n-1)d] = 0$$

$$\Rightarrow \quad 2a + (n-1)d = 0$$

$$\Rightarrow \quad 2 \times 18 + (n-1)(-2) = 0$$

$$\Rightarrow \quad n - 1 = 18 \Rightarrow n = 19$$

22. First 8 multiples of 3 are 3, 6, 9, 12, 15, 18, 21, 24.

∴ The sum of first 8 multiples of 3

$$= \frac{n}{2}[a + l] = \frac{8}{2}[3 + 24] = 4 \times 27 = 108$$

23. The annual salary received by Subha Rao in the years 1995, 1996, 1997 etc., is ₹ 5000, ₹ 5200, ₹ 5400, ..., ₹ 7000

Hence, the list of numbers 5000, 5200, 5400, ..., 7000 forms an AP

$$\because \qquad a_2 - a_1 = a_3 - a_2 = 200$$

Let nth term of an AP, $a_n = 7000$

$$\Rightarrow \qquad 7000 = a + (n-1)d \quad [\because a_n = a + (n-1)d]$$

$$\Rightarrow \qquad 7000 = 5000 + (n-1)(200)$$

$$\Rightarrow \qquad 200(n-1) = 7000 - 5000 = 2000$$

$$\Rightarrow \qquad n - 1 = \frac{2000}{200} = 10$$

$$\Rightarrow \qquad n = 10 + 1 = 11$$

Thus, 11th year of his service or in 2005 Subha Rao received an annual salary ₹ 7000.

24. Ramkali' savings in the subsequent weeks are respectively ₹ 5, ₹ 5 + ₹ 1.75, ₹ 5 + 2 × ₹ 1.75, ₹ 5 + 3 × 1.75 ...

In nth week her saving will be ₹ 5 + $(n-1)$ × ₹ 1.75

$$\Rightarrow \qquad 5 + (n-1) \times 1.75 = 20.75 \qquad \text{[given]}$$

$$\Rightarrow \qquad (n-1) \times 1.75 = 20.75 - 5 = 15.75$$

$$\Rightarrow \qquad n - 1 = \frac{15.75}{1.75} = 9$$

$$\Rightarrow \qquad n = 9 + 1 = 10$$

25. Given, $\dfrac{1 + 3 + 5 + \ldots \text{ upto } n \text{ terms}}{2 + 5 + 8 + \ldots \text{ upto } 8 \text{ term}} = 9$

$$\Rightarrow \qquad \frac{\dfrac{n}{2}[2(1) + (n-1)2]}{\dfrac{8}{2}[2(2) + (8-1)3]} = 9$$

$$\Rightarrow \qquad \frac{n(2n)}{8(25)} = 9$$

$$\Rightarrow n^2 = 9 \times 100 \Rightarrow n^2 = 900 \Rightarrow n = 30$$

26. $\because$ nth term of an AP,

$$a_n = S_n - S_{n-1}$$

$$= 3n^2 + 5n - 3(n-1)^2 - 5(n-1)$$

$$[\because S_n = 3n^2 + 5n \text{ (given)}]$$

$$= 3n^2 + 5n - 3n^2 - 3 + 6n - 5n + 5$$

$$a_n = 6n + 2 \qquad \ldots\text{(i)}$$

or $\qquad a_k = 6k + 2 = 164 \qquad [\because a_k = 164 \text{ (given)}]$

$$\Rightarrow \qquad 6k = 164 - 2 = 162$$

$$\therefore \qquad k = 27$$

27. Given series is $(-5) + (-8) + (-11) + \ldots + (-230)$

Here, first term, $a = -5$ and common difference,

$$d = -8 - (-5) = -8 + 5 = -3$$

$$\because \qquad a_n = a + (n-1)d$$

$$\therefore \qquad (-230) = -5 + (n-1)(-3)$$

$$\Rightarrow \qquad (n-1)(-3) = -230 + 5$$

$$\Rightarrow \qquad (n-1) = \frac{-225}{-3}$$

$$\Rightarrow \qquad n - 1 = 75$$

$$\Rightarrow \qquad n = 75 + 1 = 76$$

$\because$ The sum of n th term is

$$S_n = \frac{n}{2}[a + l]$$

$$\therefore \qquad S_n = \frac{76}{2}[-5 + (-230)]$$

$$= 38[-235] = -8930$$

28. $\qquad S_n = 5n^2 - 3n$

Now, $\quad a_n = S_n - S_{n-1}$

$$= 5n^2 - 3n - [5(n-1)^2 - 3(n-1)]$$

$$= 5n^2 - 3n - [5(n^2 + 1 - 2n) - 3n + 3]$$

$$\Rightarrow \qquad a_n = 10n - 8 \qquad \ldots\text{(i)}$$

Clearly, $a_{16} = 10 \times 16 - 8 = 160 - 8 = 152$

Now, for finding AP, put $n = 1, 2, 3, 4 \ldots\ldots$ in Eq. (i).

So, from Eq. (i), we have

$$a_1 = 2, \ a_2 = 12, \ a_3 = 22$$

The AP is 2, 12, 22, ...

29. Given, $a_1 = 8$, $d_1 = 20$, $a_2 = -30$, $d_2 = 8$

$$S_n = S_{2n}$$

$$\frac{n}{2}[2 \times 8 + (n-1) \times 20] = \frac{2n}{2}[2 \times (-30) \times 30 + (2n-1) \times 8]$$

$$\Rightarrow \qquad [16 + (n-1)20] = 2[-60 + (2n-1)8]$$

$$\Rightarrow \qquad 16 + 20n - 20 = -120 + 32n - 16$$

$$\Rightarrow \qquad 12n = 132 \Rightarrow n = 11$$

30. Here, $\quad a_1 = \sqrt{2}, \ a_2 = \sqrt{8} = 2\sqrt{2}, \ a_3 = 3\sqrt{2}$

$$\therefore \qquad a = \sqrt{2}, \ d = a_2 - a_1 = 2\sqrt{2} - \sqrt{2} = \sqrt{2}$$

$$\therefore \qquad S_{10} = \frac{10}{2}[2 \times \sqrt{2} + (10-1)(\sqrt{2})]$$

$$= 5[2\sqrt{2} + 9\sqrt{2}] = 55\sqrt{2}$$

31. The multiples of 7 lying between 500 and 900 are 504, 511, 518, ..., 896.

Clearly, it forms an AP.

Here, $a = 504$ and $d = 511 - 504 = 7$

Let there are n terms, i.e. $a_n = 896$

$$\Rightarrow \qquad a + (n-1)d = 896$$

$$\Rightarrow \qquad 504 + (n-1)7 = 896$$

$$\Rightarrow \qquad (n-1)7 = 392$$

$$\Rightarrow \qquad n - 1 = 56$$

$$\Rightarrow \qquad n = 57$$

Now, $\qquad S_{57} = \frac{n}{2}(a + l) = \frac{57}{2}(504 + 896)$

$$= \frac{57}{2} \times 1400 = 39900$$

32. The sequence of two digit number which divided by 5 and leave the remainder 2 is

12, 17, 22, ..., 97 which is an AP

Here, $a = 12$, $d = 17 - 12 = 5$ and $l = 97$

$\therefore \qquad l = a + (n - 1)\, d$

$\therefore \qquad 97 = 12 + (n - 1)5$

$\Rightarrow \qquad 85 = (n - 1)\, 5$

$\Rightarrow \qquad (n - 1) = 17$

$\Rightarrow \qquad n = 17 + 1 = 18$

$\therefore$ Required sum of two digit number which divided by

5 and leave the remainder 2 is $\dfrac{n}{2}(a + l)$

$$= \dfrac{18}{2}(12 + 97) = 9 \times 109 = 981$$

33. $\because$ Sum of n terms of an AP,

$$S_n = \dfrac{n}{2}[2a + (n - 1)\, d]\qquad \ldots(i)$$

$\therefore \qquad S_8 = \dfrac{8}{2}[2a + (8 - 1)\, d]$

$$= 4(2a + 7d) = 8a + 28d$$

and $\qquad S_4 = \dfrac{4}{2}[2a + (4 - 1)\, d]$

$$= 2(2a + 3d) = 4a + 6d$$

Now, $\qquad S_8 - S_4 = 8a + 28d - 4a - 6d = 4a + 22d \qquad \ldots(ii)$

and $\qquad S_{12} = \dfrac{12}{2}[2a + (12 - 1)\, d] = 6(2a + 11\, d)$

$$= 3(4a + 22d) = 3(S_8 - S_4) \quad [\text{from Eq. (ii)}]$$

$\therefore \qquad S_{12} = 3(S_8 - S_4) \qquad\qquad$ **Hence proved.**

34. For finding, the sum of last ten terms, we write the given AP in reverse order.

i.e. 126, 124, 122, ..., 12, 10, 8

Here, first term $(a) = 126$,

common difference,

$\qquad (d) = 124 - 126 = -2$

$\therefore \qquad S_{10} = \dfrac{10}{2}[2a + (10 - 1)\, d] \left[\because S_n = \dfrac{n}{2}[2a + (n - 1)\, d] \right]$

$$= 5\,\{2(126) + 9(-2)\}$$

$$= 5\,(252 - 18)$$

$$= 5 \times 234$$

$$= 1170$$

35. Let the sequence of 100 natural numbers be 1, 2, 3, ..., 100

Here, $a = 1$, $d = 2 - 1 = 3 - 2 = 1$

Thus, natural number sequence is an AP.

Now, sum of first 100 natural number is

$$S_{100} = \dfrac{100}{2}[2 \times 1 + (100 - 1)1] \left[S_n = \dfrac{n}{2}[2a + (n - 1)d] \right]$$

$$= 50[2 + 99]$$

$$= 50 \times 101 = 5050$$

36. For finding, the sum of first seven numbers which are multiples of 2 as well as of 9. Take LCM of 2 and 9 which is 18.

So, the series becomes 18, 36, 54,...

Here, first term $(a) = 18$,

common difference $(d) = 36 - 18 = 18$

$\therefore \qquad S_7 = \dfrac{n}{2}[2a + (n - 1)\, d]$

$$= \dfrac{7}{2}[2(18) + (7 - 1)\, 18]$$

$$= \dfrac{7}{2}[36 + 6 \times 18]$$

$$= 7\,(18 + 3 \times 18)$$

$$= 7\,(18 + 54)$$

$$= 7 \times 72 = 504$$

37. Given, first term of an AP, $a = 5$

Common difference, $d = 3$

nth term of an AP, $a_n = 50$

$\therefore \qquad a + (n - 1)d = 50$

$\Rightarrow \qquad 5 + (n - 1)3 = 50$

$\Rightarrow \qquad (n - 1)3 = 50 - 5$

$\Rightarrow \qquad n - 1 = \dfrac{45}{3}$

$\Rightarrow \qquad n - 1 = 15$

$\Rightarrow \qquad n = 15 + 1 = 16$

$\therefore$ The sum of nth term of an AP is

$$S_n = \dfrac{n}{2}[2a + (n - 1)d]$$

$\therefore \qquad S_{16} = \dfrac{16}{2}[2 \times 5 + (16 - 1) \times 3]$

$$= 8[10 + 15 \times 3]$$

$$= 8[10 + 45]$$

$$= 8 \times 55 = 440$$

38. Let a and d be the first term and common difference of an AP. Then,

$$a_4 = -15 \text{ and } a_9 = -30$$

$\Rightarrow \qquad a + (4 - 1)\, d = -15$

and $\qquad a + (9 - 1)d = -30$

$\Rightarrow \qquad a + 3d = -15 \qquad\qquad \ldots(i)$

and $\qquad a + 8d = -30 \qquad\qquad \ldots(ii)$

On subtracting Eq. (i) from Eq. (ii), we get

$$8d - 3d = -30 - (-15)$$

$\Rightarrow \qquad 5d = -30 + 15$

$\Rightarrow \qquad d = -\dfrac{15}{5}$

$\Rightarrow \qquad d = -3$

Put $d = -3$ in Eq. (i), we get

$$a + 3(-3) = -15$$

$\Rightarrow \qquad a = -15 + 9$

$\Rightarrow \qquad a = -6$

$\therefore$ The sum of first 16 terms of an AP is

$$S_n = \dfrac{n}{2}[2a + (n - 1)d]$$

$\Rightarrow \qquad S_{16} = \dfrac{16}{2}[2(-6) + 15\,(-3)]$

$$= 8[-12 - 45]$$

$$= 8 \times (-57) = -456$$

39. Let a and d be the first term and common difference of an AP. Then,

$$S_{14} = 1050 \text{ and } T_4 = 40 \qquad \text{[given]}$$

$$\Rightarrow \quad \frac{14}{2}[2a + (14 - 1)d] = 1050 \text{ and } a + (4 - 1)d = 40$$

$$\Rightarrow \quad 7[2a + 13d] = 1050 \text{ and } a + 3d = 40$$

$$\Rightarrow \quad 2a + 13d = 150 \qquad \text{...(i)}$$

$$\text{and} \qquad a + 3d = 40 \qquad \text{...(ii)}$$

Multiply Eq. (ii) by 2 and subtract Eq. (ii) from Eq. (i),

$$13d - 6d = 150 - 80$$

$$\Rightarrow \quad 7d = 70$$

$$\Rightarrow \quad d = 10$$

Put $d = 10$ in Eq. (i), we get

$$2a + 13 \times 10 = 150$$

$$\Rightarrow \quad 2a = 150 - 130$$

$$\Rightarrow \quad 2a = 20$$

$$\Rightarrow \quad a = 10$$

$\therefore$ The 20th term of an AP is

$$a_{20} = a + (20 - 1)d$$

$$= 10 + 19 \times 10$$

$$= 10 + 190 = 200$$

40. Let the first term, common difference and number of terms of the AP 9, 7, 5, ... are a_1, d_1 and n_1, respectively.

i.e. first term $(a_1) = 9$ and common difference (d_1)

$$= 7 - 9 = -2.$$

$\therefore$ Its nth term, $\quad T'_n = a_1 + (n - 1)d_1$

$$\Rightarrow \quad T'_n = 9 + (n - 1)(-2)$$

$$\Rightarrow \quad T'_n = 9 - 2n + 2$$

$$\Rightarrow \quad T'_n = 11 - 2n \qquad \text{...(i)}$$

Let the first term, common difference and the number of terms of the AP 24, 21, 18, ... are a_2, d_2 and n_2, respectively.

i.e. first term, $(a_2) = 24$ and common difference $(d_2) = 21 - 24 = -3$.

$\therefore$ Its nth term, $\quad T''_n = a_2 + (n - 1)d_2$

$$\Rightarrow \quad T''_n = 24 + (n - 1)(-3)$$

$$\Rightarrow \quad T''_n = 24 - 3n + 3$$

$$\Rightarrow \quad T''_n = 27 - 3n \qquad \text{...(ii)}$$

Now, by given condition,

nth terms of the both APs are same,

i.e. $\qquad T'_n = T''_n$

$$11 - 2n = 27 - 3n \qquad \text{[from Eqs. (i) and (ii)]}$$

$$\Rightarrow \quad n = 16$$

$\therefore$ nth term of first AP,

$$T'n = 11 - 2n = 11 - 2(16)$$

$$= 11 - 32 = -21$$

and nth term of second AP,

$$T''n = 27 - 3n$$

$$= 27 - 3(16) = 27 - 48 = -21$$

Hence, the value of n is 16 and that term i.e. nth term is –21.

41. Let the first term, common difference and number of terms of an AP are a, d and n, respectively.

We know that, if last term of an AP is known, then

$$l = a + (n - 1)d \qquad \text{...(i)}$$

and nth term of an AP is

$$T_n = a + (n - 1)d \qquad \text{...(ii)}$$

Given that, 26th term of an AP = 0

$$\Rightarrow \quad T_{26} = a + (26 - 1)d = 0 \qquad \text{[from Eq. (i)]}$$

$$\Rightarrow \quad a + 25d = 0 \qquad \text{...(iii)}$$

11th term of an AP = 3

$$\Rightarrow \quad T_{11} = a + (11 - 1)d = 3 \qquad \text{[from Eq. (ii)]}$$

$$\Rightarrow \quad a + 10d = 3 \qquad \text{... (iv)}$$

and last term of an AP $= -1/5$

$$\Rightarrow \quad l = a + (n - 1)d \qquad \text{[from Eq. (i)]}$$

$$\Rightarrow \quad -1/5 = a + (n - 1)d \qquad \text{...(v)}$$

Now, subtracting Eq. (iv) from Eq. (iii),

$$a + 25d = 0$$
$$a + 10d = 3$$
$$\underline{\quad - \quad - \qquad - \quad}$$
$$15d = -3$$

$$\Rightarrow \quad d = -\frac{1}{5}$$

Put the value of d in Eq. (iii), we get

$$a + 25\left(-\frac{1}{5}\right) = 0$$

$$\Rightarrow \quad a - 5 = 0$$

$$\Rightarrow \quad a = 5$$

Now, put the value of a, d in Eq. (v), we get

$$-1/5 = 5 + (n - 1)(-1/5)$$

$$\Rightarrow \quad -1 = 25 - (n - 1)$$

$$\Rightarrow \quad -1 = 25 - n + 1$$

$$\Rightarrow \quad n = 25 + 2 = 27$$

Hence, the common difference and number of terms are $-1/5$ and 27, respectively.

42. Let a and d be the first term and common difference of the given AP, respectively.

Given $\qquad a_4 = 0$

$$\Rightarrow \quad a + 3d = 0$$

$$\Rightarrow \quad a = -3d \qquad \text{...(i)}$$

Now, $\qquad a_{25} = a + 24d$

$$= -3d + 24d \qquad \text{[from Eq. (i)]}$$

$$\Rightarrow \quad a_{25} = 21d \qquad \text{...(ii)}$$

Also, $\qquad a_{11} = a + 10d$

$$= -3d + 10d \qquad \text{[From Eq. (i)]}$$

$$\Rightarrow \quad a_{11} = 7d$$

$$\Rightarrow \quad 3a_{11} = 21d \qquad \text{...(iii)}$$

From Eqs. (ii) and (iii), we get

$$a_{25} = 3a_{11} \qquad \textbf{Hence proved.}$$

43. Let a and d be the first term and common difference of an AP.

Then, $T_m = \dfrac{1}{n}$

$$\Rightarrow \quad a + (m - 1)d = \frac{1}{n} \qquad \text{...(i)}$$

and $\qquad T_n = \dfrac{1}{m}$

$$\Rightarrow \quad a + (n - 1)d = \frac{1}{m} \qquad \text{...(ii)}$$

Subtracting Eq. (ii) from Eq. (i), we get

$$[(m-1)-(n-1)]d = \frac{1}{n} - \frac{1}{m}$$

$$\Rightarrow \qquad (m-n)d = \frac{m-n}{mn}$$

$$\Rightarrow \qquad d = \frac{1}{mn}$$

Put $d = \dfrac{1}{mn}$ in Eq (i), we get

$$a + (m-1)\frac{1}{mn} = \frac{1}{n}$$

$$\Rightarrow \quad a = \frac{1}{n} - \frac{1}{mn}(m-1) = \frac{1}{mn}$$

$$\therefore \quad a_{mn} = a + (mn-1)d$$

$$= \frac{1}{mn} + (mn-1) \times \frac{1}{mn}$$

$$= \frac{1}{mn}[1 + mn - 1] = \frac{mn}{mn} = 1$$

44. Given first term of an AP, $a = 54$

Common difference, $d = -3$

and nth term of an AP,

$$a_n = 0$$

$$\Rightarrow \qquad a + (n-1)d = 0$$

$$\Rightarrow \qquad 54 + (n-1)(-3) = 0$$

$$\Rightarrow \qquad 54 - 3n + 3 = 0$$

$$\Rightarrow \qquad 3n = 57$$

$$\Rightarrow \qquad n = \frac{57}{3}$$

$$\Rightarrow \qquad n = 19$$

Now, sum of first 19 terms of given AP is

$$S_n = \frac{n}{2}[2a + (n-1)d]$$

$$\therefore \qquad S_{19} = \frac{19}{2}[2 \times 54 + (19-1)(-3)]$$

$$= \frac{19}{2}[108 - 54]$$

$$= 513$$

45. Given equation is $1 + 4 + 7 + 10 + ... + x = 287$

Consider series, $1 + 4 + 7 + 10 + ... + x$

Here, $a_1 = 1, a_2 = 4, a_3 = 7$

Now, $a_2 - a_1 = 4 - 1 = 3$

$$a_3 - a_2 = 7 - 4 = 3$$

It implies that common difference is constant say 3. So, it is an AP series, whose first term is $a = 1$ and common difference $d = 3$.

Here, last term of an AP is $l = x$

$$\because \qquad l = a + (n-1)d$$

$$\therefore \qquad x = 1 + (n-1) \times 3$$

$$\Rightarrow \qquad x = 1 + 3n - 3$$

$$\Rightarrow \qquad x = 3n - 2$$

$$\Rightarrow \qquad n = \frac{x+2}{3}$$

Now, sum of AP series is

$$S_n = \frac{n}{2}[2a + (n-1)d]$$

$$= \frac{1}{2}\left(\frac{x+2}{3}\right)\left[2 \times 1 + \left(\frac{x+2}{3} - 1\right)3\right]$$

$$= \frac{x+2}{6}[2 + x - 1]$$

$$\Rightarrow \qquad 287 = \frac{x+2}{6} \times (x+1)$$

$$\Rightarrow \qquad 1722 = x^2 + 3x + 2$$

$$\Rightarrow \qquad x^2 + 3x - 1720 = 0$$

$$\Rightarrow \quad x^2 + (43-40)x - 1720 = 0 \quad \text{[splitting middle term]}$$

$$\Rightarrow \qquad x^2 + 43x - 40x - 1720 = 0$$

$$\Rightarrow \qquad x(x+43) - 40(x+43) = 0$$

$$\Rightarrow \qquad (x-40)(x+43) = 0$$

$$\Rightarrow \qquad x = 40, -43$$

But $x = -43$ is not possible, because it is an increasing AP.

Hence, required value of x is 40.

46. Given, equation is $1 + 5 + 9 + 13 + ... + x = 1326$

Here, first term is $a_1 = 1$

last term is $a_n = l = x$

Difference of two consecutive terms,

$$5 - 1 = 4 \text{ and } 9 - 5 = 4, \text{ which is same.}$$

Thus, given series is an AP.

Then, nth term of given AP is

$$a_n = a + (n-1)d$$

$$\therefore \qquad x = 1 + (n-1)4$$

$$\Rightarrow \qquad (n-1)4 = x - 1$$

$$\Rightarrow \qquad n - 1 = \frac{x-1}{4}$$

$$\Rightarrow \qquad n = \frac{x-1}{4} + 1$$

$$\Rightarrow \qquad n = \frac{x+3}{4}$$

Now, sum of given AP is

$$S_n = \frac{n}{2}[2a + (n-1)d]$$

$$\therefore \qquad 1326 = \frac{x+3}{4 \times 2}\left[2 \times 1 + \frac{x+3}{4} \times 4\right]$$

$$\Rightarrow \qquad 1326 \times 8 = (x+3)[2 + x + 3]$$

$$\Rightarrow \qquad 10608 = (x+3)(x+5)$$

$$\Rightarrow \qquad x^2 + 8x + 15 - 10608 = 0$$

$$\Rightarrow \qquad x^2 + 8x - 10593 = 0$$

$$\Rightarrow \qquad x^2 + (107-99)x - 10593 = 0$$

$$\text{[by splitting middle term]}$$

$$\Rightarrow \qquad x^2 + 107x - 99x - 10593 = 0$$

$$\Rightarrow \qquad x(x+107) - 99(x+107) = 0$$

$$\Rightarrow \qquad (x-99)(x+107) = 0$$

$$\Rightarrow \qquad x = 99, -107$$

47. (i) Here, first term $(a) = 1$
and common difference
$$(d) = (-2) - 1 = -3$$
$\because$ Sum of n terms of an AP,
$$S_n = \frac{n}{2}[2a + (n-1)d]$$
$$\Rightarrow \qquad S_n = \frac{n}{2}[2 \times 1 + (n-1) \times (-3)]$$
$$\Rightarrow \qquad S_n = \frac{n}{2}(2 - 3n + 3)$$
$$\Rightarrow \qquad S_n = \frac{n}{2}(5 - 3n) \qquad \ldots(i)$$
We know that, if the last term (l) of an AP is known, then
$$l = a + (n-1)d$$
$$\Rightarrow \qquad -236 = 1 + (n-1)(-3) \; [\because l = -236, \text{ given}]$$
$$\Rightarrow \qquad -237 = -(n-1) \times 3$$
$$\Rightarrow \qquad n - 1 = 79$$
$$\Rightarrow \qquad n = 80$$
Now, put the value of n in Eq. (i), we get
$$S_n = \frac{80}{2}[5 - 3 \times 80]$$
$$= 40(5 - 240)$$
$$= 40 \times (-235)$$
$$= -9400$$
Hence, the required sum is -9400.
Alternate Method
Given, $a = 1$, $d = -3$ and $l = -236$
$\therefore$ Sum of n terms of an AP,
$$S_n = \frac{n}{2}[a + l]$$
$$= \frac{80}{2}[1 + (-236)] \qquad [\because n = 80]$$
$$= 40 \times (-235)$$
$$= -9400$$
(ii) Here, first term, $\quad a = 4 - \dfrac{1}{n}$

Common difference,
$$d = \left(4 - \frac{2}{n}\right) - \left(4 - \frac{1}{n}\right) = \frac{-2}{n} + \frac{1}{n} = \frac{-1}{n}$$
$\because$ Sum of n terms of an AP,
$$S_n = \frac{n}{2}[2a + (n-1)d]$$
$$\Rightarrow \quad S_n = \frac{n}{2}\left[2\left(4 - \frac{1}{n}\right) + (n-1)\left(\frac{-1}{n}\right)\right]$$
$$= \frac{n}{2}\left\{8 - \frac{2}{n} - 1 + \frac{1}{n}\right\}$$
$$= \frac{n}{2}\left(7 - \frac{1}{n}\right)$$
$$= \frac{n}{2} \times \left(\frac{7n-1}{n}\right)$$
$$= \frac{7n-1}{2}$$

48. Given AP sequence is $-\dfrac{4}{3}, -1, -\dfrac{2}{3}, \ldots, 4\dfrac{1}{3}$

Here, first term $(a) = -\dfrac{4}{3}$,

common difference $(d) = -1 + \dfrac{4}{3} = \dfrac{1}{3}$

and the last term $(l) = 4\dfrac{1}{3} = \dfrac{13}{3}$

$\because$ nth term of an AP,
$$l = a_n = a + (n-1)d$$
$$\Rightarrow \qquad \frac{13}{3} = -\frac{4}{3} + (n-1)\frac{1}{3}$$
$$\Rightarrow \qquad 13 = -4 + (n-1)$$
$$\Rightarrow \qquad n - 1 = 17$$
$$\Rightarrow \qquad n = 18 \qquad \text{[even]}$$
So, the two middle most terms are $\left(\dfrac{n}{2}\right)$th and $\left(\dfrac{n}{2} + 1\right)$th.

i.e. $\left(\dfrac{18}{2}\right)$th and $\left(\dfrac{18}{2} + 1\right)$th terms

i.e. 9th and 10th terms.
$$\therefore \qquad a_9 = a + 8d = -\frac{4}{3} + 8\left(\frac{1}{3}\right) = \frac{-4+8}{3} = \frac{4}{3}$$
$$\text{and} \qquad a_{10} = a + 9d = \frac{-4}{3} + 9\left(\frac{1}{3}\right) = \frac{-4+9}{3} = \frac{5}{3}$$
So, sum of the two middle most terms
$$= a_9 + a_{10}$$
$$= \frac{4}{3} + \frac{5}{3} = \frac{9}{3} = 3$$

49. Let the first term, common difference and the number of terms in an AP are a, d and n, respectively.
We know that, the nth term of an AP,
$$T_n = a + (n-1)d \qquad \ldots (i)$$
$\therefore$ 4th term of an AP,
$$T_4 = a + (4-1)d = -15 \qquad \text{[given]}$$
$$\Rightarrow \qquad a + 3d = -15 \qquad \ldots(ii)$$
and 9th term of an AP,
$$T_9 = a + (9-1)d = -30 \qquad \text{[given]}$$
$$\Rightarrow \qquad a + 8d = -30 \qquad \ldots(iii)$$
Now, subtract Eq. (ii) from Eq. (iii), we get
$$\begin{array}{r} a + 8d = -30 \\ a + 3d = -15 \\ \underline{- \quad - \quad \quad +} \\ 5d = -15 \end{array}$$
$$\Rightarrow \qquad d = -3$$
Put the value of d in Eq. (ii), we get
$$a + 3(-3) = -15$$
$$\Rightarrow \qquad a - 9 = -15$$
$$\Rightarrow \qquad a = -15 + 9$$
$$\Rightarrow \qquad a = -6$$
$\because$ Sum of first n terms of an AP,
$$S_n = \frac{n}{2}[2a + (n-1)d]$$

$\therefore$ Sum of first 17 terms of an AP,

$$S_{17} = \frac{17}{2}[2 \times (-6) + (17 - 1)(-3)]$$

$$= \frac{17}{2}[-12 + (16)(-3)]$$

$$= \frac{17}{2}(-12 - 48)$$

$$= \frac{17}{2} \times (-60)$$

$$= 17 \times (-30)$$

$$= -510$$

Hence, the required sum of first 17 terms of an AP is -510.

50. Given first term of each sum of an AP is 1 and common ratio of each sum are 1, 2 and 3, respectively.

$$\therefore \qquad S_1 = \frac{n}{2}[2(1) + (n - 1)1]$$

$$= \frac{n}{2}[2 + n - 1]$$

$$= \frac{n}{2}(n + 1)$$

$$\therefore \qquad S_2 = \frac{n}{2}[2(1) + (n - 1)2]$$

$$= \frac{n}{2}[2 + 2n - 2]$$

$$= n^2$$

and $\qquad S_3 = \frac{n}{2}[2(1) + (n - 1)3]$

$$= \frac{n}{2}[2 + 3n - 3]$$

$$= \frac{n}{2}(3n - 1)$$

$$\text{LHS} = S_1 + S_3$$

$$= \frac{n}{2}(n + 1) + \frac{n}{2}(3n - 1)$$

$$= \frac{n}{2}[n + 1 + 3n - 1]$$

$$= \frac{n}{2} \times 4n$$

$$= 2n^2 = 2S_2 \qquad \textbf{Hence proved.}$$

51. Given, $S_4 = 40$ and $S_{14} = 280$

Let a be the first term and d be the common difference of given AP. Then, $S_4 = 40 \Rightarrow \frac{4}{2}[2a + (4-1)d] = 40$

$$\left[\because S_n = \frac{n}{2}\{2a + (n - 1)d\}\right]$$

$$\Rightarrow \quad 2[2a + 3d] = 40 \Rightarrow 2a + 3d = 20 \qquad \ldots(i)$$

and $\qquad S_{14} = 280$

$$\Rightarrow \qquad \frac{14}{2}[2a + (14 - 1)d] = 280$$

$$\Rightarrow \qquad 2a + 13d = 40 \qquad \ldots(ii)$$

On subtracting Eq. (i) from Eq. (ii), we get

$$10d = 20 \Rightarrow d = 2$$

On substituting $d = 2$ in Eq. (i), we get

$$\Rightarrow \qquad 2a + 3 \times 2 = 20$$

$$\Rightarrow \qquad 2a = 14$$

$$a = 7$$

Now, $S_n = \frac{n}{2}[2a + (n - 1)d] = \frac{n}{2}[2(7) + (n - 1)2]$

$$= \frac{n}{2}[14 + 2n - 2] = n[6 + n] = 6n + n^2$$

Hence, the sum of first n terms is $n^2 + 6n$.

52. Let a and d be the first term and common difference of an AP.

Given that, $\qquad a_{11} : a_{18} = 2 : 3$

$$\Rightarrow \qquad \frac{a + 10d}{a + 17d} = \frac{2}{3}$$

$$\Rightarrow \qquad 3a + 30d = 2a + 34d$$

$$\Rightarrow \qquad a = 4d \qquad \ldots(i)$$

Now, $\qquad a_5 = a + 4d = 4d + 4d = 8d \quad$ [from Eq. (i)]

and $\qquad a_{21} = a + 20d = 4d + 20d = 24d$ [from Eq. (i)]

$$\therefore \qquad a_5 : a_{21} = 8d : 24d = 1 : 3$$

Now, sum of the first five terms,

$$S_5 = \frac{5}{2}[2a + (5 - 1)d]$$

$$= \frac{5}{2}[2(4d) + 4d] \qquad \text{[from Eq. (i)]}$$

$$= \frac{5}{2}(8d + 4d) = \frac{5}{2} \times 12d = 30d$$

and sum of the first 21 terms,

$$S_{21} = \frac{21}{2}[2a + (21 - 1)d]$$

$$= \frac{21}{2}[2(4d) + 20d] \qquad \text{[from Eq. (i)]}$$

$$= \frac{21}{2}(28d) = 294d$$

So, ratio of the sum of the first five terms to the sum of the first 21 terms

$$S_5 : S_{21} = 30d : 294d = 5 : 49$$

53. Let the four consecutive number of an AP be $a, a + d, a + 2d$ and $a + 3d$.

Since, sum of four consecutive number in AP is 32.

$$\therefore \quad a + a + d + a + 2d + a + 3d = 32$$

$$\Rightarrow \qquad 4a + 6d = 32$$

$$\Rightarrow \qquad 2a + 3d = 16 \qquad \text{[divide by 2]}$$

$$\Rightarrow \qquad a = \frac{16 - 3d}{2} \qquad \ldots(i)$$

According to the question,

$$\frac{\text{Product of first and last terms}}{\text{Product of two middle terms}} = \frac{7}{15}$$

$$\frac{a(a + 3d)}{(a + d)(a + 2d)} = \frac{7}{15}$$

$$\Rightarrow \qquad 15a(a + 3d) = 7(a + d)(a + 2d)$$

$$\Rightarrow \qquad 15a^2 + 45ad = 7a^2 + 21ad + 14d^2$$

$$\Rightarrow \qquad 8a^2 + 24ad - 14d^2 = 0$$

$$\Rightarrow \qquad 4a^2 + 12ad - 7d^2 = 0 \qquad \text{[divide by 2]}$$

$\Rightarrow \qquad 4a^2 + (14 - 2)ad - 7d^2 = 0$

$$[\text{by splitting middle term}]$$

$\Rightarrow \qquad 4a^2 + 14ad - 2ad - 7d^2 = 0$

$\Rightarrow \qquad 2a(2a + 7d) - d(2a + 7d) = 0$

$\Rightarrow \qquad (2a + 7d)(2a - d) = 0$

$\Rightarrow \qquad a = -\dfrac{7d}{2} \text{ and } a = \dfrac{d}{2} \qquad \qquad …(ii)$

Put $a = -\dfrac{7d}{2}$ in Eq. (i), we get

$$-\frac{7d}{2} = \frac{16 - 3d}{2}$$

$\Rightarrow \qquad -7d = 16 - 3d$

$\Rightarrow \qquad 4d = -16 \Rightarrow d = -4$

Now, put $a = \dfrac{d}{2}$ in Eq. (i), we get

$$\frac{d}{2} = \frac{16 - 3d}{2}$$

$\Rightarrow \qquad d = 16 - 3d$

$\Rightarrow \qquad 4d = 16 \Rightarrow d = 4$

For $a = -\dfrac{7d}{2}$ and $d = -4$, then

$$a = -\frac{7 \times (-4)}{2} = 14$$

For $a = \dfrac{d}{2}$ and $d = 4$, then $a = \dfrac{4}{2} = 2$

Therefore, the four consecutive numbers in an AP are
$14, [14 + (-4)], [14 + (2 \times -4)], [14 + (3 \times -4)]$
or $2, (2 + 4), (2 + 2 \times 4), (2 + 3 \times 4)$.

Hence, the numbers are 14, 10, 6, 2 or 2, 6, 10, 14.

54. Given that, the AP is a, b, c.

Here, first term $= a$, common difference $= b - a$

and last term, $l = a_n = c$

$\because \qquad a_n = l = a + (n - 1)\,d$

$\Rightarrow \qquad c = a + (n - 1)(b - a)$

$\Rightarrow \qquad (n - 1) = \dfrac{c - a}{b - a}$

$\Rightarrow \qquad n = \dfrac{c - a}{b - a} + 1$

$\Rightarrow \qquad n = \dfrac{c - a + b - a}{b - a} = \dfrac{c + b - 2a}{b - a} \qquad …(i)$

$\therefore$ Sum of an AP,

$$S_n = \frac{n}{2}[2a + (n - 1)\,d]$$

$$= \frac{(b + c - 2a)}{2(b - a)}\left[2a + \left\{\frac{b + c - 2a}{b - a} - 1\right\}(b - a)\right]$$

$$= \frac{(b + c - 2a)}{2(b - a)}\left[2a + \frac{c - a}{b - a} \cdot (b - a)\right]$$

$$= \frac{(b + c - 2a)}{2(b - a)}(2a + c - a)$$

$$= \frac{(b + c - 2a)}{2(b - a)} \cdot (a + c) \qquad \textbf{Hence proved.}$$

55. Given AP is $20, 19\dfrac{1}{3}, 18\dfrac{2}{3}, … .$

Here, $a = 20$ and $d = 19\dfrac{1}{3} - 20 = \dfrac{58}{3} - 20 = \dfrac{58 - 60}{3} = \dfrac{-2}{3}$

Let n terms of given AP be required to get sum 300.

We know that, $\quad S_n = \dfrac{n}{2}[2a + (n - 1)d]$

$\Rightarrow \qquad 300 = \dfrac{n}{2}\left[2(20) + (n - 1)\left(\dfrac{-2}{3}\right)\right]$

$$[\because a = 20 \text{ and } d = -2/3]$$

$\Rightarrow \qquad 600 = n\left[40 - \dfrac{2}{3}n + \dfrac{2}{3}\right]$

$\Rightarrow \qquad 600 = \dfrac{1}{3}[120n - 2n^2 + 2n]$

$\Rightarrow \qquad 600 \times 3 = 122n - 2n^2$

$\Rightarrow \qquad 1800 + 2n^2 - 122n = 0$

$\Rightarrow \qquad 2[n^2 - 61n + 900] = 0$

$\Rightarrow \qquad n^2 - 61n + 900 = 0 \qquad [\text{divide by 2}]$

$\Rightarrow \qquad n^2 - 36n - 25n + 900 = 0$

$\Rightarrow \qquad n(n - 36) - 25(n - 36) = 0$

$\Rightarrow \qquad (n - 36)(n - 25) = 0 \Rightarrow n = 36 \text{ or } 25$

Since, a is positive and d is negative, so both values of n are possible.

Hence, sum of 25 terms of given AP

$$= \text{Sum of 36 terms of given AP} = 300.$$

56. (i) Now, she takes ₹ 1 on day 1, ₹ 2 on day 2, ₹ 3 on day 3 and so on till the end of the month, from this money.

i.e. $1 + 2 + 3 + 4 + … + 31$.

which form an AP in which terms are 31 and first term $(a) = 1$, common difference $(d) = 2 - 1 = 1$

$\therefore$ Sum of first 31 terms $= S_{31}$

Sum of n terms,

$$S_n = \frac{n}{2}[2a + (n - 1)\,d]$$

$\therefore \qquad S_{31} = \dfrac{31}{2}[2 \times 1 + (31 - 1) \times 1]$

$$= \frac{31}{2}(2 + 30) = \frac{31 \times 32}{2} = 31 \times 16 = 496$$

So, Kanika takes ₹ 496 till the end of the month from this money.

(ii) Let her pocket money be ₹ x.

Now, she spent ₹ 204 of her pocket money and found that at the end of the month she still has ₹ 100 with her.

Now, according to the condition,

$$(x - 496) - 204 = 100$$

$\Rightarrow \qquad x - 700 = 100$

$\therefore \qquad x = ₹\ 800$

Hence, ₹ 800 was her pocket money for the month.

(iii) Here, $a = 1, d = 1, n = 13$

Now, $a_n = a + (n - 1)d$

$\Rightarrow \quad a_{13} = 1 + 12(1) = 1 + 12 = 13$

So, Kanika, saved ₹ 13 till January 13th, 2008.

Chapter Test

Multiple Choice Questions

1. The list of numbers $-10, -6, -2, 2, ...$ is

[**NCERT Exemplar**]

(a) an AP with $d = -16$ (b) an AP with $d = 4$
(c) an AP with $d = -4$ (d) not an AP

2. In an AP, if $a = 3.5$, $d = 0$ and $n = 101$, then a_n will be

(a) 0   (b) 3.5
(c) 103.5   (d) 104.5

3. Is an sequence defined by $a_n = 2n^2 + 1$ forms an AP?
(a) Yes
(b) Not
(c) Cannot be determined
(d) None of the above

4. The sum of first 20 terms of an AP in which $a = 1$ and 20th term $= 58$ is
(a) 590   (b) 580
(c) 570   (d) 560

5. The 10th term of an AP is 52 and 16th term is 82, then 32nd term of the AP is   [**NCERT Exemplar**]

(a) 152   (b) 159
(c) 162   (d) 156

Case Based MCQs

6. Kartik starts repaying a loan as first installment of
₹100. He increases the installment by ₹5 every month.
(i) AP formed from the given situation is
(a) 105, 110, 115, ...   (b) 100, 105, 110, ...
(c) 95, 100, 105, ...   (d) 110, 115, 120, ...

(ii) The amount Kartik will pay in 30th installment is
(a) ₹ 265   (b) ₹ 235
(c) ₹ 255   (d) ₹ 245

(iii) If Kartik pays ₹ 795, then it is
(a) 140th installment
(b) 150th installment
(c) 160th installment
(d) 170th installment

(iv) Total amount paid in 13th and 17th installment is
(a) ₹ 380
(b) ₹ 300
(c) ₹ 360
(d) ₹ 340

(v) If he increases the installment by ₹ 6 every month, then the amount he will pay in 53th installment is
(a) ₹ 314   (b) ₹ 360
(c) ₹ 412   (d) ₹ 416

Short Answer Type Questions

7. Two AP's have the same common difference. The first term of one AP is 2 and that of the other is 7.

The difference between their 10th terms is the same as the difference between their 21st terms, which is the same as the difference between any two corresponding terms? Why?   [**NCERT Exemplar**]

8. Determine the AP whose fifth term is 19 and the difference of the eighth term from the thirteenth term is 20.

9. Find the sum of all the 11 terms of an AP whose middle most term is 30.

Long Answer Type Questions

10. An AP consists of 37 terms. The sum of the three middle most terms is 225 and the sum of the last three terms is 429. Find the AP.

11. If sum of first 6 terms of an AP is 36 and that of the first 16 terms is 256, then find the sum of first 10 terms.

12. Which term of the AP : 121, 117, 113, ... is its second negative term?

13. The sum of the third and the seventh terms of an AP is 6 and their product is 8. Find the sum of first sixteen terms of the AP.

14. Solve the equation $-4 + (-1) + 2 + ... + x = 437$.

Answers

1. (b)   **2.** (b)   **3.** (b)   **4.** (c)   **5.** (a)   **6.** (i) (b) (ii) (d) (iii) (a) (iv) (d) (v) (c)

7. (37)   **8.** 3, 7, 11, 15   **9.** 330   **10.** 3, 7, 11, 15

11. 100   **12.** 33rd term   **13.** 20 or 76   **14.** $x = 50$

For Detailed Solutions

Scan the code

CHAPTER 03

Circles

In this Chapter...

- Circle
- Tangent of a Circle
- Theorem Related to Tangent of a Circle

A circle is a collection of all points in a plane which are at a constant distance i.e. radius from a fixed point i.e. centre.

In the given figure, O is the centre of circle and OA is the radius of the circle. Also, AB is the diameter of the circle.

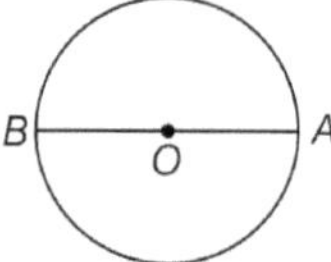

Two or more circles having the same centre are called concentric circles.

Some Important Terms Related to Circle

Chord

A line segment joining any two points on the circumference of the circle is called a **chord** of the circle. If this chord passes through the centre, then this chord (or diamter) is the longest chord of the circle.

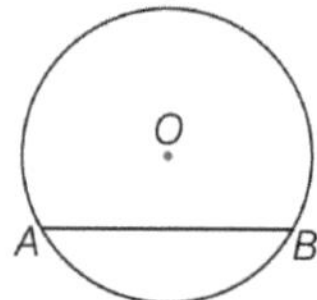

Semi-circle

A diameter of a circle divides it into two equal parts or in two equal arcs. Each of these two arcs is called a **semi-circle**.

Circumference

The length of the complete circle is called the circumference of the circle.

Arc

A continuous piece of a circle is called an **arc**. In adjoining figure, P and Q are two points on a circle which divide it into two parts, called the arcs. The larger part is called the **major arc** $\overparen{QRP}$ and the smaller part is called the **minor arc** $\overparen{PMQ}$.

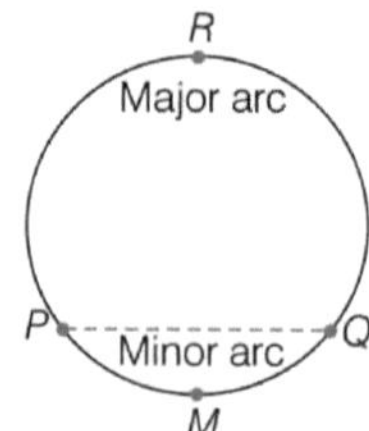

Segment

The region between a chord and either of its arcs is called a **segment** of the circular region or simply a segment of the circle. The segment formed by minor arc along with chord, is called **minor segment** and the segment formed by major arc, is called the **major segment**.

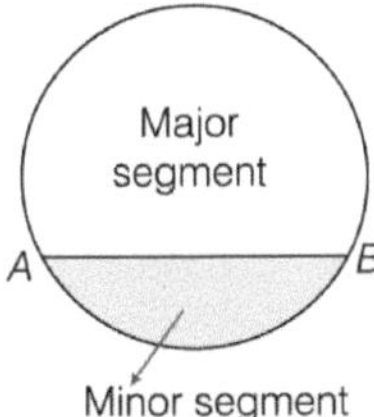

Sector

The region between an arc and the two radii, joining the ends of the arc to the centre, is called a **sector**.

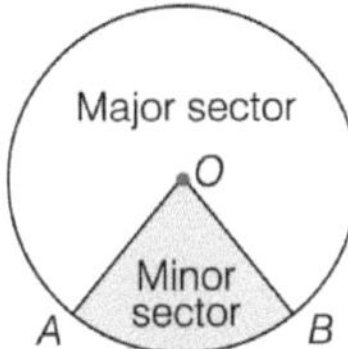

The sector formed by minor arc, is called **minor sector** and the sector formed by major arc, is called **major sector**.

Important Results Related to Circle

(i) The perpendicular drawn from the centre of a circle to a chord bisects it and *vice-versa*.

(ii) Equal chords of a circle are equidistant from the centre.

(iii) The angle subtended by an arc (or corresponding chord) at the centre of the circle is twice the angle subtended by the same arc at any point on the remaining part of the circle.

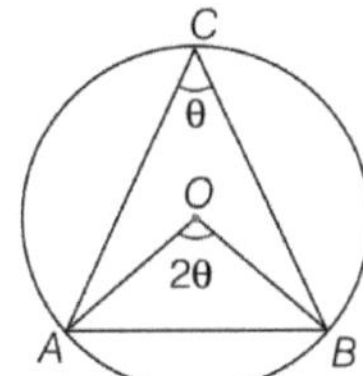

(iv) Equal chords of a circle subtend equal angles at the centre.

(v) The angle in a semi-circle is a right angle.

(vi) Angles in the same segment of a circle are equal.

(vii) The sum of any pair of opposite angles of a cyclic quadrilateral is $180°$.

(viii) If two circles intersect at two points, then the line through the centres is the perpendicular bisector of the common chord.

Tangent to a Circle

A line which touches the circle at a point, is called tangent to a circle.

In the figure, O is the centre of circle, AB is a tangent line and P is a point of contact.

- There is only one tangent at a point of the circle.
- A circle can have maximum two parallel tangents which can be drawn to the opposite sides of the centre.

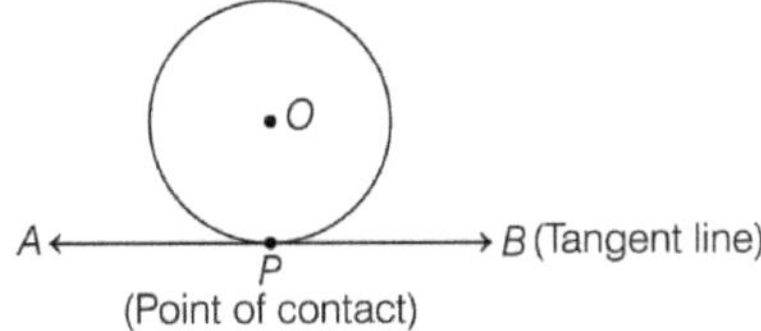

Length of a Tangent

The length of the segment of the tangent, between the given point (on the tangent) and the point of contact, is called the length of tangent from the given point.

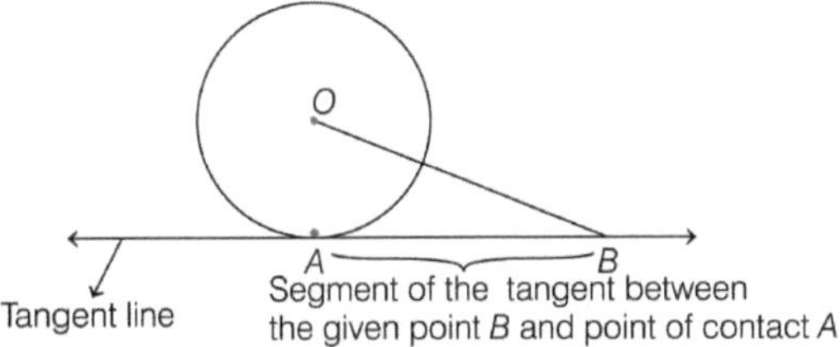

In the above figure, AB is called the length of tangent.

$\therefore$ Length of tangent to the circle from an exterior point,

$$AB = \sqrt{(\text{Distance of exterior point from centre})^2 - (\text{Radius})^2}$$

Number of Tangent from a Point on a Circle

(i) If point P lies outside the circle, then two tangents can be drawn to the circle, i.e. PT_1 and PT_2.

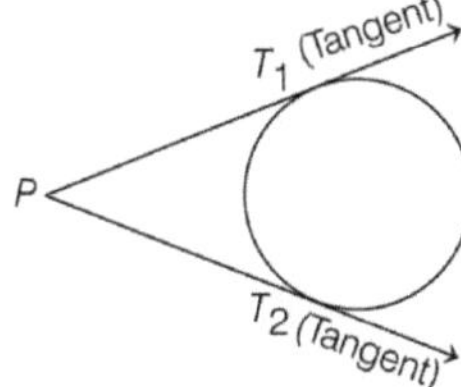

(ii) If point P lies on the circle, then there is one and only one tangent to a circle passing through point P.

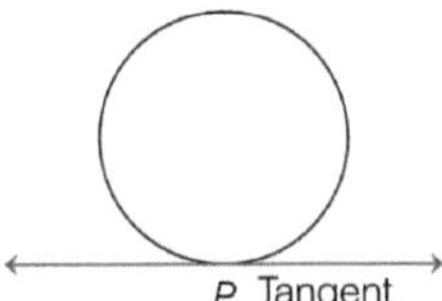

(iii) If a point P lies inside the circle, then there is no tangent to a circle passing through a point lying inside the circle.

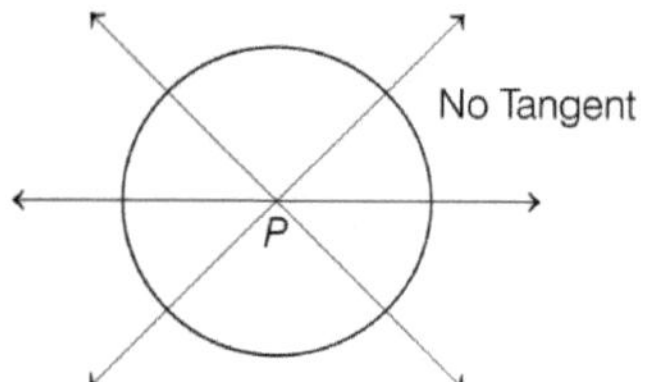

Theorems Related to Tangent of Circle

Theorem 1 The tangent at any point of a circle is perpendicular to the radius through the point of contact.

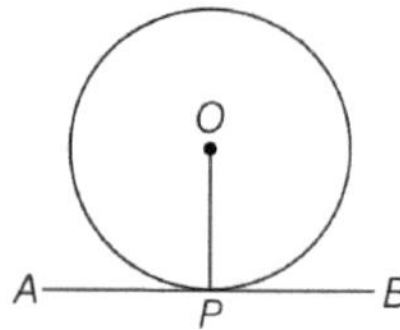

Here, O is centre of circle and AB is tangent of circle at P and it is point of contact and OP is radius.

$\therefore \qquad OP \perp AB.$

Theorem 2 A perpendicular drawn from the end point of radius is tangent to the circle. If $OP \perp AB$, then AB is tangent to circle.

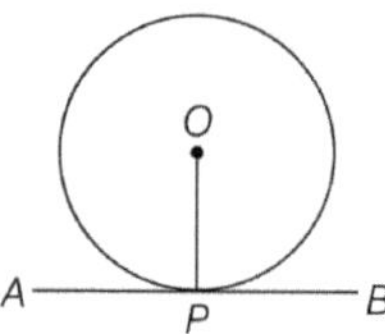

Theorem 3 The lengths of two tangents drawn from an external point to a circle are equal.

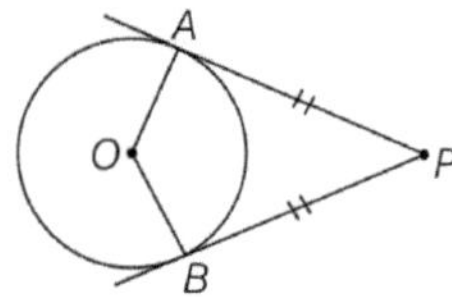

Here, P is exterior point and PA and PB are tangents.

$\therefore \qquad PA = PB$

Important Results Related to Tangent to a Circle

(i) If two circles touch internally or externally, then point of contact lies on the straight line through the two centres.

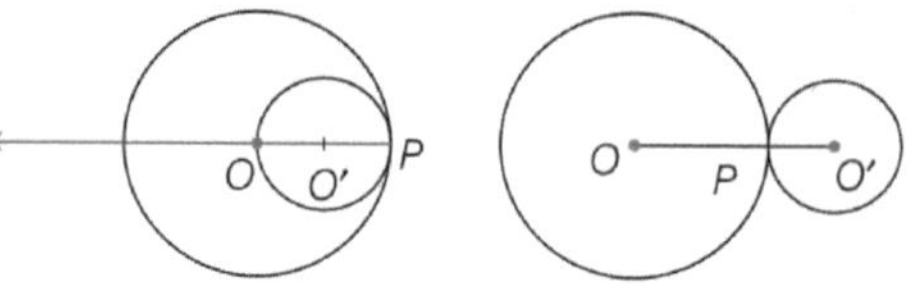

(ii) A pair of tangents drawn at two points of a circle are either parallel or they intersect each other at a point outside the circle.

(iii) If two tangents drawn to a circle are parallel to each other, then the line segment joining their point of contact is a diameter of the circle.

(iv) If two tangents are drawn to a circle from an external point, then

   (a) They subtend equal angles at the centre,

   i.e. $\quad \angle POA = \angle POB.$

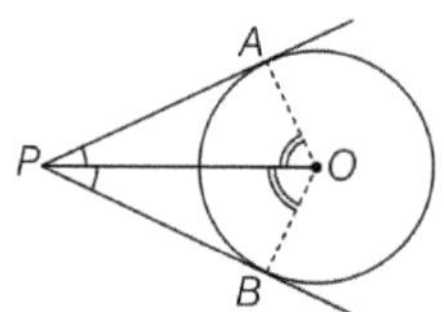

   (b) They are equally inclined to the segment joining the centre to that point,

   i.e. $\quad \angle APQ = \angle BPQ.$

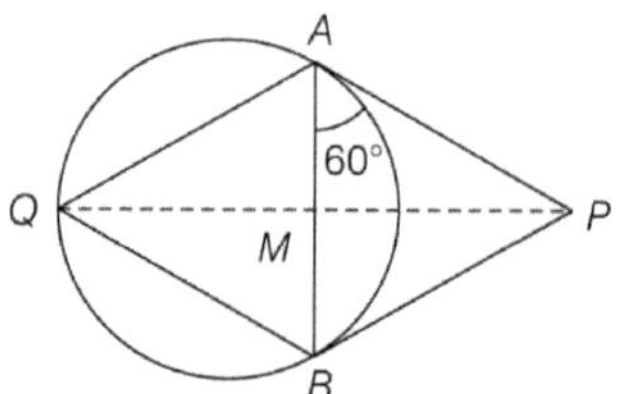

(v) The opposite sides of a quadrilateral circumscribing a circle subtend supplementary angles at the centre of the circle.

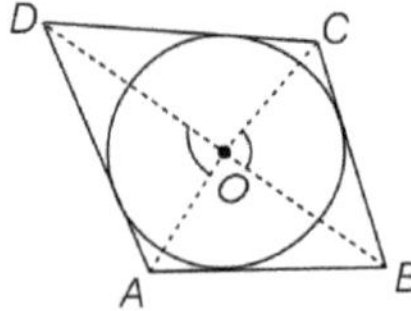

Solved Examples

Example 1. Prove that a tangent to a circle is perpendicular to the radius through the point of contact. **[CBSE 2020 (Standard)]**

Sol. **Given** A circle with centre O and a tangent AB at a point P on the circle.

To prove $OP \perp AB$

Construction Take any point Q, other than P on the tangent AB and join OQ.

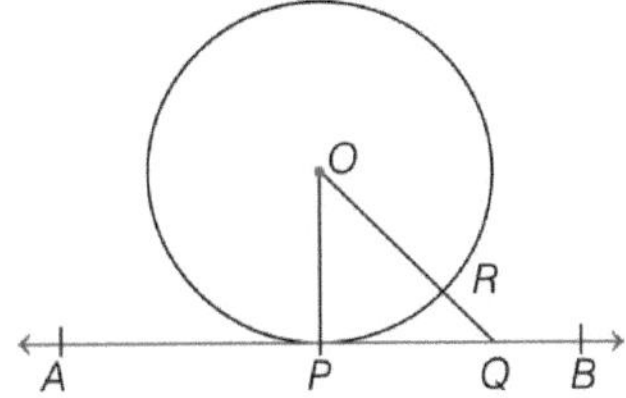

Proof Here, Q is a point on the tangent AB, other than the point of contact P. So, Q lies outside the circle (if Q lies inside the circle, then AB becomes a secant and not a tangent to the circle).

Let OQ intersects the circle at R.

Then,	$OP = OR$	[radii of the circle]
Now,	$OQ = OR + RQ$	
$\Rightarrow$	$OQ > OR$	
$\Rightarrow$	$OQ > OP$ or $OP < OQ$	$[\because OP = OR]$

Thus, OP is shorter than any other segment joining O to any point of AB. Also, we know that the shortest distance between a point and a line is perpendicular distance from the point to the line.

So, OP is perpendicular to AB.

i.e. $OP \perp AB$ **Hence proved.**

Example 2. In given figure, two circles touch each other at the point C. Prove that the common tangent to the circles at C, bisects the common tangent at P and Q.

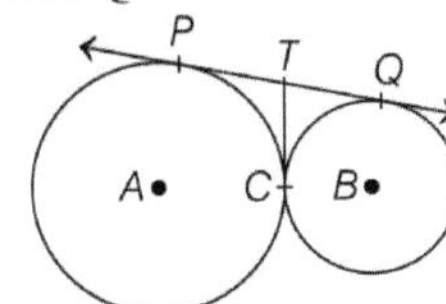

Sol. We know that, tangents drawn from an external point are of equal length. Therefore, according to the given figure,

$$TP = TC \quad …(i) [\because \text{point } T \text{ is external}]$$

and

$$TQ = TC \quad …(ii) [\because \text{point } T \text{ is external}]$$

From Eqs. (i) and (ii), we get

$$TP = TQ$$

Hence, T is the mid-point of the line segment PQ.

Example 3. In figure, PQ is tangent to the circle with centre O, at the point B. If $\angle AOB = 100°$, then find $\angle ABP$. **[CBSE 2020 (Standard)]**

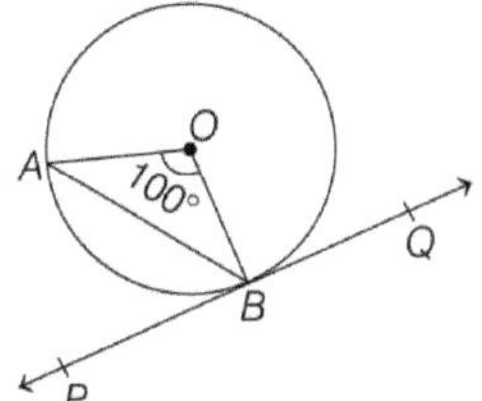

Sol. Given, $\angle AOB = 100°$,

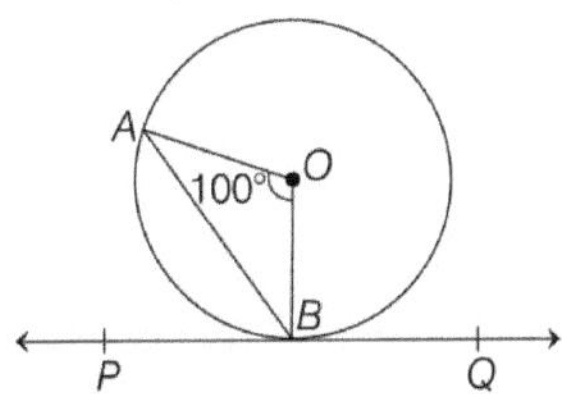

In ΔOAB,

	$OA = OB$	[radii of the circle]
$\Rightarrow$	$\angle OBA = \angle OAB$	

[angles opposite to equal sides are equal] …(i)

In ΔOAB,

$$\angle AOB + \angle OAB + \angle OBA = 180°$$

[by angle sum property of triangle]

$\Rightarrow$	$100° + \angle OBA + \angle OBA = 180°$	[from Eq. (i)]
$\Rightarrow$	$2\angle OBA = 180° - 100°$	
$\Rightarrow$	$\angle OBA = \dfrac{80°}{2}$	
$\Rightarrow$	$\angle OBA = 40°$	…(ii)

We know that, radius of circle is perpendicular to the tangent.

$\therefore$	$\angle OBP = 90° \Rightarrow \angle OBA + \angle ABP = 90°$
$\Rightarrow$	$40° + \angle ABP = 90°$
$\Rightarrow$	$\angle ABP = 90° - 40° \Rightarrow \angle ABP = 50°$

Example 4. In below figure, PA is a tangent from an external point P to a circle with centre O. If $\angle POB = 115°$, find $\angle APO$. **[CBSE 2020 (Standard)]**

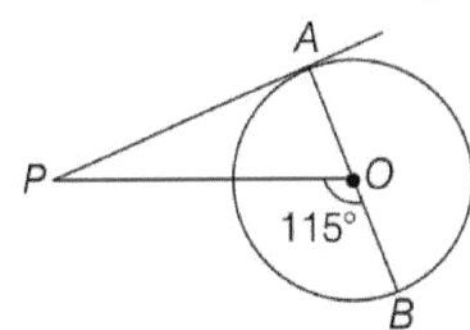

Sol. Given, $\angle POB = 115°$

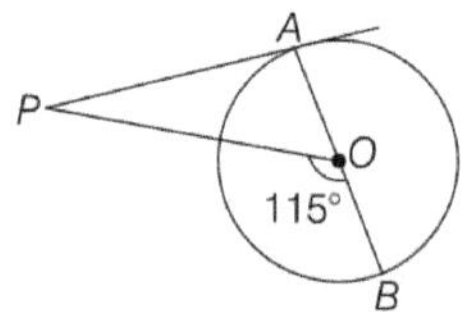

Since, AB is a straight line.

$\therefore$ $\qquad \angle POB + \angle AOP = 180°$

$\Rightarrow \qquad 115° + \angle AOP = 180°$

$\Rightarrow \qquad\qquad \angle AOP = 180° - 115°$

$\Rightarrow \qquad\qquad \angle AOP = 65°$

We know that, radius line is perpendicular to the tangent.

$\therefore \ \angle PAO = 90°$

In $\triangle AOP$,

$$\angle PAO + \angle AOP + \angle APO = 180°$$

$$[\because \text{ sum of all angles of a triangle is } 180°]$$

$\therefore \qquad 90° + 65° + \angle APO = 180°$

$\Rightarrow \qquad \angle APO = 180° - (65° + 90°)$

$$= 180° - 155° = 25°$$

Example 5. Prove that the length of tangents drawn from an external point to a circle are equal.

[CBSE 2020 (Standard)]

Sol. Let AP and AQ are two tangents drawn from a point A to a circle with centre O.

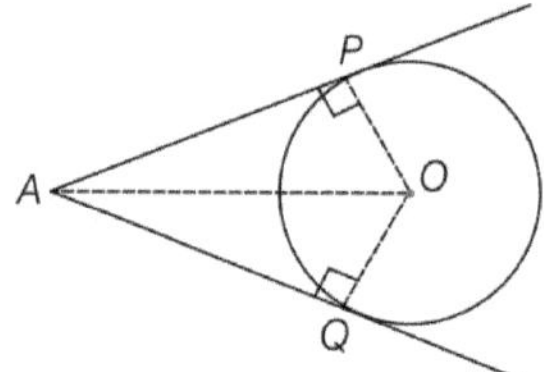

To prove $AP = AQ$

Construction Join OP, OQ and OA.

Proof We know that, a tangent at any point of a circle is perpendicular to the radius through the point of contact.

Here, AP is a tangent and OP is the radius of the circle through P.

$\therefore \qquad OP \perp AP$

Similarly, $\qquad OQ \perp AQ$

$\Rightarrow \qquad \angle OPA = \angle OQA = 90° \qquad$ ...(i)

First Method

In $\triangle OPA$ and $\triangle OQA$, we have

$$OP = OQ \qquad [\text{radii of a circle}]$$

$$\angle OPA = \angle OQA = 90° \qquad [\text{from Eq. (i)}]$$

$$OA = OA \qquad [\text{common sides}]$$

So, $\qquad \triangle OPA \cong \triangle OQA \quad [\text{by RHS congruence rule}]$

$\therefore \qquad AP = AQ \qquad\qquad [\text{by CPCT}]$

Second Method

In right angled $\triangle OPA$,

$$OA^2 = OP^2 + AP^2$$

$$[\text{by Pythagoras theorem}]$$

$\Rightarrow \qquad AP^2 = OA^2 - OP^2$

$\Rightarrow \qquad AP^2 = OA^2 - OQ^2$

$$[\because OP = OQ = \text{radii of a circle}] \text{ ...(ii)}$$

Now, in right angled $\triangle OQA$,

$$OA^2 = OQ^2 + AQ^2$$

$\Rightarrow \qquad AQ^2 = OA^2 - OQ^2 \qquad\qquad \text{...(iii)}$

From Eqs. (ii) and (iii), we get

$$AP^2 = AQ^2$$

$\Rightarrow \qquad AP = AQ \qquad\qquad$ **Hence proved.**

Example 6. Prove that the angle between the two tangents drawn from an external point to a circle is supplementary to the angle subtended by the line segment joining the points of contact at the centre.

Sol. Let PQ and PR be two tangents drawn from an external point P to a circle with centre O.

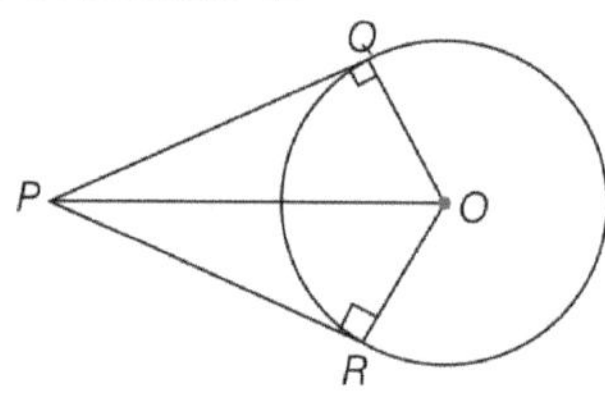

To prove $\angle QOR = 180° - \angle QPR$

or $\angle QOR + \angle QPR = 180°$

Proof In $\triangle OQP$ and $\triangle ORP$,

$$PQ = PR \qquad [\because \text{ tangents drawn from an}$$
$$\text{external point are equal in length}]$$

$$OQ = OR \qquad [\text{radii of circle}]$$

$$OP = OP \qquad [\text{common sides}]$$

$\therefore \qquad \triangle OQP \cong \triangle ORP \qquad [\text{by SSS congruence rule}]$

Then, $\qquad \angle QPO = \angle RPO \qquad [\text{by CPCT}]$

and $\qquad \angle POQ = \angle POR \qquad [\text{by CPCT}]$

$\Rightarrow \qquad \angle QPR = 2 \angle OPQ$

and $\qquad \angle QOR = 2 \angle POQ \qquad\qquad$ ...(i)

Now, in right angled $\triangle OQP$,

$$\angle QPO + \angle QOP = 90°$$

$\Rightarrow \qquad \angle QOP = 90° - \angle QPO$

$\Rightarrow \qquad 2\angle QOP = 180° - 2 \angle QPO$

$$[\text{multiplying both sides by 2}]$$

$\Rightarrow \qquad \angle QOR = 180° - \angle QPR \qquad [\text{from Eq. (i)}]$

$\Rightarrow \qquad \angle QOR + \angle QPR = 180° \qquad$ **Hence proved.**

Example 7. In figure, find the perimeter of $\triangle ABC$, if $AP = 12$ cm.

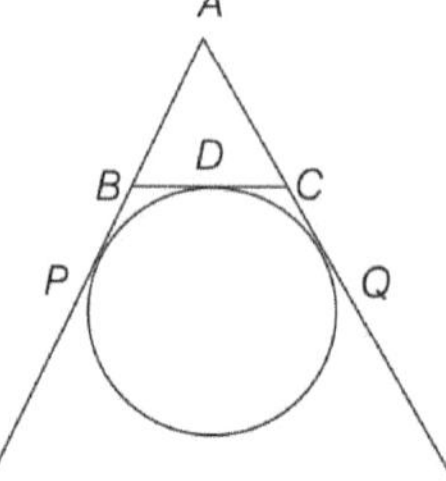

Sol. Given, $AP = 12\,\text{cm}$

$\Rightarrow \quad AQ = AP = 12\,\text{cm}$

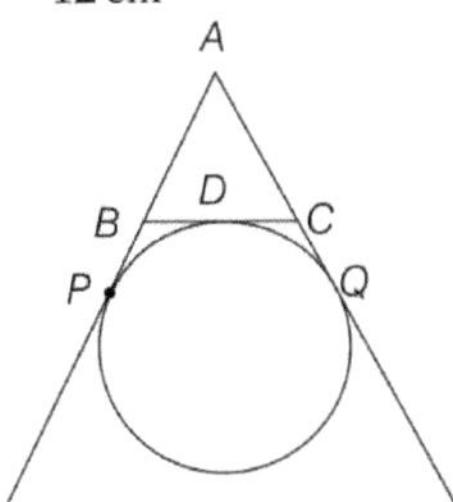

$[\because$ tangents drawn from an external point are equal in lengths$]$

Also, $\qquad\qquad BD = BP$

$\qquad\qquad [\because B$ is an external point$]\ \dots(i)$

and $\qquad\qquad CD = CQ$

$\qquad\qquad [\because C$ is an external point$]\ \dots(ii)$

Now, $\quad AP = AB + BP$

$\Rightarrow \qquad 12 = AB + BD \qquad$ [from Eq. (i)] $\dots(iii)$

and $\qquad AQ = AC + CQ$

$\Rightarrow \qquad 12 = AC + CD \qquad$ [from Eq. (i)] $\dots(iv)$

Perimeter of $\triangle ABC$

$\qquad = AB + BC + AC$

$\qquad = AB + BD + DC + AC$

$\qquad = 12 + 12 \qquad$ [from Eqs. (iii) and (iv)]

$\qquad = 24\,\text{cm}$

Hence, perimeter of a $\triangle ABC$ is 24 cm.

Example 8. In below figure, $\triangle ABC$ is circumscribing a circle, the length of BC is …… cm.

[CBSE 2020 (Standard)]

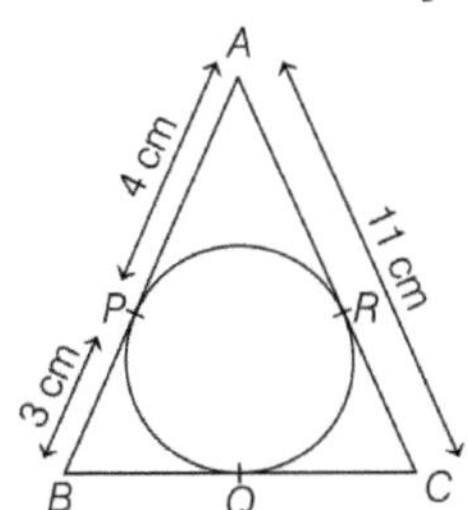

Sol. We know that, the tangents drawn from an external point to a circle are equal. Therefore,

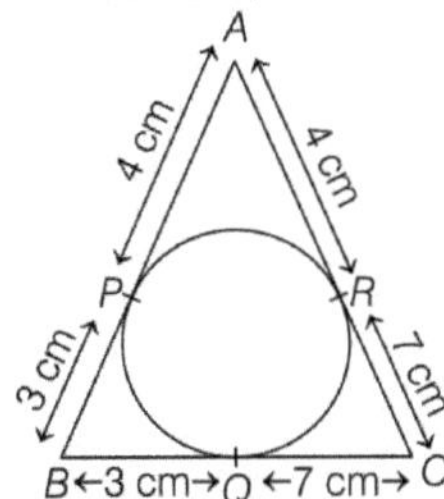

$\qquad BP = BQ, \qquad$ [point B is an external]

$\qquad AP = AR \qquad$ [point A is an external]

and $\qquad CQ = CR \qquad$ [point C is an external]

$\therefore \qquad\qquad AC = AR + RC$

$\Rightarrow \qquad\qquad 11 = 4 + RC$

$\Rightarrow \qquad\qquad RC = 11 - 4 = 7\,\text{cm}$

Now, $\qquad\qquad BC = BQ + QC$

$\qquad\qquad\qquad = 3 + 7 = 10\,\text{cm}$

Hence, length of BC is 10 cm.

Example 9. In the given figure, from an external point P, two tangents PQ and PR are drawn to a circle of radius 4 cm with centre O. If $\angle QPR = 90°$, then find the length of PQ.

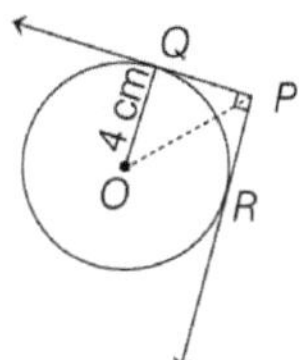

Sol. We know that, if pair of tangents are drawn from an external point P, then line joining from centre O to the point P, bisects the angle P.

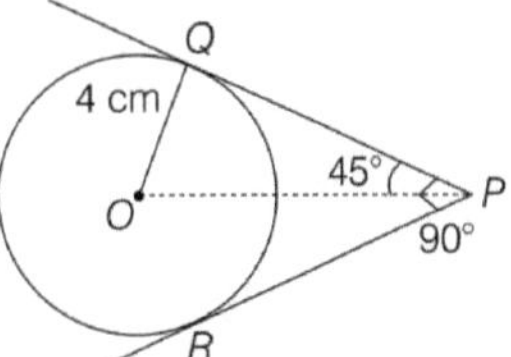

$\therefore \qquad \angle OPQ = \dfrac{\angle QPR}{2}$

$\qquad\qquad\qquad = \dfrac{90°}{2} = 45°$

Also, radius of circle OQ is perpendicular to the tangent line QP.

Now, in right angled $\triangle OQP$,

$\qquad\qquad \tan 45° = \dfrac{OQ}{QP}$

$\Rightarrow \qquad\qquad 1 = \dfrac{4}{QP}$

$\Rightarrow \qquad\qquad QP = 4\,\text{cm}$

Hence, length of PQ is 4 cm.

Example 10. In the given figure, if tangents PA and PB from an external point P to a circle with centre O, are inclined to each other at an angle of $80°$, then find $\angle AOB$. **[CBSE 2020 (Standard)]**

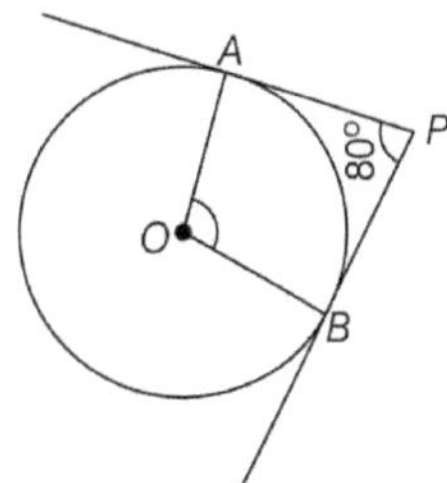

Sol. Given, $\angle APB = 80°$.

We know that, line drawn from centre of a circle to the tangent is perpendicular.
Since, $OA \perp PA$ and $OB \perp PB$.
Then, $\angle OAP = \angle OBP = 90°$ ...(i)

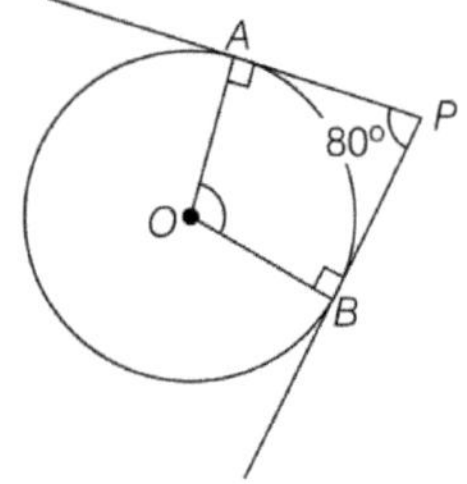

Since, $OAPB$ is a quadrilateral.
By using angle sum property of a quadrilateral,
$$\angle AOB + \angle OBP + \angle APB + \angle OAP = 360°$$
$$\Rightarrow \quad \angle AOB + 90° + 80° + 90° = 360°$$
$$\Rightarrow \quad \angle AOB = 360° - 260°$$
$$\Rightarrow \quad \angle AOB = 100°$$

Example 11. In given figure, PA and PB are tangents to the circle with centre O, such that $\angle APB = 50°$, then the measure of $\angle OAB$ is ......

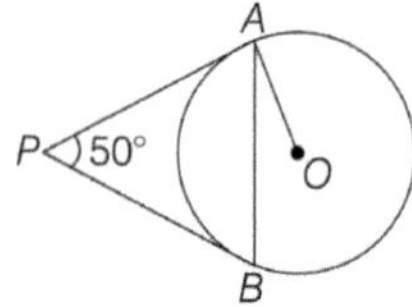

Sol. Given, $\angle APB = 50°$

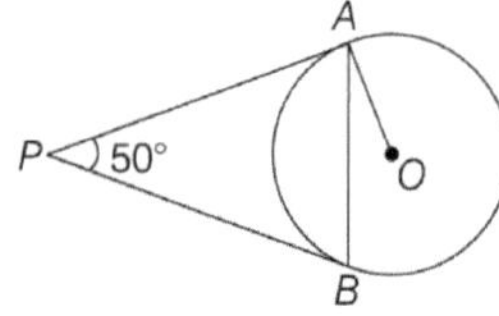

Since, P is an external point of a circle.
Therefore, $PA = PB$
  [$\because$ tangents drawn from an external to a circle are equal]
$$\Rightarrow \quad \angle PBA = \angle PAB$$
  [$\because$ angles opposite to equal sides are equal] ...(i)
In $\triangle APB$,
$$\angle APB + \angle PBA + \angle PAB = 180°$$
  [$\because$ sum of all angles of a triangle is 180°]
$$\therefore \quad 50° + 2\angle PAB = 180° \quad \text{[from Eq. (i)]}$$
$$\Rightarrow \quad 2\angle PAB = 130°$$
$$\Rightarrow \quad \angle PAB = 65° \quad \text{...(ii)}$$
Also, radius OA is perpendicular to the tangent of a circle.
Therefore,
$$\angle OAP = 90°$$
$$\Rightarrow \quad \angle OAB + \angle PAB = 90°$$
$$\Rightarrow \quad \angle OAB + 65° = 90° \quad \text{[from Eq. (ii)]}$$
$$\Rightarrow \quad \angle OAB = 90° - 65° = 25°$$

Example 12. In given figure, two tangents TP and TQ are drawn to a circle with centre O from an external point T. Prove that $\angle PTQ = 2\angle OPQ$.

[CBSE 2020 (Standard)]

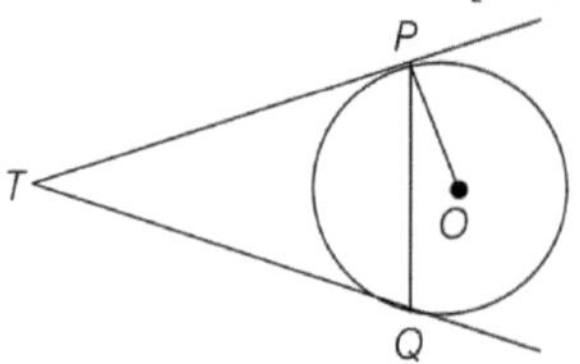

Sol. Given, TP and TQ are two tangents of a circle with centre O and points P and Q are point of contact.

To prove $\angle PTQ = 2\angle OPQ$

Proof Let $\angle PTQ = \theta$

As we know that, the length of tangents drawn from an external point to a circle are equal.
So, $\triangle TPQ$ is an isosceles triangle.
Therefore, according to the given figure,
$$\angle TPQ = \angle TQP = \frac{1}{2}(180° - \theta) = 90° - \frac{\theta}{2}$$

As we know that, the tangents at any point of a circle is perpendicular to the radius through the point of contact.

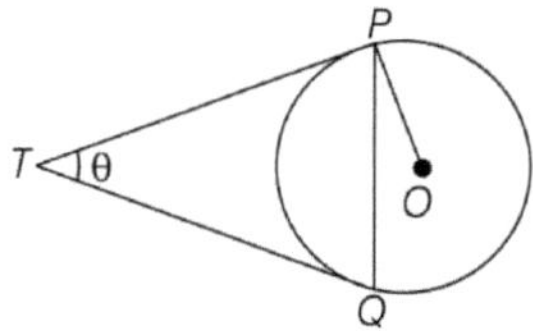

$$\therefore \quad \angle OPT = 90°$$
Now, $\angle OPQ = \angle OPT - \angle TPQ$
$$= 90° - \left(90° - \frac{\theta}{2}\right) = \frac{\theta}{2} = \frac{\angle PTQ}{2}$$
$$\Rightarrow \quad \angle PTQ = 2\angle OPQ \qquad \textbf{Hence proved.}$$

Example 13. In figure, a quadrilateral $ABCD$ is drawn to circumscribe a circle. Prove that
$$AB + CD = BC + AD$$
[CBSE 2020 (Standard)]

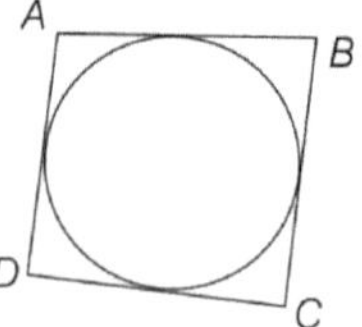

Sol. **Given** A quadrilateral $ABCD$ is circumscribing a circle.
To prove $AB + CD = AD + BC$
Proof Let P, Q, R and S be the point of contact.

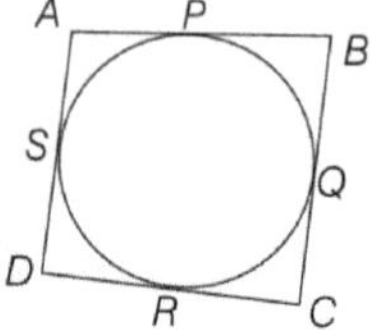

We know that, the length of tangents drawn from an external point to a circle are equal.

$\therefore \qquad AP = AS$

$\qquad$ [$\because$ both are tangents to a circle from point A] ...(i)

Similarly, $\quad BP = BQ,$ $\qquad\qquad$ ...(ii)

$\qquad CR = CQ$ $\qquad\qquad$ ...(iii)

and $\qquad DR = DS$ $\qquad\qquad$ ...(iv)

Adding Eqs. (i), (ii), (iii) and (iv), we get

$(AP + BP) + (CR + DR) = (AS + BQ) + (CQ + DS)$

$\Rightarrow \qquad AB + CD = (AS + DS) + (BQ + CQ)$

$\Rightarrow \qquad AB + CD = AD + BC$ $\quad$ **Hence proved.**

Example 14. Prove that the tangents at the extremities of any chord of a circle make equal angles with the chord. **[CBSE 2020 (Standard)]**

Sol. Let AB be a chord of a circle having centre O. Let AP and BP be the tangents at A and B, which intersect at point P.

To prove $\angle PAC = \angle PBC$

Construction Join points C and P.

Proof We know that, tangents drawn from an external point are equal.

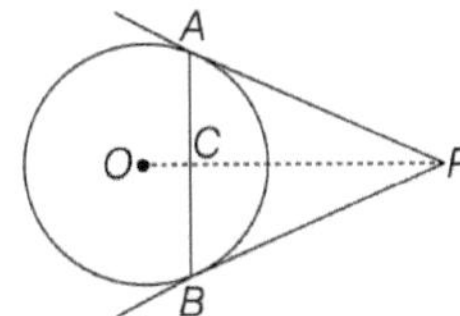

$\therefore$ In $\triangle PCA$ and $\triangle PCB$,

$\qquad PA = PB,$ $\qquad$ [$\because$ P is an external point of a circle]

$\qquad \angle APC = \angle BPC$

$\qquad\qquad$ [$\because$ AP and BP are equally inclined to OP]

and $\qquad PC = PC$ $\qquad$ [common sides]

$\therefore \qquad \triangle PAC \sim \triangle PBC$ $\qquad$ [by SAS similarity rule]

$\Rightarrow \qquad \angle PAC = \angle PBC$ $\qquad$ [by CPCT]

Example 15. In given figure, PQ is a chord of a circle and PT is tangent at P such that $\angle QPT = 60°$, then the measure of $\angle PRQ$ is .... **[CBSE 2020 (Standard)]**

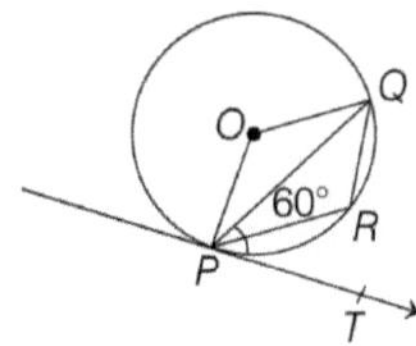

Sol. Take a point Q' on circle and join PQ' and QQ'.

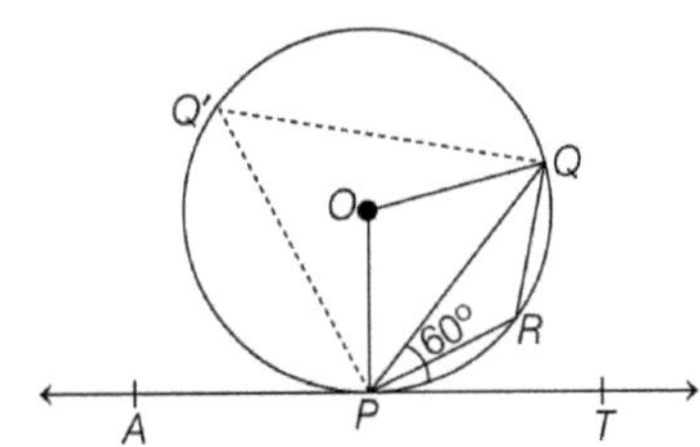

Now, $\angle OPQ = 90° - 60° = 30°$

$\qquad$ [$\because$ $\angle OPT = 90°$, as radius line OP is perpendicular to the tangent]

$\Rightarrow \qquad \angle OQP = 30°$

$\qquad$ [angles opposite to equal sides are equal]

In $\triangle OPQ$, using angle sum property of a triangle,

$\angle POQ + \angle OPQ + \angle OQP = 180°$

$\Rightarrow \qquad \angle POQ + 30° + 30° = 180°$

$\Rightarrow \qquad \angle POQ = 180° - 60° = 120°$

$\Rightarrow \qquad \angle PQ'Q = 60°$

$\qquad$ [angle subtended by an arc at centre is twice the angle subtended at remaining part of circle]

$\Rightarrow \angle PRQ = 180° - \angle PQ'Q = 120°$

$\qquad$ [$\because$ opposite angles are supplementary in a cyclic quadrilateral $PQ'QR$]

Example 16. In given figure, AB is a chord of circle with centre O, AOC is diameter and AT is tangent at A. Prove that $\angle BAT = \angle ACB$.

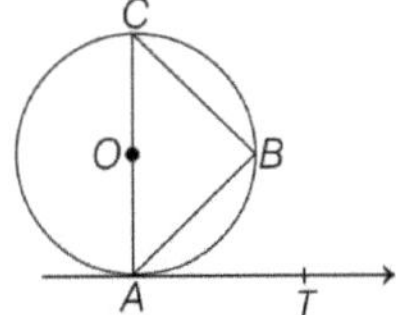

Sol. Given AB is a chord of a circle, AOC is a diameter of the circle having centre O and line AT is tangent at A.

To prove $\angle BAT = \angle ACB$

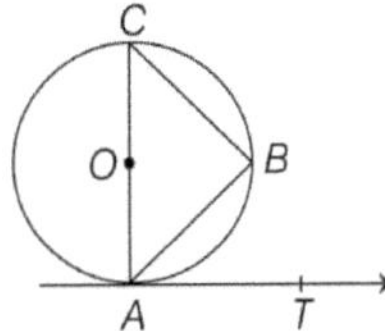

Proof We know that, diameter of a circle subtends 90° to the semi-circle.

$\therefore \qquad \angle ABC = 90°$

Let $\quad \angle ACB = \theta,$

then $\angle CAB = 180° - (90° + \theta)$

$\qquad\qquad$ [by using angle sum property of triangle]

$\Rightarrow \qquad \angle CAB = 90° - \theta$ $\qquad\qquad$ ...(i)

We know that, radius of a circle is perpendicular to the tangent.

$\therefore \qquad \angle OAT = 90°$

$\Rightarrow \qquad \angle OAB + \angle BAT = 90°$

$\Rightarrow \qquad \angle CAB + \angle BAT = 90°$ $\qquad$ [$\because$ $\angle OAT = \angle CAT$]

$\Rightarrow \qquad 90° - \theta + \angle BAT = 90°$

$\Rightarrow \qquad \angle BAT = \theta$

$\Rightarrow \qquad \angle BAT = \angle ACB$ $\qquad$ **Hence proved.**

Chapter Practice

Objective Questions

• Multiple Choice Questions

1. If radii of two concentric circles are 4 cm and 5 cm, then length of each chord of one circle, which is tangent to the other circle, is **[NCERT Exemplar]**
(a) 3 cm   (b) 6 cm   (c) 9 cm   (d) 1 cm

2. The length of tangent from an external point P on a circle with centre O is always less than OP. **[NCERT Exemplar]**
(a) True   (b) False
(c) Can't determined   (d) None of these

3. The length of the tangents to the circle from a point at any distance of 5 cm from centre of the circle of radius 3 cm is
(a) 2 cm   (b) 4 cm
(c) 8 cm   (d) None of these

4. The length of the tangent drawn from a point 8 cm away from the centre of circle of radius 6 cm is
(a) $\sqrt{7}$ cm   (b) $2\sqrt{7}$ cm   (c) 10 cm   (d) 5 cm

5. PQ is a tangent to a circle with centre O at the point P. If ΔOPQ is an isosceles triangle, then $\angle OPQ$ is equal to
(a) 30°   (b) 45°   (c) 60°   (d) 90°

6. In figure, if O is the centre of a circle, PQ is a chord and the tangent PR at P makes an angle of 50° with PQ, then $\angle POQ$ is equal to **[NCERT Exemplar]**

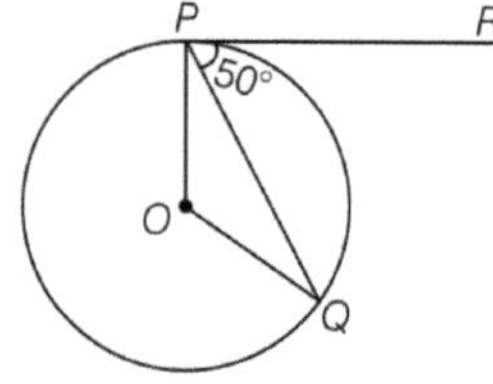

(a) 100°   (b) 80°   (c) 90°   (d) 75°

7. In the given figure, PA is a tangent from an external point P to a circle with centre O. If $\angle POB = 115°$, then $\angle APO$ is

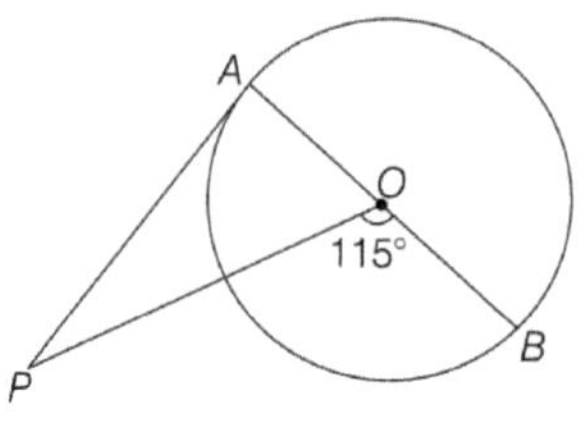

(a) 25°   (b) 20°   (c) 30°   (d) 65°

8. In figure, AT is a tangent to the circle with centre O such that $OT = 4$ cm and $\angle OTA = 30°$. Then, AT is equal to **[NCERT Exemplar]**

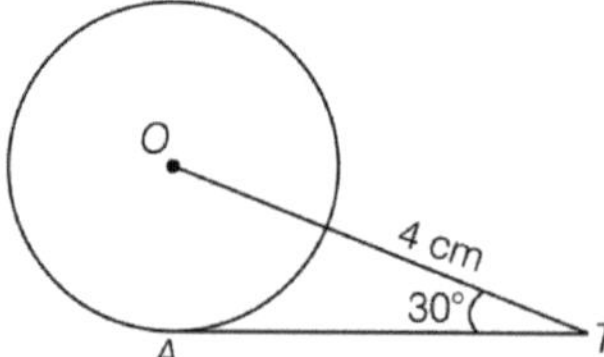

(a) 4 cm   (b) 2 cm   (c) $2\sqrt{3}$ cm   (d) $4\sqrt{3}$ cm

9. PQ is a tangent drawn from a point P to a circle with centre O and QOR is a diameter of the circle such that $\angle POR = 135°$, then $\angle OPQ$ is
(a) 60°   (b) 45°   (c) 30°   (d) 90°

10. A tangent PQ at a point P of a circle of radius 6 cm meets a line through the centre O at a point Q, so that $OQ = 14$ cm, then length of PQ is
(a) $4\sqrt{10}$ cm   (b) $6\sqrt{10}$ cm
(c) $5\sqrt{10}$ cm   (d) $7\sqrt{10}$ cm

11. In figure, if PA and PB are tangents to the circle with centre O such that $\angle APB = 50°$, then $\angle OAB$ is equal to **[NCERT Exemplar]**

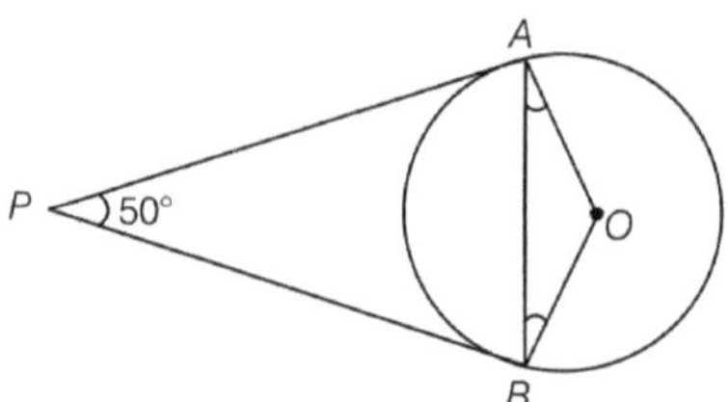

(a) 25°   (b) 30°
(c) 40°   (d) 50°

12. If angle between two tangents drawn from a point P to a circle of radius a and centre O is 90°, then $OP = a\sqrt{2}$. **[NCERT Exemplar]**

(a) True   (b) False
(c) Can't say   (d) Partially true or false

13. In the given figure, find the value of $x°$.

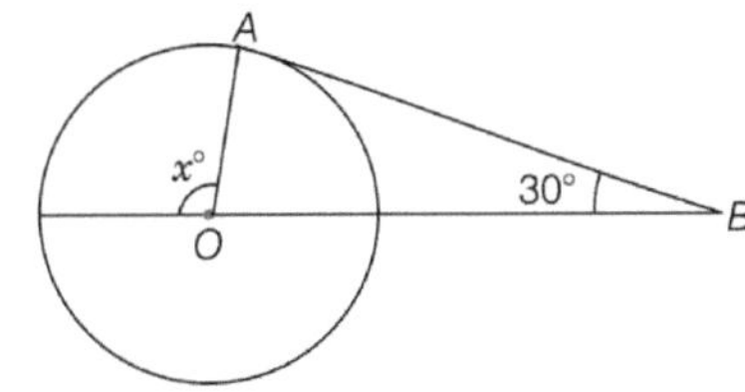

(a) 130°   (b) 75°   (c) 120°   (d) 60°

14. From the given figure, find the value of $x° + y°$.

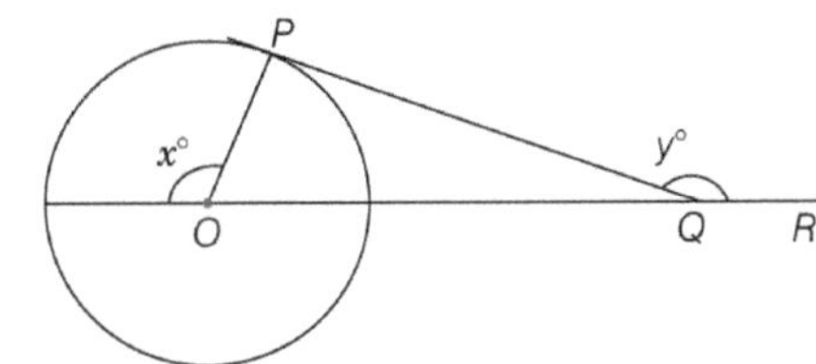

(a) 270°   (b) 180°
(c) 90°   (d) None of these

15. At one end A of a diameter AB of a circle of radius 5 cm, tangent XAY is drawn to the circle. The length of the chord CD parallel to XY and at a distance 8 cm from A is **[NCERT Exemplar]**

(a) 4 cm   (b) 5 cm   (c) 6 cm   (d) 8 cm

16. In figure, AB is a chord of the circle and AOC is its diameter such that $\angle ACB = 50°$. If AT is the tangent to the circle at the point A, then $\angle BAT$ is equal to **[NCERT Exemplar]**

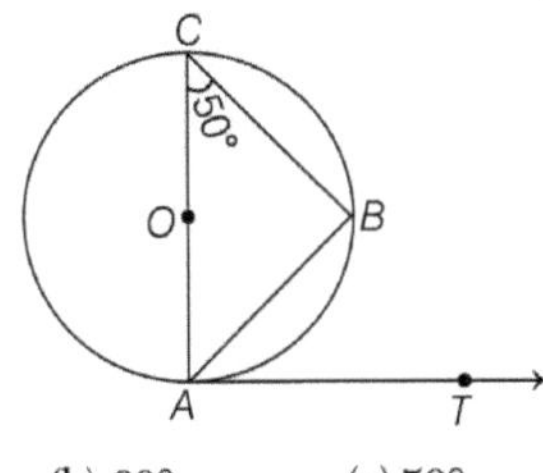

(a) 45°   (b) 60°   (c) 50°   (d) 55°

17. In the adjoining figure, $AD = 8$ cm, $AC = 6$ cm and TB is the tangent at B to the circle with centre O. If BT is 4 cm, then $OT =$ **[CBSE 2013]**

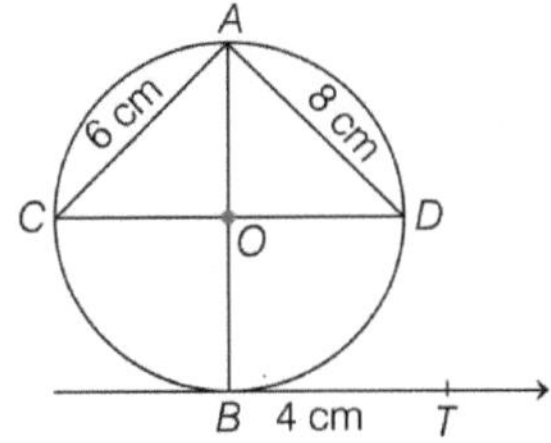

(a) 41 cm   (b) $\sqrt{41}$ cm
(c) 40 cm   (d) $\sqrt{40}$ cm

18. PA is a tangent to the circle with centre O. If $BC = 3$ cm, $AC = 4$ cm and $\triangle ACB \sim \triangle PAO$, then OA is equal to **[CBSE 2013]**

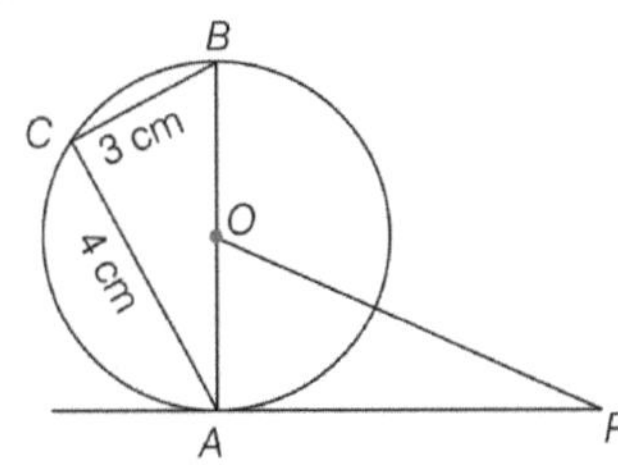

(a) 2.7 cm   (b) $\sqrt{5}$ cm
(c) 5 cm   (d) $\dfrac{5}{2}$ cm

19. In the given figure, if $\angle ACB = 50°$, then $\angle ATO$ is

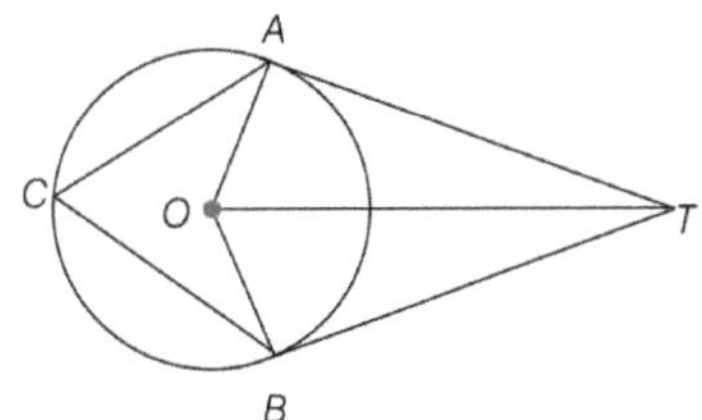

(a) 30°
(b) 50°
(c) 40°
(d) Can't be determined

20. In the adjoining figure, PQ is a chord of a circle with centre O and PT is a tangent at P such that $\angle QPT = 60°$, then $\angle PRQ =$

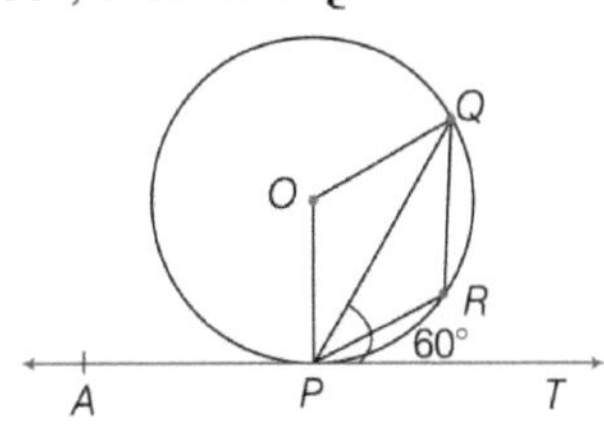

(a) 120°   (b) 160°   (c) 130°   (d) 150°

21. In figure, if PQR is the tangent to a circle at Q, whose centre is O, AB is a chord parallel to PR and $\angle BQR = 70°$, then $\angle AQB$ is equal to **[NCERT Exemplar]**

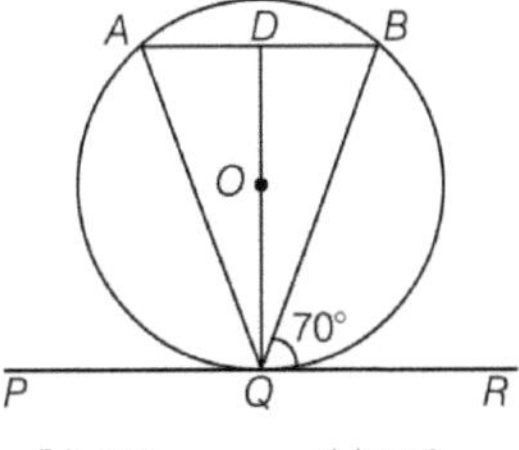

(a) 20°   (b) 40°   (c) 35°   (d) 45°

22. From an external point P, tangents PA and PB are drawn to a circle with centre O. If CD is the tangent to the circle at a point E and $PA = 14$ cm, then perimeter of ΔPCD is

(a) 14 cm   (b) 21 cm   (c) 28 cm   (d) 35 cm

23. Tangents AP and AQ are drawn to circle with centre O from an external point A, then $\angle PAQ$ is equal to

(a) $2\angle OPQ$ (b) $\dfrac{\angle OPQ}{2}$ (c) $\dfrac{\angle OPQ}{3}$ (d) $\dfrac{\angle OPQ}{4}$

24. In the given figure, two tangents AB and AC are drawn to a circle with centre O such that $\angle BAC = 120°$, then OA is equal to

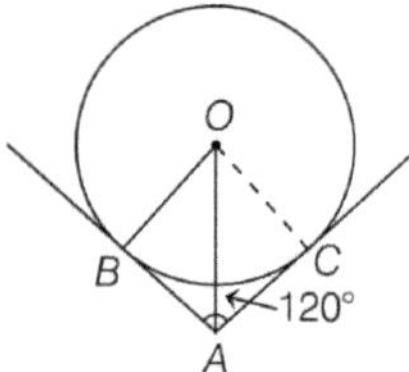

(a) $2AB$ (b) $3AB$ (c) $4AB$ (d) $5AB$

25. In the given figure, O is the centre of a circle, BOA is its diameter and the tangent at the point P meets BA extended at T. If $\angle PBO = 30°$, then $\angle PTA =$

[**CBSE 2016**]

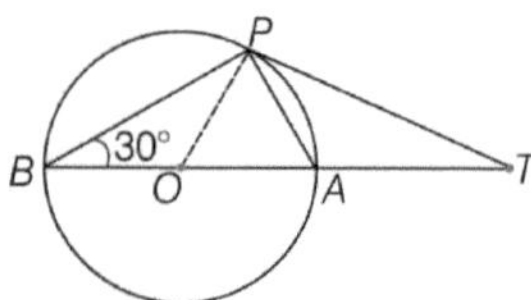

(a) $40°$ (b) $50°$ (c) $30°$ (d) $20°$

26. In adjoining figure, PQ and PR are tangents to the circle with centre O and S is a point on the circle such that $\angle SQL = 50°$ and $\angle SRM = 60°$. Then, $\angle QSR$ [**NCERT Exemplar**]

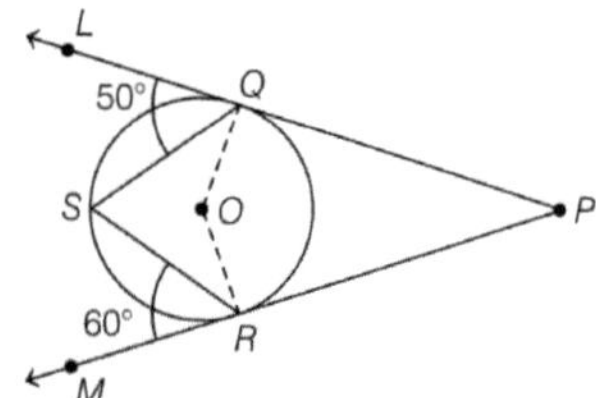

(a) $40°$ (b) $50°$ (c) $60°$ (d) $70°$

27. In given figure, AB is diameter of a circle with centre O and AT is tangent. If $\angle AOQ = 58°$, then $\angle ATQ =$ [**CBSE 2015**]

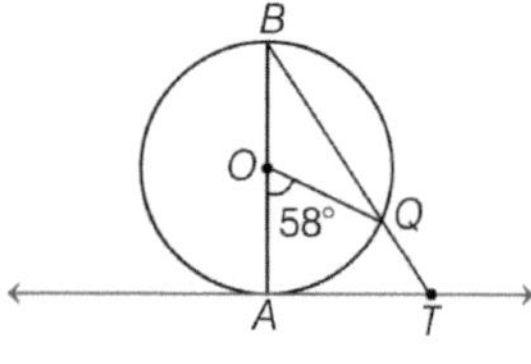

(a) $52°$ (b) $58°$ (c) $61°$ (d) $62°$

28. In figure, if $\angle AOB = 125°$, then $\angle COD$ is equal to

[**NCERT Exemplar**]

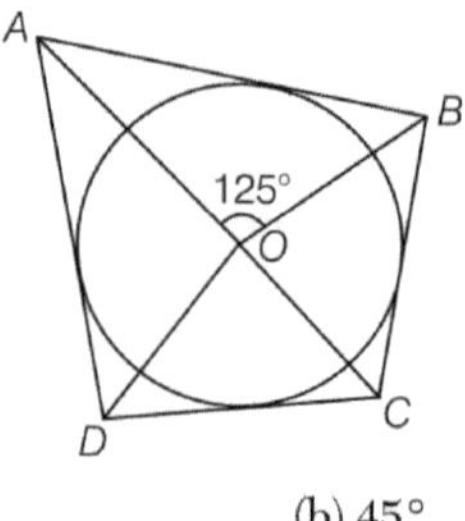

(a) $62.5°$ (b) $45°$
(c) $35°$ (d) $55°$

• Case Based MCQs

29. A playground is in the shape of a triangle with right angle at B, $AB = 3$ m and $BC = 4$ m. A pit was dig inside it such that it touches the walls AC, BC and AB at P, Q and R, respectively such that $AP = x$ m.

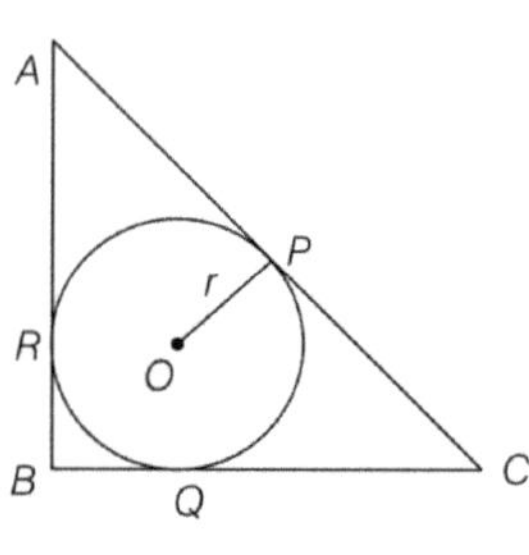 

Based on the above information, answer the following questions.

(i) The value of $AR =$
   (a) $2x$ m   (b) $x / 2$ m
   (c) x m   (d) $3x$ m

(ii) The value of $BQ =$
   (a) $2x$ m   (b) $(3 - x)$ m
   (c) $(2 - x)$ m   (d) $4x$ m

(iii) The value of $CQ =$
   (a) $(4 + x)$ m   (b) $(5 - x)$ m
   (c) $(1 + x)$ m   (d) Both (b) and (c)

(iv) Which of the following is correct?
   (a) Quadrilateral $AROP$ is a square
   (b) Quadrilateral $BROQ$ is a square
   (c) Quadrilateral $CQOP$ is a square
   (d) None of the above

(v) Radius of the pit is
   (a) 1 m   (b) 3 m
   (c) 4 m   (d) 5 m

30. A student draws two circles that touch each other externally at point K with centres A and B and radii 6 cm and 4 cm, respectively as shown in the figure.

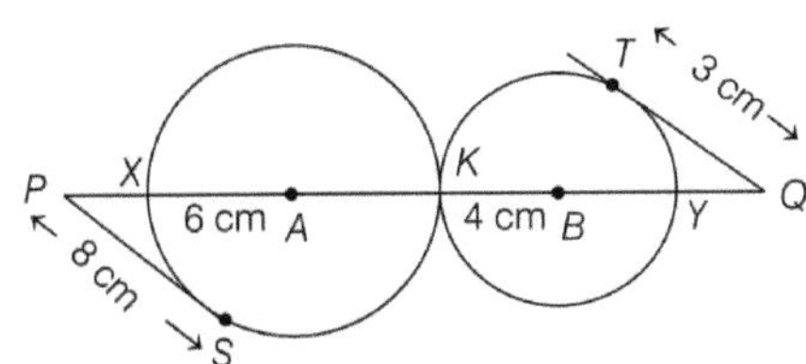

Based on the above information, answer the following questions.

(i) The value of $PA =$
  - (a) 10 cm
  - (b) 5 cm
  - (c) 13 cm
  - (d) Can't be determined

(ii) The value of $BQ =$
  - (a) 4 cm
  - (b) 5 cm
  - (c) 6 cm
  - (d) 18 cm

(iii) The value of $PK =$
  - (a) 13 cm
  - (b) 15 cm
  - (c) 16 cm
  - (d) 18 cm

(iv) The value of $QY =$
  - (a) 2 cm
  - (b) 5 cm
  - (c) 1 cm
  - (d) 3 cm

(v) If two circles touch externally, then the number of common tangents can be drawn is
  - (a) 1
  - (b) 2
  - (c) 3
  - (d) None of these

PART 2
Subjective Questions

• Short Answer Type Questions

1. If PQ is a tangent to a circle with centre O and radius 6 cm such that $\angle PQO = 60°$, then find the length of a tangent PQ and a line OQ.

2. The tangent to the circumcircle of an isosceles $\triangle ABC$ at A, in which $AB = AC$, is parallel to BC.
                                        [NCERT Exemplar]

3. If AB is a chord of a circle with centre O, AOC is a diameter and AT is the tangent at A as shown in figure. Prove that $\angle BAT = \angle ACB$.   **[NCERT Exemplar]**

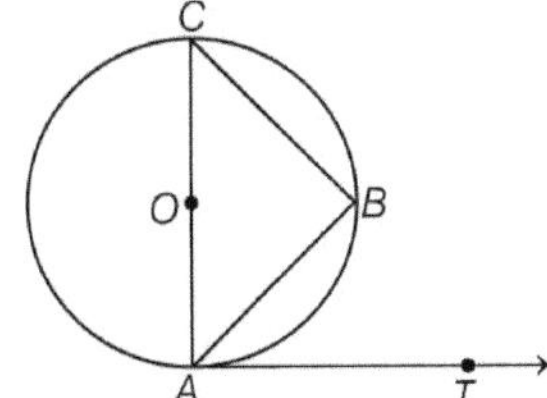

4. Prove that a diameter AB of a circle bisects all those chords, which are parallel to the tangent at the point A.   **[NCERT Exemplar]**

5. If a number of circles touch a given line segment PQ at a point A, then their centres lie on the perpendicular bisector of PQ. Why or why not?
                                        [NCERT Exemplar]

6. Out of the two concentric circles, the radius of the outer circle is 5 cm and the chord AC of length 8 cm is a tangent to the inner circle. Find the radius of the inner circle.

7. If a chord AB subtends an angle of 60° at the centre of a circle, then find the angle between the tangents at A and B.   **[NCERT Exemplar]**

8. From an external point P, two tangents, PA and PB are drawn to a circle with centre O. At one point E on the circle tangent is drawn, which intersects PA and PB at C and D, respectively. If $PA = 10$ cm, find the perimeter of the trianlge PCD.

9. Prove that the centre of a circle touching two intersecting lines lies on the angle bisector of the lines.   **[NCERT Exemplar]**

10. If from an external point B of a circle with centre O, two tangents BC and BD are drawn, such that $\angle DBC = 120°$, prove that $BC + BD = BO$ i.e. $BO = 2\,BC$.

11. In figure, AB and CD are common tangents to two circles of equal radii. Prove that $AB = CD$.
                                        [NCERT Exemplar]

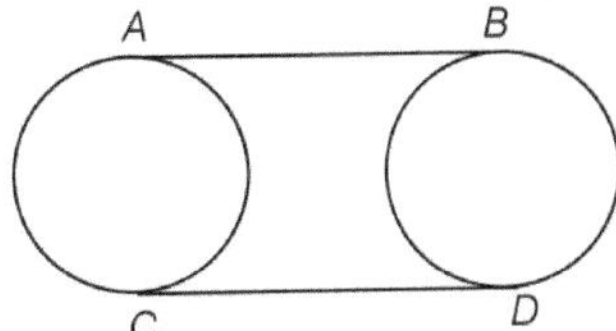

12. In figure, common tangents AB and CD to two circles intersect at E. Prove that $AB = CD$.
                                        [NCERT Exemplar]

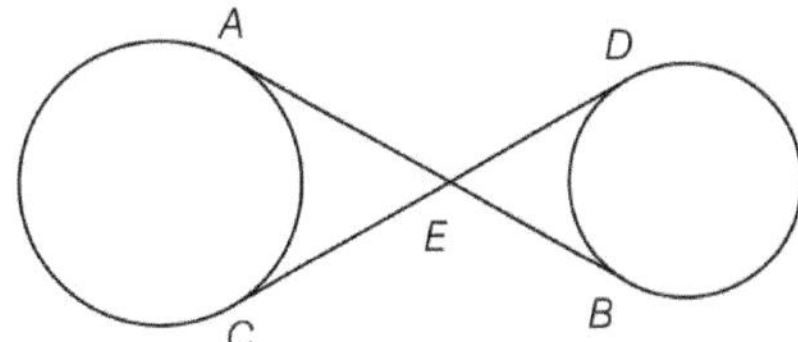

13. If PA and PB are two tangents drawn from a point P to a circle with centre O touching it at A and B, prove that OP is perpendicular bisector of AB.
                                        [CBSE 2008]

14. Tangents AP and AQ are drawn to circle with centre O from an external point A. Prove that $\angle PAQ = 2\angle OPQ$.   **[CBSE 2013, 12,11, 09]**

15. In the given figure, $\angle ADC = 90°$, $BC = 38$ cm, $CD = 28$ cm and $BP = 25$ cm, then find the radius of the circle. **[CBSE 2011]**

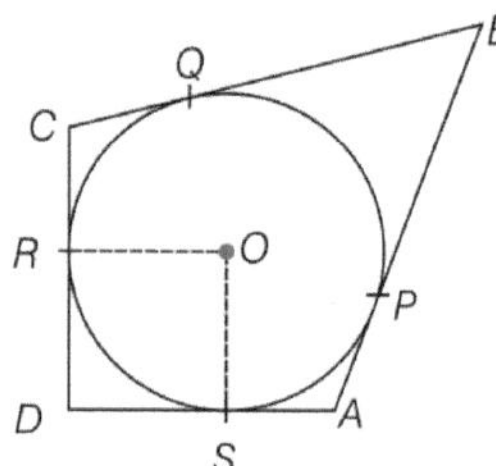

16. $\triangle ABC$ is a right angled triangle with $\angle B = 90°$, $BC = 3$ cm and $AB = 4$ cm. A circle with centre O and radius r cm has been inscribed in $\triangle ABC$. Find the radius of the incircle.

17. The radii of two concentric circles are 13 cm and 8 cm. AB is a diameter of the bigger circle. BD is a tangent to the smaller circle touching it at D. Find the length of AD. **[CBSE 2010]**

18. A circle is inscribed in a $\triangle ABC$ having sides $AB = 8$ cm, $BC = 10$ cm and $CA = 12$ cm, as shown in figure. Find AD, BE and CF. **[CBSE 2012]**

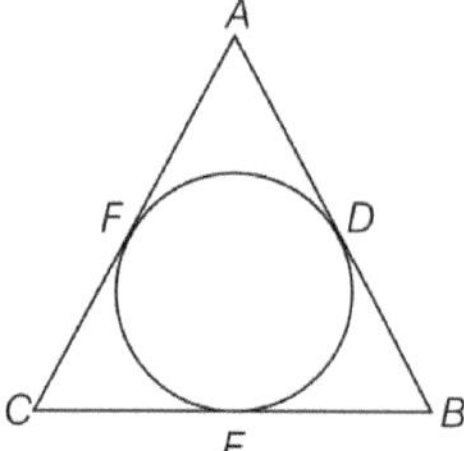

• Long Answer Type Questions

19. Let s denotes the semi-perimeter of a $\triangle ABC$, in which $BC = a$, $CA = b$ and $AB = c$. If a circle touches the sides BC, CA, AB at D, E, F, respectively. Prove that $BD = s - b$. **[NCERT Exemplar]**

20. AC and AD are tangents at C and D, respectively. If $\angle BCD = 44°$, then find $\angle CAD$, $\angle ADC$, $\angle CBD$ and $\angle ACD$.

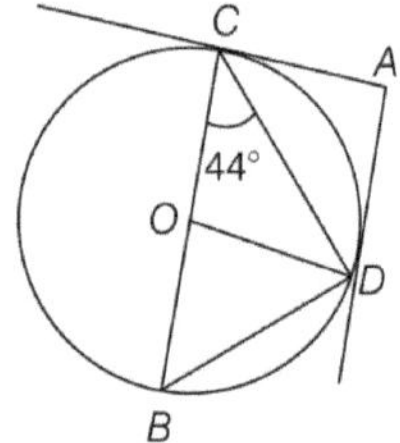

21. If a hexagon $ABCDEF$ circumscribe a circle, prove that

$$AB + CD + EF = BC + DE + FA \quad \text{[NCERT Exemplar]}$$

22. In the given figure, AD is a diameter of a circle with centre O and AB is a tangent at A. C is a point on the circle such that DC produced intersects the tangent at B and $\angle ABD = 50°$. Find $\angle COA$. **[CBSE 2015]**

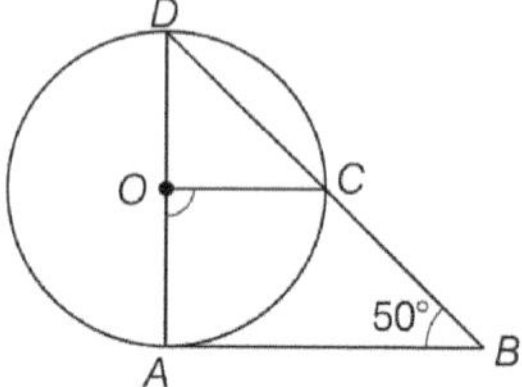

23. Tangents PQ and PR are drawn to a circle such that $\angle RPQ = 30°$. A chord RS is drawn parallel to the tangent PQ. Find $\angle RQS$. **[CBSE 2015]**

24. PA and PB are the tangents to a circle, which circumscribes an equilateral $\triangle ABQ$. If $\angle PAB = 60°$, as shown in the figure, prove that QP bisects AB at right angle. **[CBSE 2015]**

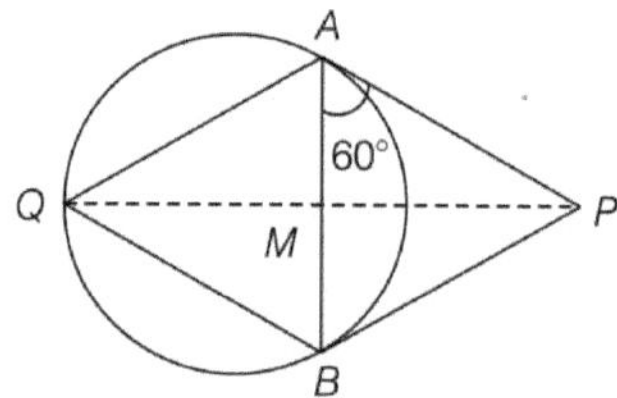

25. Two circles with centres O and O' of radii 3 cm and 4 cm, respectively intersect at two points P and Q, such that OP and $O'P$ are tangents to the two circles. Find the length of the common chord PQ. **[NCERT Exemplar]**

26. If an isosceles $\triangle ABC$ in which $AB = AC = 6$ cm, is inscribed in a circle of radius 9 cm, find the area of the triangle.

27. In a figure, the common tangents AB and CD of two circles with centres O and O' intersect at E. Prove that the points O, E and O' are collinear. **[NCERT Exemplar]**

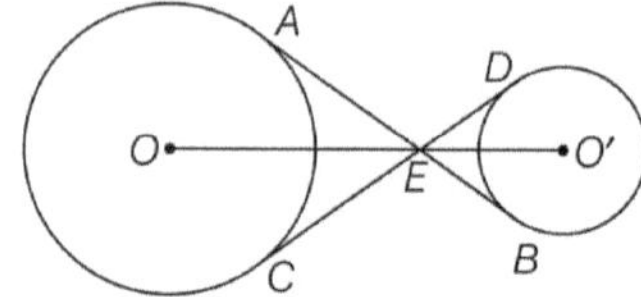

28. In figure, O is the centre of a circle of radius 5 cm, T is a point such that $OT = 13$ and OT intersects the circle at E, if AB is the tangent to the circle at E, find the length of AB. **[NCERT Exemplar]**

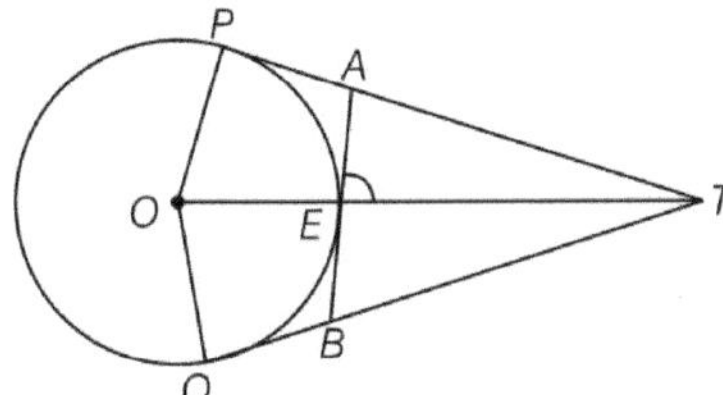

• Case Based Questions

29. Dheeraj loves geometry. So, he was curious to know more about the concepts of circles. His grand father is a mathematicians. So, he reached to his grand father to learn something interesting about tangents and circles. His grand father gave him knowledge on circles and tangents and ask him to solve the following questions.

(i) In the given figure, AP, AQ and BC are tangents to the circle such that $AB = 7$ cm, $BC = 4$ cm and $AC = 9$ cm. Find AP

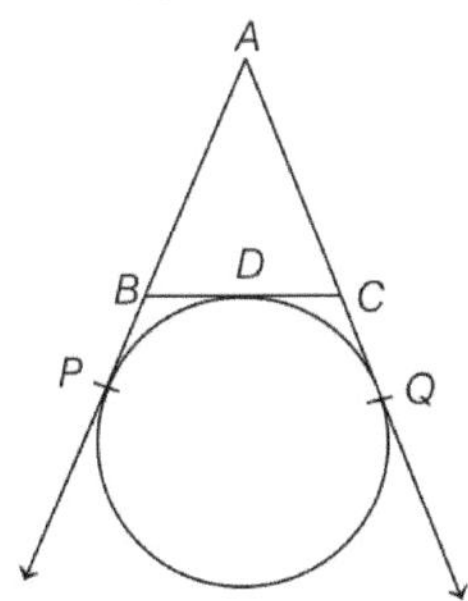

(a) 12 cm   (b) 15 cm   (c) 13 cm   (d) 10 cm

(ii) A circle of radius 3 cm is inscribed in a right angled $\triangle BAC$ such that $BD = 9$ cm and $DC = 3$ cm. Find the length of AB.

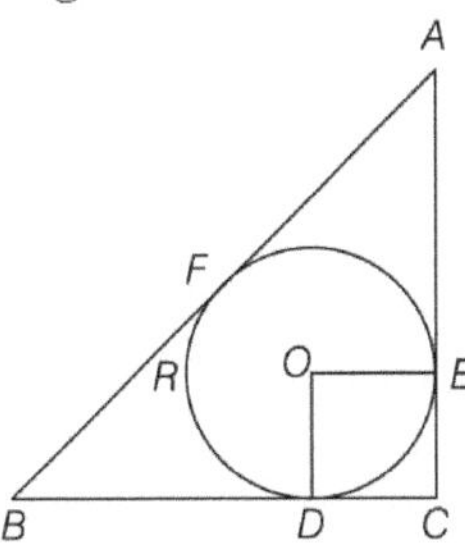

(a) 6 cm   (b) 12 cm
(c) 15 cm   (d) 10 cm

(iii) In the given figure, what is the length of CD?

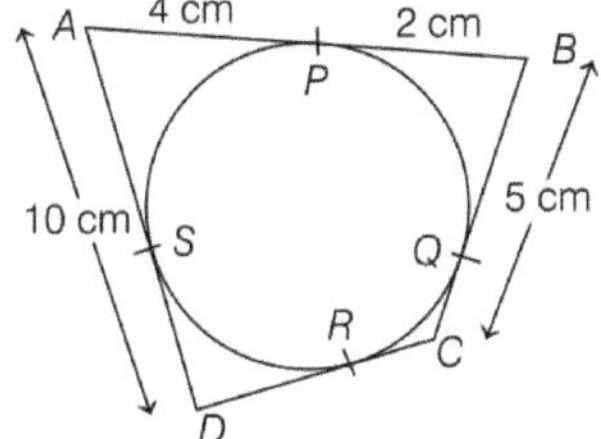

(a) 11 cm   (b) 9 cm
(c) 7 cm   (d) 13 cm

(iv) If PA and PB are two tangents to a circle with centre O from an external point P such that $\angle OPB = 50°$, then find $\angle BPA$
(a) 60°   (b) 50°
(c) 120°   (d) 100°

(v) In the given figure, P is an external point from, which tangents are drawn to two externally touching circles. If $PA = 11$ cm, then find PC.

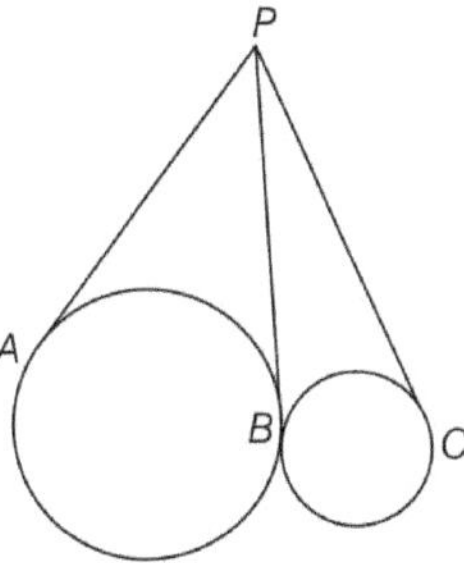

(a) 3.5 cm   (b) 4 cm
(c) 11 cm   (d) Can't be determined

SOLUTIONS

Objective Questions

1. (b) Let O be the centre of two concentric circles C_1 and C_2, whose radii are $r_1 = 4$ cm and $r_2 = 5$ cm. Now, we draw a chord AC of circle C_2, which touches the circle C_1 at B.

Also, join OB, which is perpendicular to AC.

[∵ tangent at any point of circle is perpendicular to radius through the point of contact]

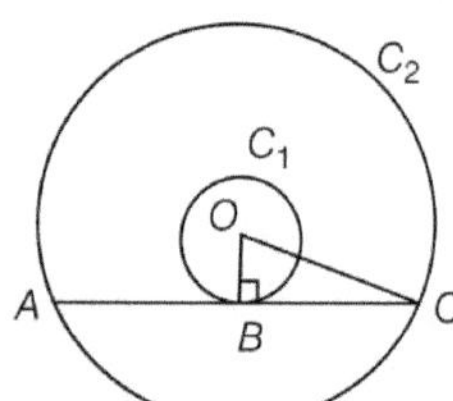

Now, in right angled ΔOBC, by using Pythagoras theorem,

$$OC^2 = BC^2 + BO^2$$

[∵ (hypotenuse)^2 = (base)^2 + (perpendicular)^2]

$$\Rightarrow \quad 5^2 = BC^2 + 4^2$$
$$\Rightarrow \quad BC^2 = 25 - 16 = 9$$
$$\Rightarrow \quad BC = 3 \text{ cm}$$
$$\therefore \quad \text{Length of chord } AC = 2\,BC$$
$$= 2 \times 3 = 6 \text{ cm}$$

2. (a)

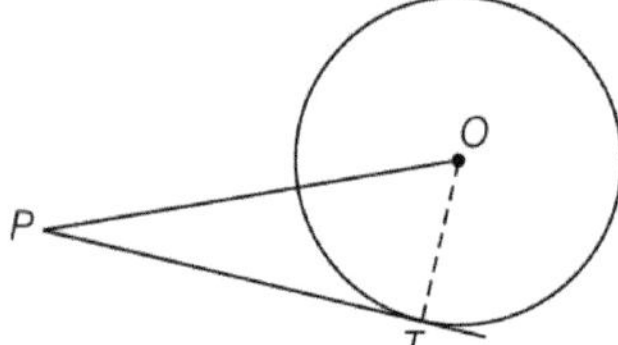

PT is a tangent drawn from external point P. Join OT.

$$\because \qquad OT \perp PT$$

So, ΔOPT is a right angled triangle formed.

In right angled triangle, hypotenuse is always greater than any of the two sides of the triangle.

$$\therefore \qquad OP > PT$$
$$\text{or} \qquad PT < OP$$

3. (b) Given, $OB = 5$ cm and radius $OA = 3$ cm

By Pythagoras theorem, in right angled ΔOAB,

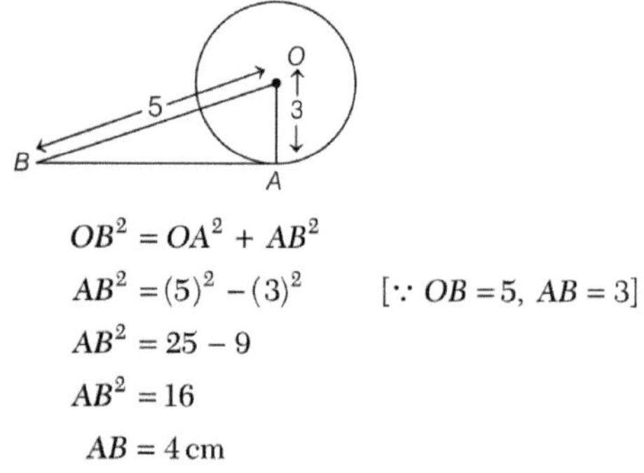

$$OB^2 = OA^2 + AB^2$$
$$AB^2 = (5)^2 - (3)^2 \qquad [\because OB = 5,\ AB = 3]$$
$$AB^2 = 25 - 9$$
$$AB^2 = 16$$
$$AB = 4 \text{ cm}$$

4. (b) Since, tangent to a circle is perpendicular to the radius through the point of contact.

$$\therefore \qquad \angle OTP = 90°$$

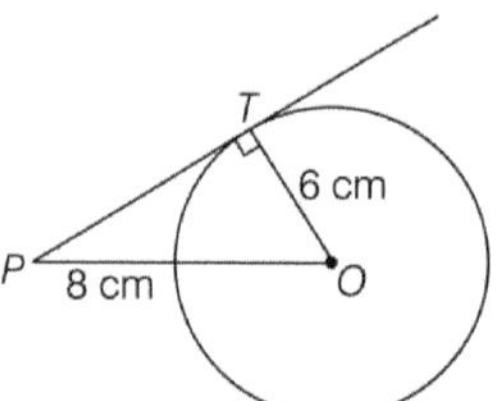

In ΔOTP, we have

$$OP^2 = OT^2 + PT^2$$
$$\Rightarrow \quad (8)^2 = (6)^2 + PT^2$$
$$\Rightarrow \quad PT^2 = 64 - 36 = 28$$
$$\Rightarrow \quad PT = \sqrt{28} = 2\sqrt{7} \text{ cm}$$

5. (b) Since, PQ is a tangent to a circle from a point P and centre of circle is O.

$\therefore \Delta OPQ$ is an isosceles triangle.

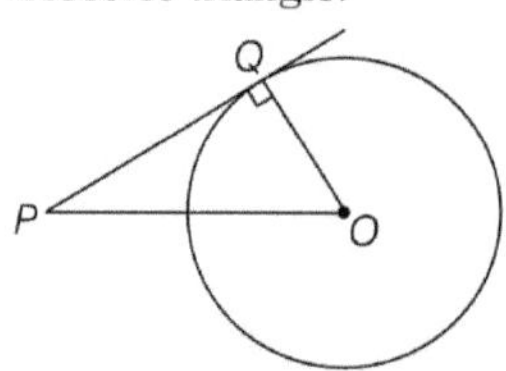

$$\angle OQP = 90°$$
$$OP = QP$$
$$\therefore \qquad \angle POQ = \angle OPQ$$

In ΔOPQ,
$$\angle POQ + \angle OQP + \angle OPQ = 180°$$
$$\Rightarrow \quad 2\angle OPQ = 180° - 90° \quad [\because \angle POQ = \angle OPQ]$$
$$\Rightarrow \quad 2\angle OPQ = 90° \Rightarrow \angle OPQ = 45°$$

6. (a) Given, $\angle QPR = 50°$

We know that, the tangent at any point of a circle is perpendicular to the radius through the point of contact.

$$\therefore \qquad \angle OPR = 90°$$
$$\Rightarrow \quad \angle OPQ + \angle QPR = 90° \qquad \text{[from figure]}$$
$$\Rightarrow \quad \angle OPQ = 90° - 50° = 40° \qquad [\because \angle QPR = 50°]$$
$$\text{Now,} \qquad OP = OQ = \text{Radius of circle}$$
$$\therefore \qquad \angle OQP = \angle OPQ = 40°$$

[since, angles opposite to equal sides are equal]

In ΔOPQ, $\angle O + \angle P + \angle Q = 180°$

[since, sum of all angles of a triangle = 180°]

$$\Rightarrow \quad \angle O = 180° - (40° + 40°) \quad [\because \angle P = 40° = \angle Q]$$
$$= 180° - 80° = 100°$$

7. (a) Here, $\angle OAP = 90°$ [∵ tangent at any point of a circle is perpendicular to the radius]

Now, $\angle AOP + \angle BOP = 180°$

$$\Rightarrow \quad \angle AOP + 115° = 180°$$
$$\Rightarrow \quad \angle AOP = (180° - 115°) = 65°$$

And also, $\angle OAP + \angle AOP + \angle APO = 180°$

[angle sum property of triangle]

$\Rightarrow \quad 90° + 65° + \angle APO = 180°$

$\Rightarrow \quad 155° + \angle APO = 180°$

$\Rightarrow \angle APO = 180° - 155° = 25°$

8. (c) Join OA.

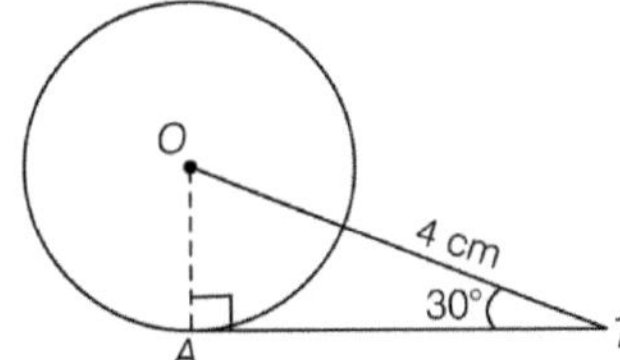

We know that, the tangent at any point of a circle is perpendicular to the radius through the point of contact.

$\therefore \qquad\qquad\qquad \angle OAT = 90°$

In $\triangle OAT, \qquad \cos 30° = \dfrac{AT}{OT}$

$\Rightarrow \qquad\qquad \dfrac{\sqrt{3}}{2} = \dfrac{AT}{4}$

$\Rightarrow \qquad\qquad AT = 2\sqrt{3}$ cm

9. (b) Given, PQ is a tangent from point P, centre O and QOR as diameter.

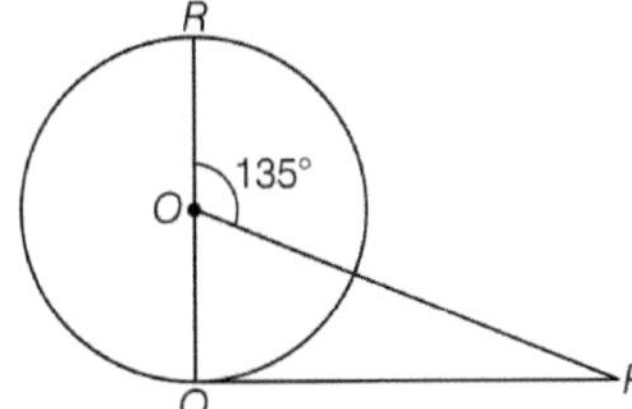

In $\triangle PQO, \qquad \angle ROP = \angle OPQ + 90°$

[$\because$ exterior angle of a triangle is equal to the sum of opposite angles]

$\angle OPQ = 135° - 90°$

$= 45°$

10. (a) Here, $OP = 6$ cm and $OQ = 14$ cm

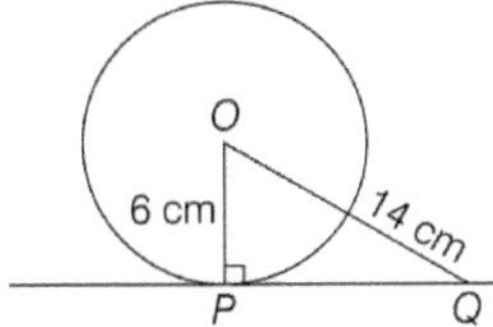

We know that, tangent at any point of a circle is perpendicular to the radius through the point of contact.

So, $OP \perp PQ$

Now, in right angled $\triangle OPQ$,

$OQ^2 = OP^2 + PQ^2$ [by Pythagoras theorem]

$\Rightarrow \qquad (14)^2 = (6)^2 + PQ^2$

$\Rightarrow \qquad PQ^2 = 196 - 36$

$\Rightarrow \qquad\qquad PQ^2 = 160$

$\Rightarrow \qquad\qquad PQ = \sqrt{16 \times 10} = 4\sqrt{10}$ cm

11. (a) Given, PA and PB are tangent lines.

$\therefore \qquad\qquad\qquad PA = PB$

[since, the length of tangents drawn from an external point to a circle is equal]

$\Rightarrow \qquad\qquad \angle PBA = \angle PAB = \theta$ [say]

In $\triangle PAB, \ \angle P + \angle A + \angle B = 180°$

[since, sum of all angles of a triangle $= 180°$]

$\Rightarrow \qquad\qquad 50° + \theta + \theta = 180°$

$\Rightarrow \qquad\qquad 2\theta = 180° - 50° = 130°$

$\Rightarrow \qquad\qquad\qquad \theta = 65°$

Also, $\qquad\qquad\qquad OA \perp PA$

[since, tangent at any point of a circle is perpendicular to the radius through the point of contact]

$\therefore \qquad\qquad\qquad \angle PAO = 90°$

$\Rightarrow \qquad \angle PAB + \angle BAO = 90°$

$\Rightarrow \qquad 65° + \angle BAO = 90°$

$\Rightarrow \qquad \angle BAO = 90° - 65° = 25°$

12. (a) From point P, two tangents are drawn.

Given, $\qquad\qquad OT = a$

Also, line OP bisects the $\angle RPT$.

$\therefore \qquad\qquad \angle TPO = \angle RPO = 45°$

Also, $\qquad\qquad OT \perp PT$

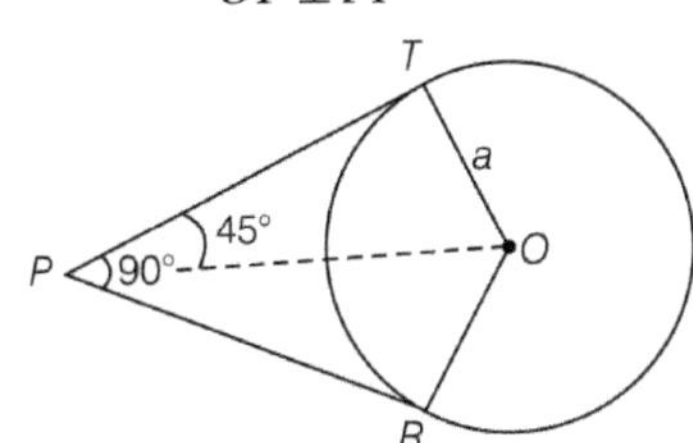

In right angled $\triangle OTP$,

$\sin 45° = \dfrac{OT}{OP}$

$\Rightarrow \qquad \dfrac{1}{\sqrt{2}} = \dfrac{a}{OP}$

$\Rightarrow \qquad OP = a\sqrt{2}$

13. (c) Given, $\angle OBA = 30°$

In $\triangle ABO$,

$x° = \angle ABO + 90°$

[$\because$ external angle = sum of opposite internal angles]

$x° = 30° + 90° = 120°$

14. (a) In $\triangle POQ$,

$x° = \angle PQO + 90°$

[$\because$ external angle = sum of opposite internal angles]

$= (180° - y°) + 90°$

$= 270° - y°$

$x° + y° = 270°$

15. (d) First, draw a circle of radius 5 cm having centre O. A tangent XY is drawn at point A.

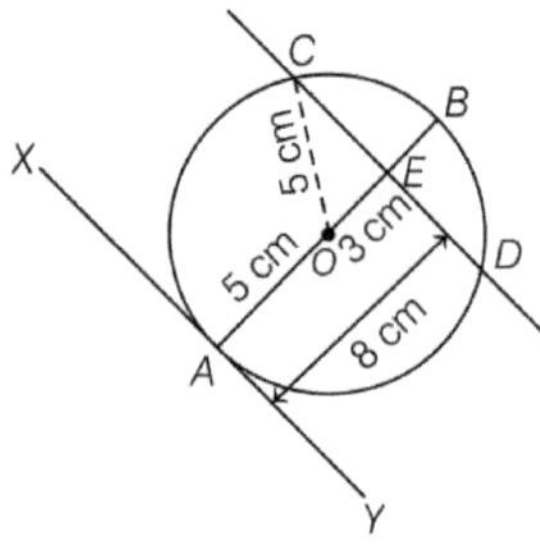

A chord CD is drawn, which is parallel to XY and at a distance of 8 cm from A.

Also, $\qquad AE = 8$ cm. Join OC

Now, in right angled ΔOEC,

$$OC^2 = OE^2 + EC^2$$
$$\Rightarrow \qquad EC^2 = OC^2 - OE^2$$

[by Pythagoras theorem]

$$= 5^2 - 3^2$$

$[\because OC = \text{radius} = 5 \text{ cm}, OE = AE - AO = 8 - 5 = 3 \text{ cm}]$

$$= 25 - 9 = 16$$
$$\Rightarrow \qquad EC = 4 \text{ cm}$$

Hence, length of chord $CD = 2\,CE$

$$= 2 \times 4 = 8 \text{ cm}$$

[since, perpendicular from centre to the chord bisects the chord]

16. (c) In figure, AOC is a diameter of the circle. We know that, diameter subtends an angle 90° at the circle.

So, $\qquad \angle ABC = 90°$

In ΔACB, $\quad \angle A + \angle B + \angle C = 180°$

[since, sum of all angles of a triangle is 180°]

$$\Rightarrow \qquad \angle A + 90° + 50° = 180°$$
$$\Rightarrow \qquad \angle A + 140 = 180$$
$$\Rightarrow \qquad \angle A = 180° - 140° = 40°$$
$$\angle A \text{ or } \angle OAB = 40°$$

Now, AT is the tangent to the circle at point A. So, OA is perpendicular to AT.

$\therefore \qquad \angle OAT = 90°$ \qquad [from figure]

$$\Rightarrow \qquad \angle OAB + \angle BAT = 90°$$

On putting $\angle OAB = 40°$, we get

$$\Rightarrow \qquad \angle BAT = 90° - 40° = 50°$$

Hence, the value of $\angle BAT$ is 50°.

17. (b) Clearly, $\angle CAD = 90°$ \qquad [angle in a semi-circle]

So, in ΔACD, $\;CD^2 = AC^2 + AD^2 = 36 + 64 = 100$

[by Pythagoras theorem]

$$\Rightarrow \qquad CD = 10 \text{ cm}$$

Therefore, $\quad OC = OD = OB = 5$ cm $\quad [\because$ radius of a circle]

Since, $\quad \angle OBT = 90°$

[angle between radius and tangent]

So, in ΔOBT, $\;OT^2 = OB^2 + BT^2$

$$= 25 + 16 = 41 \quad \text{[by Pythagoras theorem]}$$
$$\Rightarrow \qquad OT = \sqrt{41} \text{ cm}$$

18. (d) In ΔACB,

$$\angle BCA = 90° \qquad \text{[angle in a semi-circle]}$$

$\therefore \qquad AB^2 = AC^2 + BC^2 \qquad$ [by Pythagoras theorem]

$$\Rightarrow \qquad AB^2 = 4^2 + 3^2$$
$$\Rightarrow \qquad AB^2 = 16 + 9 \text{ cm}$$
$$\Rightarrow \qquad AB^2 = 25 \text{ cm}$$
$$\Rightarrow \qquad AB = 5 \text{ cm}$$
$$\Rightarrow \qquad OA = \frac{5}{2} \text{ cm}$$

19. (c) $\quad \angle OAT = 90° \qquad [\because$ angle between radius and tangent]

Now, $\angle BOA = 100°$ \qquad [angle subtended by an arc at centre is twice the angle subtended at remaining part of circle]

$\Rightarrow \quad \angle ATO = 180° - (\angle TOA + \angle OAT)$

[angles property of a triangle]

$$= 180° - (50° + 90°)$$
$$= 180° - 140° = 40°$$

20. (a) Take a point Q' on circle and join PQ' and QQ'.

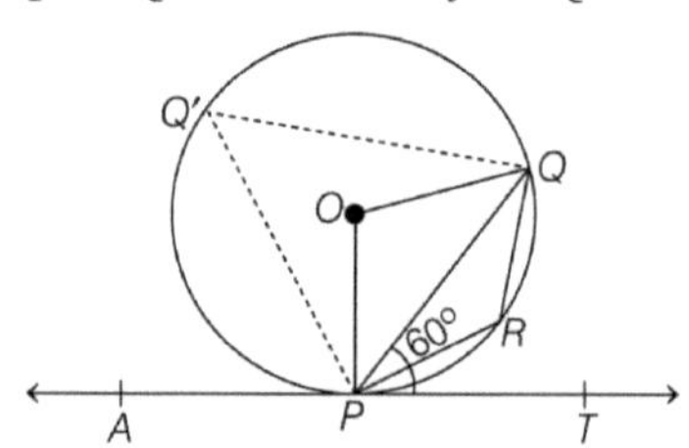

Now, $\angle OPQ = 90° - 60° = 30° \qquad [\because \angle OPT = 90°]$

$\Rightarrow \quad \angle OQP = 30° \qquad$ [angles opposite to equal sides are equal]

$\Rightarrow \qquad\qquad \angle POQ = 120°$

[angle sum property of a triangle]

$\Rightarrow \qquad \angle PQ'Q = 60°$

[angle subtended by an arc at centre is twice the angle subtended at remaining part of circle]

$\Rightarrow \qquad \angle PRQ = 120° \qquad [\because$ opposite angles are

supplementary in a cyclic quadrilateral $PQQ'R$]

21. (b) Given, $AB \parallel PR$

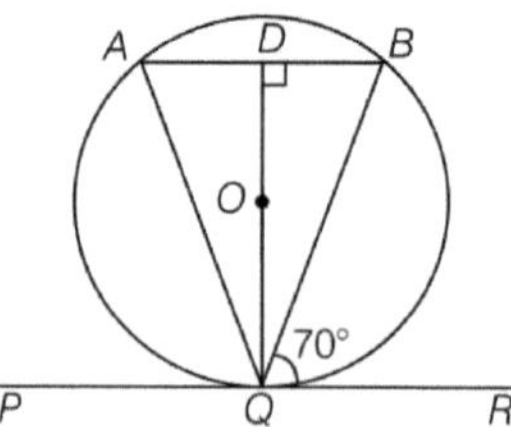

$\therefore \qquad \angle ABQ = \angle BQR = 70°$ \quad [alternate angles]

Also, QD is perpendicular to AB and QD bisects AB.

In ΔQDA and ΔQDB,

$$\angle QDA = \angle QDB \qquad \text{[each 90°]}$$
$$AD = BD$$
$$QD = QD \qquad \text{[common side]}$$

$\therefore \qquad \Delta ADQ \sim \Delta BDQ$

[by SAS similarity criterion]

Then, $\qquad \angle QAD = \angle QBD \qquad$ [by CPCT] ...(i)

Also,　　　$\angle ABQ = \angle BQR$ [alternate interior angle]

$\therefore$　　　$\angle ABQ = 70°$　　　$[\because \angle BQR = 70°]$

Hence,　　　$\angle QAB = 70°$　　　[from Eq. (i)]

Now, in $\triangle ABQ$, $\angle A + \angle B + \angle Q = 180°$

$\Rightarrow$　$\angle Q = 180° - (70° + 70°) = 40°$

22. (c) We have, $PA = PB = 14$ cm

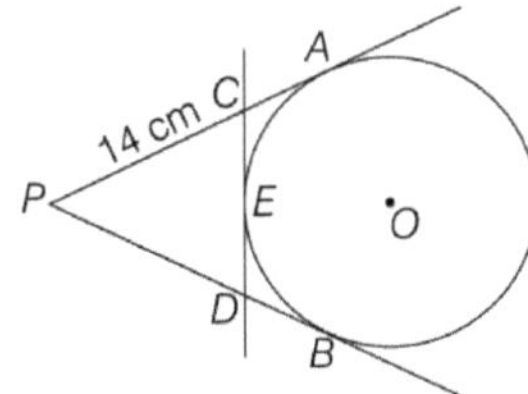

Also, CD is tangent at point E on the circle.

So, CA and CE are tangents to the circle from point C.

Therefore, $CA = CE$, similarly $DB = DE$

Now, perimeter of $\triangle PCD$

$$= PC + CD + PD = PC + CE + ED + PD$$
$$= PC + CA + PD + DB$$
$$[\because CA = CE \text{ and } DE = DB]$$
$$= PA + PB = 14 + 14 = 28 \text{ cm}$$

23. (a) Here, $AP = AQ$

$\Rightarrow$　　　$\angle AQP = \angle APQ = x$ (say)

　　　$[\because$ angles opposite to equal sides of a triangle are equal]

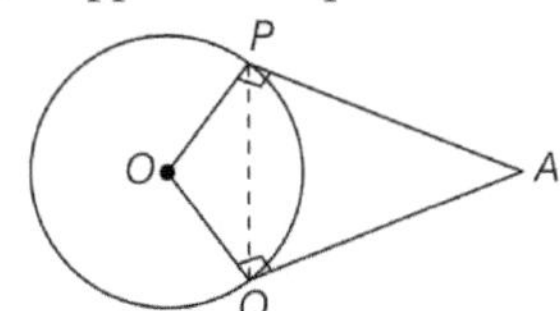

In $\triangle APQ$, $\angle PAQ = 180° - (\angle APQ + \angle AQP)$
$$= 180° - (x + x) = 180° - 2x$$

$\because$　　　$OP \perp AP$

$\therefore$　　　$\angle OPA = 90°$

$\Rightarrow \angle OPQ + \angle APQ = 90°$

$\Rightarrow$　　$\angle OPQ + x = 90°$

$\Rightarrow$　　　$\angle OPQ = 90° - x$

$\Rightarrow$　　$2\angle OPQ = 180° - 2x$　　　[multiplying by 2]

$\Rightarrow$　　　$\angle PAQ = 2\angle OPQ$

24. (a) In $\triangle OAB$ and $\triangle OAC$, we have
$$\angle OBA = \angle OCA = 90°$$
$$OA = OA \qquad \text{[common]}$$

and　　　$OB = OC$　　　[radii of circle]

So, by RHS congruence criterion,
$$\triangle OBA \cong \triangle OCA$$

$\Rightarrow$　　　$\angle OAB = \angle OAC$
$$= \frac{1}{2} \times 120° = 60°$$

In $\triangle OBA$, we have
$$\cos 60° = \frac{AB}{OA}$$

$\Rightarrow$　　　$\dfrac{1}{2} = \dfrac{AB}{OA}$

$\Rightarrow$　　　$OA = 2AB$

25. (c)　　　$\angle OPB = 30°$

　　　$[\because$ angles opposite to equal sides are equal]

and　　$\angle OPT = 90°$

Now,　　$\angle PTA = 180° - (\angle OBP + \angle BPT)$

　　　　[angle sum property of a $\triangle BPT$]
$$= 180° - (30° + 120°)$$
$$[\because \angle BPT = 90° + 30° = 120°]$$
$$= 180° - 150°$$
$$= 30°$$

26. (d) $\angle OQS = \angle OQL - \angle SQL$　[since, $OQ \perp LP$]
$$= 90° - 50° = 40°$$

Similarly, $\angle ORS = 30°$

Now, $\angle QSR = \angle OSR + \angle OSQ = \angle ORS + \angle OQS$

　　　　[$\because$ angle opposite to equal sides are equal]
$$= 30° + 40°$$
$$= 70°$$

27. (c) $\angle ABQ = \dfrac{1}{2} \angle AOQ = \dfrac{1}{2}(58°) = 29°$

　　　[angle subtended by an arc at the centre is twice the angle subtended at remaining part of circle]

and　$\angle BAT = 90°$　　　[angle between radius and tangent]

In $\triangle ABT$, we get,
$$\angle ATQ = 180° - (29° + 90°) = 61°$$

　　　　[angle sum property of a triangle]

28. (d) We know that, the opposite sides of a quadrilateral circumscribing a circle subtend supplementary angles at the centre of the circle.

i.e.　$\angle AOB + \angle COD = 180°$

$\Rightarrow$　　　$\angle COD = 180° - \angle AOB$
$$= 180° - 125° = 55°$$

29. Here, in right angled $\triangle ABC$, $AB = 3$ m and $BC = 4$ m.

$\therefore$ By Pythagoras theorem,
$$AC = \sqrt{(AB)^2 + (BC)^2}$$
$$= \sqrt{(3)^2 + (4)^2}$$
$$= \sqrt{9 + 16} = \sqrt{25} = 5 \text{ m}$$

Also, $AP = x$ m

(i) (c) $AR = AP = x$ m　　　　　　　... (i)

　　　　[since, length of tangents drawn from an external point are equal]

(ii) (b) $BQ = BR = AB - AR = (3 - x)$ m　　[using Eq. (i)]

(iii) (d) $CQ = CP = AC - AP = (5 - x)$ m

　　　Also, $CQ = BC - BQ = BC - BR$
$$= 4 - (3 - x) = 1 + x$$

(iv) (b) Since, $CQ = 5 - x = 1 + x$

$\Rightarrow$　　　$4 = 2x \Rightarrow x = 2$

$\therefore$　　　$AR = AP = 2$ m, $BR = BQ = 1$ m

and　　$CP = CQ = 3$ m

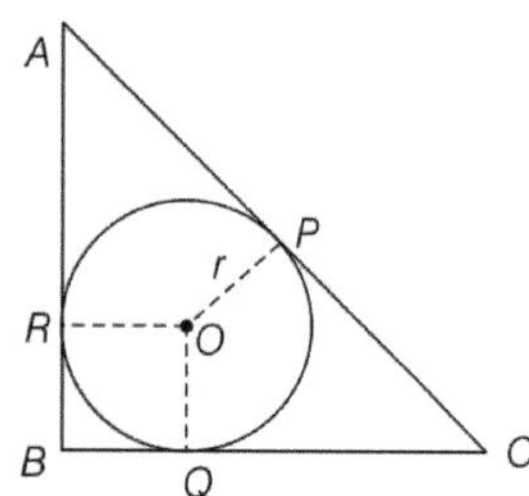

Also, $OQ \perp BQ$ and $OR \perp BR$

∴ $BROQ$ is a square.

(v) (a) Radius of the pit, $OR = BR = 1\, m$

30. Here, $AS = 6\, cm,\ BT = 4\, cm$ [∵ radii of circles]

  (i) (c) Since, radius at point of contact is perpendicular to tangent.

    ∴ By Pythagoras theorem, we have

$$PA = \sqrt{PS^2 + AS^2}$$
$$= \sqrt{8^2 + 6^2}$$
$$= \sqrt{64 + 36}$$
$$= \sqrt{100} = 10\, cm$$

  (ii) (b) Again, by Pythagoras theorem, we have

$$BQ = \sqrt{TQ^2 + BT^2} = \sqrt{3^2 + 4^2}$$
$$= \sqrt{9 + 16} = \sqrt{25} = 5\, cm$$

  (iii) (c) $PK = PA + AK = 10 + 6 = 16\, cm$

  (iv) (c) $QY = BQ - BY = 5 - 4 = 1\, cm$

  (v) (b) If two circles touch externally, then the number of common tangents can be drawn is 2.

Subjective Questions

1. Given, PQ is a tangent, $OP = 6\, cm$ and $\angle PQO = 60°$

We know that, tangent at any point of a circle is perpendicular to the radius through the point of contact.

∴ $OP \perp PQ$

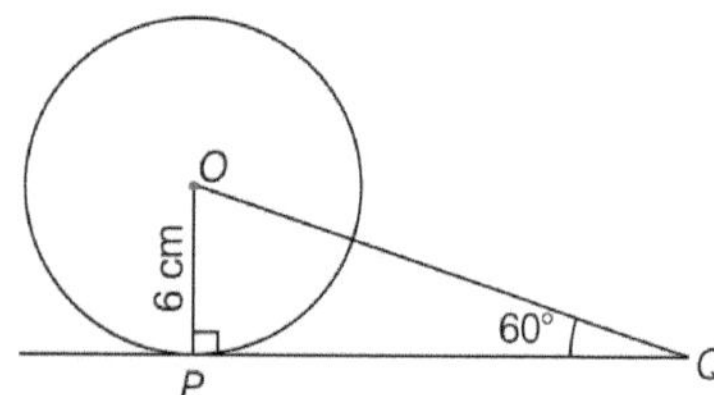

Now, in right angled $\triangle OPQ$,

$$\tan 60° = \frac{OP}{PQ} \qquad \left[∵ \tan\theta = \frac{\text{perpendicular}}{\text{base}}\right]$$

$$\Rightarrow \quad \sqrt{3} = \frac{6}{PQ} \qquad [∵ \tan 60° = \sqrt{3}]$$

$$\Rightarrow \quad PQ = \frac{6}{\sqrt{3}} \times \frac{\sqrt{3}}{\sqrt{3}} \qquad [\text{rationalising}]$$

$$\Rightarrow \quad PQ = 2\sqrt{3}\, cm \ \text{and}\ \sin 60° = \frac{OP}{OQ}$$

$$\left[∵ \sin\theta = \frac{\text{perpendicular}}{\text{hypotenuse}}\right]$$

$$\Rightarrow \qquad \frac{\sqrt{3}}{2} = \frac{6}{OQ} \qquad \left[∵ \sin 60° = \frac{\sqrt{3}}{2}\right]$$

$$\Rightarrow \qquad OQ = \frac{2 \times 6}{\sqrt{3}} \times \frac{\sqrt{3}}{\sqrt{3}} \qquad [\text{rationalising}]$$

$$\Rightarrow \qquad OQ = 4\sqrt{3}\, cm$$

Hence, length of a tangent PQ is $2\sqrt{3}\, cm$ and a line OQ is $4\sqrt{3}\, cm$.

2. Let EAF be tangent to the circumcircle of $\triangle ABC$.

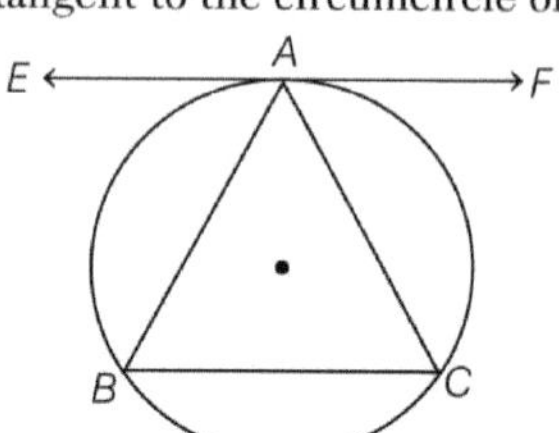

To prove $EAF \parallel BC$

                 $\angle EAB = \angle ABC$

Here, $AB = AC$

$\Rightarrow$ $\angle ACB = \angle ABC$ ...(i)

[angle between tangent and its chord equal to angle made by chord in the alternate segment]

∴ Also, $\angle EAB = \angle BCA$ ...(ii)

From Eqs. (i) and (ii), we get

$$\angle EAB = \angle ABC$$

$\Rightarrow$ $EAF \parallel BC$

3. Since, AC is a diameter line, so angle in semi-circle makes an angle 90°.

∴ $\angle ABC = 90°$

In $\triangle ABC,\ \angle CAB + \angle ABC + \angle ACB = 180°$

        [∵ sum of all interior angles of any triangle is 180°]

$\Rightarrow$ $\angle CAB + \angle ACB = 180° - 90° = 90°$ ...(i)

Since, diameter of a circle is perpendicular to the tangent.

i.e. $CA \perp AT$

∴ $\angle CAT = 90°$

$\Rightarrow$ $\angle CAB + \angle BAT = 90°$ ...(ii)

From Eqs. (i) and (ii), we get

$$\angle CAB + \angle ACB = \angle CAB + \angle BAT$$

$\Rightarrow$ $\angle ACB = \angle BAT$ **Hence proved.**

4. Given, AB is a diameter of the circle.

A tangent is drawn from point A. Draw a chord CD parallel to the tangent MAN.

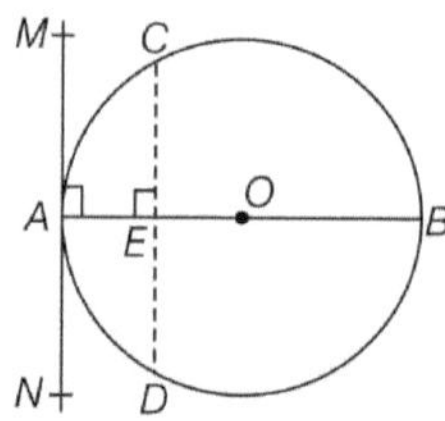

So, CD is a chord of the circle and OA is a radius of the circle.

$$\angle MAO = 90°$$

[tangent at any point of a circle is perpendicular to the radius through the point of contact]

$$\angle CEO = \angle MAO \quad [\text{corresponding angles}]$$
$$\therefore \qquad \angle CEO = 90°$$

Thus, OE bisects CD, [perpendicular from centre of circle to the chord bisects the chord]

Similarly, the diameter AB bisects all chords, which are parallel to the tangent at the point A.

5. Given that, PQ is any line segment and S_1, S_2, S_3, S_4, ... circles are touch a line segment PQ at a point A. Let the centres of the circles S_1, S_2, S_3, S_4, ... be C_1, C_2, C_3, C_4,... respectively.

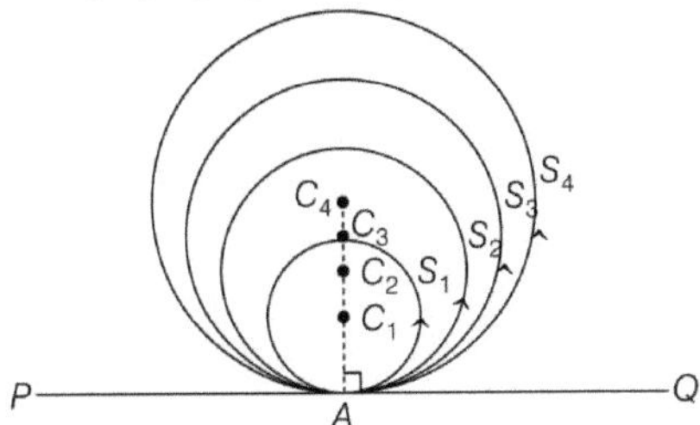

To prove Centres of these circles lie on the perpendicular bisector of PQ.

Now, joining each centre of the circles to the point A on the line segment PQ by a line segment, i.e.

C_1A, C_2A, C_3A, C_4A,... so on.

We know that, if we draw a line from the centre of a circle to its tangent line, then the line is always perpendicular to the tangent line. But it not bisect the line segment PQ.

So,
$$\begin{aligned}
C_1A \perp PQ && [\text{for } S_1] \\
C_2A \perp PQ && [\text{for } S_2] \\
C_3A \perp PQ && [\text{for } S_3] \\
C_4A \perp PQ && [\text{for } S_4]
\end{aligned}$$
... so on.

Since, each circle is passing through a point A. Therefore, all the line segments C_1A, C_2A, C_3A, C_4A,..., so on are coincident.

So, centre of each circle lies on the perpendicular line of PQ but they do not lie on the perpendicular bisector of PQ.

Hence, a number of circles touch a given line segment PQ at a point A, then their centres lie.

6. Let C_1 and C_2 be the two circles having same centre O. AC is a chord which touches the C_1 at point D.

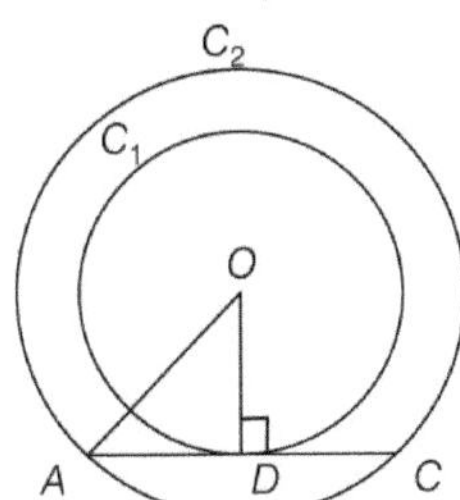

Join OD.

Also, $\qquad OD \perp AC$

$\therefore \qquad AD = DC = 4$ cm

[perpendicular line OD bisects the chord]

In right angled $\triangle AOD$,

$$OA^2 = AD^2 + DO^2 \quad [\text{by Pythagoras theorem,}$$
$$\text{i.e. } (\text{hypotenuse})^2 = (\text{base})^2 + (\text{perpendicular})^2]$$

$$\Rightarrow \qquad DO^2 = 5^2 - 4^2 = 25 - 16 = 9$$
$$\Rightarrow \qquad DO = 3 \text{ cm}$$
$\therefore$ Radius of the inner circle $OD = 3$ cm

7. Since, a chord AB subtends an angle of $60°$ at the centre of a circle.

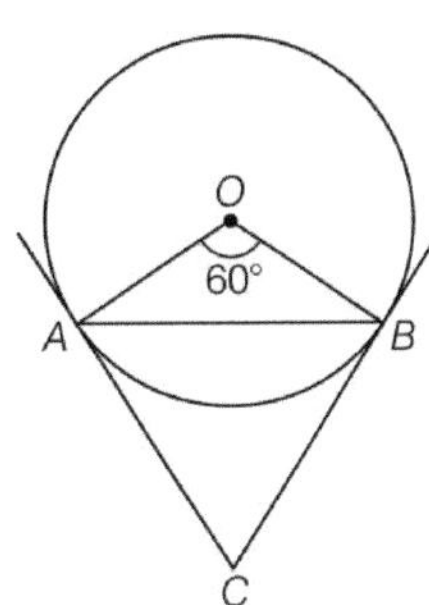

i.e. $\qquad \angle AOB = 60°$

As, $\qquad OA = OB = $ Radius of the circle

$\therefore \qquad \angle OAB = \angle OBA = 60°$

The tangent at points A and B is drawn, which intersects at C.

We know, $OA \perp AC$ and $OB \perp BC$.

$\therefore \qquad \angle OAC = 90°$ and $\angle OBC = 90°$

$\Rightarrow \qquad \angle OAB + \angle BAC = 90°$

and $\qquad \angle OBA + \angle ABC = 90°$

$\Rightarrow \qquad \angle BAC = 90° - 60° = 30°$

and $\qquad \angle ABC = 90° - 60° = 30°$

In $\triangle ABC$, $\angle BAC + \angle CBA + \angle ACB = 180°$

[since, sum of all interior angles of a triangle is $180°$]

$\Rightarrow \quad \angle ACB = 180° - (30° + 30°) = 120°$

8. Two tangents PA and PB are drawn to a circle with centre O from an external point P.

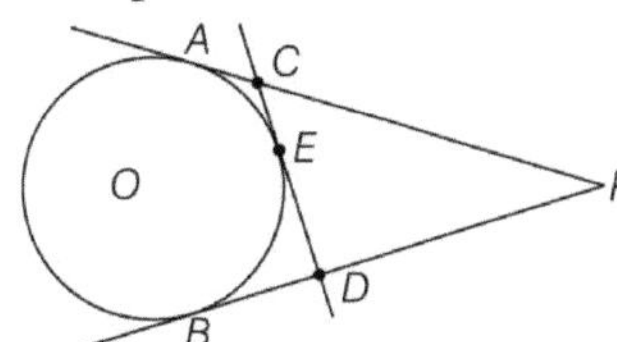

Perimeter of $\triangle PCD = PC + CD + PD$
$$= PC + CE + ED + PD$$
$$= PC + CA + DB + PD$$
$$\qquad\qquad [\because CE = CA, DE = DB]$$
$$= PA + PB$$
$$= 2PA = 2(10) \quad [PA = PB \text{ tangents from}$$
$$\text{external point to a circle are equal}]$$
$$= 20 \text{ cm}$$

9. Given Two tangents PQ and PR are drawn from an external point P to a circle with centre O.

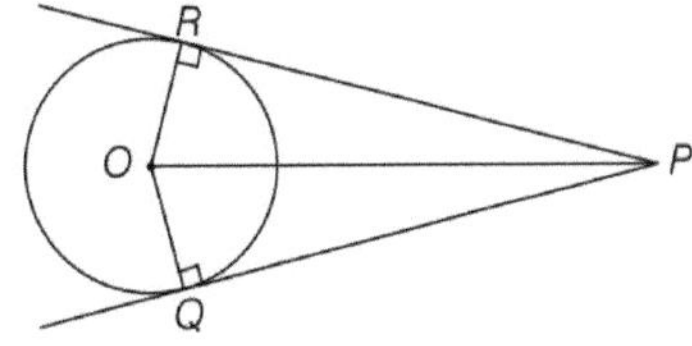

To prove Centre of a circle touching two intersecting lines lies on the angle bisector of the lines.

In $\angle RPQ$.

Construction Join OR and OQ.

In ΔPOR and ΔPOQ,
$$\angle PRO = \angle PQO = 90°$$
[tangent at any point of a circle is perpendicular to the radius through the point of contact]
$$OR = OQ \qquad \text{[radii of same circle]}$$
Since, OP is common.
$$\therefore \qquad \Delta PRO \cong \Delta PQO \qquad \text{[by RHS]}$$
Hence, $\qquad \angle RPO = \angle QPO \qquad \text{[by CPCT]}$

Thus, O lies on angle bisecter of PR and PQ. **Hence proved.**

10. Two tangents BD and BC are drawn from an external point B.

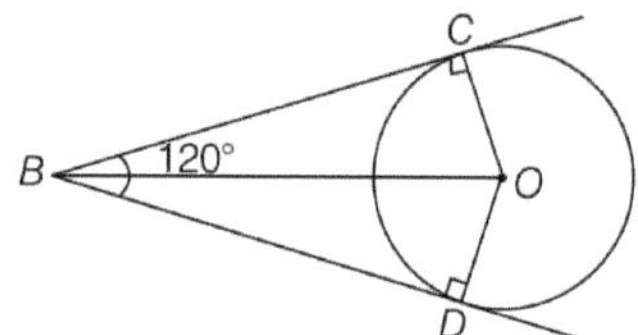

To prove $\qquad BO = 2BC$

Given, $\qquad \angle DBC = 120°$

Join OC, OD and BO.

Since, BC and BD are tangents.
$$\therefore \qquad OC \perp BC \text{ and } OD \perp BD$$
We know, OB is a angle bisector of $\angle DBC$.
$$\therefore \qquad \angle OBC = \angle DBO = 60°$$
In right angled ΔOBC,
$$\cos 60° = \frac{BC}{OB}$$
$$\Rightarrow \qquad \frac{1}{2} = \frac{BC}{OB}$$
$$\Rightarrow \qquad OB = 2\,BC$$
Also, $\qquad BC = BD$
[tangents drawn from external point to circle are equal]
$$\therefore \qquad OB = BC + BC$$
$$\Rightarrow \qquad OB = BC + BD$$

11. Given AB and CD are tangents to two circles of equal radii.

To prove $\qquad AB = CD$

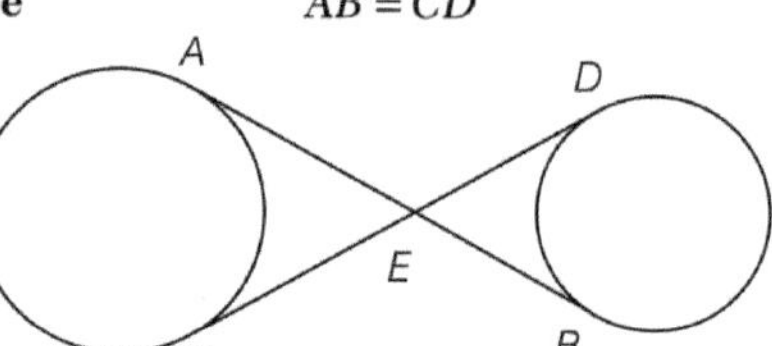

Construction Join $O'A$, $O'C$, OB and OD

Proof $\qquad$ Now, $\angle OAB = 90°$

[tangent at any point of a circle is perpendicular to radius through the point of contact]

Thus, AC is a straight line.

Also, $\qquad \angle OAB + \angle OCD = 180°$
$$\therefore \qquad AB \parallel CD$$
Similarly, BD is a straight line.

and $\qquad \angle O'BA = \angle O'DC = 90°$

Also, $\qquad AC = BD \qquad$ [radii of two circles are equal]

In quadrilateral $ABCD$,
$$\angle A = \angle B = \angle C = \angle D = 90°$$
and $\qquad AC = BD$

$ABCD$ is a rectangle

Hence, $\qquad AB = CD$

[opposite sides of rectangle are equal]

12. Given Common tangents AB and CD of two circles intersecting at E.

To prove $\qquad AB = CD$

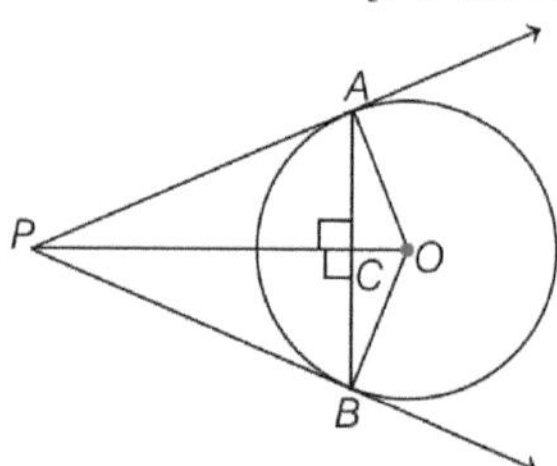

Proof $\qquad EA = EC \qquad$ ...(i)

[the lengths of tangents drawn from an external point to a circle are equal]
$$EB = ED \qquad \text{...(ii)}$$
On adding Eqs. (i) and (ii), we get
$$EA + EB = EC + ED$$
$$\Rightarrow \qquad AB = CD \qquad \textbf{Hence proved.}$$

13. Let OP intersect AB at a point C.

Clearly, $\qquad \angle APO = \angle BPO \qquad$ ...(i)

[$\because O$ lies on bisector of $\angle APB$]

Now, in ΔACP and ΔBCP,
$$AP = BP$$
[$\because$ length of tangents drawn from an external point to a circle are equal]
$$PC = PC \qquad \text{[common sides]}$$
and $\qquad \angle APO = \angle BPO \qquad$ [from Eq. (i)]
$$\therefore \qquad \Delta ACP \cong \Delta BCP \text{ [by SAS congruence rule]}$$
Then, $\qquad AC = BC \qquad$ [by CPCT]

and $\qquad \angle ACP = \angle BCP \qquad$ [by CPCT]
$$= \frac{1}{2} \times 180° = 90°$$

[$\because AB$ is a straight line]

Hence, OP is perpendicular bisector of AB. **Hence proved.**

14.

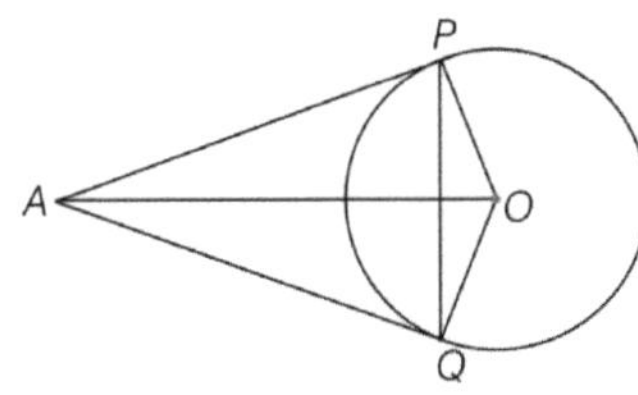

$$AP = AQ$$
$$\Rightarrow \quad \angle APQ = \angle AQP = x \qquad \text{[say]}$$
[∵ angles opposite to equal sides are equal]

In $\triangle APQ$, $\quad \angle PAQ = 180° - (\angle APQ + \angle AQP)$
[angle sum property of a triangle]
$$= 180° - (x + x) = 180° - 2x$$

∵ $\qquad OP \perp AP$

[∵ radius is perpendicular to the tangent
at the point of contact]

∴ $\qquad \angle OPA = 90°$
$\Rightarrow \qquad \angle OPQ + \angle APQ = 90°$
$\Rightarrow \qquad \angle OPQ + x = 90°$
$\Rightarrow \qquad \angle OPQ = 90° - x$
∴ $\qquad \angle PAQ = 2\angle OPQ$ **Hence proved.**

15. $\qquad CR = CQ = BC - BQ$
$$= 38 - 25 = 13 \text{ cm}$$
∴ $\qquad RD = CD - CR = 28 - 13 = 15 \text{ cm}$
Here, $OR \perp RD$ and $OS \perp DA$.

[∵ tangent is perpendicular to the radius
through the point of contact]

Also, $\angle ADC = 90°$, then fourth angle in quadrilateral $ORDS$
will be $90°$. Thus, $ORDS$ will be a rectangle.

∵ D is an external point of a circle.

∴ $\qquad DR = DS$

Also, opposites sides of rectangle are equal.

∴ $\qquad RD = OR = OS = SD$

Hence, quadrilateral $DROS$ is a square.

∴ $\qquad$ Radius $= OR = RD = 15$ cm

16. Let D, E and F are the points, where the incircle touches the
sides AB, BC and CA, respectively. Join OA, OB and OC.

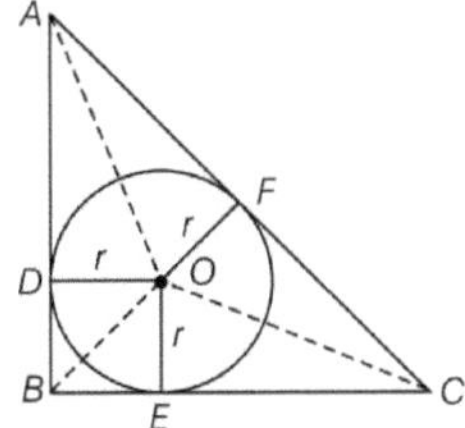

In $\triangle ABC$, $\qquad AC^2 = AB^2 + BC^2$ [by Pythagoras theorem]
$$= 4^2 + 3^2 = 16 + 9 = 25$$

∴ $\qquad AC = 5$ cm

[taking positive square root, as length cannot be negative]

Now, ar $(\triangle OAB) = \dfrac{1}{2} \times OD \times AB = \dfrac{1}{2} \times r \times 4 = \dfrac{4r}{2} \text{ cm}^2$,

ar $(\triangle OBC) = \dfrac{1}{2} \times OE \times BC = \dfrac{1}{2} \times r \times 3 = \dfrac{3r}{2} \text{ cm}^2$

and ar $(\triangle OAC) = \dfrac{1}{2} \times OF \times AC = \dfrac{1}{2} \times r \times 5 = \dfrac{5r}{2} \text{ cm}^2$

∴ ar $(\triangle ABC) =$ ar $(\triangle OAB) +$ ar $(\triangle OBC) +$ ar $(\triangle OAC)$
$$\Rightarrow \quad \dfrac{1}{2} AB \times BC = \dfrac{4r}{2} + \dfrac{3r}{2} + \dfrac{5r}{2} \Rightarrow \dfrac{1}{2} \times 3 \times 4 = \dfrac{12r}{2}$$
$$\Rightarrow \qquad r = 1 \text{ cm}$$

17. Produce BD to meet the bigger circle at E. Join AE.
Then, $\qquad \angle AEB = 90°$ $\qquad$ [∵ angle in semi-circle]

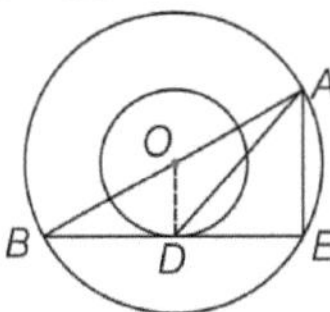

Clearly, $\qquad OD \perp BE$ $\qquad$ [∵ BE is tangent to the smaller
circle at D and OD is its radius]

∴ $\qquad BD = DE$

[∵ BE is a chord of the bigger circle and $OD \perp BE$]

Now, in $\triangle AEB$, O and D are the mid-points of AB and BE,
respectively.

Therefore, by mid-point theorem, we have
$$OD = \dfrac{1}{2} AE \Rightarrow AE = 2 \times OD = 2 \times 8 = 16 \text{ cm}$$

[∵ $OD =$ radius of smaller circle = 8 cm]

In right angled $\triangle ODB$,
$$OB^2 = OD^2 + BD^2 \qquad \text{[by Pythagoras theorem]}$$
$$\Rightarrow \qquad BD^2 = 169 - 64 = 105$$
$$\Rightarrow \qquad BD = \sqrt{105} \text{ cm} = DE \qquad [∵ BD = DE]$$

Now, in right angled $\triangle AED$,
$$AD^2 = AE^2 + ED^2 \qquad \text{[by Pythagoras theorem]}$$
$$\Rightarrow \qquad AD = \sqrt{(16)^2 + (\sqrt{105})^2}$$
$$= \sqrt{256 + 105} = \sqrt{361} = 19 \text{ cm}$$

18. We know that, tangents drawn from an exterior point to a
circle are equal in length.

∴ $\qquad AD = AF = x$ cm $\qquad$ [say]
$\qquad BD = BE = y$ cm $\qquad$ [say]
$\qquad CE = CF = z$ cm $\qquad$ [say]

Given, $\qquad AB = 8$ cm
$\Rightarrow \qquad AD + BD = 8$ cm
$\Rightarrow \qquad x + y = 8$ $\qquad$ ...(i)
$\qquad BC = 10$ cm
$\Rightarrow \qquad BE + CE = 10$ cm
$\Rightarrow \qquad y + z = 10$ $\qquad$ ...(ii)
and $\qquad CA = 12$ cm
$\Rightarrow \qquad CF + AF = 12$ cm
$\Rightarrow \qquad z + x = 12$ $\qquad$ ...(iii)

On adding Eqs. (i), (ii) and (iii), we get
$$2(x + y + z) = 30$$
$$\Rightarrow \qquad x + y + z = 15 \qquad \text{...(iv)}$$

On subtracting Eq. (ii) from Eq. (iv), we get
$$x = 15 - 10 = 5$$

On subtracting Eq. (iii) from Eq. (iv), we get
$$y = 15 - 12 = 3$$

On subtracting Eq. (i) from Eq. (iv), we get
$$z = 15 - 8 = 7$$
$$\therefore \quad AD = x \text{ cm} = 5 \text{ cm},$$
$$BE = y \text{ cm} = 3 \text{ cm}$$
and
$$CF = z \text{ cm} = 7 \text{ cm}$$

Hence, the length of AD, BE and CE are 5 cm, 3 cm and 7 cm, respectively.

19. A circle is inscribed in the $\triangle ABC$, which touches the BC, CA and AB.

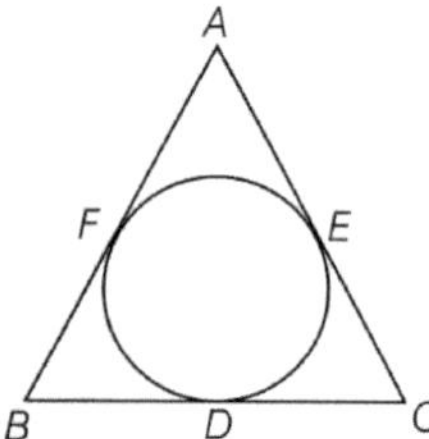

Given, $\quad BC = a$, $CA = b$ and $AB = c$

By using the property, tangents are drawn from an external point to the circle are equal in length.
$$\therefore \quad BD = BF = x \text{ [say]}$$
$$DC = CE = y \text{ [say]}$$
and
$$AE = AF = z \text{ [say]}$$

Now, $BC + CA + AB = a + b + c$
$$\Rightarrow (BD + DC) + (CE + EA) + (AF + FB) = a + b + c$$
$$\Rightarrow \quad (x + y) + (y + z) + (z + x) = a + b + c$$
$$\Rightarrow \quad 2(x + y + z) = 2s$$
$$[\because 2s = a + b + c = \text{perimeter of } \triangle ABC]$$
$$\Rightarrow \quad s = x + y + z \Rightarrow x = s - (y + z)$$
$$\Rightarrow \quad BD = s - b \quad [\because b = AE + EC = z + y]$$
Hence proved.

20. $\quad \angle OCA = 90°$ [angle between tangent and radius]

Now, $\quad \angle OCA = \angle OCD + \angle ACD$
$$\Rightarrow \quad \angle ACD = \angle OCA - \angle OCD$$
$$\Rightarrow \quad \angle ACD = 90° - 44° = 46°$$
As, $\quad AC = AD$

[tangents drawn from an external point are equal in length]

So, $\quad \angle ADC = \angle ACD = 46°$

[$\because$ angles opposite to the equal sides are equal]

Also, $\angle CAD + \angle ADC + \angle ACD = 180°$

[angle sum property of a $\triangle ACD$]
$$\Rightarrow \quad \angle CAD = 180° - (46° + 46°) = 88°$$
Again, $\quad \angle COD = 180° - \angle CAD = 92°$

Further, $\quad \angle OBD = \angle ODB \quad [OB = OD \text{ radii of circle}]$

In $\triangle OBD$, use exterior angle theorem

exterior angle $\angle COD = \angle OBD + \angle ODB$
$$= \angle OBD + \angle OBD$$
$$\Rightarrow \quad 2\angle OBD = \angle COD \quad \text{[exterior angle theorem]}$$
$$\Rightarrow \quad \angle CBD = \frac{1}{2} \times 92° = 46°$$

Hence, $\angle CAD = 88°$, $\angle ADC = 46°$, $\angle CBD = 46°$ and $\angle ACD = 46°$

21. Given, hexagon $ABCDEF$ circumscribe a circle.

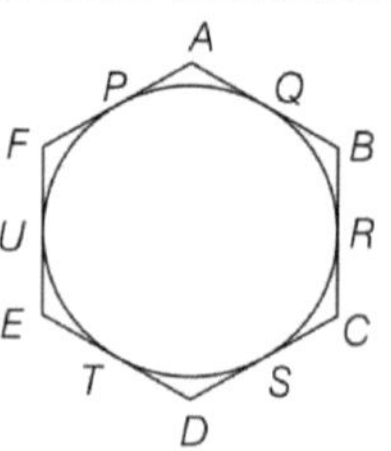

Since, tangents drawn from an external point to a circle are equal in length
$$\therefore \ AQ = AP, \ BQ = BR, \ CR = CS, \ DS = DT,$$
$$ET = EU, \ FP = FU$$
So, $\ AB + CD + EF = (AQ + QB) + (CS + SD) + (EU + UF)$
$$= AP + BR + CR + DT + ET + FP$$
$$= (AP + FP) + (BR + CR) + (DT + ET)$$
$$\Rightarrow \quad AB + CD + EF = AF + BC + DE \qquad \textbf{Hence proved.}$$

22. $\angle DAB = 90°$

In $\triangle ABD$, $\angle DAB + \angle ABD + \angle ADB = 180°$
$$\Rightarrow \quad \angle ADB = 180° - 140° = 40°$$
In $\triangle ODC$, $\quad OD = OC \qquad \text{[radii of same circle]}$
$$\Rightarrow \quad \angle OCD = \angle CDO = 40°$$
[$\because$ angles opposite to equal sides are equal]
$$\therefore \quad \angle DOC + \angle OCD + \angle CDO = 180°$$
[$\because$ sum of all angles in a triangle is 180°]
$$\Rightarrow \quad \angle DOC = 100°$$
Since, AD is a straight line.
$$\therefore \quad \angle DOC + \angle COA = 180° \Rightarrow \angle COA = 80°$$

23. Let O be the centre of circle.

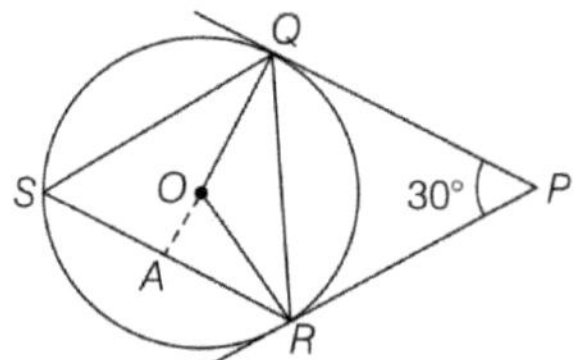

Join OQ and OR. Then,
$$OQ \perp PQ \text{ and } OR \perp PR$$
[$\because$ tangent is perpendicular to the radius at the point of contact]

So, $\quad \angle ROQ + \angle RPQ = 180°$

[$\because$ sum of all interior angles of quadrilateral is 360°]
$$\Rightarrow \quad \angle ROQ = 150°$$
But $\angle RSQ = \frac{1}{2} \angle ROQ$
$$= \frac{1}{2} \times 150° = 75°$$

Now, on extending QO to intersect RS at A, we get
$$\angle OQP = \angle QAS = 90° \quad \text{[alternate interior angle]}$$
[$\because PQ \| RS$ and $\angle OQP = 90°$]

Therefore, from $\triangle QSA$,
$$\angle SQA = 180° - 90° - 75° = 15°$$

Also, $\angle PQR + \angle PRQ + \angle QPR = 180°$
$\Rightarrow$ $\angle PQR + \angle PQR + 30° = 180°$
                    $[\because \angle PQR = \angle PRQ \text{ because } PQ = PR]$
$\Rightarrow$ $\angle PQR = \dfrac{150°}{2} = 75°$
$\Rightarrow$ $\angle AQR = \angle AQP - \angle PQR$
                    $= 90° - 75° = 15°$
So, $\angle RQS = \angle SQA + \angle AQR$
                    $= 15° + 15° = 30°$

24. Clearly, $\angle QAB = 60°$ and $\angle QBA = 60°$
                    $[\because \triangle ABQ \text{ is an equilateral}]$
So, $\angle PAQ = \angle PAB + \angle QAB = 120°$
Similarly, $\angle PBQ = 120°$
                    $[\because \angle PAB = \angle PBA, \text{ as } PA = PB] \ldots(i)$
Now, in $\triangle PAQ$ and $\triangle PBQ$,
          $PA = PB$
                    [tangents drawn from external point]
$\Rightarrow$ $AQ = BQ$ $[\triangle ABQ \text{ is an equilateral}]$
$\Rightarrow$ $\angle PAQ = \angle PBQ$ [each 120°, shown above]
So, $\triangle PAQ \cong \triangle PBQ$ [by SAS similarity rule]
$\Rightarrow$ $\angle APQ = \angle BPQ$ [by CPCT] $\ldots(ii)$
Let QP intersect AB at M.
Now, in $\triangle PAM$ and $\triangle PBM$,
          $\angle APM = \angle BPM$ [from Eq. (ii)]
$\Rightarrow$ $PA = PB$
                    [tangents drawn from an external point]
$\Rightarrow$ $PM = PM$ [common side]
So, $\triangle PAM \cong \triangle PBM$ [by SAS congruence rule]
$\Rightarrow$ $AM = BM$
and $\angle AMP = \angle BMP$ [by CPCT] $\ldots(iii)$
But $\angle AMP + \angle BMP = 180°$
$\Rightarrow$ $\angle AMP + \angle AMP = 180°$
$\Rightarrow$ $\angle AMP = 90°$ **Hence Proved.**

25. Here, two circles are of radii $OP = 3$ cm and $PO' = 4$ cm.
These two circles intersect at P and Q.

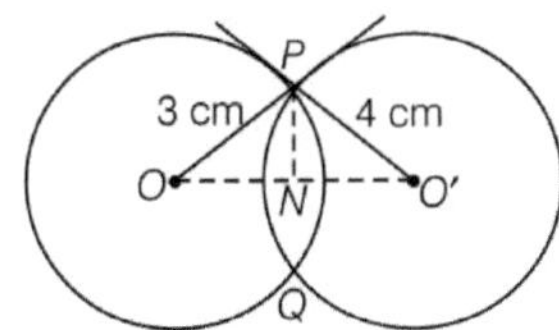

Here, OP and PO' are two tangents drawn at point P.
          $\angle OPO' = 90°$
          [tangent at any point of circle is perpendicular to radius
                    through the point of contact]
Join OO' and PN.
In right angled $\triangle OPO'$,
          $(OO')^2 = (OP)^2 + (PO')^2$ [by Pythagoras theorem]
i.e. $(\text{Hypotenuse})^2 = (\text{Base})^2 + (\text{Perpendicular})^2$
                    $= (3)^2 + (4)^2 = 25$
$\Rightarrow$ $OO' = 5$ cm
Also, $PN \perp OO'$

Let $ON = x$, then $NO' = 5 - x$
In right angled $\triangle OPN$,
          $(OP)^2 = (ON)^2 + (NP)^2$ [by Pythagoras theorem]
$\Rightarrow$ $(NP)^2 = 3^2 - x^2 = 9 - x^2$ $\ldots(i)$
and in right angled $\triangle PNO'$,
          $(PO')^2 = (PN)^2 + (NO')^2$ [by Pythagoras theorem]
$\Rightarrow$ $(4)^2 = (PN)^2 + (5 - x)^2$
$\Rightarrow$ $(PN)^2 = 16 - (5 - x)^2$ $\ldots(ii)$
From Eqs. (i) and (ii), we get
          $9 - x^2 = 16 - (5 - x)^2$
$\Rightarrow$ $7 + x^2 - (25 + x^2 - 10x) = 0 \Rightarrow 10x = 18$
$\therefore$ $x = 1.8$
Again, in right angled $\triangle OPN$,
          $OP^2 = (ON)^2 + (NP)^2$ [by Pythagoras theorem]
$\Rightarrow$ $3^2 = (1.8)^2 + (NP)^2$
$\Rightarrow$ $(NP)^2 = 9 - 3.24 = 5.76$
$\therefore$ $(NP) = 2.4$
$\therefore$ Length of common chord, $PQ = 2\,PN = 2 \times 2.4 = 4.8$ cm

26. In a circle, $\triangle ABC$ is inscribed.
Join OB, OC and OA.
Conside $\triangle ABO$ and $\triangle ACO$

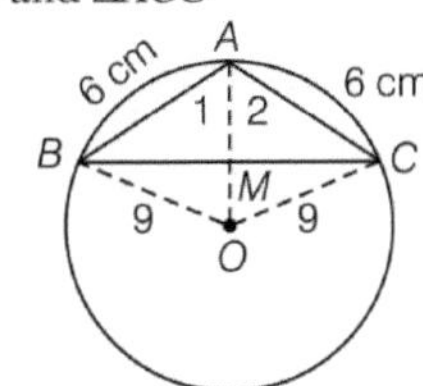

          $AB = AC$ [given]
          $BO = CO$ [radii of same circle]
          $AO = AO$ [common side]
$\therefore$ $\triangle ABO \cong \triangle ACO$ [by SSS congruence rule]
$\Rightarrow$ $\angle 1 = \angle 2$ [CPCT]
Now, in $\triangle ABM$ and $\triangle ACM$,
          $AB = AC$ [given]
          $\angle 1 = \angle 2$ [proved above]
          $AM = AM$ [common side]
$\therefore$ $\triangle AMB \cong \triangle AMC$ [by SAS congruence rule]
$\Rightarrow$ $\angle AMB = \angle AMC$ $\ldots(i)$ [CPCT]
Also, $\angle AMB + \angle AMC = 180°$ [linear pair]
$\Rightarrow$ $\angle AMB + \angle AMB = 180°$ [from Eq. (i)]
$\Rightarrow$ $\angle AMB = 90°$
We know that a perpendicular from centre of circle bisects
the chord. So, OA is perpendicular bisector of BC.
Let $AM = x$, then $OM = 9 - x$ $[\because OA = \text{radius} = 9 \text{ cm}]$
In right angled $\triangle AMC$,
          $AC^2 = AM^2 + MC^2$ [by Pythagoras theorem]
i.e. $(\text{Hypotenuse})^2 = (\text{Base})^2 + (\text{Perpendicular})^2$
$\Rightarrow$ $MC^2 = 6^2 - x^2$ $\ldots(i)$
and in right angled $\triangle OMC$,
          $OC^2 = OM^2 + MC^2$ [by Pythagoras theorem]
$\Rightarrow$ $MC^2 = 9^2 - (9 - x)^2$ $\ldots(ii)$

From Eqs. (i) and (ii),
$$6^2 - x^2 = 9^2 - (9 - x)^2$$
$$\Rightarrow \quad 36 - x^2 = 81 - (81 + x^2 - 18x)$$
$$\Rightarrow \quad 36 = 18x \Rightarrow x = 2$$
$$\therefore \quad AM = x = 2$$

In right angled $\triangle ABM$,
$$AB^2 = BM^2 + AM^2 \quad \text{[by Pythagoras theorem]}$$
$$6^2 = BM^2 + 2^2$$
$$\Rightarrow \quad BM^2 = 36 - 4 = 32 \Rightarrow BM = 4\sqrt{2}$$
$$\therefore \quad BC = 2\,BM = 2 \times 4\sqrt{2} = 8\sqrt{2}\ \text{cm}$$

$$\therefore \quad \text{Area of } \triangle ABC = \frac{1}{2} \times \text{Base} \times \text{Height}$$
$$= \frac{1}{2} \times BC \times AM$$
$$= \frac{1}{2} \times 8\sqrt{2} \times 2 = 8\sqrt{2}\ \text{cm}^2$$

Hence, the required area of $\triangle ABC$ is $8\sqrt{2}\ \text{cm}^2$.

27. In the given figure, join AO, OC and $O'D$, $O'B$.

Now, in $\triangle EO'D$ and $\triangle EO'B$,
$$O'D = O'B \quad \text{[radius]}$$
$$O'E = O'E \quad \text{[common side]}$$
$$ED = EB$$
[since, tangents drawn from an external point to the circle
are equal in length]

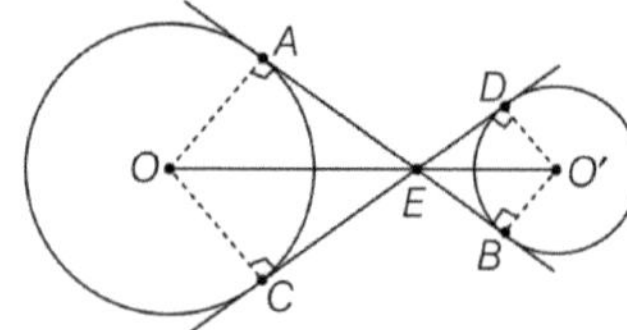

$$\therefore \quad \triangle EO'D \cong \triangle EO'B \quad \text{[by SSS similarity rule]}$$
$$\Rightarrow \quad \angle O'ED = \angle O'EB \quad \text{[by CPCT]}$$
$O'E$ is the angle bisector of $\angle DEB$. $\qquad$ ...(i)
Similarly, OE is the angle bisector of $\angle AEC$.
Now, in quadrilateral $DEBO'$,
$$\angle O'DE = \angle O'BE = 90°$$
[since, CED is a tangent to the circle and $O'D$ is the radius,
i.e. $O'D \perp CED$]
$$\Rightarrow \quad \angle O'DE + \angle O'BE = 180°$$
$$\therefore \quad \angle DEB + \angle DO'B = 180°$$
$\qquad\qquad$ [since, $DEBO'$ is cyclic quadrilateral] ...(ii)
Since, AB is a straight line.
$$\therefore \quad \angle AED + \angle DEB = 180°$$
$$\Rightarrow \quad \angle AED + 180° - \angle DO'B = 180° \quad \text{[from Eq. (ii)]}$$
$$\Rightarrow \quad \angle AED = \angle DO'B \qquad \text{...(iii)}$$
Similarly, $\qquad \angle AED = \angle AOC \qquad$ ...(iv)
Again from Eq. (ii),
$$\angle DEB = 180° - \angle DO'B$$
Divided by 2 on both sides, we get
$$\frac{1}{2}\angle DEB = 90° - \frac{1}{2}\angle DO'B$$

$$\Rightarrow \quad \angle DEO' = 90° - \frac{1}{2}\angle DO'B \qquad \text{...(v)}$$
[since, $O'E$ is the angle bisector of $\angle DEB$ i.e.
$$\frac{1}{2}\angle DEB = \angle DEO']$$
Similarly, $\qquad \angle AEC = 180° - \angle AOC$
Divided by 2 on both sides, we get
$$\frac{1}{2}\angle AEC = 90° - \frac{1}{2}\angle AOC$$
$$\Rightarrow \quad \angle AEO = 90° - \frac{1}{2}\angle AOC \qquad \text{...(vi)}$$
[since, OE is the angle bisector of $\angle AEC$
i.e. $\frac{1}{2}\angle AEC = \angle AEO]$

Now, $\angle AED + \angle DEO' + \angle AEO = \angle AED + \left(90° - \frac{1}{2}\angle DO'B\right)$
$$+ \left(90° - \frac{1}{2}\angle AOC\right)$$
$$= \angle AED + 180° - \frac{1}{2}(\angle DO'B + \angle AOC)$$
$$= \angle AED + 180° - \frac{1}{2}(\angle AED + \angle AED)$$
$$\text{[from Eqs. (iii) and (iv)]}$$
$$= \angle AED + 180° - \frac{1}{2}(2 \times \angle AED)$$
$$= \angle AED + 180° - \angle AED = 180°$$
$$\therefore \quad \angle AEO + \angle AED + \angle DEO' = 180°$$
So, OEO' is straight line.

Hence, O, E and O' are collinear. $\qquad$ **Hence proved.**

28. Given, $OT = 13$ cm and $OP = 5$ cm
Since, if we draw a line from the centre to the tangent of the circle, then it is always perpendicular to the tangent i.e. $OP \perp PT$.

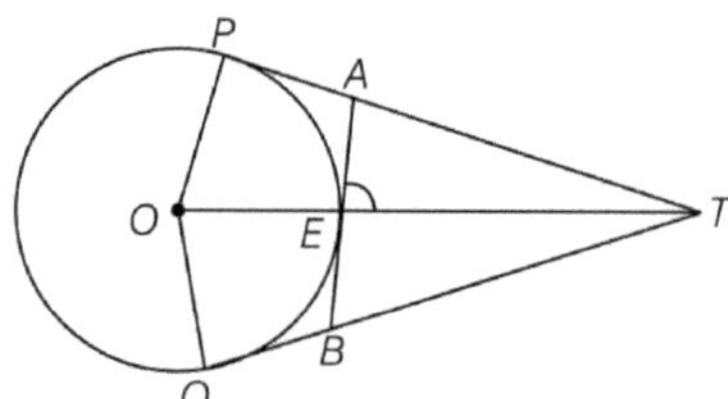

In right angled $\triangle OPT$,
$$OT^2 = OP^2 + PT^2$$
[by Pythagoras theorem,
$$(\text{hypotenuse})^2 = (\text{base})^2 + (\text{perpendicular})^2]$$
$$\Rightarrow \quad PT^2 = (13)^2 - (5)^2$$
$$= 169 - 25 = 144$$
$$\Rightarrow \quad PT = 12\ \text{cm}$$
Since, the length of pair of tangents from an external point T is equal.
$$\therefore \quad QT = 12\ \text{cm}$$
Now, $\qquad TA = PT - PA$
$$\Rightarrow \quad TA = 12 - PA \qquad \text{...(i)}$$
and $\qquad TB = QT - QB$
$$\Rightarrow \quad TB = 12 - QB \qquad \text{...(ii)}$$

Again, using the property, length of pair of tangents from an external point is equal.

$\therefore \qquad PA = AE$ and $QB = EB$ $\qquad$ ...(iii)

$\therefore \qquad OT = 13\,cm$

$\therefore \qquad ET = OT - OE$ $\qquad$ [$\because OE = 5\,cm = $ radius]

$\Rightarrow \qquad ET = 13 - 5 \Rightarrow ET = 8\,cm$

Since, AB is a tangent and OE is the radius.

$\therefore \qquad OE \perp AB$

$\Rightarrow \qquad \angle OEA = 90°$

$\therefore \qquad \angle AET = 180° - \angle OEA$ $\qquad$ [linear pair]

$\Rightarrow \qquad \angle AET = 90°$

Now, in right angled $\triangle AET$,

$$(AT)^2 = (AE)^2 + (ET)^2$$

$\qquad\qquad\qquad$ [by Pythagoras theorem]

$\Rightarrow \qquad (PT - PA)^2 = (AE)^2 + (8)^2$

$\Rightarrow \qquad (12 - PA)^2 = (PA)^2 + (8)^2$ $\qquad$ [from Eq. (iii)]

$\Rightarrow 144 + (PA)^2 - 24 \cdot PA = (PA)^2 + 64$

$\Rightarrow \qquad 24 \cdot PA = 80 \Rightarrow PA = \dfrac{10}{3}\,cm$

$\therefore \qquad AE = \dfrac{10}{3}\,cm$ $\qquad$ [from Eq. (iii)]

Similarly $\qquad BE = \dfrac{10}{3}\,cm$

Hence, $\qquad AB = AE + EB = \dfrac{10}{3} + \dfrac{10}{3} = \dfrac{20}{3}\,cm$

Hence, the required length AB is $\dfrac{20}{3}\,cm$.

29. (i) (d) We have, $AP = AQ, BP = BD, CQ = CD$ $\qquad$ ... (i)

$\qquad\qquad$ [$\because$ tangents drawn from an external point are equal in length]

Now, $AB + BC + AC = 7 + 4 + 9 = 20\,cm$

$\Rightarrow AB + BD + CD + AC = 20\,cm$

$\Rightarrow \qquad AP + AQ = 20\,cm$

$\Rightarrow \qquad 2AP = 20\,cm \Rightarrow AP = 10\,cm$

(ii) (c) Let $AF = AE = x\,cm$

$\qquad\qquad$ [$\because$ tangents drawn from an external point to a circle are equal in length]

Given, $BD = FB = 9\,cm, CD = CE = 3\,cm$

In $\triangle ABC$, $AB^2 = AC^2 + BC^2$

$\Rightarrow (AF + FB)^2 = (AE + EC)^2 + (BD + CD)^2$

$\Rightarrow \qquad (x + 9)^2 = (x + 3)^2 + 12^2$

$\Rightarrow \qquad x^2 + 81 + 18x = x^2 + 9 + 6x + 144$

$\Rightarrow \qquad 18x + 81 = 6x + 9 + 144$

$\Rightarrow \qquad 12x = 72 \Rightarrow x = 6\,cm$

$\therefore \qquad AB = 6 + 9 = 15\,cm$

(iii) (b) As we know that, tangents drawn from an external point are equal in length. Therefore, $AP = AS = 4\,cm$

$\therefore DS = DR = 10 - 4 = 6\,cm$

And $BP = BQ = 2\,cm$. So, $CR = CQ = 5 - 2 = 3\,cm$

So, $CD = DR + CR = 6 + 3 = 9\,cm$

(iv) (d) Here $\angle OAP = 90°$

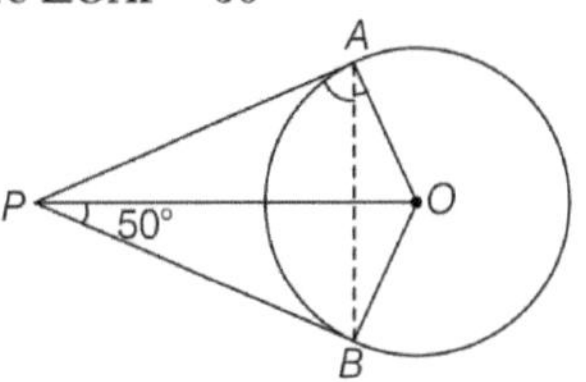

In $\triangle AOP$ and $\triangle BOP$,

$\qquad\qquad \angle OAP = \angle OBP$ $\qquad$ [90° each]

$\qquad\qquad OA = OB$ $\qquad$ [radii of circle]

$\qquad\qquad PA = PB$

$\qquad$ [tangents drawn from an external point are equal]

$\therefore \qquad \triangle AOP \sim \triangle BOP$ $\qquad$ [by SAS similarity]

$\therefore \qquad \angle APO = \angle OPB$ $\qquad$ [by CPCT]

$\qquad\qquad\quad = 50°$

$\therefore \angle BPA = 50° + 50° = 100°$

(v) (c) For bigger circle, $PA = PB$ $\qquad$ ... (i)

$\qquad$ [$\because$ tangents drawn from an external point are equal in length] ... (ii)

Similarly, for smaller circle, $PB = PC$

From Eqs. (i) and (ii), we get

$\qquad\qquad PA = PB = PC = 11\,cm$

Multiple Choice Questions

1. Two concentric circles are of radii 10 cm and 8 cm, then the length of the chord of the larger circle, which touches the smaller circle is
(a) 6 cm   (b) 12 cm
(c) 18 cm   (d) 9 cm

2. From a point P, which is at a distance of 13 cm from the centre O of a circle of radius 5 cm, the pair of tangents PQ and PR to the circle is drawn. Then, the area of the quadrilateral $PQOR$ is   **[NCERT Exemplar]**
(a) 60 cm^2 (b) 65 cm^2
(c) 30 cm^2 (d) 32.5 cm^2

3. If two tangents inclined at an angle 60° are drawn to a circle of radius 3 cm, then the length of each tangent is   **[NCERT Exemplar]**
(a) $\dfrac{3}{2}\sqrt{3}$ cm   (b) 6 cm
(c) 3 cm   (d) $3\sqrt{3}$ cm

Case Based MCQs

4. For revision of chapter circles, a teacher planned a game with some questions written on the paper, which are to be answered by the students. For each correct answer, a student will get a prize. Some of the questions are given below.

Answer the questions to check your knowledge.

(i) In the given figure, $x + y$ is
    (a) 60°
    (b) 90°
    (c) 120°
    (d) 145°

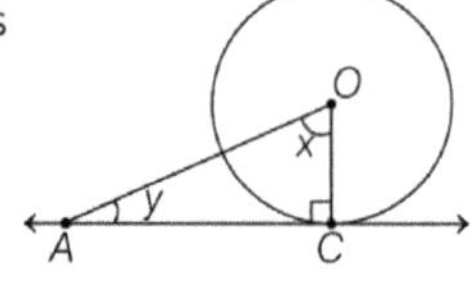

(ii) In the given figure, PQ and PR are two tangents to the circle, then $\angle ROQ$ is

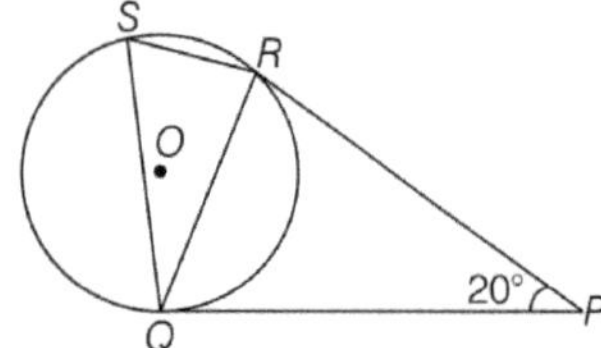

    (a) 30°   (b) 60°   (c) 105°   (d) 160°

(iii) In the adjoining figure, AB is a chord of the circle and AOC is its diameter such that $\angle ACB = 45°$, then $\angle BAT$ is
    (a) 35°
    (b) 45°
    (c) 125°
    (d) 110°

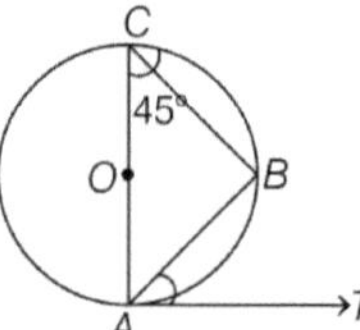

(iv) In PA and PB are two tangents, drawn to a circle with centre O from P such that $\angle PBA = 60°$, then $\angle OAB$ is
    (a) 50°   (b) 25°   (c) 30°   (d) 130°

(v) In the adjoining figure, if PC is the tangent at A of the circle with $\angle PAB = 62°$ and $\angle AOB = 132°$, then $\angle ABC$ is

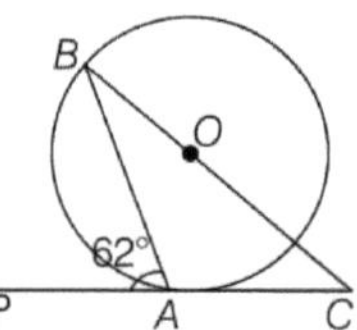

(a) 18°   (b) 20°
(c) 60°   (d) Can't be determined

Short Answer Type Questions

5. Two tangents PQ and PR are drawn from an external point to a circle with centre O. Prove that $QORP$ is a cyclic quadrilateral.

6. In figure, AB and CD are common tangents to two circles of unequal radii. Prove that $AB = CD$.   **[NCERT Exemplar]**

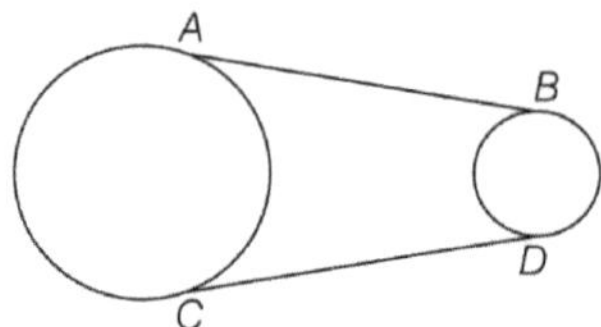

Long Answer Type Questions

7. A is a point at a distance 13 cm from the centre O of a circle of radius 5 cm. AP and AQ are the tangents to the circle at P and Q. If a tangent BC is drawn at a point R lying on the minor arc PQ to intersect AP at B and AQ at C, find the perimeter of the $\triangle ABC$.   **[NCERT Exemplar]**

8. If a chord and a tangent intersect externally, then the product of the lengths of the segments of the chord is equal to the square of the length of the tangent from the point of contact to the point of intersection.

Answers

1. (b)   **2.** (a)   **3.** (d)
4. (i) (b) (ii) (d) (iii) (b) (iv) (c) (v) (b)   **7.** 24 cm

For Detailed Solutions

Scan the code

CHAPTER 04

Constructions

In this Chapter...

- Division of a Line Segment Internally in the Given Ratio
- Construction of a Tangent to a Circle at a Point that lies on it
- Construction of Tangent to a Circle from a Point Outside the Circle
- Construction of Tangents to a Circle When Angle

Constructions 1

Division of a Line Segment Internally in the Given Ratio

To divide a line segment AB (say) internally in the given ratio $m : n$, where m and n are both positive integers, we use the following steps

Step I Draw the given line segment AB and any ray AX, making an acute angle with the line segment AB. This ray AX can be drawn above or below AB.

Step II Mark $m + n = p$ points

(i.e. $A_1, A_2, ..., A_m, ..., A_p$) on the ray AX, such that $AA_1 = A_1 A_2 = ... = A_{p-1} A_p$

Step III Join BA_p.

Step IV Through the point A_m, draw a line parallel to $A_p B$ (by making an angle equal to $\angle AA_p B$ at A_m) which intersects the line segment AB at point C. Thus, point C divides the line segment AB internally in the ratio $m : n$, i.e. $AC : CB = m : n$.

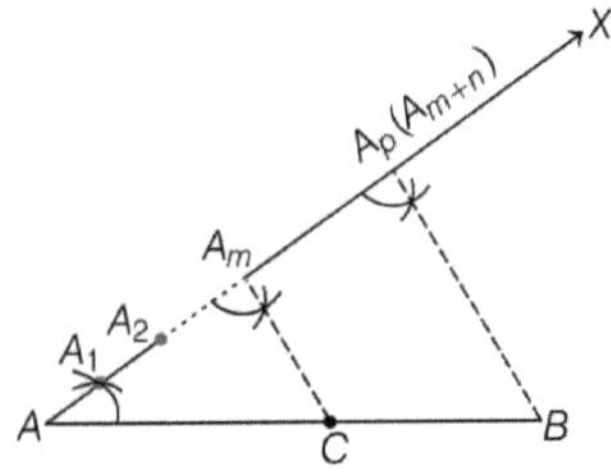

Justification

Since, $A_m C \| A_p B$, so use the basic proportionality theorem in $\triangle ABA_p$.

Then,
$$\frac{AA_m}{A_m A_p} = \frac{AC}{CB} \qquad \text{...(i)}$$

By using construction, the ratio is
$$\frac{AA_m}{A_m A_p} = \frac{m}{(p-m)} \qquad \text{...(ii)}$$

$\therefore$ From Eqs. (i) and (ii),
$$\frac{AC}{CB} = \frac{m}{(p-m)}$$

Alternate Method

To divide a line segment in the given ratio $m : n$, where m and n are both positive integers, we can also use the following steps.

Step I Draw the given line segment AB (say) and any ray AX making an acute angle with the line segment AB.

Step II Draw another ray $BY \| AX$ by making $\angle ABY = \angle BAX$.

Step III Mark m points i.e. $A_1, A_2, ..., A_m$ on AX and n points i.e. $B_1, B_2, ..., B_n$ on BY such that
$$AA_1 = A_1 A_2 = ... = A_{m-1} A_m$$
$$= BB_1 = B_1 B_2 = ... = B_{n-1} B_n$$

Step IV Join $A_m B_n$ which intersects line segment AB at the point C.

Now, C is the required point which divides line segment AB internally in the ratio $m : n$.

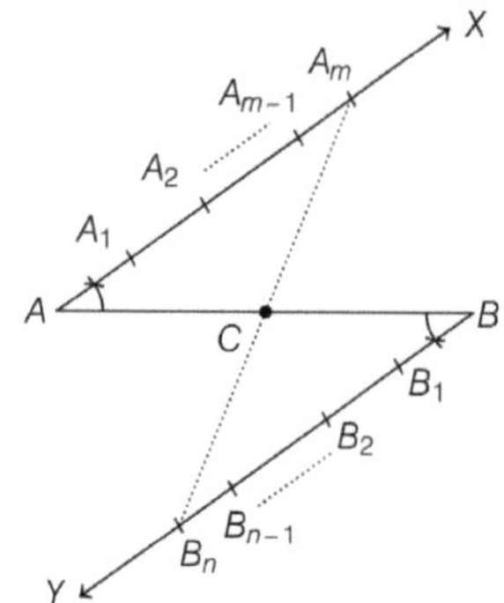

Justification

Step V Use the condition of similarity of two triangles in $\Delta AA_m C$ and $\Delta BB_n C$. Then, $\dfrac{AA_m}{BB_n} = \dfrac{AC}{BC}$ ...(i)

Step VI Write the ratio by using construction,

$$\dfrac{AA_m}{BB_n} = \dfrac{m}{n} \qquad ..(ii)$$

Step VII Equating Eqs. (i) and (ii), we get $\dfrac{AC}{BC} = \dfrac{m}{n}$

Example 1. Draw a line segment $AB = 8$ cm and divide it internally in the ratio $3 : 2$ and also justify it.

Sol. **Steps of Construction**

(i) First, draw line segment, $AB = 8$ cm and draw a ray AX, which makes an acute angle with line segment AB.

(ii) Mark $m + n = 3 + 2 = 5$ points i.e. A_1, A_2, A_3, A_4 and A_5 on the ray AX such that
$$AA_1 = A_1 A_2 = A_2 A_3 = A_3 A_4 = A_4 A_5$$

(iii) Join BA_5.

(iv) Through the point A_3 ($\because m = 3$), draw a line $A_3 C \parallel A_5 B$ (by making an angle equal to $\angle AA_5 B$ at A_3), which intersects the line segment AB at C.

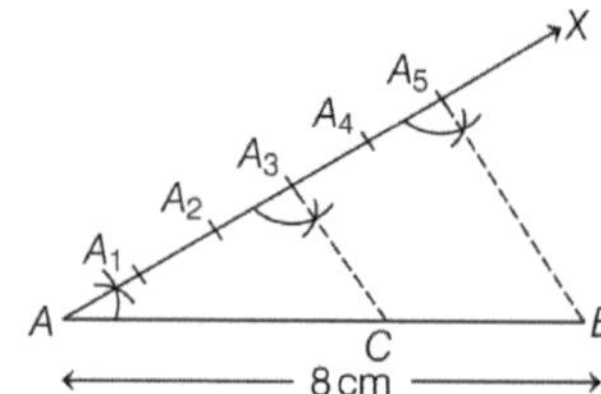

Thus, point C divides the line segment AB internally in the ratio $3 : 2$.

Justification

Since, $A_3 C \parallel A_5 B$.

So, in ΔABA_5, by basic proportionality theorem, we get

$$\dfrac{AA_3}{A_3 A_5} = \dfrac{AC}{CB} \qquad ...(i)$$

By construction, we have

$$\dfrac{AA_3}{A_3 A_5} = \dfrac{3}{(5-3)} = \dfrac{3}{2} \qquad ...(ii)$$

On equating Eqs. (i) and (ii), we get

$$\dfrac{AC}{BC} = \dfrac{3}{2}$$

This shows that C divides AB internally in the ratio $3 : 2$.

Construction 2

Construction of a Tangent to a Circle at a Point that lies on it

We can construct a tangent to a circle at a point that lies on it by two cases which are given below

Case I *By using the centre of circle*

To construct a tangent to a circle by using the centre, we use the following steps.

Step I Take a point O as centre and draw a circle of given radius.

Step II Take a point P on the circle, at which we want to draw tangent.

Step III Join OP, which is the radius of circle.

Step IV Take OP as base and construct $\angle OPT = 90°$ at P.

Step V Draw a ray PT and produce TP to T' to get the required tangent TPT'.

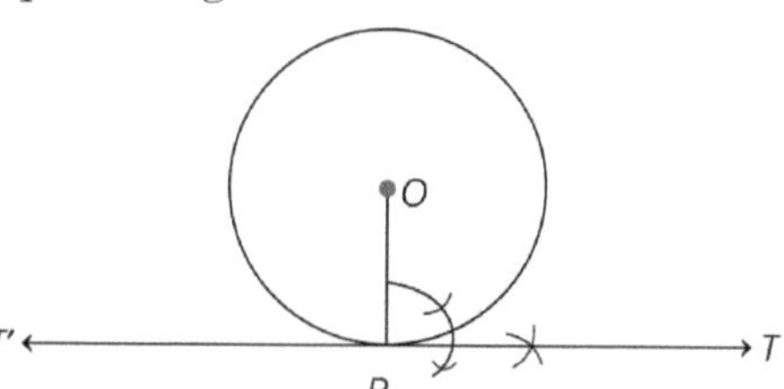

Example 2. Draw a circle of diameter $AB = 5$ cm with centre O and then draw a tangent to the circle at point A or B.

Sol. Given, diameter of circle $= AB = 5$ cm and centre is O.

$$\therefore \text{Radius} = OA = OB = \dfrac{5}{2} = 2.5 \text{ cm}$$

Steps of Construction

(i) Take a point O as centre and draw a circle of radius 2.5 cm.

(ii) Draw diameter AOB.

(iii) Take OA as base and construct $\angle OAT = 90°$ at A.

(iv) Produce TA to T' to get the required tangent TAT'. Similarly, we can draw a tangent at point B or any other point on the circle.

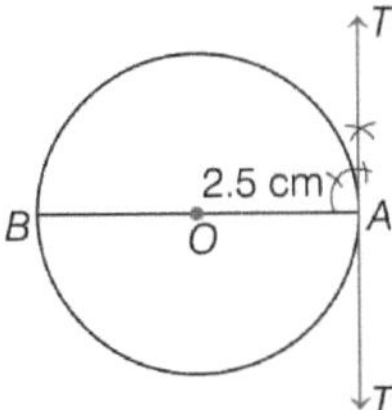

Case II *Without using the centre of circle*

To construct a tangent to a circle without using the centre of circle, we use the following steps.

Step I Draw a circle of given radius and take a point P (at which we want to draw tangent) on the circle.

Step II Draw any chord PQ through the given point P on the circle.

Step III Take a point R in either the major arc or minor arc and join PR and QR.

Step IV On taking PQ as base, construct $\angle QPY$ equal to $\angle PRQ$ and on the opposite side of R.

Step V Draw a ray PY and produce YP upto X to get the required tangent YPX.

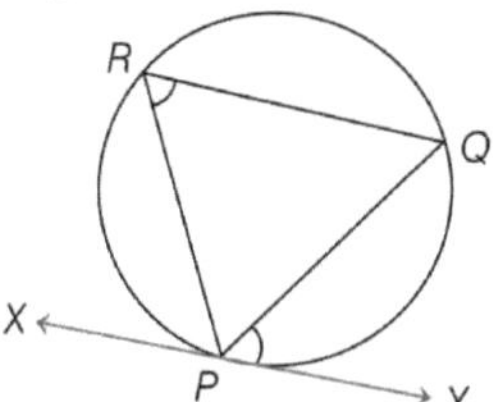

Example 3. Draw a circle of radius 6 cm. Take a point P on it. Without using the centre of the circle, draw a tangent to the circle at point P.

Sol. Given, radius of circle = 6 cm

Steps of Construction

(i) Draw a circle of radius 6 cm and take a point P on the circle.

(ii) Draw a chord PQ through the point P on the circle.

(iii) Take a point R in the major arc and join PR and RQ.

(iv) On taking PQ as base, construct $\angle QPY$ equal to $\angle PRQ$ on the opposite side of the point R.

(v) Produce YP to X. Then, YPX is the required tangent at point P.

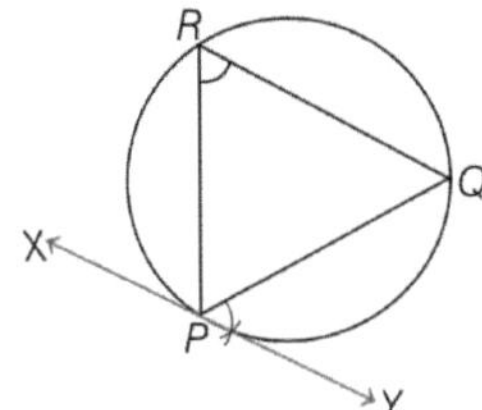

Construction 3

Construction of Tangents to a Circle from a Point Outside the Circle

If a point lies outside the circle, then there will be two tangents to the circle from this point.

Case I *When centre of circle is known*

If centre of circle is known, then to draw tangents from a given external point, we use the following steps

Step I Draw a circle with centre O of given radius and take a point P outside it.

Step II Join OP and bisect it. Let its mid-point be M. Then, $MP = MO$.

Step III On taking M as centre and MO or MP as radius, draw a dotted circle, which intersects the given circle at points Q and Q' (say).

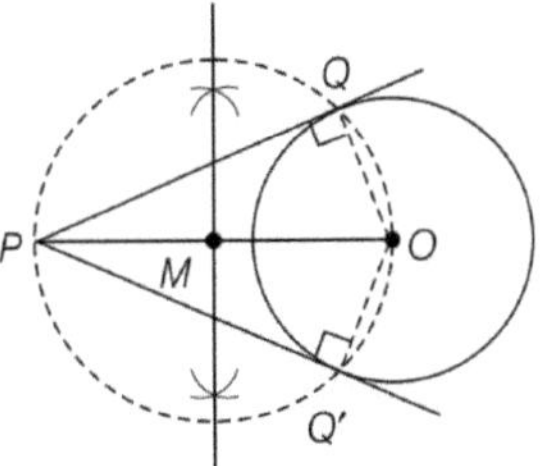

Step IV Join PQ and PQ'. Thus, PQ and PQ' are the required tangents drawn to the circle from the external point P. Here, we observe that $PQ = PQ'$.

Justification

Join OQ. Then, $\angle PQO = 90°$, since it is constructed in the semi-circle of dotted circle. It shows that $OQ \perp PQ$. Also, OQ is radius of given circle, so PQ has to be a tangent of given circle. Similarly, PQ' is also a tangent to the given circle.

Example 4. Draw a circle of radius 3.5 cm. From a point P, 6 cm from its centre, draw two tangents of the circle.

Sol. Given, a circle of radius 3.5 cm whose centre is O (say) and a point P, 6 cm away from its centre.

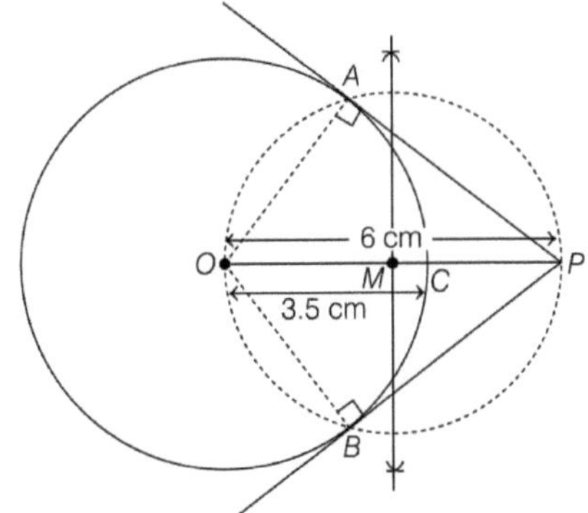

Steps of Construction

(i) Draw a circle with O as centre and radius $OC = 3.5$ cm. Take a point P such that $OP = 6$ cm.

(ii) Draw the bisector of OP which intersect OP at M.

(iii) Take M as centre and MO as radius, draw a dotted circle. Let this circle cuts the given circle at A and B.

(iv) Join PA and PB.

Hence, PA and PB are the required tangents.

Case II When centre of circle is unknown

If centre of the circle is unknown, then to draw tangents of the circle, by using the following steps

Step I Firstly, draw the circle and then draw two non-parallel chords of the circle.

Step II Draw the perpendicular bisectors of both chords which intersect each other at a point, say O. Then, this point O gives the centre of given circle. Now, we further use the steps given in case I to draw tangents.

Alternate Method

If centre of circle is unknown, then we can draw tangents without finding centre of the circle. For this, we use the following steps of construction.

Step I Draw a circle of given radius and take a point P outside it.

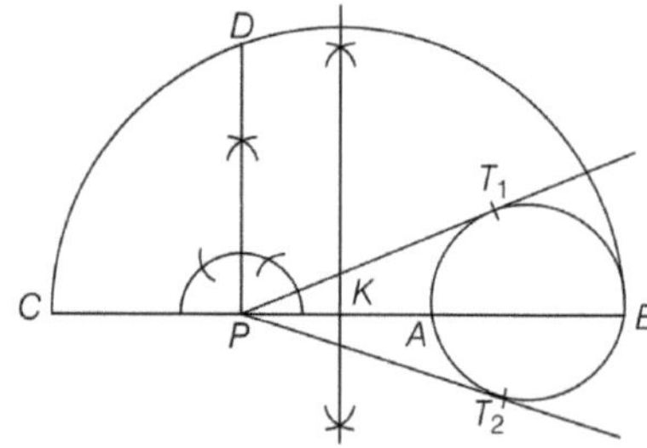

Step II Through P, draw a line (i.e. secant) intersecting the given circle at points A and B, respectively and produce it to C in opposite direction of AB such that $AP = CP$.

Step III Now, bisect the segment CB at K. Then, take K as centre and KB (or KC) as radius, draw a semi-circle.

Step IV At point P, draw $PD \perp CB$ which cuts the semi-circle at D.

Step V Take P as centre and PD as radius draw arcs to intersect the given circle at points T_1 and T_2.

Step VI Join PT_1 and PT_2 which are the required tangents.

Example 5. Draw a circle of radius 2 cm with centre O and take a point P outside the circle such that $OP = 6.5$ cm. From P, draw two tangents to the circle.

Sol. Given, radius of circle = 2 cm and distance between point P and centre = 6.5 cm

Steps of Construction

(i) Draw a circle of radius 2 cm with centre O.

(ii) Take a point P outside it, such that its distance from centre O is 6.5 cm.

(iii) Consider O and P as centre and draw arcs of radius more than half of OP on both sides of OP which intersect each other at R and S. Join RS which bisects OP at M. Then, $MP = MO$.

(iv) Consider M as centre and MO as radius, draw a dotted circle which intersects given circle at Q and Q'.

(v) Join PQ and PQ'.

Hence, we get the required tangents drawn from point P to the given circle.

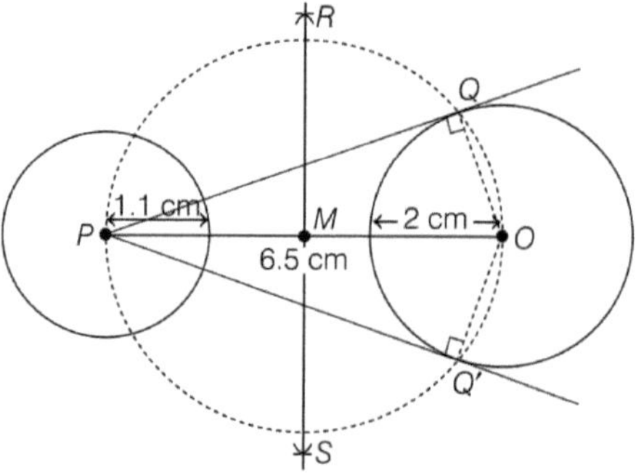

Construction 4

Construction of Tangents to a Circle When Angle between Them is Given

Sometimes, angle between two tangents (or pair of tangents) is given and we have to draw these tangents. Then, we use the following steps of construction.

Step I First, draw the given circle with centre O and radius r cm.

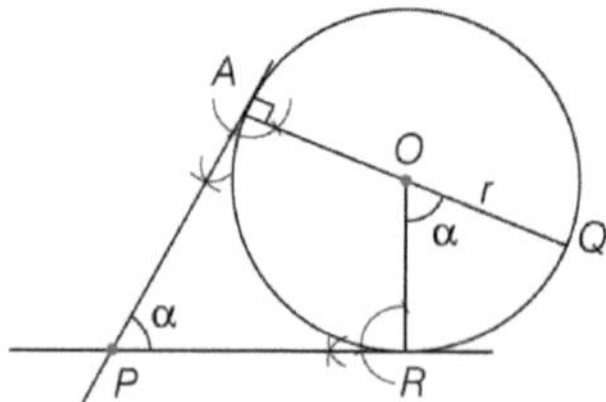

Step II Draw any diameter say AOQ of this circle.

Step III Make given angle α at centre O with OQ (say) as base which intersect the circle at point R (say) or draw the radius OR meets the circle at R such that $\angle QOR = \alpha$.

Step IV Now, draw perpendiculars to OA at A and to OR at R, which intersect the tangents each other at a point say P.

Then, AP and RP are the required pair of tangents to given circle, inclined at an angle α, i.e. angle between pair of tangents is α.

Justification

By construction, $\angle OAP = 90°$ and OA is radius.

So, PA is a tangent to the circle.

Similarly, PR is a tangent to the circle.

Also, $\angle AOR = 180° - \angle QOR$ $[\because AOQ$ is a straight line$]$

$\qquad\qquad = 180° - \alpha$

Now, in quadrilateral $AORP$,

$$\angle APR + \angle PAO + \angle AOR + \angle PRO = 360°$$

$\Rightarrow \qquad\quad \angle APR + 90° + 180° - \alpha + 90° = 360°$

$\Rightarrow \qquad\qquad\qquad\qquad\qquad\qquad \angle APR = \alpha$

Example 6. Draw a pair of tangents to a circle of radius 4 cm which are inclined to each other at an angle of 30°.

Sol. Given, a circle of radius 4 cm. We have to construct a pair of tangents, which are inclined to each other at an angle of 30°.

Steps of Construction

(i) Draw a circle with O as centre and radius 4 cm.

(ii) Draw any diameter POQ of this circle.

(iii) Draw the radius OR meets the circle at R such that $\angle QOR = 30°$.

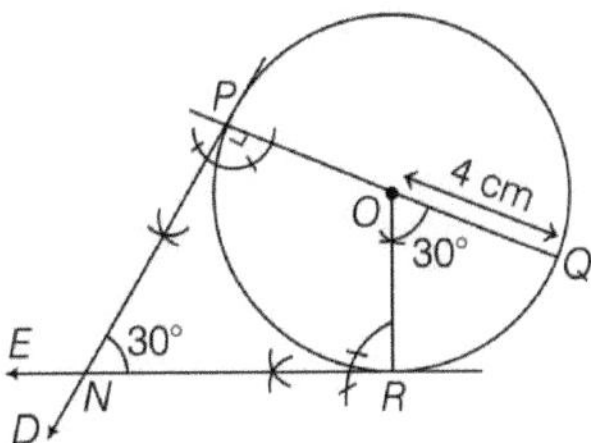

(iv) Draw $PD \perp PQ$ and $RE \perp OR$, which intersect each other at point N. Then, NP and NR are the required tangents to the given circle inclined to each other at an angle of 30°.

Justification

By construction, $\angle OPN = 90°$ and OP is radius.

$\therefore$ PN is a tangent to the circle.

Similarly, NR is a tangent to the circle.

Now, $\qquad \angle POR = 180° - 30° = 150°$

$\qquad\qquad [\because POQ$ is a straight line and $\angle QOR = 45°]$

In quadrilateral $OPNR$,

$\qquad \angle OPN = 90°,\ \angle POR = 150°$ and $\angle ORN = 90°$

$\therefore \qquad \angle PNR = 360° - (90° + 150° + 90°) = 30°$

Chapter Practice

Objective Questions

- ### Multiple Choice Questions

1. To divide a line segment AB in ratio $m : n$ (m and n are positive integers), draw a ray AX to that $\angle BAX$ is an acute angle and the mark point on ray AX at equal distances such that the minimum number of these points is

(a) greater of m and n (b) $m + n$
(c) $m + n - 1$ (d) mn

2. To divide a line segment AB in the ratio $5 : 7$, first a ray AX is drawn, so that $\angle BAX$ is an acute angle and then at equal distances points are marked on the ray AX such that the minimum number of these points is

(a) 8   (b) 10   (c) 11   (d) 12

3. To divide a line segment AB in the ratio $3 : 5$ first a ray AX is drawn so that $\angle BAX$ is an acute angle and then at equal distances points are marked on the ray AX such that the minimum number of these points is

(a) 8   (b) 9   (c) 10   (d) 11

4. To divide a line segment AB in the ratio $4 : 5$, first a ray AX is drawn making $\angle BAX$ an acute angle and then points $A_1, A_2, A_3, ..$ at equal distances are marked on the ray AX and the point B is joined to

(a) A_4 (b) A_5
(c) A_9 (d) A_7

5. The ratio of division of the line segment AB by the point P from A in the following figure is **[CBSE 2012]**

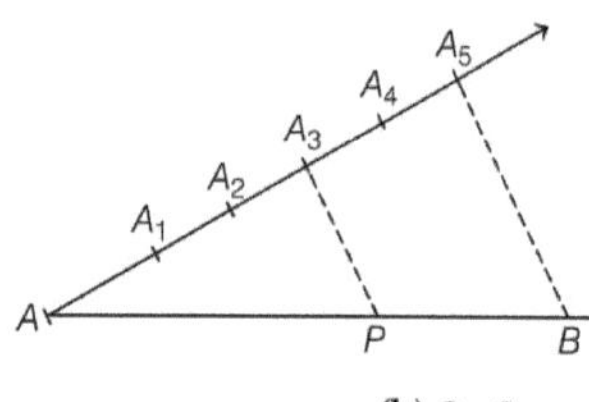

(a) $2 : 3$ (b) $3 : 2$
(c) $3 : 5$ (d) $2 : 5$

6. To divide a line segment AB in the ratio $4 : 7$, a ray AX is drawn first such that $\angle BAX$ is an acute angle and then points $A_1, A_2, A_3, ...$ are located at equal distances on the ray AX and the point B is joined to

(a) A_{12} (b) A_{11}
(c) A_{10} (d) A_9

7. To divide a line segment AB in the ratio $5 : 6$, draw a ray AX such that $\angle BAX$ is an acute angle, then draw a ray BY parallel to AX and the points $A_1, A_2, A_3, ...$ and $B_1, B_2, B_3, ...$ are located to equal distances on ray AX and BY, respectively. Then, the points joined are

(a) A_5 and B_6 (b) A_6 and B_5
(c) A_4 and B_5 (d) A_5 and B_4

8. To divide a line segment AB in the ratio $6 : 7$, a ray AX is drawn first such that $\angle BAX$ is an acute angle and then points $A_1, A_2, A_3, ...$ are located equal distances on the ray AX and the point B is joined with

(a) A_{12} (b) A_{13} (c) A_{10} (d) A_{11}

9. In the given figure, find the ratio, when P divides AB internally.

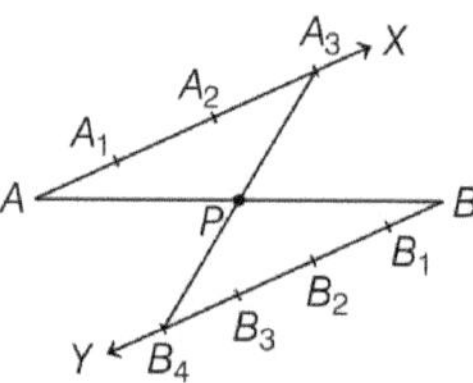

(a) $3 : 2$ (b) $2 : 3$ (c) $4 : 3$ (d) $3 : 4$

10. From the following ratios, a line segment cannot be divided into $\underline{A}$ ratio.

(a) $A \to \sqrt{5} : \dfrac{1}{\sqrt{5}}$ (b) $A \to \dfrac{1}{\sqrt{5}} : \dfrac{1}{\sqrt{5}}$

(c) $A \to \dfrac{2}{\sqrt{5}} : \dfrac{\sqrt{5}}{\sqrt{2}}$ (d) $A \to \dfrac{1}{5} : 1$

11. To draw a pair of tangents to a circle, which are inclined to each other at an angle of $60°$, it is required to draw tangents at end points of those two radii of the circle, the angle between them should be

(a) $135°$ (b) $90°$ (c) $60°$ (d) $120°$

12. A pair of tangents can be constructed from a point P to a circle of radius 3.5 cm, situated at a distance of 3 cm from the centre.

(a) True
(b) False
(c) Can't determined
(d) None of the above

13. A pair of tangents can be constructed to a circle inclined at an angle of 170°.

(a) True
(b) False
(c) Can't determined
(d) None of the above

PART 2
Subjective Questions

• Short Answer Type Questions

1. Draw a line segment of length 7 cm. Find a point P on it, which divides it in the ratio 3 : 5.

2. Draw a circle of diameter $AB = 6$ cm with centre O and then draw a tangent to the circle at point A or B.

3. Draw a circle of radius 5 cm. Take a point P on it. Without using the centre of the circle, draw a tangent to the circle at point P.

4. Draw a circle of radius 6 cm and draw a tangent to this circle, making an angle of 30° with a line passing through the centre.

5. Draw a circle of radius 4 cm. From a point 6 cm away from its centre, construct a pair of tangents to the circle and measure their lengths.
[CBSE 2019]

6. Draw a circle of radius 1cm. From a point P, 2.2 cm apart from the centre of the circle, draw tangents to the circle.

7. Draw a circle of radius 3.5 cm. Take a point P outside the circle at a distance of 7 cm from the centre of the circle and construct a pair of tangents to the circle from that point.
[CBSE 2020 (Standard)]

8. Draw a line segment AB of length 9 cm. Taking A as centre, draw a circle of radius 5 cm and taking B as centre, draw another circle of radius 3 cm. Construct tangents to each circle from the centre of the other circle.
[CBSE 2020 (Standard)]

9. Draw a circle with the help of circular solid ring. Construct a pair of tangents from a point P outside the circle. Also, justify the construction.

• Long Answer Type Questions

10. Draw a circle of radius 4 cm. Construct a pair of tangents to it, the angle between which is 60°. Also, justify the construction. Measure the distance between the centre of the circle and the point of intersection of tangents.

11. Construct a tangent to a circle of radius 1.8 cm from a point on the concentric circle of radius 2.8 cm and measure its length. Also, verify the measurement by actual calculation.

12. Draw a circle of radius 2.8 cm. From an external point P, draw tangents to the circle without using the centre of the circle.

13. Draw a pair of tangents to a circle of radius 3 cm, which are inclined to each other at an angle of 45°.

14. Let ABC be a right angled triangle, in which $AB = 6$ cm, $BC = 8$ cm and $\angle B = 90°$. BD is the perpendicular from B on AC. The circle through B, C and D is drawn. Construct the tangents from A to this circle. Also, justify the construction.

15. Draw a circle of radius 3 cm. Take two points P and Q on one of its extended diameter each at a distance of 7 cm from its centre. Draw tangents to the circle from these two points P and Q.
[NCERT]

SOLUTIONS

Objective Questions

1. (b) To divide a line segment in the ratio $m : n$, the maximum number of the points to mark are $m + n$.

2. (d) We know that, to divide a line segment AB in the ratio $m : n$, first draw a ray AX, which makes an acute angle $\angle BAX$, then marked $m + n$ points at equal distance.

Here, $m = 5, n = 7$

So, minimum number of these points $= m + n = 5 + 7 = 12$.

3. (a) Minimum number of points $= 3 + 5 = 8$

4. (c) Here, $4 + 5 = 9$ points are located at equal distances on the ray AX, so B is joined to last point A_9.

5. (b) The ratio of division of the line segment AB by the point P from A is $AP : BP = 3 : 2$.

6. (b) Here, minimum $4 + 7 = 11$ points are located at equal distances on the ray AX and then B is joined to last point is A_{11}.

7. (a) Given, a line segment AB and we have to divide it in the ratio $5 : 6$.

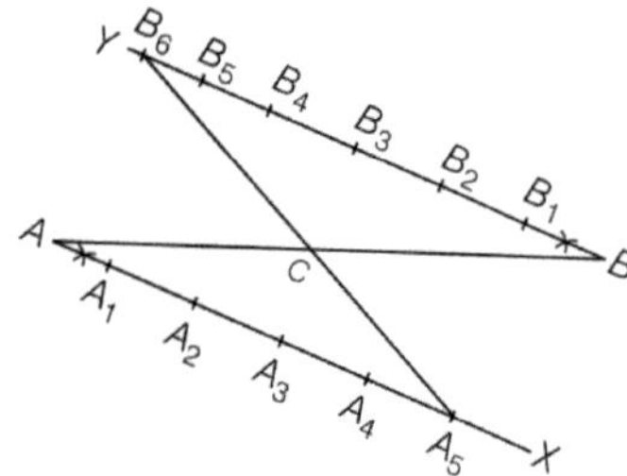

Steps of Construction

1. Draw a ray AX, making an acute $\angle BAX$.
2. Draw a ray BY parallel to AX by making $\angle ABY$ equal to $\angle BAX$.
3. Now, locate the points A_1, A_2, A_3, A_4 and A_5 ($m = 5$) on AX and B_1, B_2, B_3, B_4, B_5 and B_6 ($n = 6$) such that all the points are at equal distance from each other.
4. Join $B_6 A_5$, which intersect AB at a point C.

Then, $AC : BC = 5 : 6$

8. (b) A_{6+7} i.e. A_{13} is joined to the point B.

9. (d) From given figure, it is clear that there are three points at equal distances on AX and four points at equal distances on BY. Here, P divides AB on joining $A_3 B_4$. So, P divides AB internally in the ratio $3 : 4$.

10. (c) Since,

(a) $\sqrt{5} : \dfrac{1}{\sqrt{5}} = 5 : 1$

(b) $\dfrac{1}{\sqrt{5}} : \dfrac{1}{\sqrt{5}} = 1 : 1$

(c) $\dfrac{2}{\sqrt{5}} : \dfrac{\sqrt{5}}{\sqrt{2}} = 2\sqrt{2} : 5$

(d) $\dfrac{1}{5} : 1 = 1 : 5$

Since, (a), (b) and (d) are the ratio of both integers. So, it is possible to divide a line segment into these points. Hence, option (c) is correct.

11. (d) The angle between them should be $120°$ because in that case the figure formed by the intersection point of pair of tangent, the two end points of those two radii (at which tangents are drawn) and the centre of the circle is a quadrilateral.

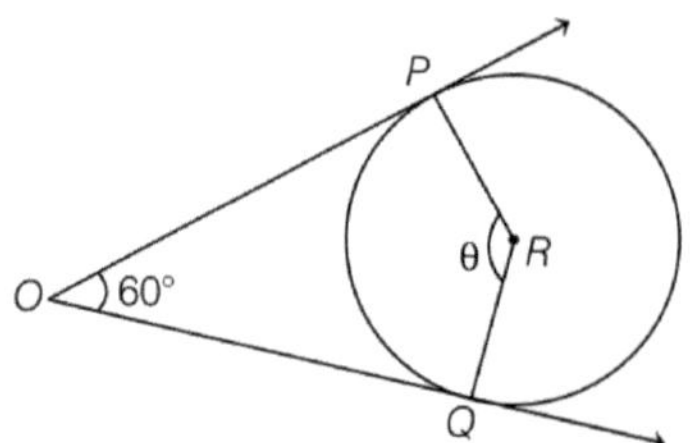

From figure, it is quadrilateral

$$\angle POQ + \angle PRQ = 180°$$
$$[\because \text{ sum of opposite angles are } 180°]$$
$$60° + \theta = 180°$$
$$\therefore \qquad \theta = 120$$

Hence, the required angle between them is $120°$.

12. (b) False, since, the radius of the circle is 3.5 cm i.e. $r = 3.5$ cm and a point P is situated at a distance of 3 cm from the centre i.e. $d = 3$ cm

We see that, $r > d$

i.e. a point P lies inside the circle. So, no tangent can be drawn to a circle from a point lying inside it.

13. True

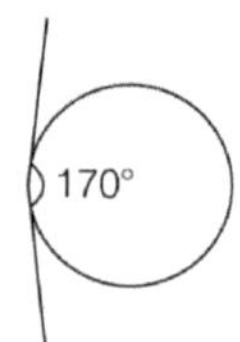

If the angle between the pair of tangents is always greater than 0 or less than $180°$, then we can construct a pair of tangents to a circle.

Hence, we can draw a pair of tangents to a circle inclined at an angle of $170°$.

Subjective Questions

1. **Steps of Construction**

1. Draw a line segment $AB = 7$ cm.
2. Draw a ray AX, making an acute $\angle BAX$.
3. Along AX, mark $3 + 5 = 8$ points

i.e. $A_1, A_2, A_3, A_4, A_5, A_6, A_7$ and A_8 such that
$$AA_1 = A_1 A_2 = A_2 A_3 = A_3 A_4$$
$$= A_4 A_5 = A_5 A_6 = A_6 A_7 = A_7 A_8$$

4. Join $A_8 B$.
5. From A_3, draw $A_3 C \parallel A_8 B$, meeting AB at C.

[by making an angle equal to $\angle BA_8 A$ at A_3]

Then, C is the point on AB, which divides it in the ratio $3 : 5$.

Thus, $AC : CB = 3 : 5$

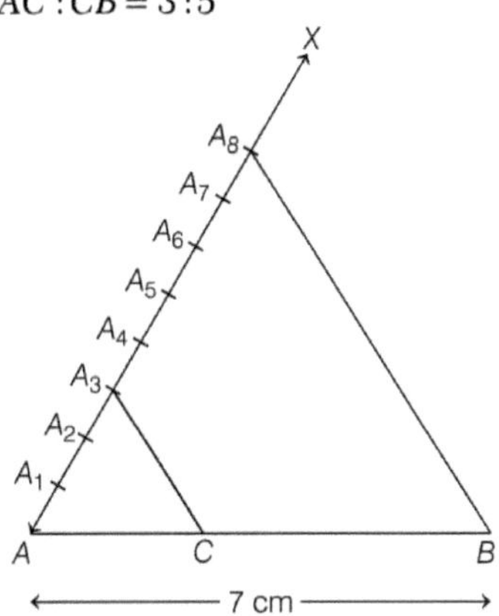

2. Given, diameter of circle $= AB = 6$ cm and centre is O.

$\therefore$ Radius $= OA = OB = \dfrac{6}{2} = 3$ cm

Steps of Construction

(i) Take a point O as centre and draw a circle of radius 3 cm.

(ii) Draw diameter AOB.

(iii) Take OA as base and construct $\angle OAT = 90°$ at A.

(iv) Draw a ray AT and produce TA to T' to get the required tangent TAT'.

Similarly, we can draw a tangent at point B or any other point on the circle.

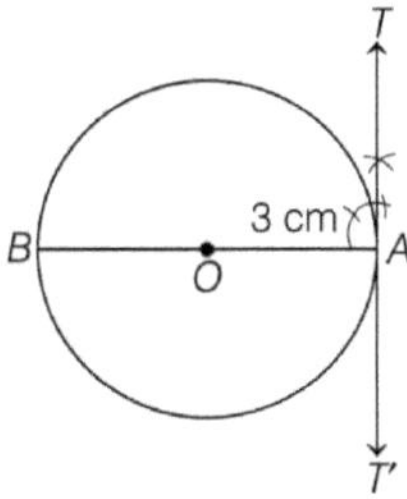

3. Given, radius of circle $= 5$ cm

Steps of Construction

(i) Draw a circle of radius 5 cm and take a point P on the circle.

(ii) Draw a chord PQ through the point P on the circle.

(iii) Take a point R in the major arc and join PR and RQ.

(iv) On taking PQ as base, construct $\angle QPY$ equal to $\angle PRQ$ on the opposite side of the point R.

(v) Draw a ray PY and produce YP to X. Then, YPX is the required tangent at point P.

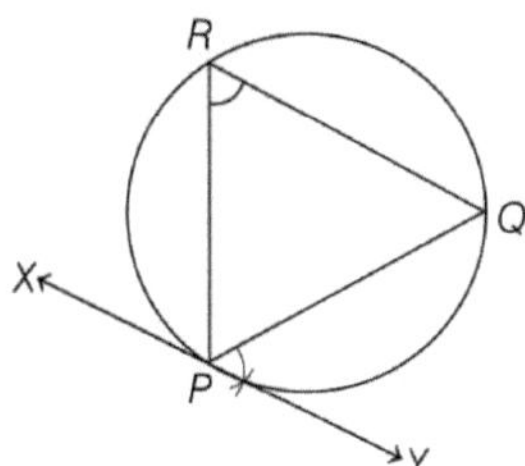

4. Steps of Construction

(i) Draw a circle with centre O and radius 6 cm.

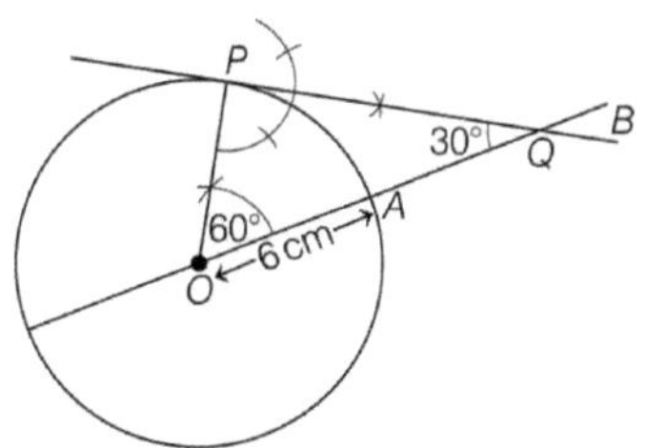

(ii) Draw a radius OA and produce it to B.

(iii) Construct an $\angle AOP$ equal to the complement of $30°$ i.e. equal to $60°$.

(iv) Draw a perpendicular to OP at P, which intersects OB at point Q.

Hence, PQ is the required tangent such that $\angle OQP = 30°$.

5. Given, a point M' is at a distance of 6 cm from the centre of a circle of radius 4 cm.

Steps of Construction

(i) Draw a circle of radius 4 cm. Let centre of this circle is O.

(ii) Join OM' and bisect it. Let M be mid-point of OM'.

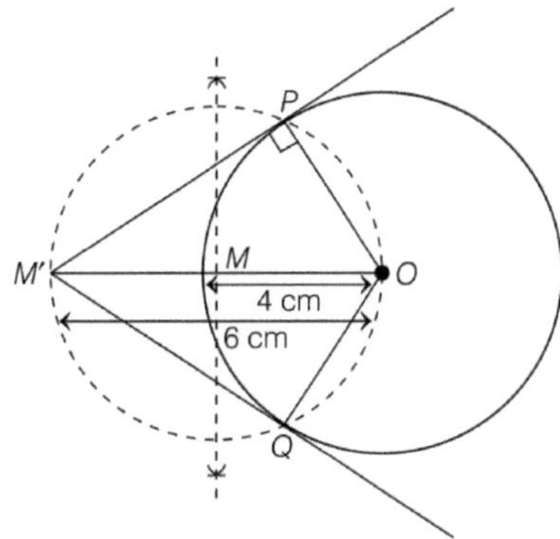

(iii) Taking M as centre and MO as radius, draw a circle to intersect circle $(0, 4)$ at two points, P and Q.

(iv) Join PM' and QM'. PM' and QM' are the required tangents from M' to circle $C\,(0,\,4)$.

The measure length of the tangents are 4.48 cm.

6. Given, radius of circle $= 1$ cm and distance between point P and centre $= 2.2$ cm.

Steps of Construction

(i) Draw a circle of radius 1 cm with centre O.

(ii) Take a point P outside it such that its distance from centre O is 2.2 cm.

(iii) Take O and P as centre and draw arcs of radius more than half of OP on both sides of OP, which intersect each other at R and S. Join RS, which bisects OP at M. Then, $MP = MO$.

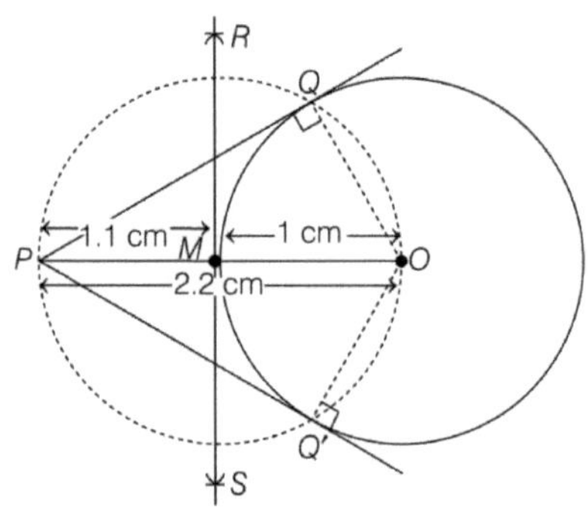

(iv) On taking M as centre and MO as radius, draw a dotted circle, which intersects given circle at Q and Q'.

(v) Join PQ and PQ'. Thus, we get the required tangents drawn from point P to the given circle.

7. Steps of Construction

(i) Draw a circle with O as centre and radius $OC = 3.5$ cm. Take a point P such that $OP = 7$ cm.

(ii) Draw the bisector of OP, which intersects OP at M.

(iii) On taking M as centre and MO as radius, draw a dotted circle. Let this circle cuts the given circle at A and B.

(iv) Join PA and PB.

Thus, PA and PB are the required tangents.

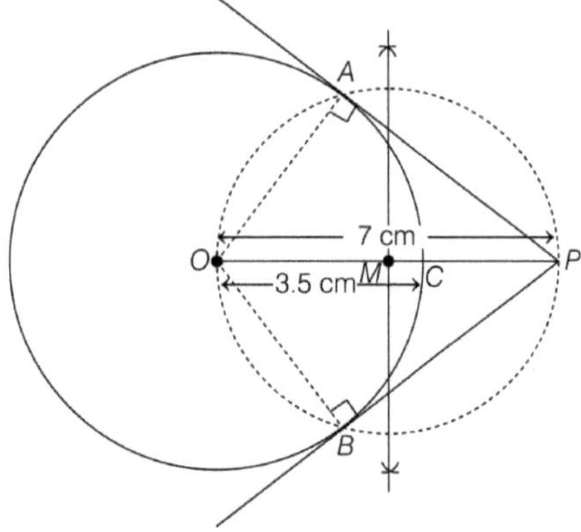

8. Given, a line segment $AB = 9$ cm, two circles with centres A and B of radii 5 cm and 3 cm, respectively.

We have to construct two tangents to each circle from the centre of the other circle.

Steps of Construction

(i) Draw a line segment $AB = 9$ cm.

(ii) Draw a circle with centre A and radius 5 cm and another circle with centre B and radius 3 cm.

(iii) Now, bisect AB. Let O be the mid-point of AB.

(iv) Take O as centre and AO as radius and draw a dotted circle, which intersects the two given circles at N, Q, M and P.

(v) Join AN, AQ, BM and BP. These are the required tangents to each circle from the centre of the other circle.

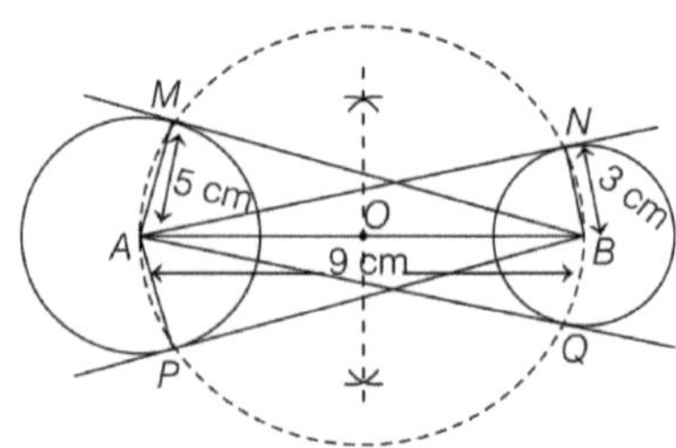

9. Steps of Construction

(i) First, draw a circle with the help of given circular solid ring and then draw two non-parallel chords AB and CD.

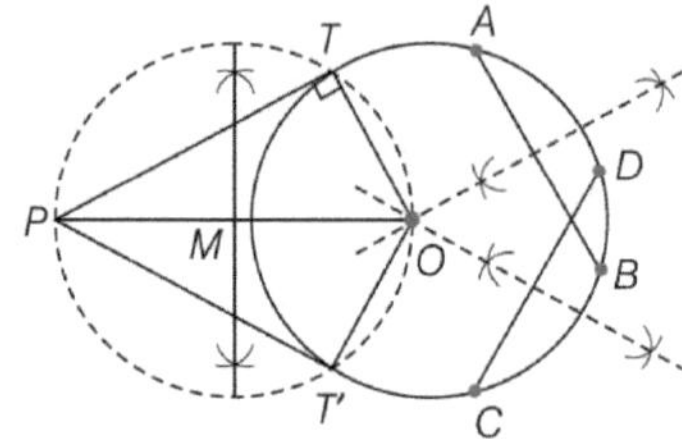

(ii) Draw perpendicular bisectors of AB and CD, which intersect each other at point O. Then, O is the centre of the circle.

(iii) Now, take a point P outside the circle and join OP.

(iv) Draw bisector of OP. Let its mid-point be M.

(v) On taking M as centre and MP as radius, draw a dotted circle which intersect the given circle at T and T'.

(vi) Join PT and PT'.

Then, PT and PT' are the required pair of tangents drawn to the circle from P.

Justification

Join OT.

Then, $\quad \angle PTO = 90°$ $\quad$ [angle in semi-circle of dotted circle]

This shows that $OT \perp PT$.

Also, OT is radius of given circle, so PT has to be a tangent of given circle. Similarly, PT' is also a tangent of given circle.

10. Steps of Construction

(i) Take a point O on the plane of the paper and draw a circle with centre O and radius $OA = 4$ cm.

(ii) At O construct radii OA and OB such that $\angle AOB$ equal to $120°$ i.e. supplement of the angle between the tangents.

(iii) Draw perpendiculars to OA and OB at A and B, respectively. Suppose these perpendiculars intersect at P. Then, PA and PB are required tangents.

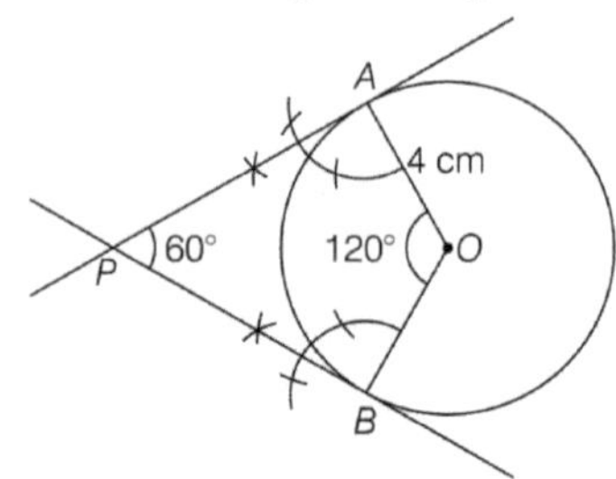

The distance between the centre of the circle and the point of intersection of tangents is 8 cm.

Justification

In quadrilateral $OAPB$, we have

$$\angle OAP = \angle OBP = 90°$$

and

$$\angle AOB = 120°$$

$$\therefore\ \angle OAP + \angle OBP + \angle AOB + \angle APB = 360°$$

$$\Rightarrow\quad 90° + 90° + 120° + \angle APB = 360°$$

$$\therefore\quad \angle APB = 360° - (90° + 90° + 120°)$$

$$= 360° - 300° = 60°$$

11. Given, two concentric circles of radii 2.8 cm and 1.8 cm with common centre say, O.

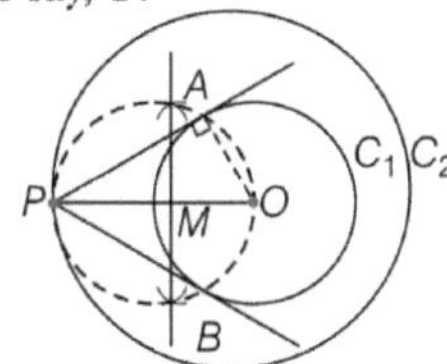

Steps of Construction

(i) Draw two circles with common centre O and radii 2.8 cm and 1.8 cm, respectively.

(ii) Take a point P on the outer circle and join OP.

(iii) Draw bisector of OP. Let mid-point of OP be M.

(iv) Taking M as centre and PM as radius, draw a dotted circle, which intersects the inner circle at two points say A and B.

(v) Join AP and BP. Then, AP and BP are required tangents. On measuring the lengths, we get $PA = PB = 2.14$ cm

Calculation

Join OA. Then, $OA = 1.8$ cm   [radius of inner circle C_1]

$$OP = 2.8 \text{ cm} \qquad [\text{radius of outer circle } C_2]$$

and $\angle PAO = 90°$

[∵ angle in semi-circle of constructed circle]

So, in $\triangle PAO$, by Pythagoras theorem,

$$OP^2 = OA^2 + AP^2$$

$$\Rightarrow\quad (2.8)^2 = (1.8)^2 + AP^2$$

$$\Rightarrow\quad 7.84 = 3.24 + AP^2$$

$$\Rightarrow\quad AP^2 = 7.84 - 3.24 = 4.6$$

$$\Rightarrow\quad AP = 2.14 \text{ cm}$$

[taking positive square root, as length cannot be negative]

$$\Rightarrow\quad PA = PB = 2.14 \text{ cm}$$

Hence, the length of tangents is 2.14 cm.

12. Given, a circle of radius 2.8 cm and we have to draw tangents without using the centre.

Steps of Construction

(i) First, draw a circle of radius 2.8 cm and take a point P outside the circle.

(ii) Through P, draw a secant PAB, which intersects the circle at A and B and extend it to C in opposite direction of AB such that $PC = PA$.

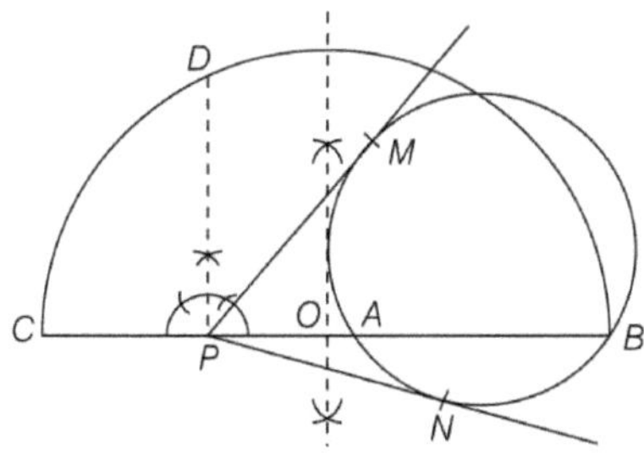

(iii) Now, bisect BC and take its mid-point as O. Draw a semi-circle with centre O and radius OB (or OC).

(iv) Draw $PD \perp BC$, which intersects the semi-circle at D.

(v) With centre P and radius PD draw two arcs, which intersects the given circle at points M and N.

(vi) Join PM and PN. Thus, PM and PN are the required tangents to the given circle.

13. Given, a circle of radius 3 cm. We have to construct a pair of tangents, which are inclined to each other at an angle of 45°.

Steps of Construction

(i) Draw a circle with O as centre and radius 3 cm.

(ii) Draw any diameter POQ of this circle.

(iii) Draw the radius OR meets the circle at R such that $\angle QOR = 45°$.

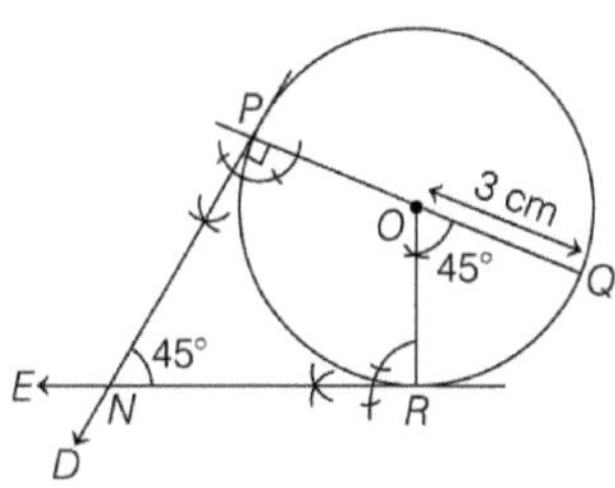

(iv) Draw $PD \perp PQ$ and $RE \perp OR$, which intersects each other at point N.

Then, NP and NR are the required tangents to the given circle inclined to each other at an angle of 45°.

Justification

By construction, $\angle OPN = 90°$ and OP is radius.

$\therefore\ PN$ is a tangent to the circle.

Similarly, NR is a tangent to the circle.

Now, $\angle POR = 180° - 45° = 135°$

[∵ POQ is a straight line and $\angle QOR = 45°$]

In quadrilateral $OPNR$,

$$\angle OPN = 90°, \ \angle POR = 135°$$

and $\angle ORN = 90°$

$$\therefore\quad \angle PNR = 360° - (90° + 135° + 90°) = 45°$$

14. Given, ABC is a right angled triangle, in which $AB = 6$ cm, $BC = 8$ cm, $\angle B = 90°$ and BD is perpendicular to AC.

Then, $\angle ADB = \angle CDB = 90°$

Steps of Construction

(i) Draw the line segments $AB = 6$ cm and $BC = 8$ cm perpendicular to each other. Join AC. Thus, $\triangle ABC$ is the given right angled triangle.

(ii) Draw perpendicular bisector of BC, which meets BC at O.

(iii) With O as centre and OB as radius draw a circle, which intersects AC at D, then $\angle BDC = 90°$. Thus, BD is perpendicular to AC.

(iv) With A as centre and AB as radius draw an arc, cutting the circle at M.

(v) Join AM. Thus, AB and AM are required tangents.

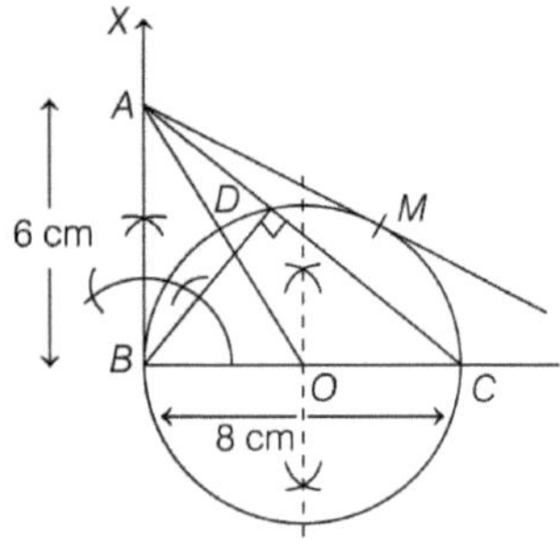

Justification

Since $\triangle ABC$ is right angled triangle with $\angle ABC = 90°$
$\therefore BO \perp AB$.

Also, BO is the radius of circle. So, AB has to be tangent of the circle. Similarly, AM is also a tangent to the circle.

15. Given, two points P and Q on the extended diameter of a circle with radius 3 cm such that $OP = OQ = 7$ cm

We have to construct the tangents to the circle from the given points P and Q.

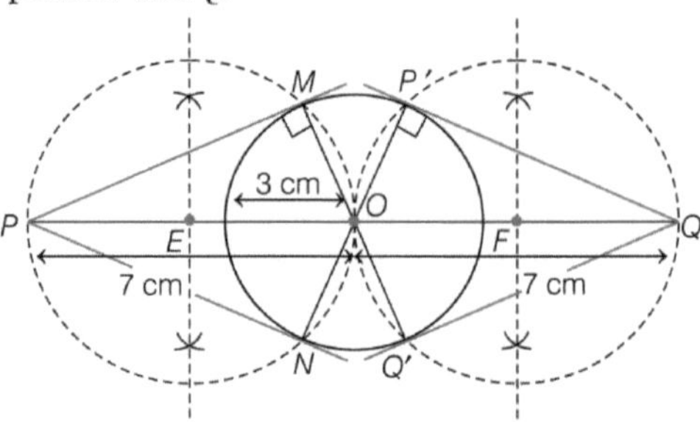

Steps of Construction

(i) Draw a circle of radius 3 cm with centre at O.

(ii) Produce its diameter on both sides and take points P and Q on it such that $OP = OQ = 7$ cm

(iii) Draw bisector of OP and OQ, which intersect OP and OQ at and F, respectively.

(iv) Now, take E as centre and OE as radius, draw a dotted circle which intersects the given circle at two points M, N. Again, take F as centre and OF as radius, draw another dotted circle which intersects the given circle at two points P' and Q'.

(v) Join PM, PN, QP' and QQ'. These are the required tangents from P and Q to the given circle.

Justification

Join OM and ON. The $\angle OMP$ is the angle that lies in the semi-circle of the dotted circle with centre E. Therefore,
$$\angle OMP = 90° \Rightarrow OM \perp PM$$

Since, OM is radius of the circle. So, MP has to be a tangent to the circle. Similarly, PN, QP' and QQ' are also tangents to the given circle.

Chapter Test

Multiple Choice Questions

1. To divide a line segment AB in the ratio $2 : 5$, first a ray AX is drawn, so that $\angle BAX$ is an acute angle and then at equal distances, then the number of points located on the ray AX is
[CBSE 2011]

   (a) 7　　　　　　　(b) 10
   (c) 2　　　　　　　(d) 5

2. To divide a line segment AB in the ratio $7 : 5$, first a ray AX is drawn, so that $\angle BAX$ is acute angle and then at equal distance points are marked. Then, the minimum number of these points is
   (a) 5　　　　　　　(b) 35
   (c) 7　　　　　　　(d) 12

3. By geometrical construction, it is possible to divide a line segment in the ratio $\sqrt{3} : \dfrac{1}{\sqrt{3}}$.

   (a) True　　　　　　(b) False
   (c) Can't determined　(d) None of these

4. To draw a pair of tangents to a circle, which are inclined to each other at an angle of $55°$, it is required to draw tangents at the end points of these two radii of the circle, the angle between two radii is
   (a) $105°$
   (b) $70°$
   (c) $125°$
   (d) $135°$

Short Answer Type Questions

5. Draw a line segment $AB = 6.5\,\text{cm}$ and divide it internally in the ratio $3 : 5$.

6. Draw two tangents at the end points of the diameter of a circle of radius 3.5 cm. Are these tangents parallel?

Long Answer Type Questions

7. Draw two concentric circles of radii 3 cm and 5 cm. Taking a point on outer circle construct the pair of tangents to the other. Measure the length of a tangent and verify it by actual calculation.

8. Draw a line segment AB of length 7 cm. Taking A as centre, draw a circle of radius 3 cm and taking B as centre, draw another circle of radius 2 cm. Construct tangents to each circle from the centre of the other circle.

Answers

1. (a)　2. (d)　3. (a)　4. (c)　6. These are parallel.　7. 4 cm

For Detailed Solutions
Scan the code

CHAPTER 05

Applications of Trigonometry

In this Chapter...

- Line of Sight & Horizontal Line
- Angle of Elevation
- Angle of Depression

Line of Sight

The line of sight is the line drawn from the eye of an observer to the point where the object is viewed by the observer.

Horizontal Line

The line which goes parallel from eye to ground, is called horizontal line.

Angle of Elevation

The angle of elevation of an object viewed, is the angle formed by the line of sight with the horizontal, when it is above the horizontal level, i.e. the case when we raise our head to look at the object.

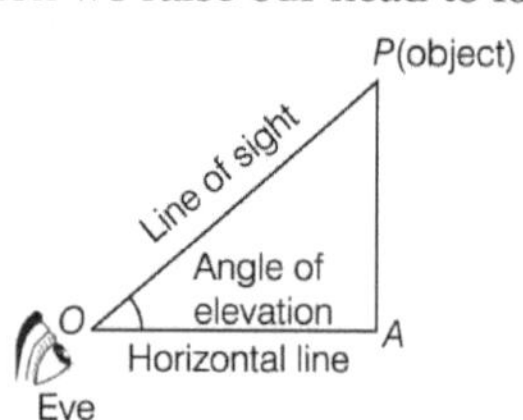

Angle of Depression

The angle of depression of an object viewed, is the angle formed by the line of sight with the horizontal, when it is below the horizontal level, i.e. the case when we lower our head to look at the object.

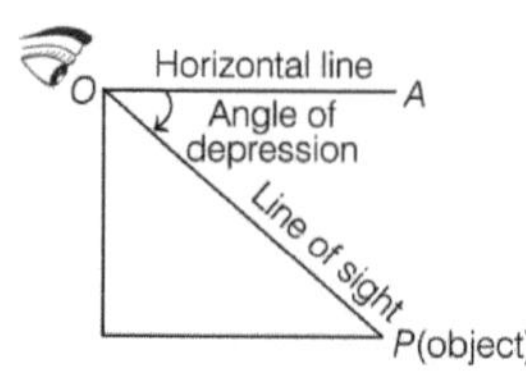

Some Important Points

(i) The angle of elevation of a point P as seen from a point O is always equal to the angle of depression of O as seen from P.

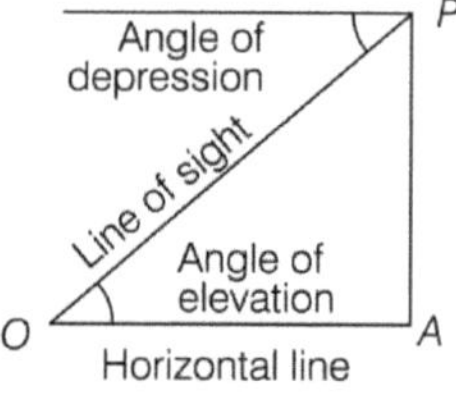

(ii) The angles of elevation and depression are always acute angles.

(iii) If the observer moves towards the perpendicular line (tower/building), then angle of elevation increases and if the observer moves away from the perpendicular line (tower/building), then angle of elevation decreases.

(iv) If the height of tower is doubled and the distance between the observer and foot of the tower is also doubled, then the angle of elevation remains same.

(v) If the angle of elevation of Sun, above a tower decreases, then the length of shadow of a tower increases and *vice-versa.*

Solved Examples

Example 1. In figure, a tightly stretched rope of length 20 m is tied from the top of a vertical pole to the ground. Find the height of the pole, if the angle made by the rope with the ground is 30°.

[CBSE 2020 (Standard)]

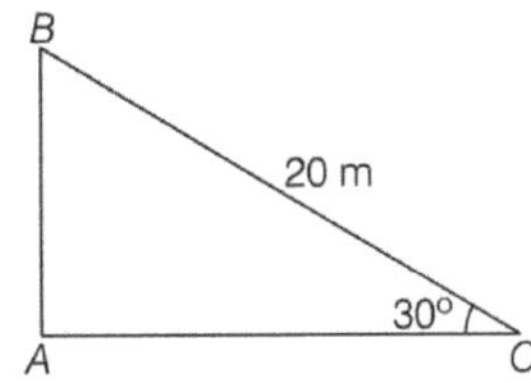

Sol. Let $AB = h$ be the height of the pole.

Given, length of rope, $BC = 20$ m

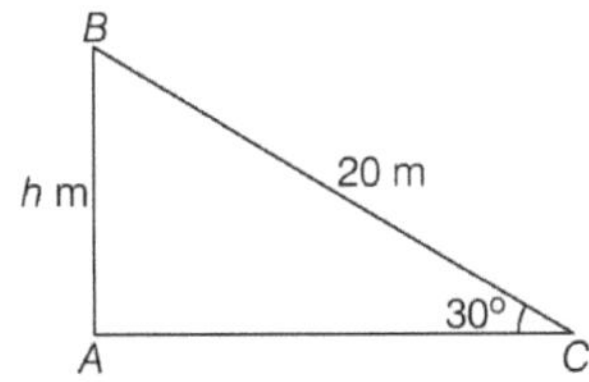

In right angled $\triangle ACB$,

$$\sin 30° = \frac{\text{Perpendicular}}{\text{Hypotenuse}}$$

$$\therefore \qquad \frac{1}{2} = \frac{h}{20}$$

$$\Rightarrow \qquad h = \frac{20}{2} = 10 \text{ m}$$

Hence, height of the pole is 10 m.

Example 2. In figure, the angle of elevation of the top of a tower from a point C on the ground, which is 30 m away from the foot of the tower, is 30°. Find the height of the tower. [CBSE 2020 (Standard)]

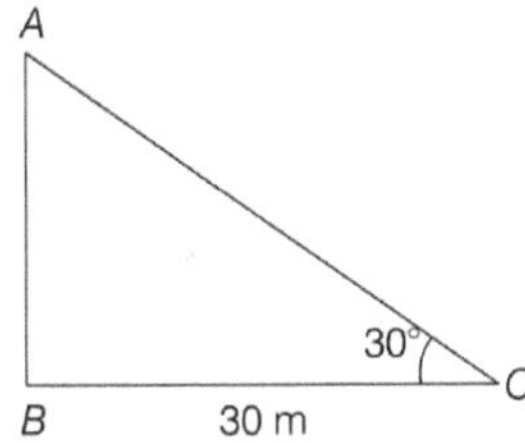

Sol. Let height of a tower be $AB = h$ m

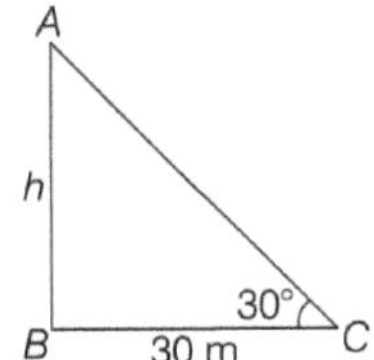

In right angled $\triangle ACB$,

$$\tan 30° = \frac{AB}{BC}$$

$$\Rightarrow \qquad \frac{1}{\sqrt 3} = \frac{h}{30}$$

$$\Rightarrow \qquad h = \frac{30}{\sqrt 3} \times \frac{\sqrt 3}{\sqrt 3}$$

[multiply numerator and denominator by $\sqrt 3$]

$$= \frac{30 \times \sqrt 3}{3}$$

$$= 10\sqrt 3 \text{ m}$$

Hence, height of the tower is $10\sqrt 3$ m.

Example 3. The ratio of the length of a vertical rod and the length of its shadow is $1 : \sqrt 3$. Find the angle of elevation of the Sun at that moment?

[CBSE 2020 (Standard)]

Sol. Let AB be the vertical rod and BC be its shadow and θ be the angle of elevation of the Sun.

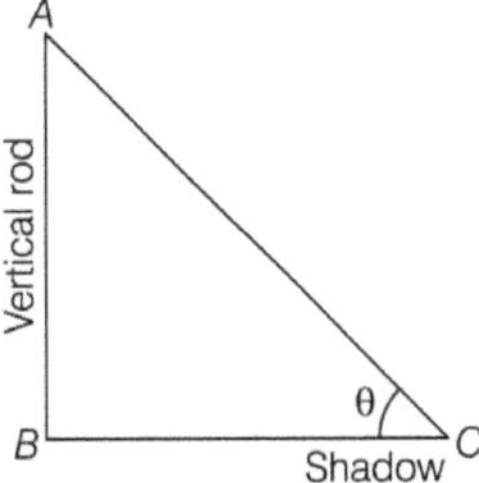

We have, $AB : BC = 1 : \sqrt 3$

Let $AB = x$, then $BC = x\sqrt 3$

In $\triangle ABC$, $\tan\theta = \dfrac{AB}{BC}$

$$\Rightarrow \qquad \tan\theta = \frac{x}{x\sqrt 3} = \frac{1}{\sqrt 3}$$

$$\Rightarrow \qquad \tan\theta = \tan 30°$$

$$\Rightarrow \qquad \theta = 30°$$

Example 4. A vertical tower stands on a horizontal plane and is surmounted by a vertical flag-staff of height 6 m. At a point on the plane, the angle of elevation of the bottom and top of the flag-staff are 30° and 45°, respectively. Find the height of the tower. (take, $\sqrt 3 = 1.73$) [CBSE 2020 (Standard)]

Sol. Let $BC = h$ be the height of the tower, $CD = 6$ m be the height of the flag-staff and A is any point on the ground. Consider, $AB = x$ m.

Given, the angle of elevation from point A to the points C and D are $\angle CAB = 30°$ and $\angle DAB = 45°$.

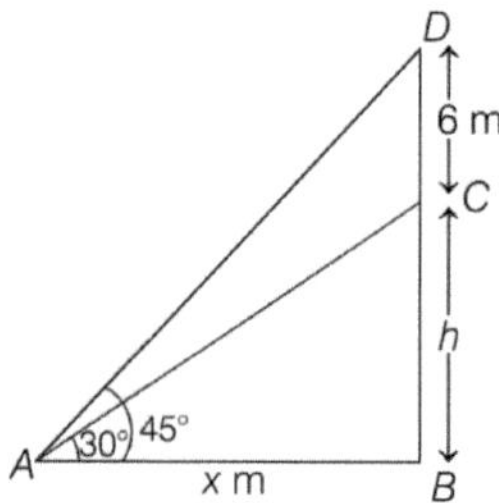

In right angled $\triangle ABC$,

$$\tan 30° = \frac{BC}{AB}$$

$$\Rightarrow \quad \frac{1}{\sqrt{3}} = \frac{h}{x}$$

$$\Rightarrow \quad x = \sqrt{3}\, h \text{ m} \qquad \qquad \qquad …(i)$$

Now, in right angled $\triangle ABD$,

$$\tan 45° = \frac{BD}{AB}$$

$$\Rightarrow \quad 1 = \frac{6+h}{x} \qquad [\because BD = BC + CD = 6 + h]$$

$$\Rightarrow \quad x = 6 + h \qquad \qquad \qquad …(ii)$$

$$\Rightarrow \quad \sqrt{3}h = 6 + h \qquad \qquad [\text{from Eq. (i)}]$$

$$\Rightarrow \quad h(\sqrt{3} - 1) = 6$$

$$\Rightarrow \quad h = \frac{6}{(\sqrt{3}-1)} \times \frac{\sqrt{3}+1}{\sqrt{3}+1} \qquad \text{(rationalisation)}$$

$$= \frac{6(\sqrt{3}+1)}{(\sqrt{3})^2 - (1)^2} \quad [\because (a-b)(a+b) = a^2 - b^2]$$

$$= \frac{6(1.73 + 1)}{3 - 1} = \frac{6 \times 2.73}{2}$$

$$= 3 \times 2.73 = 8.19 \text{ m}$$

Hence, height of tower is 8.19 m.

Example 5. A statue 1.6 m tall, stands on the top of a pedestal. From a point on the ground, the angle of elevation of the top of the statue is 60° and from the same point the angle of elevation of the top of the pedestal is 45°. Find the height of the pedestal. (use $\sqrt{3} = 1.73$)

Sol. Let $BC = h$ m be the height of the pedestal and $CD = 1.6$ m be the length of the statue, which is standing on the pedestal.

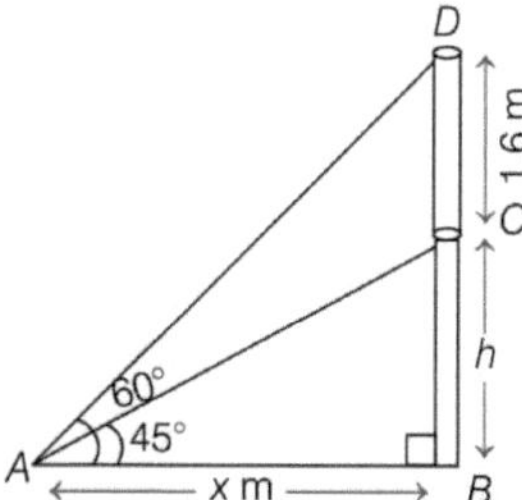

Again, let point A be a fixed point on the ground such that the angles of elevation of the top of the statue and bottom of the statue (i.e. top of the pedestal) are

$$\angle DAB = 60° \text{ and } \angle CAB = 45°.$$

Also, let $AB = x$ m.

In right angled $\triangle ABD$,

$$\tan 60° = \frac{\text{Perpendicular}}{\text{Base}} = \frac{BD}{AB}$$

$$\Rightarrow \quad \sqrt{3} = \frac{BC + CD}{x} \qquad [\because \tan 60° = \sqrt{3}]$$

$$\Rightarrow \quad \sqrt{3} = \frac{h + 1.6}{x}$$

$$\sqrt{3}x = h + 1.6$$

$$\Rightarrow \quad h = \sqrt{3}x - 1.6 \qquad \qquad …(i)$$

In right angled $\triangle CBA$,

$$\tan 45° = \frac{BC}{AB}$$

$$\Rightarrow \quad 1 = \frac{h}{x} \qquad \qquad [\because \tan 45° = 1]$$

$$\Rightarrow \quad x = h$$

On putting $x = h$ in Eq. (i), we get

$$h = \sqrt{3}h - 1.6$$

$$\Rightarrow \quad h(\sqrt{3} - 1) = 1.6$$

$$\Rightarrow \quad h = \frac{1.6}{(\sqrt{3}-1)} \times \frac{\sqrt{3}+1}{\sqrt{3}+1} \qquad [\text{rationalising}]$$

$$= \frac{1.6(\sqrt{3}+1)}{(\sqrt{3})^2 - (1)^2} [\because (a+b)(a-b) = a^2 - b^2]$$

$$= \frac{1.6}{2}(\sqrt{3} + 1)$$

$$= 0.8(1.73 + 1)$$

$$= 0.8 \ (2.73) = 2.184 \text{ m}$$

Hence, the height of the pedestal is 2.184 m.

Example 6. From a point on the ground, the angles of elevation of the bottom and the top of a transmission tower fixed at the top of a 20 m high building are 45° and 60°, respectively. Find the height of the tower. (use $\sqrt{3} = 1.73$)

Sol. Let $AB = 20$ m be the height of the building and $BC = h$ m be the height of transmission tower. The angles of elevation from a ground point D to the points B and C are $\angle ADB = 45°$ and $\angle ADC = 60°$

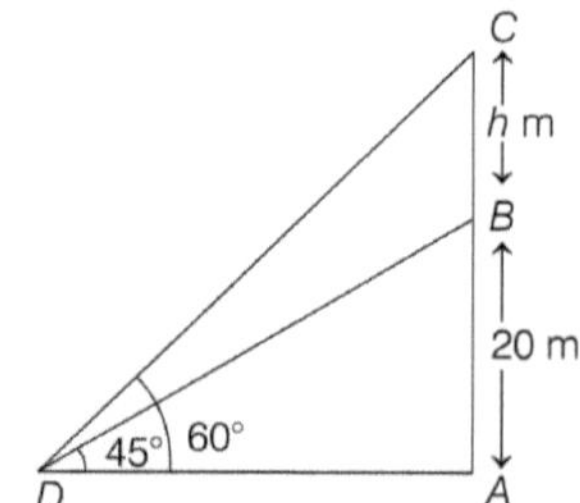

In right angled $\triangle ADB$,

$$\tan 45° = \frac{AB}{AD}$$

$$\Rightarrow \quad 1 = \frac{20}{AD}$$

$$\Rightarrow \quad AD = 20 \text{ m} \qquad \qquad …(i)$$

Now, in right angled ΔADC,

$$\tan 60° = \frac{AC}{AD}$$

$$\Rightarrow \qquad \sqrt{3} = \frac{AB + BC}{20} \qquad [\because \text{from Eq. (i)}]$$

$$\Rightarrow \qquad 20\sqrt{3} = 20 + h$$

$$\Rightarrow \qquad h = 20(\sqrt{3} - 1) = 20(1.73 - 1)$$

$$= 20 \times 0.73 = 14.60 \text{ m}$$

Hence, height of the transmission tower is 14.6 m.

Example 7. Two poles of equal heights are standing opposite to each other on either side of the road, which is 100 m wide. From a point between them on the road, the angles of elevation of the top of the poles are 60° and 30°, respectively. Find the height of the poles and the distance of the point from the poles. **[CBSE 2020 (Standard)]**

Sol. Let $AB = 100$ m be the width of the road. On both sides of the road, poles $AE = BD = h$ m are standing. Let C be any point on AB such that from point C, angles of elevation are $\angle BCD = 60°$ and $\angle ACE = 30°$

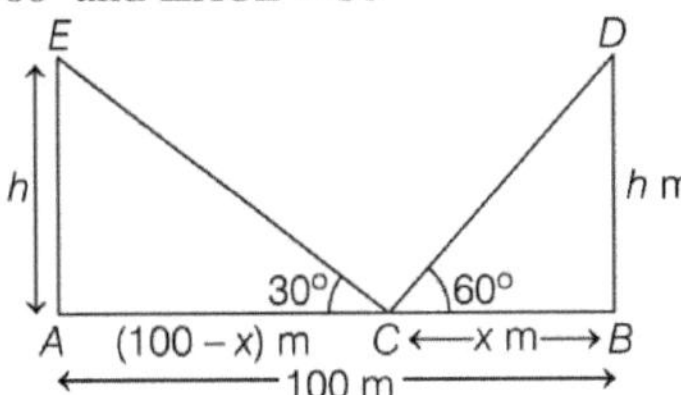

Let $BC = x$ m, then $AC = AB - BC = (100 - x)$ m

In right angled ΔCAE,

$$\tan 30° = \frac{\text{Perpendicular}}{\text{Base}}$$

$$\therefore \qquad \frac{1}{\sqrt{3}} = \frac{AE}{AC} \Rightarrow \frac{1}{\sqrt{3}} = \frac{h}{(100 - x)}$$

$$\Rightarrow \qquad h = \frac{(100 - x)}{\sqrt{3}}$$

$$\Rightarrow \qquad h\sqrt{3} = 100 - x \qquad \ldots\text{(i)}$$

and in right angled ΔBCD,

$$\tan 60° = \frac{BD}{BC}$$

$$\Rightarrow \qquad \sqrt{3} = \frac{h}{x}$$

$$\Rightarrow \qquad h = \sqrt{3}x \qquad \ldots\text{(ii)}$$

Put $h = \sqrt{3}x$ in Eq. (i), we get

$$\sqrt{3}x \times \sqrt{3} = 100 - x$$

$$\Rightarrow \qquad 3x + x = 100 \Rightarrow 4x = 100$$

$$\Rightarrow \qquad x = \frac{100}{4} = 25 \text{ m}$$

$\therefore BC = 25$ m and $AC = 100 - x = 100 - 25 = 75$ m

Put $x = 25$ in Eq. (i), we get

$$\Rightarrow \qquad h\sqrt{3} = 100 - 25$$

$$\Rightarrow \qquad h = \frac{75}{\sqrt{3}} \times \frac{\sqrt{3}}{\sqrt{3}} = \frac{75\sqrt{3}}{3}$$

$$\Rightarrow \qquad h = 25\sqrt{3} \text{ m}$$

Hence, height of the pole is $25\sqrt{3}$ m and distances of the point from the poles are 25 m and 75 m.

Example 8. The angle of elevation of the top of a building from the foot of a tower is 30° and the angle of elevation of the top of a tower from the foot of the building is 60°. If the tower is 50 m high, then find the height of the building.

Sol. Let $AB = 50$ m, $CD = h$ be the height of the tower and building. Then,

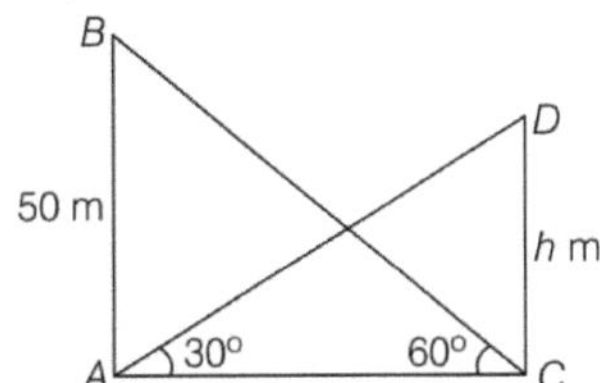

$$\angle CAD = 30° \text{ and } \angle ACB = 60°$$

In right angled ΔACD,

$$\tan 30° = \frac{CD}{AC} \Rightarrow \frac{1}{\sqrt{3}} = \frac{h}{AC}$$

$$\Rightarrow \qquad AC = \sqrt{3}\, h \qquad \ldots\text{(i)}$$

In right angled ΔCAB,

$$\tan 60° = \frac{AB}{AC}$$

$$\Rightarrow \qquad \sqrt{3} = \frac{50}{AC}$$

$$\Rightarrow \qquad \sqrt{3} = \frac{50}{\sqrt{3}h} \qquad [\text{from Eq. (i)}]$$

$$\Rightarrow \qquad h = \frac{50}{3} = 16.67 \text{ m}$$

Hence, the height of the building is 16.67 m.

Example 9. From the top of a 7 m high building the angle of elevation of the top of a tower is 60° and the angle of depression of its foot is 45°. Determine the height of the tower. **[CBSE 2020 (Standard)]**

Sol. Let $AB = 7$ m be the height of the building and EC be the height of tower.

A is the point from where elevation of tower is 60° and the angle of depression of its foot is 45°.

Here, $EC = DE + CD$

Also, $CD = AB = 7$ m

and $BC = AD$

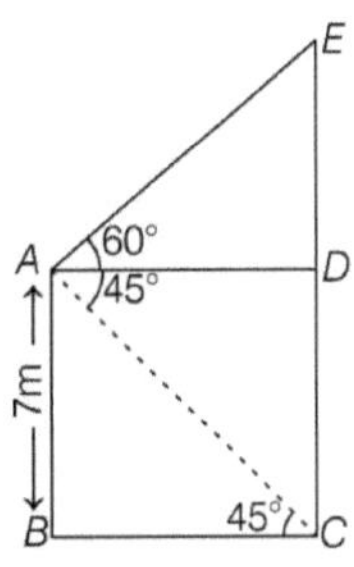

Now, in right angled $\triangle ABC$,

$$\tan 45° = \frac{AB}{BC}$$

$$\Rightarrow \qquad 1 = \frac{7}{BC}$$

$$\Rightarrow \qquad BC = 7\,\text{m}$$

Also, in right angled $\triangle ADE$,

$$\tan 60° = \frac{DE}{AD}$$

$$\Rightarrow \qquad \sqrt{3} = \frac{DE}{7} \qquad [\because AD = BC]$$

$$\Rightarrow \qquad DE = 7\sqrt{3}\ \text{m}$$

$\therefore$ Height of the tower,

$$EC = DE + CD$$
$$= (7\sqrt{3} + 7)\ \text{m}$$
$$= 7(\sqrt{3} + 1)\ \text{m}$$

Hence, height of the tower is $7(\sqrt{3} + 1)$ m.

Example 10. If the angle of elevation of a cloud from a point 10 m above a lake is 30° and the angle of depression of its reflection in the lake is 60°, find the height of the cloud from the surface of lake.

[CBSE 2020 (Standard)]

Sol. Let AB be the surface of the lake and P be the point of observation such that $AP = 10$ m. Let C be the position of the cloud and C' be the reflection in the lake, then $CB = C'B$.

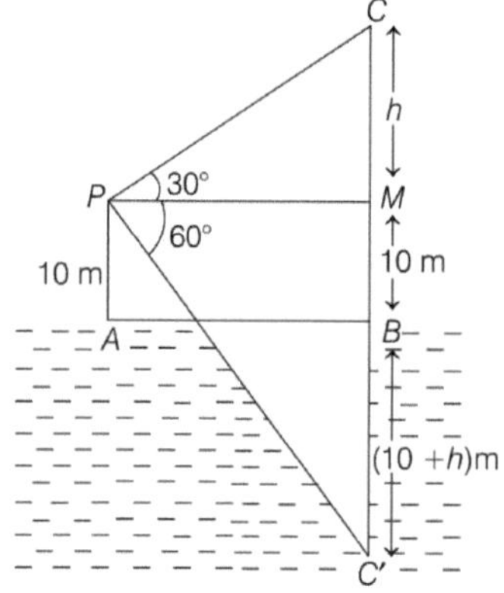

Let $CM = h$, then $CB = 10 + h$

$$\Rightarrow \qquad C'B = 10 + h$$

In right angled $\triangle CMP$,

$$\tan 30° = \frac{CM}{PM}$$

$$\Rightarrow \qquad \frac{1}{\sqrt{3}} = \frac{h}{PM}$$

$$\Rightarrow \qquad PM = \sqrt{3}h \qquad \qquad \text{...(i)}$$

In right angled $\triangle PMC'$,

$$\tan 60° = \frac{C'M}{PM}$$

$$\Rightarrow \qquad \sqrt{3} = \frac{C'B + BM}{PM}$$

$$\Rightarrow \qquad \sqrt{3} = \frac{10 + h + 10}{\sqrt{3}h} \qquad \text{[from Eq. (i)]}$$

$$\Rightarrow \qquad 3h = 20 + h$$
$$\Rightarrow \qquad 2h = 20$$
$$\Rightarrow \qquad h = 10\ \text{m}$$

Now, the height of the cloud from the surface of lake

$$= BC$$
$$= BM + h$$
$$= 10 + 10 = 20\ \text{m}$$

Example 11. From a point on a bridge across a river, the angles of depression of the banks on opposite sides of the river are 30° and 45°, respectively. If the bridge is at a height of 30 m from sea level, then find the width of the river. (use $\sqrt{3} = 1.73$)

Sol. Let A be a point on the bridge and points B and D are on the opposite side of the banks. Then, angles of depression from point A to the opposite banks are

$$\angle EAB = 30° \text{ and } \angle FAD = 45°$$

$$\Rightarrow \qquad \angle CBA = 30° \text{ and } \angle CDA = 45°$$

$$[\because \text{ alternate angles are equal}]$$

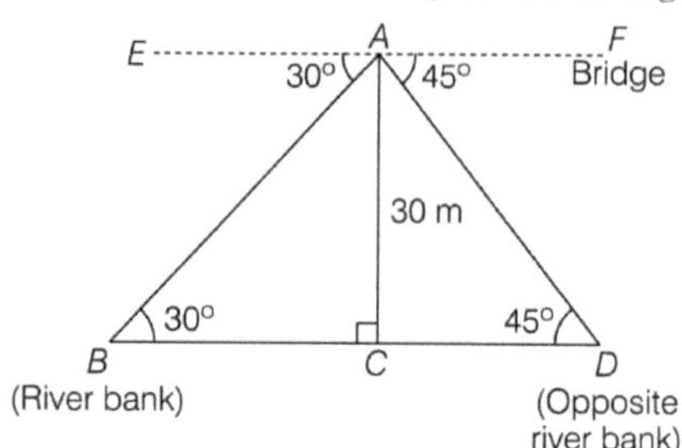

In right angled $\triangle ACB$,

$$\tan 30° = \frac{AC}{BC}$$

$$\Rightarrow \qquad \frac{1}{\sqrt{3}} = \frac{30}{BC}$$

$$\Rightarrow \qquad BC = 30\sqrt{3}\ \text{m}$$

and in right angled $\triangle ACD$,

$$\tan 45° = \frac{AC}{CD}$$

$$\Rightarrow \qquad 1 = \frac{AC}{30}$$

$$\Rightarrow \qquad AC = 30\ \text{m}$$

Hence, width of the river is

$$BD = BC + CD$$
$$= 30\sqrt{3} + 30$$
$$= 30 \times 1.73 + 30$$
$$= 51.9 + 30$$
$$= 81.9$$

Hence, width of the river is 81.9 m.

Example 12. From the top of a 7 m building, the angle of elevation of the top of a cable tower is $60°$ and the angle of depression of its foot is $45°$. Determine the height of the tower. (use $\sqrt{3} = 1.73$).

[**CBSE 2020 (Standard)**]

Sol. Let $AB = 7$ m be the height of the building and $DE = h$ m be the height of cable tower.

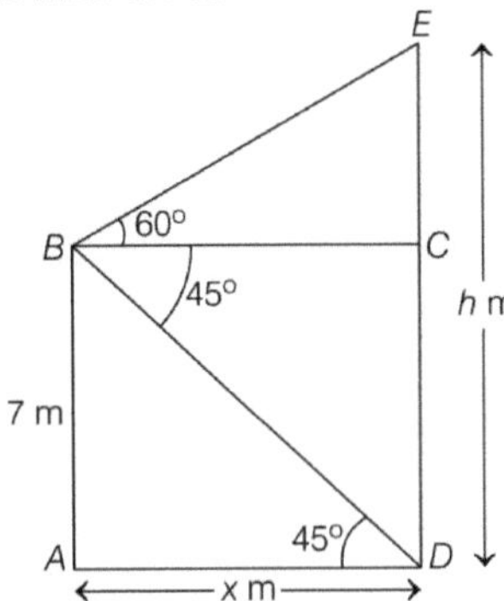

Then, $\angle CBE = 60°$
and $\angle CBD = 45° \Rightarrow \angle ADB = 45°$ (alternate angle)
Let distance between two towers be
$$AD = BC = x \text{ m}$$
In right angled ΔBCE, $\tan 60° = \dfrac{CE}{BC}$
$$\Rightarrow \qquad \sqrt{3} = \dfrac{CE}{x} \Rightarrow x = \dfrac{CE}{\sqrt{3}} \qquad \dots \text{(i)}$$
and in right angled ΔADB,
$$\tan 45° = \dfrac{AB}{AD} \Rightarrow 1 = \dfrac{7}{x} \Rightarrow x = 7 \text{ m}$$
Put $x = 7$ in Eq. (i), we get
$$7 = \dfrac{CE}{\sqrt{3}} \Rightarrow CE = 7\sqrt{3} \text{ m}$$
Now, height of cable tower,
$$h = DC + CE$$
$$= 7 + 7\sqrt{3} = 7(1 + \sqrt{3})$$
$$= 7(1 + 1.73) = 7 \times 2.73 = 19.11 \text{ m}$$

Example 13. The angle of elevation of an aeroplane from point O on the ground is $60°$. After a flight of 10 s, on the same height, the angle of elevation from point O becomes $30°$. If the aeroplane is flying at the speed of 720 km/h, find the constant height at which the aeroplane is flying. [**CBSE 2020 (Standard)**]

Sol. Let OX be the horizontal ground, A and B be the two positions of the plane and O be the points of observation.
Let height of an aeroplane from A to the ground is
$$AC = BD = h \text{ m}$$

Given, speed of plane is 720 km/h and time of flight is 10 s.
Also, given $\angle AOC = 60°$ and $\angle BOD = 30°$
In right angled ΔOCA,
$$\cot 60° = \dfrac{OC}{AC}$$
$$\Rightarrow \qquad \dfrac{1}{\sqrt{3}} = \dfrac{OC}{h}$$
$$\Rightarrow \qquad OC = \dfrac{h}{\sqrt{3}} \text{ m}$$
In right angled ΔODB,
$$\cot 30° = \dfrac{OD}{BD}$$
$$\Rightarrow \qquad \sqrt{3} = \dfrac{OD}{h}$$
$$\Rightarrow \qquad OD = h\sqrt{3}$$
Now, $CD = OD - OC$
$$= h\sqrt{3} - \dfrac{h}{\sqrt{3}} = \dfrac{2h}{\sqrt{3}} \text{ m}$$
Thus, distance covered by aeroplane in 10 s is $\dfrac{2h}{\sqrt{3}}$ m.

$\because$ Speed of aeroplane $= \dfrac{\text{Distance}}{\text{Time}}$

$\therefore \qquad 720 \times \dfrac{5}{18} = \dfrac{\frac{2h}{\sqrt{3}}}{10}$ $\left[\because 1 \text{ km} = \dfrac{5}{18} \text{ m/s} \right]$

$\Rightarrow \qquad 40 \times 5 \times 10\sqrt{3} = 2h$
$\Rightarrow \qquad h = 1000\sqrt{3} \text{ m}$

Hence, height at which the aeroplane is flying is $1000\sqrt{3}$ m.

Example 14. A straight highway leads to the foot of a tower. A man standing at the top of the tower observes a car at an angle of depression of $30°$, which is approaching the foot of the tower with a uniform speed. After covering a distance of 50 m, the angle of depression of the car becomes $60°$.

Find the height of the tower. (use $\sqrt{3} = 1.73$).

[**CBSE 2020 (Standard)**]

Sol. Let $AB = h$ m be the height of the tower. Let C be the initial position of the car and D be the final position of the car, when it covers a distance, $CD = 50$ m.

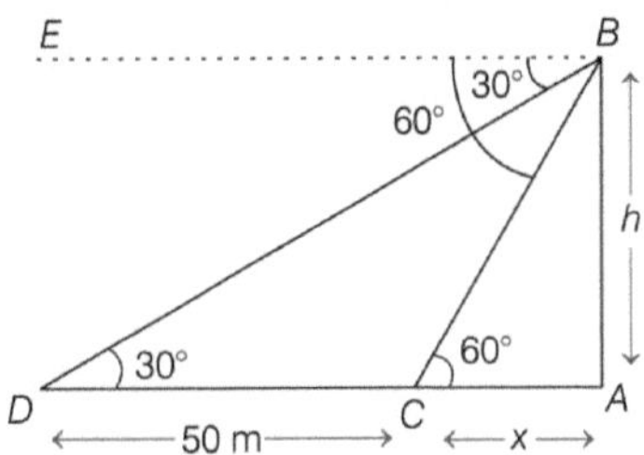

Given, the angle of depressions from point B to the points C and D are
$$\angle EBC = 60° \text{ and } \angle EBD = 30°$$
$$\Rightarrow \qquad \angle BCA = 60° \text{ and } \angle BDA = 30° \text{ [alternate angles]}$$

In right angled ΔCAB,

$$\tan 60° = \frac{AB}{AC}$$

$$\Rightarrow \quad \sqrt{3} = \frac{h}{x}$$

$$\Rightarrow \quad x = \frac{h}{\sqrt{3}} \text{ m} \qquad \ldots\text{(i)}$$

And in right angled ΔDAB,

$$\tan 30° = \frac{AB}{AD}$$

$$\Rightarrow \quad \frac{1}{\sqrt{3}} = \frac{h}{50 + x}$$

$$\Rightarrow \quad 50 + x = h\sqrt{3}$$

$$\Rightarrow \quad x = h\sqrt{3} - 50 \qquad \ldots\text{(ii)}$$

From Eqs. (i) and (ii), we have

$$\frac{h}{\sqrt{3}} = h\sqrt{3} - 50$$

$$\Rightarrow \quad h = 3h - 50\sqrt{3}$$

$$\Rightarrow \quad 2h = 50\sqrt{3}$$

$$\Rightarrow \quad h = 25\sqrt{3}$$

$$\Rightarrow \quad h = 25 \times 1.73$$

$$\Rightarrow \quad h = 43.25 \text{ m}$$

Hence, height of the tower is 43.25 m.

Example 15. The angles of depression of the top and bottom of a tower as seen from the top of a $60\sqrt{3}$ m high cliff are 45° and 60°, respectively. Find the height of the tower. (use $\sqrt{3} = 1.73$)

Sol. Let $AC = 60\sqrt{3}$ m be the height of the cliff, $DE = h$ m be the height of the tower and distance between tower and cliff be $CD = BE = x$ m.

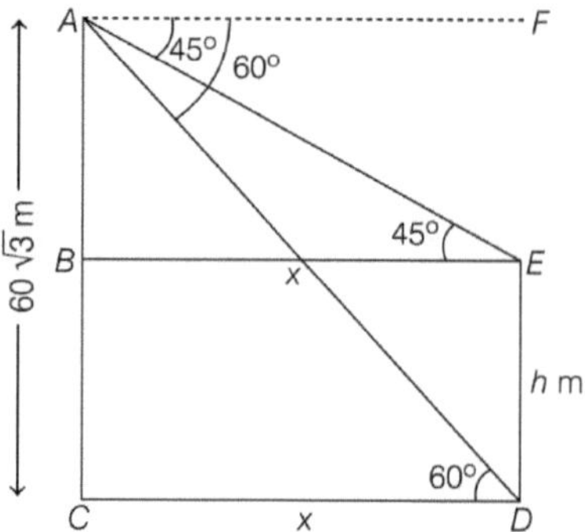

Given, the angle of depressions from point A are

$$\angle FAE = 45° \text{ and } \angle FAD = 60°$$

$$\Rightarrow \quad \angle BEA = 45° \text{ and } \angle CDA = 60° \text{ [alternate angles]}$$

In right angled ΔAEB,

$$\tan 45° = \frac{AB}{BE} \Rightarrow 1 = \frac{AB}{x}$$

$$\Rightarrow \quad x = AB \qquad \ldots\text{(i)}$$

and in right angled ΔADC,

$$\tan 60° = \frac{AC}{CD} \Rightarrow \sqrt{3} = \frac{60\sqrt{3}}{x} \Rightarrow x = \frac{60\sqrt{3}}{\sqrt{3}}$$

$$\Rightarrow \quad x = 60 \text{ m} \qquad \ldots\text{(ii)}$$

$\therefore$ From Eqs. (i) and (ii), we get

$$AB = x = 60 \text{ m}$$

Now height of cliff,

$$h = AC - AB$$

$$= 60\sqrt{3} - 60$$

$$= 60(\sqrt{3} - 1)$$

$$= 60(1.73 - 1)$$

$$= 60 \times 0.73 = 43.8 \text{ m}$$

Hence, height of the cliff is 43.8 m.

Chapter Practice

Objective Questions

- ### Multiple Choice Questions

1. The angle of elevation of the Sun when the shadow of a pole h m high is $\sqrt{3}\,h$ m long is
   (a) 0° (b) 30° (c) 45° (d) 60°

2. If a pole 6 m high casts a shadow $2\sqrt{3}$ m long on the ground, then the Sun's elevation is
   (a) 60° (b) 45°
   (c) 30° (d) 90°

3. If $300\sqrt{3}$ m high tower makes an angle of elevation at a point on ground which is 300 m away from its foot, then the angle of elevation is
   (a) 0° (b) 30°
   (c) 45° (d) 60°

4. From the top of a 60 m high tower, the angle of depression of a point on the ground is 30°. The distance of the point from the foot of tower is
   (a) 180 m (b) $60\sqrt{3}$ m
   (c) 150 m (d) $30\sqrt{3}$ m

5. The figure shows the observation of point C from point A. The angle of depression from A is
   [CBSE 2013]

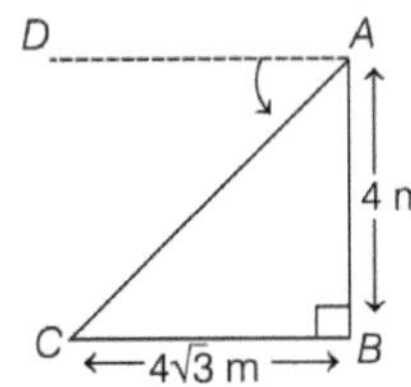

   (a) 30° (b) 45° (c) 60° (d) 90°

6. A circus artist is climbing a 20 m long rope, which is tightly stretched and tied from the top of a vertical pole to the ground, then the height of pole, if the angle made by the rope with the ground level is 30°, is
   (a) 5 m (b) 10 m
   (c) 15 m (d) 20 m

7. A ladder, leaning against a wall, makes an angle of 60° with the horizontal. If the foot of the ladder is 9.5 m away from the wall. The length of the ladder is
   [NCERT Exemplar]
   (a) 10 m (b) 16 m
   (c) 18 m (d) 19 m

8. A ramp for disabled people in a hospital have slope 30°. If the height of the ramp be 1 m, then the length of ramp is
   (a) 2 m (b) 0.5 m
   (c) $2\sqrt{3}$ m (d) 1 m

9. A kite is flying at a height of 80 m above the ground. The string attached to the kite is temporarily tied to a point on the ground. The inclination of the string with ground is 60°, then the length of the string is
   (a) 62.37 m (b) 92.37 m
   (c) 52.57 m (d) 72.57 m

10. The length of a string between a kite and a point on the ground is 85 m. If the string makes an angle θ with the ground level such that $\tan\theta = \dfrac{15}{8}$, then the height of kite is
    (a) 75 m (b) 78.05 m
    (c) 226 m (d) None of these

11. A tower stands near an airport. The angle of elevation θ of the tower from a point on the ground is such that its tangent is 5/12. The height of the tower, if the distance of the observer from the tower is 120 m is
    [CBSE 2015]
    (a) 40 m (b) 50 m
    (c) 60 m (d) 70 m

12. The top of two poles of height 20 m and 14 m are connected by a wire. If the wire makes an angle of 30° with the horizontal, then the length of the wire is
    (a) 12 m (b) 10 m (c) 8 m (d) 6 m

13. An observer, 1.5 m tall is 20.5 m away from a tower 22 m high, then the angle of elevation of the top of the tower from the eye of the observer is
    (a) 30° (b) 45° (c) 60° (d) 90°

14. The angle of elevation of the top of the tower from a point, which is 40 m away from the base of the tower in the horizontal level, is 45°. Find the height of the tower.

(a) 70 m
(b) 60 m
(c) 40 m
(d) 30 m

15. The angle of elevation of the top of a building 150 m high, from a point on the ground is 45°. The distance of the point from foot of the building is

(a) 120 m
(b) 130 m
(c) 140 m
(d) 150 m

16. The angle of depression of the car parked on the road from the top of a 150 m high tower is 30°. The distance of the car from the tower is　　[**CBSE 2014**]

(a) 150 m
(b) 75 m
(c) $150\sqrt{3}$ m
(d) $\dfrac{150}{\sqrt{3}}$ m

17. From a point on the ground, the angles of elevation of the bottom and the top of a transmission tower fixed at the top of a 20 m high building are 45° and 60° respectively, then the height of the tower is

(a) 14.64 m
(b) 28.64 m
(c) 38.64 m
(d) 19.64 m

18. A bridge on a river makes an angle of 45° with its edge. If the length along the bridge from one edge to the other is 150 m, then the width of the river is

(a) 107.75 m
(b) 105 m
(c) 75 m
(d) 106.05 m

• Case Based MCQs

19. There are two balcony in a house. First balcony is at a height of 3 m above the ground and other balcony is 6 m vertically above the lower balcony. Ankit and Radha are sitting inside the two balcony at points G and F, respectively. At any instant, the angles of elevation of a Parachute from these balcony are observed to be 60° and 45° as shown below

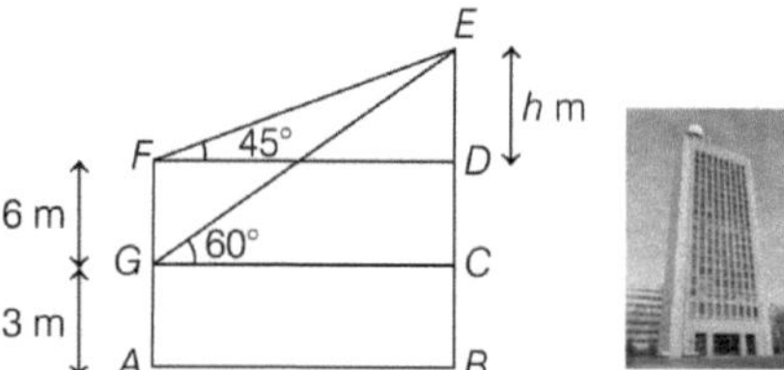

Based on the above information, answer the following questions.

(i) Who is more closer to the Parachute.

(a) Ankit
(b) Radha
(c) Both are at equal distance
(d) Can't be determined

(ii) Value of DF is equal to

(a) $\dfrac{h}{\sqrt{3}}$ m
(b) $h\sqrt{3}$ m
(c) $\dfrac{h}{2}$ m
(d) h m

(iii) Value of h is

(a) 2
(b) $3(\sqrt{3}+1)$
(c) 4
(d) $3(\sqrt{3}-1)$

(iv) Height of the Parachute from the ground is

(a) 4 m
(b) $3(4-\sqrt{3})$
(c) 8 m
(d) $3(4+\sqrt{3})$

(v) If the Parachute is moving towards the building, then both angles of elevation will

(a) remain same
(b) increases
(c) decreases
(d) Can't be determined

20. A cyclist is climbing through a 20 m long rope which is highly stretched and tied from the top of a vertical pole to the ground as shown below

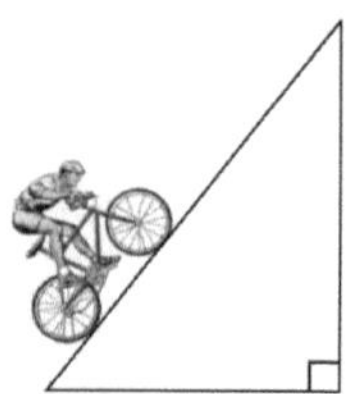

Based on the above information, answer the following questions.

(i) The height of the pole, if angle made by rope with the ground level is 60°, is

(a) 15 m
(b) $10\sqrt{3}$ m
(c) $\dfrac{10}{\sqrt{3}}$ m
(d) $\dfrac{15}{\sqrt{2}}$ m

(ii) If the angle made by the rope with the ground level is 60°, then the distance between artist and pole at ground level is

(a) $\dfrac{10}{\sqrt{2}}$ m
(b) $10\sqrt{2}$ m
(c) 10 m
(d) $10\sqrt{3}$ m

(iii) If the angle made by the rope with the ground level is 45°. The height of the pole is

(a) 2.5 m
(b) 10 m
(c) 7.5 m
(d) $10\sqrt{2}$ m

(iv) If the angle made by the rope with the ground level is 45° and 3 m rope is broken, then the height of the pole is

(a) $\dfrac{17}{\sqrt{2}}$ m
(b) 7 m
(c) 14 m
(d) $7\sqrt{2}$ m

(v) Which mathematical concept is used here?

(a) Similar triangles
(b) Pythagoras theorem
(c) Application of trigonometry
(d) None of the above

21. A group of students of class X visited India Gate on an educational trip. The teacher and students had interest in history as well. The teacher narrated that India Gate, official name Delhi Memorial, originally called All-India War Memorial, monumental sandstone arch in New Delhi, dedicated to the troops of British India who died in wars fought between 1914 and 1919.The teacher also said that India Gate, which is located at the eastern end of the Rajpath (formerly called the Kingsway), is about 138 feet (42 m) in height.

(i) What is the angle of elevation if they are standing at a distance of 42 m away from the monument?
(a) 30° (b) 45°
(c) 60° (d) 0°

(ii) They want to see the tower at an angle of 60°. So, they want to know the distance where they should stand and hence find the distance.
(a) 25.24 m (b) 20.12 m
(c) 42 m (d) 24.24 m

(iii) If the altitude of the Sun is at 60°, then the height of the vertical tower that will cast a shadow of length 20 m is
(a) $20\sqrt{3}$ m (b) $\dfrac{20}{\sqrt{3}}$ m
(c) $\dfrac{15}{\sqrt{3}}$ m (d) $15\sqrt{3}$ m

(iv) The ratio of the length of a rod and its shadow is 1 : 1. The angle of elevation of the Sun is
(a) 30° (b) 45°
(c) 60° (d) 90°

(v) The angle formed by the line of sight with the horizontal when the object viewed is below the horizontal level is
(a) corresponding angle
(b) angle of elevation
(c) angle of depression
(d) complete angle

22. A Satellite flying at height h is watching the top of the two tallest mountains in Uttarakhand and Karnataka ,they being Nanda Devi (height 7,816m) and Mullayanagiri (height 1,930 m). The angles of depression from the satellite to the top of Nanda Devi and Mullayanagiri are 30° and 60°, respectively. If the distance between the peaks of two mountains is 1937 km, and the satellite is vertically above the mid-point of the distance between the two mountains. (use $\sqrt{3} = 1.73$)

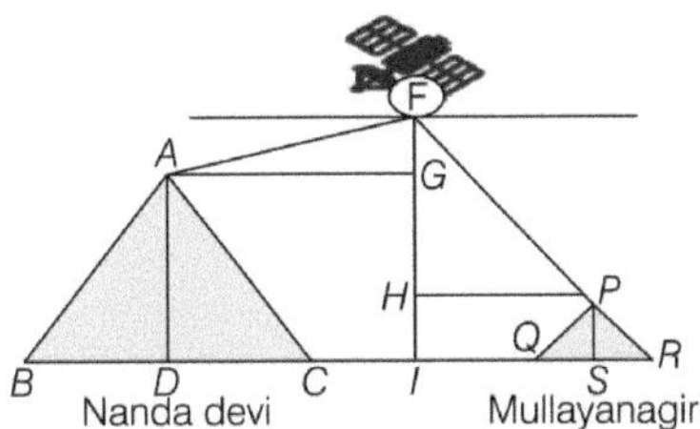

(i) The distance of the satellite from the top of Nanda Devi is
(a) 1139.4 km (b) 1119.65 km
(c) 1937 km (d) 1025.36 km

(ii) The distance of the satellite from the top of Mullayanagiri is
(a) 1139.4 km (b) 577.52 km
(c) 1937 km (d) 1025.36 km

(iii) The distance of the satellite from the ground is
(a) 1139.4 km (b) 567.64 km
(c) 1937 km (d) 1025.36 km

(iv) What is the angle of elevation, if a man is standing at a distance of 7816 m from Nanda Devi?
(a) 30° (b) 45°
(c) 60° (d) 0°

(v) If a mile stone very far away, makes 45° to the top of Mullayanagiri mountain. Hence, find the distance of this mile stone from the mountain.
(a) 1118.327 m (b) 566.976 m
(c) 1930 m (d) 1025.36 m

PART 2

Subjective Questions

• Short Answer Type Questions

1. If the height of a tower and the distance of the point of observation from its foot, both are increased by 10%, then the angle of elevation of its top remains unchanged. Explain.

2. A straight tree is broken due to thunderstorm. The broken part is bent in such a way that the peak of the tree touches the ground at an angle of 60° at a distance of $2\sqrt{3}$ m. Find the whole height of the tree.

3. Determine the height of a mountain, if the elevation of its top at an unknown distance from the base is 30° and at a distance 10 km farther off from the mountain, along the same line, the angle of elevation is 15°. (take $\tan 15° = 0.27$)

4. There is a flag staff on a tower of height 20 m. At a point on the ground, the angles of elevation of the foot and top of the flag are 45° and 60°, respectively. Find the height of the flag staff.

5. If the length of the shadow of a tower is increasing, then the angle of elevation of the Sun is also increasing. Why or why not?

6. A window in a building is at a height of 10 m from the ground. The angle of depression of a point P on the ground from the window is 30°. The angle of elevation of the top of the building from the point P is 60°. Find the height of the building.   **[CBSE 2007]**

7. A player sitting on the top of a tower of height 20 m observes the angle of depression of a ball lying on the ground as 60°. Find the distance between the foot of the tower and the ball.

8. If two towers of height x m and y m subtend angles of 30° and 60°, respectively at the centre of the line joining their feet, then find $x : y$.   **[CBSE 2015]**

9. If a man standing on a platform 3 m above the surface of a lake observes a cloud and its reflection in the lake, then the angle of elevation of the cloud is equal to the angle of depression of its reflection. State true or false. Justify.

10. From the top of a hill, the angles of depression of two consecutive kilometre stones due East are found to be 30° and 45°. Find the height of the hill.
[CBSE 2015]

11. The shadow of a tower is 30 m long, when the Sun's angle of elevation is 30°. What is the length of the shadow, when Sun's elevation is 60°?

12. Two ships are there in the sea on either side of a light house in such a way that the ships and the base of the light house are in the same straight line. The angle of depression of two ships as observed from the top of the light house are 60° and 45°. If the height of the light house is 200 m, then find the distance between the two ships.   **[CBSE 2014]**

13. From the top of a tower of height 50 m, the angles of depression of the top and bottom of a pole are 30° and 45°, respectively. Find   **[CBSE 2015]**
(i) how far the pole is from the bottom of the tower.
(ii) the height of the pole. [take, $\sqrt{3} = 1.732$]

14. A man standing on the deck of a ship, which is 10 m above the water level. He observes that the angle of elevation of the top of a hill is 60° and the angle of depression of the base of the hill is 30°. Calculate the distance of the hill from the ship and height of the hill.   **[CBSE 2016]**

15. The angle of elevation of an aeroplane from a point on the ground is 45°. After flying for 15 s, the angle of elevation changes to 30°. If the aeroplane is flying at a constant height of 2500 m, then find the average speed of the aeroplane.   **[CBSE 2013]**

16. The shadow of a flag staff is three times as long as the shadow of the flag staff, when the Sun rays meet the ground at an angle of 60°. Find the angle between the Sun rays and the ground at the time of longer shadow.

17. An aeroplane, when flying at a height of 4000 m from the ground, passes vertically above another aeroplane at an instant when the angles of elevation of two planes from the same point on the ground are 60° and 45°, respectively. Find the vertical distance between the aeroplanes at that instant.

18. There is a small island in the middle of a 100 m wide river and a tall tree stands on the island. P and Q are points directly opposite to each other on two banks and in line with the tree. If the angles of elevation of the top of the tree from P and Q are respectively 30° and 45°, then find the height of the tree. [take, $\sqrt{3} = 1.732$]

• Long Answer Type Questions

19. An aeroplane is at an altitude of 1200 m. If two ships are sailing towards it in the same direction. The angles of depression of the ships as observed from the aeroplane are 60° and 30°, respectively. Find the distance between both ships.

20. The angles of depression of two consecutive kilometre stones on the road on right and left of an aeroplane are 60° and 45°, respectively as observed from the aeroplane. Find the height of the aeroplane.

21. The angle of elevation of the top of a tower at a distance of 120 m from a point A on the ground is 45°. If the angle of elevation of the top of a flag staff fixed at the top of the tower, at A is 60°, then find the height of the flag staff. [use, $\sqrt{3} = 1.73$]
[CBSE 2014]

22. A balloon is connected to an electric pole. It is inclined at 60° to the horizontal by a cable of length 215 m. Determine the height of the balloon from the ground. Also, find the height of the balloon, if the angle of inclination is changed from 60° to 30°.
[CBSE 2015]

23. A man in a boat rowing away from a light house 100 m high takes 2 min to change the angle of elevation of the light house from 60° to 45°. Find the speed of boat.

24. The angle of elevation of the top of a tower from certain point is 30°. If the observer moves 20 m towards the tower, the angle of elevation of the top increases by 15°. Find the height of the tower.

25. The shadow of a tower standing on a level plane is found to be 50 m longer when Sun's elevation is 30° than when it is 60°. Find the height of the tower.

26. A vertical tower stands on a horizontal plane and is surmounted by a vertical flag staff of height h. At a point on the plane, the angles of elevation of the bottom and the top of the flag staff are α and β respectively. Prove that the height of the tower is

$$\left(\frac{h\,\tan\alpha}{\tan\beta-\tan\alpha}\right).$$

27. The angle of elevation of the top of a tower 30 m high from the foot of another tower in the same plane is 60° and the angle of elevation of the top of the second tower from the foot of the first tower is 30°. Find the distance between the two towers and also the height of the tower.

28. From the top of a tower h m high, angles of depression of two objects, which are in line with the foot of the tower are α and β $(\beta>\alpha)$. Find the distance between the two objects.

29. A ladder against a vertical wall at an inclination α to the horizontal. Its foot is pulled away from the wall through a distance p, so that its upper end slides a distance q down the wall and then the ladder makes an angle β with the horizontal. Show that

$$\frac{p}{q}=\frac{\cos\beta-\cos\alpha}{\sin\alpha-\sin\beta}.$$

30. The angle of elevation of the top of a vertical tower from a point on the ground is 60°. From another point 10 m vertically above the first, its angle of elevation is 45°. Find the height of the tower.

31. A window of a house is h m above the ground. From the window, the angles of elevation and depression of the top and the bottom of another house situated on the opposite side of the lane are found to be α and β, respectively. Prove that the height of the other house is $h(1+\tan\alpha\cot\beta)$ m.

32. The lower window of a house is at a height of 2 m above the ground and its upper window is 4 m vertically above the lower window. At any instant the angles of elevation of a balloon from these windows are observed to be 60° and 30°, respectively. Find the height of the balloon above the ground.

• Case Based Questions

33. A girl 8 m tall spots a parrot sitting on the top of a building of height 58 m from the ground. The angle of elevation of the parrot from the eyes of girl at any instant is 60°. The parrot flies away horizontally in such a way that it remained at a constant height from the ground. After 8 s, the angle of elevation of the parrot from the same point is 30°.

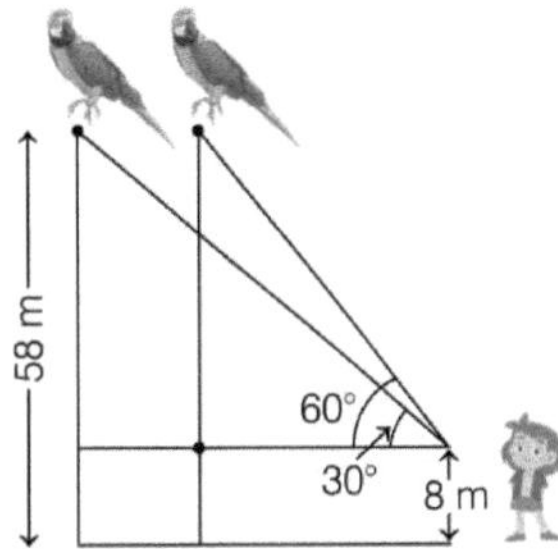

Based on the above information, answer the following questions. (Take $\sqrt{3}=1.73$)

(i) Find the distance of first position of the parrot from the eyes of the girl.

(ii) If the distance between the position of parrot increases, then the angle of elevation decreases. Justify with girl.

(iii) Find the distance between the girl and the building.

(iv) How much distance covers parrot covers?

(v) Find the speed of the parrot in 8s.

SOLUTIONS

Objective Questions

1. (b) Let the angle of elevation of the Sun is θ.

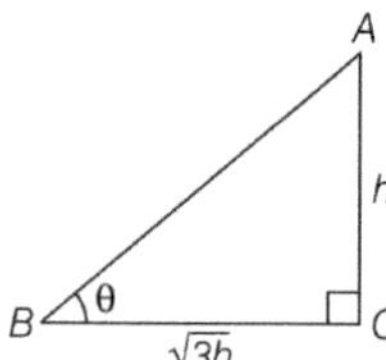

Given, height of pole $= h$

Now, in $\triangle ABC$, $\tan\theta = \dfrac{AC}{BC} = \dfrac{h}{\sqrt{3}h}$

$\Rightarrow \qquad \tan\theta = \dfrac{1}{\sqrt{3}} = \tan 30°$

$\Rightarrow \qquad \theta = 30°$

Hence, the angle of elevation of the Sun is $30°$.

2. (a) Let $BC = 6$ m be the height of the pole and $AB = 2\sqrt{3}$ m be the length of the shadow on the ground.

Let the Sun makes an angle θ on the ground.

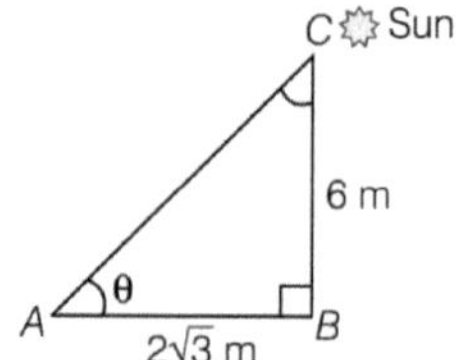

Now, in $\triangle BAC$, $\tan\theta = \dfrac{BC}{AB}$

$\Rightarrow \qquad \tan\theta = \dfrac{6}{2\sqrt{3}} = \dfrac{3}{\sqrt{3}} \cdot \dfrac{\sqrt{3}}{\sqrt{3}}$ [by rationalising]

$\Rightarrow \qquad \tan\theta = \dfrac{3\sqrt{3}}{3} = \sqrt{3} = \tan 60°$ $[\because \tan 60° = \sqrt{3}]$

$\therefore \qquad \theta = 60°$

Hence, the Sun's elevation is $60°$.

3. (d) Let AB be the tower whose height is $300\sqrt{3}$ m,

i.e. $AB = 300\sqrt{3}$ m. Again, let C be the point at a distance of 300 m from the foot of the tower, i.e. $AC = 300$ m.

Here, the angle of elevation is unknown, so let it be θ.

Since, here base and perpendicular are given.

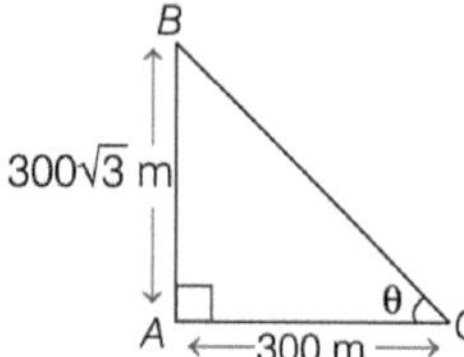

So, in right angled $\triangle BAC$,

$\tan\theta = \dfrac{\text{Perpendicular}}{\text{Base}} = \dfrac{AB}{AC} = \dfrac{300\sqrt{3}}{300}$

$\Rightarrow \qquad \tan\theta = \sqrt{3} = \tan 60°$

$\therefore \qquad \theta = 60°$

Hence, the required angle of elevation is $60°$.

4. (b) Let the distance of the foot of tower from the point be $QR = x$ m.

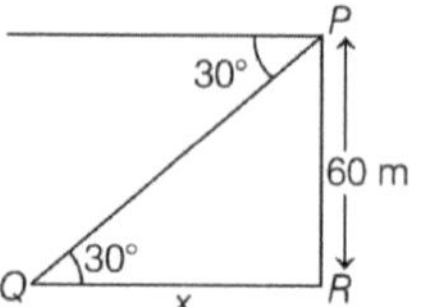

and height $PR = 60$ m and $\angle PQR = 30°$

In $\triangle PRQ$, $\tan 30° = \dfrac{PR}{QR} = \dfrac{60}{x}$

$\Rightarrow \qquad \dfrac{1}{\sqrt{3}} = \dfrac{60}{x} \Rightarrow x = 60\sqrt{3}$ m

5. (a) In right angled $\triangle ABC$, $\angle B = 90°$

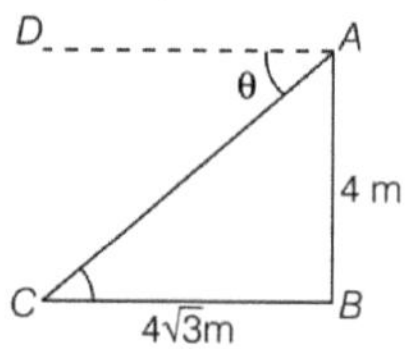

Let $\qquad \angle DAC = \theta$

Then, $\quad \angle ACB = \angle DAC = \theta$ [alternate angles]

Now, $\quad \tan\theta = \dfrac{\text{Perpendicular}}{\text{Base}} = \dfrac{AB}{BC} = \dfrac{4}{4\sqrt{3}} = \dfrac{1}{\sqrt{3}} = \tan 30°$

$\therefore$ The angle of depression from A is $30°$.

6. (b) Let AB be the vertical pole and CA be the 20 m long rope such that its one end A is tied from the top of the vertical pole AB and the other end C is tied to a point C on the ground.

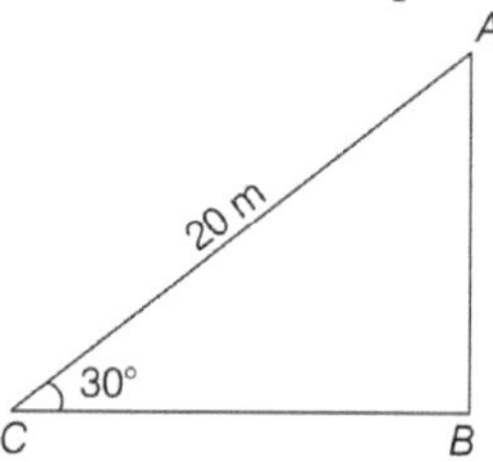

In $\triangle ABC$, we have

$\sin 30° = \dfrac{AB}{AC}$

$\Rightarrow \qquad \dfrac{1}{2} = \dfrac{AB}{20}$

$\Rightarrow \qquad AB = 10$ m

Hence, the height of the pole is 10 m.

7. (d) Let the length of ladder $AB = h$ m.

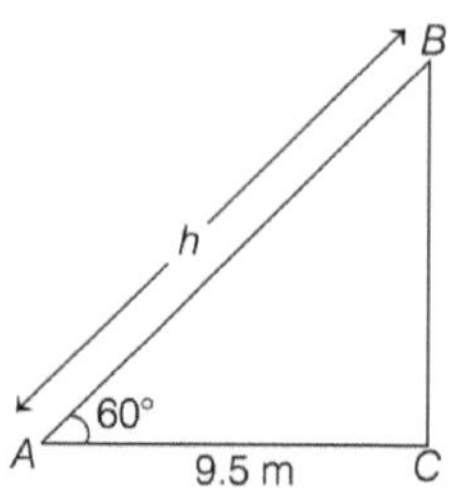

Here, $AC = 9.5$ m, $\angle BAC = 60°$

In $\triangle ABC$, $\cos 60° = \dfrac{AC}{AB} \Rightarrow \dfrac{1}{2} = \dfrac{9.5}{h}$

$\Rightarrow \qquad h = 2 \times 9.5 = 19$ m

Hence, length of ladder is 19 m.

8. (a) Let XZ be the length and YZ be the height of the ramp.

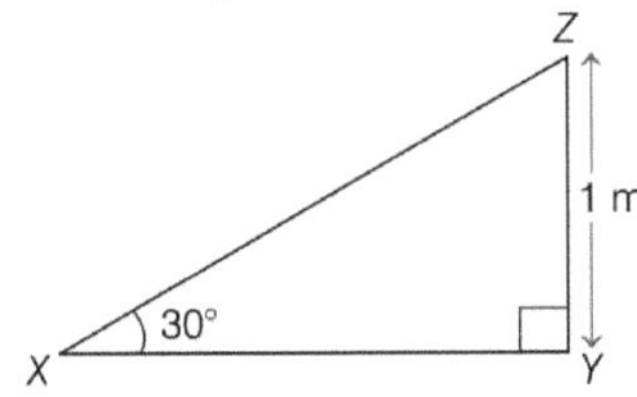

Then, $\angle ZXY = 30°$ and $YZ = 1$ m

In right angled $\triangle XYZ$,

$$\sin 30° = \dfrac{\text{Perpendicular}}{\text{Hypotenuse}} = \dfrac{YZ}{XZ}$$

$\Rightarrow \qquad \dfrac{1}{2} = \dfrac{1}{XZ} \Rightarrow XZ = 2$ m

Hence, the length of ramp is 2 m.

9. (b) Let C be the position of the kite and AC be the length of the string which makes an angle of $60°$ with the ground. The height of the kite from the ground is $BC = 80$ m.

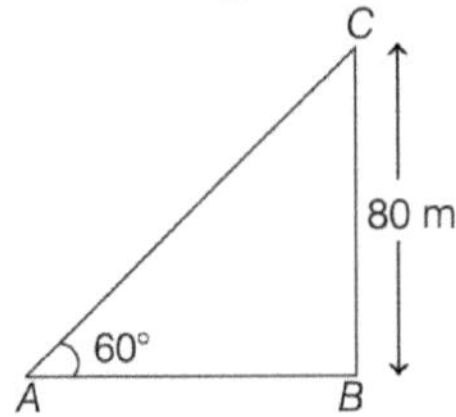

In right angled $\triangle ABC$,

$$\sin 60° = \dfrac{\text{Perpendicular}}{\text{Hypotenuse}} = \dfrac{BC}{AC}$$

$\Rightarrow \qquad \dfrac{\sqrt{3}}{2} = \dfrac{80}{AC}$

$\Rightarrow \qquad AC = \dfrac{80 \times 2}{\sqrt{3}} \times \dfrac{\sqrt{3}}{\sqrt{3}} \qquad$ [by rationalising]

$$= \dfrac{160\sqrt{3}}{3} = \dfrac{160 \times 1.732}{3} = 92.37 \text{ m}$$

Hence, the length of the string is 92.37 m.

10. (a) Given, length of the string of the kite,

$$AB = 85 \text{ m}$$

and $\qquad \tan\theta = \dfrac{15}{8}$

$\Rightarrow \qquad \cot\theta = \dfrac{8}{15}$

$\because \qquad \operatorname{cosec}^2\theta - 1 = \cot^2\theta$

$\therefore \qquad \operatorname{cosec}^2\theta - 1 = \dfrac{64}{225}$

$\Rightarrow \qquad \operatorname{cosec}^2\theta = 1 + \dfrac{64}{225} = \dfrac{289}{225}$

$\Rightarrow \qquad \operatorname{cosec}\theta = \sqrt{\dfrac{289}{225}} = \dfrac{17}{15}$

$\Rightarrow \qquad \sin\theta = \dfrac{15}{17}$

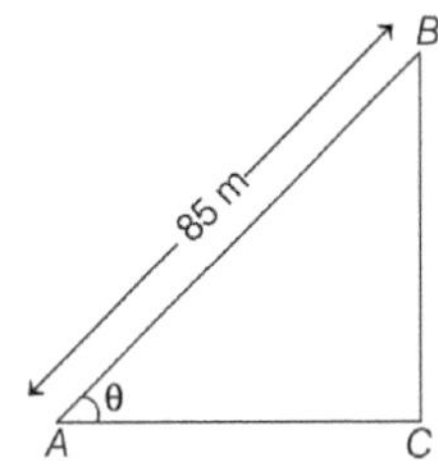

In $\triangle ABC$, $\qquad \sin\theta = \dfrac{BC}{AB}$

$\Rightarrow \qquad \dfrac{15}{17} = \dfrac{BC}{85}$

$\Rightarrow \qquad BC = 75$ m

Hence, height of kite is 75 m

11. (b) Let $BC = h$ m be the height of the tower and A be the point on the ground such that, $\angle BAC = \theta$.

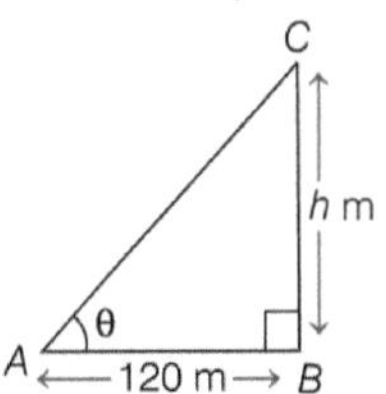

Then, $\qquad AB = 120$ m

In right angled $\triangle ABC$,

$$\tan\theta = \dfrac{\text{Perpendicular}}{\text{Base}} = \dfrac{BC}{AB} = \dfrac{h}{120}$$

$\Rightarrow \qquad \dfrac{5}{12} = \dfrac{h}{120} \qquad \left[\because \tan\theta = \dfrac{5}{12}, \text{ given}\right]$

$\Rightarrow \qquad h = 50$ m

Hence, height of the tower is 50 m.

12. (a) Here, $CD = 20$ m $\qquad$ [height of big pole]

$\qquad\qquad AB = 14$ m $\qquad$ [height of small pole]

$\therefore \qquad\qquad DE = CD - CE$

$\Rightarrow \qquad\qquad DE = CD - AB \qquad [\because AB = CE]$

$\Rightarrow \qquad\qquad DE = 20 - 14 = 6$ m

In $\triangle BDE$, $\qquad \sin 30° = \dfrac{DE}{BD}$

$\Rightarrow \qquad \dfrac{1}{2} = \dfrac{6}{BD} \Rightarrow BD = 12$ m

$\therefore$ Length of wire $= 12$ m

13. (b) Let $BE = 22$ m be the height of the tower and $AD = 1.5$ m be the height of the observer. The point D be the observer's eye. Draw $DC \parallel AB$.

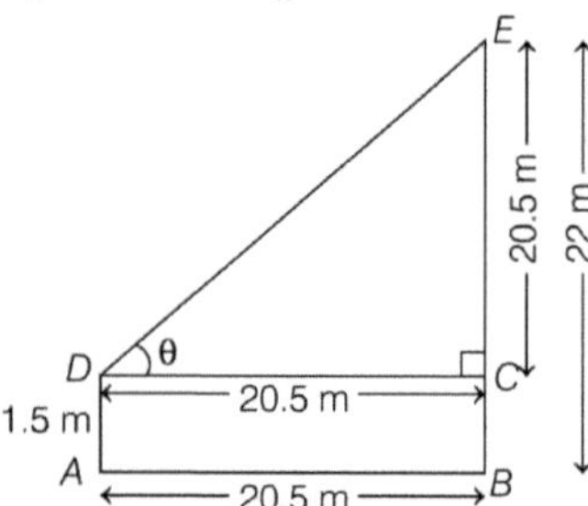

Then, $AB = 20.5$ m $= DC$

and $EC = BE - BC = BE - AD$

$$= 22 - 1.5 = 20.5 \text{ m} \qquad [\because BC = AD]$$

Let θ be the angle of elevation made by observer's eye with the top of the tower i.e. $\angle EDC = \theta$.

In right angled ΔDCE,

$$\tan\theta = \frac{\text{Perpendicular}}{\text{Base}} = \frac{CE}{DC} = \frac{20.5}{20.5}$$

$\Rightarrow$ $\tan\theta = 1$

$\Rightarrow$ $\tan\theta = \tan 45°$

$\Rightarrow$ $\theta = 45°$

14. (c) In the figure, let AB be a tower which has height h m. The angle of elevation from point C at a distance of 40 m from point B is $\angle ACB = 45°$ and $BC = 40$ m.

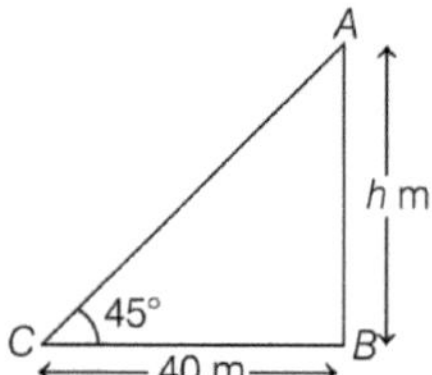

Then, in right angled ΔABC,

$$\tan 45° = \frac{\text{Perpendicular}}{\text{Base}} = \frac{AB}{BC}$$

$\Rightarrow$ $\tan 45° = \dfrac{h}{40} \Rightarrow 1 = \dfrac{h}{40}$ $[\because \tan 45° = 1]$

$\therefore$ $h = 40$ m

Hence, the height of tower is 40 m.

15. (d) Let $AB = 150$ m be the height of building and C be a point on the ground such that $\angle ACB = 45°$.

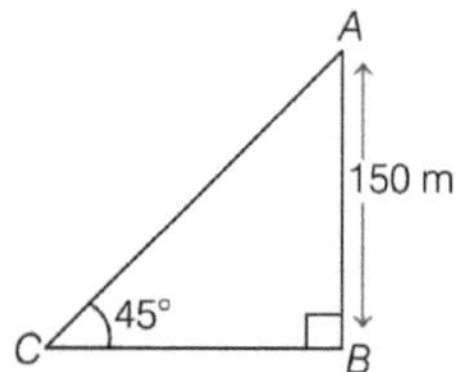

In right angled ΔABC,

$$\tan 45° = \frac{\text{Perpendicular}}{\text{Base}} = \frac{AB}{BC}$$

$\Rightarrow$ $1 = \dfrac{150}{BC} \Rightarrow BC = 150$ m

Hence, the distance of the point from foot of the building is 150 m.

16. (c) Let $AB = 150$ m be the height of the tower and angle of depression is $\angle DAC = 30°$.

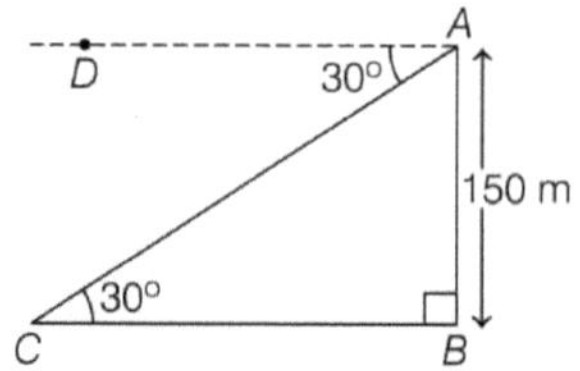

Then, $\angle ACB = \angle DAC = 30°$ [alternate angles]

Now, in right angled ΔABC,

$$\tan 30° = \frac{\text{Perpendicular}}{\text{Base}} = \frac{AB}{BC}$$

$\Rightarrow$ $\dfrac{1}{\sqrt{3}} = \dfrac{150}{BC}$

$\Rightarrow$ $BC = 150\sqrt{3}$ m

Hence, the distance of the car from the tower is $150\sqrt{3}$ m.

17. (a) Let the height of the building be, $BC = 20$ m

and height of the tower be $CD = x$ m

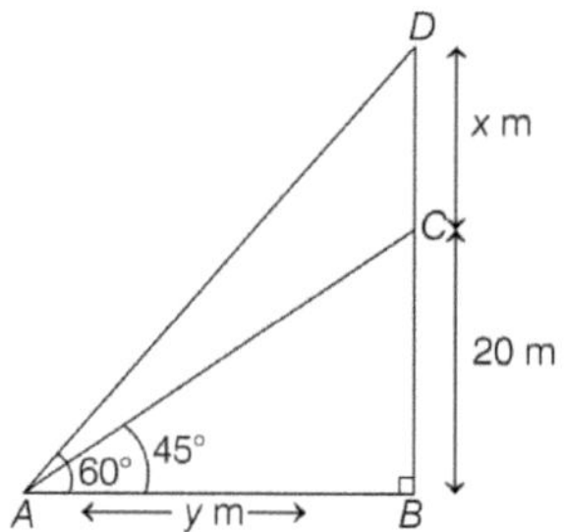

Let the point A be at a distance y m from the foot of the building.

Now, in ΔABC,

$$\frac{BC}{AB} = \tan 45° = 1$$

$\Rightarrow$ $\dfrac{20}{y} = 1$

$\Rightarrow$ $y = 20$ m

i.e. $AB = 20$ m

Now, in ΔABD, $\dfrac{BD}{AB} = \tan 60° = \sqrt{3}$

$\Rightarrow$ $\dfrac{BD}{AB} = \sqrt{3}$

$\Rightarrow$ $\dfrac{20 + x}{20} = \sqrt{3}$

$\Rightarrow$ $20 + x = 20\sqrt{3}$

$\Rightarrow$ $x = 20\sqrt{3} - 20$

$$= 20(\sqrt{3} - 1)$$

$$= 20(1.732 - 1)$$

$\Rightarrow$ $x = 20 \times 0.732 = 14.64$ m

18. (d) Let BC be the width of the river and A, B be the ends of river such that $AB = 150$ m = Length of the bridge　　[given] and $\angle BAC = 45°$.

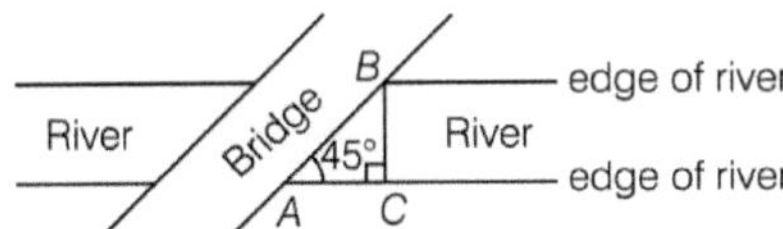

In right angled $\triangle ACB$,

$$\sin 45° = \frac{\text{Perpendicular}}{\text{Hypotenuse}}$$

$\Rightarrow \qquad \dfrac{1}{\sqrt{2}} = \dfrac{BC}{AB} = \dfrac{BC}{150} \qquad \left[\because \sin 45° = \dfrac{1}{\sqrt{2}}\right]$

$\therefore \qquad BC = \dfrac{150}{\sqrt{2}} \times \dfrac{\sqrt{2}}{\sqrt{2}} \qquad$ [by rationalising]

$\qquad\qquad = \dfrac{150}{2}\sqrt{2} = 75\sqrt{2}$

$\qquad\qquad = 75 \times 1.414 \qquad [\because \sqrt{2} = 1.414]$

$\qquad\qquad = 106.05$ m (approx.)

Hence, width of the river is 106.05 m.

19. (i) (b) Radha is more closer to the Parachute because the angles of elevation of Parachute from these balcony are observed to be $45°$. So, Radha is more closer to the Parachute than Ankit.

(ii) (d) In $\triangle DEF$, $\angle D = 90°$, $\angle DFE = 45°$, $\tan 45° = \dfrac{DE}{DF}$

$\Rightarrow \qquad 1 = \dfrac{DE}{DF}$

$\Rightarrow \qquad DE = DF = h$ m

(iii) (b) In $\triangle EGC$, $\angle EGC = 60°$, $\angle C = 90°$

$\tan 60° = \dfrac{CE}{CG}$

$\sqrt{3} = \dfrac{CD + DE}{CG} \Rightarrow \sqrt{3} = \dfrac{h + 6}{DF} \quad [\because CG = DF]$

$\Rightarrow \qquad \sqrt{3} = \dfrac{h + 6}{h}$

$\Rightarrow \qquad \sqrt{3} = 1 + \dfrac{6}{h} \Rightarrow (\sqrt{3} - 1) = \dfrac{6}{h}$

$\therefore \qquad h = \dfrac{6}{(\sqrt{3} - 1)} \times \dfrac{\sqrt{3} + 1}{\sqrt{3} + 1} \qquad$ [by rationalising]

$\qquad\qquad = \dfrac{6(\sqrt{3} + 1)}{(\sqrt{3})^2 - (1)^2} \quad [\because (a + b)(a - b) = a^2 - b^2]$

$\qquad\qquad = \dfrac{6(\sqrt{3} + 1)}{3 - 1} = \dfrac{6(\sqrt{3} + 1)}{2} = 3(\sqrt{3} + 1)$ m

(iv) (d) Height of the Parachute from the ground is BE, then

$\qquad BE = BC + CD + DE$

$\qquad BE = 3 + 6 + 3(\sqrt{3} + 1)$

$\qquad\qquad = 9 + 3(\sqrt{3} + 1)$

$\qquad\qquad = 9 + 3\sqrt{3} + 3$

$\qquad\qquad = 12 + 3\sqrt{3}$

$\qquad\qquad = 3(4 + \sqrt{3})$ m

(v) (c) If the Parachute is moving towards the building, then both angles of elevation will decreases.

20. (i) (b) Let in $\triangle ABC$, AC will be rope and AB be a vertical pole.

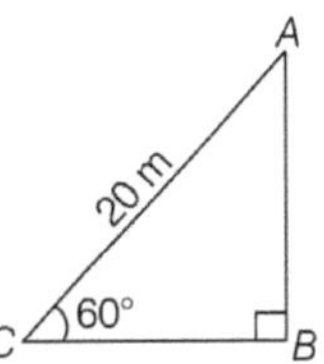

Then, $AC = 20$ m, $\angle C = 60°$, $\angle B = 90°$

In $\triangle ABC$, $\qquad \sin 60° = \dfrac{AB}{AC}$

$\qquad\qquad \dfrac{\sqrt{3}}{2} = \dfrac{AB}{20}$

$\qquad\qquad AB = 10\sqrt{3}$ m

(ii) (c) $\cos 60° = \dfrac{BC}{AC} \Rightarrow \dfrac{1}{2} = \dfrac{BC}{20}$

$\qquad\qquad BC = 10$ m

(iii) (d) $\sin 45° = \dfrac{AB}{AC} \qquad [\angle C = 45°]$

$\qquad \dfrac{1}{\sqrt{2}} = \dfrac{AB}{20} \Rightarrow \dfrac{20}{\sqrt{2}} = AB$

$\Rightarrow \qquad AB = \dfrac{20}{\sqrt{2}} \times \dfrac{\sqrt{2}}{\sqrt{2}} \qquad$ [by rationalising]

$\qquad\qquad = 10\sqrt{2}$ m

(iv) (a) Length of rope = $20 - 3 = 17$ m

$\qquad \sin 45° = \dfrac{AB}{AC} \qquad [\angle C = 45°]$

$\qquad \dfrac{1}{\sqrt{2}} = \dfrac{AB}{17} \Leftrightarrow AB = \dfrac{17}{\sqrt{2}}$ m

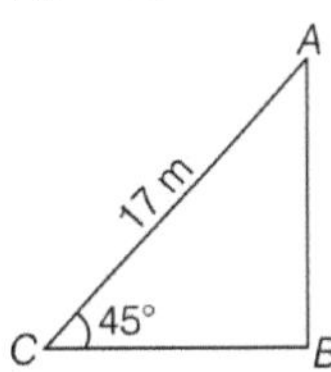

(v) (c) in this, mathematical concept trigonometric ratio is used here, which is application of trigonometry.

21. (i) (b) Let AB be the monument of height 42 m and C is the point where they are standing, such that $BC = 42$ m.

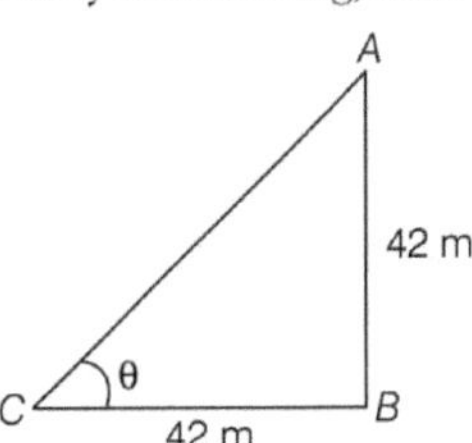

Now, in $\triangle ABC$,

$\qquad\qquad \tan\theta = \dfrac{AB}{BC}$

$\Rightarrow \qquad \tan\theta = \dfrac{42}{42} = 1$

$\Rightarrow \qquad \tan\theta = 1 \quad \Rightarrow \quad \theta = 45°$

(ii) (d) In $\triangle ABC$,

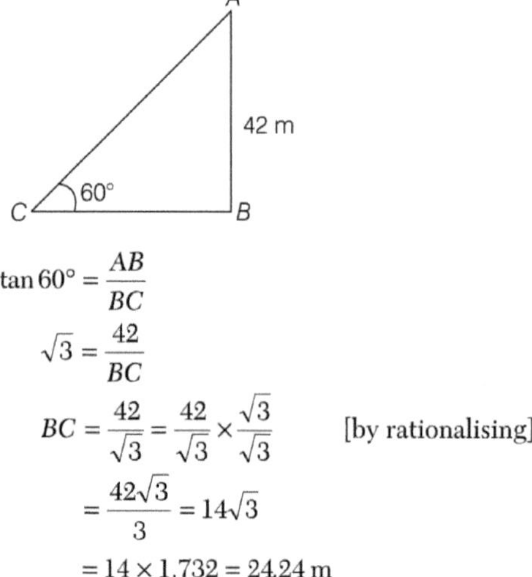

$$\tan 60^\circ = \frac{AB}{BC}$$

$$\sqrt{3} = \frac{42}{BC}$$

$$BC = \frac{42}{\sqrt{3}} = \frac{42}{\sqrt{3}} \times \frac{\sqrt{3}}{\sqrt{3}} \qquad \text{[by rationalising]}$$

$$= \frac{42\sqrt{3}}{3} = 14\sqrt{3}$$

$$= 14 \times 1.732 = 24.24 \text{ m}$$

(iii) (a) Let $AB = h$ be the height of the tower.

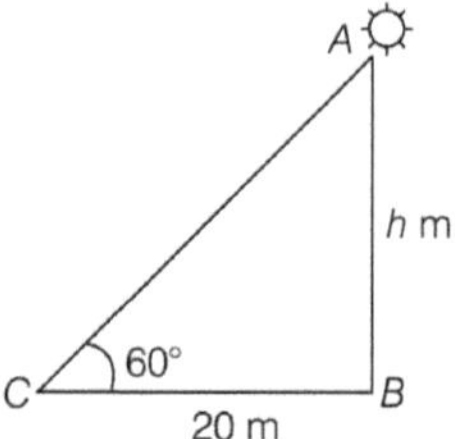

Now, in $\triangle ABC$, $\tan 60^\circ = \dfrac{AB}{BC} \Rightarrow \sqrt{3} = \dfrac{h}{20} \Rightarrow h = 20\sqrt{3}$ m

(iv) (b) Let h and x be the height and length of shadow of the vertical tower.

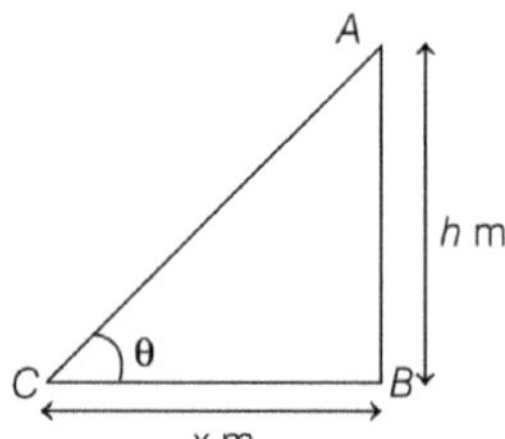

Now, in $\triangle ABC$,

$$\tan\theta = \frac{AB}{BC} \Rightarrow \tan\theta = \frac{h}{x}$$

$$\Rightarrow \qquad \tan\theta = 1 \qquad [\because h : x = 1 : 1]$$

$$\Rightarrow \qquad \theta = 45^\circ$$

(v) (c) The angle of depression of the object viewed, is the angle formed by the line of sight with the horizontal, when it is below the horizontal level.

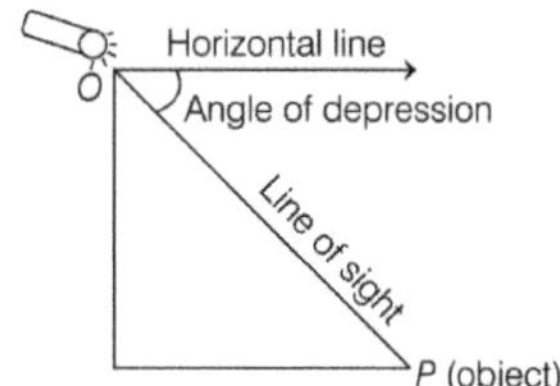

22. As it is given that satellite is the mid-point of the two mountain hills i.e. I is the mid-point of DS.

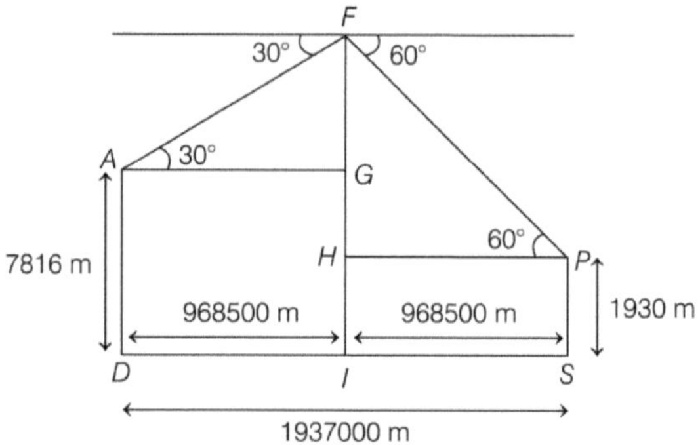

(i) (b) We have, $AG = DI = 968500$ m

Now, in $\triangle FAG$,

$$\cos 30^\circ = \frac{AG}{AF}$$

$$\Rightarrow \qquad \frac{\sqrt{3}}{2} = \frac{968500}{AF}$$

$$\Rightarrow \qquad AF = \frac{968500 \times 2}{\sqrt{3}} = \frac{1937000}{1.73}$$

$$= 1119653.18 \text{ m}$$

$$= 1119.65 \text{ km}$$

(ii) (c) We have, $HP = IS = 968500$ m

Now, in $\triangle FHP$,

$$\cos 60^\circ = \frac{HP}{FP}$$

$$\frac{1}{2} = \frac{968500}{FP}$$

$$FP = 968500 \times 2 = 1937000 \text{ m} = 1937 \text{ km}$$

(iii) (b) In $\triangle FAG$, $\tan 30^\circ = \dfrac{FG}{AG} \Rightarrow \dfrac{1}{\sqrt{3}} = \dfrac{FG}{968500}$

$$\Rightarrow \qquad FG = \frac{968500}{\sqrt{3}} = 559826.59 \text{ m}$$

$$= 559.82 \text{ km}$$

$\therefore$ Height of satellite from ground $= FI = FG + GI$

$$= 559.82 + 7.816$$

$$[\because GI = AD = 7816 \text{ m} = 7.816 \text{ km}]$$

$$= 567.64 \text{ km}$$

(iv) (b) Let E be the position of man.

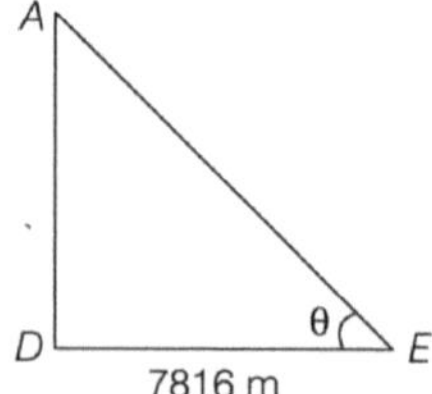

Then, $DE = 7816$ m

In $\triangle ADE$, $\tan\theta = \dfrac{AD}{DE} = \dfrac{7816}{7816} = 1$

$$[\because \text{ height of mountain } AD = 7816 \text{ m}]$$

$$\therefore \qquad \theta = 45^\circ$$

(v) (c) Let T be the point where mile stone is kept.

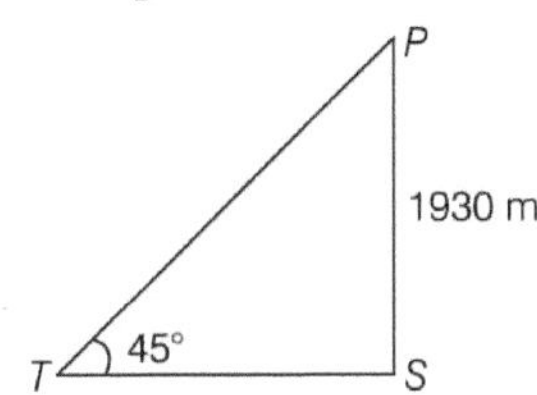

So, In ΔPST, $\tan 45° = \dfrac{PS}{TS}$

$\Rightarrow \qquad 1 = \dfrac{1930}{TS} \Rightarrow TS = 1930$ m

Subjective Questions

1. *Case* I Let the height of a tower be h and the distance of the point of observation from its foot be x.

In ΔABC,

$$\tan \theta_1 = \dfrac{AC}{BC} = \dfrac{h}{x}$$

$$\Rightarrow \qquad \theta_1 = \tan^{-1}\left(\dfrac{h}{x}\right) \qquad \text{...(i)}$$

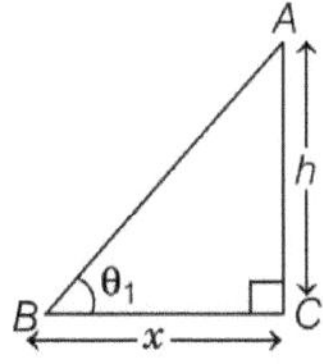

Case II Now, the height of the tower increased by 10%

$$= h + 10\% \text{ of } h = h + h \times \dfrac{10}{100} = \dfrac{11 h}{10}$$

and the distance of the point of observation from its foot

$$= x + 10\% \text{ of } x$$

$$= x + x \times \dfrac{10}{100} = \dfrac{11x}{10}$$

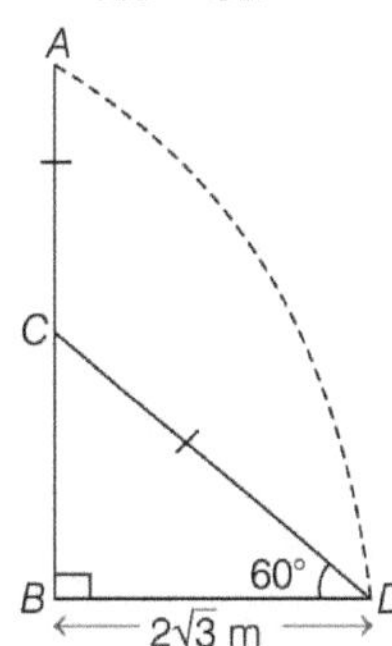

In ΔPQR, $\tan \theta_2 = \dfrac{PR}{QR} = \dfrac{\left(\dfrac{11h}{10}\right)}{\left(\dfrac{11x}{10}\right)}$

$$\Rightarrow \qquad \tan \theta_2 = \dfrac{h}{x}$$

$$\Rightarrow \qquad \theta_2 = \tan^{-1}\left(\dfrac{h}{x}\right) \qquad \text{...(ii)}$$

From Eqs. (i) and (ii),

$$\theta_1 = \theta_2$$

Hence, the required angle of elevation of its top remains unchanged.

2. Let AB be the tree whose part AC breaks and touches the ground at D.

Then, $\qquad BD = 2\sqrt{3}$ m $\qquad$ [given]

and $\qquad AC = CD$

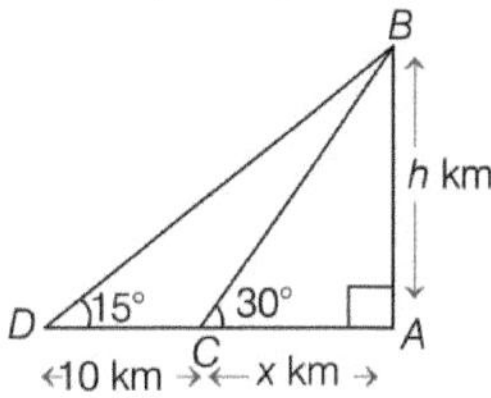

In right angled ΔCBD,

$$\cos 60° = \dfrac{BD}{CD}$$

$$\Rightarrow \qquad \dfrac{1}{2} = \dfrac{2\sqrt{3}}{CD} \qquad \left[\because \cos 60° = \dfrac{1}{2} \text{ and } BD = 2\sqrt{3} \text{ m}\right]$$

$$\Rightarrow CD = 2 \times 2\sqrt{3} = 4\sqrt{3}$$

$$= 4 \times 1.732 = 6.928 \text{ m} \qquad [\because \sqrt{3} = 1.732]$$

$$\therefore \qquad AC = CD = 6.928 \text{ m}$$

Again, in right angled ΔCBD,

$$\tan 60° = \dfrac{BC}{BD}$$

$$\Rightarrow \qquad \sqrt{3} = \dfrac{BC}{2\sqrt{3}} \qquad [\because \tan 60° = \sqrt{3} \text{ and } BD = 2\sqrt{3} \text{ m}]$$

$$\Rightarrow \qquad BC = \sqrt{3} \times 2\sqrt{3} = 6 \text{ m}$$

Now, $\qquad AB = AC + BC$

$$= 6.928 + 6 = 12.928 \text{ m (approx.)}$$

Hence, whole height of the tree is 12.928 m.

3. Let $AB = h$ km be the height of the mountain. Let C be a point at a distance of x km from the base of the mountain such that $\angle ACB = 30°$ and let D be a point at a distance of 10 km from C along the same line. Then, $\angle ADB = 15°$ and $AD = AC + DC = (x + 10)$ km

In right angled ΔBAC,

$$\tan 30° = \dfrac{AB}{AC}$$

$$\Rightarrow \qquad \dfrac{1}{\sqrt{3}} = \dfrac{h}{x} \qquad \left[\because \tan 30° = \dfrac{1}{\sqrt{3}}\right]$$

$$\Rightarrow \qquad x = h\sqrt{3} \qquad \text{...(i)}$$

In right angled ΔBAD,

$$\tan 15° = \dfrac{AB}{AD}$$

$\Rightarrow \qquad 0.27 = \dfrac{h}{x + 10} \qquad$ [given, $\tan 15° = 0.27$]

$\Rightarrow \qquad 0.27(x + 10) = h \qquad$ ...(ii)

On putting $x = \sqrt{3}h$ from Eq. (i) in Eq. (ii), we get

$\qquad 0.27(\sqrt{3}h + 10) = h$

$\Rightarrow \quad 0.27 \times \sqrt{3}h + 0.27 \times 10 = h$

$\Rightarrow \qquad h(1 - 0.27 \times \sqrt{3}) = 0.27 \times 10$

$\Rightarrow \qquad h(1 - 0.27 \times 1.732) = 2.7 \qquad$ [$\because \sqrt{3} = 1.732$]

$\Rightarrow \qquad h(1 - 0.47) = 2.7$

$\Rightarrow \qquad 0.53h = 2.7$

$\Rightarrow \qquad h = \dfrac{2.7}{0.53} = 5.09 \approx 5 \ \text{km}$

Hence, the height of mountain is 5 km.

4. Let AB be the tower and AC be the flag staff on the tower. Let D be a point on the ground such that the angles of elevation of foot A and top C of the flag staff are $45°$ and $60°$, respectively.

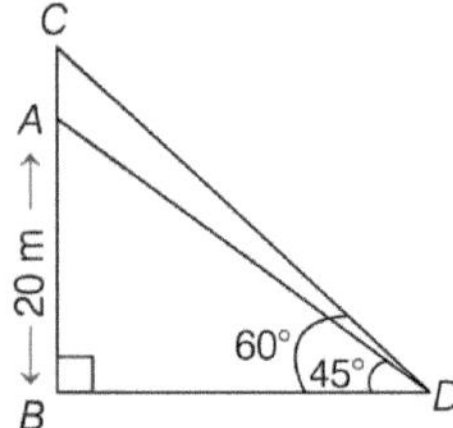

Then, we have $AB = 20$ m, $\angle ADB = 45°$ and $\angle CDB = 60°$

In right angled $\triangle ABD$,

$\qquad \tan 45° = \dfrac{AB}{BD} \qquad \left[\because \tan\theta = \dfrac{\text{Perpendicular}}{\text{Base}}\right]$

$\Rightarrow \qquad 1 = \dfrac{20}{BD}$

$\Rightarrow \qquad BD = 20 \ \text{m} \qquad$ [$\because \tan 45° = 1$]

and in right angled $\triangle CBD$,

$\qquad \tan 60° = \dfrac{BC}{BD} \Rightarrow \sqrt{3} = \dfrac{BC}{20} \qquad$ [$\because \tan 60° = \sqrt{3}$]

$\Rightarrow \qquad BC = 20\sqrt{3} = 20 \times 1.732 \qquad$ [$\because \sqrt{3} = 1.732$]

$\qquad = 34.64 \ \text{m (approx.)}$

Now, $\qquad AC = BC - AB = 34.64 - 20$

$\qquad = 14.64 \ \text{m (approx.)}$

Hence, the height of the flag staff is 14.64 m.

5. To understand the fact of this question, consider the following example

I. A tower $2\sqrt{3}$ m high casts a shadow 2 m long on the ground, when the Sun's elevation is $60°$.

In $\triangle ACB$, $\qquad \tan\theta = \dfrac{BC}{AB} = \dfrac{2\sqrt{3}}{2}$

$\Rightarrow \qquad \tan\theta = \sqrt{3} = \tan 60°$

$\therefore \qquad \theta = 60°$

II. A same hight of tower casts a shadow 4m long from preceding shadow, when the Sun's elevation is $30°$.

In $\triangle APB$, $\qquad \tan\theta = \dfrac{AB}{PB}$

$\qquad = \dfrac{AB}{PC + CB}$

$\Rightarrow \qquad \tan\theta = \dfrac{2\sqrt{3}}{4 + 2} = \dfrac{2\sqrt{3}}{6}$

$\Rightarrow \qquad \tan\theta = \dfrac{\sqrt{3}}{3} \cdot \dfrac{\sqrt{3}}{\sqrt{3}} = \dfrac{3}{3\sqrt{3}}$

$\Rightarrow \qquad \tan\theta = \dfrac{1}{\sqrt{3}} = \tan 30°$

$\therefore \qquad \theta = 30°$

Hence, we conclude from above two examples that if the length of the shadow of a tower is increasing, then the angle of elevation of the Sun is decreasing.

6. Let QS be the building and R be the position of window.

Given, height of the window, $QR = 10$ m

$\qquad \angle QPR = \angle XRP = 30° \qquad$ [alternate angles]

and $\qquad \angle SPQ = 60°$

In right angled $\triangle PQR$,

$\qquad \tan 30° = \dfrac{QR}{PQ}$

$\Rightarrow \qquad \dfrac{1}{\sqrt{3}} = \dfrac{10}{PQ} \qquad \left[\because \tan 30° = \dfrac{1}{\sqrt{3}}\right]$

$\Rightarrow \qquad PQ = 10\sqrt{3} \ \text{m} \qquad$ ...(i)

In right angled $\triangle PQS$,

$\qquad \tan 60° = \dfrac{QS}{PQ}$

$\Rightarrow \qquad \sqrt{3} = \dfrac{QS}{10\sqrt{3}} \quad$ [$\because \tan 60° = \sqrt{3}$ and from Eq. (i)]

$\Rightarrow \qquad QS = 10 \times 3 = 30 \ \text{m}$

Hence, height of the building is 30 m.

7. Let $AB = 20$ m be the height of tower and let the ball lying on the ground at point C.

Given, angle of depression,

$$\angle TAC = 60° = \angle ACB \qquad \text{[alternate angles]}$$

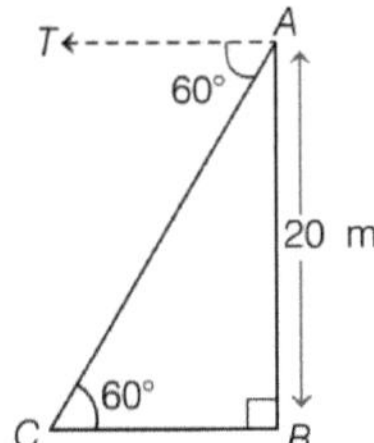

In right angled $\triangle ABC$,

$$\tan 60° = \frac{AB}{BC}$$

$$\Rightarrow \qquad \sqrt{3} = \frac{20}{BC}$$

$$\Rightarrow \qquad BC = \frac{20}{\sqrt{3}} = \frac{20}{1.732} = 11.55 \text{ m}$$

Hence, the distance between the foot of the tower and the ball is 11.55 m.

8. Let AB be the tower of height x m, and CD be the tower of height y m.

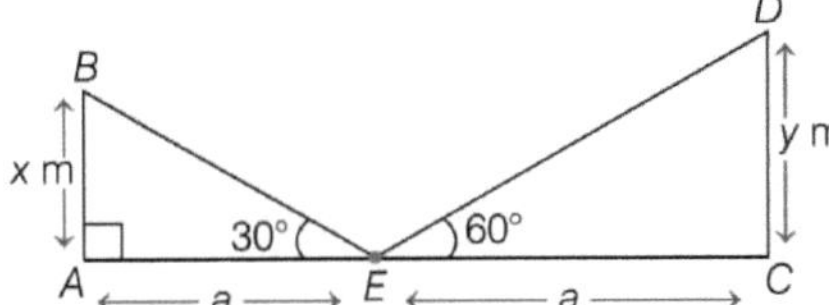

Let E be the mid-point of the line AC. Then, $\angle AEB = 30°$ and $\angle CED = 60°$.

Also, $\quad AE = EC = a$ m (let)

In right angled $\triangle BAE$,

$$\tan 30° = \frac{AB}{AE} = \frac{x}{a}$$

$$\Rightarrow \qquad \frac{1}{\sqrt{3}} = \frac{x}{a} \Rightarrow x = \frac{a}{\sqrt{3}} \qquad \ldots(i)$$

and in right angled $\triangle DCE$,

$$\tan 60° = \frac{DC}{CE} = \frac{y}{a}$$

$$\Rightarrow \qquad \sqrt{3} = \frac{y}{a} \Rightarrow y = \sqrt{3}a \qquad \ldots(ii)$$

$$[\because \text{Eq. (i) divide by Eq. (ii)}]$$

$$\therefore \qquad \frac{x}{y} = \frac{\frac{a}{\sqrt{3}}}{\sqrt{3}a} = \frac{1}{\sqrt{3}\times\sqrt{3}} = \frac{1}{3}$$

Hence, $x : y = 1 : 3$

9. From figure, we observe that, a man standing on a platform at point P, 3 m above the surface of a lake observes a cloud at point C. Let the height of the cloud from the surface of the platform is h and angle of elevation of the cloud is θ_1.

Now at same point P, a man observes a cloud reflection in the lake at this time the height of reflection of cloud in lake is $(h + 3)$ because in lake platform height is also added to reflection of cloud.

So, angle of depression is different in the lake from the angle of elevation of the cloud above the surface of a lake.

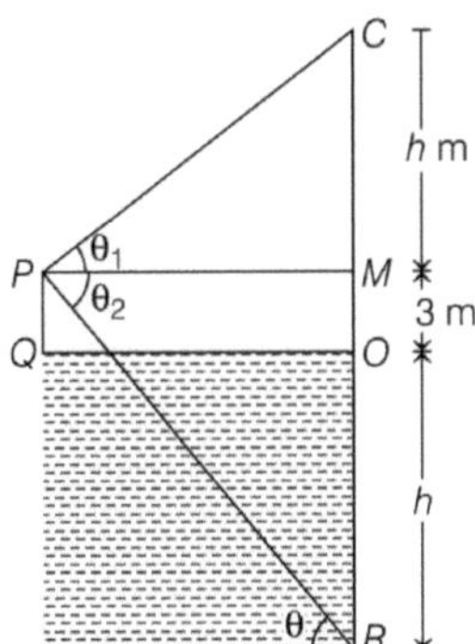

In $\triangle MPC$, $\qquad \tan \theta_1 = \frac{CM}{PM} = \frac{h}{PM}$

$$\Rightarrow \qquad \frac{\tan \theta_1}{h} = \frac{1}{PM} \qquad \ldots(i)$$

In $\triangle RPM$, $\qquad \tan \theta_2 = \frac{RM}{PM} = \frac{OR + OM}{PM} = \frac{h + 3}{PM}$

$$\Rightarrow \qquad \frac{\tan \theta_2}{h + 3} = \frac{1}{PM} \qquad \ldots(ii)$$

From Eqs. (i) and (ii),

$$\frac{\tan \theta_1}{h} = \frac{\tan \theta_2}{h + 3} \Rightarrow \tan \theta_2 = \left(\frac{h + 3}{h}\right)\tan \theta_1$$

So, $\qquad\qquad \theta_1 \neq \theta_2$

Hence, it is a false statement.

10. Let $AB = h$ km be the height of the hill and C, D be two consecutive stones such that $CD = 1$ km.

Let BC be x km, then $BD = BC + CD = (x + 1)$ km

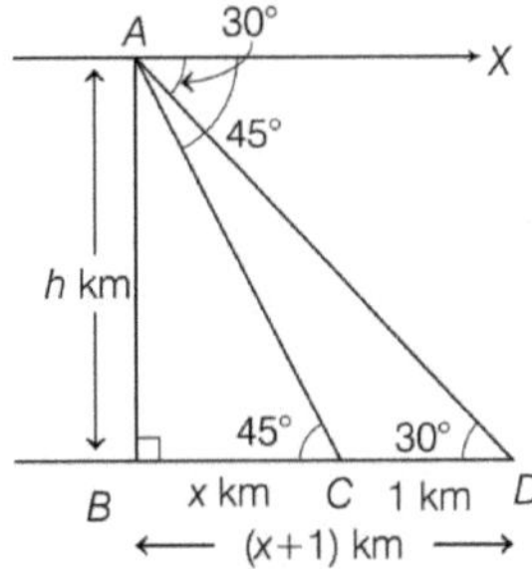

Now, $\qquad \angle ADB = \angle XAD = 30°$ $\qquad$ [alternate angles]

and $\qquad \angle ACB = \angle XAC = 45°$ $\qquad$ [alternate angles]

In right angled $\triangle ABC$,

$$\tan 45° = \frac{\text{Perpendicular}}{\text{Base}} = \frac{AB}{BC}$$

$$\Rightarrow \qquad 1 = \frac{h}{x} \Rightarrow x = h \qquad \ldots(i)$$

Now, in right angled $\triangle ABD$, $\tan 30° = \frac{AB}{BD}$

$$\Rightarrow \qquad \frac{1}{\sqrt{3}} = \frac{h}{x + 1} \qquad \left[\because \tan 30° = \frac{1}{\sqrt{3}}\right]$$

$$\Rightarrow \qquad \frac{1}{\sqrt{3}} = \frac{h}{h + 1} \qquad \text{[from Eq. (i)]}$$

$$\Rightarrow \qquad h + 1 = \sqrt{3}h$$
$$\Rightarrow \qquad h(\sqrt{3} - 1) = 1$$
$$\Rightarrow \qquad h = \frac{1}{\sqrt{3} - 1} \times \frac{\sqrt{3} + 1}{\sqrt{3} + 1} = \left(\frac{\sqrt{3} + 1}{2}\right) \text{ km}$$

Hence, height of the hill is $\dfrac{\sqrt{3} + 1}{2}$ km.

11. Let AB be the tower, BC be the shadow of tower, when angle of elevation of Sun is $30°$ and BD be the shadow of tower, when angle of elevation of Sun is $60°$.

Then, we have
$$BC = 30 \text{ m}, \angle ACB = 30° \text{ and } \angle ADB = 60°$$

Now, let $AB = h$ m and $BD = x$ m

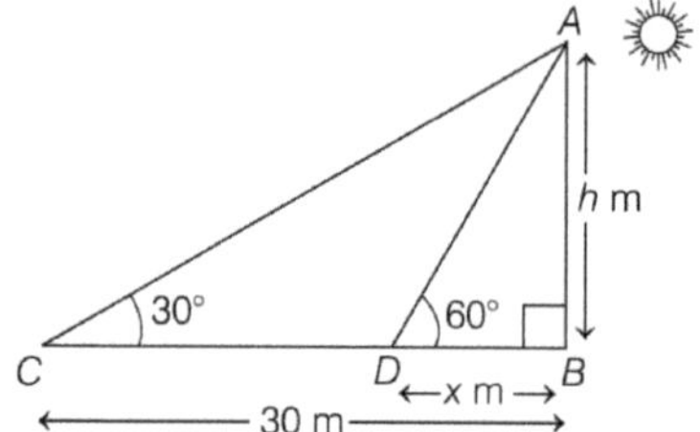

Clearly, in $\triangle ABC$, we have
$$\tan 30° = \frac{\text{Perpendicular}}{\text{Base}} = \frac{AB}{BC} = \frac{h}{30}$$
$$\Rightarrow \qquad \frac{1}{\sqrt{3}} = \frac{h}{30} \Rightarrow h = \frac{30}{\sqrt{3}}$$
$$\Rightarrow \qquad \frac{30}{\sqrt{3}} \times \frac{\sqrt{3}}{\sqrt{3}} = \frac{30\sqrt{3}}{3} = 10\sqrt{3} \text{ m}$$

Also, in $\triangle ABD$, $\tan 60° = \dfrac{AB}{BD} = \dfrac{h}{x}$
$$\Rightarrow \qquad \sqrt{3} = \frac{10\sqrt{3}}{x} \Rightarrow x = 10 \text{ m}$$

Hence, length of shadow is 10 m, when angle of elevation is $60°$.

12. Let PM be the light house of height 200 m and let A and B be two ships on either sides of light house such that the angles of depression of A and B are $60°$ and $45°$, respectively.

Let $\qquad AM = x$ m and $BM = y$ m

Then, $\quad \angle XPB = \angle MBP = 45°$ [alternate angles]

and $\qquad \angle YPA = \angle MAP = 60°$ [alternate angles]

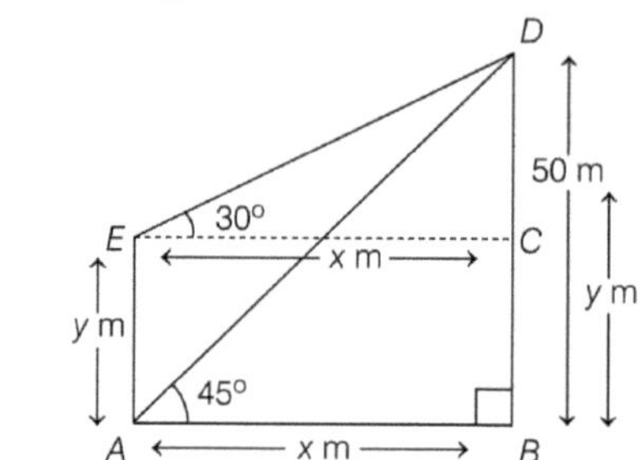

In right angled $\triangle AMP$,
$$\tan 60° = \frac{\text{Perpendicular}}{\text{Base}} = \frac{PM}{AM}$$
$$\Rightarrow \qquad \sqrt{3} = \frac{200}{x} \qquad [\because \tan 60° = \sqrt{3}]$$
$$\Rightarrow \qquad x = \frac{200}{\sqrt{3}} \text{ m} = \frac{200}{1.732} \text{ m} = 115.47 \text{ m}$$

In right angled $\triangle BMP$,
$$\tan 45° = \frac{PM}{BM}$$
$$\Rightarrow \qquad 1 = \frac{200}{y} \qquad [\because \tan 45° = 1]$$
$$\Rightarrow \qquad y = 200 \text{ m}$$

Now, distance between the two ships $= AB = x + y$
$$= 115.47 + 200$$
$$= 315.47 \text{ m}$$

13. Let distance of the pole, say AE, from the bottom of the tower, say BD, be x m and let the height of the pole, $AE = y$ m

Now, draw $EC \parallel AB$.

Then, $\angle DEC = 30°$, $\angle DAB = 45°$

and $\qquad DC = DB - BC = DB - AE$ $[\because BC = AE]$

$\Rightarrow \qquad DC = (50 - y) \text{ m}$

(i) In right angled $\triangle ABD$,
$$\tan 45° = \frac{\text{Perpendicular}}{\text{Base}} = \frac{BD}{AB}$$
$$\Rightarrow \qquad 1 = \frac{50}{x} \Rightarrow x = 50 \text{ m} \qquad \text{...(i)}$$

$\therefore$ The pole is 50 m away from the foot of the tower.

(ii) In right angled $\triangle ECD$,
$$\tan 30° = \frac{\text{Perpendicular}}{\text{Base}} = \frac{DC}{EC}$$
$$\Rightarrow \qquad \frac{1}{\sqrt{3}} = \frac{50 - y}{x} \qquad \left[\tan 30° = \frac{1}{\sqrt{3}}\right]$$
$$\Rightarrow \qquad \frac{1}{\sqrt{3}} = \frac{50 - y}{50} \qquad [\because x = 50 \text{ m from Eq. (i)}]$$
$$\Rightarrow \qquad \sqrt{3}(50 - y) = 50$$
$$\Rightarrow \qquad 50 - y = \frac{50}{\sqrt{3}}$$
$$\Rightarrow \qquad y = 50\left(1 - \frac{1}{\sqrt{3}}\right)$$
$$= 50\left(1 - \frac{1}{1.732}\right)$$
$$= 50(1 - 0.57737)$$
$$= 50 \times 0.4226$$
$$= 21.13 \text{ m}$$

$\therefore$ Height of the pole $= 21.13$ m

14. Let a man is standing on the deck of a ship at point A such that $AB = 10$ m and let CD be the hill.

Then, $\angle EAD = 60°$

and $\qquad \angle CAE = \angle BCA = 30°$ [alternate angles]

Let $\quad BC = x$ m $= AE$ and $DE = h$ m

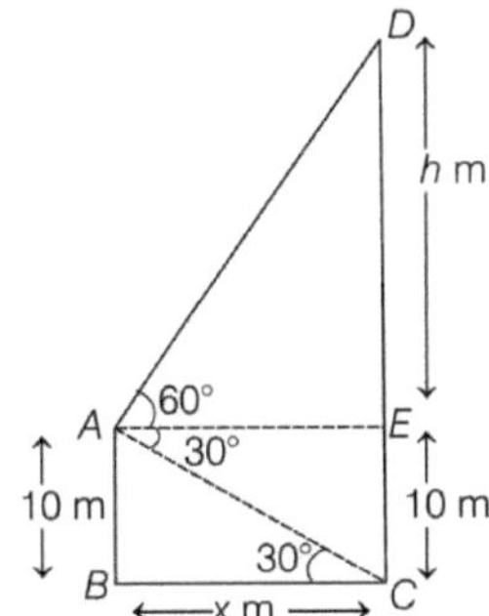

In right angled $\triangle AED$,

$$\tan 60° = \frac{\text{Perpendicular}}{\text{Base}} = \frac{DE}{EA} = \frac{h}{x}$$

$$\Rightarrow \quad \sqrt{3} = \frac{h}{x} \Rightarrow h = \sqrt{3}\,x$$

In right angled $\triangle ABC$,

$$\tan 30° = \frac{AB}{BC} \Rightarrow \frac{1}{\sqrt{3}} = \frac{10}{x} \quad \left[\because \tan 30° = \frac{1}{\sqrt{3}}\right]$$

$$\Rightarrow \quad x = 10\sqrt{3} \text{ m}$$

$$\Rightarrow \quad h = 10\sqrt{3} \times \sqrt{3} = 30 \text{ m}$$

$\therefore$ The height of hill, $CD = h + 10 = 30 + 10 = 40$ m

Hence, The distance of the hill from the ship is $10\sqrt{3}$ m and height of the hill is 40 m.

15. Let OX be the horizontal ground; A and B be the two positions of the plane and O be the point of observation.

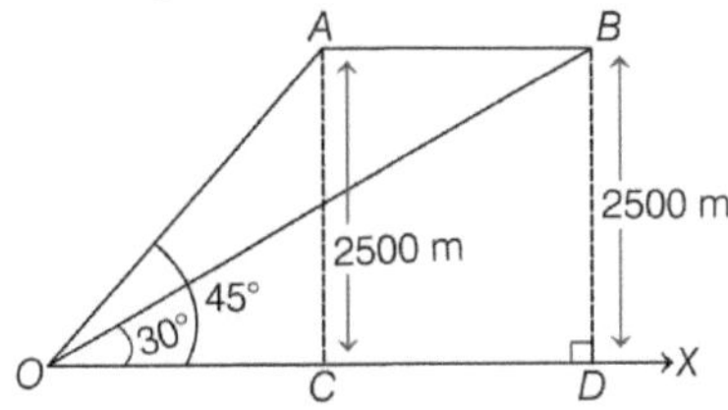

Here, $AC = BD = 2500$ m, $\angle AOC = 45°$

and $\quad \angle BOD = 30°$

In right angled $\triangle OCA$,

$$\cot 45° = \frac{\text{Base}}{\text{perpendicular}} = \frac{OC}{AC}$$

$$\Rightarrow \quad 1 = \frac{OC}{AC} \quad [\because \cot 45° = 1]$$

$$\Rightarrow \quad OC = AC = 2500 \text{ m}$$

In right angled $\triangle ODB$,

$$\cot 30° = \frac{OD}{BD} \Rightarrow \sqrt{3} = \frac{OD}{2500}$$

$$\Rightarrow \quad OD = 2500\sqrt{3} \text{ m}$$

Now, $CD = OD - OC = 2500\sqrt{3} - 2500$

$$= 2500(\sqrt{3} - 1) = 2500(1.732 - 1)$$

$$= 2500 \times 0.732 = 1830 \text{ m}$$

Thus, distance covered by plane in 15 s is 1830 m.

$\therefore$ Speed of plane $= \dfrac{1830}{15} \times \dfrac{60 \times 60}{1000} = 439.2$ km/h

16. Let AB be the flag staff of height h units and $AC = x$ units be length of its shadow, when the Sun rays meet the ground at an angle of 60°.

Also, let θ be the angle between the Sun rays and the ground, when the length of the shadow of the flag staff is $AD = 3x$ units.

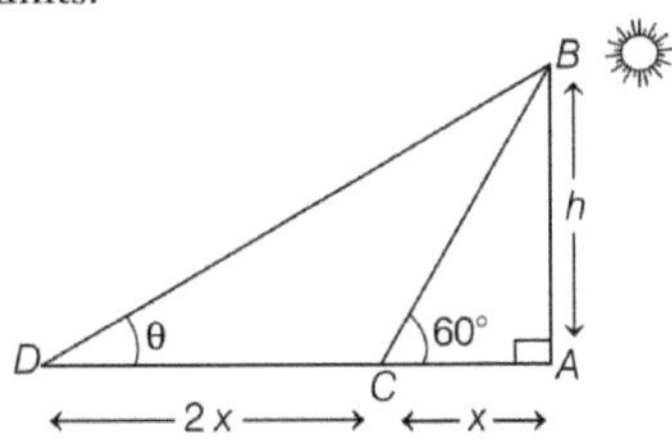

In right angled $\triangle CAB$,

$$\tan 60° = \frac{\text{Perpendicular}}{\text{Base}} = \frac{AB}{AC}$$

$$\Rightarrow \quad \sqrt{3} = \frac{h}{x} \quad [\because \tan 60° = \sqrt{3}]$$

$$\Rightarrow \quad h = \sqrt{3}x \qquad \text{...(i)}$$

Now, in right angled $\triangle DAB$,

$$\tan\theta = \frac{AB}{AD} = \frac{AB}{DC + CA} \quad [\because AD = DC + CA]$$

$$\Rightarrow \quad \tan\theta = \frac{h}{2x + x} = \frac{h}{3x}$$

$$= \frac{\sqrt{3}x}{3x} \qquad [\text{from Eq. (i)}]$$

$$= \frac{1}{\sqrt{3}} = \tan 30° \quad \left[\because \tan 30° = \frac{1}{\sqrt{3}}\right]$$

$$\therefore \qquad \theta = 30°$$

Hence, the angle between the sun rays and the ground at the time of longer shadow is 30°.

17. Let P and Q be the positions of two aeroplanes, where P is vertically above Q and $OP = 4000$ m.

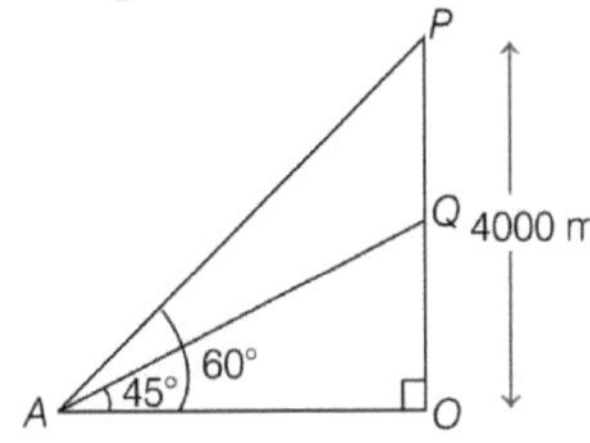

Here, $\angle PAO = 60°$ and $\angle QAO = 45°$

Now, in right angled $\triangle AOP$,

$$\tan 60° = \frac{\text{Perpendicular}}{\text{Base}} = \frac{OP}{AO}$$

$$\Rightarrow \quad \sqrt{3} = \frac{4000}{AO} \quad [\because \tan 60° = \sqrt{3}]$$

$$\Rightarrow \quad AO = \frac{4000}{\sqrt{3}} \qquad \text{...(i)}$$

In right angled $\triangle AOQ$,

$$\tan 45° = \frac{OQ}{OA} \Rightarrow 1 = \frac{OQ}{OA} \quad [\because \tan 45° = 1]$$

$$\Rightarrow \quad OA = OQ \qquad \text{...(ii)}$$

From Eqs. (i) and (ii), we get
$$OQ = \frac{4000}{\sqrt{3}}\ \text{m}$$

∴vertical distance between the aeroplanes
$$= PQ = OP - OQ = 4000 - \frac{4000}{\sqrt{3}}$$
$$= 4000\left(1 - \frac{1}{\sqrt{3}}\right) = 4000\left(1 - \frac{1}{1.732}\right)$$
$$= 4000\,(1 - 0.577)$$
$$= 4000 \times 0.423 = 1692\ \text{m}$$

18. Let OA be the tree of height h m.

Given, $PQ = 100$ m and angles of elevation are $\angle APO = 30°$ and $\angle OQA = 45°$.

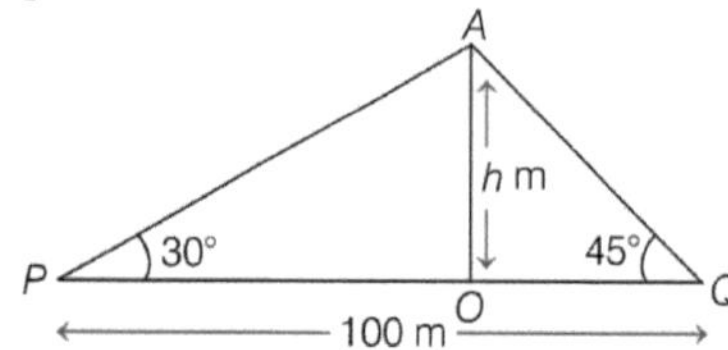

In right angled $\triangle POA$, $\tan 30° = \dfrac{\text{Perpendicular}}{\text{Base}} = \dfrac{OA}{OP}$

$\Rightarrow \qquad \dfrac{1}{\sqrt{3}} = \dfrac{h}{OP} \qquad \left[\because \tan 30° = \dfrac{1}{\sqrt{3}}\right]$

$\Rightarrow \qquad OP = \sqrt{3}h \qquad \qquad \text{...(i)}$

Now, in right angled $\triangle QOA$,
$$\tan 45° = \frac{OA}{OQ}$$

$\Rightarrow \qquad 1 = \dfrac{h}{OQ} \qquad [\because \tan 45° = 1]$

$\Rightarrow \qquad OQ = h \qquad \qquad \text{...(ii)}$

On adding Eqs. (i) and (ii), we get
$$OP + OQ = \sqrt{3}h + h$$

$\Rightarrow \qquad PQ = (\sqrt{3} + 1)h \qquad [\because OP + OQ = PQ]$

$\Rightarrow \qquad 100 = (\sqrt{3} + 1)h \ [\because PQ = 100\,\text{m, given}]$

$\Rightarrow \qquad h = \dfrac{100}{\sqrt{3} + 1} \times \dfrac{\sqrt{3} - 1}{\sqrt{3} - 1} \ \text{[by rationalising]}$

$$= \frac{100\,(1.732 - 1)}{2}$$
$$= 50 \times 0.732 = 36.6\ \text{m}$$

Hecne, height of the tree is 36.6 m.

19. Let the aeroplane be at B and two ships be at C and D such that their angles of depression from B are 60° and 30°, respectively. Then, the angles of elevation of B from D and C are 30° and 60°, respectively.

We have, $\quad AB = 1200$ m

Let $\qquad AC = x$ m and $CD = y$ m.

In right angled $\triangle BAC$, we have
$$\tan 60° = \frac{\text{Perpendicular}}{\text{Base}} = \frac{AB}{AC}$$

$\Rightarrow \qquad \sqrt{3} = \dfrac{1200}{x} \qquad [\because \tan 60° = \sqrt{3}]$

$\Rightarrow \qquad x = \dfrac{1200}{\sqrt{3}} \times \dfrac{\sqrt{3}}{\sqrt{3}} \qquad \text{[rationalising]}$

$\Rightarrow \qquad x = \dfrac{1200\sqrt{3}}{3} = 400\,\sqrt{3}\ \text{m} \qquad \text{...(i)}$

In right angled $\triangle BAD$, we have
$$\tan 30° = \frac{AB}{AD} = \frac{AB}{DC + CA} \qquad [\because AD = DC + CA]$$

$\Rightarrow \qquad \dfrac{1}{\sqrt{3}} = \dfrac{1200}{x + y}$

$\Rightarrow \qquad x + y = 1200\sqrt{3} \qquad \left[\because \tan 30° = \dfrac{1}{\sqrt{3}}\right]$

$\Rightarrow \qquad y = 1200\sqrt{3} - x \qquad \text{...(ii)}$

On putting the value of x from Eq. (i) in Eq. (ii), we get
$$y = 1200\sqrt{3} - 400\sqrt{3}$$
$$= 800\sqrt{3}$$
$$= 800 \times 1.732 \qquad [\because \sqrt{3} = 1.732]$$
$$= 1385.6\ \text{m}$$

Hence, the distance between both ships is 1385.6 m.

20. Let A be the aeroplane and AD be its height. Again, let B and C be two consecutive kilometre stones on the road on the left and right of plane A and the angles of depression of C and B from plane A are 60° and 45°, respectively.

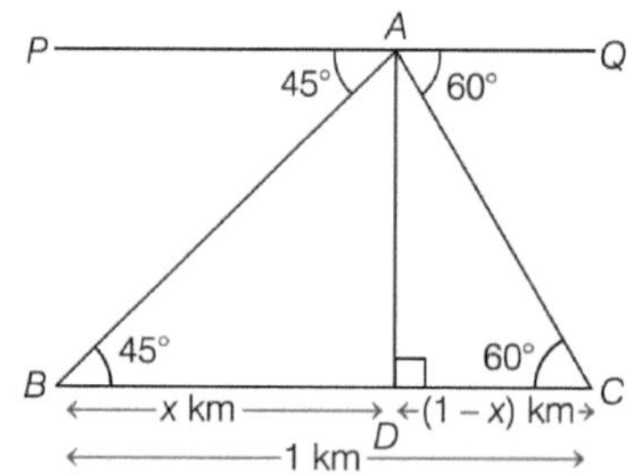

Then, $\quad \angle ABC = \angle PAB = 45°$ $\qquad$ [alternate angles]

and $\quad \angle ACB = \angle QAC = 60°$ $\qquad$ [alternate angles]

Also, $\quad BC = 1$ km

Let $\qquad BD = x$ km, then

$\qquad DC = BC - BD = (1 - x)\,\text{km} \qquad \text{...(i)}$

In right angled $\triangle ADB$,
$$\tan 45° = \frac{\text{Perpendicular}}{\text{Base}} = \frac{AD}{BD}$$

$\Rightarrow \qquad 1 = \dfrac{AD}{x} \qquad [\because \tan 45° = 1]$

$\Rightarrow \qquad AD = x$

and in right angled $\triangle ADC$,
$$\tan 60° = \frac{AD}{DC}$$

$$\Rightarrow \qquad \sqrt{3} = \frac{x}{1-x}$$

$$[\because \tan 60° = \sqrt{3} \text{ and from Eq. (i)}]$$

$$\Rightarrow \qquad \sqrt{3} - \sqrt{3}x = x$$

$$\Rightarrow \qquad \sqrt{3} = \sqrt{3}x + x$$

$$\Rightarrow \qquad (\sqrt{3}+1)\,x = \sqrt{3}$$

$$\Rightarrow \qquad x = \frac{\sqrt{3}}{\sqrt{3}+1} = \frac{\sqrt{3}}{\sqrt{3}+1} \times \frac{\sqrt{3}-1}{\sqrt{3}-1}$$

$$[\text{by rationalising}]$$

$$= \frac{3-\sqrt{3}}{(\sqrt{3})^2 - (1)^2}$$

$$[\because (a+b)(a-b) = a^2 - b^2]$$

$$= \frac{3-\sqrt{3}}{2} = \frac{3-1.732}{2} \; [\because \sqrt{3} = 1.732]$$

$$= \frac{1.268}{2} = 0.634 \text{ km}$$

Hence, the height of the aeroplane is 0.634 km.

21. Let height of the tower, $BC = h$ m and height of the flagstaff $CD = H$ m.

$$\therefore \qquad BD = BC + CD = (h+H)\,\text{m} \qquad \qquad …(i)$$

Given, $AB = 120$ m, $\angle CAB = 45°$ and $\angle DAB = 60°$

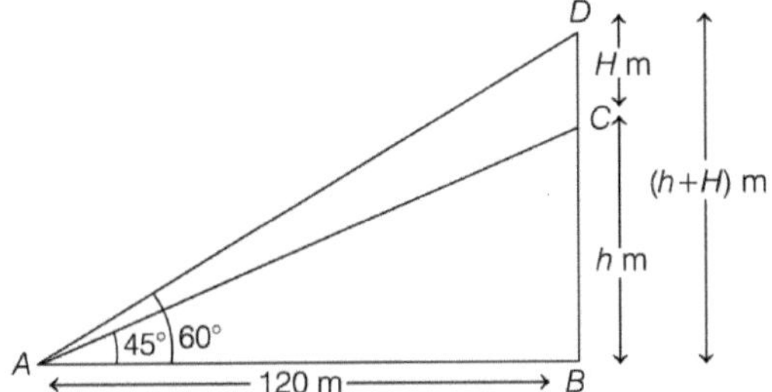

In right angled $\triangle ABC$, we get

$$\tan 45° = \frac{BC}{AB} \qquad \left[\because \tan\theta = \frac{\text{Perpendicular}}{\text{Base}}\right]$$

$$\Rightarrow \qquad 1 = \frac{h}{120} \qquad [\because \tan 45° = 1]$$

$$\Rightarrow \qquad h = 120 \text{ m} \qquad \qquad …(ii)$$

Now, in right angled $\triangle ABD$, we get $\tan 60° = \dfrac{BD}{AB}$

$$\Rightarrow \qquad \sqrt{3} = \frac{h+H}{120} \qquad \qquad …(iii)$$

$$[\because \tan 60° = \sqrt{3} \text{ and from Eq. (i)}]$$

From Eqs. (ii) and (iii),

$$\sqrt{3} = \frac{120+H}{120}$$

$$\Rightarrow \qquad 120\sqrt{3} = 120 + H$$

$$\Rightarrow \qquad H = 120\,(\sqrt{3}-1)$$

$$= 120(1.732 - 1)$$

$$= 120 \times 0.732 = 87.84 \text{ m}$$

Hence, height of flag staff is 87.84 m.

22. Let D be the position of the balloon, when it is inclined at angle of 60° and AB be the height of the pole.

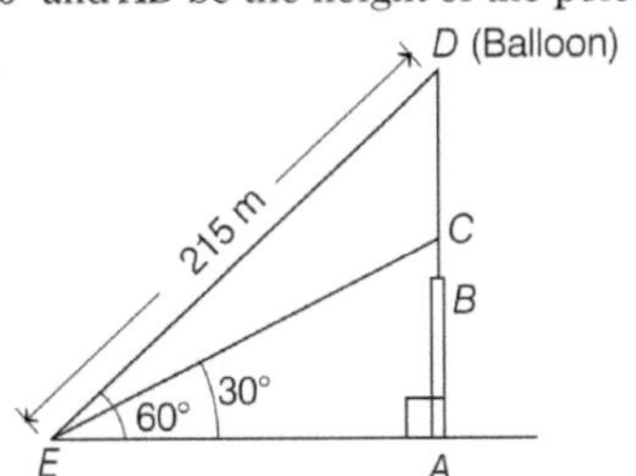

Given, length of cable, $DE = 215$ m

In right angled $\triangle EAD$,

$$\sin 60° = \frac{\text{Perpendicular}}{\text{Hypotenuse}} = \frac{AD}{ED}$$

$$\Rightarrow \qquad \frac{\sqrt{3}}{2} = \frac{AD}{215} \qquad \left[\because \sin 60° = \frac{\sqrt{3}}{2}\right]$$

$$\Rightarrow \qquad AD = \frac{215\sqrt{3}}{2} \text{ m}$$

Hence, initial height of the balloon from the ground is $\dfrac{215\sqrt{3}}{2}$ m.

Again, in right angled $\triangle EAD$,

$$\cos 60° = \frac{\text{Base}}{\text{Hypotenuse}} = \frac{AE}{DE} = \frac{AE}{215}$$

$$\Rightarrow \qquad \frac{1}{2} = \frac{AE}{215} \qquad \left[\because \cos 60° = \frac{1}{2}\right]$$

$$\Rightarrow \qquad AE = \frac{215}{2} \text{ m} \qquad \qquad …(i)$$

Now, the angle of inclination is changed, say $\angle CEA = 30°$.

In right angled $\triangle EAC$,

$$\tan 30° = \frac{\text{Perpendicular}}{\text{Base}} = \frac{AC}{EA}$$

$$\Rightarrow \qquad \frac{1}{\sqrt{3}} = \frac{AC \times 2}{215}$$

$$\Rightarrow \qquad 2\sqrt{3}AC = 215$$

$$\Rightarrow \qquad AC = \frac{215}{2\sqrt{3}} \text{ m}$$

23. Let the height of the light house AB be 100 m. C and D be the positions of man when angle of elevation changes from 60° to 45°, respectively. The man has covered a distance CD in 2 min.

$$\because \qquad \text{Speed} = \frac{\text{Distance}}{\text{Time}} \Rightarrow \text{Speed} = \frac{CD}{2} \qquad …(i)$$

In right angled $\triangle ABC$,

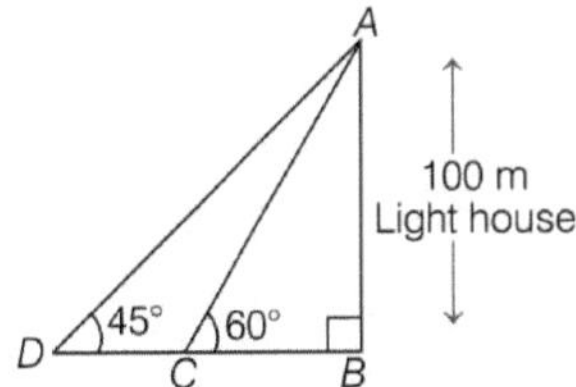

$$\tan 60° = \frac{\text{Perpendicular}}{\text{Base}} = \frac{AB}{BC}$$

$$\Rightarrow \quad \sqrt{3} = \frac{100}{BC} \qquad [\because \tan 60° = \sqrt{3}]$$

$$\Rightarrow \quad BC = \frac{100\sqrt{3}}{3} \text{ m} \qquad \ldots(ii)$$

In right angled $\triangle ABD$,

$$\tan 45° = \frac{AB}{BD}$$

$$\Rightarrow \quad 1 = \frac{100}{BD} \qquad [\because \tan 45° = 1]$$

$$\Rightarrow \quad BD = 100 \text{ m}$$

Now, $\qquad CD = BD - BC = 100 - \dfrac{100\sqrt{3}}{3}$

and Speed $= \dfrac{CD}{2} = \dfrac{100\left(\dfrac{3-\sqrt{3}}{3}\right)}{2} = \dfrac{50}{3}(3 - \sqrt{3})$ m/min

24. Let the height of the tower be h.

Also, $\qquad SR = x$ m, $\angle PSR = \theta$

Given that, $\quad QS = 20$ m

and $\qquad \angle PQR = 30°$

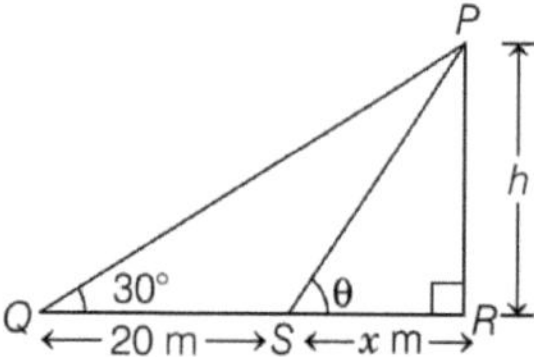

Now, in $\triangle PSR$,

$$\tan \theta = \frac{PR}{SR} = \frac{h}{x}$$

$$\Rightarrow \quad \tan \theta = \frac{h}{x}$$

$$\Rightarrow \quad x = \frac{h}{\tan \theta} \qquad \ldots(i)$$

Now, in $\triangle PQR$,

$$\tan 30° = \frac{PR}{QR} = \frac{PR}{QS + SR}$$

$$\Rightarrow \quad \tan 30° = \frac{h}{20 + x}$$

$$\Rightarrow \quad 20 + x = \frac{h}{\tan 30°} = \frac{h}{1/\sqrt{3}}$$

$$\Rightarrow \quad 20 + x = h\sqrt{3}$$

$$\Rightarrow \quad 20 + \frac{h}{\tan \theta} = h\sqrt{3} \qquad [\text{from Eq. (i)}] \ldots(ii)$$

Since, after moving 20 m towards the tower the angle of elevation of the top increases by 15°.

i.e. $\qquad \angle PSR = \theta = \angle PQR + 15°$

$$\Rightarrow \quad \theta = 30° + 15 = 45°$$

$\therefore$ From Eq. (i) $20 + \dfrac{h}{\tan 45°} = h\sqrt{3}$

$$\Rightarrow \quad 20 + \frac{h}{1} = h\sqrt{3}$$

$$\Rightarrow \quad 20 = h\sqrt{3} - h$$

$$\Rightarrow \quad h(\sqrt{3} - 1) = 20$$

$$\therefore \qquad h = \frac{20}{\sqrt{3} - 1} \cdot \frac{\sqrt{3} + 1}{\sqrt{3} + 1} \qquad [\text{by rationalisation}]$$

$$\Rightarrow \qquad = \frac{20(\sqrt{3} + 1)}{3 - 1}$$

$$= \frac{20(\sqrt{3} + 1)}{2}$$

$$\Rightarrow \qquad = 10(\sqrt{3} + 1) \text{ m}$$

Hence, the required height of tower is $10(\sqrt{3} + 1)$ m.

25. Let the height of the tower be h and $RQ = x$ m

Given that, $\qquad PR = 50$ m

and $\qquad \angle SPQ = 30°, \angle SRQ = 60°$

Now, in $\triangle SRQ$, $\tan 60° = \dfrac{SQ}{RQ}$

$$\Rightarrow \quad \sqrt{3} = \frac{h}{x} \quad \Rightarrow \quad x = \frac{h}{\sqrt{3}} \qquad \ldots(i)$$

and in $\triangle SPQ$, $\tan 30° = \dfrac{SQ}{PQ} = \dfrac{SQ}{PR + RQ} = \dfrac{h}{50 + x}$

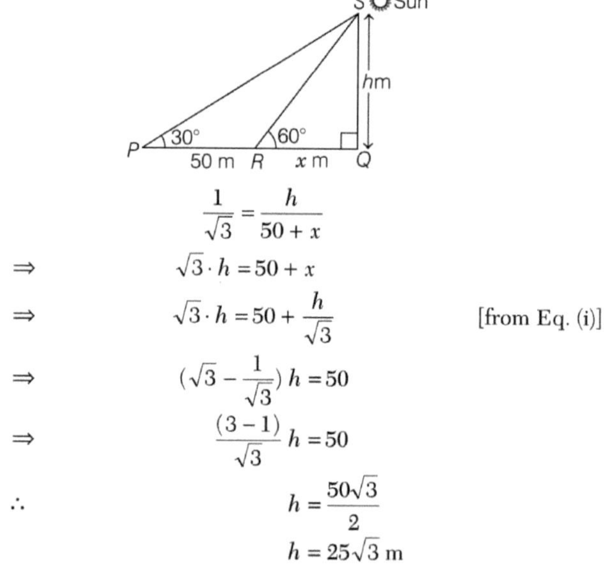

$$\frac{1}{\sqrt{3}} = \frac{h}{50 + x}$$

$$\Rightarrow \quad \sqrt{3} \cdot h = 50 + x$$

$$\Rightarrow \quad \sqrt{3} \cdot h = 50 + \frac{h}{\sqrt{3}} \qquad [\text{from Eq. (i)}]$$

$$\Rightarrow \quad \left(\sqrt{3} - \frac{1}{\sqrt{3}}\right) h = 50$$

$$\Rightarrow \quad \frac{(3 - 1)}{\sqrt{3}} h = 50$$

$$\therefore \qquad h = \frac{50\sqrt{3}}{2}$$

$$h = 25\sqrt{3} \text{ m}$$

Hence, the required height of tower is $25\sqrt{3}$ m.

26. Let the height of the tower be H and $OR = x$

Given that, height of flag staff $= h = FP$ and $\angle PRO = \alpha$, $\angle FRO = \beta$

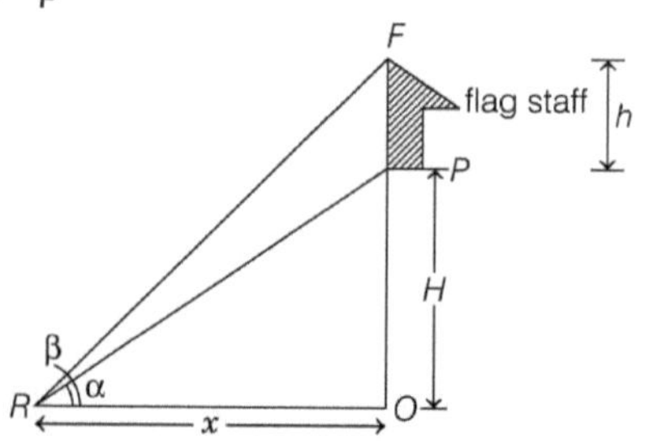

Now, in ΔPRO, $\quad \tan \alpha = \dfrac{PO}{RO} = \dfrac{H}{x}$

$\Rightarrow \qquad x = \dfrac{H}{\tan \alpha} \qquad \qquad \text{...(i)}$

and in ΔFRO, $\quad \tan \beta = \dfrac{FO}{RO}$

$$= \dfrac{FP + PO}{RO}$$

$\Rightarrow \qquad \tan \beta = \dfrac{h + H}{x}$

$\Rightarrow \qquad x = \dfrac{h + H}{\tan \beta} \qquad \qquad \text{...(ii)}$

From Eqs. (i) and (ii),

$$\dfrac{H}{\tan \alpha} = \dfrac{h + H}{\tan \beta}$$

$\Rightarrow \qquad H \tan \beta = h \tan \alpha + H \tan \alpha$

$\Rightarrow \qquad H \tan \beta - H \tan \alpha = h \tan \alpha$

$\Rightarrow \qquad H (\tan \beta - \tan \alpha) = h \tan \alpha$

$\Rightarrow \qquad H = \dfrac{h \tan \alpha}{\tan \beta - \tan \alpha}$

Hence, the required height of tower is $\dfrac{h \tan \alpha}{\tan \beta - \tan \alpha}$

Hence proved.

27. Let distance between the two towers $= AB = x$ m

and height of the other tower $= PA = h$ m

Given that, height of the tower $= QB = 30$ m and $\angle QAB = 60°$, $\angle PBA = 30°$

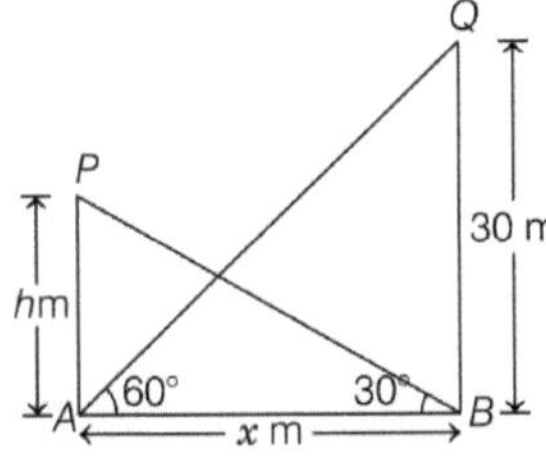

Now, in ΔQAB, $\quad \tan 60° = \dfrac{QB}{AB} = \dfrac{30}{x}$

$\Rightarrow \qquad \sqrt{3} = \dfrac{30}{x}$

$\therefore \qquad x = \dfrac{30}{\sqrt{3}} \cdot \dfrac{\sqrt{3}}{\sqrt{3}} \qquad \text{[by rationalising]}$

$$= \dfrac{30\sqrt{3}}{3} = 10\sqrt{3} \text{ m}$$

and in ΔPBA,

$$\tan 30° = \dfrac{PA}{AB} = \dfrac{h}{x}$$

$\Rightarrow \qquad \dfrac{1}{\sqrt{3}} = \dfrac{h}{10\sqrt{3}} \qquad [\because x = 10\sqrt{3} \text{ m}]$

$\Rightarrow \qquad h = 10 \text{ m}$

Hence, the required distance and height are $10\sqrt{3}$ m and 10 m, respectively.

28. Let the distance between two objects is x m. and $CD = y$ m.

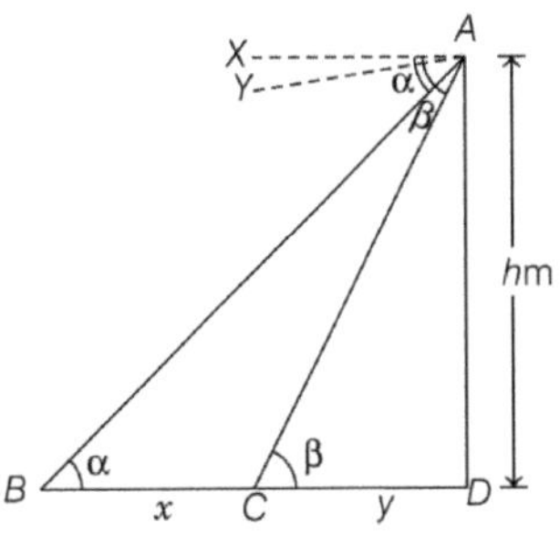

Given that, $\quad \angle BAX = \alpha = \angle ABD,$ [alternate angle]

$\angle CAY = \beta = \angle ACD$ [alternate angle]

and the height of tower, $\quad AD = h$ m

Now, in ΔACD,

$$\tan \beta = \dfrac{AD}{CD} = \dfrac{h}{y}$$

$\Rightarrow \qquad y = \dfrac{h}{\tan \beta} \qquad \qquad \text{...(i)}$

and in ΔABD,

$$\tan \alpha = \dfrac{AD}{BD} = \dfrac{AD}{BC + CD}$$

$\Rightarrow \qquad \tan \alpha = \dfrac{h}{x + y}$

$\Rightarrow \qquad x + y = \dfrac{h}{\tan \alpha}$

$\Rightarrow \qquad y = \dfrac{h}{\tan \alpha} - x \qquad \qquad \text{...(ii)}$

From Eqs. (i) and (ii),

$$\dfrac{h}{\tan \beta} = \dfrac{h}{\tan \alpha} - x$$

$\therefore \qquad x = \dfrac{h}{\tan \alpha} - \dfrac{h}{\tan \beta}$

$$= h \left(\dfrac{1}{\tan \alpha} - \dfrac{1}{\tan \beta} \right)$$

$$= h (\cot \alpha - \cot \beta) \qquad \left[\because \cot \theta = \dfrac{1}{\tan \theta} \right]$$

which is the required distance between the two objects.

Hence proved.

29. Let $\qquad OQ = x$ and $OA = y$

Given that, $\quad BQ = q$, $SA = P$ and $AB = SQ = $ Length of ladder

Also, $\qquad \angle BAO = \alpha$ and $\angle QSO = \beta$

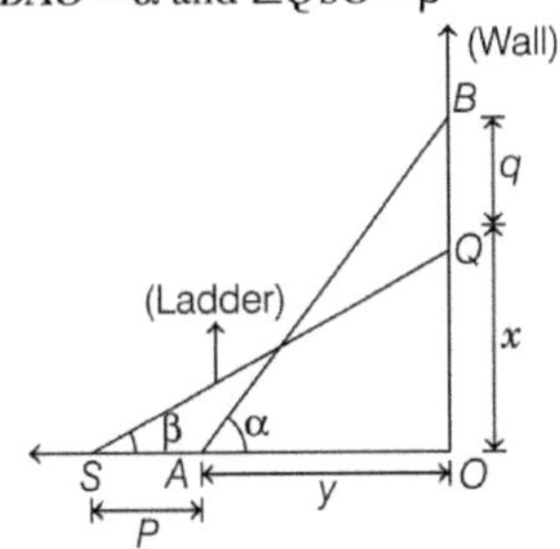

Now, in ΔBAO,

$$\cos \alpha = \frac{OA}{AB}$$

$\Rightarrow \qquad OA = AB \cos \alpha \qquad \ldots\text{(i)}$

and $\qquad \sin \alpha = \dfrac{OB}{AB}$

$\Rightarrow \qquad OB = BA \sin \alpha \qquad \ldots\text{(ii)}$

Now, in ΔQSO,

$$\cos \beta = \frac{OS}{SQ}$$

$\Rightarrow \qquad OS = SQ \cos \beta = AB \cos \beta$

$$[\because AB = SQ] \ldots\text{(iii)}$$

and $\qquad \sin \beta = \dfrac{OQ}{SQ}$

$\Rightarrow \qquad OQ = SQ \sin \beta = AB \sin \beta$

$$[\because AB = SQ] \ldots\text{(iv)}$$

Now, $\qquad SA = OS - AO$

$\qquad\qquad P = AB \cos \beta - AB \cos \alpha$

$\Rightarrow \qquad P = AB (\cos \beta - \cos \alpha) \qquad \ldots\text{(v)}$

and $\qquad BQ = BO - QO$

$\Rightarrow \qquad q = BA \sin \alpha - AB \sin \beta$

$\Rightarrow \qquad q = AB (\sin \alpha - \sin \beta) \qquad \ldots\text{(vi)}$

On dividing Eq. (v) by Eq. (vi), we get

$$\frac{p}{q} = \frac{AB (\cos \beta - \cos \alpha)}{AB (\sin \alpha - \sin \beta)} = \frac{\cos \beta - \cos \alpha}{\sin \alpha - \sin \beta}$$

$\Rightarrow \qquad \dfrac{p}{q} = \dfrac{\cos \beta - \cos \alpha}{\sin \alpha - \sin \beta}$ **Hence proved.**

30. Let the height of vertical tower be,

$$OT = H \text{ and } OP = AB = x \text{ m}$$

Given that, $\quad AP = 10 \text{ m}$

and $\qquad \angle TPO = 60°, \angle TAB = 45°$

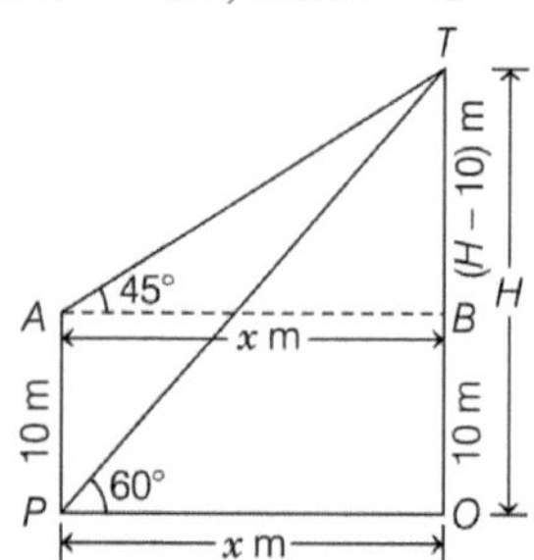

Now, in ΔTPO,

$$\tan 60° = \frac{OT}{OP} = \frac{H}{x}$$

$\Rightarrow \qquad \sqrt{3} = \dfrac{H}{x} \Rightarrow x = \dfrac{H}{\sqrt{3}} \qquad \ldots\text{(i)}$

and in ΔTAB,

$$\tan 45° = \frac{TB}{AB} = \frac{H - 10}{x}$$

$\Rightarrow \qquad 1 = \dfrac{H - 10}{x} \Rightarrow x = H - 10$

$\Rightarrow \qquad \dfrac{H}{\sqrt{3}} = H - 10 \qquad \text{[from Eq. (i)]}$

$\Rightarrow \qquad H - \dfrac{H}{\sqrt{3}} = 10 \Rightarrow H \left(1 - \dfrac{1}{\sqrt{3}}\right) = 10$

$\Rightarrow \qquad H \left(\dfrac{\sqrt{3} - 1}{\sqrt{3}}\right) = 10$

$\therefore \qquad H = \dfrac{10\sqrt{3}}{\sqrt{3} - 1} \cdot \dfrac{\sqrt{3} + 1}{\sqrt{3} + 1} \qquad \text{[by rationalisation]}$

$$= \frac{10\sqrt{3}\,(\sqrt{3} + 1)}{3 - 1} = \frac{10\sqrt{3}\,(\sqrt{3} + 1)}{2}$$

$\Rightarrow \qquad = 5\sqrt{3}\,(\sqrt{3} + 1) = 5(\sqrt{3} + 3) \text{ m}.$

Hence, the required height of the tower is $5\,(\sqrt{3} + 3)$ m.

31. Let the height of the other house $= OQ = H$

and $\qquad OB = MW = x \text{ m}$

Given that, height of the first house $= WB = h = MO$

and $\quad \angle QWM = \alpha, \angle OWM = \beta = \angle WOB \qquad \text{[alternate angle]}$

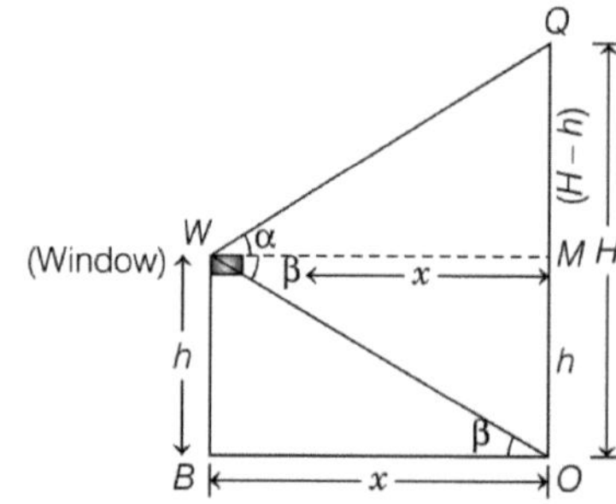

Now, in ΔWOB, $\qquad \tan \beta = \dfrac{WB}{OB} = \dfrac{h}{x}$

$\Rightarrow \qquad x = \dfrac{h}{\tan \beta} \qquad \ldots\text{(i)}$

And in ΔQWM, $\qquad \tan \alpha = \dfrac{QM}{WM} = \dfrac{OQ - MO}{WM}$

$\Rightarrow \qquad \tan \alpha = \dfrac{H - h}{x}$

$\Rightarrow \qquad x = \dfrac{H - h}{\tan \alpha} \qquad \ldots\text{(ii)}$

From Eqs. (i) and (ii),

$$\frac{h}{\tan \beta} = \frac{H - h}{\tan \alpha}$$

$\Rightarrow \qquad h \tan \alpha = (H - h) \tan \beta$

$\Rightarrow \qquad h \tan \alpha = H \tan \beta - h \tan \beta$

$\Rightarrow \qquad H \tan \beta = h(\tan \alpha + \tan \beta)$

$\therefore \qquad H = h \left(\dfrac{\tan \alpha + \tan \beta}{\tan \beta}\right)$

$$= h \left(1 + \tan \alpha \cdot \frac{1}{\tan \beta}\right)$$

$$= h \,(1 + \tan \alpha \cdot \cot \beta)$$

$$\left[\because \cot \theta = \frac{1}{\tan \theta}\right]$$

Hence, the required height of the other house is
$h\,(1 + \tan \alpha \cdot \cot \beta)$ m. **Hence proved.**

32. Let the height of the balloon above the ground is H

and $\qquad OP = W_2R = W_1Q = x$

Given that, height of lower window from above the ground

$$= W_2P = 2\text{ m} = OR$$

Height of upper window from above the lower window

$$= W_1W_2 = 4\text{ m} = QR$$

$\therefore \qquad BQ = OB - (QR + RO)$

$$= H - (4 + 2) = H - 6$$

and $\qquad \angle BW_1Q = 30°$

$\Rightarrow \qquad \angle BW_2R = 60°$

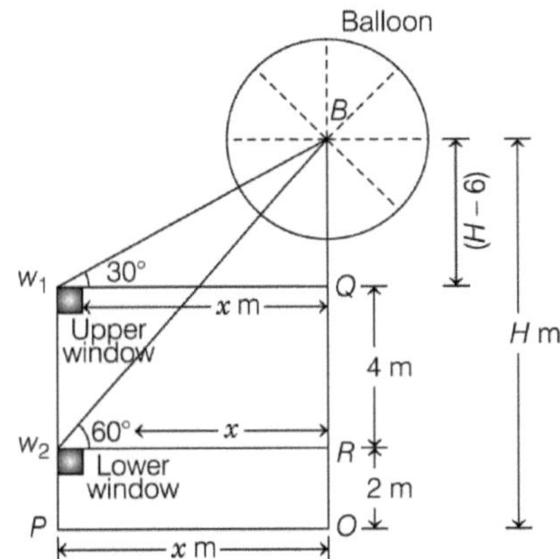

Now, in ΔBW_2R,

$$\tan 60° = \frac{BR}{W_2R} = \frac{BQ + QR}{x}$$

$\Rightarrow \qquad \sqrt{3} = \dfrac{(H-6)+4}{x}$

$\Rightarrow \qquad x = \dfrac{H-2}{\sqrt{3}} \qquad \qquad \text{...(i)}$

and in ΔBW_1Q,

$$\tan 30° = \frac{BQ}{W_1Q}$$

$\Rightarrow \qquad \tan 30° = \dfrac{H-6}{x} = \dfrac{1}{\sqrt{3}}$

$\Rightarrow \qquad x = \sqrt{3}(H-6) \qquad \qquad \text{...(ii)}$

From Eqs. (i) and (ii),

$$\sqrt{3}(H-6) = \frac{(H-2)}{\sqrt{3}}$$

$$3(H-6) = H - 2$$

$\Rightarrow \qquad 3H - 18 = H - 2$

$\Rightarrow \qquad\qquad 2H = 16$

$\Rightarrow \qquad\qquad H = 8$

So, the required height is 8 m.

Hence, the required height of the balloon above the ground is 8 m.

33. (i) Distance of first position of parrot from the eyes of girl

$$= AC$$

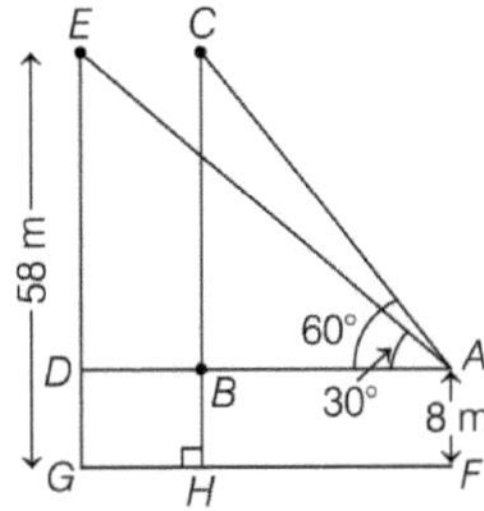

In ΔABC,

$$\sin 60° = \frac{BC}{AC}$$

$\Rightarrow \qquad AC = \dfrac{CH - BH}{\sin 60°}$

$$= \frac{58 - 8}{\sqrt{3}/2} = \frac{100}{\sqrt{3}}\text{ m}$$

(ii) If the distance increases, then the angle of elevation decreases.

(iii) Distance between girl and building $= AB$

Now, in ΔABC,

$$\tan 60° = \frac{BC}{AB} \Rightarrow \sqrt{3}\, AB = 50 \Rightarrow AB = \frac{50}{\sqrt{3}}\text{ m}$$

(iv) In ΔAED, $\tan 30° = \dfrac{DE}{AD}$

$\Rightarrow \qquad AD = \sqrt{3}\, BC = 50\sqrt{3}\text{ m}$

$$[\because ED = BC = 58 - 8 = 50]$$

Now, distance between two position of parrot $= EC$

$$= BD = AD - AB$$

$$= \left(50\sqrt{3} - \frac{50}{\sqrt{3}}\right)\text{ m}$$

$$= \frac{50(3-1)}{1.73} = \frac{100}{1.73} = 57.80\text{ m}$$

(v) Speed of parrot $= \dfrac{\text{Distance covered}}{\text{Time taken}}$

$$= \left(\frac{57.80}{8}\right)\text{ m/s} = 7.225\text{ m/s}$$

Chapter Test

Multiple Choice Questions

1. A circus artist is climbing from the ground along a rope stretched from the top of a vertical pole and tied at the ground. The height of the pole is 12 m and the angle made by the rope with ground level is 30°. The distance covered by the artist in climbing to the top of the pole is

(a) 12 m   (b) 6 m
(c) 24 m   (d) 32 m

2. A ladder 15 m long just reaches the top of a vertical wall. If the ladder makes an angle of 60° with the wall, then the height of the wall is

(a) 30 m   (b) $\dfrac{15}{2}$ m
(c) 15 m   (d) 25 m

3. A kite is flying at a height of 30 m from the ground. The length of string from the kite to the ground is 60 m. Assuming that there is no slack in the string, then the angle of elevation of the kite at the ground is

(a) 30°   (b) 45°
(c) 60°   (d) None of these

4. The tops of two poles of height 30 m and 24 m are connected by a wire. If the wire makes an angle of 45° with the horizontal, then find the length of the wire.

(a) 14 m   (b) 3 m
(c) 4 m   (d) $6\sqrt{2}$ m

5. An observer 3.5 m tall is 38.5 m away from a tower 42 m high. The angle of elevation of the top of the tower from the eye of the observer is

(a) 30°
(b) 90°
(c) 45°
(d) 60°

Case Based MCQs

6. A boy is standing on the top of mountain. He observed that boat P and boat Q are approaching towards mountain from opposite directions. He finds that angle of depression of boat P is 60° and angle of depression of boat Q is 45°. He also knows that height of the mountain is 50 m.

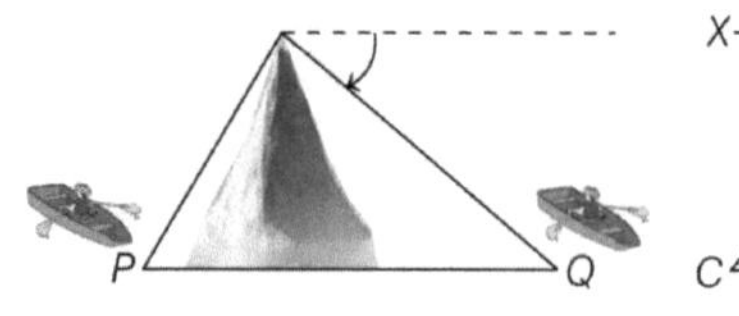

Based on the above information, answer the following questions.

(i) Measure of $\angle ACD$ is equal to

(a) 30°   (b) 45°
(c) 60°   (d) 90°

(ii) If $\angle YAB = 45°$, then $\angle ABD$ is also 45°, Why?

(a) vertically opposite angles
(b) alternate interior angles
(c) alternate exterior angles
(d) corresponding angles

(iii) Length of CD is equal to

(a) 90 m   (b) $50\sqrt{3}$ m
(c) $50/\sqrt{3}$ m   (d) 100 m

(iv) Length of BD is equal to

(a) 50 m   (b) 100 m
(c) $100\sqrt{2}$ m   (d) $100\sqrt{3}$ m

(v) Length of AC is equal to

(a) $100/\sqrt{3}$ m   (b) $100\sqrt{3}$ m
(c) 50 m   (d) 100 m

Short Answer Type Questions

7. The angle of elevation of the top of a tower is 30°. If the height of the tower is doubled, then the angle of elevation of its top will also be doubled. State true or false. Explain.

8. A peacock is sitting on the top of a tree. It observes a serpent on the ground making an angle of depression of 30°. The peacock catches the serpent in 12 s with the speed of 300 m/min. What is the height of the tree? **[CBSE 2015]**

9. The angles of elevation and depression of the top and bottom of a light house from the top of a 60 m high building are 30° and 60°, respectively. Find the difference between the heights of the light house and building.

10. As observed from the top of a 100 m high light house from the sea-level, the angles of depression of two ships are 30° and 45°. If one ship is exactly behind the other on the same side of the light house, find the distance between the two ships. **[CBSE 2018]**

Long Answer Type Questions

11. Two ships are sailing in the sea on either side of the light house. The angles of depression of two ships as observed from the top of the light house are 60° and 45°, respectively. If the distance between the ships is $100\left(\dfrac{\sqrt{3}+1}{\sqrt{3}}\right)$ m, then find the height of the light house.

Answers

1. (c)   *2. (b)*   *3. (a)*   *4. (d)*   *5. (c)*   *6. (i) (c) (ii) (b) (iii) (c) (iv) (a) (v) (a)*

7. False   *8. 30 m*   *9. 20 m*   *10. $100(\sqrt{3}-1)$ m*   *11. 100 m*

For Detailed Solutions

Scan the code

CHAPTER 06

Surface Areas and Volumes

In this Chapter...

- Solid Figures
- Surface Area
- Volume
- Combination of Two Figures
- Conversion of Solid from One Shape to Another

Solid Figures

The objects having definite shape, size and occupies a fixed amount of space in three dimensions are called **solids** such as cube, cuboid, cylinder, cone, sphere and hemisphere, etc.

Surface Area (SA)

Surface area of a solid body is the area of all of its surfaces together and it is always measured in **square unit.**

e.g. A cube has 6 surfaces and each surface is in a square shape. Therefore, its surface area will be $6a^2$ sq units, where a^2 is the area of each surface of the cube.

Volume

Space occupied by an object/solid body is called the **volume** of that particular object/solid. Volume is always measured in **cube unit.**

e.g. Suppose, a cube has edge of length a units. Volume of a cube is equal to the product of area of base and height of a cube i.e. $a^2 \times a = a^3$ cu units.

Different Types of Solid Figures

1. Cuboid

A cuboid is a solid figure having 6 rectangular faces. Let its length = l units, breadth = b units and height = h units.

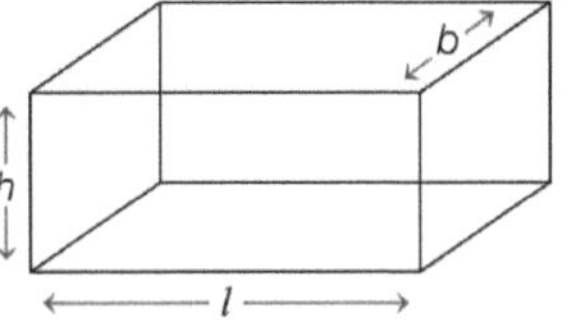

Then,

(i) Total surface area of cuboid (TSA)
$$= 2(lb + bh + hl) \text{ sq units}$$

(ii) Lateral surface area of cuboid $= 2(l + b)h$ sq units

or Lateral surface area = Area of the 4 vertical faces

(iii) Diagonal of the cuboid $= \sqrt{l^2 + b^2 + h^2}$ units

(iv) Volume of cuboid $= l \times b \times h$ cu units

2. Cube

Cube is a special case of cuboid which has 6 equal square faces.

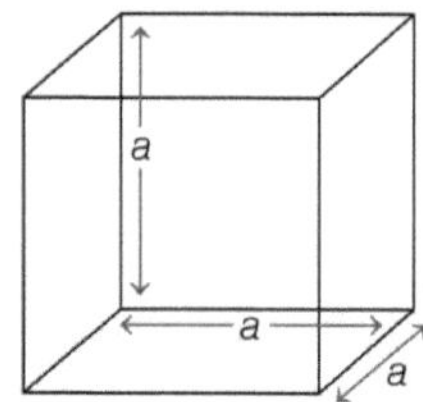

Let its length = breadth = height = a units

$\therefore$ Each edge of cube = a units

Then,

(i) Total surface area (TSA) of a cube
$$= 6 \times (\text{Edge})^2 = 6a^2 \text{ sq units}$$

(ii) Lateral surface area of cube = $4 \times (\text{Edge})^2 = 4a^2$ sq units

(iii) Diagonal of a cube = $\sqrt{3} \times \text{Edge} = \sqrt{3}\,a$ units

(iv) Volume of a cube = $(\text{Edge})^3 = a^3$ cu units

3. Right Circular Cylinder

Cylinder is a solid figure obtained by revolving the rectangle, say $ABCD$, about its one side, say BC. Let base radius of right circular cylinder be r units and its height be h units. Then,

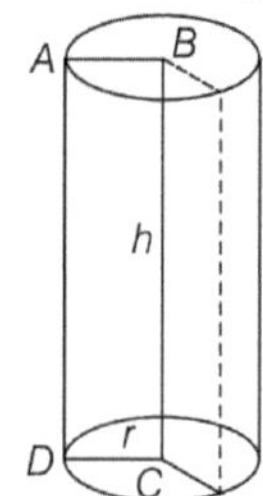

(i) Curved surface area (CSA)
$$= \text{Circumference of the base} \times \text{Height} = 2\pi rh \text{ sq units}$$

(ii) Total surface area (TSA)
$$= \text{Curved surface area (CSA)} + \text{Area of two ends}$$
$$= 2\pi rh + 2\pi r^2 = 2\pi r(h + r) \text{ sq units}$$

(iii) Volume of the cylinder = Area of base × Height
$$= \pi r^2 h \text{ cu units}$$

4. Right Circular Hollow Cylinder

Let R units and r units be the external and internal radii of the hollow cylinder, respectively and h units be its height.

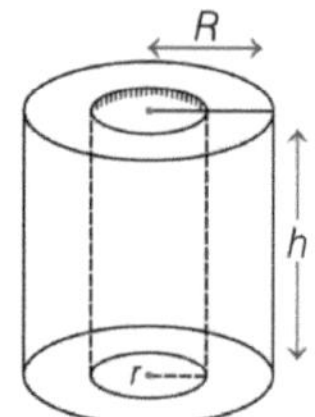

Then,

(i) Curved surface area (CSA)
$$= \text{CSA of outer cylinder} + \text{CSA of inner cylinder}$$
$$= 2\pi Rh + 2\pi rh$$
$$= 2\pi(R + r)h \text{ sq units}$$

(ii) Total surface area (TSA)
$$= \text{CSA of hollow cylinder} + \text{Area of both ends}$$
$$= 2\pi(R + r)h + 2\pi(R^2 - r^2)$$
$$= 2\pi(R + r)h + 2\pi(R + r)(R - r)$$
$$= 2\pi(R + r)[h + R - r] \text{ sq units}$$

(iii) Total outer surface area = $2\pi Rh + 2\pi(R^2 - r^2)$ sq units

(iv) Volume of hollow cylinder
$$= \text{Volume of outer cylinder}$$
$$\qquad - \text{Volume of inner cylinder}$$
$$= \pi R^2 h - \pi r^2 h$$
$$= \pi(R^2 - r^2)h \text{ cu units}$$

5. Sphere

A sphere is a solid generated by the revolution of a semi-circle about its diameter. Let radius of sphere be r units.

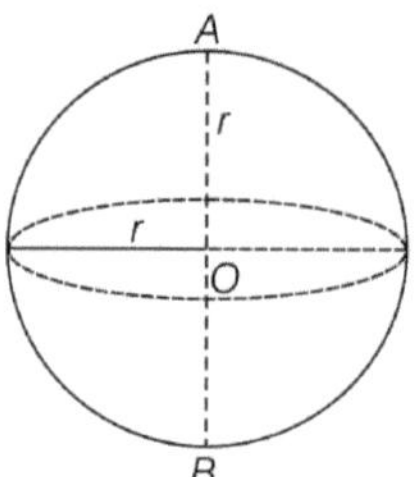

Then,

(i) Surface area (SA) of sphere = $4\pi r^2$ sq units

(ii) Volume of sphere = $\dfrac{4}{3}\pi r^3$ cu units

6. Spherical Shell

If R and r are respectively the outer and inner radii of a spherical shell, then

(i) Outer surface area = $4\pi R^2$ sq units

(ii) Inner surface area = $4\pi r^2$ sq units

(iii) Volume of a hollow sphere = $\dfrac{4}{3}\pi(R^3 - r^3)$ cu units

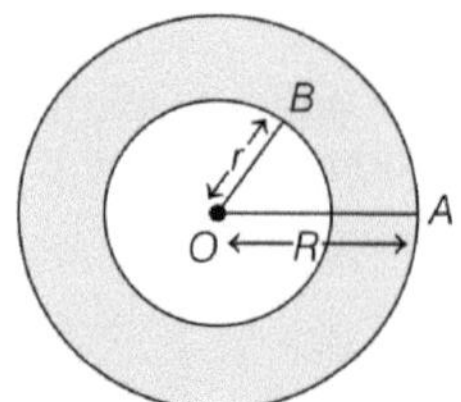

7. Hemisphere

A plane passing through the centre, cuts the sphere in two equal parts, each part is called a hemisphere. Let radius of hemisphere be r units. Then,

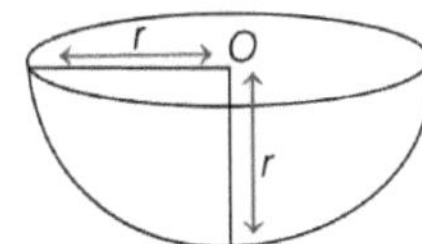

(i) Curved surface area (CSA) of hemisphere $= 2\pi r^2$ sq units

(ii) Total surface area (TSA) of hemisphere

$$= \text{CSA of hemisphere} + \text{Area of one end}$$
$$= 2\pi r^2 + \pi r^2 = 3\pi r^2 \text{ sq units.}$$

(iii) Volume of hemisphere $= \dfrac{2}{3}\pi r^3$ cu units

8. Right Circular Cone

A right circular cone is a solid generated by the revolution of a right angled triangle about one of its sides containing the right angle as axis as shown in figure. Let height of a right circular cone be h units and its radius be r units. Then,

(i) Slant height of the cone,
$$l = AC = \sqrt{r^2 + h^2} \text{ units}$$

(ii) Curved surface area (CSA) of cone $= \pi r l$ sq units

(iii) Total surface area (TSA) of a cone
$$= \text{Curved surface area (CSA)} + \text{Area of the base}$$
$$= \pi r l + \pi r^2 = \pi r(l + r) \text{ sq units}$$

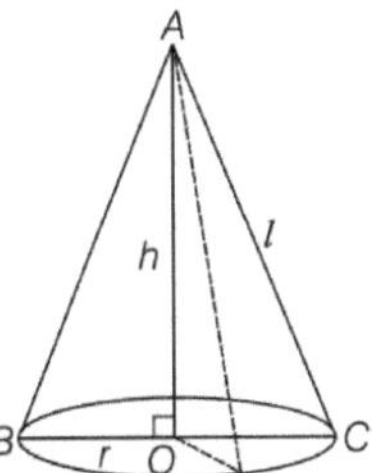

(iv) Volume of cone $= \dfrac{1}{3}\pi r^2 h$ cu units

Combination of Two Solids

Sometimes, we have to find the curved surface area and volume of a solid, which is a combination of two solids. Then, for finding the surface area, we add the curved surface areas of individual solids and for finding the volume of this solid, we add the volumes of individual solids.

e.g. A combined solid is formed by joining hemisphere and right circular cone.

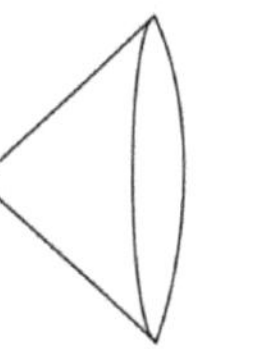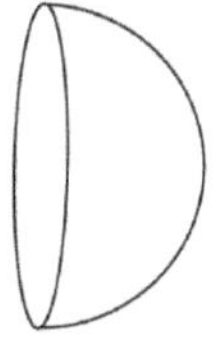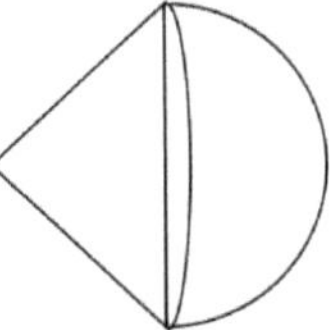

(i) Surface area of combined solid figure
$$= \text{CSA of cone } + \text{CSA of hemisphere}$$

(ii) Volume of combined solid figure
$$= \text{Volume of cone} + \text{Volume of hemisphere}$$

While calculating the surface area, we have not added the surface areas of the two individual solids, rather we have added curved surface area because some part of the surface area disappeared in the process of joining them. But this will not be in the case, when we calculate the volume.

Conversion of Solid from One Shape to Another

Sometimes, we need to convert solid figure of one shape to another. When we come across objects which are converted from one shape to another or when a liquid which is originally filled in one container of a particular shape is poured into another container of a different shape or size, the volume remains same. e.g.

(i) If a solid metallic sphere is melted and recast into more than one spherical balls, then volume of metallic sphere $= \text{Sum of volumes of all spherical balls.}$

(ii) If the Earth taken out by digging a well and spreading it uniformly around the well to form an embankment in the shape of a cylindrical shell from its original shape of right circular cylinder, then volume of embankment $= \text{Volume of Earth taken out by digging a well.}$

Important Results or Formulae

If a solid of one shape is converted into solid (or solids) of another shape, then

(i) Volume of the solid to be converted $=$ Total volume of the solids into which the given solid is to be converted

(ii) Number of solids of a given shape in which a given solid is to be converted
$$= \frac{\text{Volume of the solid to be converted}}{\text{Volume of one converted solid}}$$

Solved Examples

Example 1. Three metallic solid cubes whose edges are 3 cm, 4 cm and 5 cm are melted and formed into a single cube. Find the edge of the cube so formed.

Sol. Given, edges of three solid cubes are 3 cm, 4 cm and 5 cm, respectively.

$\therefore$ Volume of first cube $= (3)^3 = 27$ cm^3

$$[\because \text{ volume of cube} = (\text{side})^3]$$

Volume of second cube $= (4)^3 = 64$ cm^3

and volume of third cube $= (5)^3 = 125$ cm^3

$\therefore$ Sum of volume of three cubes $= (27 + 64 + 125)$

$$= 216 \text{ cm}^3$$

Let the edge of the resulting cube $= R$ cm

Then, volume of the resulting cube, $R^3 = 216 \Rightarrow R = 6$ cm

Example 2. The volume of a right circular cylinder with its height equal to the radius is $25\dfrac{1}{7}$ cm^3. Find the height of the cylinder. (Use $\pi = \dfrac{22}{7}$)

Sol. Let h and r be the height and radius of right circular cylinder, respectively.

Given, height of cylinder = Radius of cylinder

i.e. $h = r$

$\because$ Volume of cylinder $= \pi r^2 h$

$\therefore \qquad 25\dfrac{1}{7} = \dfrac{22}{7} \times h^2 \times h \quad [\because h = r \text{ and } V = 25\dfrac{1}{7}, \text{ given}]$

$\Rightarrow \qquad \dfrac{176}{7} = \dfrac{22}{7} \times h^3$

$\Rightarrow \qquad h^3 = 8$

$\Rightarrow \qquad h^3 = 2^3 \Rightarrow h = 2 \qquad \text{[taking cube root]}$

Hence, height of cylinder is 2 cm.

Example 3. An iron pole consists of a cylinder of height 240 cm and base diameter 26 cm, which is surmounted by another cylinder of height 66 cm and radius 10 cm. Find the mass of the pole given that 1 cm^3 of iron has approximately 8 g mass.

$$[\text{take, } \pi = 3.14]$$

Sol. Here, solid iron pole is a combination of two cylinders.

For first cylinder,

Height $= 240$ cm

Base diameter $= 26$ cm

$\therefore$ Base radius $= \dfrac{26}{2}$ cm $= 13$ cm

For second cylinder,

Height $= 66$ cm

Radius $= 10$ cm

We know that,

Volume of cylinder $= \pi r^2 h$

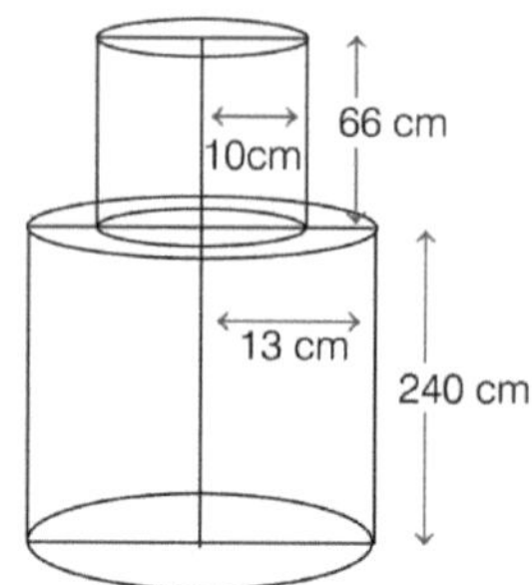

$\therefore$ Total volume of iron pole = Volume of first cylinder

$$+ \text{ Volume of second cylinder}$$

$$= \pi (13)^2 \times 240 + \pi (10)^2 \times 66$$

$$= \pi [169 \times 240 + 100 \times 66]$$

$$= 3.14 [40560 + 6600]$$

$$= 3.14 \times 47160$$

$$= 148082.4 \text{ cm}^3$$

Hence, total mass of the iron pole

$$= 148082.4 \times 8 \text{ g} = 1184659.2 \text{ g}$$

$$[\text{given, } 1 \text{ cm}^3 \approx 8 \text{ g}]$$

$$= \dfrac{1184659.2}{1000} \text{ kg}$$

$$= 1184.66 \text{ kg} \qquad \left[\because 1g = \dfrac{1}{1000} \text{kg}\right]$$

Example 4. A spherical metal ball of radius 8 cm is melted to make 8 smaller identical balls. The radius of each new ball is .... cm.

Sol. Let radius of larger sphere be $R = 8$ cm

and radius of smaller sphere be r cm

Let number of smaller sphere be $n = 8$

According to the given condition,

Volume of larger sphere $= n \times$ volume of smaller sphere

$\therefore \qquad \dfrac{4}{3}\pi R^3 = n \times \dfrac{4}{3}\pi r^3$

$\therefore \qquad (8)^3 = 8 \times r^3$

$\Rightarrow \qquad r^3 = 8^2 \Rightarrow r^3 = 64 = (4)^3$

$\Rightarrow \qquad r = 4 \text{ cm} \qquad \text{[taking cube root]}$

Hence, radius of new ball is 4 cm.

Example 5. A solid is in the shape of a cone mounted on a hemisphere of same base radius. If the curved surface areas of the hemispherical part and the conical part are equal, then find the ratio of the radius and the height of the conical part.

Sol. Let radius, height and slant height of a cone are r, h and l, respectively. Then, radius of hemisphere will be r.

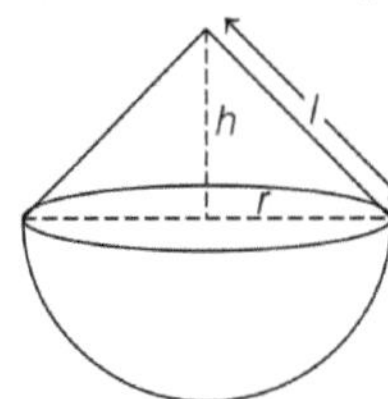

Now, curved surface area of cone $C_1 = \pi r l$

and curved surface area of hemisphere, $C_2 = 2\pi r^2$

According to the question,
$$C_1 = C_2$$
$$\therefore \qquad \pi r l = 2\pi r^2 \implies l = 2r \qquad \ldots(i)$$

Also, $l = \sqrt{r^2 + h^2}$

$$\implies \qquad (2r) = \sqrt{r^2 + h^2} \qquad [\because \text{ from Eq. (i)}]$$

On squaring both sides, we get
$$(2r)^2 = (\sqrt{r^2 + h^2})^2 \implies 4r^2 = r^2 + h^2$$
$$\implies \qquad 3r^2 = h^2 \implies (\sqrt{3}r)^2 = h^2$$

Taking square root both sides, we get
$$\sqrt{3}r = h \implies \frac{r}{h} = \frac{1}{\sqrt{3}}$$

Hence, the ratio of the radius and height of the conical part is $1 : \sqrt{3}$.

Example 6. A solid is in the shape of a hemisphere surmounted by a cone. If the radius of hemisphere and base radius of cone is 7 cm and height of cone is 3.5 cm, find the volume of the solid.

$$\left[\text{take, } \pi = \frac{22}{7}\right]$$

Sol. Given, radius of hemisphere and cone is $r = 7$ cm.

And height of cone $(h) = 3.5$ cm

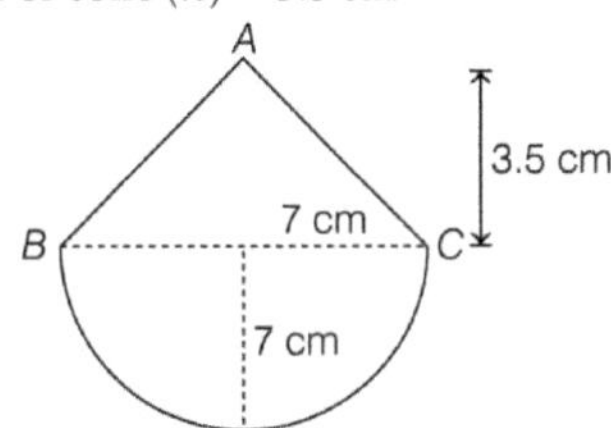

Now, volume of cone $V_1 = \dfrac{1}{3}\pi r^2 h = \dfrac{1}{3} \times \dfrac{22}{7} \times (7)^2 \times 3.5$

$$= 179.67 \text{ cm}^3$$

and Volume of hemisphere, $V_2 = \dfrac{2}{3}\pi r^3 = \dfrac{2}{3} \times \dfrac{22}{7} \times (7)^3$

$$= 718.67 \text{ cm}^3$$

$\therefore$ The volume of solid figure
$$= \text{Volume of cone} + \text{Volume of hemisphere}$$
$$= V_1 + V_2$$
$$= 179.67 + 718.67 = 898.34 \text{ cm}^3$$

Hence, volume of solid shape is 898.34 cm^3.

Example 7. In figure, a tent is in the shape of a cylinder surmounted by a conical top. The cylindrical part is 2.1 m high and conical part has slant height 2.8 m. Both the parts have same radius 2 m. Find the area of the canvas used to make the tent.

$$\left[\text{Use } \pi = \frac{22}{7}\right]$$

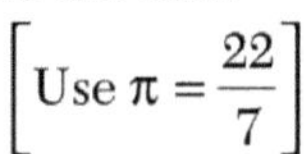
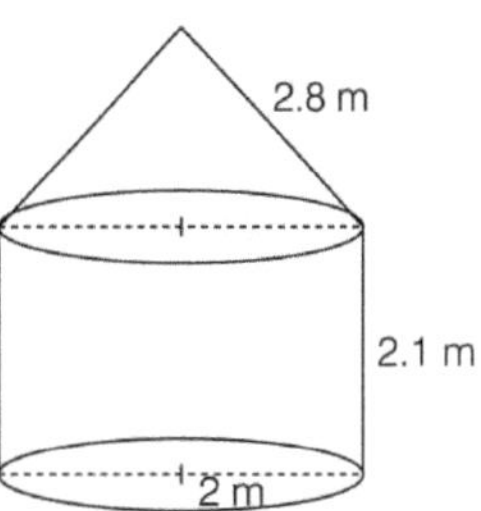

Sol. Given radius of conical and cylindrical part is $r = 2$ m.

Slant height of cone is $l = 2.8$ m

And height of cylinder is $h = 2.1$ m

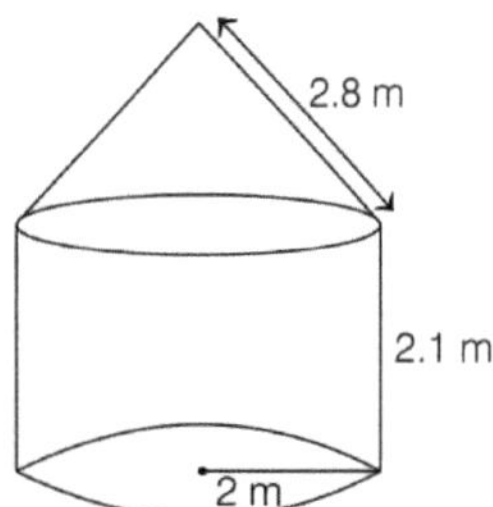

$\therefore$ The area of the canvas used, to make the tent = curve surface area of cone + curve surface area of cylinder
$$= \pi r l + 2\pi r h$$
$$= \frac{22}{7} \times 2 \times 2.8 + 2 \times \frac{22}{7} \times 2 \times 2.1$$
$$= 17.6 + 26.4 = 44 \text{ cm}^2$$

Hence, the area of the canvas used to make the tent is 44 cm^2.

Example 8. From a solid right circular cylinder of height 14 cm and base radius 6 cm, a right circular cone of same height and same base radius is removed. Find the volume of the remaining solid.

Sol. Given radius and height of cylinder are
$$r = 6 \text{ cm and } h = 14 \text{ cm}$$

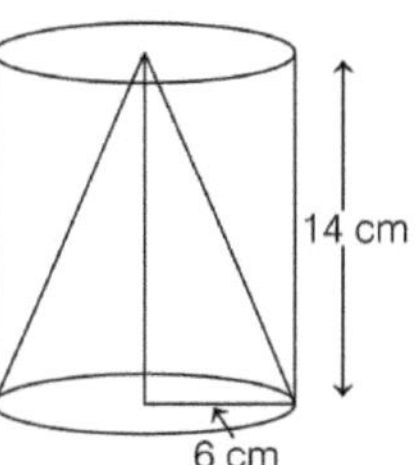

Also, radius and height of cone will be
$$r_1 = 6 \text{ cm and } h_1 = 14 \text{ cm}$$

Now, volume of cylinder,

$$V_1 = \pi r_1^{2} h$$
$$= \frac{22}{7} \times (6)^2 \times 14 = 1584 \text{ cm}^3$$

Volume of cone, $V_2 = \dfrac{1}{3} \pi r_1^{2} h_1$

$$= \frac{1}{3} \times \frac{22}{7} \times (6)^2 \times 14 = 528 \text{ cm}^3$$

∴ Volume of remaining solid

$$= \text{Volume of cylinder} - \text{Volume of cone}$$
$$= V_1 - V_2$$
$$= 1584 - 528 = 1056 \text{ cm}^3$$

Hence, volume of the remaining solid is 1056 cm^3.

Example 9. An ice-cream cone full of ice-cream having radius 5 cm and height 10 cm as shown in figure

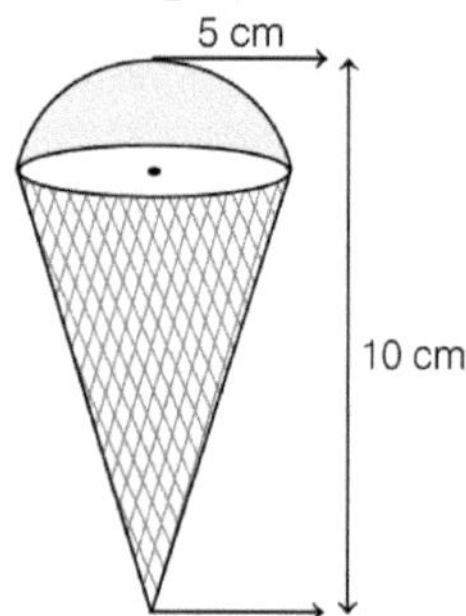

Calculate the volume of ice-cream, provided that its $\dfrac{1}{6}$ part is left unfilled with ice-cream.

Sol. Given, ice-cream cone is the combination of a hemisphere and a cone.

Also ,   radius of hemisphere $= 5$ cm

∴   Volume of hemisphere $= \dfrac{2}{3} \pi r^3 = \dfrac{2}{3} \times \dfrac{22}{7} \times (5)^3$

$$= \frac{5500}{21} = 261.90 \text{ cm}^3$$

Now,   radius of the cone $= 5$ cm

and   height of the cone $= 10 - 5 = 5$ cm

∴   Volume of the cone $= \dfrac{1}{3} \pi r^2 h$

$$= \frac{1}{3} \times \frac{22}{7} \times (5)^2 \times 5$$
$$= \frac{2750}{21} = 130.95 \text{ cm}^3$$

Now, total volume of ice-cream cone

$$= 261.90 + 130.95 = 392.85 \text{ cm}^3$$

Since, $\dfrac{1}{6}$ part is left unfilled with ice-cream.

∴ Required volume of ice-cream $= 392.85 - 392.85 \times \dfrac{1}{6}$

$$= 392.85 - 65.475$$
$$= 327.4 \text{ cm}^3$$

Example 10. Two cones with same base radius 8 cm and height 15 cm are joined together along their bases. Find the surface area of the shape so formed.

Sol. If two cones with same base and height are joined together along their bases, then the shape so formed is look like as figure shown.

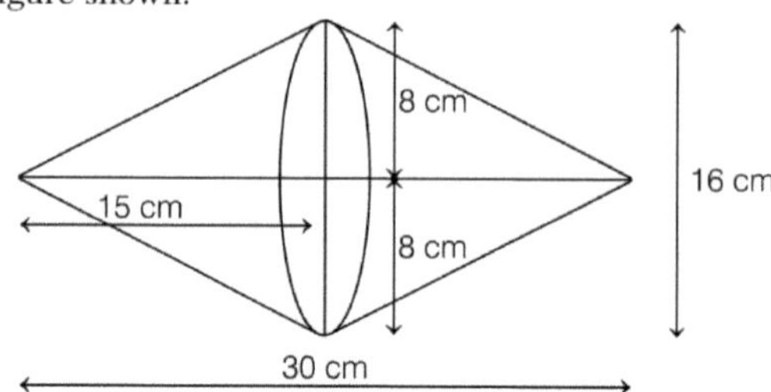

Given that, radius of cone, $r = 8$ cm and height of cone,

$$h = 15 \text{ cm}$$

So, surface area of the shape so formed

$$= \text{Curved area of first cone}$$
$$+ \text{Curved surface area of second cone}$$
$$= 2 \cdot \text{Surface area of cone} \quad [\text{since, both cones are identical}]$$
$$= 2 \times \pi r l = 2 \times \pi \times r \times \sqrt{r^2 + h^2}$$
$$= 2 \times \frac{22}{7} \times 8 \times \sqrt{(8)^2 + (15)^2} = \frac{2 \times 22 \times 8 \times \sqrt{64 + 225}}{7}$$
$$= \frac{44 \times 8 \times \sqrt{289}}{7} = \frac{44 \times 8 \times 17}{7}$$
$$= \frac{5984}{7} = 854.85 \text{ cm}^2$$
$$= 855 \text{ cm}^2 \text{ (approx.)}$$

Hence, the surface area of shape so formed is 855 cm^2.

Example 11. The barrel of a fountain pen, cylindrical in shape, is 7 cm long and 0.5 cm in diameter. A full barrel of ink in the pen can be used for writing 275 words on an average. How many words would be written using a bottle of ink containing one-fourth of a litre?   **[CBSE 2015, 14]**

Sol. Given, height of cylindrical pen $= 7$ cm

$$\text{Radius} = \frac{\text{Diameter}}{2} = \frac{0.5}{2} \text{ cm}$$

∴ Volume of barrel of a fountain pen $= \pi r^2 h$

$$= \frac{22}{7} \times \left(\frac{0.5}{2}\right)^2 \times 7 = \frac{22}{16} \text{ cm}^3$$

It is given that, a pen can write 275 words by using the ink $\dfrac{22}{16}$ cm^3.

∴   Volume of ink $= 275$ words

⇒ $\dfrac{22}{16}$ cm^3 $= 275$ words

⇒ $\dfrac{1}{4} \times 1000$ cm$^3 = \dfrac{275 \times 16}{22} \times \dfrac{1}{4} \times 1000 = 50000$

$$\left[\because \text{he will use } \frac{1}{4} \text{ L of ink to write words}\right]$$

Hence, the pen can write 50000 words by $\dfrac{1}{4}$ L of ink.

Example 12. 500 persons are taking a dip into a cuboidal pond which is 80 m long and 50 m broad. What is the rise of water level in the pond, if the average displacement of the water by a person is 0.04 m^3?

Sol. Let the rise of water level in the pond be h m when 500 persons are taking a dip into a cuboidal pond.

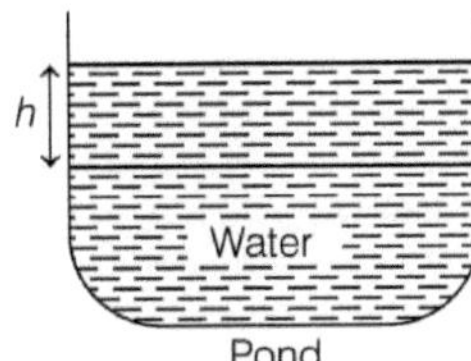

Given that,

Length of the cuboidal pond $= 80$ m

Breadth of the cuboidal pond $= 50$ m

Now, volume for the rise of water level in the pond

$$= \text{Length} \times \text{Breadth} \times \text{Height}$$
$$= 80 \times 50 \times h$$
$$= 4000 \, h \text{ m}^3$$

and the average displacement of the water by a person
$$= 0.04 \text{ m}^3$$

So, the average displacement of the water by 500 persons
$$= 500 \times 0.04 \text{ m}^3$$

Now, by given condition,

Volume for the rise of water level in the pond $=$ Average displacement of the water by 500 persons

$$\Rightarrow \qquad 4000 \, h = 500 \times 0.04$$

$$\therefore \qquad h = \frac{500 \times 0.04}{4000} = \frac{20}{4000} = \frac{1}{200} \text{ m}$$
$$= 0.005 \text{ m}$$
$$= 0.005 \times 100 \text{ cm}$$
$$[\because 1 \text{ m} = 100 \text{ cm}]$$
$$= 0.5 \text{ cm}$$

Hence, the required rise of water level in the pond is 0.5 cm.

Example 13. A small terrace at a hockey ground comprises of 10 steps each of which 20 m long and built of solid concrete. Each step has a rise of $\dfrac{1}{4}$ m and a tread of $\dfrac{1}{2}$ m. Calculate the total volume of concrete required to build the terrace.

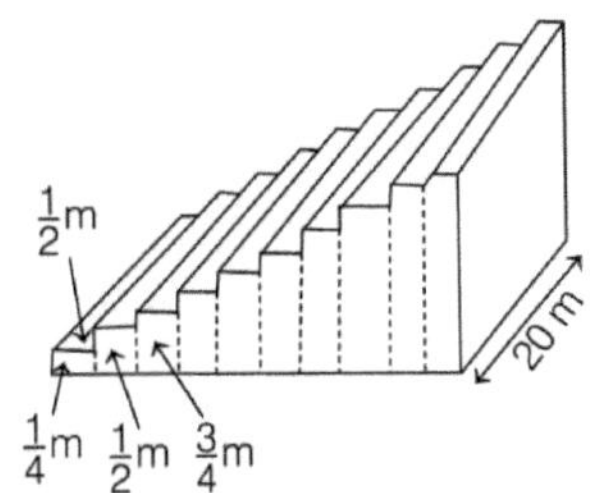

Sol. It is clear, from the figure, length $= 20$ m

and width $= \dfrac{1}{2}$ m of each step.

and height of Ist step which is in the bottom $= \dfrac{1}{4}$ m

$\therefore$ Height of second step $= 2 \times \dfrac{1}{4} = \dfrac{1}{2}$ m

Height of third step $= 3 \times \dfrac{1}{4} = \dfrac{3}{4}$ m

$\vdots \qquad \qquad \vdots$

Height of tenth step $= 10 \times \dfrac{1}{4} = \dfrac{10}{4}$ m

Total volume of the concrete used

$$= 20 \times \frac{1}{2} \times \frac{1}{4} + 20 \times \frac{1}{2} \times \frac{2}{4} + 20 \times \frac{1}{2} \times \frac{3}{4} + \ldots + 20 \times \frac{1}{2} \times \frac{10}{4}$$
$$[\because \text{ volume of cuboid} = l \times b \times h]$$

$$= 20 \times \frac{1}{2} \times \frac{1}{4} [1 + 2 + 3 + \ldots + 10]$$

$$= 20 \times \frac{1}{2} \times \frac{1}{4} \times \frac{10 \times 11}{2} \qquad \left[\because 1 + 2 + \ldots + n = \frac{n(n+1)}{2} \right]$$

$$= 137.5 \text{ m}^3$$

Example 14. A wall 24 m long, 0.4 m thick and 6 m high is constructed with the bricks each of dimensions $25 \text{ cm} \times 16 \text{ cm} \times 10 \text{ cm}$. If the mortar occupies $\dfrac{1}{10}$ th of the volume of the wall, then find the number of bricks used in constructing the wall.

Sol. Given that, a wall is constructed with the help of bricks and mortar.

$\therefore$ Number of bricks

$$= \frac{(\text{Volume of wall}) - \left(\dfrac{1}{10} \text{ th volume of wall} \right)}{\text{Volume of a brick}} \qquad \ldots\text{(i)}$$

Also, given that

Length of a wall $(l) = 24$ m,

Thickness of a wall $(b) = 0.4$ m,

Height of a wall $(h) = 6$ m

So, volume of a wall constructed with the bricks $= l \times b \times h$

$$= 24 \times 0.4 \times 6$$
$$= \frac{24 \times 4 \times 6}{10} \text{ m}^3$$

Now, $\dfrac{1}{10}$ th volume of a wall $= \dfrac{1}{10} \times \dfrac{24 \times 4 \times 6}{10}$

$$= \frac{24 \times 4 \times 6}{10^2} \text{ m}^3$$

and Length of a brick $(l_1) = 25$ cm $= \dfrac{25}{100}$ m

Breadth of a brick $(b_1) = 16$ cm $= \dfrac{16}{100}$ m

Height of a brick $(h_1) = 10$ cm $= \dfrac{10}{100}$ m

So, volume of a brick $= l_1 \times b_1 \times h_1$

$$= \frac{25}{100} \times \frac{16}{100} \times \frac{10}{100} = \frac{25 \times 16}{10^5} \text{ m}^3$$

From Eq. (i),

$$\text{Number of bricks} = \frac{\left(\dfrac{24 \times 4 \times 6}{10} - \dfrac{24 \times 4 \times 6}{100}\right)}{\left(\dfrac{25 \times 16}{10^5}\right)}$$

$$= \frac{24 \times 4 \times 6}{100} \times 9 \times \frac{10^5}{25 \times 16}$$

$$= \frac{24 \times 4 \times 6 \times 9 \times 1000}{25 \times 16}$$

$$= 24 \times 6 \times 9 \times 10 = 12960$$

Hence, the required number of bricks used in constructing the wall is 12960.

Example 15. Water is flowing at the rate of 5 km/h through a pipe of diameter 14 cm into a rectangular tank which is 50 m long and 44 m wide. Determine the time in which the level of the water in the tank will rise by 7 cm.

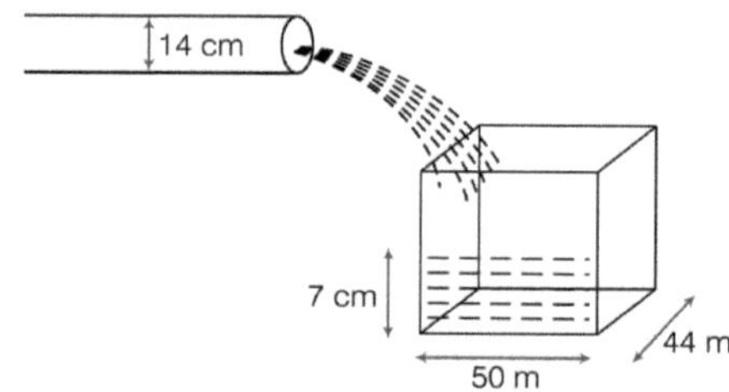

Sol. Suppose, the level of the water in the tank will rise by 7 cm in x h.

Since, the water is flowing at the rate of 5 km/h.

Therefore, length of the water flow in x h $= 5x$ km $= 5000x$ m

$$[\because 1 \text{ km} = 1000 \text{ m}]$$

We have, diameter of cylindrical pipe $= 14$ cm

$\therefore$ Radius of cylindrical pipe, $r = \dfrac{14}{2} = 7$ cm $= \dfrac{7}{100}$ m

Volume of the water flowing through the cylindrical pipe in

$$x\,h = \pi r^2 h = \frac{22}{7} \times \left(\frac{7}{100}\right)^2 \times 5000x$$

$$= 77x \text{ m}^3$$

Also, volume of the water that falls into the tank in x h

$$= l \times b \times h$$

$$= 50 \times 44 \times \frac{7}{100}$$

$$= 154 \text{ m}^3$$

$$\left[\because l = 50 \text{ m}, b = 44 \text{ m and } h = \text{radius} = \frac{7}{100} \text{ m}\right]$$

$\because$ Volume of the water flowing through the cylindrical pipe in x h $=$ Volume of water that falls in the tank in x h

$$\Rightarrow \qquad 77x = 154$$

$$\Rightarrow \qquad x = 2$$

Hence, the level of water in the tank will rise by 7 cm in 2 h.

Chapter Practice

Objective Questions

• Multiple Choice Questions

1. Three cubes each of side 5 cm are joined end to end, then the surface area of the resulting solid is
(a) 250 cm^2 (b) 180 cm^2
(c) 350 cm^2 (d) None of these

2. A solid ball is exactly fitted inside the cubical box of side a. The volume of the ball is
(a) $\dfrac{1}{6}\pi a^3$ (b) $\dfrac{4}{3}\pi a^3$
(c) $\dfrac{1}{3}\pi a^3$ (d) None of these

3. A cubical icecream brick of edge 22 cm is to be distributed among some children by filling icecream cones of radius 2 cm and height 7 cm upto its brim. How many children will get icecream cones?
(a) 163   (b) 263
(c) 363   (d) 463

4. A right circular cylinder of radius r cm and height h cm (where, $h > 2r$) just encloses a sphere of diameter
(a) r cm   (b) $2r$ cm
(c) h cm   (d) $2h$ cm

5. If two solid hemispheres of same base radius r are joined together along their bases, then curved surface area of this new solid is
(a) $4\pi r^2$ (b) $6\pi r^2$
(c) $3\pi r^2$ (d) $8\pi r^2$

6. A solid cylinder of radius r and height h is placed over other cylinder of same height and radius. The total surface area of the shape so formed is
(a) $4\pi r(h^2 + r^2)$
(b) $4\pi r[h + r]$
(c) $4\pi(h^2 + r^2)$
(d) None of the above

7. A cylindrical pencil sharpened at one edge is the combination of
(a) a cone and a cylinder
(b) cube and a cylinder
(c) a hemisphere and a cylinder
(d) two cylinders

8. A surahi is the combination of
(a) a sphere and a cylinder
(b) a hemisphere and a cylinder
(c) two hemispheres
(d) a cylinder and a cone

9. Two cones have their heights in the ratio 1 : 3 and radii in the ratio 3 : 1, then the ratio of their volumes is
(a) 1 : 3   (b) 3 : 1
(c) 2 : 3   (d) 3 : 2

10. The shape of a gilli, in the gilli-danda game (see figure) is a combination of

(a) two cylinders
(b) a cone and a cylinder
(c) two cones and a cylinder
(d) two cylinders and a cone

11. A plumbline (sahul) is the combination of (see figure)

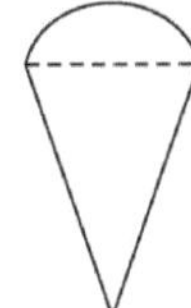

(a) a cone and a cylinder   (b) a hemisphere and a cone
(c) cube and a cylinder   (d) sphere and cylinder

12. A solid cone of radius r and height h is placed over a solid cylinder having same base radius and height as that of a cone. The total surface area of the combined solid is
(a) $\pi r l + 2\pi r h$ (b) $\pi r^2(l + 2h)$
(c) $\pi r[\sqrt{r^2 + h^2} + 2h + r]$ (d) None of these

13. The capacity of a cylindrical vessel with a hemispherical portion raised upward at the bottom as shown in the figure is $\dfrac{\pi r^2}{3}[3h - 2r]$.

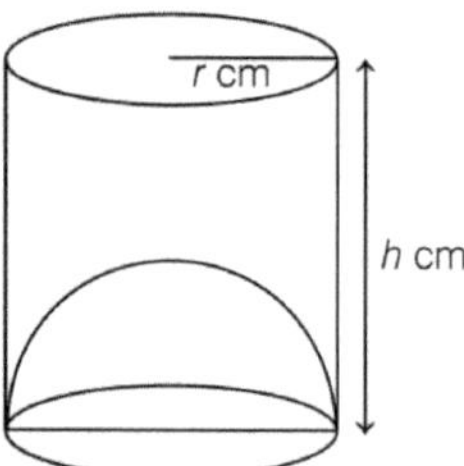

(a) $\dfrac{1}{3}\pi r^2[2h - 3r]$

(b) $\dfrac{2}{3}\pi r^2[3h - 2r]$

(c) $\dfrac{1}{3}\pi r^2[3h - 2r]$

(d) None of these

14. The diameter of a sphere is 6 cm. It is melted and drawn into a wire of diameter 2 mm.
The length of the wire is
(a) 12 m
(b) 18 m
(c) 36 m
(d) 66 m

15. During conversion of a solid from one shape to another, the volume of the new shape will
(a) increase
(b) decrease
(c) remain unaltered
(d) be doubled

16. From a solid circular cylinder with height 10 cm and radius of the base 6 cm, a right circular cone of the same height and same base is removed, then the volume of remaining solid is
(a) $280\,\pi$ cm^3
(b) $330\,\pi$ cm^3
(c) $240\,\pi$ cm^3
(d) $440\,\pi$ cm^3

17. A 20 m deep well, with diameter 7 m is dug and the earth from digging is evenly spread out to form a platform 22 m by 14 m. The height of the platform is
(a) 2.5 m
(b) 3.5 m
(c) 3 m
(d) 2 m

18. If the radius of the base of a right circular cylinder is halved, keeping the height same, then find the ratio of the volume of the cylinder thus obtained to the volume of original cylinder. **[CBSE 2009]**
(a) $\dfrac{1}{3}$
(b) $\dfrac{1}{4}$
(c) $\dfrac{1}{2}$
(d) $\dfrac{1}{5}$

19. Marbles of diameter 1.4 cm are dropped into a cylindrical beaker of diameter 7 cm containing some water. The water level rises by 5.6 cm. When marble dropped into the beaker, then the number of marble is
(a) 150
(b) 160
(c) 175
(d) 235

20. A wooden article was made by scooping out a hemisphere from each end of a solid cylinder, as shown in figure. If the height of the cylinder is 10 cm and its base is of radius 3.5 cm. Find the total surface area of the article.

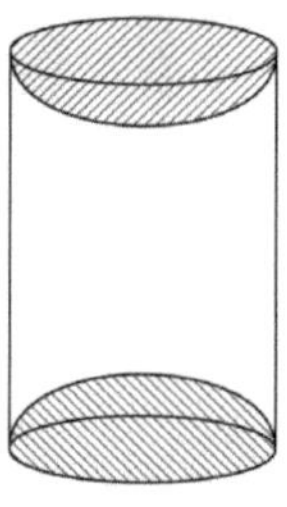

[CBSE 2018]

(a) 374 cm^2
(b) 370 cm^2
(c) 475 cm^2
(d) None of these

21. A heap of rice is in the form of a cone of base diameter 24 m and height 3.5 m. Find the volume of the rice. How much canvas as cloth is required to just cover the heap? **[CBSE 2018]**
(a) 105.5 m^2
(b) 471.42 m^2
(c) 173.5 m^2
(d) None of these

22. A mason constructs a wall of dimensions 270 cm × 300 cm × 350 cm with the bricks each of size 22.5 cm × 11.25 cm × 8.75 cm and it is assumed that $\dfrac{1}{8}$ space is covered by the mortar. Then, the number of bricks used to construct the wall is
(a) 11100
(b) 11200
(c) 11000
(d) 11300

• Case Based MCQs

23. To make the learning process more interesting creative and innovative Shavya's class teacher brings clay in the classroom, to teach the topic. Surface Areas and Volumes. With clay, she forms a cylinder of radius 4 cm and height 18 cm. Then, she moulds the cylinder into a sphere and ask some question to students.

(i) The radius of the sphere so formed is
(a) 4 cm
(b) 6 cm
(c) 7 cm
(d) 8 cm

(ii) The volume of the sphere so formed is
  (a) 905.14 cm^3 (b) 903.27 cm^3
  (c) 1296.5 cm^3 (d) 1156.63 cm^3

(iii) Find the ratio of the volume of sphere to the volume of cylinder.
  (a) 2 : 1 (b) 1 : 2
  (c) 1 : 1 (d) 3 : 1

(iv) Total surface area of the cylinder is
  (a) 553.14 cm^2 (b) 751.52 cm^2
  (c) 625 cm^2 (d) 785.38 cm^2

(v) During the conversion of a solid from one shape to another the volume of new shape will
  (a) be increase (b) be decrease
  (c) remain unaltered (d) be double

24. Geeta and Meena have 10 and 6 CD respectively, each of radius 4 cm and thickness 1 cm. They place their CD one above the other to form solid cylinders.

Based on the above information, answer the following questions.

(i) Curved surface area of the cylinder made by Geeta is
  (a) 308.17 cm^2 (b) 132 cm^2
  (c) 154 cm^2 (d) 251.42 cm^2

(ii) The ratio of curved surface area of the cylinder made by Geeta and Meena is
  (a) 3 : 5 (b) 3 : 2
  (c) 5 : 3 (d) 5 : 7

(iii) The volume of the cylinder made by Meena is
  (a) 301.44 cm^3 (b) 144 cm^3
  (c) 132 cm^3 (d) 208.42 cm^3

(iv) The ratio of the volume of the cylinders made by Geeta and Meena is
  (a) 1 : 2 (b) 2 : 5
  (c) 3 : 5 (d) 5 : 3

(v) When two CD Cassette are shifted from Geeta cylinder to Meena's cylinder, then
  (a) Volume of two cylinder become equal
  (b) Volume of Geeta's cylinder > Volume of Meena's cylinder
  (c) Volume of Meena's cylinder > Volume of Geeta's cylinder
  (d) None of the above

25. The Great Stupa at Sanchi is one of the oldest stone structures in India, and an important monument of Indian Architecture. It was originally commissioned by the emperor Ashoka in the 3rd century *BCE*. Its nucleus was a simple hemispherical brick structure built over the relics of the Buddha. It is a perfect example of combination of solid figures. A big hemispherical dome with a cuboidal structure mounted on it. $\left(\text{take } \pi = \dfrac{22}{7}\right)$

[CBSE Question Bank]

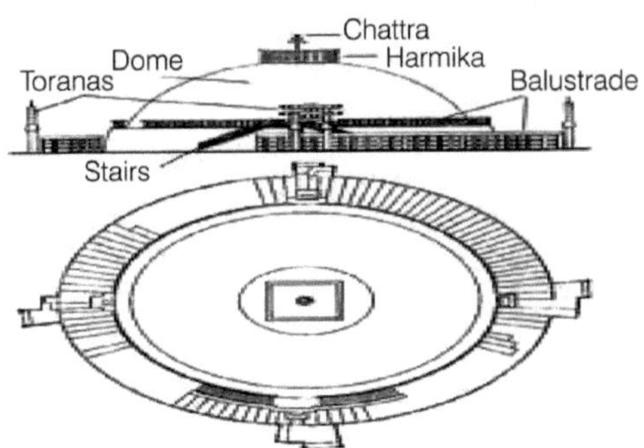

(i) Calculate the volume of the hemispherical dome if the height of the dome is 21 m.
  (a) 19404 cu m (b) 2000 cu m
  (c) 15000 cu m (d) 19000 cu m

(ii) The formula to find the volume of sphere is
  (a) $\dfrac{2}{3}\pi r^3$ (b) $\dfrac{4}{3}\pi r^3$
  (c) $4\pi r^2$ (d) $2\pi r^2$

(iii) The cloth require to cover the hemispherical dome if the radius of its base is 14m is
  (a) 1222 sq m (b) 1232 sq m
  (c) 1200 sq m (d) 1400 sq m

(iv) The total surface area of the combined figure i.e. hemispherical dome with radius 14 m and cuboidal shaped top with dimensions 8 m × 6 m × 4 m is
  (a) 1200 sq m (b) 1232 sq m
  (c) 1392 sq m (d) 1932 sq m

(v) The volume of the cuboidal shaped top is with dimensions mentioned in question (iv).
  (a) 182.45 m^3 (b) 282.45 m^3
  (c) 292 m^3 (d) 192 m^3

PART 2
Subjective Questions

• Short Answer Type Questions

1. Two identical cubes each of volume 64 cm^3 are joined together end to end. What is the surface area of the resulting cuboid?

2. How many shots each having diameter 3 cm can be made from a cuboidal lead solid of dimensions 9 cm × 11 cm × 12 cm?

3. 16 glass spheres each of radius 2 cm are packed into a cuboidal box of internal dimensions 16 cm × 8 cm × 8 cm and then the box is filled with water. Find the volume of water filled in the box.

4. If a solid piece of iron in the form of a cuboid of dimensions 49 cm × 33 cm × 24 cm, is moulded to form a solid sphere. Then, find radius of the sphere.

5. If volumes of two spheres are in the ratio 64 : 27, then find the ratio of their surface areas.

6. The decorative block shown in the following figure is made of two solids, a cube and a hemisphere. The base of the block is a cube with edge 6 cm and the hemisphere fixed on the top has a diameter of 2.1 cm, then find the total surface area of the block and find the total area to be painted.

$$\left[\text{take, } \pi = \frac{22}{7}\right]$$

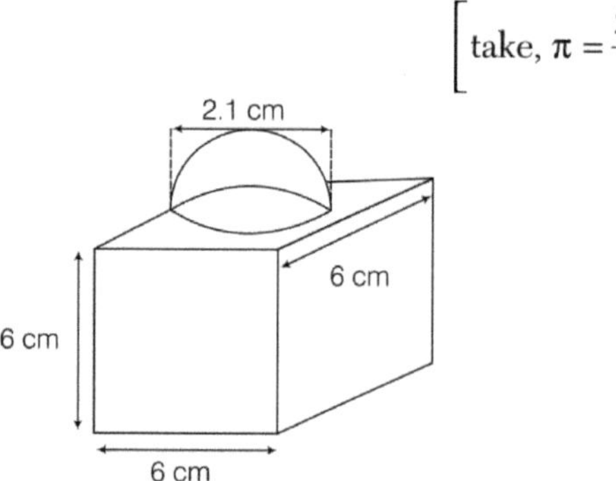

7. From a solid cube of side 7 cm, a conical cavity of height 7 cm and radius 3 cm is hollowed out. Find the volume of the remaining solid.

8. A hemispherical bowl of internal radius 9 cm is full of liquid. The liquid is to be filled into cylindrical shaped bottles each of radius 1.5 cm and height 4 cm. How many bottles are needed to empty the bowl?

9. A building is in the form of a cylinder surmounted by a hemispherical dome (see the figure). The base diameter of the dome is equal to $\frac{2}{3}$ of the total height of the building. Find the height of the building, if it contains $67\frac{1}{21}$ m^3 of air.

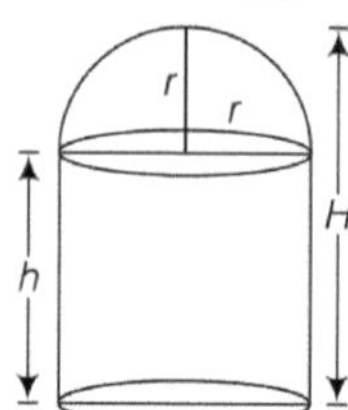

10. Twelve solid spheres of the same size are made by melting a solid metallic cylinder of base diameter 2 cm and height 16 cm. Find the diameter of each sphere.

11. A solid is composed of a cylinder with hemispherical ends. If the whole length of the solid is 104 cm and the radius of each hemispherical end is 7 cm, then find the cost of polishing its surface at the rate of ₹ 2 per dm^2.

$$\left[\text{take, } \pi = \frac{22}{7}\right]$$

12. A solid metallic hemisphere of radius 8 cm is melted and recasted into a right circular cone of base radius 6 cm. Determine the height of the cone.

13. A rectangular water tank of base 11 m × 6 m contains water upto a height of 5 m. If the water in the tank is transferred to a cylindrical tank of radius 3.5 m, find the height of the water level in the tank.

14. A copper rod of diameter 1 cm and length 8 cm is drawn into a wire of length 8 m of uniform thickness. Find the thickness of the wire.

15. The rain water from a roof of dimensions 22 m × 20 m drains into a cylindrical vessel having diameter of base 2 m and height 3.5 m. If the rain water collected from the roof just fill the cylindrical vessel, then find the rainfall (in cm).

16. A cylindrical bucket of height 32 cm and base radius 18 cm is filled with sand. This bucket is emptied on the ground and a conical heap of sand is formed. If the height of the conical heap is 24 cm, find the radius and slant height of the heap.

17. The barrel of a fountain pen, cylindrical in shape, is 7 cm long and 5 mm in diameter. A full barrel of ink in the pin is used up on writing 3300 words on an average. How many words can be written in a bottle of ink containing one-fifth of a litre?

18. Water flows at the rate of 10 m min^{-1} through a cylindrical pipe 5 mm in diameter. How long would it take to fill a conical vessel whose diameter at the base is 40 cm and depth 24 cm?

19. Water flows through a cylindrical pipe, whose inner radius is 1 cm, at the rate of 80 cms^{-1} in an empty cylindrical tank, the radius of whose base is 40 cm. What is the rise of water level in tank in half an hour?

20. A factory manufactures 120000 pencils daily. The pencils are cylindrical in shape each of length 25 cm and circumference of base as 1.5 cm. Determine the cost of colouring the curved surfaces of the pencils manufactured in one day at ₹ 0.05 per dm^2.

21. A well of diameter 10 m is dug 14 m deep. The Earth taken out of it is spread evenly all around to a width of 5 m to form an embankment. Find the height of embankment.

22. Marbles of diameter 1.4 cm are dropped into a cylindrical beaker of diameter 7 cm containing some water. Find the number of marbles that should be dropped into the beaker, so that the water level rises by 5.6 cm.

• Long Answer Type Questions

23. If a hollow cube of internal edge 22 cm is filled with spherical marbles of diameter 0.5 cm and it is assumed that $\dfrac{1}{8}$ space of the cube remains unfilled.

Then, the number of marbles that the cube can accomodate is

24. A solid iron cuboidal block of dimensions 4.4 m × 2.6 m × 1 m is recast into a hollow cylindrical pipe of internal radius 30 cm and thickness 5 cm. Find the length of the pipe.

25. A building is in the form of a cylinder surmounted by a hemispherical vaulted dome and contains $41\dfrac{19}{21}$ m^3 of air. If the internal diameter of dome is equal to its total height above the floor, find the height of the building?

26. A medicine-capsule is in the shape of a cylinder of diameter 0.5 cm with two hemispheres stuck to each of its ends. The length of entire capsule is 2 cm. The capacity of the capsule is

27. A rocket is in the form of a right circular cylinder closed at the lower end and surmounted by a cone with the same radius as that of the cylinder. The diameter and height of the cylinder are 6 cm and 12 cm, respectively. If the slant height of the conical portion is 5 cm, then find the total surface area and volume of the rocket. [use $\pi = 3.14$]

28. A solid toy is in the form of a hemisphere surmounted by a right circular cone. The height of the cone is 3 cm and the diameter of the base is 4 cm. Determine the volume of the solid toy. If a right circular cylinder circumscribes the toy, then find the difference of the volumes of the cylinder and the toy. [take, $\pi = 3.14$]

29. A wooden toy rocket is in the shape of a cone mounted on a cylinder, as shown in figure. The height of the entire rocket is 24 cm, while the height of the conical part is 4 cm.

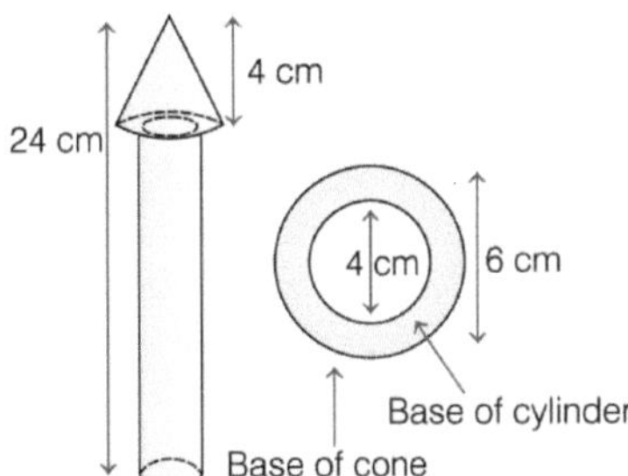

The base of the conical portion has a diameter of 6 cm, while the base diameter of the cylindrical portion is 4 cm. If the conical portion is to be painted orange and the cylindrical portion yellow, then find the area of the rocket painted with each of these colours. [take, $\pi = 3.14$]

30. Two solid cones A and B are placed in a cylindrical tube as shown in the figure. The ratio of their capacities is 2 : 1. Find the heights and capacities of cones. Also, find the volume of the remaining portion of the cylinder.

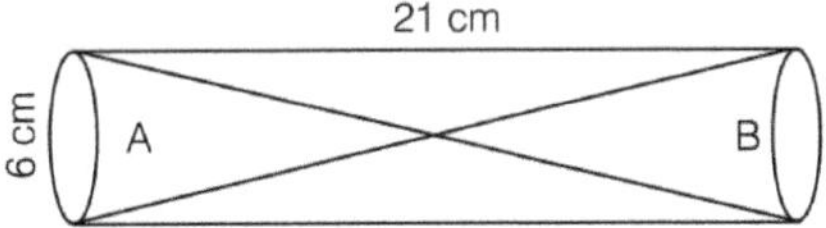

31. How many spherical lead shots of diameter 4 cm can be made out of a solid cube of lead whose edge measures 44 cm.

32. A metallic spherical shell of internal and external diameters 4 cm and 8 cm, respectively is melted and recast into the form of a cone of base diameter 8 cm. Find the height of the cone.

33. How many spherical lead shots each of diameter 4.2 cm can be obtained from a solid rectangular lead piece with dimensions 66 cm, 42 cm and 21 cm?

34. Find the number of metallic circular disc with 1.5 cm base diameter and of height 0.2 cm to be melted to form a right circular cylinder of height 10 cm and diameter 4.5 cm.

35. A heap of rice is in the form of a cone of diameter 9 m and height 3.5 m. Find the volume of the rice. How much canvas cloth is required to just cover heap?

36. How many cubic centimetres of iron is required to construct an open box whose external dimensions are 36 cm, 25 cm and 16.5 cm provided the thickness of the iron is 1.5 cm. If one cubic centimetre of iron weights 7.5 g, then find the weight of the box.

37. Water is flowing at the rate of 15 kmh^{-1} through a pipe of diameter 14 cm into a cuboidal pond which is 50 m long and 44 m wide. In what time will the level of water in pond rise by 21 cm?

• Case Base Questions

38. Mathematics teacher of a school took her 10th standard students to show Ram Mandir. It was a part of their Educational trip. The teacher had interest in history as well. She narrated the facts of Ram Mandir to students.

Ram mandir is a Hindu temple that is being built in Ayodhya, which is in Uttar Pradesh. The temple construction is being supervised by the Shri Ram Janmabhoomi Teerth Kshetra.

Then the teacher said in this monuments one can find combination of solid figures. She pointed that there are cubical bases and in centre cylinder with the cone shape structure on the top is constructed.

(i) Ram Mandir is constructed in the form of the cubical base of 30 cm × 20 cm × 10 cm, then find the area covered.

(ii) If the radius of the cylinder is 7 cm and Height of the cylinder is 60 cm and the radius of the cone is similar to that of cylinder and Height of the cone is 24 cm, then the ratio of curved surface area of cylinder to curved surface area of the cone.

(iii) Given structure in based on the concept of

(a) Area and perimeter

(b) Surface area and volume

(c) Both (a) and (b)

(d) None of the above

39. Adventure camps are the perfect place for the children to practice decision making for themselves without parents and teachers guiding their every move. Some students of a school reached for adventure at Sakleshpur. At the camp, the waiters served some students with a welcome drink in a cylindrical glass and some students in a hemispherical cup whose dimensions are shown below.

After that they went for a jungle trek. The jungle trek was enjoyable but tiring. As dusk fell, it was time to take shelter. Each group of four students was given a canvas of area 551m². Each group had to make a conical tent to accommodate all the four students. Assuming that all the stitching and wasting incurred while cutting, would amount to 1 m², the students put the tents. The radius of the tent is 7 m.　　　**[CBSE Question Bank]**

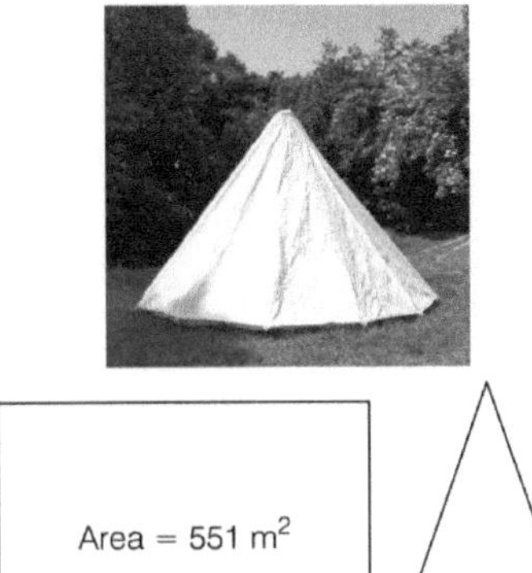

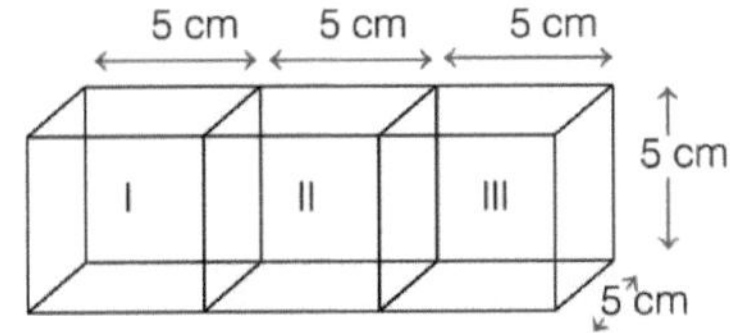

(i) Find the volume of cylindrical cup.

(ii) Find the volume of hemispherical cup.

(iii) Find the height of the conical tent prepared to accommodate four students.

40. On a Sunday, your Parents took you to a fair. You could see lot of toys displayed, and you wanted them to buy a RUBIK's cube and strawberry ice-cream for you.

Observe the figures and answer the questions.
　　　[CBSE Question Bank]

(i) Find the length of the diagonal if each edge measures 6cm.

(ii) Find volume of the solid figure if the length of the edge is 7cm.

(iii) What is the curved surface area of hemisphere (ice-cream) if the base radius is 7 cm?

(iv) Find the slant height of a cone if the radius is 7 cm and the height is 24 cm

(v) Find the total surface area of cone with hemispherical ice cream.

SOLUTIONS

Objective Questions

1. (c) Here, on joining three cubes, we get a cuboid whose length, $l = 5 + 5 + 5 = 15$ cm, breadth, $b = 5$ cm and height, $h = 5$ cm

∴ Required surface area of the resulting solid

= Surface area of new cuboid

$= 2(lb + bh + hl) = 2(15 \times 5 + 5 \times 5 + 5 \times 15)$

$= 2(75 + 25 + 75) = 2(175) = 350 \text{ cm}^2$

2. (a) Because solid ball is exactly fitted inside the cubical box of side a. So, a is the diameter for the solid ball.

∴　　　Radius of the ball $= \dfrac{a}{2}$

So,　　volume of the ball $= \dfrac{4}{3}\pi\left(\dfrac{a}{2}\right)^3 = \dfrac{1}{6}\pi a^3$

3. (c) Given, volume of brick $= 22^3 \text{ cm}^3$

∴Volume of 1 cone $= \dfrac{1}{3}\pi r^2 h$

$= \dfrac{1}{3} \times \dfrac{22}{7} \times 2 \times 2 \times 7 = \dfrac{22 \times 4}{3}$

Let number of cones $= n$

Then, $n \times 22 \times \dfrac{4}{3} = 22 \times 22 \times 22$

$\Rightarrow$　　　$n = \dfrac{22 \times 22 \times 3}{4}$

∴　　　$n = 121 \times 3 = 363$

4. (b) Because the sphere encloses in the cylinder, therefore the diameter of sphere is equal to diameter of cylinder which is $2r$ cm.

5. (a) Because curved surface area of a hemisphere is $2\pi r^2$ and here, we join two solid hemispheres along their bases of radius r, from which we get a solid sphere.

Hence, the curved surface area of new solid

$= 2\pi r^2 + 2\pi r^2 = 4\pi r^2$

6. (d) Since, the total surface area of cylinder of radius r and height $h = 2\pi rh + 2\pi r^2$

When one cylinder is placed over the other cylinder of same height and radius,

then height of the new cylinder $= 2h$

and radius of the new cylinder $= r$

$\therefore$ Total surface area of the new cylinder $= 2\pi r(2h) + 2\pi r^2$

$$= 4\pi rh + 2\pi r^2$$

$$= 2\pi r(2h + r)$$

7. (a) Because the shape of sharpened pencil is

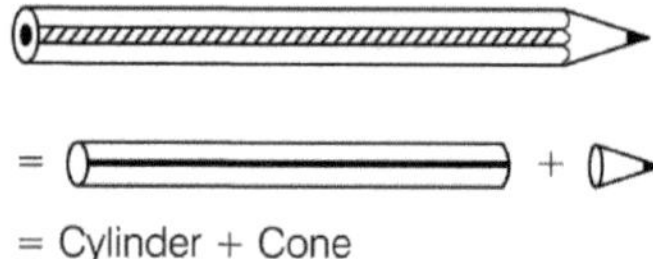

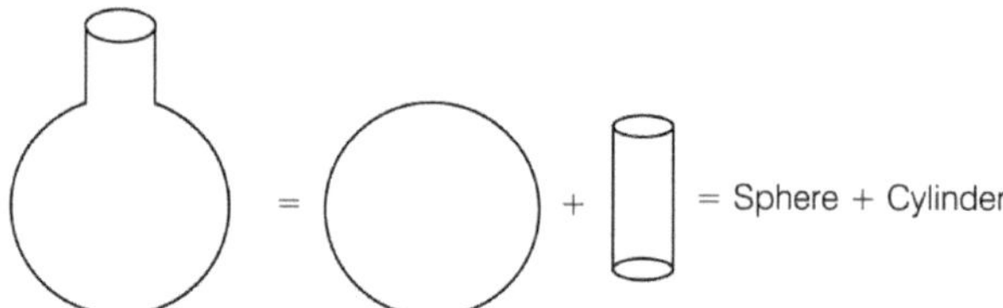

$$= \text{Cylinder} + \text{Cone}$$

8. (a) Because the shape of surahi is

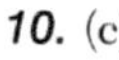

$$= \text{Sphere} + \text{Cylinder}$$

9. (b) Let the radii of two cones are r_1, r_2 and their heights are h_1 and h_2.

Given, $\dfrac{r_1}{r_2} = \dfrac{3}{1}$ and $\dfrac{h_1}{h_2} = \dfrac{1}{3}$

Now, the ratio of their volumes, $\dfrac{V_1}{V_2} = \dfrac{\frac{1}{3}\pi r_1^2 h_1}{\frac{1}{3}\pi r_2^2 h_2} = \left(\dfrac{r_1}{r_2}\right)^2\left(\dfrac{h_1}{h_2}\right)$

$$= \left(\dfrac{3}{1}\right)^2 \times \left(\dfrac{1}{3}\right) = 9 \times \dfrac{1}{3} = \dfrac{3}{1} = 3:1$$

Hence, the ratio of their volumes is $3:1$.

10. (c)

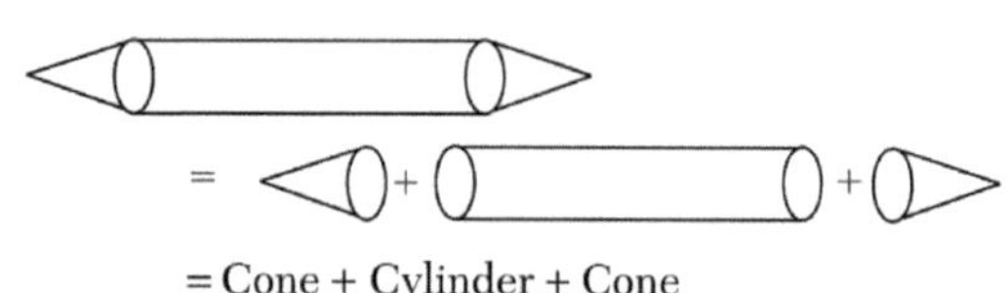

$$= \text{Cone} + \text{Cylinder} + \text{Cone}$$

$$= \text{Two cones and a cylinder}$$

11. (b)

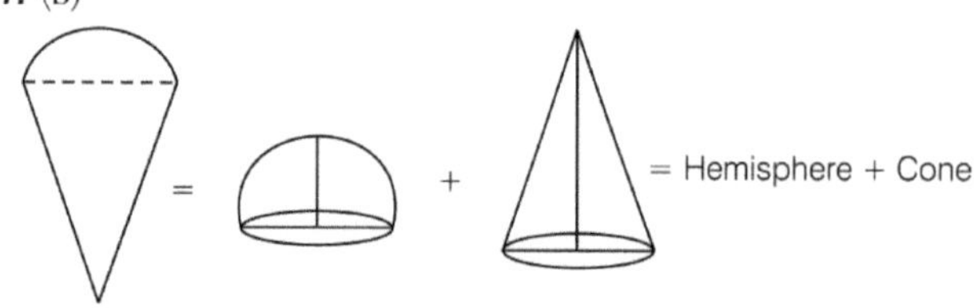

$$= \text{Hemisphere} + \text{Cone}$$

12. (c) We know that, total surface area of a cone of radius, r and height, h = Curved surface Area + area of base

$$= \pi rl + \pi r^2$$

where, $\qquad l = \sqrt{h^2 + r^2}$

and total surface area of a cylinder of base radius, r and height, h

$$= \text{Curved surface area} + \text{Area of both base}$$

$$= 2\pi rh + 2\pi r^2$$

Here, when we placed a cone over a cylinder, then one base is common for both.

So, total surface area of the combined solid

$$= \pi rl + 2\pi rh + \pi r^2$$

$$= \pi r\,[\,l + 2h + r\,]$$

$$= \pi r\left[\sqrt{r^2 + h^2} + 2h + r\right]$$

13. (c) We know that, capacity of cylindrical vessel $= \pi r^2 h$ cm^3

and capacity of hemisphere $= \dfrac{2}{3}\pi r^3$ cm

From the figure, capacity of the cylindrical vessel

$$= \pi r^2 h - \dfrac{2}{3}\pi r^3 = \dfrac{1}{3}\pi r^2[\,3h - 2r\,]$$

14. (c) We have, diameter of metallic sphere $= 6$ cm

$\therefore$ Radius of metallic sphere, $r_1 = 3$ cm

Also, diameter of cross-section of cylindrical wire $= 0.2$ cm

$\therefore$ Radius of cross-sections of cylindrical wire, $r_2 = 0.1$ cm

Let the length of the wire be h cm.

Since, metallic sphere is converted into a cylindrical shaped wire of length h cm.

$\therefore$ Volume of the metal used in wire = Volume of the sphere

$$\Rightarrow \qquad \pi r_2^2 h = \dfrac{4}{3}\pi r_1^3$$

$$\Rightarrow \qquad \pi \times \left(\dfrac{1}{10}\right)^2 \times h = \dfrac{4}{3} \times \pi \times 27$$

$$\Rightarrow \qquad \pi \times \dfrac{1}{100} \times h = 36\pi$$

$$\Rightarrow \qquad h = \dfrac{36\pi \times 100}{\pi}$$

$$= 3600 \text{ cm} = 36 \text{ m}$$

$$[\because 1\text{m} = 100\text{cm}]$$

15. (c) During conversion of a solid from one shape to another, the volume of the new shape will remain unaltered.

16. (c) Volume of the remaining solid

$$= \text{Volume of the cylinder} - \text{Volume of the cone}$$

$$= \left\{\pi \times 6^2 \times 10 - \dfrac{1}{3} \times \pi \times 6^2 \times 10\right\}$$

$$= (360\pi - 120\pi) = 240\pi \text{ cm}^3$$

17. (a) $\because$ Radius of the well $= \dfrac{7}{2}$ m $= 3.5$ m

$\therefore$ Volume of the earth dug out $= \dfrac{22}{7} \times (3.5)^2 \times 20$

$$= \dfrac{22}{7} \times 3.5 \times 3.5 \times 20$$

$$= 770 \text{ m}^3$$

Area of platform $= (22 \times 14)$ m^2 $= 308$ m^2

$$\therefore \qquad \text{Height} = \dfrac{770}{308} = 2.5 \text{ m}$$

18. (b) Let the radius of original right circular cylinder be 'r' cm. and height be 'h' cm. Then,

Volume of original cylinder $V_1 = (\pi r^2 h)\,\text{cm}^3$

Volume of circular cylinder, when radius is halved

$$V_2 = \pi \left(\frac{r}{2}\right)^2 h\,\text{cm}^3 = \frac{\pi r^2 h}{4}\,\text{cm}^3$$

Thus, $\dfrac{V_2}{V_1} = \dfrac{\pi r^2 h}{4} \times \dfrac{1}{\pi r^2 h} = \dfrac{1}{4}$.

19. (a) So, volume of one spherial marble $= \dfrac{4}{3}\pi (0.7)^3$

$$\left[\because \text{ volume of sphere} = \frac{4}{3}\pi r^3\right]$$

$$= \frac{1.372}{3}\pi\,\text{cm}^3$$

$\therefore$ Volume of the raised water in beaker $= \pi\,(3.5)^2 \times 5.6$

$$[\because \text{ volume of cylinder} = \pi r^2 h]$$

$$= 68.6\,\pi\,\text{cm}^3$$

Now, required number of marbles

$$= \frac{\text{Volume of the raised water in beaker}}{\text{Volume of one spherical marble}}$$

$$= \frac{68.6\,\pi}{1.372\,\pi} \times 3 = 150 \text{ marbles}$$

20. (a) Given, wooden article is a combination of a cylinder and two hemispheres.

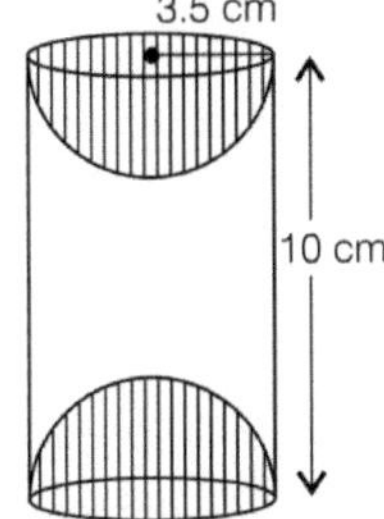

Here, height of the cylinder, $h = 10\,\text{cm}$

$\because$ Radius of base of the cylinder

$$= \text{Radius of hemisphere}, r = 3.5\text{ cm}$$

Now, required TSA of the wooden article

$$= 2 \times \text{CSA of one hemisphere} + \text{CSA of cylinder}$$

$$= 2 \times (2\pi r^2) + 2\pi r h$$

$$= 2\,\pi r\,(2r + h)$$

$$= 2 \times \frac{22}{7} \times 3.5 \times (2 \times 3.5 + 10)$$

$$= \frac{22}{7} \times 7 \times (7 + 10) = 22 \times 17 = 374\,\text{cm}^2$$

21. (b) Given diameter $d = 24\,\text{m}$

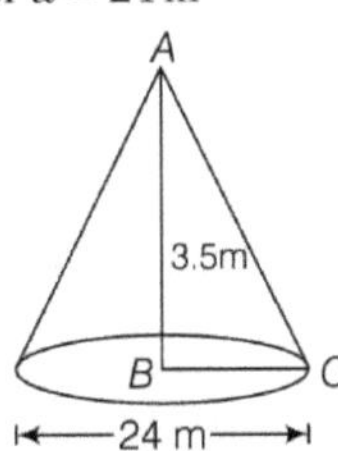

Now, volume of rice = volume of cone $= \dfrac{1}{3}\pi r^2 h$

$$= \frac{1}{3} \times \frac{22}{7} \times (12)^2 \times 3.5 \quad \left[\because r = \frac{d}{2} = \frac{24}{2} = 12\text{ m}\right]$$

$$= \frac{22 \times 144 \times 3.5}{21}$$

$$= \frac{11088}{21} = 528\,\text{m}^3$$

Now, slant height $l = \sqrt{h^2 + r^2}$

$$= \sqrt{(3.5)^2 + (12)^2} = \sqrt{12.25 + 144}$$

$$= \sqrt{156.25} = 12.5\,\text{m}$$

$\therefore$ The canvas required to cover the heap $= \pi r l$

$$= \frac{22}{7} \times 12 \times 12.5 = \frac{3300}{7} = 471.42\,\text{m}^2$$

22. (b) Volume of the wall $= 270 \times 300 \times 350 = 28350000\,\text{cm}^3$

$$[\because \text{ volume of cuboid} = \text{length} \times \text{breadth} \times \text{height}]$$

Since, $\dfrac{1}{8}$ space of wall is covered by mortar.

So, remaining space of wall = Volume of wall

$$- \text{Volume of mortar}$$

$$= 28350000 - 28350000 \times \frac{1}{8}$$

$$= 28350000 - 3543750$$

$$= 24806250\,\text{cm}^3$$

Now, volume of one brick $= 22.5 \times 11.25 \times 8.75$

$$= 2214.844\,\text{cm}^3$$

$$[\because \text{ volume of cuboid} = \text{length} \times \text{breadth} \times \text{height}]$$

$\therefore$ Required number of bricks $= \dfrac{24806250}{2214.844} = 11200$ (approx.)

Hence, the number of bricks used to construct the wall is 11200.

23. (i) (b) Since, volume of sphere = Volume of cylinder

$$\Rightarrow \frac{4}{3}\pi R^3 = \pi r^2 h, \text{ where } R, r \text{ are the radii of sphere and}$$

cylinder, respectively.

$$\Rightarrow \quad R^3 = r^2 \times h \times \frac{3}{4}$$

$$\Rightarrow \quad R^3 = \frac{4 \times 4 \times 18 \times 3}{4} = 8 \times 27 \Rightarrow R^3 = (2 \times 3)^3$$

$$\therefore \quad R = 6\text{ cm}$$

(ii) (a) Volume of sphere $= \dfrac{4}{3}\pi R^3 = \dfrac{4}{3} \times \dfrac{22}{7} \times 6 \times 6 \times 6$

$$= 905.14\,\text{cm}^3$$

(iii) (c) Since the volume of sphere is equal to volume of cylinder, then the ratio of volume of the sphere to the volume of cylinder $= 1 : 1$

(iv) (a) Total surface area of cylinder $= 2\pi r(r + h)$

$$= 2 \times \frac{22}{7} \times 4(4 + 18) = 2 \times \frac{22}{7} \times 4 \times 22$$

$$= 553.14\,\text{cm}^2$$

(v) (c) During the conversion of a solid from one shape to another the volume of new shape will remain unaltered.

24. We have radius of each CD cassette $= 4$ cm

and thickness of each cassette $= 1$ cm

So, height of cylindrical made by Geeta, $h_1 = 10 \times 1 = 10$ cm

and height of cylindrical made by Meena, $h_2 = 6 \times 1 = 6$ cm

(i) (d) Curved surface area of cylinder made by Geeta

$$= 2\pi r h = 2 \times \frac{22}{7} \times 4 \times 10 = 251.42 \text{ cm}^2$$

(ii) (c) $\therefore$ Required ratio $= \dfrac{\begin{bmatrix} \text{Curved surface area of} \\ \text{cylinder made by Geeta} \end{bmatrix}}{\begin{bmatrix} \text{Curved surface area of} \\ \text{cylinder made by Meena} \end{bmatrix}}$

$$= \frac{2\pi r h_1}{2\pi r h_2} = \frac{h_1}{h_2} = \frac{10}{6} = 5 : 3$$

(iii) (a) Volume of cylinder made by Meena

$$= \pi r^2 h_2 = \frac{22}{7} \times 4 \times 4 \times 6$$

$$= 301.44 \text{ cm}^3$$

(iv) (d) Required ratio

$$= \frac{\text{Volume of the cylinder made by Geeta}}{\text{Volume of the cylinder made by Meena}}$$

$$= \frac{\pi r^2 h_1}{\pi r^2 h_2} = \frac{h_1}{h_2} = 5 : 3$$

(v) (a) When two CD Cassette are shifted from Geeta's cylinder to Meena's cylinder, then length of both cylinders become equal.

So, volume of both cylinders become equal.

25. (i) (a) As, we know that hemisphere is a type of solid in which radius is the height. So, radius $= 21$ m

$\therefore$ Required volume $= \dfrac{2}{3}\pi r^3$

$$= \frac{2}{3} \times \frac{22}{7} \times 21 \times 21 \times 21$$

$$= 19404 \text{ cu m}$$

(ii) (b) Volume of sphere $= \dfrac{4}{3}\pi r^3$

(iii) (b) Given, radius $(r) = 14$ m

$\therefore$ Curved surface area of hemisphere dome $= 2\pi r^2$

$$= 2 \times \frac{22}{7} \times 14 \times 14$$

$$= 1232 \text{ sq m}$$

(iv) (c) Here, radius of hemispherical dome $(r) = 14$ m

Surface area of dome $= 2\pi r^2$

$$= 2 \times \frac{22}{7} \times 14 \times 14 = 1232 \text{ m}^2$$

and CSA of cuboidal shaped top $= 2 \times h(l+b) + lb$

$$= 2 \times 4(8+6) + 8 \times 6$$

$$= 8(14) + 48$$

$$= 112 + 48 = 160 \text{ m}^2$$

$\therefore$ Total surface area $= 1232 + 160 = 1392 \text{ m}^2$

(v) (d) Volume of cuboidal shape $= lbh$

$$= 8 \times 6 \times 4 = 192 \text{ m}^3$$

Subjective Questions

1. Let the length of a side of a cube $= a$ cm

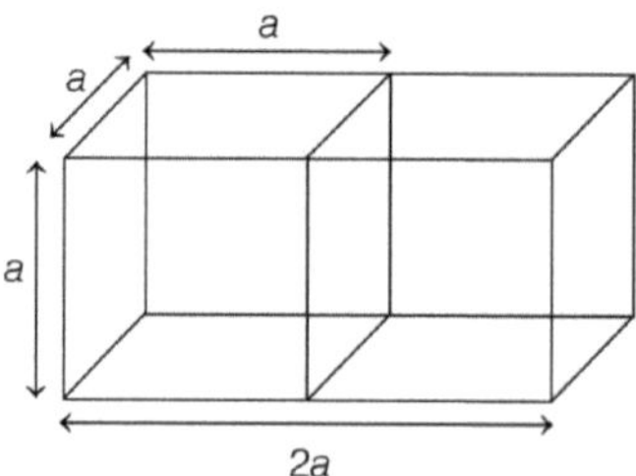

Given, volume of the cube, $a^3 = 64 \text{ cm}^3 \Rightarrow a = 4$ cm

On joining two cubes, we get a cuboid whose

$$\text{length, } l = 2a \text{ cm}$$

$$\text{breadth, } b = a \text{ cm}$$

and $\qquad\qquad$ height, $h = a$ cm

Now, surface area of the resulting cuboid

$$= 2(lb + bh + hl)$$

$$= 2(2a \cdot a + a \cdot a + a \cdot 2a)$$

$$= 2(2a^2 + a^2 + 2a^2) = 2(5a^2)$$

$$= 10a^2 = 10(4)^2 = 160 \text{ cm}^2$$

2. Given, dimensions of cuboidal $= 9 \text{ cm} \times 11 \text{ cm} \times 12 \text{ cm}$

$\therefore$ Volume of cuboidal $= 9 \times 11 \times 12 = 1188 \text{ cm}^3$

and diameter of shot $= 3$ cm

$\therefore$ Radius of shot, $r = \dfrac{3}{2} = 1.5$ cm

$$\text{Volume of shot} = \frac{4}{3}\pi r^3 = \frac{4}{3} \times \frac{22}{7} \times (1.5)^3$$

$$= \frac{297}{21} = 14.143 \text{ cm}^3$$

$\therefore$ Required number of shots $= \dfrac{1188}{14.143} = 84$ (approx.)

3. Given, dimensions of the cuboidal $= 16 \text{ cm} \times 8 \text{ cm} \times 8 \text{ cm}$

$\therefore$ Volume of the cuboidal $= 16 \times 8 \times 8 = 1024 \text{ cm}^3$

Also, given radius of one glass sphere $= 2$ cm

$\therefore$ Volume of one glass sphere $= \dfrac{4}{3}\pi r^3 = \dfrac{4}{3} \times \dfrac{22}{7} \times (2)^3$

$$= \frac{704}{21} = 33.523 \text{ cm}^3$$

Now, volume of 16 glass spheres $= 16 \times 33.523 = 536.37 \text{ cm}^3$

$\therefore$ Required volume of water $=$ Volume of cuboidal

$$- \text{ Volume of 16 glass spheres}$$

$$= 1024 - 536.37$$

$$= 487.6 \text{ cm}^3$$

4. Given, dimensions of the cuboid $= 49 \text{ cm} \times 33 \text{ cm} \times 24 \text{ cm}$

$\therefore$ Volume of the cuboid $= 49 \times 33 \times 24 = 38808 \text{ cm}^3$

$$[\because \text{ volume of cuboid} = \text{length} \times \text{breadth} \times \text{height}]$$

Let the radius of the sphere is r, then

Volume of the sphere $= \dfrac{4}{3}\pi r^3$

$$\left[\because \text{ volume of the sphere} = \frac{4}{3}\pi \times (\text{radius})^3\right]$$

According to the question,

Volume of the sphere = Volume of the cuboid

$$\Rightarrow \quad \frac{4}{3}\pi r^3 = 38808$$

$$\Rightarrow \quad 4 \times \frac{22}{7} r^3 = 38808 \times 3$$

$$\Rightarrow \quad r^3 = \frac{38808 \times 3 \times 7}{4 \times 22} = 441 \times 21$$

$$\Rightarrow \quad r^3 = 21 \times 21 \times 21$$

$$\therefore \quad r = 21 \text{ cm}$$

Hence, the radius of the sphere is 21 cm.

5. Let the radii of the two spheres are r_1 and r_2, respectively.

$$\therefore \quad \text{Volume of the sphere of radius, } r_1 = V_1 = \frac{4}{3}\pi r_1^3 \qquad \text{...(i)}$$

$$\left[\because \text{volume of sphere} = \frac{4}{3}\pi \,(\text{radius})^3\right]$$

and volume of the sphere of radius, $r_2 = V_2 = \frac{4}{3}\pi \, r_2^3 \qquad \text{...(ii)}$

Given, ratio of volumes $= V_1 : V_2 = 64 : 27 \Rightarrow \dfrac{\frac{4}{3}\pi r_1^3}{\frac{4}{3}\pi r_2^3} = \dfrac{64}{27}$

$$[\text{using Eqs. (i) and (ii)}]$$

$$\Rightarrow \quad \frac{r_1^3}{r_2^3} = \frac{64}{27} \Rightarrow \frac{r_1}{r_2} = \frac{4}{3} \qquad \text{...(iii)}$$

Now, ratio of surface area $= \dfrac{4\pi r_1^2}{4\pi r_2^2}$

$$[\because \text{surface area of a sphere} = 4\pi \,(\text{radius})^2]$$

$$= \frac{r_1^2}{r_2^2}$$

$$= \left(\frac{r_1}{r_2}\right)^2 = \left(\frac{4}{3}\right)^2 = \frac{16}{9} \qquad [\text{using Eq. (iii)}]$$

Hence, the required ratio of their surface area is 16 : 9.

6. Here, the decorative block is a combination of a cube and a hemisphere.

For cubical portion,

Each edge = 6 cm

For hemispherical portion,

$$\text{Diameter} = 2.1 \text{ cm}$$

$$\therefore \quad \text{Radius, } r = \frac{2.1}{2} \text{ cm}$$

Now, total surface area of the cube

$$= 6 \times (\text{Edge})^2 = 6 \times 6 \times 6 = 216 \text{ cm}^2$$

Here, the part of the cube where the hemisphere is attached, is not included in the surface area.

So, the total surface area of the decorative block

= Total surface area of cube − Area of base of hemisphere

$$\qquad\qquad\qquad + \text{Curved surface area of hemisphere}$$

$$= 216 - \pi r^2 + 2\pi r^2 = 216 + \pi r^2$$

$$= 216 + \frac{22}{7} \times \frac{2.1}{2} \times \frac{2.1}{2}$$

$$= 216 + 3.465 = 219.465 \text{ cm}^2$$

Clearly, the total area to be painted = Total surface area of

$$\text{the decorative block} - \text{Area of base of cube}$$

$$= 219.465 - 6^2 = 219.465 - 36 = 183.465 \text{ cm}^2$$

7. Given that, side of a solid cube $(a) = 7$ cm

Height of conical cavity i.e. cone, $h = 7$ cm

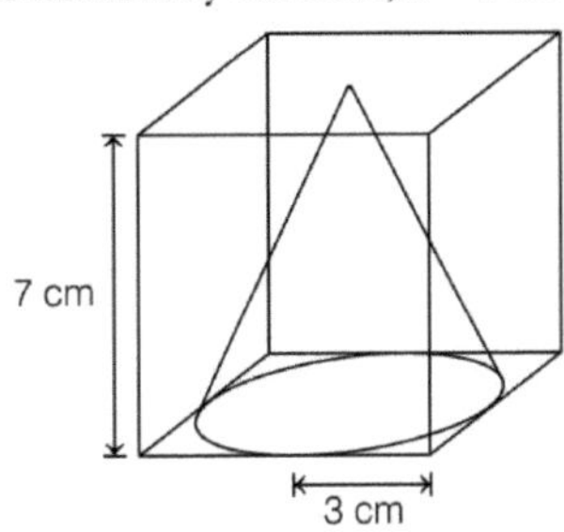

Since, the height of conical cavity and the side of cube is equal that means the conical cavity fit vertically in the cube.

Radius of conical cavity i.e. cone, $r = 3$ cm

$$\Rightarrow \qquad \text{Diameter} = 2 \times r = 2 \times 3 = 6 \text{ cm}$$

Since, the diameter is less than the side of a cube that means the base of a conical cavity is not fit inhorizontal face of cube.

Now, volume of cube $= (\text{side})^3 = a^3 = (7)^3 = 343 \text{ cm}^3$

and volume of conical cavity i.e. cone $= \dfrac{1}{3}\pi \times r^2 \times h$

$$= \frac{1}{3} \times \frac{22}{7} \times 3 \times 3 \times 7$$

$$= 66 \text{ cm}^3$$

$\therefore$ Volume of remaining solid = Volume of cube

$$- \text{Volume of conical cavity}$$

$$= 343 - 66 = 277 \text{ cm}^3$$

Hence, the required volume of solid is 277 cm^3.

8. Given, radius of hemispherical bowl, $r = 9$ cm

and radius of cylindrical bottles, $R = 1.5$ cm and height, $h = 4$ cm

$\therefore$ Number of required cylindrical bottles

$$= \frac{\text{Volume of hemispherical bowl}}{\text{Volume of one cylindrical bottle}}$$

$$= \frac{\frac{2}{3}\pi r^3}{\pi R^2 h}$$

$$= \frac{\frac{2}{3} \times \pi \times 9 \times 9 \times 9}{\pi \times 1.5 \times 1.5 \times 4} = 54$$

9. Let r be the radius of the hemispherical dome and total height of building be H m.

It is given that diameter of dome

$$= \frac{2}{3} \times \text{Total height of the building}$$

$$\Rightarrow \qquad r = \frac{1}{3}H \text{ m}$$

Let h m be the height of the cylinder.

$$\therefore \qquad h = H - r = H - \frac{1}{3}H = \frac{2}{3}H\text{m}$$

Volume of the air inside the building = Volume of air
inside the dome + Volume of air inside the cylinder

$$= \frac{2}{3}\pi r^3 + \pi r^2 h$$

$$= \pi\left[\frac{2}{3}\left(\frac{1}{3}H\right)^3 + \left(\frac{1}{3}H\right)^2\left(\frac{2}{3}H\right)\right]$$

$$= \pi\left[\frac{2H^3}{81} + \frac{2}{27}H^3\right]$$

$$= \frac{8}{81}\pi H^3 \text{ m}^3$$

Given, volume of the air inside the building $= 67\frac{1}{21}$ m^3

$$\therefore \qquad \frac{8}{81}\pi H^3 = \frac{1408}{21}$$

$$\Rightarrow \qquad H^3 = \frac{1408}{21} \times \frac{81}{8\pi}$$

$$\Rightarrow \qquad H^3 = \frac{1408 \times 81 \times 7}{21 \times 8 \times 22}$$

$$\Rightarrow \qquad H^3 = 216 \Rightarrow H = 6 \text{ m}$$

10. Given, diameter of the cylinder = 2 cm

$\therefore$ Radius = 1 cm and height of the cylinder = 16 cm

$$[\because \text{ diameter} = 2 \times \text{radius}]$$

$\therefore$ Volume of the cylinder $= \pi \times (1)^2 \times 16 = 16\pi$ cm^3

$$[\because \text{ volume of cylinder} = \pi \times (\text{radius})^2 \times \text{height}]$$

Now, let the radius of solid sphere $= r$ cm

Then, its volume $= \frac{4}{3}\pi r^3$ cm^3

$$[\because \text{ volume of sphere} = \frac{4}{3} \times \pi \times (\text{radius})^3]$$

According to the question,

Volume of the twelve solid sphere = Volume of cylinder

$$\Rightarrow \qquad 12 \times \frac{4}{3}\pi r^3 = 16\pi$$

$$\Rightarrow \qquad r^3 = 1 \Rightarrow r = 1 \text{ cm}$$

$\therefore$ Diameter of each sphere, $d = 2r = 2 \times 1 = 2$ cm

Hence, the required diameter of each sphere is 2 cm.

11. Given, whole length of the solid = 104 cm

and the radius of each hemisphere = 7 cm

Therefore, the length of the cylindrical part of the solid

$$= (104 - 2 \times 7) = 90 \text{ cm}$$

For hemispherical portion,

Radius, $r = 7$ cm

For cylindrical portion,

Radius, $r = 7$ cm

Height, $h = 90$ cm

$\therefore$ Total surface area of the solid

$$= 2 \times \text{Curved surface area of a hemisphere}$$
$$+ \text{Curved surface area of cylindrical part}$$

$$= 2\left[2\pi r^2\right] + 2\pi r h$$

$$= 2 \times \left[2\pi\,(7)^2\right] + 2\pi\,(7)\,(90)$$

$$= 2 \times \left[2 \times \frac{22}{7} \times (7)^2\right] + 2 \times \frac{22}{7} \times (7)\,(90)$$

$$= 4 \times 22 \times 7 + 2 \times 22 \times 90 = 22\,[28 + 180]$$

$$= 4576 \text{ cm}^2$$

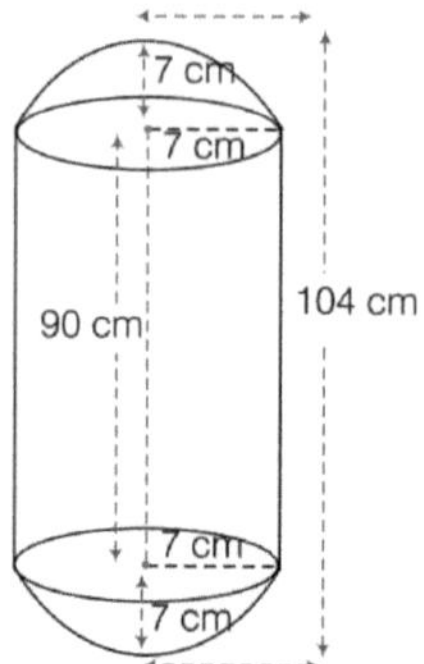

Then, the cost of polishing at the rate of ₹ 2 per dm^2

$$= ₹ \frac{4576 \times 2}{100} = ₹ 91.52 \qquad [\because 1 \text{ dm}^2 = 100 \text{ cm}^2]$$

12. Let height of the cone be h.

Given, radius of the base of the cone = 6 cm

$$\therefore \quad \text{Volume of circular cone} = \frac{1}{3}\pi r^2 h = \frac{1}{3}\pi\,(6)^2\,h$$

$$= \frac{36\,\pi\,h}{3} = 12\,\pi\,h \text{ cm}^3$$

Also, given radius of the hemisphere = 8 cm

$$\therefore \text{Volume of the hemisphere} = \frac{2}{3}\pi\,r^3 = \frac{2}{3}\pi\,(8)^3$$

$$= \frac{512 \times 2\pi}{3} \text{ cm}^3$$

According to the question,

Volume of the cone = Volume of the hemisphere

$$\Rightarrow \qquad 12\pi h = \frac{512 \times 2\pi}{3}$$

$$\therefore \qquad h = \frac{512 \times 2\pi}{12 \times 3\,\pi} = \frac{256}{9} = 28.44 \text{ cm}$$

13. Given, dimensions of base of rectangular tank = 11 m $\times$ 6 m

and height of water = 5 m

Volume of the water in rectangular tank $= 11 \times 6 \times 5$

$$= 330 \text{ m}^3$$

Also, given radius of the cylindrical tank = 3.5 m

Let height of water level in cylindrical tank be h.

Then, volume of the water in cylindrical tank $= \pi r^2 h$

$$= \pi\,(3.5)^2 \times h$$

$$= \frac{22}{7} \times 3.5 \times 3.5 \times h = 11.0 \times 3.5 \times h = 38.5\,h \text{ m}^3$$

According to the question,

$$330 = 38.5\,h$$

[since, volume of water is same in both tanks]

$$\therefore \qquad h = \frac{330}{38.5} = \frac{3300}{385}$$

$$\therefore \qquad = 8.57 \text{ m or } 8.6 \text{ m}$$

Hence, the height of water level in cylindrical tank is 8.6 m.

14. Here, a rod of cylindrical shape is converted into a wire of cylindrical shape.

For rod,

Diameter $= 1$ cm $\Rightarrow$ Radius, $r_1 = \dfrac{1}{2}$ cm and length,

$h = 8$ cm

$\therefore$ Volume of the rod $= \pi r_1^2 h = \pi \times \left(\dfrac{1}{2}\right)^2 \times 8 = 2\pi$ cm^3

For wire,

Length $= 8$ m $= 800$ cm $\qquad\qquad$ [$\because 1$ m $= 100$ cm]

Let r be the radius (in cm) of cross-section of the wire, then

Volume of wire $= \pi \times r^2 \times 800$ cm^3

Since, the rod is converted into wire, so

$\qquad$ Volume of wire $=$ Volume of rod

$\Rightarrow \qquad \pi \times r^2 \times 800 = 2\pi \Rightarrow r^2 = \dfrac{1}{400} \Rightarrow r = \dfrac{1}{20}$ cm

Then, diameter $= \dfrac{2}{20} = \dfrac{1}{10}$ cm

Hence, the diameter of the cross-section, i.e. the thickness of the wire is $\dfrac{1}{10}$ cm, i.e. 1 mm [$\because 1$ cm $= 10$ mm]

15. Given, length of roof $= 22$ m and breadth of roof $= 20$ m

Let the rainfall be a cm.

$\therefore$ Volume of water on the roof $= 22 \times 20 \times \dfrac{a}{100} = \dfrac{22a}{5}$ m^3

Also, we have radius of base of the cylindrical vessel, $r = 1$ m and height of the cylindrical vessel, $h = 3.5$ m

$\therefore$ Volume of water in the cylindrical vessel when it is just full

$$= \pi r^2 h = \left(\dfrac{22}{7} \times 1 \times 1 \times \dfrac{7}{2}\right) = 11 \text{ m}^3$$

Now, volume of water on the roof $=$ Volume of water in the vessel

$\Rightarrow \qquad\qquad \dfrac{22a}{5} = 11$

$\therefore \qquad\qquad a = \dfrac{11 \times 5}{22} = 2.5$ cm

$\qquad\qquad$ [$\because$ volume of cylinder $= \pi \times (\text{radius})^2 \times \text{height}$]

Hence, the rainfall is 2.5 cm.

16. Given, radius of the base of the bucket $= 18$ cm

Height of the bucket $= 32$ cm

So, volume of the sand in cylindrical bucket $= \pi r^2 h$

$$= \pi (18)^2 \times 32 = 10368\,\pi$$

Also, given height of the conical heap $(h) = 24$ cm

Let radius of heap be r cm.

Then, volume of the sand in the heap $= \dfrac{1}{3}\pi r^2 h$

$$= \dfrac{1}{3}\pi r^2 \times 24 = 8\,\pi\, r^2$$

According to the question,

Volume of the sand in cylindrical bucket $=$ Volume of the sand in conical heap

$\Rightarrow \qquad\qquad 10368\,\pi = 8\pi r^2$

$\Rightarrow \qquad\qquad 10368 = 8\,r^2$

$\Rightarrow \qquad\qquad r^2 = \dfrac{10368}{8} = 1296 \Rightarrow r = 36$ cm

Again, let the slant height of the conical heap $= l$

Now, $\qquad l^2 = h^2 + r^2 = (24)^2 + (36)^2$

$$= 576 + 1296 = 1872$$

$\therefore \qquad\qquad l = 43.267$ cm

Hence, radius of conical heap of sand $= 36$ cm

and $\qquad$ slant height of conical heap $= 43.267$ cm

17. Given, length of the barrel of a fountain pen $= 7$ cm

and diameter $= 5$ mm $= \dfrac{5}{10}$ cm $= \dfrac{1}{2}$ cm $\quad \left[\because 1 \text{ mm} = \dfrac{1}{10} \text{ cm}\right]$

$\therefore$ Radius of the barrel $= \dfrac{1}{2 \times 2} = 0.25$ cm

$\qquad$ Volume of the barrel $= \pi r^2 h$ [since, its shape is cylindrical]

$$= \dfrac{22}{7} \times (0.25)^2 \times 7$$

$$= 22 \times 0.0625 = 1.375 \text{ cm}^3$$

Also, given volume of ink in the bottle $= \dfrac{1}{5}$ of litre

$$= \dfrac{1}{5} \times 1000 \text{ cm}^3 = 200 \text{ cm}^3$$

Now, 1.375 cm^3 ink is used for writing number of words

$$= 3300$$

$\therefore 1$ cm^3 ink is used for writing number of words $= \dfrac{3300}{1.375}$

$\therefore 200$ cm^3 ink is used for writing number of words

$$= \dfrac{3300}{1.375} \times 200 = 480000$$

18. Given, speed of water flow $= 10$ m min$^{-1} = 1000$ cm/min

and diameter of the pipe $= 5$ mm $= \dfrac{5}{10}$ cm $\quad \left[\because 1 \text{ mm} = \dfrac{1}{10} \text{ cm}\right]$

$\therefore \qquad$ Radius of the pipe $= \dfrac{5}{10 \times 2} = 0.25$ cm

$\therefore$ Area of the face of pipe

$$= \pi r^2 = \dfrac{22}{7} \times (0.25)^2 = 0.1964 \text{ cm}^2$$

Also, given diameter of the conical vessel $= 40$ cm

$\therefore$ Radius of the conical vessel $= \dfrac{40}{2} = 20$ cm

and depth of the conical vessel $= 24$ cm

$\therefore$ Volume of conical vessel $= \dfrac{1}{3}\pi r^2 h = \dfrac{1}{3} \times \dfrac{22}{7} \times (20)^2 \times 24$

$$= \dfrac{211200}{21} = 10057.14 \text{ cm}^3$$

$\therefore$ Required time $= \dfrac{\text{Volume of the conical vessel}}{\text{Area of the face of pipe} \times \text{Speed of water}}$

$$= \dfrac{10057.14}{0.1964 \times 1000}$$

$$= 51.20 \text{ min} = 51 \text{ min} \dfrac{20}{100} \times 60 \text{ s}$$

$$= 51 \text{ min } 12 \text{ s}$$

19. Given, radius of tank, $r_1 = 40$ cm

Let height of water level in tank in half an hour $= h_1$

Also, given internal radius of cylindrical pipe, $r_2 = 1$ cm

and speed of water $= 80$ cm/s i.e. in 1s water flow $= 80$ cm

$\therefore$ In 30 (min) water flow $= 80 \times 60 \times 30 = 144000$ cm

According to the question,

Volume of water in cylindrical tank = Volume of water flow from the circular pipe in half an hour

$$\Rightarrow \qquad \pi r_1^2\, h_1 = \pi r_2^2\, h_2$$

$$\Rightarrow \qquad 40 \times 40 \times h_1 = 1 \times 1 \times 144000$$

$$\therefore \qquad h_1 = \frac{144000}{40 \times 40} = 90 \text{ cm}$$

Hence, the level of water in cylindrical tank rises 90 cm in half an hour.

20. Given, pencils are cylindrical in shape.

Length of one pencil $= 25$ cm

and circumference of base, $2\pi r = 1.5$ cm

$$\Rightarrow \qquad r = \frac{1.5 \times 7}{22 \times 2} = 0.2386 \text{ cm}$$

Now, curved surface area of one pencil $= 2\pi rh$

$$= 2 \times \frac{22}{7} \times 0.2386 \times 25$$

$$= \frac{262.46}{7} = 37.49 \text{ cm}^2$$

$$= \frac{37.49}{100} \text{ dm}^2 \qquad \left[\because 1 \text{ cm} = \frac{1}{10} \text{ dm}\right]$$

$$= 0.375 \text{ dm}^2$$

$\therefore$ Curved surface area of 120000 pencils $= 0.375 \times 120000$

$$= 45000 \text{ dm}^2$$

Now, cost of colouring 1 dm^2 curved surface of the pencils manufactured in one day $= ₹\, 0.05$

$\therefore$ Cost of colouring 45000 dm^2 curved surface

$$= 45000 \times 0.05 = ₹\, 2250$$

21. Here, a well is dug and Earth taken out of it is used to form an embankment.

Given, Diameter of well $= 10$ m

$$\therefore \quad \text{Radius} = \frac{10}{2} = 5 \text{ m}$$

Also, depth $= 14$ m

$\therefore$ Volume of Earth taken out on digging the well

$$= \pi r^2 h = \frac{22}{7} \times (5)^2 \times 14 = 1100 \text{ m}^3$$

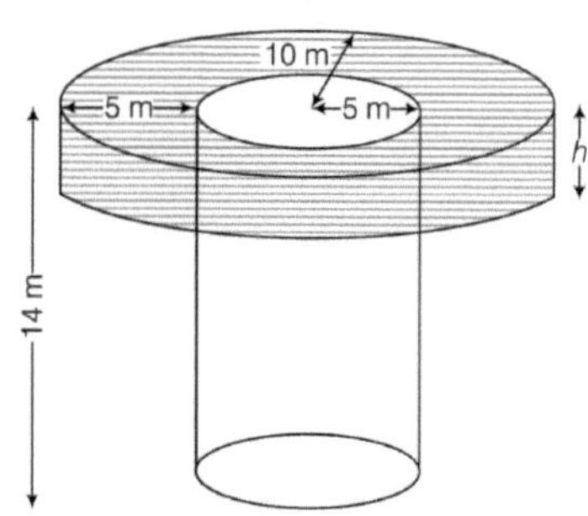

The embankment is in the form of cylindrical shell, so area of embankment $= \pi(R^2 - r^2) = \pi(10^2 - 5^2)$

$$= \pi\,(100 - 25) = \frac{22}{7} \times 75 \text{ m}^2$$

Since, Earth taken out from well is used to form embankment.

$\therefore$ Volume of embankment

$$= \text{Volume of Earth taken out on digging the well}$$

$$\Rightarrow \quad \text{Area of embankment} \times \text{Height of embankment}$$

$$= \text{Volume of Earth dugout}$$

$$\Rightarrow \text{Height of embankment} = \frac{\text{Volume of Earth dugout}}{\text{Area of the embankment}}$$

$$= \frac{1100}{\dfrac{22}{7} \times 75} = 4.67 \text{ m}$$

22. Given, diameter of a marble $= 1.4$ cm

$$\therefore \qquad \text{Radius of marble } (r) = \frac{1.4}{2} = 0.7 \text{ cm}$$

So, volume of one marble $= \dfrac{4}{3}\pi r^3 = \dfrac{4}{3}\pi(0.7)^3$

$$= \frac{4}{3}\pi \times 0.343 = \frac{1.372}{3}\pi \text{ cm}^3$$

Also, given diameter of beaker $= 7$ cm

$\therefore$ Radius of beaker $= \dfrac{7}{2} = 3.5$ cm

Height of water level raised $= 5.6$ cm

$\therefore$ Volume of the raised water in beaker

$$= \pi\,(3.5)^2 \times 5.6 = 68.6\pi \text{ cm}^3$$

Now, required number of marbles

$$= \frac{\text{Volume of the raised water in beaker}}{\text{Volume of one spherical marble}}$$

$$= \frac{68.6\,\pi}{1.372\,\pi} \times 3 = 150$$

23. Given, edge of the cube $= 22$ cm

$$\therefore \quad \text{Volume of the cube} = (22)^3 = 10648 \text{ cm}^3$$

$$[\because \text{ volume of cube} = (\text{side})^3]$$

Also, given diameter of marble $= 0.5$ cm

$$\therefore \quad \text{Radius of a marble, } r = \frac{0.5}{2} = 0.25 \text{ cm}$$

$$[\because \text{ diameter} = 2 \times \text{radius}]$$

$$\text{Volume of one marble} = \frac{4}{3}\pi r^3 = \frac{4}{3} \times \frac{22}{7} \times (0.25)^3$$

$$\left[\because \text{ volume of sphere} = \frac{4}{3} \times \pi \times (\text{radius})^3\right]$$

$$= \frac{1.375}{21} = 0.0655 \text{ cm}^3$$

Filled space of cube $= \text{Volume of the cube} - \dfrac{1}{8}$

$$\times \text{ Volume of cube}$$

$$= 10648 - 10648 \times \frac{1}{8}$$

$$= 10648 \times \frac{7}{8} = 9317 \text{ cm}^3$$

$\therefore$ Required number of marbles

$$= \frac{\text{Total space filled by marbles in a cube}}{\text{Volume of one marble}}$$

$$= \frac{9317}{0.0655} = 142244 \text{ (approx.)}$$

Hence, the number of marbles that the cube can accomodate is 142244.

24. Given that, a solid iron cuboidal block is recast into a hollow cylindrical pipe.

Length of cuboidal pipe $(l) = 4.4\,\text{m}$

Breadth of cuboidal pipe $(b) = 2.6\,\text{m}$ and height of cuboidal pipe $(h) = 1\,\text{m}$

So, volume of a solid iron cuboidal block $= l \cdot b \cdot h$
$$= 4.4 \times 2.6 \times 1 = 11.44\,\text{m}^3$$

Also, internal radius of hollow cylindrical pipe $(r_i) = 30\,\text{cm}$
$$= 0.3\,\text{m}$$

and thickness of hollow cylindrical pipe $= 5\,\text{cm} = 0.05\,\text{m}$

So, external radius of hollow cylindrical pipe
$(r_e) = r_i + \text{Thickness}$
$$= 0.3 + 0.05 = 0.35\,\text{m}$$

$\therefore$ Volume of hollow cylindrical pipe

$\quad$ = Volume of cylindrical pipe with external radius

$\qquad$ − Volume of cylindrical pipe with internal radius

$$= \pi r_e^2 h_1 - \pi r_i^2 h_1 = \pi (r_e^2 - r_i^2)\, h_1$$

$$= \frac{22}{7} [(0.35)^2 - (0.3)^2] \cdot h_1$$

$$= \frac{22}{7} [0.1225 - 0.09] \cdot h_1 = \frac{22}{7} [0.0325] \cdot h_1$$

$$= 0.715 \times h_1 / 7$$

where, h_1 be the length of the hollow cylindrical pipe.

Now, by given condition,

Volume of solid iron cuboidal block = Volume of hollow cylindrical pipe

$$\Rightarrow \qquad 11.44 = 0.715 \times h / 7$$

$$\therefore \qquad h = \frac{11.44 \times 7}{0.715} = 112\,\text{m}$$

Hence, required length of pipe is 112 m.

25. Let total height of the building = Internal diameter of the dome $= 2r$ m

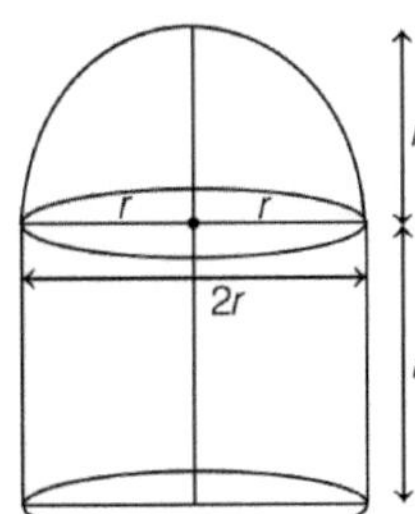

$$\therefore \quad \text{Radius of building (or dome)} = \frac{2r}{2} = r\,\text{m}$$

$$\text{Height of cylinder} = 2r - r = r\,\text{m}$$

$$\therefore \qquad \text{Volume of the cylinder} = \pi\, r^2\, (r) = \pi r^3\,\text{m}^3$$

and volume of hemispherical dome on cylinder $= \dfrac{2}{3}\pi r^3\,\text{m}^3$

$\therefore$ Total volume of the building = Volume of the cylinder
$$\qquad\qquad\qquad\qquad + \text{Volume of hemispherical dome}$$

$$= \left(\pi r^3 + \frac{2}{3}\pi r^3 \right) \text{m}^3 = \frac{5}{3}\pi r^3\,\text{m}^3$$

According to the question,

Volume of the building = Volume of the air

$$\Rightarrow \qquad \frac{5}{3}\pi r^3 = 41\frac{19}{21}$$

$$\Rightarrow \qquad \frac{5}{3}\pi r^3 = \frac{880}{21}$$

$$\Rightarrow \qquad r^3 = \frac{880 \times 7 \times 3}{21 \times 22 \times 5}$$

$$= \frac{40 \times 21}{21 \times 5} = 8$$

$$\Rightarrow \qquad r^3 = 8 \Rightarrow r = 2\,\text{m}$$

$\therefore$ Height of the building $= 2r = 2 \times 2 = 4\,\text{m}$

26. Given, diameter of cylinder = Diameter of hemisphere
$$= 0.5\,\text{cm}$$

$\qquad$ [since, both hemispheres are attach with cylinder]

$\therefore$ Radius of cylinder (r) = radius of hemisphere

$$(r) = \frac{0.5}{2} = 0.25\,\text{cm}$$

$\qquad\qquad\qquad\qquad$ [$\because$ diameter $= 2 \times$ radius]

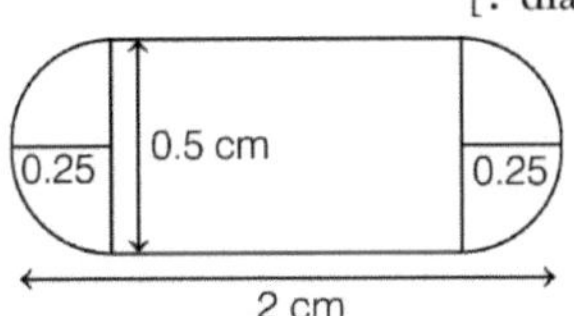

and total length of capsule = 2 cm

$\therefore$ Length of cylindrical part of capsule,

$$h = \text{Length of capsule} - \text{Radius of both hemispheres}$$
$$= 2 - (0.25 + 0.25) = 1.5\,\text{cm}$$

Now, capacity of capsule = Volume of cylindrical part
$$\qquad\qquad\qquad + 2 \times \text{Volume of hemisphere}$$

$$= \pi r^2 h + 2 \times \frac{2}{3}\pi r^3$$

$\qquad$ [$\because$ volume of cylinder $= \pi \times (\text{radius})^2$

$\qquad\qquad \times$ height and volume of hemisphere $= \dfrac{2}{3}\pi(\text{radius})^3$]

$$= \frac{22}{7} [(0.25)^2 \times 1.5 + \frac{4}{3} \times (0.25)^3]$$

$$= \frac{22}{7} [0.09375 + 0.0208]$$

$$= \frac{22}{7} \times 0.11455 = 0.36\,\text{cm}^3$$

Hence, the capacity of capsule is $0.36\,\text{cm}^3$.

27. Since, rocket is the combination of a right circular cylinder and a cone.

Given, diameter of the cylinder = 6 cm

$$\therefore \qquad \text{Radius of the cylinder} = \frac{6}{2} = 3\,\text{cm}$$

and height of the cylinder = 12 cm

$$\therefore \quad \text{Volume of the cylinder} = \pi r^2 h = 3.14 \times (3)^2 \times 12$$
$$= 339.12\,\text{cm}^3$$

and curved surface area $= 2\pi r h$
$$= 2 \times 3.14 \times 3 \times 12 = 226.08$$

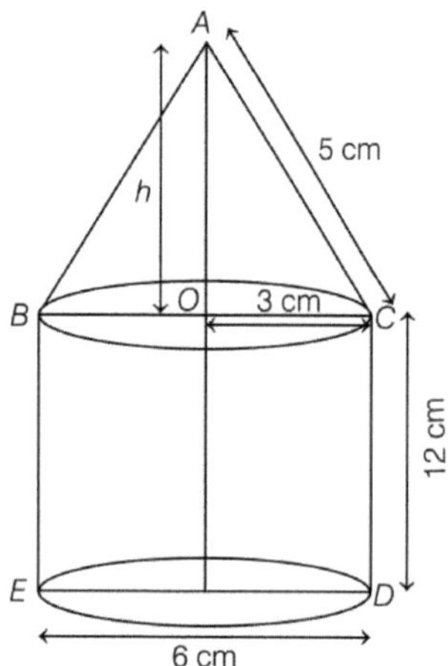

Now, in right angled ΔAOC,

$$h = \sqrt{5^2 - 3^2}$$
$$= \sqrt{25 - 9} = \sqrt{16} = 4$$

$\therefore$ Height of the cone, $h = 4$ cm

and radius of the cone, $r = 3$ cm

Now, volume of the cone

$$= \frac{1}{3}\pi r^2 h = \frac{1}{3} \times 3.14 \times (3)^2 \times 4$$
$$= \frac{113.04}{3} = 37.68 \text{ cm}^3$$

and curved surface area $= \pi r l = 3.14 \times 3 \times 5 = 47.1$

Hence, total volume of the rocket

$$= 339.12 + 37.68 = 376.8 \text{ cm}^3$$

and total surface area of the rocket

$= $ CSA of cone $+$ CSA of cylinder $+$ Area of base of cylinder

$= 47.1 + 226.08 + 28.26$

$= 301.44 \text{ cm}^2$

28. Here, given solid toy is a combination of a right circular cone and a hemisphere.

Let BPC be the hemisphere and ABC be the cone standing on the base of the hemisphere as shown in the figure.

For conical portion, height, $h = 3$ cm

Diameter, $d = 4$ cm

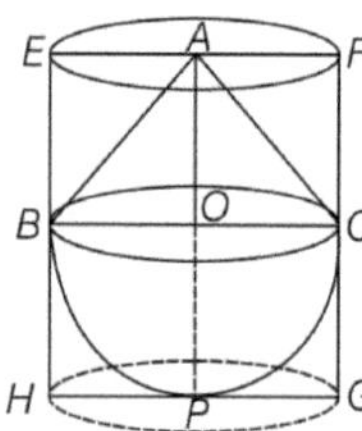

$\therefore$ Radius, $r = \dfrac{4}{2}$ cm $= 2$ cm

For hemispherical portion,

Radius, $r = 2$ cm $[\because$ radii of hemisphere and cone are same]

So, volume of the solid toy

$= $ Volume of hemisphere $+$ Volume of cone

$$= \frac{2}{3}\pi r^3 + \frac{1}{3}\pi r^2 h$$
$$= \left[\frac{2}{3} \times 3.14 \times (2)^3 + \frac{1}{3} \times 3.14 \times (2)^2 \times 3 \right]$$
$$= 16.75 + 12.56 = 29.31 \text{ cm}^3$$

Hence, volume of the solid toy is 29.31 cm^3.

Now, let the right circular cylinder $EFGH$ circumscribe the given solid toy. Then, radius of the base of the right circular cylinder $= HP = BO = 2$ cm and its height,

$$EH = AP = AO + OP = 3 + 2 = 5 \text{ cm}$$

So, volume of the cylinder $= \pi\, r^2 h$

$$= 3.14 \times 2^2 \times 5$$
$$= 62.8 \text{ cm}^3$$

Now, required difference of the volume of the cylinder and the solid toy $= $ Volume of cylinder $-$ Volume of solid toy

$$= 62.8 - 29.31 = 33.49 \text{ cm}^3$$

29. Here, the given wooden toy rocket is combination of a cone and a cylinder.

For conical portion,

Diameter $= 6$ cm

$\therefore\qquad$ Radius, $r_1 = \dfrac{6}{2}$ cm $= 3$ cm

Height, $h_1 = 4$ cm

Then, slant height, $l = \sqrt{(3)^2 + 4^2}$ $\qquad [\because l = \sqrt{r^2 + h^2}]$

$$= \sqrt{9 + 16} = \sqrt{25} = 5 \text{ cm}$$

For cylindrical portion,

Diameter $= 4$ cm

$\therefore\qquad$ Radius, $r_2 = \dfrac{4}{2}$ cm $= 2$ cm

Height, $h_2 = $ Total height of rocket $-$ Height of cone

$$= 24 - 4 \quad [\because \text{ total height of rocket} = 24 \text{ cm}]$$
$$= 20 \text{ cm}$$

Here, we have to find the area of the rocket painted with orange and yellow colours separately.

Since, radius of base of cone is larger than radius of base of cylinder and cone is mounted on cylinder.

$\therefore$ Area to be painted orange $= $ Curved surface area of cone

$\qquad\qquad + $ Area of base of cone $-$ Area of base of cylinder

$\qquad\qquad [\because$ area of base of cylinder is common

$\qquad\qquad\qquad$ in area of base of cone]

$$= \pi r_1 l + \pi r_1^2 - \pi r_2^2$$
$$= 3.14 \times 3 \times 5 + 3.14 \times (3)^2 - 3.14 \times (2)^2$$
$$= 3.14\,[15 + 9 - 4]$$
$$= 3.14 \times 20 = 62.8 \text{ cm}^2$$

Now, area to be painted yellow

$\qquad\qquad = $ Curved surface area of cylinder

$\qquad\qquad\qquad + $ Area of base of the cylinder $= 2\pi r_2 h_2 + \pi r_2^2$

$$= 2 \times 3.14 \times 2 \times 20 + 3.14 \times (2)^2$$
$$= 3.14\,[80 + 4]$$
$$= 3.14 \times 84 = 263.76 \text{ cm}^2$$

30. Let volume of cone A be $2V$ and volume of cone B be V.

Again, let height of the cone $A = h_1$ cm, then height of cone $B = (21 - h_1)$ cm

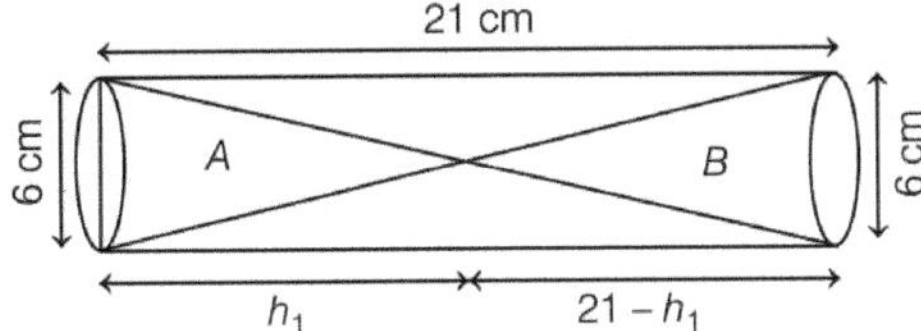

Given, diameter of the cone = 6 cm

$\therefore$ Radius of the cone $= \dfrac{6}{2} = 3$ cm

Now, volume of the cone, $A = 2V = \dfrac{1}{3}\pi r^2 h = \dfrac{1}{3}\pi(3)^2 h_1$

$\Rightarrow \qquad V = \dfrac{1}{6}\pi \, 9h_1 = \dfrac{3}{2}h_1\pi$ ...(i)

and volume of the cone,

$B = V = \dfrac{1}{3}\pi\,(3)^2\,(21 - h_1) = 3\pi\,(21 - h_1)$ ...(ii)

From Eqs. (i) and (ii),

$$\dfrac{3}{2}h_1\pi = 3\pi\,(21 - h_1)$$

$\Rightarrow \qquad h_1 = 2\,(21 - h_1)$

$\Rightarrow \qquad 3h_1 = 42$

$\Rightarrow \qquad h_1 = \dfrac{42}{3} = 14$ cm

$\therefore$ Height of cone, $B = 21 - h_1 = 21 - 14 = 7$ cm

Now, volume of the cone, $A = 3 \times 14 \times \dfrac{22}{7} = 132$ cm^3

[using Eq. (i)]

and volume of the cone, $B = \dfrac{1}{3} \times \dfrac{22}{7} \times 9 \times 7 = 66$ cm^3

[using Eq. (ii)]

Now, volume of the cylinder $= \pi r^2 h = \dfrac{22}{7}(3)^2 \times 21 = 594$ cm^3

$\therefore$ Required volume of the remaining portion

= Volume of the cylinder

$\qquad$ – (Volume of cone A + Volume of cone B)

$= 594 - (132 + 66) = 396$ cm^3

31. Given that, lots of spherical lead shots made out of a solid cube of lead.

$\therefore$ Number of spherical lead shots

$= \dfrac{\text{Volume of a solid cube of lead}}{\text{Volume of a spherical lead shot}}$ ...(i)

Given that, diameter of a spherical lead shot i.e. sphere = 4 cm

$\Rightarrow \qquad$ Radius of a spherical lead shot $(r) = \dfrac{4}{2}$

$\qquad\qquad r = 2$ cm $[\because$ diameter $= 2 \times$ radius$]$

So, volume of a spherical lead shot i.e. sphere

$= \dfrac{4}{3}\pi\,r^3$

$= \dfrac{4}{3} \times \dfrac{22}{7} \times (2)^3 = \dfrac{4 \times 22 \times 8}{21}$ cm^3

Now, since edge of a solid cube $(a) = 44$ cm

So, volume of a solid cube $= (a)^3$

$\qquad\qquad = (44)^3$

$\qquad\qquad = 44 \times 44 \times 44$ cm^3

From Eq. (i),

Number of spherical lead shots $= \dfrac{44 \times 44 \times 44}{4 \times 22 \times 8} \times 21$

$\qquad\qquad = 11 \times 21 \times 11$

$\qquad\qquad = 121 \times 21$

$\qquad\qquad = 2541$

Hence, the required number of spherical lead shots is 2541.

32. Given, internal diameter of spherical shell = 4 cm

and external diameter of shell = 8 cm

$\therefore$ Internal radius of spherical shell, $r_1 = \dfrac{4}{2}$ cm = 2 cm

$[\because$ diameter $= 2 \times$ radius$]$

and external radius of shell, $r_2 = \dfrac{8}{2} = 4$ cm

$[\because$ diameter $= 2 \times$ radius$]$

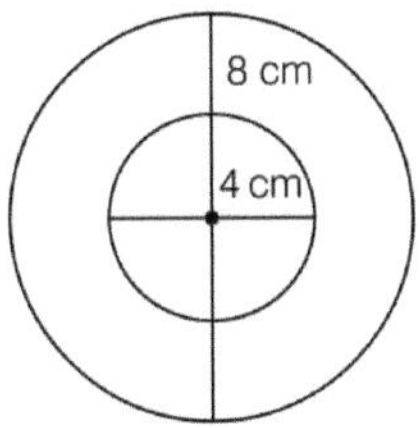

Spherical shell

Now, volume of the spherical shell $= \dfrac{4}{3}\pi[r_2^3 - r_1^3]$

$[\because$ volume of the spherical shell $= \dfrac{4}{3}\pi$

$\{(\text{external radius})^3 - (\text{internal radius})^3\}]$

$= \dfrac{4}{3}\pi\,(4^3 - 2^3)$

$= \dfrac{4}{3}\pi\,(64 - 8)$

$= \dfrac{224}{3}\pi$ cm^3

Let height of the cone = h cm

Diameter of the base of cone = 8 cm

$\therefore$ Radius of the base of cone $= \dfrac{8}{2} = 4$ cm

$[\because$ diameter $= 2 \times$ radius$]$

According to the question,

Volume of cone = Volume of spherical shell

$\Rightarrow \qquad \dfrac{1}{3}\pi(4)^2 h = \dfrac{224}{3}\pi$

$\Rightarrow \qquad h = \dfrac{224}{16} = 14$ cm

$[\because$ volume of cone $= \dfrac{1}{3} \times \pi \times (\text{radius})^2 \times (\text{height})]$

Hence, the height of the cone is 14 cm.

33. Given that, lots of spherical lead shots made from a solid rectangular lead piece.

$\therefore$ Number of spherical lead shots

$$= \frac{\text{Volume of solid rectangular lead piece}}{\text{Volume of a spherical lead shot}} \qquad ...(i)$$

Also, given that diameter of a spherical lead shot i.e. sphere = 4.2 cm

$\therefore$ Radius of a spherical lead shot, $r = \dfrac{4.2}{2} = 2.1$ cm

$$\left[\because \ \text{radius} = \frac{1}{2}\ \text{diameter}\right]$$

So, volume of a spherical lead shot i.e. sphere

$$= \frac{4}{3}\,\pi\,r^3$$

$$= \frac{4}{3} \times \frac{22}{7} \times (2.1)^3$$

$$= \frac{4}{3} \times \frac{22}{7} \times 2.1 \times 2.1 \times 2.1$$

$$= \frac{4 \times 22 \times 21 \times 21 \times 21}{3 \times 7 \times 1000}$$

Now, length of rectangular lead piece, $l = 66$ cm

Breadth of rectangular lead piece, $b = 42$ cm

Height of rectangular lead piece, $h = 21$ cm

$\therefore$ Volume of a solid rectangular lead piece i.e. cuboid

$$= l \times b \times h$$

$$= 66 \times 42 \times 21$$

From Eq. (i),

Number of spherical lead shots

$$= \frac{66 \times 42 \times 21}{4 \times 22 \times 21 \times 21 \times 21} \times 3 \times 7 \times 1000$$

$$= \frac{3 \times 22 \times 21 \times 2 \times 21 \times 21 \times 1000}{4 \times 22 \times 21 \times 21 \times 21}$$

$$= 3 \times 2 \times 250$$

$$= 6 \times 250 = 1500$$

Hence, the required number of spherical lead shots is 1500.

34. Given that, lots of metallic circular disc to be melted to form a right circular cylinder. Here, a circular disc work as a circular cylinder.

Base diameter of metallic circular disc = 1.5 cm

$\therefore$ Radius of metallic circular disc = $\dfrac{1.5}{2}$ cm

$$[\because \ \text{diameter} = 2 \times \text{radius}]$$

and height of metallic circular disc i.e. = 0.2 cm

$\therefore$ Volume of a circular disc = $\pi \times (\text{Radius})^2 \times \text{Height}$

$$= \pi \times \left(\frac{1.5}{2}\right)^2 \times 0.2$$

$$= \frac{\pi}{4} \times 1.5 \times 1.5 \times 0.2$$

Now, height of a right circular cylinder $(h) = 10$ cm

and diameter of a right circular cylinder = 4.5 cm

$\Rightarrow$ Radius of a right circular cylinder $(r) = \dfrac{4.5}{2}$ cm

$\therefore$ Volume of right circular cylinder = $\pi r^2 h$

$$= \pi \left(\frac{4.5}{2}\right)^2 \times 10$$

$$= \frac{\pi}{4} \times 4.5 \times 4.5 \times 10$$

$\therefore$ Number of metallic circular disc

$$= \frac{\text{Volume of a right circular cylinder}}{\text{Volume of a metallic circular disc}}$$

$$= \frac{\dfrac{\pi}{4} \times 4.5 \times 4.5 \times 10}{\dfrac{\pi}{4} \times 1.5 \times 1.5 \times 0.2}$$

$$= \frac{3 \times 3 \times 10}{0.2} = \frac{900}{2} = 450$$

Hence, the required number of metallic circular disc is 450.

35. Given that, a heap of rice is in the form of a cone.

Height of a heap of rice i.e. cone $(h) = 3.5$ m

and diameter of a heap of rice i.e. cone = 9 m

Radius of a heap of rice i.e. cone $(r) = \dfrac{9}{2}$ m

So, volume of rice $= \dfrac{1}{3}\,\pi \times r^2 h$

$$= \frac{1}{3} \times \frac{22}{7} \times \frac{9}{2} \times \frac{9}{2} \times 3.5$$

$$= \frac{6237}{84} = 74.25 \ \text{m}^3$$

Now, canvas cloth required to just cover heap of rice

$$= \text{Surface area of a heap of rice}$$

$$= \pi r l$$

$$= \frac{22}{7} \times r \times \sqrt{r^2 + h^2}$$

$$= \frac{22}{7} \times \frac{9}{2} \times \sqrt{\left(\frac{9}{2}\right)^2 + (3.5)^2}$$

$$= \frac{11 \times 9}{7} \times \sqrt{\frac{81}{4} + 12.25}$$

$$= \frac{99}{7} \times \sqrt{\frac{130}{4}} = \frac{99}{7} \times \sqrt{32.5}$$

$$= 14.142 \times 5.7 = 80.61 \ \text{m}^2$$

Hence, 80.61 m^2 canvas cloth is required to just cover heap.

36. Let the length(l), breadth (b) and height (h) be the external dimension of an open box and thickness be x.

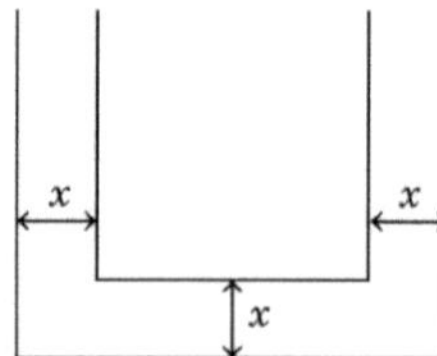

Given that,

external length of an open box $(l) = 36$ cm

external breadth of an open box $(b) = 25$ cm

and external height of an open box $(h) = 16.5$ cm

$\therefore$ External volume of an open box $= lbh$

$$= 36 \times 25 \times 16.5 = 14850 \text{ cm}^3$$

Since, the thickness of the iron $(x) = 1.5$ cm

So, internal length of an open box $(l_1) = l - 2x$

$$= 36 - 2 \times 1.5$$
$$= 36 - 3 = 33 \text{ cm}$$

Therefore, internal breadth of an open box $(b_2) = b - 2x$

$$= 25 - 2 \times 1.5$$
$$= 25 - 3 = 22 \text{ cm}$$

and internal height of an open box $(h_2) = (h - x)$

$$= 16.5 - 1.5 = 15 \text{ cm}$$

So, internal volume of an open box

$$= (l - 2x) \cdot (b - 2x) \cdot (h - x)$$
$$= 33 \times 22 \times 15$$
$$= 10890 \text{ cm}^3$$

Therefore, required iron to construct an open box

$=$ External volume of an open box

$\qquad\qquad -$ Internal volume of an open box

$= 14850 - 10890 = 3960 \text{ cm}^3$

Hence, required iron to construct an open box is 3960 cm^3.

Given that, 1 cm^3 of iron weights $= 7.5 \text{ g} = \dfrac{7.5}{1000} \text{ kg}$

$$= 0.0075 \text{ kg}$$

$\therefore$ 3960 cm^3 of iron weights $= 3960 \times 0.0075 = 29.7 \text{ kg}$

37. Given, length of the pond $= 50$ m and width of the pond

$$= 44 \text{ m}$$

Depth required of water $= 21 \text{ cm} = \dfrac{21}{100} \text{ m}$

$\therefore$ Volume of water in the pond $= l \times b \times h$

$$= \left(50 \times 44 \times \dfrac{21}{100}\right)$$
$$= 462 \text{ m}^3$$

Also, given radius of the pipe $= 7 \text{ cm} = \dfrac{7}{100} \text{ m}$

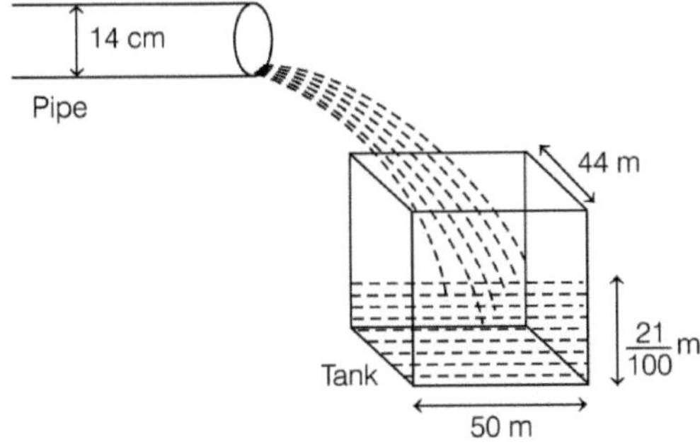

and speed of water flowing through the pipe $= (15 \times 1000)$

$$= 15000 \text{ mh}^{-1}$$

Now, volume of water flow in 1 h $= \pi R^2 H$

$$= \left(\dfrac{22}{7} \times \dfrac{7}{100} \times \dfrac{7}{100} \times 15000\right)$$
$$= 231 \text{ m}^3$$

Since, 231 m^3 of water falls in the pond in 1 h.

So, 1 m^3 water falls in the pond in $\dfrac{1}{231}$ h.

Also, 462 m^3 of water falls in the pond in $\left(\dfrac{1}{231} \times 462\right)$ h $= 2$ h

Hence, the required time is 2 h.

38. (i) Length of the cuboid $(L) = 30$ cm

Breadth of the cuboid $(B) = 20$ cm

Height of the cuboid $(H) = 10$ cm

Then,

Area covered by the cuboid

$$= L \times B + 2H(L + B)$$
$$= 30 \times 20 + 2 \times 10(30 + 20)$$
$$= 600 + 1000$$
$$= 1600 \text{ cm}^2$$

(ii) We know that,

C.S.A of the cylinder $= 2\pi R H_1$

C.S.A of the cylinder $= 2 \times \dfrac{22}{7} \times 7 \times 60$

$$= 2 \times 22 \times 60$$
$$= 2640 \text{ cm}^2$$

In cone, height is given and radius of the cone is equal to radius of the cylinder,

$\because \qquad\qquad L^2 = H_2^2 + R^2$

$\Rightarrow \qquad\qquad L^2 = 7 \times 7 + 24 \times 24$

$\Rightarrow \qquad\qquad L^2 = 49 + 576 = 625$

$\therefore \qquad\qquad L = 25 \text{ cm}$

C.S.A. of cone $= \pi r l = \dfrac{22}{7} \times 7 \times 25 = 550 \text{ cm}^2$

$\Rightarrow \quad \dfrac{\text{C.S.A of the cylinder}}{\text{C.S.A. of the cone}} = \dfrac{2640}{550} = 24:5$

(iii) (b) Given structure is based on the concept of surface area and volume.

39. (i) Given, $r = \dfrac{7}{2}$ cm, $h = 10.5 \text{ cm} = \dfrac{21}{2}$ cm

Volume of cylindrical cup $= \pi r^2 h$

$$= \dfrac{22}{7} \times \dfrac{7}{2} \times \dfrac{7}{2} \times \dfrac{21}{2}$$
$$= \dfrac{11 \times 7 \times 21}{4}$$
$$= 404.25 \text{ cm}^3$$

(ii) Given, $r = \dfrac{7}{2}$ cm

$\therefore$ Volume of hemispherical cup $= \dfrac{2}{3} \times \dfrac{22}{7} \times \dfrac{7}{2} \times \dfrac{7}{2} \times \dfrac{7}{2}$

$\qquad\qquad = 89.83 \text{ cm}^3$

(iii) Area of canvas provided $= 551 \text{ m}^2$

Area of remained after westage $= 551 - 1 = 550 \text{ m}^2$

So, area of conical tent $= \pi r l$

Here, $r = 7 \text{ m}$

$\therefore \quad \pi r l = 550 \Rightarrow \dfrac{22}{7} \times 7 \times l = 550 \Rightarrow l = 25 \text{ m}$

Now, $h = \sqrt{l^2 - r^2} = \sqrt{625 - 49}$

$\qquad = \sqrt{576} = 24 \text{ m}$

40. (i) Given, edge of cube $= 6 \text{ cm}$

$\therefore$ Diagonal of cube $= \sqrt{3} \times$ edge of cube

$\qquad\qquad\qquad = \sqrt{3} \times 6 = 6\sqrt{3} \text{ cm}$

(ii) Given edge of cube $= 7 \text{ cm}$

$\therefore$ Volume of cube $= 7 \times 7 \times 7 = 343 \text{ cm}^3$

(iii) Given, radius $(r) = 7 \text{ cm}$

$\therefore$ Curved surface area of hemisphere $= 2\pi r^2$

$\qquad\qquad = 2 \times \dfrac{22}{7} \times 7 \times 7$

$\qquad\qquad = 44 \times 7 = 308 \text{ cm}^2$

(iv) Given, radius $(r) = 7 \text{ cm}$ and height $(h) = 24 \text{ cm}$

Slant height $(l) = ?$

$\therefore \quad l^2 = r^2 + h^2 = (7)^2 + (24)^2$

$\qquad = 49 + 576 = 625$

$\Rightarrow \quad l = \sqrt{625} = 25 \text{ cm}$

(v) TSA of cone $= \pi r l + 2\pi r^2$

$\qquad\qquad = \dfrac{22}{7} \times 7 \times 25 + 2 \times \dfrac{22}{7} \times 7 \times 7$

$\qquad\qquad = 550 + 308 = 858 \text{ cm}^2$

Chapter Test

Multiple Choice Questions

1. How many cubes of side 2 cm can be made from a solid cube of side 10 cm?
(a) 100   (b) 125   (c) 175   (d) 200

2. 2 cubes, each of volume 125 cm^3, are joined end to end. Find the surface area of the resulting cuboid.
(a) 100 cm^2 (b) 200 cm^2 (c) 225 cm^2 (d) 250 cm^2

3. The radius of a sphere (in cm) whose volume is 12π cm^3, is
(a) 3   (b) $3\sqrt{3}$ (c) $3^{2/3}$ (d) $3^{1/3}$

4. A solid spherical ball fits exactly inside the cubical box of side 2a. The volume of the ball is
(a) $\dfrac{16}{3}\pi a^3$ (b) $\dfrac{1}{6}\pi a^3$
(c) $\dfrac{32}{3}\pi a^3$ (d) $\dfrac{4}{3}\pi a^3$

5. A cone and a cylinder have the same radii but the height of the cone is 3 times that of the cylinder, then the ratio of their volumes.
(a) 1 : 2   (b) 2 : 1
(c) 1 : 1   (d) None of these

Case Based MCQs

6. One day Aakash was going home from market saw a carpenter working on wood. He found that he is carving out a cone of same height and same diameter from a cylinder. The height of the cylinder is 48 cm and base radius is 14 cm. While watching this, some questions came into Aakash's mind. Help Aakash to find the answer of the following questions.

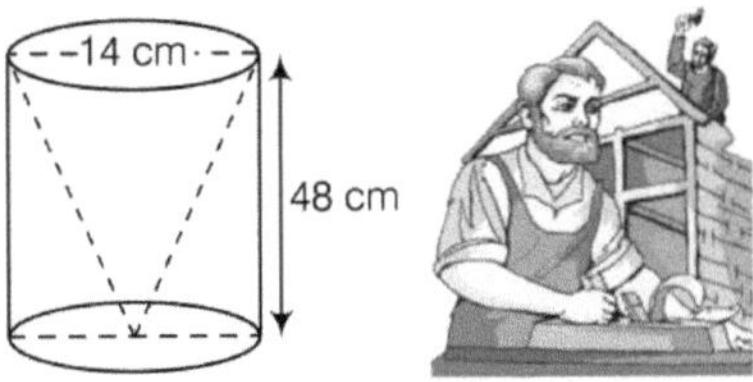

(i) After carving out cone from the cylinder,
(a) Volume of the cylindrical wood will decrease
(b) Height of the cylindrical wood will increase
(c) Volume of cylindrical wood will increase
(d) Radius of the cylindrical wood will decrease

(ii) Find the slant height of the conical cavity so formed.
(a) 28 cm   (b) 60 cm
(c) 40 cm   (d) 50 cm

(iii) The curved surface area of the conical cavity so formed is
(a) 2250 cm^2 (b) 2200 cm^2
(c) 1800 cm^2 (d) 2400 cm^2

(iv) External curved surface area of the cylinder is
(a) 2876 cm^2 (b) 1250 cm^2
(c) 4224 cm^2 (d) 3824 cm^2

(v) Volume of conical cavity is
(a) 6232 cm^3
(b) 7248 cm^3
(c) 5380 cm^3
(d) 9856 cm^3

Short Answer Type Questions

7. A hemispherical depression is cut out from one face of a cuboidal block of side 7 cm such that the diameter of the hemisphere is equal to the edge of the cube. Find the surface area of the remaining solid.

8. The capacity of a cylindrical glass tumbler is 125.6 cm^3. If the radius of the glass tumbler is 2 cm, then find its height. (Use $\pi = 3.14$)

9. In given figure, a solid toy is in the form of a hemisphere surmounted by a right circular cone. The height of the cone is 2 cm and the diameter of the base is 4 cm. Determine the volume of the toy. $\left[\text{take } \pi = \dfrac{22}{7}\right]$

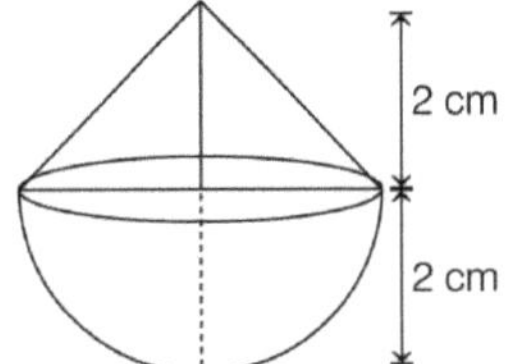

Long Answer Type Questions

10. From a solid cylinder whose height is 2.4 cm and diameter 1.4 cm, a conical cavity of the same height and same diameter is hollowed out. Find the total surface area of the remaining solid to the nearest cm^2.

11. A well of diameter 3 m is dug 14 m deep. The earth taken out of it has been spread evenly all around it in the shape of a circular ring of width 4 m to form a platform. Find the height of the platform. $\left[\text{take } \pi = \dfrac{22}{7}\right]$

Answers

1. (b)   *2.* (d)   *3.* (c)   *4.* (d)   *5.* (c)   *6.* (i) (a) (ii) (d) (iii) (b) (iv) (c) (v) (d)
7. 332.465 cm^2 *8.* 10 cm   *9.* 25.12 cm^3 *10.* 18 cm^2 *11.* 1.125 m

For Detailed Solutions
Scan the code

CHAPTER 07

Statistics

In this Chapter...

- Mean of Grouped Data
- Mode of Grouped Data
- Median of Grouped Data

Arithmetic Mean or Mean or Average

The arithmetic mean of a set of observations is obtained by dividing the sum of the values of all observations by the total number of observations.

Thus, the mean of n observations $x_1, x_2, x_3, ..., x_n$, is defined as

$$\text{Mean } (\bar{x}) = \frac{x_1 + x_2 + x_3 + ... + x_n}{n} = \frac{\sum\limits_{i=1}^{n} x_i}{n}$$

where, the Greek letter 'Σ' (sigma) means 'Summation.'

Let $x_1, x_2, ..., x_n$ be n observations with respective frequencies $f_1, f_2, ..., f_n$. This means observation x_1 occurs f_1 times, x_2 occurs f_2 times and so on.

$$\therefore \quad \text{Mean } (\bar{x}) = \frac{\sum\limits_{i=1}^{n} f_i x_i}{\sum\limits_{i=1}^{n} f_i} = \frac{\Sigma f_i x_i}{\Sigma f_i}$$

Method of Calculating Mean of Grouped Data

1. Direct Method

In this method, we find the class marks of each class interval. These class marks would serve as the representative of whole class and are represented by x_i.

In general, for the ith class interval, we have frequency f_i corresponding to the class mark x_i. The sum of the values in the last column gives us $\Sigma f_i x_i$, so the mean $\bar{x}$ of the given data is given by

$$\bar{x} = \frac{\Sigma f_i x_i}{\Sigma f_i}.$$

2. Assumed Mean Method

The cases, in which numerical values of x_i and f_i are large and computation of product of x_i and f_i becomes tedious and time consuming, assumed mean method is used. In this method, first of all, one among x_i's is chosen as the **assumed mean** denoted by 'a'. After that, the difference d_i between a and each of the x_i's, i.e. $d_i = x_i - a$ is calculated. Then, arithmetic mean is given by

$$\bar{x} = a + \frac{\Sigma f_i d_i}{\Sigma f_i}$$

where, $\quad d_i = x_i - a$

Mode

The observation, which occurs most frequently among the given observations, i.e. the value of the observation having maximum frequency is called **mode**. e.g. Mode of the numbers 2, 3, 4, 4, 6, 6, 6, 6, 7 and 9 is 6 because it is repeated maximum number of times, i.e. 4 times.

Modal Class

In a grouped frequency distribution, it is not possible to determine the mode by looking at the frequencies. So, here we first locate a class with the maximum frequency. This class is called modal class. e.g.

Class interval	0-10	10-20	20-30	30-40	40-50	50-60
Number of students	2	9	14	20	22	8

Here, the highest frequency is of the class 40-50, which is 22. Hence, the modal class is 40-50.

Mode of Grouped Data

In grouped data, mode is a value that lies in the modal class and it is given by the formula,

$$\text{Mode} = l + \left\{ \frac{f_1 - f_0}{2f_1 - f_0 - f_2} \right\} \times h$$

where, l = lower limit of the modal class

h = size of the class intervals (assuming all class sizes to be equal)

f_1 = frequency of the modal class

f_0 = frequency of the class preceding the modal class

f_2 = frequency of the class succeeding the modal class

Median

Median is defined as the middle-most or the central observation, when the observations are arranged either in ascending or descending order of their magnitudes.

Median divides the arranged series into two equal parts, i.e. 50% of the observations lie below the median and the remaining are above the median.

Let n be the total number of observations and suppose that they are arranged in ascending or descending order.

Median of the data depends on the number of observations (n).

Case I If n is odd, then

$$\text{Median} = \text{Value of} \left(\frac{n+1}{2} \right) \text{th observation}$$

e.g. If five girls of different heights are made to stand in a row, in descending order of their heights, then the height of the third girl from either end is median height.

Since, $n = 5$ is odd.

$$\therefore \ \text{Median} = \left(\frac{n+1}{2} \right) \text{th observation} = \frac{5+1}{2}$$

$$= \frac{6}{2} = \text{3rd observation}$$

Case II If n is even, then

$$\text{Median} = \text{Mean of value of} \left(\frac{n}{2} \right) \text{th and} \left(\frac{n}{2} + 1 \right) \text{th}$$

observations

$$= \frac{1}{2} \times \text{Value of} \left[\left(\frac{n}{2} \right) \text{th} + \left(\frac{n}{2} + 1 \right) \text{th} \right]$$

observations

e.g. If six girls of different heights are made to stand in a row, in descending order of their heights, then the mean height of third and fourth girl from either end is the median height.

Since, $n = 6$ is even.

So, $\dfrac{n}{2} = \dfrac{6}{2} = $ 3rd observation

and $\left(\dfrac{n}{2} + 1 \right) = \dfrac{6}{2} + 1 = \dfrac{6+2}{2} = $ 4th observation

$\therefore$ Median = Mean of 3rd and 4th observations

Cumulative Frequency

The frequency of an observation in a data refers to how many times that observation occur in the data. Cumulative frequency of a class is defined as the sum of all frequencies upto the given class.

Less than type and **more than type**. Formation of these two distributions can be understood with the help of following example.

e.g. Consider a grouped frequency distribution of marks obtained out of 100, by 58 students, in a certain examination, as follows:

Marks	Number of students
0-10	5
10-20	7
20-30	4
30-40	2
40-50	3
50-60	6
60-70	7
70-80	9
80-90	8
90-100	7

Cumulative frequency distribution of the less than type
Here, the number of students who have scored marks less than 10 are 5. The number of students who have scored marks less than 20 includes the number of students who have scored marks from 0-10 as well as the number of students who have scored marks from 10-20.

Thus, the total number of students with marks less than 20 is $5 + 7$, i.e. 12. So, the cumulative frequency of the class 10-20 is 12.

Similarly, on computing the cumulative frequencies of the other classes, which is shown in the table.

Marks obtained	Number of students (cumulative frequency)
Less than 10	5
Less than 20	$5 + 7 = 12$
Less than 30	$12 + 4 = 16$
Less than 40	$16 + 2 = 18$
Less than 50	$18 + 3 = 21$
Less than 60	$21 + 6 = 27$
Less than 70	$27 + 7 = 34$
Less than 80	$34 + 9 = 43$
Less than 90	$43 + 8 = 51$
Less than 100	$51 + 7 = 58$

Cumulative frequency distribution of the more than type
For this type of distribution, we make the table for the number of students with scores, more than or equal to 0, more than or equal to 10, more than or equal to 20 and so on. From the example, we observed that all 58 students have scored marks more than or equal to 0.

There are 5 students scoring marks in the interval 0-10, it shows that there are $58 - 5 = 53$ students getting more than or equal to 10 marks. In the same manner, the number of students scoring 20 marks or above $= 53 - 7 = 46$ students, and so on.

Marks obtained	Number of students (cumulative frequency)
More than or equal to 0	58
More than or equal to 10	$58 - 5 = 53$
More than or equal to 20	$53 - 7 = 46$
More than or equal to 30	$46 - 4 = 42$
More than or equal to 40	$42 - 2 = 40$
More than or equal to 50	$40 - 3 = 37$
More than or equal to 60	$37 - 6 = 31$
More than or equal to 70	$31 - 7 = 24$
More than or equal to 80	$24 - 9 = 15$
More than or equal to 90	$15 - 8 = 7$

Median for Discrete Series

A series having observations $x_1, x_2, x_3, \ldots, x_n$ with respective frequencies $f_1, f_2, f_3 \ldots, f_n$ is known as **discrete series.**

Method to Find the Median of the Discrete Series

Firstly, we arrange the data in the ascending or descending order of x_i, then we find the cumulative frequencies of all the observations.

Let n be the total number of observations (sum of frequencies), then median of the data depends on the number of observations (n).

If n is odd, then $\text{Median} = \text{Value of} \left(\dfrac{n+1}{2}\right)\text{th observation.}$

If n is even, then

$$\text{Median} = \text{Mean of} \left(\dfrac{n}{2}\right)\text{th and} \left(\dfrac{n}{2}+1\right)\text{th observations}$$

$$= \frac{1}{2} \times \text{Value of} \left[\left(\dfrac{n}{2}\right)\text{th} + \left(\dfrac{n}{2}+1\right)\text{th}\right] \text{observations}$$

Here, for the value of observation, first look at the cumulative frequency just greater than (and nearest to) the position of required observations. Then, determine the corresponding value of the observation.

Median for Grouped Data

In a grouped data, we may not find the middle observation by looking at the cumulative frequencies, since the middle observation will be some value in a class interval, so it is necessary to find the value inside a class that divides the whole distribution into two halves.

For this, we find the cumulative frequencies of all the classes and then determine $\dfrac{n}{2}$, where $n = $ number of observations.

Now, locate the class whose cumulative frequency is greater than (i.e. nearest to) $\dfrac{n}{2}$ and this class is called **median class.**

After finding the median class, use the following formula for calculating the median.

$$\text{Median} = l + \left\{\dfrac{\dfrac{N}{2} - cf}{f}\right\} \times h$$

where, $l = $ lower limit of median class

     $N = $ sum of frequencies

     $cf = $ cumulative frequency of the class preceding the median class

     $f = $ frequency of the median class

     $h = $ class width (assuming class sizes to be equal)

Relationship among Mean, Median and Mode

There is an empirical relationship among the three measures of central tendency, which is given by

$$\text{Mode} = 3(\text{Median}) - 2(\text{Mean})$$

or $$\text{Mean} = \dfrac{3 \, (\text{Median}) - \text{Mode}}{2}$$

or $$\text{Median} = \dfrac{\text{Mode} + 2 \, (\text{Mean})}{3}$$

Solved Examples

Example 1. Find the mean of the following data.

x	10	30	50	70	89
f	7	8	10	15	10

Sol. Table for the given data is

x_i	f_i	$f_i x_i$
10	7	70
30	8	240
50	10	500
70	15	1050
89	10	890
Total	$\Sigma f_i = 50$	$\Sigma f_i x_i = 2750$

Here, $\quad \Sigma f_i = 50$ and $\Sigma f_i x_i = 2750$

$\therefore \quad$ Mean $(\bar{x}) = \dfrac{\Sigma f_i x_i}{\Sigma f_i}$

$\qquad = \dfrac{2750}{50} = 55$

Hence, mean of the given data is 55.

Example 2. Calculate the mean of the scores of 20 students in a mathematics test

Marks	10-20	20-30	30-40	40-50	50-60
Number of students	2	4	7	6	1

Sol. We first, find the class marks x_i of each class and then proceed as follows

Marks	Class marks (x_l)	Frequency (f_i)	$f_i x_i$
10-20	15	2	30
20-30	25	4	100
30-40	35	7	245
40-50	45	6	270
50-60	55	1	55
		$\Sigma f_i = 20$	$\Sigma f_i x_i = 700$

Therefore, mean $(\bar{x}) = \dfrac{\Sigma f_i x_i}{\Sigma f_i} = \dfrac{700}{20} = 35$

Hence, the mean of scores of 20 students in mathematics test is 35.

Example 3. Find the value of p, if the mean of the following distribution is 7.5.

Classes	2-4	4-6	6-8	8-10	10-12	12-14
Frequency (f_i)	6	8	15	p	8	4

Sol. The table for given data is

Class	Frequency (f_i)	Mid-value (x_i)	$f_i x_i$
2-4	6	3	18
4-6	8	5	40
6-8	15	7	105
8-10	p	9	$9p$
10-12	8	11	88
12-14	4	13	52
	$\Sigma f_i = p + 41$		$\Sigma f_i x_i$ $= 9p + 303$

Given, mean $= 7.5$

$\therefore \quad \dfrac{\Sigma f_i x_i}{\Sigma f_i} = 7.5 \Rightarrow \dfrac{9p + 303}{p + 41} = 7.5$

$\Rightarrow \qquad 9p + 303 = 7.5p + 307.5$

$\Rightarrow \qquad 9p - 7.5p = 307.5 - 303$

$\Rightarrow \qquad 1.5p = 4.5$

$\Rightarrow \qquad p = \dfrac{4.5}{1.5} = 3$

Hence, value of p is 3.

Example 4. The weights of tea in 70 packets are shown in the following table

Weight (in gm)	Number of packets
200-201	13
201-202	27
202-203	18
203-204	10
204-205	1
205-206	1

Find the mean weight of packets.

Sol. First, we find the class marks of the given data as follows.

Weight (in gm)	Number of Packets (f_i)	Class marks (x_i)	Deviation $(d_i = x_i - a)$	$f_i d_i$
200-201	13	200.5	-3	-39
201-202	27	201.5	-2	-54
202-203	18	202.5	-1	-18
203-204	10	$a = 203.5$	0	0
204-205	1	204.5	1	1
205-206	1	205.5	2	2
$N = \Sigma f_i = 70$				$\Sigma f_i d_i = -108$

Here, assume mean $(a) = 203.5$

$$\therefore \quad \text{Mean } (\bar{x}) = a + \frac{\Sigma f_i d_i}{\Sigma f_i}$$

$$= 203.5 - \frac{108}{70}$$

$$= 203.5 - 1.54$$

$$= 201.96$$

Hence, the required mean weight is 201.96 gm.

Example 5. The following distribution gives cumulative frequencies of 'more than type':

Marks obtained (More than or equal to)	5	10	15	20
Number of students (cumulative frequency)	30	23	8	2

Change the above data into a continuous grouped frequency distribution. **[CBSE 2015]**

Sol. Given, distribution is the more than type distribution.

Here, we observe that, all 30 students have obtained marks more than or equal to 5. Further, since 23 students have obtained score more than or equal to 10. So, $30 - 23 = 7$ students lie in the class 5-10. Similarly, we can find the other classes and their corresponding frequencies. Now, we construct the continuous grouped frequency distribution as

Class (Marks obtained)	Number of students
5-10	$30 - 23 = 7$
10-15	$23 - 8 = 15$
15-20	$8 - 2 = 6$
More than or equal to 20	2

Example 6. Consider a grouped frequency distribution of marks obtained out of 100, by 70 students in a certain examination, as follows:

Marks	Number of students
0-10	10
10-20	8
20-30	7
30-40	4
40-50	6
50-60	8
60-70	5
70-80	9
80-90	5
90-100	8

Form the cumulative frequency distribution of less than type.

Sol. Here, the number of students who have scored marks less than 10 are 10. The number of students who have scored marks less than 20 includes the number of students who have scored marks from 0-10 as well as the number of students who have scored marks from 10-20.

Thus, the total number of students with marks less than 20 is $10 + 8$, i.e. 18. So, the cumulative frequency of the class 10-20 is 18.

Similarly, on computing the cumulative frequencies of the other classes, i.e. the number of students with marks less than 30, less than 40, … less than 100, we get the distribution which is called the *cumulative frequency distribution of the less than type.*

Marks obtained	Number of students (cumulative frequency)
Less than 10	10
Less than 20	$10 + 8 = 18$
Less than 30	$18 + 7 = 25$
Less than 40	$25 + 4 = 29$
Less than 50	$29 + 6 = 35$
Less than 60	$35 + 8 = 43$
Less than 70	$43 + 5 = 48$
Less than 80	$48 + 9 = 57$
Less than 90	$57 + 5 = 62$
Less than 100	$62 + 8 = 80$

Here, 10, 20, 30,…, 100 are the upper limits of the respective class intervals.

Example 7. In a class of 72 students, marks obtained by the students in a class test (out of 10) are given below:

Marks obtained (Out of 10)	1	2	3	4	6	7	9	10
Number of students	3	5	12	18	23	8	2	1

Find the mode of the data.

Sol. The mode of the given data is 6 as it has the maximum frequency, i.e. 23 among all the observations.

Example 8. The weight of coffee in 70 packets are shown in the following table

Weight (in gm)	Number of packets
200-201	12
201-202	26
202-203	20
203-204	9
204-205	2
205-206	1

Determine the modal weight.

Sol. In the given data, the highest frequency is 26, which lies in the interval 201-202

Here, $l = 201$, $f_1 = 26$, $f_0 = 12$, $f_2 = 20$ and $h = 1$

$$\therefore \text{Mode} = l + \left(\frac{f_1 - f_0}{2f_1 - f_0 - f_2}\right) \times h$$

$$= 201 + \left(\frac{26 - 12}{2 \times 26 - 12 - 20}\right) \times 1$$

$$= 201 + \left(\frac{14}{52 - 32}\right) = 201 + \frac{14}{20}$$

$$= 201 + 0.7 = 201.7 \text{ gm}$$

Hence, the modal weight is 201.7 gm.

Example 9. Find the mode of the following distribution

Marks	0-10	10-20	20-30	30-40	40-50	50-60
Number of students	4	6	7	12	5	6

Sol. Given, distribution table is

Marks	Number of students
0-10	4
10-20	6
20-30	$7\,(f_0)$
30-40	$12\,(f_1)$
40-50	$5\,(f_2)$
50-60	6

The highest frequency in the given distribution is 12, whose corresponding class is 30 - 40.

Thus, 30-40 is the required modal class.

Here, $l = 30$, $f_1 = 12$, $f_0 = 7$, $f_2 = 5$ and $h = 10$

$$\therefore \quad \text{Mode} = l + \frac{f_1 - f_0}{2f_1 - f_0 - f_2} \times h$$

$$= 30 + \frac{12 - 7}{2 \times 12 - 7 - 5} \times 10$$

$$= 30 + \frac{50}{24 - 12} = 30 + \frac{50}{12} = 30 + 4.17 = 34.17$$

Hence, mode of the given distribution is 34.17.

Example 10. The monthly income of 100 families are given as below

Income (in ₹)	Number of families
0-5000	8
5000-10000	26
10000-15000	41
15000-20000	16
20000-25000	3
25000-30000	3
30000-35000	2
35000-40000	1

Calculate the modal income.

Sol. In a given data, the highest frequency is 41, which lies in the interval 10000-15000.

Here, $l = 10000$, $f_1 = 41$, $f_0 = 26$, $f_2 = 16$ and $h = 5000$

$$\therefore \quad \text{Mode} = l + \left(\frac{f_1 - f_0}{2f_1 - f_0 - f_2}\right) \times h$$

$$= 10000 + \left(\frac{41 - 26}{2 \times 41 - 26 - 16}\right) \times 5000$$

$$= 10000 + \left(\frac{15}{82 - 42}\right) \times 5000$$

$$= 10000 + \left(\frac{15}{40}\right) \times 5000$$

$$= 10000 + 15 \times 125$$

$$= 10000 + 1875$$

$$= ₹\, 11875$$

Hence, the modal income is ₹ 11875.

Example 11. Find the median of the following data.

Marks obtained	20	29	28	42	19	35	51
Number of students	3	4	5	7	9	2	3

Sol. Let us arrange the data in ascending order of x_i and make a cumulative frequency table.

Marks obtained (x_i)	Number of students (f_i)	Cumulative frequency (cf)
19	9	9
20	3	$9 + 3 = 12$
28	5	$12 + 5 = 17$
29	4	$17 + 4 = 21$
35	2	$21 + 2 = 23$
42	7	$23 + 7 = 30$
51	3	$30 + 3 = 33$

Here, $n = 33$ (odd)

$$\therefore \quad \text{Median} = \text{Value of} \left(\frac{n+1}{2}\right) \text{th observation}$$

$$= \text{Value of} \left(\frac{33+1}{2}\right) \text{th observation}$$

$$= \text{Value of 17th observation}$$

Corresponding value of 17th observation of cumulative frequency in x_i is 28. Hence, median is 28.

Example 12. 200 surnames were randomly picked up from a local telephone directory and the frequency distribution of the number of letters in English alphabets in the surnames was obtained as follows:

Number of letters	0-5	5-10	10-15	15-20	20-25
Number of surnames	20	60	80	32	8

Find the median of the above data.

Sol. The cumulative frequency table of given data is

Number of letters	Number of surnames (f_i)	Cumulative frequency (cf)
0-5	20	20
5-10	60	$20 + 60 = 80\,(cf)$
10-15	$80\,(=f)$	$80 + 80 = 160$
15-20	32	$160 + 32 = 192$
20-25	8	$192 + 8 = 200$
Total	$N = 200$	

Since, the cumulative frequency just greater than 100 is 160 and the corresponding class interval is 10-15.

$$\therefore \quad N = 200; \quad \therefore \quad \frac{N}{2} = \frac{200}{2} = 100$$

Here, $l = 10$, $cf = 80$, $h = 5$ and $f = 80$

$$\text{Now, median} = l + \left\{\frac{\dfrac{N}{2} - cf}{f}\right\} \times h = 10 + \left\{\frac{100 - 80}{80}\right\} \times 5$$

$$= 10 + \left(\frac{20}{80}\right) \times 5 = 10 + 1.25 = 11.25$$

Example 13. The median of the following data is 50. Find the values of p and q, if the sum of all the frequencies is 90.

Marks	Frequency
20-30	p
30-40	15
40-50	25
50-60	20
60-70	q
70-80	8
80-90	10

Sol.

Marks	Frequency (f_i)	Cumulative frequency (cf)
20-30	p	p
30-40	15	$15 + p$
40-50	25	$40 + p = cf$
50-60	$20\,(=f)$	$60 + p$
60-70	q	$60 + p + q$
70-80	8	$68 + p + q$
80-90	10	$78 + p + q$

Given, $N = 90$

$$\therefore \quad \frac{N}{2} = \frac{90}{2} = 45$$

which lies in the interval 50-60.

Here, $l = 50$, $f = 20$, $cf = 40 + p$ and $h = 10$

$$\because \qquad \text{Median} = l + \frac{\left(\dfrac{N}{2} - cf\right)}{f} \times h$$

$$= 50 + \frac{(45 - 40 - p)}{20} \times 10$$

$$\Rightarrow \quad 50 = 50 + \left(\frac{5 - p}{2}\right) \Rightarrow 0 = \frac{5 - p}{2} \qquad [\text{Median} = 50]$$

$$\therefore \qquad\qquad p = 5$$

Also, $\qquad 78 + p + q = 90 \qquad\qquad [\text{given}]$

$$\Rightarrow \qquad\qquad 78 + 5 + q = 90$$

$$\Rightarrow \qquad\qquad q = 90 - 83$$

$$\therefore \qquad\qquad q = 7$$

Example 14. The median of the following data is 525. Find the values of x and y, if total frequency is 100.

Class	0-100	100-200	200-300	300-400	400-500	500-600	600-700	700-800	800-900	900-1000
Frequency	2	5	x	12	17	20	y	9	7	4

Sol. Given, frequency table is

Class	Frequency (f_i)	Cumulative Frequency (cf)
0-100	2	2
100-200	5	7
200-300	x	$7 + x$
300-400	12	$19 + x$
400-500	17	$36 + x\,(cf)$
500-600	$20\,(f)$	$56 + x$
600-700	y	$56 + x + y$
700-800	9	$65 + x + y$
800-900	7	$72 + x + y$
900-1000	4	$76 + x + y$

Given, total frequency is 100.

$$\therefore \; 2 + 5 + x + 12 + 17 + 20 + y + 9 + 7 + 4 = 100$$

$$\Rightarrow \qquad\qquad 76 + x + y = 100$$

$$\Rightarrow \qquad\qquad x + y = 24 \qquad\qquad \dots(i)$$

It is given that the median is 525.

Clearly, 525 lies in the class 500-600. So, 500-600 is the median class.

Here, $\quad l = 500$, $h = 100$, $f = 20$ and $cf = 36 + x$

$$\therefore \qquad N = 100$$

$$\because \text{ Median} = l + \frac{\dfrac{N}{2} - cf}{f} \times h$$

$$\Rightarrow \quad 525 = 500 + \frac{50 - 36 - x}{20} \times 100$$

$$\Rightarrow \quad 525 = 500 + (14 - x) \times 5$$

$$\Rightarrow \quad 525 = 500 + 70 - 5x$$

$$\Rightarrow \quad 5x = 570 - 525$$

$$\Rightarrow \quad 5x = 45 \Rightarrow x = \frac{45}{5} = 9$$

Put $x = 9$ in Eq. (i), we get

$$9 + y = 24 \Rightarrow y = 24 - 9 = 15$$

Hence, $x = 9$ and $y = 15$

Chapter Practice

Objective Questions

• Multiple Choice Questions

1. Which of the following is a measure of central tendency?
(a) Frequency   (b) Cumulative frequency
(c) Mean   (d) Class-limit

2. While computing mean of grouped data, we assume that the frequencies are
(a) evenly distributed over all the class
(b) centred at the class marks of the class
(c) centred at the upper limits of the class
(d) centred at the lower limits of the class

3. While computing the mean of grouped data, we assume that the frequencies are
(a) evenly distributed over all the class
(b) centred at the class marks of the class
(c) centred at the upper limits of the class
(d) centred at the lower limits of the class

4. If the difference of mode and median of a data is 24, then the difference of median and mean is
(a) 12   (b) 24   (c) 8   (d) 36

5. If $\bar{x}$ is the mean of x's, then the value of $\displaystyle\sum_{i=1}^{n} x_i$ is
(a) $\dfrac{\bar{x}}{2}$ (b) $2\bar{x}$ (c) $n\bar{x}$ (d) $\dfrac{\bar{x}}{n}$

6. If x_i's are the mid-points of the class intervals of grouped data, f_i's are the corresponding frequencies and $\bar{x}$ is the mean, then $\Sigma(f_i x_i - \bar{x})$ is equal to
(a) 0   (b) −1   (c) 1   (d) 2

7. In the formula $\bar{x} = a + \dfrac{\Sigma f_i d_i}{\Sigma f_i}$, for finding the mean of grouped data d_i's are deviation from a of
(a) lower limits of the class
(b) upper limits of the class
(c) mid-points of the class
(d) frequencies of the class marks

8. If the arithmetic mean of the following distribution is 47, then the value of p is

Class interval	0-20	20-40	40-60	60-80	80-100
Frequency	8	15	20	p	5

(a) 10   (b) 11   (c) 13   (d) 12

9. The times (in seconds) taken by 150 atheletes to run a 110 m hurdle race are tabulated below

Class	13.8-14	14-14.2	14.2-14.4	14.4-14.6	14.6-14.8	14.8-15
Frequency	2	4	5	71	48	20

The number of atheletes who completed the race in less than 14.6 s is
(a) 11   (b) 71   (c) 82   (d) 130

10. For the following distribution

Marks	Number of students
Below 10	3
Below 20	12
Below 30	27
Below 40	57
Below 50	75
Below 60	80

The modal class is
(a) 10-20   (b) 20-30   (c) 30-40   (d) 50-60

11. Consider the following distribution

Marks obtained	Number of students
More than or equal to 0	63
More than or equal to 10	58
More than or equal to 20	55
More than or equal to 30	51
More than or equal to 40	48
More than or equal to 50	42

The frequency of the class 30-40 is
(a) 3   (b) 4   (c) 48   (d) 51

12. For the following distribution

Marks	Number of students	Marks	Number of students
Below 10	3	Below 40	57
Below 20	12	Below 50	75
Below 30	28	Below 60	80

The modal class is

(a) 0-20   (b) 20-30   (c) 30-40   (d) 50-60

13. A student noted the number of cars passing through a spot on a road for 100 periods each of 3 min and summarised in the table given below.

Number of cars	Frequency
0-10	7
10-20	14
20-30	13
30-40	12
40-50	20
50-60	11
60-70	15
70-80	8

Then, the mode of the data is

(a) 34.7   (b) 44.7   (c) 54.7   (d) 64.7

14. Mode of the following grouped frequency distribution is

Class	3-6	6-9	9-12	12-15	15-18	18-21	21-24
Frequency	2	5	10	23	21	12	3

(a) 13.6   (b) 15.6   (c) 14.6   (d) 16.6

15. If the number of runs scored by 11 players of a cricket team of India are 5, 19, 42, 11, 50, 30, 21, 0, 52, 36, 27, then median is

(a) 30   (b) 32   (c) 36   (d) 27

16. Consider the following frequency distribution

Class	0-5	6-11	12-17	18-23	24-29
Frequency	13	10	15	8	11

The upper limit of the median class is

(a) 17   (b) 17.5   (c) 18   (d) 18.5

17. Consider the following frequency distribution

Class	65-85	85-105	105-125	125-145	145-165	165-185	185-205
Frequency	4	5	13	20	14	7	4

The difference of the upper limit of the median class and the lower limit of the modal class is

(a) 0   (b) 19   (c) 20   (d) 38

18. The mean, mode and median of grouped data will always be

(a) same
(b) different
(c) depends on the type of data
(d) None of the above

19. The mean and median of a distribution are 14 and 15 respectively. The value of mode is

(a) 16   (b) 17
(c) 13   (d) 18

• Case Based Study

20. **Analysis of Water Consumption in a Society**

An inspector in an enforcement squad of department of water resources visit to a society of 100 families and record their monthly consumption of water on the basis of family members and wastage of water, which is summarise in the following table.

Monthly Consumption (in kWh)	0-10	10-20	20-30	30-40	40-50	50-60	Total
Number of Families	10	x	25	30	y	10	100

payTM   **B BHARAT BILLPAY**

Payment Receipt

Receipt Number: 9496737194   Receipt Date : 24-07-2019
Bill Date : 2019-07-02

Service Provider   **Payer**
National Payment corporation of India (BBPS Dept.)   9113298110
National Payment corporation of India (BBPS Dept.)   Vaishali Sinha
1001A, The Capital 8 Wing, 10th Floor, Bandra Kurla Complex, Bandra (E), Mumbai

BBPS Biller Id: BWSSB0000KAR01
BBPS Transaction Id: PT01GRD8B3S1
Payment Mode:
Payment Channel: androidapp 8.2.11

Description	Amount	Convenience Fee	Total Amount
Bill Payment for Bangalore Water Supply and Sewerage Board (BWSSB) Consumer Number SE312541	2703	0	2703

Total Amount in Words: Two Thousand Seven Hundred Three Rupees Only

Please Note:
Dear Consumer, the bill payment will reflect in next 48 hours or in the next billing cycle, at your service provider's end. Please contact paytm customer support for any queries regarding this order.

DECLARATION:
This is not an invoice but only a confirmation of the receipt of the amount paid against for the service as described above. Subject to terms and conditions mentioned at paytm.com

(This is computer generated receipt and does not require physical signature.)
B-121 Sector 5, Noida, Uttar Pradesh 201301.
Service tax registration number: AAACO4007ASD002
Paytm Order ID :8824333026

Based on the above information, answer the following questions.

(i) The value of $x + y$ is

    (a) 50   (b) 42
    (c) 25   (d) 200

(ii) If the median of the above data is 32, then x is equal to

    (a) 10   (b) 8
    (c) 9   (d) None of these

(iii) What will be the upper limit of the modal class?

    (a) 40   (b) 60
    (c) 65   (d) 70

(iv) If A be the assumed mean, then A is always
(a) > (Actual mean)
(b) < (Actual Mean)
(c) = (Actual Mean)
(d) Can't say

(v) The class mark of the modal class is
(a) 25   (b) 35
(c) 30   (d) 45

21. As the demand for the products grew a manufacturing company decided to purchase more machines. For which they want to know the mean time required to complete the work for a worker.

The following table shows the frequency distribution of the time required for each machine to complete a work.

Time (in hours)	15-19	20-24	25-29	30-34	35-39
Number of machines	20	35	32	28	25

Based on the above information, answer the following questions.

(i) The class mark of the modal class 30-34 is
(a) 17   (b) 22
(c) 27   (d) 32

(ii) If x_i's denotes the class mark and f_i's denotes the corresponding frequencies for the given data, then the value of $\Sigma x_i f_i$ equals to
(a) 3600
(b) 3205
(c) 3670
(d) 3795

(iii) The mean time required to complete the work for a worker is
(a) 27.10 h
(b) 23 h
(c) 24 h
(d) None of the above

(iv) If a machine work for 10 h in a day, then approximate time required to complete the work for a machine is
(a) 3 days   (b) 4 days
(c) 5 days   (d) 6 days

(v) The measure of central tendency is
(a) Mean   (b) Median
(c) Mode   (d) All of these

22. Direct income in India was drastically impacted due to the COVID-19 lockdown. Most of the companies decided to bring down the salaries of the employees upto 50%.

The following table shows the salaries (in percent) received by 50 employees during lockdown.

Salaries received (in %)	50-60	60-70	70-80	80-90
Number of employees	18	12	16	4

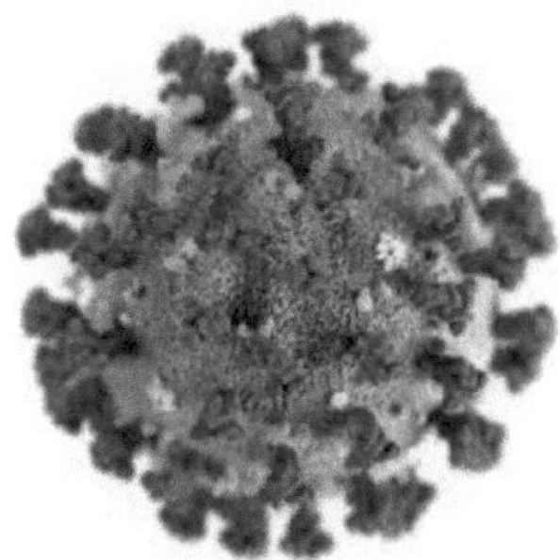

Based on the above information, answer the following questions.

(i) Total number of persons whose salary is reduced by more than 20% is
(a) 40   (b) 46   (c) 30   (d) 22

(ii) Total number of persons whose salary is reduced by atmost 40% is
(a) 32   (b) 40
(c) 46   (d) 18

(iii) The modal class is
(a) 50-60   (b) 60-70
(c) 70-80   (d) 80-90

(iv) The median class of the given data is
(a) 50-60   (b) 60-70
(c) 70-80   (d) 80-90

(v) The empirical relationship among mean, median and mode is
(a) 3 Median = Mode + 2 Mean
(b) 3 Median = Mode − 2 Mean
(c) Median = 3 Mode − 2 Mean
(d) Median = 3 Mode + 2 Mean

PART 2
Subjective Questions

• Short Answer Type Questions

1. Find the class marks of the class 15-35 and class 45-60.

2. What is the arithmetic mean of first n natural numbers?

3. Calculate the mean of the following data.

Class	4-7	8-11	12-15	16-19
Frequency	5	4	9	10

4. Find the mean of the distribution.

Class	1-3	3-5	5-7	7-10
Frequency	9	22	27	17

5. The following table gives the number of pages written by Sarika for completing her own book for 30 days.

Number of pages written per day	16-18	19-21	22-24	25-27	28-30
Number of days	1	3	4	9	13

Find the mean number of pages written per day.

6. The mean of the following data is 14. Find the value of k.

x	5	10	15	20	25
f	7	k	8	4	5

7. The mean of the following frequency distribution is 18. The frequency f in the class interval 19-21 is missing. Determine f.

Class interval	11-13	13-15	15-17	17-19	19-21	21-23	23-25
Frequency	3	6	9	13	f	5	4

8. The mileage (kmL^{-1}) of 50 cars of the same model was tested by a manufacturer and details are tabulated as given below.

Mileage (kmL^{-1})	10-12	12-14	14-16	16-18
Number of cars	7	12	18	13

Find the mean mileage.

The manufacturer claimed that the mileage of the model was 16 kmL^{-1}. Do you agree with this claim?

9. An NGO working for welfare of cancer patients, maintained its records as follows:

Age of patients (in years)	0-20	20-40	40-60	60-80
Number of patients	35	315	120	50

Find mode. **[CBSE 2016]**

10. Find the mode of the following distribution.

Class	10-15	15-20	20-25	25-30	30-35	35-40
Frequency	45	30	75	20	35	15

11. Find the mode of the following distribution.

Class	25-30	30-35	35-40	40-45	45-50	50-55
Frequency	20	36	53	40	28	14

12. Compute the mode for the following frequency distribution.

Size of items (in cm)	0-4	4-8	8-12	12-16	16-20	20-24	24-28
Frequency	5	7	9	17	12	10	6

13. Find the mode of the following frequency distribution.

Class	15-20	20-25	25-30	30-35	35-40	40-45
Frequency	3	8	9	10	3	2

14. The set of data given below shows the ages of participants in a certain summer camp. Draw a cumulative frequency table for the data.

Age (in years)	10	11	12	13	14	15
Frequency	3	18	13	12	7	27

15. Given below is a cumulative frequency distribution showing the marks secured by 50 students of a class

Marks	Below 20	Below 40	Below 60	Below 80	Below 100
Number of students	17	22	29	37	50

Form the frequency distribution table for the data.

16. The following table shows the cumulative frequency distribution of marks of 800 students in an examination.

Marks	Number of students
Below 10	10
Below 20	50
Below 30	130
Below 40	270
Below 50	440
Below 60	570
Below 70	670
Below 80	740
Below 90	780
Below 100	800

Construct a frequency distribution table for the data above.

17. The following distribution of weights (in kg) of 40 persons.

Weight (in kg)	Number of persons
40-45	4
45-50	4
50-55	13
55-60	5
60-65	6
65-70	5
70-75	2
75-80	1

Construct a cumulative frequency distribution (of the less than type) table for the data above.

18. Form the frequency distribution table from the following data

Marks (Out of 90)	Number of candidates
More than or equal to 80	4
More than or equal to 70	6
More than or equal to 60	11
More than or equal to 50	17
More than or equal to 40	23
More than or equal to 30	27
More than or equal to 20	30
More than or equal to 10	32
More than or equal to 0	34

19. From the following distribution, find the median

Class	Frequency
500-600	36
600-700	32
700-800	32
800-900	20
900-100	30

20. Size of agricultural holdings in a survey of 200 families is given in the following table

Size of agricultural holdings (in hectare)	Number of families
0-5	10
5-10	15
10-15	30
15-20	80
20-25	40
25-30	20
30-35	5

Compute median and modal class of the holdings.

21. If median $= 137$ units and mean $= 137.05$ units, then find the mode.

• Long Answer Type Questions

22. The weights (in kg) of 50 wrestlers are recorded in the following table.

Weight (in kg)	Number of wrestlers
100-110	4
110-120	14
120-130	21
130-140	8
140-150	3

Find the mean weight of the wrestlers.

23. If mode of the following series is 54, then find the value of f.

Class interval	0-15	15-30	30-45	45-60	60-75	75-90
Frequency	3	5	f	16	12	7

Find the modal class in which the given mode lies and find the value of f by using the formula,

$$\text{Mode} = l + \left\{ \frac{f_1 - f_0}{2f_1 - f_0 - f_2} \right\} \times h.$$

24. Find the mode of the following distribution.

Classes	0-20	20-40	40-60	60-80	80-100
Frequency	10	8	12	16	4

25. The following are the ages of 300 patients getting medical treatment in a hospital on a particular day

Age (in years)	10-20	20-30	30-40	40-50	50-60	60-70
Number of patients	60	42	55	70	53	20

Form

(i) less than type cumulative frequency distribution.

(ii) more than type cumulative frequency distribution.

26. Find the unknown entries a, b, c, d, e and f in the following distribution of heights of students in a class

Height (in cm)	Frequency	Cumulative frequency
150-155	12	a
155-160	b	25
160-165	10	c
165-170	d	43
170-175	e	48
175-180	2	f
Total	50	

27. The maximum bowling speeds (in km/h) of 33 players at a cricket coaching centre are given as follows

Speed (in km/h)	Number of players
85-100	11
100-115	9
115-130	8
130-145	5

Calculate the median bowling speed.

28. Obtain the median for the following frequency distribution.

x	1	2	3	4	5	6	7	8	9
y	8	10	11	16	20	25	15	9	6

29. Weekly income of 600 families is tabulated below

Weekly income (in ₹)	Number of families
0-1000	250
1000-2000	190
2000-3000	100
3000-4000	40
4000-5000	15
5000-6000	5
Total	600

Compute the median income.

30. A survey regarding the heights (in cm) of 51 boys of Class X of a school was conducted and the following data was obtained:

Heights (in cm)	Number of boys
Less than 140	4
Less than 145	11
Less than 150	29
Less than 155	40
Less than 160	46
Less than 165	51

Find the median height.

31. Find the missing frequencies in the following frequency distribution table, if $N = 100$ and median is 32. **CBSE 2019**

Marks obtained	0-10	10-20	20-30	30-40	40-50	50-60	Total
Number of students	10	?	25	30	?	10	100

32. The table below shows the salaries of 280 persons.

Salary (in ₹ thousand)	Number of persons
5-10	49
10-15	133
15-20	63
20-25	15
25-30	6
30-35	7
35-40	4
40-45	2
45-50	1

Calculate (i) median of the data,

(ii) mode of the data.

• Case Based Questions

33. The men's 200 m race event at the 2020 Tokyo Olympic took place 3 and 4 August. A stopwatch was used to find the time that it took a group of Athletes to run 200 m.

Time (in seconds)	0-20	20-40	40-60	60-80	80-100
Number of Students	8	10	13	6	3

(i) Estimate the mean time taken by a student to finish the race.

Time (in seconds)	Number of Students
0-20	8
20-40	10
40-60	13
60-80	6
80-100	3

(ii) What is the sum of lower limits of median class and modal class.

(iii) How many students finished the race within 1 min?

SOLUTIONS

Objective Questions

1. (c) Mean is the measure of central tendency.

2. (b) In computing the mean of grouped data, the frequencies are centred at the class marks of the class.

3. (b) While computing mean of grouped data, we assume that the frequencies are centred at the class marks of the classes.

4. (a) We have, Mode − Median = 24

We know that, Mode = 3 Median − 2 Mean

∴   Mode − Median = 2 Median − 2 Mean

⇒   24 = 2(Median − Mean)

⇒   Median − Mean = 12

5. (c) We know that,

$$\because \qquad \bar{x} = \frac{\sum\limits_{i=1}^{n} x_i}{n}$$

$$\Rightarrow \qquad \sum\limits_{i=1}^{n} x_i = n\bar{x}$$

6. (a) $\because \qquad \bar{x} = \dfrac{\sum f_i x_i}{n}$

$\therefore \; \Sigma\,(f_i x_i - \bar{x}) = \Sigma f_i x_i - \Sigma\bar{x} = n\bar{x} - n\bar{x} \qquad [\because \Sigma\bar{x} = n\bar{x}\,]$
$$= 0$$

7. (c) We know that, $d_i = x_i - a$

i.e. d_i's are the deviation from a of mid-points of the classes.

8. (d) Let us construct the following table for finding the arithmetic mean

Class interval	Frequency (f_i)	Class mark (x_i)	$f_i x_i$
0-20	8	10	80
20-40	15	30	450
40-60	20	50	1000
60-80	p	70	$70p$
80-100	5	90	450
Total	$\Sigma f_i = 48 + p$		$\Sigma f_i x_i = 1980 + 70p$

Now, $\qquad \bar{x} = \dfrac{\Sigma f_i x_i}{\Sigma f_i}$

$$= \frac{1980 + 70p}{48 + p}$$

$\Rightarrow \qquad 47 = \dfrac{1980 + 70p}{48 + p}$

⇒ $2256 + 47p = 1980 + 70p$

⇒ $276 = 23p$

⇒ $p = 12$

9. (c) The number of atheletes who completed the race in less than 14.6 = 2 + 4 + 5 + 71 = 82

10. (c)

Marks	Number of students	Cumulative frequency
Below 10	$3 = 3$	3
10-20	$12 - 3 = 9$	12
20-30	$27 - 12 = 15$	27
30-40	$57 - 27 = 30$	57
40-50	$75 - 57 = 18$	75
50-60	$80 - 75 = 5$	80

Here, we see that the highest frequency is 30, which lies in the interval 30-40.

11. (a) Given, the distribution table

Marks obtained	Number of students
0-10	$63 - 58 = 5$
10-20	$58 - 55 = 3$
20-30	$55 - 51 = 4$
30-40	$51 - 48 = 3$
40-50	$48 - 42 = 6$
50	42

Frequency of the modal class 30-40 is 3 from the above table.

12. (c) Let us first construct the following frequency distribution table.

Marks	Number of students
0-10	3
10-20	9
20-30	16
30-40	29
40-50	18
50-60	5

Since, the maximum frequency is 29 and the class corresponding to this frequency is 30-40.

So, the modal class is 30-40.

13. (b) Here, modal class is 40-50. Since, it has maximum frequency which is 20.

$\therefore l = 40,\ f_1 = 20,\ f_0 = 12,\ f_2 = 11$ and $h = 10$

$$\because \quad \text{Mode} = l + \left(\frac{f_1 - f_0}{2f_1 - f_0 - f_2}\right) \times h$$

$$= 40 + \left(\frac{20 - 12}{40 - 12 - 11}\right) \times 10$$

$$= 40 + \frac{80}{17}$$

$$= 40 + 4.7 = 44.7$$

14. (c) We observe that the class 12-15 has maximum frequency. Therefore, this is the modal class.

We have, $l = 12,\ h = 3,\ f_1 = 23,\ f_0 = 10$ and $f_2 = 21$

$$\because \quad \text{Mode} = l + \frac{f_1 - f_0}{2f_1 - f_0 - f_2} \times h$$

$$= 12 + \frac{23 - 10}{46 - 10 - 21} \times 3$$

$$= 12 + \frac{13}{15} \times 3 = 12 + \frac{13}{5} = 12 + 2.6 = 14.6$$

15. (d) Arranging the terms in ascending order,

$$0,\ 5,\ 11,\ 19,\ 21,\ 27,\ 30,\ 36,\ 42,\ 50,\ 52$$

Here $n = 11$ (odd)

$$\because \text{Median} = \left(\frac{n + 1}{2}\right)\text{th}$$

$$\text{Median value} = \left(\frac{11 + 1}{2}\right)\text{th} = 6\text{th value} = 27$$

16. (b) Given, classes are not continuous, so we make continuous by subtracting 0.5 from lower limit and adding 0.5 to upper limit of each class.

Class	Frequency	Cumulative frequency
−0.5-5.5	13	13
5.5-11.5	10	23
11.5-17.5	15	38
17.5-23.5	8	46
23.5-29.5	11	57

Here, $\dfrac{N}{2} = \dfrac{57}{2} = 28.5$, which lies in the interval 11.5-17.5.

Hence, the upper limit is 17.5.

17. (c)

Class	Frequency	Cumulative frequency
65-85	4	4
85-105	5	9
105-125	13	22
125-145	20	42
145-165	14	56
165-185	7	63
185-205	4	67

Here, $\dfrac{N}{2} = \dfrac{67}{2} = 33.5$ which lies in the interval 125 -145.

Hence, upper limit of median class is 145.

Here, we see that the highest frequency is 20 which lies in 125-145. Hence, the lower limit of modal class is 125.

$\therefore$ Required difference = Upper limit of median class

$$- \text{Lower limit of modal class}$$

$$= 145 - 125 = 20$$

18. (c) No, the value of these three measures can be the same, it depends on the type of data.

19. (b) Given, mean $= 14$ and median $= 15$

By using empirical relationship,

Mode $= 3$ Median $- 2$ Mean $= 3 \times 15 - 2 \times 14 = 45 - 28 = 17$

Case Based Study

20. (i) (c) Given x and y are the frequencies of class intervals 10-20 and 40-50, respectively. Then,

$$10 + x + 25 + 30 + y + 10 = 100$$
$$\Rightarrow \qquad x + y = 25 \qquad \ldots(1)$$

(ii) (c) Median is 32, which lies in 30-40.

So, the median class is 30-40.

$\therefore\ l = 30, h = 10, f = 30, N = 100$

and $cf = 10 + x + 25 = x + 35$

Now, median $= l + \left(\dfrac{\dfrac{N}{2} - cf}{f}\right) \times h$

$$\Rightarrow 30 + \left[\dfrac{\{50 - (x + 35)\}}{30} \times 10\right] = 32$$

$$\Rightarrow 30 + \dfrac{(15 - x)}{3} = 32$$

$$\Rightarrow \qquad (15 - x) = 6 \Rightarrow x = 9$$

Put $x = 9$ in Eq. (1), we get

$$y = 16$$

Hence, $x = 9$ and $y = 16$

(iii) (a) Since, the maximum frequency is 30, so the modal class is 30-40.

Hence, upper limit of the modal class is 40.

(iv) (d) The value of assumed mean can be less, more or equal than the actual mean.

(v) (b) The modal class is 30-40.

$\therefore\ $ Class mark $= \dfrac{30 + 40}{2} = \dfrac{70}{2} = 35$

21. (i) (d) Class mark of class 30-34

$$= \dfrac{30 + 34}{2}$$
$$= \dfrac{64}{2}$$
$$= 32$$

(ii) (d) Let's make the table

Class	Class marks (x_i)	Frequency (f_i)	$x_i f_i$
15-19	17	20	340
20-24	22	35	770
25-29	27	32	864
30-34	32	28	896
35-39	37	25	925
Total		$\Sigma f_i = 140$	$\Sigma x_i f_i = 3795$

$$\Sigma x_i f_i = 3795$$

(iii) (a) Mean time $(\overline{X}) = \dfrac{\Sigma x_i f_i}{\Sigma f_i}$

$$= \dfrac{3795}{140}$$
$$= 27.10$$

(iv) (a) Approximate time $= \dfrac{27.10}{10}$

$$= 2.710$$
$$\simeq 3 \text{ days}$$

(v) (d) Measure of central tendency are mean, median and mode.

22. (i) (b) $\therefore$ Required number of employees $= 18 + 12 + 16$

$$= 46$$

(ii) (a) $\therefore$ Required number of employees $= 12 + 16 + 4$

$$= 32$$

(iii) (a) The maximum frequency is 18 and the corresponding class is 50-60.

Hence, modal class is 50-60.

(iv) (b) Consider the table

Salaries received (in %)	Number of employees (f_i)	Cumulative frequency (cf)
50-60	18	18
60-70	12	$18 + 12 = 30$
70-80	16	$30 + 16 = 46$
80-90	4	$46 + 4 = 50$
Total	$\Sigma f_i = 50$	

Here, $\dfrac{N}{2} = \dfrac{50}{2} = 25$

The cumulative frequency more than 25 lies in 60-70.

Hence, median class is 60-70.

(v) (a) As we know, Mode $= 3$ Median $- 2$ Mean

$\therefore\ 3$ Median $=$ Mode $+ 2$ Mean

Subjective Questions

1. We know that, Class mark $= \dfrac{\text{Lower limit} + \text{Upper limit}}{2}$

$\therefore$ Class mark of 15-35 is $= \dfrac{15 + 35}{2} = \dfrac{50}{2} = 25$

Class mark of 45-60 is $\dfrac{45 + 60}{2} = \dfrac{105}{2} = 52.5$

2. Arithmetic mean $= \dfrac{\text{Sum of all the observations}}{\text{Number of observations}}$

$$= \dfrac{1 + 2 + \ldots + n}{n}$$

$$= \dfrac{\dfrac{n}{2}[2 \times 1 + (n - 1)1]}{n}$$

$[\because 1 + 2 + \ldots + n$ is an AP series whose first term is $a = 1$ and common difference is $d = 1$. We know that, the sum of nth term of an AP is $S_n = \dfrac{n}{2}[2a + (n - 1)d]]$

$$= \dfrac{2 + n - 1}{2} = \dfrac{n + 1}{2}$$

3. Since, given data is not continuous, so we subtract 0.5 from the lower limit and add 0.5 in the upper limit of each class.

Now, we first find the class mark x_i of each class and then proceed as follows

Class	Class marks (x_i)	Frequency (f_i)	$f_i x_i$
3.5-7.5	5.5	5	27.5
7.5-11.5	9.5	4	38
11.5-15.5	13.5	9	121.5
15.5-19.5	17.5	10	175
		$\Sigma f_i = 28$	$\Sigma f_i x_i = 362$

Therefore, $(\bar{x})$ mean $= \dfrac{\Sigma f_i x_i}{\Sigma f_i} = \dfrac{362}{28} = 12.93$

Hence, mean of the given data is 12.93.

4. We first, find the class mark x_i of each class and then proceed as follows.

Class	Class marks (x_i)	Frequency (f_i)	$f_i x_i$
1-3	2	9	18
3-5	4	22	88
5-7	6	27	162
7-10	8.5	17	144.5
		$\Sigma f_i = 75$	$\Sigma f_i x_i = 412.5$

Therefore, mean $(\bar{x}) = \dfrac{\Sigma f_i x_i}{\Sigma f_i} = \dfrac{412.5}{75} = 5.5$

Hence, mean of the given distribution is 5.5.

5. Since, given data is not continuous, so we subtract 0.5 from the lower limit and add 0.5 in the upper limit of each class.

Class mark	Mid-value (x_i)	Number of days (f_i)	$f_i x_i$
15.5-18.5	17	1	17
18.5-21.5	20	3	60
21.5-24.5	23	4	92
24.5-27.5	26	9	234
27.5-30.5	29	13	377
Total		30	780

$\because$ Mean $(\bar{x}) = \dfrac{\Sigma f_i x_i}{\Sigma f_i} = \dfrac{780}{30} = 26$

Hence, the mean of pages written per day is 26.

6. Table for the given data is

x_i	f_i	$f_i x_i$
5	7	35
10	k	$10k$
15	8	120
20	4	80
25	5	125
Total	$\Sigma f_i = k + 24$	$\Sigma f_i x_i = 10k + 360$

Here, $\Sigma f_i = k + 24$ and $\Sigma f_i x_i = 10k + 360$

Given, mean $= 14$

$\therefore$ $\dfrac{\Sigma f_i x_i}{\Sigma f_i} = 14 \Rightarrow \dfrac{10k + 360}{k + 24} = 14$

$\Rightarrow \quad 10k + 360 = 14(k + 24)$

$\Rightarrow \quad 10k + 360 = 14k + 336$

$\Rightarrow \quad 14k - 10k = 360 - 336$

$\Rightarrow \quad 4k = 24$

$\therefore \quad k = \dfrac{24}{4} = 6$

Hence, the value of k is 6.

7. Table of given data is

Class interval	Frequency (f_i)	Mid-value (x_i)	$x_i f_i$
11-13	3	12	36
13-15	6	14	84
15-17	9	16	144
17-19	13	18	234
19-21	f	20	$20f$
21-23	5	22	110
23-25	4	24	96
Total	$\Sigma f_i = 40 + f$		$\Sigma f_i x_i = 704 + 20f$

$\because$ Mean $= \dfrac{\Sigma f_i x_i}{\Sigma f_i}$

$\therefore$ $18 = \dfrac{704 + 20f}{40 + f}$ $[\because \text{mean} = 18, \text{given}]$

$\Rightarrow \quad 720 + 18f = 704 + 20f$

$\Rightarrow \quad 16 = 2f$

$\Rightarrow \quad f = 8$

Hence, missing frequency in the given data is 8.

8.

Mileage (kmL^{-1})	Class marks (x_i)	Number of cars (f_i)	$f_i x_i$
10-12	11	7	77
12-14	13	12	156
14-16	15	18	270
16-18	17	13	221
Total		$\Sigma f_i = 50$	$\Sigma f_i x_i = 724$

Here, $\Sigma f_i = 50$

and $\Sigma f_i x_i = 724$

$\because$ Mean $(\bar{x}) = \dfrac{\Sigma f_i x_i}{\Sigma f_i} = \dfrac{724}{50} = 14.48$

Hence, mean mileage is 14.48 kmL^{-1}.

No, the manufacturer is claiming mileage 1.52 kmL^{-1} more than average mileage.

9.

Age of patients (in years)	0-20	20-40	40-60	60-80
Number of patients	$35(f_0)$	$315(f_1)$	$120(f_2)$	50

Here, maximum frequency is 315 and the class corresponding to this frequency is 20-40. So, the modal class is 20-40.

$\therefore l = 20,\ f_1 = 315,\ f_0 = 35,\ f_2 = 120$ and $h = 20$

$$\text{Now, Mode} = l + \left(\frac{f_1 - f_0}{2f_1 - f_0 - f_2} \right) \times h$$

$$= 20 + \left(\frac{315 - 35}{2 \times 315 - 35 - 120} \right) \times 20$$

$$= 20 + \left(\frac{280}{630 - 155} \right) \times 20$$

$$= 20 + \frac{280}{475} \times 20$$

$$= 20 + 11.79 = 31.79$$

Hence, average age of maximum number of patients is 31.79.

10. Given, distribution table is

Class	Frequency
10-15	45
15-20	$30(f_0)$
20-25	$75(f_1)$
25-30	$20(f_2)$
30-35	35
35-40	15

The highest frequency in the given data is 75 and the corresponding class is 20-25, which is a modal class.

Here, $l = 20,\ f_1 = 75,\ f_0 = 30,\ f_2 = 20$ and $h = 5$

$$\because \text{Mode} = l + \frac{f_1 - f_0}{2f_1 - f_0 - f_2} \times h$$

$$= 20 + \frac{75 - 30}{2 \times 75 - 30 - 20} \times 5$$

$$= 20 + \frac{45 \times 5}{150 - 50}$$

$$= 20 + \frac{225}{100} = 20 + 2.25 = 22.25$$

11. Given, distribution table is

Class	Frequency
25-30	20
30-35	36
35-40	53
40-45	40
45-50	28
50-55	14

In the given table, the highest frequency is 53 and corresponding class of this frequency is 35-40.

Thus, 35-40 is a modal class.

Here, $l = 35,\ f_1 = 53,\ f_0 = 36,\ f_2 = 40$ and $h = 5$

$$\because \qquad \text{Mode} = l + \frac{f_1 - f_0}{2f_1 - f_0 - f_2} \times h$$

$$= 35 + \frac{53 - 36}{2 \times 53 - 36 - 40} \times 5$$

$$= 35 + \frac{17 \times 5}{106 - 76} = 35 + \frac{85}{30}$$

$$= 35 + 2.83 = 37.83 \qquad \text{(approx)}$$

Hence, mode of given data is 37.83.

12. Given frequency distribution table is

Size of items (in cm)	Frequency
0-4	5
4-8	7
8-12	9
12-16	17
16-20	12
20-24	10
24-28	6

The maximum frequency in the given distribution table is 17, which lies in the class interval 12-16.

$\therefore$ Modal class = 12-16

So, $l = 12,\ f_1 = 17,\ f_0 = 9,\ f_2 = 12$ and $h = 4$

$$\because \ \text{Mode} = l + \left(\frac{f_1 - f_0}{2f_1 - f_0 - f_2} \right) \times h$$

$$= 12 + \left(\frac{17 - 9}{2 \times 17 - 9 - 12} \right) \times 4$$

$$= 12 + \left(\frac{8}{34 - 21} \right) \times 4$$

$$= 12 + \frac{32}{13} = 12 + 2.46 = 14.46$$

Hence, mode of given distribution is 14.46.

13. Given, frequency distribution table is

Class	Frequency (f_i)
15-20	3
20-25	8
25-30	9
30-35	10
35-40	3
40-45	2

The maximum frequency in the given distribution table is 10, which lies in the class interval 30-35.

$\therefore$ Modal Class = 30-35

So, $l = 30,\ f_1 = 10,\ f_0 = 9,\ f_2 = 3$ and $h = 5$

$$\because \quad \text{Mode} = l + \frac{f_1 - f_0}{2f_1 - f_0 - f_2} \times h$$

$$= 30 + \frac{10 - 9}{2 \times 10 - 9 - 3} \times 5$$

$$= 30 + \frac{5}{8} = 30 + 0.625 = 30.625$$

Hence, mode of given distribution is 30.625.

14. The cumulative frequency of first observation is the same as its frequency, since there is no frequency before it.

Now, the cumulative frequency table is

Age (in years)	Frequency (f_i)	Cumulative frequency (cf)
10	3	3
11	18	$3 + 18 = 21$
12	13	$21 + 13 = 34$
13	12	$34 + 12 = 46$
14	7	$46 + 7 = 53$
15	27	$53 + 27 = 80$

15. Here, we observe that, 17 students have scored marks below 20 i.e. it lies between class interval 0-20 and 22 students have scored marks below 40, so $22 - 17 = 5$ students lies in the class interval 20-40 continuting in the same manner, we get the complete frequency distribution table for given data.

Marks	Number of students
0-20	17
20-40	$22 - 17 = 5$
40-60	$29 - 22 = 7$
60-80	$37 - 29 = 8$
80-100	$50 - 37 = 13$

16. Here, we observe that 10 students have scored marks below 10 i.e. it lies between class interval 0-10. Similarly, 50 students have scored marks below 20. So, $50 - 10 = 40$ students lies in the interval 10 - 20 and so on. The table of a frequency distribution for the given data is

Class interval	Number of students (f_i)
0-10	10
10-20	$50 - 10 = 40$
20-30	$130 - 50 = 80$
30-40	$270 - 130 = 140$
40-50	$440 - 270 = 170$
50-60	$570 - 440 = 130$
60-70	$670 - 570 = 100$
70-80	$740 - 670 = 70$
80-90	$780 - 740 = 40$
90-100	$800 - 780 = 20$

17. The cumulative distribution (less than type) table is shown below

Weight (in kg)	Cumulative frequency (cf)
Less than 45	4
Less than 50	$4 + 4 = 8$
Less than 55	$8 + 13 = 21$
Less than 60	$21 + 5 = 26$
Less than 65	$26 + 6 = 32$
Less than 70	$32 + 5 = 37$
Less than 75	$37 + 2 = 39$
Less than 80	$39 + 1 = 40$

18. Here, we observe that, all 34 students have scored marks more than or equal to 0. Since, 32 students have scored marks more than or equal to 10. So, $34 - 32 = 2$ students lies in the interval 0-10 and so on.

Now, we construct the frequency distribution table.

Class interval	Number of candidates (f_i)
0-10	$34 - 32 = 2$
10-20	$32 - 30 = 2$
20-30	$30 - 27 = 3$
30-40	$27 - 23 = 4$
40-50	$23 - 17 = 6$
50-60	$17 - 11 = 6$
60-70	$11 - 6 = 5$
70-80	$6 - 4 = 2$
80-90	4

19. The cumulative frequency table for given distribution is

Class	Frequency (f_i)	Cumulative Frequency (cf)
500-600	36	36
600-700	32	$36 + 32 = 68$
700-800	$32 \,(f)$	$68 + 32 = 100$
800-900	20	$100 + 20 = 120$
900-1000	30	$120 + 30 = 150$

Here, $\dfrac{N}{2} = \dfrac{150}{2} = 75$, which lies in the cumulative frequency 100, whose corresponding class is 700-800. Thus, modal class is 700-800.

Here, $l = 700$, $cf = 68$, $f = 32$ and $h = 100$

$$\because \text{Median} = l + \frac{\dfrac{N}{2} - cf}{f} \times h$$

$$= 700 + \frac{75 - 68}{32} \times 100 = 700 + \frac{700}{32}$$

$$= 700 + 21.88 = 721.88$$

Hence, median of the given distribution is 721.88.

20.

Size of agricultural holdings (in hec)	Number of families (f_i)	Cumulative frequency (cf)
0-5	10	10
5-10	15	25
10-15	30	55
15-20	80 (f)	135
20-25	40	175
25-30	20	195
30-35	5	200

I. Here, $N = 200$

Now, $\dfrac{N}{2} = \dfrac{200}{2} = 100$, which lies in the interval 15-20.

Here, $l = 15$, $h = 5$, $f = 80$ and $cf = 55$

$\therefore \qquad \text{Median} = l + \left(\dfrac{\dfrac{N}{2} - cf}{f} \right) \times h$

$$= 15 + \left(\dfrac{100 - 55}{80} \right) \times 5$$

$$= 15 + \left(\dfrac{45}{16} \right)$$

$$= 15 + 2.81 = 17.81 \text{ hec}$$

II. In a given table 80 is the highest frequency.

So, the modal class is 15-20.

21. Given, median = 137 units and mean = 137.05 units.

We know that,

$$\text{Mode} = 3(\text{Median}) - 2(\text{Mean})$$
$$= 3(137) - 2(137.05)$$
$$= 411 - 274.10$$
$$= 136.90$$

Hence, the value of mode is 136.90 units.

22. We first find the class mark x_i, of each class and then proceed as follows

Weight (in kg)	Number of wrestlers (f_i)	Class marks (x_i)	Deviations $d_i = x_i - a,$ $a = 125$	$f_i d_i$
100-110	4	105	−20	−80
110-120	14	115	−10	−140
120-130	21	$a = 125$	0	0
130-140	8	135	10	80
140-150	3	145	20	60
	$N = \Sigma f_i = 50$			$\Sigma f_i d_i = -80$

$\therefore$ Assumed mean $(a) = 125$,

Class width $(h) = 10$ and total observation $(N) = 50$

By assumed mean method,

$$\text{Mean} (\bar{x}) = a + \dfrac{\Sigma f_i d_i}{\Sigma f_i}$$

$$= 125 + \dfrac{(-80)}{50}$$

$$= 125 - 1.6 = 123.4 \text{ kg}$$

23. Here, given mode is 54, which lies between 45-60. Therefore, the modal class is 45-60.

$\therefore \qquad l = 45$, $f_1 = 16$, $f_0 = f$, $f_2 = 12$ and $h = 15$

$\because \qquad \text{Mode} = l + \left(\dfrac{f_1 - f_0}{2f_1 - f_0 - f_2} \right) \times h$

$\therefore \qquad 54 = 45 + \left(\dfrac{16 - f}{2 \times 16 - f - 12} \right) \times 15$

$\Rightarrow \qquad 9 = \dfrac{16 - f}{20 - f} \times 15$

$\Rightarrow \qquad 9(20 - f) = 15(16 - f)$

$\Rightarrow \qquad 180 - 9f = 240 - 15f$

$\Rightarrow \qquad 6f = 240 - 180 = 60$

$\Rightarrow \qquad f = 10$

Hence, required value of f is 10.

24. The given distribution table is

Class	Frequency (f)
0-20	10
20-40	8
40-60	12 (f_0)
60-80	16 (f_1)
80-100	4 (f_2)

The highest frequency in the given distribution table is 16, whose corresponding class is 60-80. Thus, 60-80 is the modal class of the given distribution.

Here, $l = 60$, $f_1 = 16$, $f_0 = 12$, $f_2 = 4$ and $h = 20$

$\because \text{Mode} = l + \dfrac{f_1 - f_0}{2f_1 - f_0 - f_2} \times h$

$$= 60 + \dfrac{16 - 12}{2 \times 16 - 12 - 4} \times 20$$

$$= 60 + \dfrac{4 \times 20}{32 - 16} = 60 + \dfrac{80}{16}$$

$$= 60 + 5 = 65$$

Hence, mode of the given distribution is 65.

25. (i) We observe that the number of patients which take medical treatment in a hospital on a particular day less than 10 is 0. Similarly, less than 20 include the number of patients which take medical treatment from 0-10 as well as the number of patients which take medical treatment from 10-20.

So, the total number of patients less than 20 is $0 + 60 = 60$, we say that the cumulative frequency of the class 10-20 is 60. Similarly, for other classes, which is shown below the table.

(ii) Also, we observe that all 300 patients which take medical treatment more than or equal to 10. Since, there are 60 patients which take medical treatment in the interval 10-20, this means that there are $300 - 60 = 240$ patients which take medical treatment more than or equal to 20. Continuing in the same manner, which is shown below the table.

(i) **Less than type**		(ii) **More than type**	
Age (in years)	**Number of students**	**Age** (in years)	**Number of students**
Less than 10	0	More than or equal to 10	300
Less than 20	60	More than or equal to 20	240
Less than 30	102	More than or equal to 30	198
Less than 40	157	More than or equal to 40	143
Less than 50	227	More than or equal to 50	73
Less than 60	280	More than or equal to 60	20
Less than 70	300		

26.

Height (in cm)	Frequency (f_i)	Cumulative frequency (given)	Cumulative frequency (cf)
150-155	12	a	12
155-160	b	25	$12 + b$
160-165	10	c	$22 + b$
165-170	d	43	$22 + b + d$
170-175	e	48	$22 + b + d + e$
175-180	2	f	$24 + b + d + e$
Total	50		

On comparing last two tables, we get

$$a = 12$$

$\therefore \qquad 12 + b = 25$

$\Rightarrow \qquad\qquad b = 25 - 12 = 13$

$$22 + b = c$$

$\Rightarrow \qquad\qquad c = 22 + 13 = 35$

$$22 + b + d = 43$$

$\Rightarrow \qquad 22 + 13 + d = 43$

$\Rightarrow \qquad\qquad d = 43 - 35 = 8$

$$22 + b + d + e = 48$$

$\Rightarrow \qquad 22 + 13 + 8 + e = 48$

$\Rightarrow \qquad\qquad e = 48 - 43 = 5$

and $\qquad\quad 24 + b + d + e = f$

$\Rightarrow \qquad 24 + 13 + 8 + 5 = f$

$\therefore \qquad\qquad\qquad f = 50$

27. First we construct the cumulative frequency table

Speed (in km/h)	Number of players (f_i)	Cumulative frequency (cf)
85-100	11	11
100-115	$9\,(f)$	$11 + 9 = 20$
115-130	8	$20 + 8 = 28$
130-145	5	$28 + 5 = 33$

It is given that, $N = 33$

$\therefore \qquad \dfrac{N}{2} = \dfrac{33}{2} = 16.5$

So, the median class is 100-115.

Here, $l = 100$, $f = 9$, $cf = 11$ and $h = 15$

$\because \qquad \text{Median} = l + \dfrac{\left(\dfrac{N}{2} - cf\right)}{f} \times h$

$\qquad\qquad = 100 + \dfrac{(16.5 - 11)}{9} \times 15$

$\qquad\qquad = 100 + \dfrac{5.5 \times 15}{9}$

$\qquad\qquad = 100 + \dfrac{82.5}{9}$

$\qquad\qquad = 100 + 9.17 = 109.17$

Hence, the median bowling speed is 109.17 km/h.

28. Here, the given data is in ascending order of x_i.

Cumulative frequency table for the given data is

x_i	f_i	cf
1	8	8
2	10	18
3	11	29
4	16	45
5	20	65
6	25	90
7	15	105
8	9	114
9	6	120

Here, $n = 120$ (even)

$\therefore \text{Median} = \dfrac{1}{2}\left[\text{Value of }\left\{\left(\dfrac{n}{2}\right)\text{th} + \left(\dfrac{n}{2} + 1\right)\text{th}\right\}\right]\text{observations}$

$= \dfrac{1}{2}\left[\text{Value of }\left\{\left(\dfrac{120}{2}\right)\text{th} + \left(\dfrac{120}{2} + 1\right)\text{th}\right\}\right]\text{observations}$

$= \dfrac{1}{2}\,[\text{Value of 60th observation} + \text{Value of 61th observation}]$

Both 60th and 61th observations lie in the cumulative frequency 65 and its corresponding value of x_i is 5.

$\therefore \qquad\qquad \text{Median} = \dfrac{1}{2}\,(5 + 5) = 5$

29. First we construct a cumulative frequency table.

Weekly income (in ₹)	Number of families (f_i)	Cumulative frequency (cf)
0-1000	250	250
1000-2000 = mid class	$190 = f$	$250 + 190 = 440$
2000-3000	100	$440 + 100 = 540$
3000-4000	40	$540 + 40 = 580$
4000-5000	15	$580 + 15 = 595$
5000-6000	5	$595 + 5 = 600$

It is given that, $N = 600$

$$\therefore \quad \frac{N}{2} = \frac{600}{2} = 300$$

Since, cumulative frequency 440 lies in the interval 1000 - 2000.

Here, $l = 1000$, $f = 190$, $cf = 250$ and $h = 1000$

$$\because \quad \text{Median} = l + \frac{\left\{\dfrac{N}{2} - cf\right\}}{f} \times h$$

$$= 1000 + \frac{(300 - 250)}{190} \times 1000$$

$$= 1000 + \frac{50}{190} \times 1000$$

$$= 1000 + \frac{5000}{19}$$

$$= 1000 + 263.15$$

$$= 1263.15$$

Hence, the median income is ₹ 1263.15.

30. To calculate the median height, we need to convert the given data in the continuous grouped frequency distribution.

Given, distribution is of less than type and 140, 145, 150, ..., 165 gives the upper limits of the corresponding class intervals. So, the classes should be below 140, 140-145, 145-150, ..., 160-165.

Clearly, the frequency of class interval below 140 is 4, since there are 4 boys with height less than 140. For the frequency of class interval 140-145 subtract the number of boys having height less than 140 from the number of boys having height less than 145.

Thus, the frequency of class interval 140 - 145 is $11 - 4 = 7$. Similarly, we can calculate the frequencies of other class intervals and get the following table

Class interval	Frequency (f_i)	Cumulative frequency (cf)
Below 140	4	4
140-145	$11 - 4 = 7$	11
145-150	$29 - 11 = 18 = f$	29
150-155	$40 - 29 = 11$	40
155-160	$46 - 40 = 6$	46
160-165	$51 - 46 = 5$	51

Here, $N = 51$

$$\therefore \quad \frac{N}{2} = \frac{51}{2} = 25.5$$

Since, the cumulative frequency just greater than 25.5 is 29 and the corresponding class interval is 145-150.

∴ Median class = 145-150

Now, $l = 145$, $f = 18$, $cf = 11$ and $h = 5$

$$\therefore \quad \text{Median} = l + \left\{\frac{\dfrac{N}{2} - cf}{f}\right\} \times h = 145 + \left\{\frac{25.5 - 11}{18}\right\} \times 5$$

$$= 145 + \frac{72.5}{18} = 145 + 4.03 = 149.03$$

Hence, the required median height is 149.03 cm.

31. Given, median = 32

and $\quad N = \Sigma f = 100$

Let f_1 and f_2 be the frequencies of the class interval 10-20 and 40-50, respectively.

Since, sum of frequencies = 100

$$\therefore \quad 10 + f_1 + 25 + 30 + f_2 + 10 = 100$$

$$\Rightarrow \quad f_1 + f_2 = 100 - 75 \Rightarrow f_1 + f_2 = 25$$

$$\Rightarrow \quad f_2 = 25 - f_1 \qquad \text{...(i)}$$

Now, the cumulative frequency table for given distribution is

Class interval	Frequency (f_i)	Cumulative frequency (cf)
0-10	10	10
10-20	f_1	$10 + f_1$
20-30	25	$35 + f_1$
30-40	$30\,(f)$	$65 + f_1$
40-50	f_2	$65 + f_1 + f_2$
50-60	10	$75 + f_1 + f_2$
Total	$N = f_1 + f_2 + 75$	

Here, $N = 100 \Rightarrow \dfrac{N}{2} = 50$

Given, median = 32, which belongs to the class 30-40. So, the median class is 30-40.

Then, $l = 30$, $h = 10$, $f = 30$ and $cf = 35 + f_1$

$$\because \quad \text{Median} = l + \left\{\frac{\dfrac{N}{2} - cf}{f}\right\} \times h$$

$$\therefore \quad 32 = 30 + \left\{\frac{50 - 35 - f_1}{30}\right\} \times 10$$

$$\Rightarrow \quad 32 - 30 = \frac{15 - f_1}{3}$$

$$\Rightarrow \quad 2 \times 3 = 15 - f_1$$

$$\Rightarrow \quad f_1 = 15 - 6 = 9$$

On putting the value of f_1 in Eq. (i), we get

$$f_2 = 25 - 9 = 16$$

Hence, the missing frequencies are $f_1 = 9$ and $f_2 = 16$.

32. First, we construct a cumulative frequency table

Salary (in ₹ thousand)	Number of persons (f_i)	Cumulative frequency (cf)
5-10	$49\,(f_0)$	$49\,(cf)$
10-15	$f_1 = 133$	$133 + 49 = 182$
15-20	$63\,(f_2)$	$182 + 63 = 245$
20-25	15	$245 + 15 = 260$
25-30	6	$260 + 6 = 266$
30-35	7	$266 + 7 = 273$
35-40	4	$273 + 4 = 277$
40-45	2	$277 + 2 = 279$
45-50	1	$279 + 1 = 280$
	$N = 280$	

$$\therefore \quad \frac{N}{2} = \frac{280}{2} = 140$$

(i) Here, median class is 10-15, because 140 lies in it.

$$\therefore l = 10, f = 133, cf = 49 \text{ and } h = 5$$

$$\because \text{ Median} = l + \frac{\left(\dfrac{N}{2} - cf\right)}{f} \times h$$

$$= 10 + \frac{(140 - 49)}{133} \times 5$$

$$= 10 + \frac{91 \times 5}{133}$$

$$= 10 + \frac{455}{133} = 10 + 3.421$$

$$= ₹\, 13.421 \text{ (in thousand)}$$

$$= 13.421 \times 1000$$

$$= ₹\, 13421$$

(ii) Here, the highest frequency is 133, which lies in the interval 10-15, called modal class.

$$\therefore l = 10, h = 5, f_1 = 133, f_0 = 49, \text{ and } f_2 = 63.$$

$$\therefore \text{ Mode} = l + \left(\frac{f_1 - f_0}{2f_1 - f_0 - f_2}\right) \times h$$

$$= 10 + \left\{\frac{133 - 49}{2 \times 133 - 49 - 63}\right\} \times 5$$

$$= 10 + \frac{84 \times 5}{266 - 112}$$

$$= 10 + \frac{84 \times 5}{154} = 10 + 2.727$$

$$= ₹\, 12.727 \text{ (in thousand)}$$

$$= 12.727 \times 1000 = ₹\, 12727$$

Hence, the median and modal salary are ₹ 13421 and ₹ 12727, respectively.

33. (i)

Time (in seconds)	Number of students (f_i)	Class mark (x_i)	$f_i x_i$
0-20	8	10	$8 \times 10 = 80$
20-40	10	30	$10 \times 30 = 300$
40-60	13	50	$13 \times 50 = 650$
60-80	6	70	$6 \times 70 = 420$
80-100	3	90	$3 \times 90 = 270$
	$\Sigma f_i = 40$		$\Sigma f_i x_i = 1720$

$$\text{Mean } (\bar{x}) = \frac{\Sigma f_i x_i}{\Sigma f_i} = \frac{1720}{40} = 43$$

$\therefore$ Mean time is 43s.

(ii)

Time (in seconds)	Number of students (f_i)	Cumulative frequency (cf)
0-20	8	8
20-40	10	$8 + 10 = 18$
40-60	13	$18 + 13 = 31$
60-80	6	$31 + 6 = 37$
80-100	3	$37 + 3 = 40$
	$\Sigma f_i = 40$	

Modal class is a class having highest frequency.

So, 40-60 is modal class

To find median class, we find cumulative frequency

$$\frac{N}{2} = \frac{40}{2} = 20$$

$\therefore$ 40-60 has cumulative frequency greater than 20.

Thus, 40-60 is the median class.

$\therefore$ Sum of lower limits of median class and modal class
$$= 40 + 40 = 80.$$

(iii) Students finished the race within 1 min

= Students between 0-20 + Students between 20-40

+ Students between 40-60

$$= 8 + 10 + 13 = 31$$

Chapter Test

Multiple Choice Questions

1. A survey conducted by a group of students is given as

Family Size	1-3	3-5	5-7	7-9	9-11
Number of families	7	8	2	2	1

The mean of the data is
(a) 6.8   (b) 4.2
(c) 5.4   (d) None of these

2. The relationship among mean, median and mode for a distribution is
(a) Mode = Median −2 mean
(b) Mode = 3 Median −2 mean
(c) Mode = 2 Median − 3 mean
(d) Mode = Median − mean

3. For the following distribution

Class	0 - 5	5 -10	10 -15	15 - 20	20 - 25
Frequency	10	15	12	20	9

The sum of lower limits of the median class and modal class is
(a) 15   (b) 25   (c) 30   (d) 35

Case Based MCQs

4. A Tesla car manufacturing industry wants to declare the mileage of their electric cars. For this, they recorded the mileage (km/charge) of 100 cars of the same model. Details of which are given in the following table.

Mileage (km/charge)	100-120	120-140	140-160	160-180
Number of Cars	14	24	36	26

Based on the above information, answer the following questions.

(i) The average mileage is
   (a) 140 km/charge
   (b) 150 km/charge
   (c) 130 km/charge
   (d) 144.8 km/charge

(ii) The modal value of the given data is
   (a) 150   (b) 150.91
   (c) 145.6   (d) 140.9

(iii) The median value of the given data is
   (a) 140   (b) 146.67   (c) 130   (d) 136.6

(iv) Assumed mean method is useful in determining the
   (a) Mean   (b) Median
   (c) Mode   (d) All of these

(v) The manufacturer can claim that the mileage for his car is
   (a) 144 km/charge   (b) 155 km/charge
   (c) 165 km/charge   (d) 175 km/charge

Short Answer Type Questions

5. Find the median of the first ten prime numbers.

6. An aircraft has 120 passenger seats. The number of seats occupied during 100 flights is given in the following table.

Number of seats	100-104	104-108	108-112	112-116	116-120
Frequency	15	20	32	18	15

Determine the mean number of seats occupied over the flights.

7. The following distribution gives the daily income of 50 workers of a factory:

Daily income (in ₹)	100-120	120-140	140-160	160-180	180-200
Number of workers	12	14	8	6	10

Write the above distribution as 'less than type' cumulative frequency distribution. **[CBSE 2015]**

8. Find the mode of the following frequency distribution. **[CBSE 2019]**

Class	0-10	10-20	20-30	30-40	40-50	50-60	60-70
Frequency	8	10	10	16	12	6	7

Long Answer Type Questions

9. Find the mean of the following frequency distribution using assumed mean method.

Class	2-8	8-14	14-20	20-26	26-32
Frequency	6	3	12	11	8

Answers

1. (b)   *2. (b)*   *3. (b)*   *4. (i) (d) (ii) (b) (iii) (b) (iv) (a) (v) (a)*
5. 12   *6. 109.92*   *8. 36,*   *9. 18.8*

For Detailed Solutions

Scan the code

Practice Paper 1*
(Solved)

Instructions

- Time : 2 Hr
- Max. Marks : 40

1. The question paper contains three sections A, B and C.
2. Section A has 5 questions with 3 internal choices.
3. Section B has 4 questions with 3 internal choices.
4. Section C has 1 Case Based MCQs comprises of 5 MCQs.
5. There is no negative marking.

As exact Blue-print and Pattern for CBSE Term II exams is not released yet. So the pattern of this paper is designed by the author on the basis of trend of past CBSE Papers. Students are advised not to consider the pattern of this paper as official, it is just for practice purpose.

Section A
(3 Marks Each)

This section consists of 5 questions of Short Answer Type.

1. Find the value of k for which the quadratic equation $(3k + 1)x^2 + 2(k + 1)x + 1 = 0$, has equal roots . Also find these roots.

2. Write the expression $a_n - a_k$ for the AP $a, a + d, a + 2d, \ldots$

   Hence, find the common difference of the AP for which 25th term is 10 more than the 23rd term.

Or If two towers of heights x m and y m subtend angles of $45°$ and $60°$, respectively at the centre of a line joining their feet, then find the ratio of $(x + y){:}y$.

3. The length of common chord of two intersecting circles is 30 cm. If the diameters of these two circles are 50 cm and 34 cm, then calculate the distance between their centres.

Or Given, a line segment AB. Divide it in the ratio $m : n$ by construction, where both m and n are positive integers and let $m = 4$ and $n = 3$.

4. From a solid cube of side 7 cm, a conical cavity of height 7 cm and radius 3 cm is hollowed out. Find the volume of the remaining solid.

5. The mode of the following series is 36. Find the missing (x) frequency in it.

Class interval	0-10	10-20	20-30	30-40	40-50	50-60	60-70
Frequency	8	10	x	16	12	6	7

Or The 8th term of an AP is 17 and its 14th term is 29. Find its common difference.

Section B
(5 Marks Each)

This section consists of 4 questions of Long Answer Type.

6. Construct a tangent to a circle of radius 4 cm from a point on the concentric circle of radius 6 cm and measure its length. Also, verify the measurement by actual calculation.

Or A decorative block as shown in figure is made of two solids, a cube and a hemisphere.

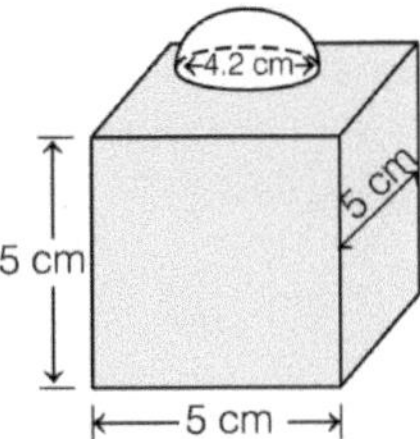

The base of the block is the cube with edge of 5 cm and the hemisphere attached on the top has a diameter of 4.2 cm. If the block is to be painted, then find the total area to be painted. [take, $\pi = 22 / 7$]

7. From the point, 36 m above the surface of a lake, the angle of elevation of a bird is observed to be 30° and angle of depression of its image in the water of the lake is observed to be 60°. Find the actual height of the bird above the surface of the lake.

Or Prove that the intercept of a tangent between two parallel tangents to a circle subtends a right angle at the centre.

8. Find the solution of the equation $\dfrac{x-1}{2x+1} + \dfrac{2x+1}{x-1} = \dfrac{5}{2}, x \neq -\dfrac{1}{2}, 1$ by factorisation method.

Or Find the median for the following frequency distribution.

Height (in cm)	**Frequency**
160-162	15
163-165	117
166-168	136
169-171	118
172-174	14

9. A girl of height 120 cm is walking away from the base of a lamp-post at a speed of 1.2 m/s. If the lamp is 4.8 m above the ground, then find the length of her shadow after 6 s.

Section C
(1 Mark Each)

This section consists of 1 Case Based comprises of 5 MCQs.

10. In a mathematic class, a teacher explain the concept for determine the mean by defining the formula $\bar{x} = \dfrac{\Sigma f_i x_i}{\Sigma f_i}$.

Further, a teacher give one example for explaining the above concepts.

The marks obtained by 30 students of class X of a certain school in a mathematics paper consisting of 100 marks are presented in table below

Class interval	10-25	25-40	40-55	55-70	70-85	85-100
Number of Students	2	3	7	6	6	6

  (i) Find the average marks obtained by the students.
    (a) 61
    (b) 62
    (c) 63
    (d) 64

 (ii) Find the cumulative frequency value in the interval (40-55).
    (a) 5   (b) 12
    (c) 2   (d) 18

(iii) Through cumulative frequency table, which central measurement can be determined.
    (a) mean   (b) mode
    (c) median   (d) None of these

(iv) Find the lower limit of the median class.
    (a) 55   (b) 40
    (c) 70   (d) 25

 (e) Find the upper limit of modal class.
    (a) 40   (b) 55
    (c) 70   (d) 25

Solutions

1. Given quadratic equation is
$$(3k + 1)x^2 + 2(k + 1)x + 1 = 0$$

On comparing with $ax^2 + bx + c = 0$, we get
$$a = 3k + 1,\ b = 2(k + 1),\ c = 1$$

Since, the roots are equal, so $b^2 - 4ac = 0$

$\therefore \qquad [2(k + 1)]^2 - 4(3k + 1)(1) = 0$

$\Rightarrow \qquad 4(k + 1)^2 - 4(3k + 1) = 0$

$\Rightarrow \qquad 4(k^2 + 2k + 1) - 4(3k + 1) = 0$

$\Rightarrow \qquad 4(k^2 + 2k + 1 - 3k - 1) = 0$

$\Rightarrow \qquad k^2 + 2k + 1 - 3k - 1 = 0$

$\Rightarrow \qquad k^2 + 2k + 1 - 3k - 1 = 0 \qquad [\because 4 \neq 0]$

$\Rightarrow \qquad k^2 - k = 0$

$\Rightarrow \qquad k(k - 1) = 0$

$\Rightarrow \qquad k = 0 \text{ or } k = 1$

We know that, if roots are equal, then roots will be the form of $\dfrac{-b}{2a}, \dfrac{-b}{2a}$.

Thus, roots are $\dfrac{-b}{2a}, \dfrac{-b}{2a}$.

$\therefore$ Equal roots are $\dfrac{-(k + 1)}{(3k + 1)}, \dfrac{-(k + 1)}{(3k + 1)}$

When $k = 0$, equal roots are $\dfrac{-(0 + 1)}{0 + 1}$ and $\dfrac{-(0 + 1)}{0 + 1}$

i.e. -1 and -1.

When $k = 1$, equal roots are $\dfrac{-(1 + 1)}{3 + 1}$ and $\dfrac{-(1 + 1)}{3 + 1}$

i.e. $-\dfrac{1}{2}$ and $-\dfrac{1}{2}$.

2. Given, first term $= a$ and common difference $= d$

$\therefore \qquad a_n = a + (n - 1)d \qquad \qquad \text{...(i)}$

and $\qquad a_k = a + (k - 1)d \qquad \qquad \text{...(ii)}$

On subtracting Eq. (ii) from Eq. (i), we get
$$a_n - a_k = [a + (n - 1)d] - [a + (k - 1)d]$$

$\Rightarrow \quad a_n - a_k = a + (n - 1)d - a - (k - 1)d$

$\Rightarrow \quad a_n - a_k = (n - 1 - k + 1)d$

$\Rightarrow \quad a_n - a_k = (n - k)d$

Now, $a_n - a_k = (n - k)d$

$\Rightarrow a_{25} - a_{23} = (25 - 23)d \qquad [\text{put } n = 25 \text{ and } k = 23]$

$\Rightarrow \qquad 10 = 2d \qquad [\because a_{25} - a_{23} = 10, \text{ given}]$

$\Rightarrow \qquad d = 5$

Hence, the common difference is 5.

Or

Let $AB = x$ m be the height of a tower and $CD = y$ m be the height of other tower and $\angle AEB = 45°$ and $\angle CED = 60°$.

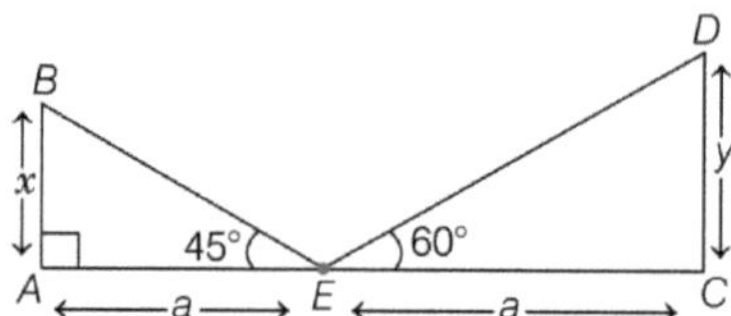

Let E be the point (centre) on the line AC.

i.e. $AE = EC = a$ m

In right angled $\triangle BAE$,

$$\tan 45° = \frac{AB}{AE} \qquad \left[\because \tan\theta = \frac{\text{perpendicular}}{\text{base}}\right]$$

$\Rightarrow \qquad \dfrac{x}{a} = 1 \qquad \qquad [\because \tan 45° = 1]$

$\Rightarrow \qquad x = a \qquad \qquad \text{...(i)}$

Again, in right angled $\triangle DCE$,

$$\tan 60° = \frac{DC}{CE}$$

$\Rightarrow \qquad \sqrt{3} = \dfrac{y}{a} \qquad \qquad [\because \tan 60° = \sqrt{3}]$

$\Rightarrow \qquad y = \sqrt{3}\,a \qquad \qquad \text{...(i)}$

$\therefore \qquad (x+y):y = (a+\sqrt{3}a):a\sqrt{3} = (1+\sqrt{3}):\sqrt{3}$

Hence, the required ratio $(x+y):y$ is $(1+\sqrt{3}):\sqrt{3}$.

3. Let, PQ be the length of the common chord of two intersecting circles.

$\therefore \qquad PQ = 30\,\text{cm}$ [given]

Diameters of two circles are 50 cm and 34 cm.

Join AB.

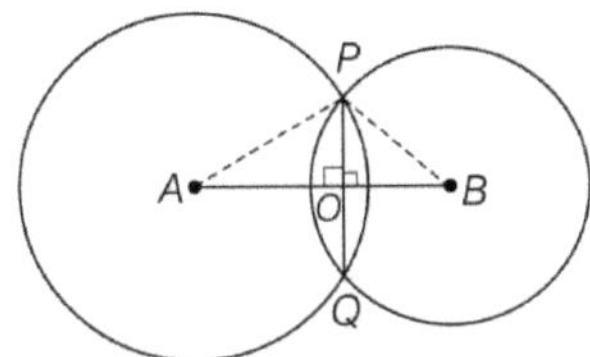

Since, AB bisects the common chord PQ perpendicularly.

$$\therefore \qquad OP = OQ = \frac{1}{2} \times PQ = \frac{1}{2} \times 30 = 15 \text{ cm}$$

Radius, $AP = \dfrac{1}{2} \times 50 = 25$ cm

and radius, $PB = \dfrac{1}{2} \times 34 = 17$ cm

In right angled $\triangle AOP$,

$$OA = \sqrt{(AP)^2 - (OP)^2}$$

[by using Pythagoras theorem]

$$= \sqrt{(25)^2 - (15)^2}$$
$$= \sqrt{625 - 225} = \sqrt{400} = 20 \text{ cm}$$

In right angled $\triangle POB$,

$$OB = \sqrt{(PB)^2 - (OP)^2} = \sqrt{(17)^2 - (15)^2}$$

[by using Pythagoras theorem]

$$= \sqrt{289 - 225}$$
$$= \sqrt{64} = 8 \text{ cm}$$

$\therefore$ Distance between centres,

$$AB = OA + OB = 20 \text{ cm} + 8 \text{ cm} = 28 \text{ cm}$$

Or

Given A line segment AB, $m = 4$ and $n = 3$.

Steps of construction

(i) Draw any ray AX making an acute angle with AB.

(ii) **Locate 7** (i.e. $m + n$) points $A_1, A_2, ..., A_7$ on AX, such that $AA_1 = A_1A_2 = ... = A_6A_7$.

(iii) Join BA_7.

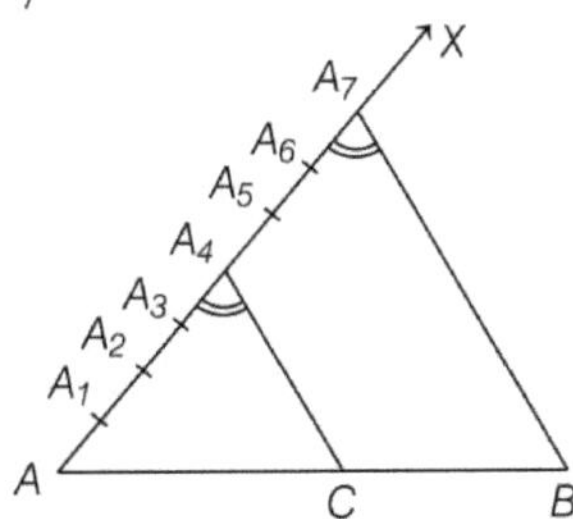

(iv) Now, through the point $A_4(m = 4)$, draw a line parallel to A_7B by making an angle equal to $\angle AA_7B$ at A_4 intersecting AB at a point C.

Then, $AC : BC = 4 : 3$

Alternative Method

(i) Draw any ray AX making an acute angle with AB.

(ii) Draw a ray BY parallel to AX by making $\angle ABY = \angle BAX$.

(iii) Locate the points A_1, A_2, A_3, A_4 (for $m = 4$) on AX and similarly B_1, B_2, B_3 (for $n = 3$) on BY, such that

$$AA_1 = A_1A_2 = A_2A_3 = A_3A_4$$
$$= BB_1 = B_1B_2 = B_2B_3$$

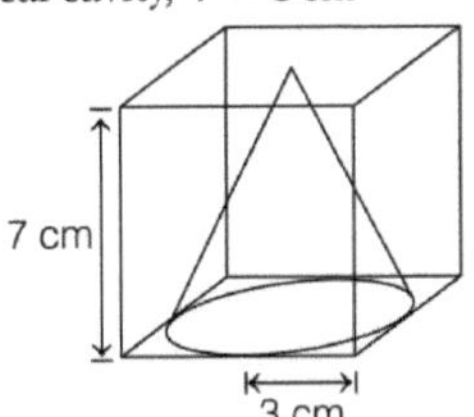

(iv) Join A_4B_3. Let it intersects AB at point C.

Then, $\dfrac{AC}{BC} = \dfrac{4}{3}$

4. Given, side of a solid cube, $a = 7$ cm

Height of conical cavity, i.e. cone, $h = 7$ cm

Radius of conical cavity, $r = 3$ cm

Now, volume of cube $= a^3 = (7)^3 = 343 \text{ cm}^3$

and volume of conical cavity $= \dfrac{1}{3}\pi \times r^2 \times h$

$$= \frac{1}{3} \times \frac{22}{7} \times 3 \times 3 \times 7 = 66 \text{ cm}^3$$

According to the question,

Volume of remaining solid

$\qquad$ = Volume of cube − Volume of conical cavity

$\qquad = 343 - 66 = 277 \text{ cm}^3$

Hence, the required volume of solid is 277 cm^3.

5. Since, the mode of the given series is 36, which lies in the class 30-40.

So, the modal class is 30-40.

Then, $l = 30,\ f_1 = 16,\ f_0 = x,\ f_2 = 12$

and $\qquad\qquad\qquad\qquad h = 10$

Also, $\quad$ mode $= 36$

$\because \qquad$ Mode $= l + \left\{ h \times \dfrac{f_1 - f_0}{2f_1 - f_0 - f_2} \right\}$

$\therefore \qquad 36 = 30 + \left\{ 10 \times \dfrac{16 - x}{2 \times 16 - x - 12} \right\}$

$\Rightarrow \qquad 36 = 30 + \dfrac{10\,(16 - x)}{(20 - x)}$

$\Rightarrow \qquad 36 - 30 = \dfrac{10\,(16 - x)}{(20 - x)} \Rightarrow \dfrac{6}{1} = \dfrac{10(16 - x)}{(20 - x)}$

$\Rightarrow \qquad 10\,(16 - x) = 6\,(20 - x)$

$\Rightarrow \qquad 160 - 10\,x = 120 - 6x$

$\Rightarrow \qquad -10x + 6x = 120 - 160$

$\Rightarrow \qquad -4x = -40$

$\therefore \qquad x = \dfrac{-40}{-4} = 10$

Hence, the missing frequency is 10.

Or

Given,

$\varepsilon_8 = 17,\ \varepsilon_{14} = 29$

Let be a first term a

$\qquad \varepsilon_n = a + (n - 1)d$

$\qquad 17 = 9 + (8 - 1)d$

$\Rightarrow \qquad 17 = a + 7d \qquad \qquad \ldots(i)$

Similarly, $29 = a + 13d \qquad \ldots(ii)$

Subtract Eq. (i) from Eq. (ii),

$\qquad a + 13d - a - 7d = 29 - 17 = d = 2$

6. Given, two concentric circles of radii 4 cm and 6 cm with common centre O.

Here, we have to draw two tangents to inner circle C_1 from a point of outer circle C_2.

Steps of construction

(i) Draw two concentric circles C_1 and C_2 with common centre O and radii 4 cm and 6 cm, respectively.

(ii) Take any point P on outer circle C_2 and join OP.

(iii) Now, bisect OP. Let M' be the mid-point of OP.

(iv) Taking M' as centre and OM' as radius, draw a dotted circle which cuts the inner circle C_1 at two points M and P'.

(v) Join PM and PP'. Thus, PM and PP' are required tangents.

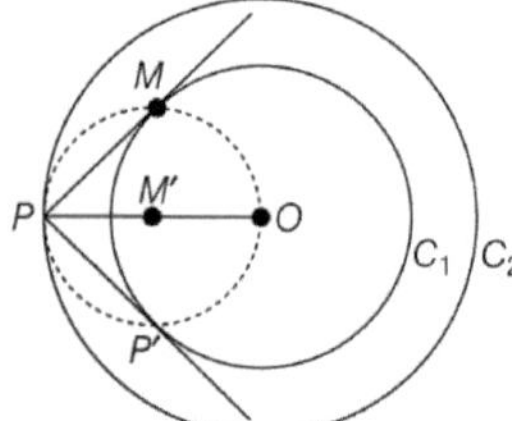

On measuring PM and PP', we get

$\qquad PM = PP' = 4.5$ cm

Calculation In right angled $\triangle OMP$, $\angle PMO = 90°$

$\therefore \qquad (PM)^2 = (OP)^2 - (OM)^2 \qquad$ [by Pythagoras theorem]

$\Rightarrow \qquad (PM)^2 = (6)^2 - (4)^2 = 36 - 16 = 20$

$\Rightarrow \qquad PM = \sqrt{20} = 4.47 \approx 4.5$

Hence, the length of tangent is 4.5 cm.

Or

Given, edge of cube $= 5$ cm

and diameter of hemisphere $= 4.2$ cm

radius of hemisphere $= \dfrac{4.2}{2}$ cm $= 2.1$ cm

Clearly, total surface area of the cube

$\qquad = 6\,(\text{Edge})^2$

$\qquad = 6 \times 5 \times 5 = 150$ cm^2

Now, area to be painted on the cube

$\qquad = $ Total surface area of cube

$\qquad \qquad \qquad - $ Base area of hemisphere

$\qquad = 150 - \pi r^2 = 150 - \dfrac{22}{7} \times \dfrac{4.2}{2} \times \dfrac{4.2}{2}$

$\qquad = 150 - 13.86 = 136.14$ cm^2

Area to be painted on the hemisphere

$\qquad = $ Curved surface area of hemisphere

$\qquad = 2\pi r^2 = 2 \times \dfrac{22}{7} \times \dfrac{4.2}{2} \times \dfrac{4.2}{2} = 27.72$ cm^2

$\therefore$ Total area to be painted

$\qquad = $ Area to be painted on the cube

$\qquad \qquad + $ Area to be painted on the hemisphere

$\qquad = 136.14 + 27.72 = 163.86$ cm^2

7. Let QR be the surface of the lake and P be point above the surface such that $PQ = 36$ m. Let B represents the bird and B' be its image in the lake.

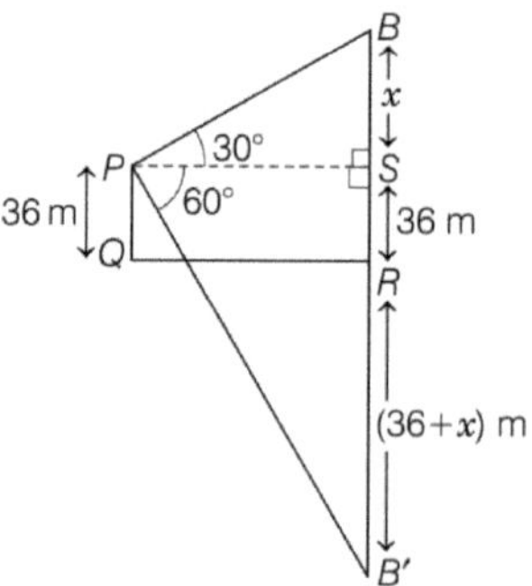

$\therefore \angle BPS = 30°$ and $\angle B'PS = 60°$

Also, $\quad SR = PQ = 36$ m

Let $\quad BS = x$

$\Rightarrow \quad B'R = BR = (36 + x)$ m

$\therefore \qquad B'S = SR + BR$

$\qquad \qquad = 36 + 36 + x = (72 + x)$ m

In right angled $\triangle PSB$,

$\qquad \dfrac{BS}{PS} = \tan 30°$

$\therefore \qquad \dfrac{x}{PS} = \dfrac{1}{\sqrt{3}} \qquad \left[\because \tan 30° = \dfrac{1}{\sqrt{3}} \right]$

$\Rightarrow \qquad PS = \sqrt{3}x \qquad \qquad \text{...(i)}$

Again, in right angled $\Delta B'SP$,

$\dfrac{B'S}{PS} = \tan 60° \Rightarrow \dfrac{72 + x}{PS} = \sqrt{3}$

$[\because \ B'S = (72+x) \text{ m and } \tan 60° = \sqrt{3} \ ]$

$\Rightarrow \qquad PS = \dfrac{72 + x}{\sqrt{3}} \qquad \qquad \text{...(ii)}$

From Eqs. (i) and (ii), we get

$\sqrt{3}x = \dfrac{72 + x}{\sqrt{3}}$

$\Rightarrow \qquad \sqrt{3} \cdot \sqrt{3}x = 72 + x$

$\Rightarrow \qquad 3x - x = 72 \Rightarrow 2x = 72$

$\Rightarrow \qquad x = \dfrac{72}{2} \Rightarrow x = 36$

$\therefore$ Height of bird above surface of the lake,

$BR = BS + SR = 36 + 36 = 72 \text{ m}$

Or

Let, AB and CD are two tangents to a circle and $AB \parallel CD$. Tangent BD subtends $\angle BOD$ at the centre.

To prove $\angle BOD = 90°$

Construction Join OP, OQ and OR.

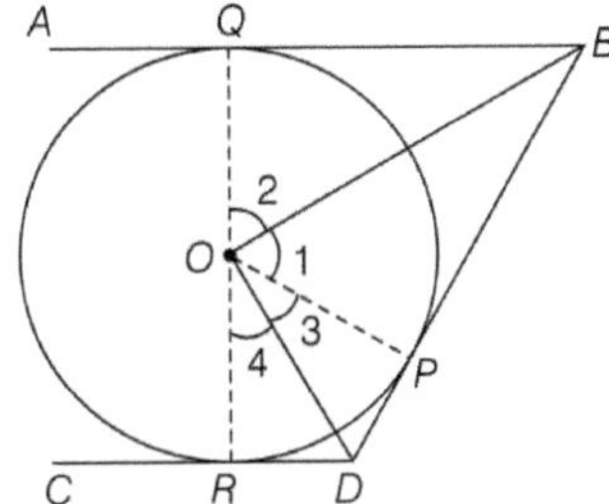

Proof Here, $OP \perp BD$

$[\because$ a tangent at any point of a circle is perpendicular to the radius through the point of contact]

In right angled ΔOQB and ΔOPB,

$BQ = BP$

$[\because$ the lengths of tangents drawn from an external point are equal]

$OQ = OP \qquad \qquad \text{[radii]}$

$OB = OB \qquad \qquad \text{[common]}$

$\therefore \qquad \Delta OQB \cong \Delta OPB \qquad \text{[by SSS congruency]}$

Then, $\qquad \angle 1 = \angle 2 \qquad \qquad \text{[by CPCT] ...(i)}$

Similarly, in right angled ΔOPD and ΔORD,

$\angle 3 = \angle 4 \qquad \qquad \text{...(ii)}$

$\therefore \qquad \angle BOD = \angle 1 + \angle 3 = \dfrac{1}{2}(2\angle 1 + 2\angle 3)$

$= \dfrac{1}{2}(\angle 1 + \angle 1 + \angle 3 + \angle 3)$

$= \dfrac{1}{2}(\angle 1 + \angle 2 + \angle 3 + \angle 4)$

[from Eqs. (i) and (ii)]

$= \dfrac{1}{2}(180°) = 90°$

$[\because QR$ is a straight line, therefore $\angle 1 + \angle 2 + \angle 3 + \angle 4 = 180°]$

Hence proved.

8. We have, $\dfrac{x-1}{2x+1} + \dfrac{2x+1}{x-1} = \dfrac{5}{2}$

Let $y = \dfrac{x-1}{2x+1}$, then given equation becomes

$y + \dfrac{1}{y} = \dfrac{5}{2} \Rightarrow \dfrac{y^2 + 1}{y} = \dfrac{5}{2} \Rightarrow 2y^2 - 5y + 2 = 0$

This is a quadratic equation.

By using factorisation method,

$2y^2 - 4y - y + 2 = 0$

$\Rightarrow \qquad 2y(y - 2) - 1(y - 2) = 0$

$\Rightarrow \qquad (2y - 1)(y - 2) = 0$

$\Rightarrow \qquad 2y - 1 = 0 \text{ or } y - 2 = 0$

$\Rightarrow \qquad y = \dfrac{1}{2} \text{ or } y = 2$

Put $y = \dfrac{x-1}{2x+1}$, we get

$\dfrac{x-1}{2x+1} = \dfrac{1}{2} \text{ or } \dfrac{x-1}{2x+1} = 2$

$\Rightarrow \qquad 2x - 2 = 2x + 1 \text{ or } x - 1 = 4x + 2$

$\Rightarrow \qquad -2 = 1, \text{ which is not true.}$

Consider, $x - 1 = 4x + 2$

$\Rightarrow \qquad 3x = -3 \Rightarrow x = -1$

Or

The given series is in inclusive form. Converting it to exclusive form and preparing the cumulative frequency table is given below

Class interval	Frequency (f_i)	Cumulative frequency
159.5-162.5	15	15
162.5-165.5	117	132
165.5-168.5	136	268
168.5-171.5	118	386
171.5-174.5	14	400
Total	$N = \Sigma f_i = 400$	

Here, $\quad N = 400$

Now, $\quad \dfrac{N}{2} = \dfrac{400}{2} = 200$

The cumulative frequency just greater than 200 is 268 and the corresponding class is 165.5-168.5.

Thus, the median class is 165.5-168.5.

$\therefore l = 165.5, h = 3$ and $f = 136$ and $C = 132$

$$\therefore \text{Median} = l + \left\{ h \times \frac{\frac{N}{2} - C.f}{f} \right\} \quad (1/2)$$

$$= 165.5 + \left\{ 3 \times \frac{(200 - 132)}{136} \right\}$$

$$= 165.5 + \frac{3 \times 68}{136} = 165.5 + 1.5 = 167$$

Hence, the median height is 167 cm.

9. Let AB be the lamp-post, CD be the girl and D be the position of girl after 6 s.

Again, let $DE = x$ m be the length of shadow of the girl.

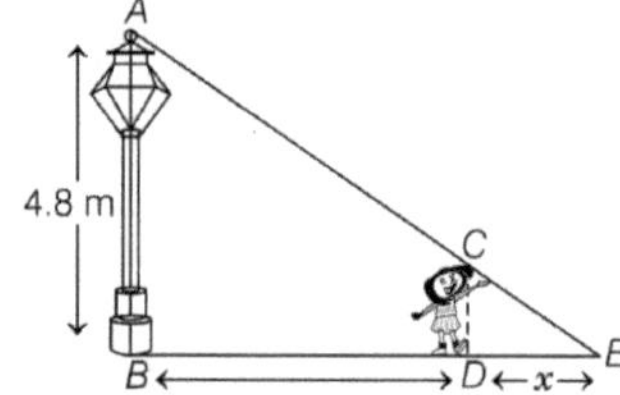

Given, $CD = 120$ cm $= 1.2$ m, $AB = 4.8$ m

and speed of the girl $= 1.2$ m/s

$\therefore$ Distance of the girl from lamp-post after 6 s.

$$BD = 1.2 \times 6 = 7.2 \text{ m} \qquad [\because \text{distance} = \text{speed} \times \text{time}]$$

In $\triangle ABE$ and $\triangle CDE$,

$$\angle B = \angle D \qquad \qquad [\text{each } 90°]$$
$$\angle E = \angle E \qquad \qquad [\text{common angle}]$$
$$\therefore \triangle ABE \sim \triangle CDE \qquad [\text{by AA similarity criterion}]$$
$$\Rightarrow \frac{BE}{DE} = \frac{AB}{CD} \qquad \qquad \dots(i)$$

On substituting all the values in Eq. (i), we get

$$\frac{7.2 + x}{x} = \frac{4.8}{1.2} \qquad [\because BE = BD + DE = 7.2 + x]$$

$$\Rightarrow \quad \frac{7.2 + x}{x} = 4$$

$$\Rightarrow \quad 7.2 + x = 4x$$

$$\Rightarrow \quad 3x = 7.2 \Rightarrow x = \frac{7.2}{3} = 2.4 \text{ m}$$

Hence, the length of her shadow after 6 s is 2.4 m.

10. (i) (b) Let us make the following table for the given data.

Class Interval	Frequency	Class marks (x_i)	$f_i x_i$	Cumulative frequency (cf)
10-25	2	$\frac{10 + 25}{2} = 17.5$	35.0	2
25-40	3	$\frac{25 + 40}{2} = 32.5$	97.5	5
40-55	7	$\frac{40 + 55}{2} = 47.5$	332.5	12
55-70	6	$\frac{55 + 70}{2} = 62.5$	375.0	18
70-85	6	$\frac{70 + 85}{2} = 77.5$	465.0	24
85-100	6	$\frac{85 + 100}{2} = 92.5$	555.0	30
Total	$\Sigma f_i = 30$		$\Sigma f_i x_i = 1860.0$	

Here, $\Sigma f_i = 30$ and $\Sigma f_i x_i = 1860.0$

$\because$ Average, $\bar{x} = \dfrac{\Sigma f_i x_i}{\Sigma f_i} = \dfrac{1860.0}{30} = 62$

Hence, average marks obtained by student is 62.

(ii) (b) The cumulative frequency value in the interval 40-55 is 12.

(iii) (c) Through cumulative frequency table, median can be determined.

(iv) (a) Here, $\dfrac{N}{2} = \dfrac{30}{2} = 15$, which lies in the cumulative frequency 18, whose corresponding frequency is 55-70. Hence, lower limit of the median class is 55.

(v) (b) In the given data, the highest frequency is 7, whose corresponding interval is 40-55. Hence, upper limit of the modal class is 55.

Practice Paper 2*
(Unsolved)

Instructions

■ Time : 2 Hr
■ Max. Marks : 40

1. The question paper contains three sections A, B and C.
2. Section A has 5 questions with 3 internal choices.
3. Section B has 4 questions with 3 internal choices.
4. Section C has 1 Case Based MCQs comprises of 5 MCQs.
5. There is no negative marking.

As exact Blue-print and Pattern for CBSE Term II exams is not released yet. So the pattern of this paper is designed by the author on the basis of trend of past CBSE Papers. Students are advised not to consider the pattern of this paper as official, it is just for practice purpose.

Section A
(3 Marks Each)

This section consists of 5 questions of Short Answer Type.

1. Find the roots of the quadratic equation $9x^2 - 9(a+b)x + (2a^2 + 5ab + 2b^2) = 0$.

2. Which term of the progression $19, 18\dfrac{1}{5}, 17\dfrac{2}{5}, \ldots$ is the first negative term?

Or From the top of a 10 m high building, the angle of elevation of the top of a tower is $60°$ and the angle of depression of its foot is $45°$. Determine the height of the tower.

3. In the given figure, AB is the diameter of a circle with centre O and QC is a tangent to the circle at C. If $\angle CAB = 30°$, then find $\angle CQA$ and $\angle CBA$.

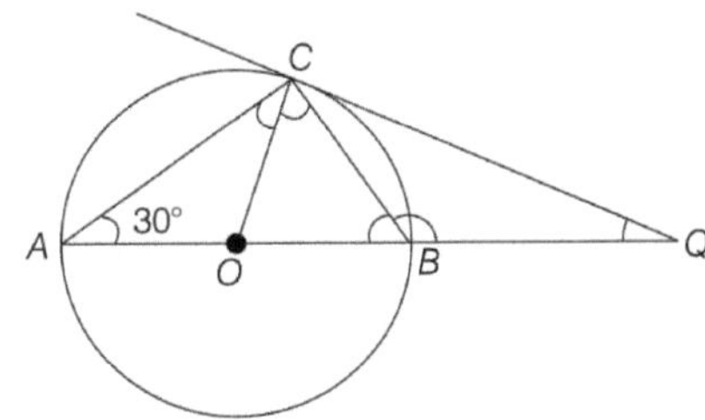

Or A copper wire 4 mm in diameter is evenly wound about a cylinder whose length is 24 cm and diameter 20 cm so as to cover the whole surface. Find the length and weight of the wire assuming the specific density to be 8.88 gm/cm^3.

4. Draw a circle of radius 6 cm. Take a point P on it. Without using the centre of the circle, draw a tangent to the circle at point P.

5. The mean of the following frequency table is 50 but the frequencies f_1 and f_2 in class intervals 20-40 and 60-80 are missing. Find the missing frequencies.

Class interval	0-20	20-40	40-60	60-80	80-100	Total
Frequency	17	f_1	32	f_2	19	120

Or Find the volume area of the largest right circular cone that can be cut out of a cube whose edge is 10 cm.

Section B
     (5 Marks Each)

This section consists of 4 questions of Long Answer Type.

6. A cone of maximum size is cut-out from a cube of edge 14 cm. Find the surface area of the remaining solid left out after the cone is cut-out.

Or The angle of elevation of a jet plane from a point A on the ground is 60°. After a flight of 15 sec, the angle of elevation changes to 30°. If the jet plane is flying at a constant height of $1500\sqrt{3}$ m, find the speed of the jet plane.

7. If α and β are the zeroes of the quadratic polynomial $f(x) = 3x^2 - 4x + 1$, find a quadratic polynomial whose zeroes are $\dfrac{\alpha^2}{\beta}$ and $\dfrac{\beta^2}{\alpha}$.

Or If m times the mth term of an AP is equal to n times its nth term, then show that $(m + n)$ th term of the AP is zero.

8. Construct a tangent to a circle of radius 1.8 cm from a point on the concentric circle of radius 2.8 cm and measure its length. Also, verify the measurement by actual calculation.

9. In the given figure, PT is a tangent and PAB is a secant. If $PT = 6$ cm and $AB = 5$ cm, then find the length of PA.

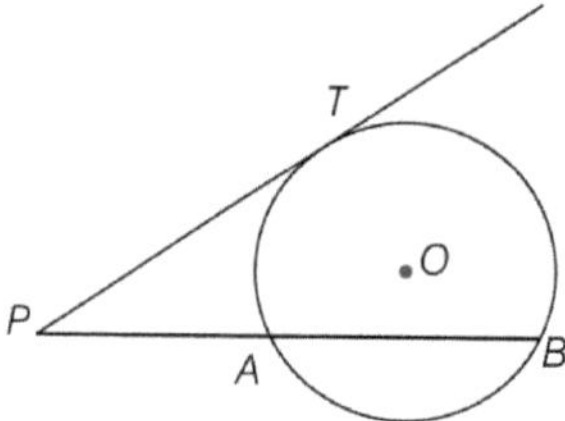

Or Find the mean, mode and median of the following data.

Class	0-10	10-20	20-30	30-40	40-50	50-60	60-70
Frequency	3	4	7	15	10	7	4

Section C
     (1 Mark Each)

This section consists of 1 Case Based comprises of 5 MCQs.

10. In one corner of the drawing room, a flower basket is kept inside the glass, lies on the table. The basket is designed in such a way that every one pleases to see it.

The shape of flower basket is hemisphere with radius 60 cm and upper shape is conical with height 120 cm from the bottom surface.

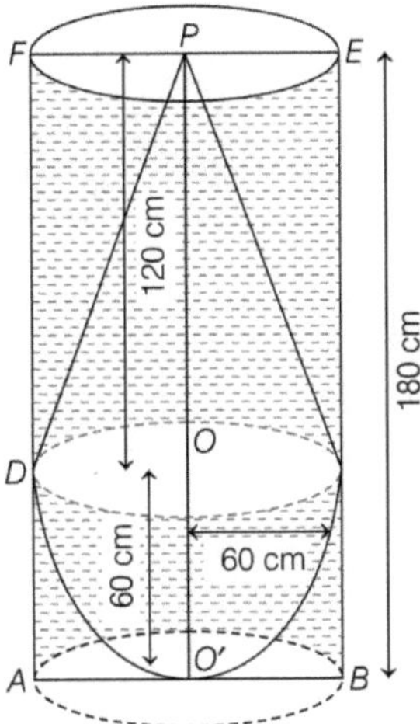

(i) Find the capacity of the glass.

    (a) $\dfrac{14.256}{7}$ m^3 (b) $\dfrac{12.256}{7}$ m^3 (c) $\dfrac{142.56}{7}$ m^3 (d) $\dfrac{14.256}{5}$ m^3

(ii) Find the volume of the cone.

    (a) 0.54 m^3 (b) 0.45 m^3 (c) 0.25 m^3 (d) 0.52 m^3

(iii) Find the curve surface area of hemisphere.

    (a) 0.201 m^2 (b) 0.104 m^2 (c) 0.102 m^2 (d) 0.401 m^2

(iv) The volume of two combined figure is equal to the sum of

    (a) two individual volumes   (b) two individual curve surface area
    (c) volumes and curve surface area   (d) None of these

(v) If the cost of painting the glass outside is ₹ 1.20 per m^2, find the total cost of painting the CSA of the glass.

    (a) ₹ 55   (b) ₹ 55.02   (c) ₹ 57   (d) ₹ 57.02

Answers

1. $\dfrac{(2a+b)}{3}, \dfrac{(a+2b)}{3}$ **2.** *25th term or* $10(\sqrt{3}+)1\,m$ **3.** $\angle CQA = 30°$ *and* $\angle CBA = 60°$ *or 4.21 kg*

5. $f_1 = 28$ *and* $f_2 = 24$ *or 261.9 cm^2*   **6.** *1022 + 154$\sqrt{5}$ cm^2 or 720 km/h*

7. $k\left(x^2 - \dfrac{28}{9}x + \dfrac{1}{3}\right)$ *where k is any non-zero real number*   **8.** *2.14 cm*

9. *4 cm or (i) 37.4, (ii) 36.15, (iii) 37.3*   **10.** *(i) (a) (ii) (b) (iii) (c) (iv) (a) (v) (d)*

Practice Paper 3*
(Unsolved)

Instructions

- Time : 2 Hr
- Max. Marks : 40

1. The question paper contains three sections A, B and C.
2. Section A has 5 questions with 3 internal choices.
3. Section B has 4 questions with 3 internal choices.
4. Section C has 1 Case Based MCQs comprises of 5 MCQs.
5. There is no negative marking.

As exact Blue-print and Pattern for CBSE Term II exams is not released yet. So the pattern of this paper is designed by the author on the basis of trend of past CBSE Papers. Students are advised not to consider the pattern of this paper as official, it is just for practice purpose.

Section A
(3 Marks Each)

This section consists of 5 questions of Short Answer Type.

1. Find the solution of the equation $\dfrac{x-3}{x+3} - \dfrac{x+3}{x-3} = \dfrac{48}{7}$, $x \neq 3$, $x \neq -3$.

2. Write the expression $a_n - a_k$ for the AP $a, a+d, a+2d, \ldots$

   Hence, find the common difference of the AP for which 25th term is 10 more than the 23rd term.

Or A statue 1.6 m tall stands on the top of a pedestal. From a point on the ground, the angle of elevation of the top of the statue is 60° and from the same point the angle of elevation of the top of the pedestal is 45°. Find the height of the pedestal.

3. In the given figure, PQ and QR are tangents to the circle centre O, at P and R, respectively. Find the value of x.

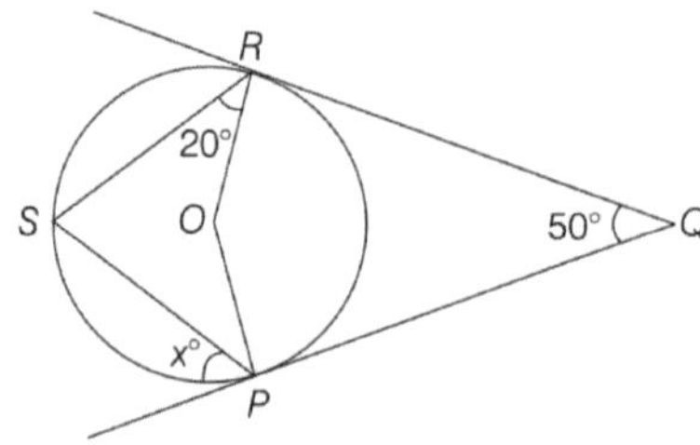

Or Draw a circle with the help of circular solid ring. Construct a pair of tangents from a point P to the circle.

4. For grouped data, if $\Sigma f_i = 20$, $\Sigma f_i x_i = 2p + 20$ and mean of distribution is 12, then find the value of p.

5. A vessel is in the form of a hollow hemisphere mounted by a hollow cylinder. The diameter of the hemisphere is 14 cm and the total height of the vessel is 13 cm. Find the inner surface area of the vessel.

Or Two pillars of equal height are on either sides of a road, which is 100 m wide. The angles of the top of the pillars are 60° and 30° at a point on the road between the pillars. Find the position of the point between the pillars. Also, find the height of each pillar.

<h1 style="text-align:center">Section B</h1>

(5 Marks Each)

This section consists of 4 questions of Long Answer Type.

6. A solid toy is in the form of a hemisphere surmounted by a right circular cone. Height of the cone is 4 cm and the diameter of the base is 8 cm. If a right circular cylinder circumscribes the solid. Find how much more space it will cover?

Or The angle of elevation of the top of a tower from certain point is 30°. If the observer moves 20 m towards the tower, the angle of elevation of the top increases by 15°. Find the height of the tower.

7. Construct a tangent to a circle of radius 1.8 cm from a point on the concentric circle of radius 2.8 cm and measure its length. Also, verify the measurement by actual calculation.

Or From an external point P, two tangents PA and PB are drawn to the circle with centre O. Prove that OP is the perpendicular bisector of AB.

8. Solve the following quadratic equation by factorisation method.

$$\frac{1}{a+b+x} = \frac{1}{a} + \frac{1}{b} + \frac{1}{x}, \ a+b \neq 0.$$

Or The angles of a triangle are in AP. If the greatest angle equals to the sum of the other two, then find the angles. Also, conclude that find these angles are multiple of which angle.

9. The median of the distribution given below is 14.4. Find the values of x and y, if the total frequency is 20.

Class interval	0-6	6-12	12-18	18-24	24-30
Frequency	4	x	5	y	1

<h1 style="text-align:center">Section C</h1>

(1 Mark Each)

This section consists of 1 Case Based comprises of 5 MCQs.

10. Suppose, there are two windows in a house. A window of the house is at a height of 1.5 m above the ground and the other window is 3 m vertically above the lower window.

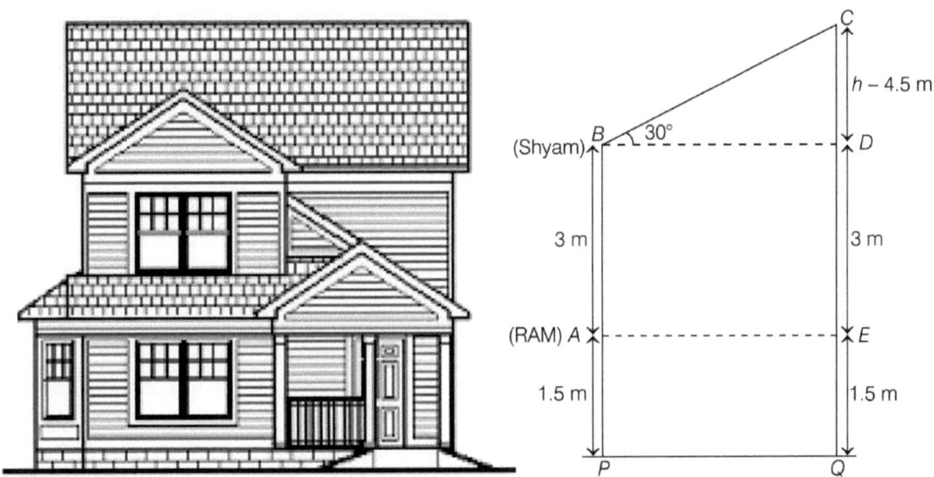

Anil and Sanjeev are sitting in the two windows. At an instant, the angles of elevation of a balloon from these windows are observed as 45° and 30°, respectively.

(i) Find the height of the balloon from the ground.
  (a) 6.8 m
  (c) 9.4 m
  (b) 8.6 m
  (d) 9.6 m

(ii) Among Anil and Sanjeev, who is more closer to the balloon?
  (a) Sanjeev
  (c) cannot say
  (b) Anil
  (d) None of these

(iii) If the balloon is moving towards the building, then will both the angles of elevation remain same?
  (a) cannot say
  (c) No
  (b) Yes
  (d) None of these

(iv) If the height of any tower is double and the distance between the observer and foot of the tower is also doubled, then the angle of elevation
  (a) remain same
  (c) become triple
  (b) become double
  (d) None of these

(v) Suppose a tower and a pole is standing on the ground. And the angle of elevation from bottom of pole is θ_1 and elevation from top of pole to the top of tower is θ_2.

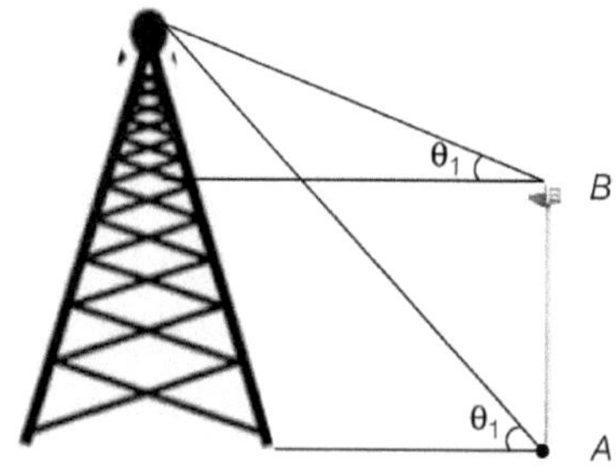

Choose the correct option.
  (a) $\theta_1 > \theta_2$
  (c) $\theta_1 < \theta_2$
  (b) $\theta_1 = \theta_2$
  (d) None of these

Answers

1. $-4, \dfrac{9}{4}$ **2.** 5 or $0.8(\sqrt{3}+1)\,m$ **3.** 45°   **4.** 110   **5.** 572 cm^2 or 25 m, 43.3 m

6. $\dfrac{128}{3}\,\pi\,cm^3$ or $10(\sqrt{3}+1)\,m$ **7.** 2.14 cm   **8.** $x = -a$ or $x = -b$ or ₹ 30°, 60° and 90° angles are the multiple of 30°

9. $x = 4$ and $y = 6$ **10.** (i) (b) (ii) (a) (iii) (c) (iv) (a) (v) (a)

Printed by Libri Plureos GmbH in Hamburg,
Germany